LAW FOR BUSINESS STUDENTS

ALIX ADAMS

Law for Business Students

NINTH EDITION

PEARSON

Harlow, England • London • New York • Boston • San Francisco • Toronto • Sydney • Auckland • Singapore • Hong Kong
Tokyo • Seoul • Taipei • New Delhi • Cape Town • São Paulo • Mexico City • Madrid • Amsterdam • Munich • Paris • Milan

PEARSON EDUCATION LIMITED
Edinburgh Gate
Harlow CM20 2JE
United Kingdom
Tel: +44 (0)1279 623623
Web: www.pearson.com/uk

First published under the Pitman Publishing imprint in Great Britain in 1996 (print)
Second edition published 2000 (print)
Third edition published 2003 (print)
Fourth edition published 2006 (print)
Fifth edition published 2008 (print)
Sixth edition published 2010 (print)
Seventh edition published 2012 (print)
Eighth edition published 2014 (print and electronic)
Ninth edition published 2016 (print and electronic)

ISBN: 978-1-292-08893-8 (print)
        978-1-29208897-6 (PDF)
        978-1-29214518-1 (ePub)

British Library Cataloguing-in-Publication Data
A catalogue record for the print edition is available from the British Library

Library of Congress Cataloguing-in-Publication Data
A catalog record for the print edition is available from the Library of Congress

10 9 8 7 6 5 4 3 2 1
20 19 18 17 16

Front cover image: Getty Images

Print edition typeset in 10/13pt ITC Giovanni Std by Lumina Datamatics
Printed in Slovakia by Neografia

NOTE THAT ANY PAGE CROSS REFERENCES REFER TO THE PRINT EDITION

For Cherry, with much love and gratitude for all her support

Brief contents

Contents

CONTENTS

Part 3: The law of tort 273

Publisher's acknowledgements

Photographs

The publisher would like to thank the following for their kind permission to reproduce their photographs:

Brand X Pictures: 16; **Digital Vision:** 312, 356, 392, 414, 472, 522, xlii; **Getty Images:** 76, 100, 122, 150, 290, 390, 474; **Ingram:** 2, 26, 74, 180, 200, 232, 252, 270, 292, 510, 544, 558, 560, 582; **John Foxx Images:** 452, 496

All other images © Pearson Education

Preface

Over 30 years of teaching law on a variety of further and higher education courses from GCSE to post-graduate level taught me much about the difficulties experienced by students in grasping legal concepts. It can be particularly hard for students following an intensive course of which law forms only one part. Hopefully, this text will meet their needs. I have tried to make it accessible, without over-simplification of the subject matter.

I have aimed to express the law, as far as possible, in accessible terms for the lay person and with a light touch, in the hope that it may not only instruct its readers, but also entertain them a little as well and maybe encourage them to pursue further study of the law. It is a subject that I love and would like to encourage others to love it at least a little.

Many thanks to all at Pearson who have helped me in the creation of this edition, especially Owen Knight, Vicky Tubb and Carole Drummond. I greatly value their support and practical assistance.

Photo: Alix Adams

Last, but definitely not least, many thanks to my partner Cherry Potts. As ever, her emotional support and encouragement have been crucial to the editing process. She has also given me lots of patient practical assistance and the technical support crucial to a somewhat Luddite author.

Table of cases

Table of statutes

Table of statutory instruments

Table of European and International legislation

PART 1

Introduction: getting started

CHAPTER 1
Study skills

Introduction

This chapter, which aims to help you to acquire the skills essential to the successful study of law, is divided into four sections:

1 starting to study;
2 good study habits;
3 writing law assignments;
4 revision and examination technique.

Starting to study

Get rid of your misconceptions

Many of you will be studying law for the first time and as one component of a course. You may be feeling nervous about it because it feels remote or difficult and even perhaps boring. In practice (and particularly if you follow the advice in this chapter), you will probably find law much more interesting than you thought when you began your studies. Contrary to common belief, the study of law is not primarily concerned with ancient, dry and precise regulations that you have to learn by heart. Most of your studies are involved with quite modern cases, that have come to court just because the law was not precise and consequently gave rise to the dispute. This book looks at how the law applies to real-life situations, which will help you to recall the legal principles on which it is based. Effective communication of your *understanding* of those principles is the main requirement for examination success.

Remembering all the cases by name and being able to quote extracts from statutes word for word is icing on the cake – impressive, but not essential.

Law is relevant to you

Remember that the law responds and develops as required by the society within which it operates. For example, until 1935 the driving test was not compulsory because road safety had not assumed the importance it enjoys today. At that time there was much less motorised traffic moving more slowly than today and consequently many fewer accidents. The law affects you personally every day of your life. For example, it determines your eligibility for a student loan, your rights to treatment under the National Health Service and your entitlements and responsibilities as a consumer, business owner, employer or employee.

Widen your horizons

Your studies will be more rewarding if you do not consider law as something to be thought about only when you are in class or reading a relevant text. The effects of many areas of the law are widely reported and discussed in the media. Such reports can help you to see how the law works (or does not work), as well as reminding you of what you have studied. Stay in touch with the news, try to look at a quality daily paper and look out for relevant TV and radio programmes. (Some suggestions for resources appear in Appendix 1.) The internet is an excellent research tool. (Try visiting the websites suggested by the web activity references at the end of Chapters 3–25.)

Make connections

The more you study, the easier it gets. Studying law is rather like doing a large jig-saw without the help of a picture – progress is initially slow while the framework is established, but patience is rewarded. Once the picture begins to reveal itself you can see more easily how the different pieces fit together and then the task gets easier and quicker.

Try not to think of each topic as a separate entity to be 'done' and neatly filed away in the memory. Exploit the links with other related topics; this aids both recollection and understanding. Exam and assignment questions may involve a problem, raising issues about a number of different topics; the ability to see connections is vital to an effective response. To help you do this, frequent cross-references appear in the text. Pondering on the questions in the 'Worth thinking about?' boxes in this work, and maybe discussing these with your classmates, will help with the process.

Read and practice, applying your knowledge

Somebody (not a lawyer) once told the author that law is a very 'paper-based subject'. This made it sound a bit like origami, but nevertheless did contain some truth. Reading thoroughly and widely is essential; practising the written skills required by the examinations is also crucial.

Hopefully you will find this book accessible, but if you are new to the study of law it would take magical powers to understand it all fully at a first reading. Be prepared to go back and re-read a section that you do not understand. (The chapter summaries may help you to grasp the main points of each chapter.) Often it is best to try to get a general picture on the first reading of a topic that you find hard, pressing on even if you do not understand it. You will still get something from it, and on each subsequent reading it will become clearer.

Get all the writing practice that you can. Homework provides safe space to make mistakes; and it is much better to make them then rather than in the exam. Try the quizzes and assignments in this book. Prepare written answers to tutorial questions and be prepared to participate when attending them. This is much more valuable (and more fun) than listening mutely to other people's answers.

Good study habits

Create a structure for learning

Success in your studies depends more on being well organised than having a flair for the subject. Settling yourself into a reasonably structured regime is very helpful but isn't necessarily all that easy when you are starting something new, maybe away from home for the first time and excited by all the attractions on offer in this new phase of

Study skills

1

your life. Possibly all this newness is a bit daunting and you are feeling a bit anxious or homesick. Either way, some structure will help.

Taking care of yourself

This is your first priority. Remember that your brain is part of your body! This very obvious statement still needs reinforcement for many students who ignore their need for proper food and sleep and relaxation. It is easy to let these apparently simple requirements slip under the pressure of a new and taxing academic course, pursuit of a social life, and the part-time job that most students will find necessary. Many of you, particularly mature students, may have caring responsibilities that may have to take priority.

However, try to eat a balanced diet and get a reasonable amount of sleep. Be prepared to acknowledge that you may from time to time need some extra support. If you are ill, or having any other problems that hinder your studies, tell your lecturers or personal tutor what is going on, as they are often able to help. Counselling services may also be available at your university or college that can be very helpful.

Time management

It is important that you set aside a sensible amount of time each week for your private study, as this is a crucial supplement to the tuition that you receive. It is not realistic to expect your lecturers to provide you with more than 5 per cent of what you need. The other 95 per cent is up to you. Attending a lecture is the first step towards understanding a topic, but you must personally reinforce this initial learning in your own time by reading and preparing for and participating in tutorials. It's what you do for yourself that really counts.

Make yourself a study timetable with realistic goals. Short bursts spread across the week may be more appropriate than aiming to study in lengthy blocks, particularly in the early stages of your course.

Be punctual for lectures and tutorials to ensure that you get the most benefit from them and do not distract the other students or lecturer by your late entrance.

Keep your diary up to date and double check dates for assignment submissions. You really don't want to find your assignment refused for late submission or discover that the exam you have come for one afternoon has already taken place that morning.

Note-taking

Your lecture notes are an essential lifeline. It is probably best not to make them 'in rough'. Your good intentions to write them up later may not be fulfilled. Use a loose-leaf folder and write on one side of the paper only. That enables you to add notes later on when you read the textbook. Do not take unnecessary notes. If your tutor provides lecture outlines, you may not need to write many extra lecture notes.

You will probably want to take some notes from your reading. Use your own words with plenty of side headings. Note the sources of any extra notes you take, you may need to cite them later in an assignment.

If you copy something, be sure to use quotation marks and indicate the source. This will ensure that you do not later represent this great thought as your own in an assignment, as you could be penalised for plagiarism (see below).

Reading

1

The library is your second home. It is very important that you always read the relevant section of the textbook, as soon as possible after each lecture, as well as any cases or other materials recommended by your tutor. At first you may find this heavy going, but if you persevere it does get easier. Do not worry about understanding every word. If you get bogged down at the beginning of the course do not struggle endlessly with the early topics. Keep up with the reading relevant to your lectures and light will eventually dawn.

While you need to read your chosen texts thoroughly, it is always useful to consult others (see Appendix 1). Make good use of the index or contents section of additional texts to find the bits you need. Do not be afraid to skim. Use the search facility when reading PDF documents online. This can be a real help in isolating the bits you want in a law report, for example.

So far this section has been a counsel of perfection. There may be times when you find a particular study topic very tough, either because it is not exciting you, or is complex, or worst of all both. Possibly your life is not going smoothly in other ways. That is the time to retire to the basic materials and try to get a grip on them. It is better to keep up basically than fall behind because you are temporarily finding it difficult to see the wood from the trees.

Checking your learning

It is a good idea to check that you have understood what you have been reading about. This book also helps you to check your progress in four ways.

1 *Chapter summary*: the bullet points should act like triggers and bring to mind more information from the chapter when you read them.

2 *Key terms*: check that you have grasped the meanings of these. Try writing them down using your own words.

3 *Quizzes*: these provide a simple way to check that you have grasped some of the important basic issues covered by the chapter.

4 *Join a study group*: getting together informally with a group of fellow students to discuss your work can be both fun and helpful. Having to voice issues is a very good way of finding out how well or otherwise you understand them. In the event of a dispute, having to provide a reasoned answer is also an excellent academic exercise and good preparation for tutorials. The group can provide valuable mutual support near the exams too. Doing stuff together is also a good way of making friends.

Writing law assignments

General advice

Before we examine the specific techniques for writing law assignments it is useful to check that you are aware of what an assignment at degree or diploma level requires.

1 Style

Remember that you are not writing a personal account. Avoid saying 'I think' or 'I believe', however passionately you feel about your argument. Get used to using the third person instead and say something like 'it may be thought/argued that . . .'

2 Evidence

Back up your arguments: indicate your sources by referring to the relevant case refer-ence, statute section, book title and page, date of newspaper article or website address. Make sure that you develop your arguments rather than just giving a string of case or other source names. You must show how the evidence you cite supports your argument.

Always use primary sources as far as possible. This means the first publication of the document. For instance, if you cite a case you should footnote the actual law report reference, not the page in the textbook where you first found it. Footnotes are a neat way to show your references and they do not usually form part of your word limit. It is best to keep to a bare reference. While you may come across texts that seem to have more footnote than content, don't be tempted into using this device as a subterfuge to exceed the word limit. It is unlikely to fool your tutors.

3 Avoid plagiarism

In simple terms, plagiarism means passing off someone else's work as your own. An obvious example is copying a chunk of text without using quote marks, but altering some words in that text while leaving the sentence structure the same may also be plagiarism.

Plagiarism is easily avoided by clearly marking any direct quotes with inverted com-mas. Otherwise anything you write should be in your own words, however difficult it is to find them. In the early stages of a new course of study it may be tempting to mir-ror someone else's text too closely but, with practice, your confidence in yourself will grow as you acquire a better grasp of new concepts and get better at self-expression.

So far we have been considering what might be called careless plagiarism, though even this may lead to your work being downgraded. Sadly a minority of students set out to profit from intentional plagiarism. This is a form of cheating and carries heavy penalties including permanent exclusion in the most serious cases. Don't fool yourself into thinking you will get away with it. Apart from the fact that your tutors will notice blatant copying from sources they have recommended, all manner of plagiarism detec-tion techniques are now being used which can spot much more subtle tricks.

4 Submission requirements

Your student handbook will spell out the submission requirements for your course work. It is crucial that you make sure that you know and understand them, as failure to comply may jeopardise your success in your course. Each institution has its own very specific requirements. The devil is in the detail, so make sure that you know when, where and in what form and format your institution wants you to deliver your assignment. Promptness is crucial, miss the deadline and your work may be rejected, or only accepted if you are able to produce a really good reason with proof for the delay. Excuses are not reasons. Give yourself enough time to avoid last-minute disasters such as a computer failure or a non-running bus, causing you a fatal delay. Although we live in an electronic age, you may still be required to deliver hard copy rather than emailing it in. A minimum font size may also be stipulated. A special cover sheet may be required. Check all the details before you submit.

Writing technique for law assignments

Your written assignments may take two forms:

1 *Problem or 'situation-based' assignments*. These involve a scenario to which you are expected to apply principles of law and draw reasoned conclusions.

2 *Discursive assignments*: essays and reports.

Very different types of answers are demanded by these two methods of testing your knowledge and abilities. However, we first need to examine the requirements which both types of work have in common at degree or diploma level.

Problem questions

A good answer to such a question will require the following:

● a clear explanation of the relevant points of law;

● an analysis of the given facts in the light of the relevant law, indicating likely outcome.

Sometimes the facts will be deliberately vague to encourage you to indicate that a decision could go either way. It is crucial that you give reasons to support your arguments. It is not good enough to write at length about the general legal principles raised by the problem, and follow that with an assertion that X or Y will win. Giving clearly analysed reasons why you are making such an assertion is what earns you marks. Here are some tips to help you.

1 *Read the problem thoroughly and think about what is involved*. This is crucial to spotting the relevant legal areas and to your grasp of the relationship of the parties and their names. Underline the 'triggers', the points of fact in the scenario which indicate the points of law to be applied. Refer to your books and notes to make sure that you understand these points of law.

2 *Briefly jot down the relevant points of law that relate to the behaviour of the parties.* If the facts of the problem are complicated, representing the relationship of the parties in diagram form may assist.

3 *Now write your answer in full.* It is a good idea to have a brief opening paragraph giving an overview of the problem faced by the parties and indicating how the law affects this. Next, proceed to the first 'trigger': stick to the point of law that it raises. Do not write about the law at large. If the examiner expressly tells you the legal situation on a particular point, this does not need to be debated. For example, if a contract question specifically states that an offer has been made and a price stipulated, you do not need to discuss the existence of offer or consideration. Link each point of law to the relevant trigger and explain its implications. There is no need to worry about the evidence that would have to be proved in real life. For instance, if postal contractual acceptance is involved, do not worry about whether the offeree can actually prove that the letter was posted. Explain the outcome if the postal rules are applied. Then proceed to the next trigger point and repeat the process.

4 *When stating a point of law indicate its primary source.* Name relevant cases or statute sections, or otherwise indicate that you know you are quoting a legal rule by saying, for example, 'in law'. There is usually no need to explain the facts of the case, though a brief reference may be useful to stress its relevance or to show how it can be distinguished from the problem facts.

5 *Conclude with a brief summary.* This gives polish to your answer and should always form part of a coursework assignment. In an exam, if you are short of time, it is not important as it should not include any new argument. Remember that there is not necessarily a right or a wrong answer. You are being tested on your reasoning. The facts of the problem may be capable of more than one interpretation, each indicating a potentially different result.

Check your answer carefully, rewriting and polishing if necessary. (See the discursive assignment tips below.)

This approach is demonstrated in the analysis of the following problem (Assignment 3 in Chapter 5). The italicised words are the 'triggers'.

Iris made an offer to sell her piano to Diana for £500 on Monday. Diana replied: 'I will buy it *if I can raise the money*'. Iris *promised that she would not sell to anyone else before Saturday*, and added that Diana could collect the piano *any time before noon on Saturday*. On Wednesday, Diana phoned and left a message with Iris's daughter, Athena, saying that *she had got the money* and *would come to collect the piano on Saturday morning*. *Athena forgot to pass on the message.* On Thursday, Iris was visited by Juno who said that she would pay £600 for the piano. *Iris accepted this offer.* Later that day Iris *posted a letter to Diana telling her that she could not have the piano.* Mercury, the postman, delivered it to the wrong address and Diana, *who never received it*, appeared with a *hired van* to collect the piano at 10 o'clock on Saturday morning.

Advise Iris of her legal position.

The issues of law raised by the problem

1 Unconditional acceptance is essential to contract formation.

2 Promises are not contractually binding without consideration.

3 Acceptance must be communicated.

4 Revocation can take place up to the moment of acceptance.

5 Notice of revocation is necessary to make it effective.

6 Note that you are told that an offer was made by Iris, so you do not need to discuss whether or not an offer exists.

The points of law pinpointed by the 'triggers'

1 *If*: conditional acceptance is not binding, therefore no contract formed yet.

2 *Promise*: Iris is not bound to keep offer open until Saturday, unless Diana pays to keep the offer open (*Routledge* v *Grant* (1828)).

3 *She had got the money, and would come to collect the piano*: intention to accept?

4 *Athena forgot to pass on the message*: has acceptance been communicated? (*Entores* v *Miles Far East Corporation; Brinkibon*).

5 *Posted a letter . . . never received it*: revocation possible up to time of acceptance (*Payne* v *Cave*). Notice essential (*Dickinson* v *Dodds*). Postal revocation is not effective until received (*Byrne* v *Van Tienhoven*).

6 *Hired van*: acceptance by conduct (*Brogden* v *Metropolitan Railway*), or does she verbally accept before she is told of the revocation? If effective acceptance, a contract results. Iris is liable for breach and must compensate Diana for resulting losses.

Writing discursive assignments

Students often incorrectly assume that writing essays and reports is easier than answering problems, but careful analysis is necessary to ensure that you discover exactly what you are being asked to do and how you are required to present the relevant information. A question will not tell you to write everything you know about a topic. Drifting from the point or failing to present the required analysis will lose you marks. The important points to remember are as follows:

1 *Make sure you understand the question*. Analyse it carefully. Look for the *key words*. These tell you what information is required and *how* to present your answer. 'How' words include: 'compare', 'discuss', 'distinguish between', 'critically assess', 'what are the advantages/disadvantages of', 'explain'. Sometimes you may be required to present information in the form of a memorandum or report. Head this appropriately with the relevant title and present it with side headings, using numbered points if appropriate.

2 *Carry out your research*. Apart from checking your existing knowledge of the topic, you will need to refer to additional sources and make notes of relevant points with source references.

3 *Plan your answer in writing*. You need to jot down the points to be made, paragraph-by-paragraph.

4 *Write your first draft.* Remember the warnings against plagiarism above and take care to use your own words. Proof-read and amend and correct, where necessary, and make sure your sources are clearly referenced.

5 *Edit thoroughly.* This is best done after a break. Going back to your work will enable you to spot accurately where improvements may be made apart from doing the obvious things like a spell check. Maybe you need to cut and paste to make your work flow more logically. Now is the time to check for repetition and anything you feel unsure about in terms of content and meaning of particular words. You may find that you still have a lot to do. Are you still within the word limit? Have you indicated all your sources?

6 *Final checks.* Read through your work one more time and check your student hand-book to make sure you have fulfilled the presentation requirements.

Revision and examination technique

Few people enjoy the examination process. However, everybody can make the process less stressful and more productive by ensuring that they both revise for and perform in the exam as effectively as possible. Much of what follows in this chapter may seem very obvious but her experience as a lecturer has informed the writer that students find it helpful to be reminded of apparently simple things that they may forget under the pressure of the circumstances. As with everything else in the study process, structure and good organisation are essential to ensuring that you fulfil your potential.

Revision

Effective preparation is essential to success: lack of it undermines your confidence and thus doubly impairs your examination performance. You may find the following tips helpful.

Time planning

1 Make yourself a realistic revision timetable

This must take into account all your other commitments and your likely concentration span. Short periods (30–45 minutes) are usually the most effective. Hours spent unre-mittingly at a desk are likely to produce little more than a sense of virtue and a headache.

2 Prioritise your study time

Where you have a choice, study at the times of day when you find it easiest to concen-trate. While you may be sacrificing time that you would probably rather spend else-where, it is important that you view this short-term loss as producing long-term gains. If you have family commitments, be aware of the need to take time for yourself at this important point in your life. What is good for you will be good for your family as well in the long term. If you go out to work, check your entitlement to study leave or even consider taking some of your holiday entitlement.

3 Stick to your timetable

It is very important to ensure that you revise across the syllabus and do not get bogged down in the areas that you are least confident about. Keep to your schedule as tightly as possible, but be prepared to adapt and rationalise if necessary. Once you have given the allotted time to a particular topic, do not tweak it, polish it or check whether you remember it. Press on to the next goal.

Revision technique

1 Thorough reading is essential

Your primary aim is to consolidate your existing knowledge. Ensure that you have the basics of each topic at your fingertips. These act as recall points: magnets and foundations to which more peripheral knowledge will stick. If you have fully covered your revision you may choose to read something new, to avoid getting stale. Possibly, if you are this well prepared, you should consider taking some time off to give yourself space for assimilation and refreshment. It is possible to over-prepare, though this is likely to be a problem for only a minority of students. If you are struggling against time constraints or the intricacies of subject matter, it may be best to stick to one clear source of information like lecture notes or handouts.

Don't be lulled into a false sense of security by an 'open book' exam. Just because you are permitted to take a specified text into the exam does not mean you can ignore it beforehand. The best students find it more of a comfort blanket than of practical use. You don't have time to ferret about looking for relevant bits in a book under the pressure of a time-constrained exam. Under these circumstances a book is generally only useful for checking things like a statute section number or case name. Check the regulations to ensure book marking or other identifying marks are permitted. If it is permissible, mark it appropriately, and be prepared to use it sparingly.

2 Note-taking while you read

This generally helps concentration and can provide useful reference points for last-minute revision. List the main points of each topic. Reduce cases to a couple of sentences, briefly conveying the essence of the facts and decision in your own words. If you can do this it proves your understanding of the essential points. Consequently, you will be much more likely to remember them. It is also good practice for the examination, when your own words are what will count.

3 Testing your knowledge

When you have covered a topic, try and find/identify some relevant specimen questions. Draft answer plans, or try writing a timed answer. Use textbook quizzes. Suggested solutions may be helpful as a guide to question-answering technique but are not necessarily reliable in terms of content, so handle with care. Get someone to ask you questions: while a fellow student is best, any long-suffering friend or family member will do. If you have a study group, encourage regular meetings. If you don't, maybe now is the time to form one. It can be very supportive and help to lend structure to work.

4 Working out your battle plan

Most of us find taking exams hard. This is largely because it is an alien experience, not something that we often do. It is possible, however, to make some plans for effective use of time in the examination. The questions you have been given in tutorials may well resemble the sort of thing you will face on the day. Past papers if available are invaluable in terms of both form and content. Observe how questions are formulated. Decide which questions in each paper you would answer, avoiding any where the examiner does not make it clear what is required. Identify the advantages and disadvantages of different types of question. Remember that although it is often easier to pick up a good mark with a question that covers a number of different topics, this will require a reasonably lengthy exposition. If a question focuses on one small area, this can be useful when you are running short of time, since you may be able to convey the main points quickly. While it is too much to hope that these skills will become second nature, there is no doubt that studying the form and content of past papers, practising effective analysis routines and considering the best use of time will help you to make the correct choices on the day.

5 Maintaining your morale

The exam season is a depressing and stressful time for most students. While this is to some extent inevitable, there are many ways of reducing the problem. Take good physical care of yourself: your brain will work more efficiently if you have enough sleep, exercise, fresh air and the right sort of food.

Give yourself rewards: try to do something you find pleasant in some of your breaks between study sessions. Get away from your desk or computer. If you can, network with your fellow students to avoid feeling isolated. It helps to know that you are not the only one who is finding things difficult. Remember that feeling stressed can be beneficial: most people work better under a degree of pressure. Feeling too relaxed can inhibit effective revision. Do not be afraid to ask for help from lecturers or personal tutors, who will have had much experience of helping students prepare for exams. You may find it helpful to use the college or university counselling service.

The examination

However thoroughly you have revised, you will not reap your just rewards unless you acquit yourself well in the exam room. There are certain survival tactics that will help to keep you calm and promote efficiency. Some are very obvious, but are worth thinking about in advance so that they do not get overlooked in the heat of the moment.

1 *Do make sure that you know the location of the exam and how to get there.*

2 *Do arrive in plenty of time with all appropriate equipment.*

3 *Do not be in too much of a hurry to start writing.* Read the exam paper thoroughly before you start. Check the instructions. How many questions must you answer? Are any of them compulsory? Mark the questions you like the look of.

4 *Do start with the question that you like best.* But check that it really is as good as you first thought; under stress it is easy to misread.

5 *Do plan your answers.* It may be advisable to spend between 20–25 per cent of your time on planning, particularly if you are dealing with a complex problem. Always re-read a question and briefly list the points you wish to make before you begin to write your answer. Make sure that you are answering the question that the examiners asked, not the one you wish they had asked. Examiners constantly remark that failure to grasp the point of a question is the biggest cause of lost marks. Embrace the full scope of the question: check that you have spotted all the 'triggers' in a problem. It is better to cover every point the question raises superficially than cover one or two points in great detail. Marks will be spread across the question so you throw them away by ignoring points raised by the question.

In essay questions, make sure that you have correctly analysed the 'key words' indicating the topics involved and the method of presentation required (see above). Do keep an eye on the time. Set a time limit for each question and stick to it. Remember that most people pick up the majority of marks in the first 50 per cent of the writing time per question. If you do find yourself running out of time, answer any remaining questions in note form. Remember that if you fail to answer the required number of questions, you are potentially throwing away a vital percentage of marks (maybe 20–25 per cent per question).

6 *Do not leave before the end of the exam.* Use any spare time to check your paper: correct clerical errors, ensure that each question is numbered properly. If you have finished with more than a very few minutes in hand the chances are that something is wrong, so use the time to try to put it right. Check what you have written and see if anything needs amending. If you have left out any questions, make a stab at some answers: you might gain the crucial few marks that separate a pass from a failure (or a distinction from a pass). Even if it is the exam paper from hell, do not run away from it. Having completed a course (usually at considerable expense) you have nothing to lose from having a go. If you write nothing, nothing is what you will get. You are in with a chance: exploit it. If you placed a bet on a horse, would you shoot it before the race?

7 *Do present your work as clearly as possible.* Never copy the question from the exam paper; this only wastes valuable time. You can answer questions in any order you like, but do make sure that each question is numbered correctly. Present each question on a fresh page, leaving space to insert any forgotten points at the end of the exam. It is best to use dark ink. Take care with your handwriting, and, if you have time, underline the cases and statutes that you have quoted. This all helps to keep the examiners on your side: remember that they may be marking hundreds of scripts and will be grateful for a clearly presented paper.

Conclusion

Hopefully you will find the above study hints useful and that they will help you to get the most out of your course, with enjoyment along the way and a happy outcome.

CHAPTER 2

The nature of law

Introduction

You may be thinking that you will skip this chapter and go straight to the 'real' law topics on your syllabus. However, it could be good to read this before you start your lectures as it will help to give you insight into the distinctive features of legal rules within the English legal system resulting from its long historical development. This can help you to make sense of how the law operates today. It will also give you a head start by introducing you to some of the essential technical terms that you will meet in your studies.

Learning objectives

When you have studied this chapter you should be able to:

▶ appreciate the distinguishing features of a legal rule;

▶ explain the characteristics of English law;

▶ state its purposes;

▶ distinguish between civil and criminal law;

▶ use basic legal terms confidently and with understanding.

What is law?

English law may be defined as a body of rules, created by the state, binding within its jurisdiction and enforced with the authority of the state through the use of sanctions. Here is an analysis of this definition.

Rules

Rules are commands aimed at regulating behaviour. Rules tell us what we can and cannot do; sometimes they may permit behaviour subject to fulfilling a condition. For example, an extension of business premises is illegal unless planning permission is obtained; a shop may not sell alcohol without a licence.

Created by the state

Parliament is responsible for creating most of the law applicable in the UK. Such law is contained in *Acts of Parliament* or *statutes*. Increasingly, the content of much of this law is determined by the European Union, and in this respect Parliament does not have complete independence. Since the Human Rights Act 1998, the European Convention on Human Rights is directly enforceable in the English courts.

The jurisdiction of the state

The law of any country is binding only within its territory. The UK Parliament may introduce laws applicable to the UK as a whole, but this book is concerned with the relevant law as it applies in England and Wales.

State enforcement

A legal dispute may require formal resolution by the court or tribunal. The state or a party to the dispute may initiate the enforcement proceedings.

A sanction or penalty may be imposed in order to compensate the injured party or punish the wrongdoer.

The characteristics of English law

English law has characteristics that make it very different from the law of other countries in the European Union.

It has evolved slowly and without interruption over many centuries

The origins of the English legal system can be traced to the Norman Conquest in 1066. Although huge changes have taken place since then, development has been gradual and piecemeal. As a result, a rather untidy and conservative evolution has taken place, with historical relics rubbing shoulders with more modern developments. For example, two divisions of the High Court today still carry traces of the names of their forebears in mediaeval times: the Court of King's Bench (now the Queen's Bench Division) and the Court of Chancery (the Chancery Division).

Lack of Roman law influence

English law has been little influenced by the Roman law principles which dominate the legal systems of other European countries and which also have some influence on Scots law.

Judges have creative powers

Judges were the principal lawmakers until their powers were superseded by Parliament in the eighteenth century; senior judges today still have some limited powers to develop principles of case law. The powers of other European judges are restricted to interpretation of the legal codes created by the relevant state legislatures.

The doctrine of binding precedent

Precedent: previous judicial decision influential and possibly binding in later cases.

When deciding a case, English judges are bound to apply any relevant **precedent** (previous decision) of a senior court, unlike their other European counterparts who are guided, rather than bound, by previous cases.

Adversarial nature

Adversarial procedure: trial in which judge acts like the referee in the contest between two opposing litigants.

Inquisitorial procedure: the judge helps to establish the evidence by actively questioning witnesses.

The procedure in the English courts is largely **adversarial**. A case in the courts is essentially a contest before an umpire (the judge) whose principal tasks are to see that the rules of evidence are obeyed and to decide who the winner is. Case names look rather like football fixture lists: *Bloggs* v *Snodgrass*. The main burden of proof is on the accuser, and the party who can produce the most convincing evidence wins the case. The judge plays very little part in drawing out that evidence; too much judicial intervention may lead to the decision being reversed at an appeal. It has been said that the adversarial system is about proving facts rather than discovering truth.

The function of judges on mainland Europe is an **inquisitorial** one; this gives the judge power to call witnesses and question them during the hearing of the case. English judges are currently being encouraged to take a more interventionist role as case managers, before the hearing of complex cases, but this extension of their function is still a long way from a truly inquisitorial approach.

Why do we need law?

Any society, or group within it, however small, will make rules for the purposes of organisation, to promote the safety and convenience of members and to regulate their relationships with each other. An affluent industrialised state requires a complex system of law that aims to fulfil a number of purposes. Figure 2.1 shows how the law may be classified.

A system of law may be needed for the following reasons:

1 to provide a governmental structure and legislative procedures: constitutional law;

2 to provide public services and to raise taxes to pay for them: administrative and revenue law;

3 to regulate and promote the economy: administrative, civil and criminal law are all involved;

4 to promote public order and preserve national security: criminal law;

5 to give individual members personal rights and duties in relation to others and to enable personal enforcement of these rights: the civil law. civil law duties may arise through agreement between the parties (the law of contract), or be imposed directly (the law of tort);

6 to give legal validity to approved relationships and transactions between members of the society: this involves the law of contract, the law of property and succession, company and partnership law, and family law.

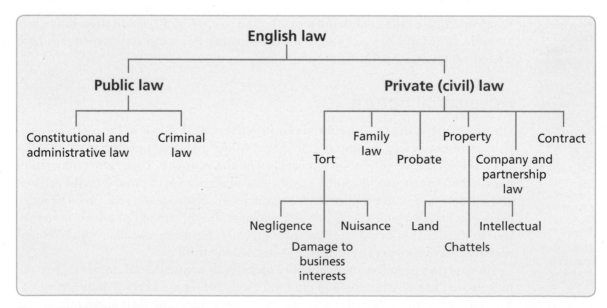

Figure 2.1 Classification of English law

The differences between criminal and civil law

It is important from the outset to understand the differences between civil and criminal law. Dual liability for a breach of both civil and criminal law may arise from the same set of facts; but since these two branches of the law have very different purposes, their procedures and penalties differ radically. The following example illustrates these crucial differences.

Real life

Alice is treated to a hot lobster lunch at 'The Fat Cat Wine Bar' by Horace. Subsequently, both Alice and Horace become ill with food poisoning, which they claim was caused by the insanitary condition of Fat Cat's kitchen.

The criminal proceedings

R[egina] v Fat Cat

Selling impure food is a criminal offence under the Food Safety Act 1990: it is in the interests of public safety to control and punish such behaviour.

In this sort of case, Fat Cat may be prosecuted in the magistrates' court by the local authority's trading standards department, rather than by the police. The burden of proving Fat Cat's guilt lies on the prosecutor, who has to prove *beyond all reasonable doubt* that the food poisoning was caused by the condition of the lobster.

If Fat Cat is found guilty, he may be fined: a fine is a sum of money payable to the court; it does not go to the victims of the crime.

The civil proceedings

Horace v Fat Cat

Alice v Fat Cat

Horace and Alice want compensation for having been made ill. Both are self-employed and, in addition to the pain and inconvenience of their illness, they have also lost earnings while they were laid low.

Two separate claims are involved: Horace, who bought the food, will sue for breach of contract, as the lobster was clearly not of satisfactory quality; Alice, who was harmed by the food but had no contract with Fat Cat, will sue in tort claiming negligence or breach of the Consumer Protection Act 1987.

Horace and Alice will take action in the county court and will have to prove that on *the balance of probabilities* Fat Cat caused their problems. This is a lower standard of proof than that required in criminal proceedings, as the court requires it to be proved only that it is more likely than not that Fat Cat was responsible.

If Horace and Alice win, damages will be payable to them by Fat Cat to compensate them for their pain and suffering and all economic loss resulting from it, including medical costs and loss of earnings. Horace will also be able to reclaim the cost of the meal.

A summary of the differences between civil and criminal law

Criminal law	Civil law
Purpose	
Regulates behaviour perceived as being anti-social and dangerous to the public.	Gives legal rights to individuals to govern their formal and informal relationships with each other.
Provides machinery by which the state may take action against offenders.	Provides the means by which they may enforce the rights arising from these relationships.
Procedure	
Generally started by the police, but some legislation is enforced by other agencies like local authorities or Revenue & Customs.	Civil proceedings are taken against the alleged lawbreaker by the party who claims that they have been wronged.
Exceptionally, a private prosecution may be brought by an individual. The victim usually plays no part in the decision to prosecute.	The case may not go to trial even if proceedings are started. Most civil law claims are settled out of court without any threat of legal action. In many others, the proceedings are abandoned before trial.
Once started, a case will proceed to trial in the magistrates' court or the Crown Court.	Most civil cases are heard in the county court and the High Court and in certain specialised tribunals.
The prosecution must prove that the accused is guilty beyond all reasonable doubt.	The claimant must prove that the defendant is liable on the balance of probability.
Penalties	
Focus on the accused and the need to protect society against criminal conduct.	Focus on the needs of the victim and generally require the wrongdoer to pay damages, which are often covered by insurance.
The ultimate aim is to control the criminal, while protecting society from future anti-social conduct.	Exceptionally, the court – by injunction or other equitable remedy – may require some practical correction of the wrong. This is usual in domestic violence cases.
A penalty may be used to contain criminals by depriving them of their freedom, or to rehabilitate them; it may be intended to deter them or others from committing future crimes.	

Changing the law

It is important to realise that the law is subject to frequent change. Very few principles actually remain constant. These changes reflect social, political, economic and technological developments taking place within society.

Social change

Changes in moral values have influenced a number of legal developments in the last 50 years, including reform of the divorce law, decriminalisation of abortion, as well as the introduction of legislation to prevent discrimination on the grounds of sex, race, sexual orientation, disability, religion or belief and age.

Political change

No government can initiate new policies unless it has legal authority to do so. This means that the law may require constant, and often radical, change. The privatisation of the water, gas and electricity utilities was achieved by repeal of previous legislation, which had introduced a policy of nationalisation.

Economic and technological change

Much of the law governing commerce and industry, including the regulation of health and safety at work, is subject to such influence. As industrial practice changes, old hazards disappear and new ones develop. For example, the commercial exploitation of the internal combustion engine has led to the development of a huge body of road traffic law.

In practice, these influences and political change may be interlinked: an economic or social issue is often the focus of a political policy.

Essential legal terms

Claimant: the party who brings a civil action.

Defendant: person against whom criminal or civil proceedings are brought.

Defence (the): the person being prosecuted in a criminal trial/their legal representatives.

Accused (the): the person being prosecuted in criminal trial.

The Prosecution/ the Crown : the prosecutor in criminal proceedings.

This book has been kept as free as possible from lawyers' jargon. However, there are a few common words and phrases explained below, which are useful shorthand. You will also find a list of the key terms arising from the particular topics under examination, at the end of each chapter. You may find it useful to look through these when you have finished reading each chapter to check your understanding.

The claimant and defendant

These are the parties in a civil case (*action*). The **claimant** *sues* (brings the case against) the **defendant**.

The prosecution and the defence

These are the parties to a criminal case. The '**defence**' is sometimes called the *defendant* or the **accused**. The prosecution is sometimes called the **Crown**, reflecting the fact that criminal proceedings are brought by the state in the name of the Crown. This is why criminal cases are usually reported as *R* v (*Snodgrass*).

The appellant and the respondent

These are the parties in a civil or criminal appeal hearing. The appellant is the party who is bringing the appeal against the decision of the court below, in which the respondent won his or her case.

The common law

This has two possible meanings. The relevant meaning is usually clear from the context.

Case law as opposed to statute law

Common law: various meanings determined by context: law applicable to the whole of England/judge-made law rather than statute/ not the law of equity.

When the **common law** first began to develop in the early centuries after the Norman Conquest, there was no centralised legal system and there were great variations in the law across England. Judges appointed by the Crown had the task of welding together a system of law applicable (and therefore *common*) to the country as a whole. This law gradually emerged from principles developed and applied to cases which came before the courts. Common law in this context means judge-made law.

Case law and statute law as opposed to principles of equity

Equity (law of): complements the common law by principles based on morality as well as legal right and practical remedies granted at the discretion of the court.

The civil law sometimes allows the court to exercise discretionary powers, which are based not just on the legal rights of the parties, but on what will produce a just and moral solution. These discretionary rules are part of the **law of equity**. They protect only those parties who are *morally* as well as *legally* entitled to a remedy.

Equitable principles govern the issue of court orders like injunctions and some contractual remedies which are described later in this book. They are the foundation of the law of mortgages and trusts, since they seek to protect the vulnerable parties to the transaction from the abuse of power by lenders and trustees respectively.

The law of equity has its origins in the fourteenth century; it was initially developed by successive Lord Chancellors to put right the defects that had become apparent in the common law system. Lord Chancellors for many years were churchmen as well as lawyers, which gave this branch of the law the emphasis on moral principle that governs its operation in the civil courts today. Its principles co-exist with other principles of common law (statute and case law in this context) and may come into play at the discretion of the court where the common law principle or remedy will cause injustice.

Chapter summary

A definition of law

A body of rules imposed by the state and with authority within it and enforceable by sanctions imposed by the courts.

Characteristics of English law

Antiquity, lengthy evolution untouched by Roman law, creative power and authority of the judiciary, adversarial procedure.

Differences between criminal and civil law

Criminal law is enforced by the state and aims to protect the public from anti-social behaviour.

Civil law enables individuals to enforce rights governing their formal and informal relationships in the courts.

Quiz 1

1 What distinguishes law from other rules?

2 What does the court hope to achieve when imposing a criminal sentence?

3 What does a civil litigant hope to achieve by taking a case to court?

4 What are the likely legal consequences in the following case? Sparrow, who has had too much to drink, carelessly crashes his taxi into Finch's lorry. Sparrow's passenger, Wren, is injured and Finch's lorry is damaged. PC Hawk witnesses the incident.

Answers to all quizzes can be found in Appendix 2.

CHAPTER 3

How the law is made

Introduction

This chapter explains where our law comes from and how it is made. There are currently three important sources of law:

1 European law;
2 Parliament;
3 The courts.

The European Union and the British Parliament are the primary sources, but the courts also have a minor (though important) law-making role. The courts also have a crucial role in the interpretation of legislation. The European Convention of Human Rights has become increasingly influential in the development of English law since its obligations became enforceable in the domestic courts.

The rights and duties of business owners, at every point from setting up and running to selling on or closing down are determined by the law in various forms. For example; the Companies Act 2006 regulates setting up and closing down a corporate business, partnership formation and dissolution are governed by the Partnership Act 1890. While running the business, the owner's relationship to employees is governed by a variety of statutes including the Employments Rights Act 1996 and the Equality Act 2010, on which European Law has been very influential. Buying and selling goods and services is governed by the law of contract, which combines a number of statutes with a fair proportion of judge-made law. Judge-made (common) law governs much of the law of tort.

Learning objectives

When you have studied this chapter you should be able to:

▶ name the sources of English law;

▶ distinguish between the functions of the institutions of the European Union;

▶ differentiate between EC regulations, directives and decisions;

▶ describe the legislative process in Parliament;

▶ explain the application of the doctrine of precedent in the English courts;

▶ describe the differing judicial approaches to interpreting statutes;

▶ appreciate the effect of the Human Rights Act 1998 on the development of English law.

European law

The law of the European Community has been a source of UK law since 1973, when the UK became a member of what was then called the European Economic Community (EEC). The 1992 Treaty on European Union (the Maastricht Treaty) officially changed the name to European Community to signify that the objectives of the Community are not just economic. The Maastricht Treaty also created the European Union (EU), which consists of three 'pillars'. In the middle pillar are the three existing Communities, i.e. the European Coal and Steel Community (ECSC), the European Atomic Energy Treaty Community (EURATOM) and the Economic Community. These three Communities are known collectively as the European Community. On either side of this central pillar are the Common Foreign and Security Policy (CFSP), and Police and Judicial Co-operation in Criminal Matters (PJCCM). These three pillars support the overarching constitutional order of the Union. However, Community law only governs the EC. The CFSP and the PJCCM pillars are governed by intergovernmental cooperation. This means that they are outside the jurisdiction of the Community institutions, particularly the Court of Justice. Also, none of the articles of the outside pillars are enforceable, or challengeable, in national courts. Thus, although the Union is wider than the European Community, it has its roots within it. EC law is an important source of business law and you will notice its impact in a number of topic areas in this book, such as product safety and employment law. The European Community (EC) is currently composed of 28 member states.

Under the European Communities Act 1972 (ECA 1972), s 2, EU law is part of UK law. In the event of conflict, EU law takes priority. Disputed points of EU law must be referred by the domestic courts for interpretation to the Court of Justice of the European Union (CJEU), or be decided in accordance with principles found in its existing decisions.

The principal institutions of the European Union

The Council of the European Union

Council of the European Union: consists of the government minister from each EU state whose portfolio reflects the business of the meeting (e.g. Internal Affairs).

(Note that rather confusingly, this may also be referred to as the 'Council of the EU' or sometimes just 'the Council'. It must not be confused with the European Council, which is entirely separate.) The **Council of the European Union** is the main legislative organ of the Community and within it the interests of member states find direct expression. It also has responsibility for approving the EU budget and developing foreign and community policies. It is made up of 'a representative of each Member State at ministerial level, authorised to commit the government of that Member State' (Treaty of Nice, Article 203). The representatives vary according to the subject matter under discussion. For General Council meetings, a member state's representative is generally its foreign minister. The ministers of state with the relevant portfolio attend all other meetings. For example, a meeting will be made up of agriculture ministers when the common agricultural policy is under discussion. The President of the Council of Ministers chairs the meetings. The presidency rotates every six months between the heads of state or heads of government of the member states.

The European Council

European Council: an EU institution composed of the foreign ministers from each member state.

The **European Council** is composed of the heads of state or of government of the member states. It meets at least twice a year in order to discuss major Community issues in a less formal atmosphere than that which prevails at the Council of the EU. It is chaired on a six-monthly rotation by the current President of the Council of the EU, assisted by the minister of foreign affairs of each of the member states and a member of the Commission. The European Council's function is to provide the Union with the necessary impetus to define the general political guidelines for its development.

The European Commission

The Commission is composed of one nominee from each member state and is an executive and policy-making body with legislative powers. Most major decisions taken by the Council must be made on the basis of proposals from the Commission. Currently there are 28 Commissioners, but once appointed they represent Community interests rather than national interests.

The European Parliament

The **European Parliament** consists of 751 members directly elected by people with the right to vote in each member state. The number of MEPs each state is entitled to elect is determined in proportion to its population size. The UK currently returns 78 members. Parliament exercises democratic supervision over the Commission, with the appointment of the President and members of the Commission subject to its approval. The Commission is thus politically answerable to the Parliament, which can pass a 'motion of censure' calling for its resignation. Together with the Council, Parliament formulates and adopts legislation proposed by the Commission.

The European Court of Justice (ECJ)

The **European Court of Justice** is made up of 28 judges assisted by advocates-general. If the court so requests, the Council may, acting unanimously, increase the number of advocates-general. The judges and advocates-general are appointed by common agreement of the governments of the member states and hold office for a renewable term of six years. They are chosen from legal experts whose independence is beyond doubt and who possess the qualifications required for appointment to the highest judicial offices in their respective countries or who are of recognised competence. The judges select one of their number to be President of the court for a renewable term of three years. The President directs the work of the court and its staff and presides at hearings and deliberations of major formations of the court.

The advocates-general assist the court in its task. They deliver independent and impartial opinions in all cases in open court, where a case does not raise any new points of law, unless the court decides otherwise. Their duties should not be confused with those of a public prosecutor or similar body.

The court has two functions:

1 to interpret any point of EU law referred by the courts of member states. It is mandatory for the highest appeal court of any member state to make a referral, if the meaning of a principle of EU law is unclear;

2 to decide the outcome of cases alleging breaches of EU legal obligations, brought by EU institutions, member states or individuals.

Once the court has reached its decision, this is immediately effective. It takes precedence over any conflicting domestic legislation. Individual states have responsibility for implementing the court's decisions by changing the relevant domestic law. Reluctance to comply may result in pressure from other member states. Since the Maastricht Treaty, a penalty may be imposed on any state which does not comply with a judgment. With the passage of time it became apparent that too many demands were being placed on the court, which is why the Single European Act 1987 introduced the Court of First Instance (CFI). The CFI is made up of one judge from each member state. The judges are appointed for a renewable term of six years by common accord of the governments of the member states. There are no permanent advocates-general attached to the CFI. All cases heard at first instance by the Court of First Instance may be subject to a right of appeal to the Court of Justice on points of law only.

The sources of European law

The treaties

The most important of these are the Treaty of Rome 1957 and the Maastricht Treaty 1992, as revised by the Treaty of Lisbon 2009, which define the constitution of the EU. The Treaty of Amsterdam 1997 and the Treaty of Nice 2003 also had an important constitutional effect as well as changing and enlarging obligations of member states. Some of these obligations are directly enforceable by individual citizens, regardless of whether the relevant member state has taken legislative action to implement them. Such directly enforceable obligations include those under Article 119 (now 141) of the Treaty of Rome, which relates to the equal treatment of men and women in employment.

Regulations

Regulation:
EU legislation which is directly effective in UK.

Regulations are intended to impose uniformity of law throughout the Community. They take effect in all member states immediately on being issued.

Directives

Directive:
EU legislation aimed at harmonising the law of member states; becomes effective once domestic law is passed to implement it.

Directives comprise the most prolific source of law in the EC. Directives apply to all member states and are intended to lead to harmonisation of law between member states, making it similar but not identical. Directives set the aims which must be achieved but leave the choice of the form and method of implementation to each member state. Thus, they have to be implemented by national parliaments. Implementation legislation may reflect the legal and social conventions of each member state.

States are required to implement directives within specified time limits, but sometimes drag their heels if a particular directive is unpopular. The Court of Justice may permit claims by individuals against an organ of a member state (though not an individual) for breaches of a directive which has not yet been implemented, provided that the wording of the directive is sufficiently clear and unconditional.

Decisions

Decision:
EU legislation binding in one state only.

A **decision** affects only particular member states, companies or individuals. It may empower the party to whom it is issued to do something, or prevent it from doing something.

The impact of EU membership on English law

The main impact so far has been felt in the areas of trade, industry, employment, the environment, provision of financial services and the promotion of equality and social justice. Membership of the EU has, therefore, had considerable influence in many areas of business law. A number of references to such developments will be found throughout this book.

As the scope of European law expands through new treaties, its impact on English law, politics and society at large increases. The Treaty of Amsterdam, which came into force on 1 May 1999, aims to place employment and citizens' rights at the heart of the Union, to remove the last remaining obstacles to freedom of movement within the Union and to strengthen security. This had a considerable impact on human rights in Britain. It required the widening of the existing principles of non-discrimination legislation in employment with regards to gender, race, ethnic origin and disability to include religious belief, age and sexual orientation. Directives on all these issues were issued to member states and implementation has taken place. (For details see Chapter 17.)

The Treaty also seeks to promote privacy of citizens' personal data. The security issues within the Treaty will also have an impact on criminal law and procedure, since the Treaty requires the police and the judiciary of all member states to coordinate action on terrorism, offences against children, drug trafficking, corruption and fraud. It also requires member states to cooperate more closely in the fight against racism and discrimination in general, while promoting equality before the law and social justice.

Parliament

Direct legislation: law made by Parliament/Acts of Parliament.

Delegated legislation: law made by a body authorised to do so by Act of Parliament.

Private Member's Bill: proposed by a backbench MP, as opposed to a minister (Government Bill).

Green Paper: discussion paper containing proposals for new legislation.

White Paper: details of proposed legislation with explanation of what it is intended to achieve.

Most English law is currently made by, or with the authority of, Parliament. **Direct (parliamentary/primary) legislation** comprises Acts of Parliament, created by the passage of a Bill through certain prescribed processes in the House of Commons and the House of Lords. Indirect **(delegated) legislation** is created by a body (usually a government department or local authority) which has been given the power to legislate by Parliament under an *enabling* Act.

How an Act of Parliament is created

Most legislation is proposed by government ministers, but backbench MPs have limited opportunities to put forward **Private Members' Bills**. These usually relate to non-party-political issues. In practice, few Private Members' Bills become Acts because of the limited amount of parliamentary time available to them.

The pre-legislative stage

A Government Bill is usually preceded by the issue of a **Green Paper**, which sets out the legislative proposals for discussion. Consultation with relevant interest groups may take place. A **White Paper** is then issued, which lays down the principles on which the draft Bill is based.

Parliamentary procedure

The first stage of a Bill's journey through Parliament is *the introduction and first reading*. Most Bills are initially processed in the House of Commons and then go through the same procedures in the House of Lords. All important and controversial Bills, including all money Bills, must start off in the Commons. The first reading is a formality to announce the existence of the Bill and to set down a date for the second reading.

The *second reading* involves a full debate which starts with a speech from the minister who is proposing the Bill. This is answered by the relevant shadow minister. After con-tributions from any interested member, a vote is taken. Provided that a majority is in its favour, the Bill passes on to the committee stage.

At the *committee stage* a standing committee of 25–45, appointed in proportion to party representation, usually examines the Bill clause by clause. Amendments may be proposed. (Some Bills require consideration by a committee of the whole House. They do not have a report stage, but progress straight to the third reading.)

Following the committee stage the committee reports on its findings (the *report stage*), debate takes place on proposed changes, and further amendments may be proposed to the Bill.

At the *third reading* of the Bill, a short debate concentrates on the main points of the Bill. In the Commons, only superficial changes (to grammar or syntax) will be made, though greater changes may take place in the House of Lords.

The processes discussed above are repeated when the Bill reaches the House of Lords (*transfer to the other House*). Note that, under the Parliament Acts 1911 and 1949, the House of Lords cannot reject a Bill outright, although it may delay any Bill except a money Bill for up to a year: a money Bill can be delayed only for a month. The power to delay may give the Lords considerable power, as the government is likely to seek a compromise to enable it to pursue its policies.

The Bill next passes on to the *consideration stage*. Each House must consider and agree to all the amendments proposed by the other before the legislative process can proceed. This may be a lengthy process if the Bill is complex and controversial as disagreement and further amendment may occur with the Bill 'ping-ponging' between the two Houses until each has agreed to the exact wording of the disputed clauses.

Before the Bill can become an Act of Parliament and pass into law, it must receive the *Royal Assent*. By convention this is just a formality: hundreds of years have passed since the Crown took an active legislative role.

The date of implementation of the whole or any part of an Act of Parliament is usually specified in it.

Delegated legislation

This is indirect or secondary legislation made by bodies outside Parliament, through the exercise of legislative power delegated to them by Act of Parliament.

In practice, the bulk of law created every year is delegated, rather than direct. Such legislation is the means by which both central and local government agencies administer their policies. Over 2,000 such regulations are enacted annually. These may, for example, limit benefit entitlements, raise the required hygiene standards in a fast-food business, and help to keep local parks free from noise pollution.

3

How the law is made

There are four main types of delegated legislation:

1 *Orders in Council*. The Emergency Powers Acts 1939 and 1984 give law-making powers to the Privy Council in times of national emergency.

2 *Statutory instruments*. These are created by government departments to execute general principles of policy set out in the enabling Act of Parliament. The Consumer Credit Act 1974 empowers the Secretary of State to make rules to safeguard users and potential users of credit facilities. About 3,000 such instruments are created annually.

3 *Regulations to implement law from the EU*. The European Communities Act 1972, s 2, empowers ministers and government departments to implement directives and treaty provisions.

4 *Bye-laws*. These are made by local authorities and other bodies with statutory powers, like London Underground and Network Rail, to regulate the facilities which they provide.

The use of delegated legislation is somewhat controversial. In general, however, its practical advantages outweigh its disadvantages. The advantages of delegated legislation are:

1 *Saving of parliamentary time*. The parliamentary legislative process is slow and protracted. Parliament finds it difficult to complete its annual legislative schedule and does not have time to debate the fine details of the regulations necessary to execute government policy.

2 *Specialist knowledge*. The creation of many regulations requires specialist knowledge not enjoyed by the average MP. They are, for example, unlikely to understand the finer points of abattoir management, or appreciate the appropriate levels of pork to be found in a sausage.

3 *Flexibility*. Such rules may be easily and quickly introduced, altered or extinguished, as and when appropriate.

4 *Legislation can take place when Parliament is not sitting*. This assists the smooth running of central and local government outside parliamentary sessions.

The disadvantages of delegated legislation are:

1 *Loss of parliamentary control*. Since details of policy administration are determined by the relevant government department, Parliament may be deprived of the opportunity to question and debate them. Scrutiny of most delegated legislation is negligible. It is laid before Parliament, but most of it is subject to a 'negative resolution' procedure. This means that it will be implemented as it stands unless an objection is sustained within the specified time limit. Exceptionally, the enabling Act may require Parliament positively to approve the regulations.

2 *Bulk and frequent change*. The huge quantity of delegated legislation produced every year makes it very difficult – even for lawyers – to keep abreast of all changes. Adapting to changes may considerably add to the burdens of running a business, despite the circulation of publicity by the regulating body.

The courts

Creative powers

The law made by the courts is case law, sometimes described as common law. Until the nineteenth century the courts were the primary law-makers, but were superseded by Parliament since social conditions required a different style of law-making. Case law evolves slowly and haphazardly, when relevant cases come before the courts with facts which justify further legal development. A point of case law may be very narrow in its effect since the courts can legislate only with regard to things that have already happened; they cannot legislate for what is to happen in future cases with different facts. This makes case law an inadequate form of law-making in a sophisticated industrial society, where blanket legislation is needed to regulate possible future problems.

Today the bulk of both civil and criminal law is statutory. New principles are most commonly developed in this way and much of the common law has been *codified* (converted into statutory form). The senior courts retain some limited creative powers, mainly in tort and contract law which are still not predominantly statutory. For example, the law of negligence (which is described in Chapters 13–14) has been, and mainly continues to be, developed by judges.

Interpretative powers

Since most law is now statutory, the courts are mainly concerned with the interpretation and application of points of law derived from Acts of Parliament and delegated legislation. When exercising this function the courts must respect the sovereignty of Parliament as a superior law-making body. A judge interpreting a statute will therefore aim to give such meaning to a disputed point of legislation as to reflect what Parliament seemed to have intended.

The words used in the statute are the main focus of the interpretation exercise and limit the freedom of the court. If the statute has an apparent gap and consequently an injustice exists, the court is not necessarily free to create the law to fill that gap, unless the context gives the necessary scope. Otherwise, all that the court can do is to recommend that Parliament amends the legislation.

Judges have a number of resources and tools, which may assist their interpretative function.

1 Intrinsic aids

These are found within the statute itself. It is common for an interpretation clause to be included which explains any special meaning to be given to words within the statute. For example, the Occupiers' Liability Act 1957 defines 'premises' as any 'fixed or moveable structure' (see Chapter 15).

3

How the law is made

2 External aids

These are materials which are not part of the statute itself. They include the following:

(a) The Interpretation Act 1978. This gives guidance on terms and phrases commonly found in legislation.

(b) Reports of the law commission or government inquiry. These may indicate why legislation is needed and thereby indicate its meaning.

(c) Parliamentary reports. Until 1993 the courts refused to admit evidence from Hansard reports of parliamentary proceedings relating to the passage of the statute. There were three main objections:

- the legislative and judicial functions of the state would be confused;
- the cut and thrust of parliamentary debate was unlikely to provide objective explanations;
- the research required to check *Hansard* would also add considerably to the cost of litigation.

Pepper v *Hart* (1993, HL)

Held (by majority): *Hansard* may be consulted by the courts if all the following circumstances exist:

- the disputed legislation is ambiguous or obscure, or the words taken at their face value produce an absurd result; and
- the *Hansard* extract consists of statements made by the relevant minister or other sponsor of the Bill; and
- the meaning of the extract is clear.

Pepper v *Hart* has been followed in a number of cases, but it is doubtful how far it is useful. The disputed section of an Act may not have been debated. Even if it was, any comments made may, in themselves, be ambiguous and confusing.

3 Judicial principles of statutory interpretation

The judiciary has developed the following practices to assist the interpretative process:

Contextual approach: vague words in a statute take their meaning from their immediate/general context.

Ejusdem generis rule: 'of the same class'. If a class of people/things is specified by the Act any person/thing within that class comes within the Act.

(a) *The contextual approach*. Any disputed words must always be interpreted within the context of the statute as a whole (a **contextual approach**). The significance of a vague, obscure or even apparently meaningless word may become crystal clear when scrutinised in relation to the surrounding text. The **ejusdem generis rule** forms part of the contextual approach. General words, like 'other animals', 'other person', or 'other thing' are meaningless in themselves. Their meaning may be clarified by reference to any specific words which precede them. Thus, if the words 'other animals' were preceded by the words 'cats, dogs and guinea pigs', it would be reasonable to assume that they include any animal commonly kept as a domestic pet. Generous interpretations are sometimes made to assist the perceived purpose of the statute. Thus in *Flack* v *Baldry* (1988) an electric shoc~~k~~ gun was held to come within the definition of 'any noxious liquid, ~~g~~ thing' under the Firearms Act 1968.

PART

Literal rule: the words of a statute must be taken at face value.

(b) *The literal rule*. A **literal rule** approach requires the court to take words at ~~t~~ value where there is no ambiguity and the meaning is clear, even if this p~~ro~~duces an absurd result.

Fisher v *Bell* (1960)

The defendant shopkeeper displayed a 'flick knife' (knife with a retractable blade) in his shop window and was charged with offering for sale an offensive weapon in breach of the Restriction of Offensive Weapons Act 1959, s 1(1).

Held: he was not guilty since, in contract law, a display of goods is an 'invitation to treat' and not 'an offer for sale' (see Chapter 5).

3

Golden rule: rule of statutory interpretation stating that if two literal meanings exist the least ridiculous be adopted.

The application of the rule in such a case has been justified by the courts on the ground that it is for Parliament to correct any practical problems arising from the statute. Any action by the courts is an unjustifiable interference with parliamentary sovereignty.

(c) *The golden rule*. The **golden rule** developed as a means of blunting the worst excesses of the literal rule. If the statute is ambiguous, the court will apply the least ridiculous meaning in order to avoid an absurd result.

Adler v *George* (1964)

A CND demonstrator who invaded a sentry post at an army base was charged with obstructing a member of HM Forces 'in the vicinity of a prohibited place' under the Official Secrets Act 1920. It was argued that since she had actually entered the base she was on it when the obstruction took place rather than in its vicinity.

Held: to dismiss the charge on the basis of a literal interpretation would produce an absurd result; 'vicinity' must be interpreted as including the place itself, not just its environs.

Smith v *Hughes* (1960)

A prostitute who, from her window, encouraged gentlemen passing in the street to avail themselves of her services was successfully prosecuted for 'soliciting in the street'.

Held: the purpose of the legislation was to prevent annoyance to people arising from the activities of prostitutes in public places. Since the effects of the defendant's conduct were felt by people in the street, that conduct clearly fell within the purpose of the Street Offences Act 1959.

(d) *The mischief rule*. The **mischief rule** is a sixteenth-century rule that allows the court to adopt a meaning which will enable the statute to fulfil its intended purpose. The court examines the law before the Act to discover the problem (mischief) which the statute was intended to correct; then the statute can be given the meaning which resolves the problem.

This rule largely fell into disfavour with the rise of the literal rule, which dominated judicial decision-making in the nineteenth century and for approximately the first 70 years of the twentieth century.

(e) The purposive approach. The purposive approach, which is somewhat similar to the mischief approach, but broader in its effect, has come into use since the UK's entry into the EC. The courts of other member states have traditionally used this approach, as does the European Court of Justice. It requires the court to interpret the statute by looking beyond its words to determine the general purpose behind it. To do this the court may examine relevant extrinsic documentary evidence such as government reports proposing the reform. The next case is a good example of this.

Royal College of Nursing v *DHSS* (1981, HL)

Under s 1(1) of the Abortion Act 1967 an abortion is legal only if carried out by a 'registered medical practitioner'. A change in abortion methods after the Act was passed meant that the procedure was largely carried out by nurses, subject to some supervision by a doctor. The courts had to decide whether abortions carried out by this procedure were legal under the Act.

The Court of Appeal (adopting a literal approach) held: the practice was unlawful since nurses do not have the necessary qualifications.

The House of Lords (by majority) held: a purposive approach should be used and that no illegality had occurred. Lord Diplock said: 'The approach of the Act seems to me to be clear. There are two aspects of it: the first, to broaden the grounds on which an abortion may be obtained; the second is to ensure that the abortion is carried out with proper skill and in hygienic conditions.'

(Before the Act legalised abortion in certain circumstances, many women died at the hands of back-street abortionists.)

The House of Lords' decision in *Pepper* v *Hart* (see above) may be seen as enabling and encouraging this approach. While the literal rule is still used today, a purposive approach is common where this assists a just outcome in the public interest. The court may use it to complement the literal rule: looking at the purpose of the statute will assist correct choice of meaning of an ambiguous word or phrase. It may be more radically used to correct an anomaly or fill a small gap.

Although called 'rules', it is more accurate to describe these judicial principles as 'tools' of interpretation. As *Royal College of Nursing* v *DHSS* (above) illustrates, they represent differing possible approaches to the interpretation process. They are not in any way superior or inferior to each other. Judges will choose what they view as the approach likely to produce the interpretation most beneficial to the public interest and which reflects current constitutional developments.

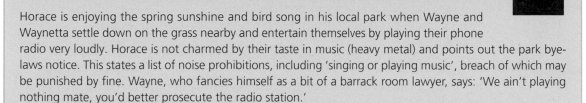

Real life

Horace is enjoying the spring sunshine and bird song in his local park when Wayne and Waynetta settle down on the grass nearby and entertain themselves by playing their phone radio very loudly. Horace is not charmed by their taste in music (heavy metal) and points out the park bye-laws notice. This states a list of noise prohibitions, including 'singing or playing music', breach of which may be punished by fine. Wayne, who fancies himself as a bit of a barrack room lawyer, says: 'We ain't playing nothing mate, you'd better prosecute the radio station.'

It would no doubt be wise of Horace to admit defeat at this point and find somewhere quieter to sit. However, he probably has the law on his side. A court considering the issue might well conclude that Wayne had breached the bye-laws. 'Playing music', even literally interpreted, is capable of including a radio transmission, so by using the golden rule approach an absurd result could be avoided by choosing the meaning of play as in 'a radio was playing music'. As the object of the bye-laws is to prevent noise pollution, a purposive approach would also include broadcast music.

4 Judicial presumptions

The courts will presume in the absence of clear evidence to the contrary that a statute will not:

(a) impose strict liability, i.e. where it is not necessary to prove that the accused intended to commit the offence;

(b) operate retrospectively, i.e. be said to apply to offences committed before the statute came into force;

(c) change the common law.

These presumptions may be contradicted (rebutted) only by express wording in the statute, or by clear implication to that effect.

Sweet v *Parsley* (1969, HL)

Miss Sweet let out a house which was raided by the police, who found cannabis in the possession of the tenants. Miss Sweet was charged with a statutory offence of 'being concerned in the management of premises' where the drugs were found.

Held: in the absence of a clear indication in the statute that she could be liable without reasonable knowledge of what was happening on her property, Miss Sweet was not guilty without proof of guilty knowledge. Strict liability was presumed not to have been intended.

The law of binding precedent

When exercising either their creative or interpretative functions, judges are bound by the law of binding precedent. This is a distinctive feature of the English legal system. In mainland European countries judges tend to follow each other's decisions in a similar way but are not obliged to do so. Their fellow judges' decisions are all **persuasive** but they are not **binding**. Under English law judges are not necessarily entitled to make their own decisions about the development or interpretation of the law. They may be bound by a decision reached in a previous case.

Two factors are crucial to determining whether a precedent (previous judicial decision) is binding:

1 the position in the court hierarchy of the court which decided the precedent, relative to the position of the court trying the current case. Inferior courts are bound by the decisions of superior courts (the letters SC, HL, CA and PC following the name of a case indicate that it involves an appeal in one of the higher courts);

2 whether the facts of the current case come within the scope of the principle of law in the previous decision.

> **Persuasive decision:** a non-binding but influential precedent.
>
> **Binding precedent:** a judicial decision which a court must follow.

The court hierarchy

1 The Supreme Court

> **Per incuriam:** a case decision found later to have been incorrectly reached, because the court did not have the opportunity to consider potentially relevant law.

Until October 2009 this court was called the House of Lords. It is the final court of appeal in England, Wales, Scotland and Northern Ireland. Its decisions (which now include all those previously reached by the House of Lords) are binding on all courts below. Before 1966, in the interests of preserving certainty, the court followed its own decisions unless a previous decision was reached *per incuriam*. Translated literally, this means 'through lack of care' caused by a failure by counsel to draw the attention of the court to crucial statutory or case law, preventing a correct decision from being reached. Since 1966 it has indicated that it is prepared to depart from existing decisions, if this is necessary to prevent injustice or unreasonable restriction of development of the common law.

Worth thinking about?

In what circumstances do you suppose that the Supreme Court would find a previous decision unjust or restrictive?

Suggested solutions can be found in Appendix 2.

---

2 The Court of Appeal

(a) The Civil Division of the Court of Appeal is bound by the decisions of the Supreme Court, and its decisions bind all the civil courts below. Subject to three exceptions laid down in *Young* v *Bristol Aeroplane Company* (1944), it is supposed to follow its own previous decisions. The exceptions are:

- two of its own previous decisions are in conflict: it must then choose which to follow; the one which is not chosen ceases to be good law;
- a previous decision conflicts with a decision of the Supreme Court: the decision of the Supreme Court must be followed;
- the previous decision was reached *per incuriam*.

(b) The Criminal Division of the Court of Appeal is bound by the decisions of the Supreme Court, and its decisions bind all the criminal courts below. It may depart from its own decisions where such flexibility is in the interests of justice.

3 The Divisional Courts

These are all bound by the Supreme Court and Court of Appeal decisions. The decisions of the Divisional Courts are binding on those courts from which they hear appeals. They follow their own decisions subject to the same exceptions as the Civil Division of the Court of Appeal.

4 The High Court

Judges in the High Court are bound by the decisions of the Supreme Court and Court of Appeal, but not by the decisions of their fellow judges. High Court decisions are binding on the Crown Court, county courts and magistrates' courts.

Decisions made in the Crown Court, the county courts and magistrates' courts are not binding in other cases or in other courts. Such courts, of course, are bound by the decisions of the relevant superior courts.

The relevance of the previous decision: the scope of the *ratio decidendi*

When judges have heard cases in the High Court or any of the courts above, they may deliver lengthy judgments. These explain their reasons for deciding in favour of one party rather than the other.

Ratio decidendi: the reasons in law and fact why a judge reached a decision.

This statement of reasons, which refers both to relevant proven facts and to the applicable principles of law, is called the **ratio decidendi** (the reason for the decision). It is the *ratio decidendi* which forms the potentially binding precedent for later cases.

A later court, when hearing a case, has to decide whether that case's facts are sufficiently relevant to the principle of the *ratio decidendi* of a previous case. If so, the previous decision must be applied, provided it was decided by a relevant court. If there are material differences, the latter case can be *distinguished* on its facts and the previous decision is not applicable.

Reversing and overruling decisions

An appeal court may decide to overturn a decision reached by a lower court. This may be on the ground that the case was incorrectly decided in the light of the current law. The lower court's decision is then said to be *reversed*. The victor at the previous trial is now the loser.

Reversing a decision does not in itself affect the validity of any precedent applied in the case. If the appeal court believes that a precedent, which bound the lower court, no longer represents the law, it may (subject to the rules explained above) **overrule** that precedent and restate the legal principle.

> **Reversing a decision:** on appeal the party who won becomes the loser.

> **Overrule:** the court declares an existing binding precedent to be no longer good law.

The importance of the law reporting system

No system of precedent can work unless there is an accurate and comprehensive collection of the key decisions of the superior courts readily accessible to all who have need of them. Authoritative reports compiled by legally qualified law reporters are produced primarily by the Council of Law Reporting. The courts may refuse to allow a non-authoritative report to be quoted in court.

Persuasive precedents

While a court may be bound to apply a precedent, other decisions called persuasive precedents are influential only. The court can choose to apply them. Persuasive precedents include:

> **Obiter dictum/ obiter dicta:** a judicial statement indicating how the judge would interpret the law in different circumstances.

1 *Obiter dicta*. In a judgment it is quite common to find statements of law relating to hypothetical facts. These are not part of the *ratio decidendi* and are called **obiter dicta** (**obiter dictum** in the singular). These indicate how the judge thinks the law should develop in the hypothetical circumstances. They are highly persuasive if they come from the Supreme Court or Court of Appeal, but a court still has a choice about applying them in a future case. Once applied, the obiter dicta become binding principles of law. Some important principles of law have originated from obiter dicta. See *Central London Property Trust* v *High Trees House* (Chapter 6).

2 The decisions of the Judicial Committee of the Privy Council. The Privy Council, which is staffed by members of the Supreme Court, hears appeals from the courts of some Commonwealth countries. As the decisions do not involve English cases they are of persuasive influence only, despite the status of the judges. The rules relating to remoteness of damage in negligence are derived from a case called *The Wagon Mound*, an appeal from the Australian courts (see Chapter 14).

The advantages and disadvantages of the binding precedent doctrine

Conflicting opinions exist about the value of the binding precedent system. The advantages are said to be:

1 *Certainty*. The system promotes valuable certainty in the law. A party can generally be given a reasonably clear prediction of the outcome of its case.

2 *Flexibility*. The necessarily firm rules are tempered by the ability of the higher courts to overrule their own decisions. A court's ability to distinguish or reconcile decisions on their facts also promotes flexibility.

3 *Practical nature*. Principles of pure case law can be developed in response to actual problems and tailored to solve them.

4 *Speed*. The law can be developed without waiting for Parliament to legislate in a new area.

The disadvantages of the system often appear correlative to the perceived advantages:

1 *Uncertainty*. The powers of the courts to distinguish and reconcile binding precedents often lead to confusing hairline distinctions and distorted applications of case law.

2 *Rigidity*. Certainty is preserved by rigid rules which arguably inhibit development of the law.

3 *Retrieval problems*. The vast amount of case law makes it easy for relevant precedents to be overlooked during preparation for litigation, and increases the time and, therefore, the cost to the client.

4 *Haphazard development*. A change in the law depends on a case with relevant facts reaching the appropriate court. This usually means the Court of Appeal or the Supreme Court; litigants do not necessarily have the means to take their cases that far.

5 *Undemocratic*. The development of pure case law by judges (not interpreting statutes) is not appropriate since they are not democratically appointed and law-making conflicts with parliamentary sovereignty.

The Human Rights Act 1998 (HRA 1998)

This important statute, which came into force in October 2000, makes most of the rights in the European Convention on Human Rights directly enforceable in the English courts. It has the potential directly and indirectly to be highly influential on the content and interpretation of legislation and on the way case law is developed.

The legal and political background to the Act

European Convention on Human Rights: the fundamental freedoms to be expected by the citizens of a democratic state and binding on its 54 state signatories. (*Not EU legislation.*)

The **European Convention on Human Rights** (the Convention) was drafted by the Council of Europe and came into force in 1953. It now has over 40 signatories, including the UK. It requires signatory states to uphold a number of fundamental civil rights, including the rights to liberty and security (Article 5), freedom of thought, conscience and religion (Article 9), freedom of expression (Article 10), and freedom of assembly and association (Article 11). The rights to life (Article 2), a fair trial (Article 6) and privacy and family life (Article 8) are also included. There is a right to manifest your religion under Article 9 and a right of access to religion (Protocol 1, Article 2). Until the HRA 1998, none of these was directly and specifically enforceable in the UK courts. Individuals had to take claims that the government had breached its duties under the Convention to the **European Court of Human Rights** (ECtHR) at Strasbourg, if no remedy had been found to exist in their case by the UK courts under domestic law.

The Convention, even when not directly binding on the English courts, was always used as an aid to statutory interpretation and to determine the scope of the common law. Decisions of the ECtHR were used as persuasive precedents.

The Convention and the ECtHR must not be confused with the law and institutions of the EU. They are different in their origins, signatories and scope of operation. However, the European Court of Justice, based at Luxembourg, which is responsible for upholding the law of the European Union, tends to reflect the principles of the Convention in its decisions.

European Court of Human Rights: hears cases concerning alleged breaches of the ECHR by citizens against their home state. (*Not* an EU institution.)

The operation of the HRA 1998

Section 6 of the HRA 1998 requires 'public authorities' to act compatibly with the Convention. Public authorities include central government departments and local authorities, as well as the courts, tribunals and police forces. A breach of the Convention by a **public authority** is therefore now actionable in the domestic courts.

Public authority: HRA 1998, s 6 includes the courts and any organisation or body with public functions.

The judges' functions

Interpretation of Convention rights: s 2

When the court is deciding any issue which has, 'arisen in connection with human rights' it must take into account the case law of the ECtHR

Interpretation of legislation: s 3

The court must, 'so far as it is possible to do so', interpret legislation so that it is compatible with Convention rights. Note that the duty under s 3 is not an absolute one. To preserve parliamentary sovereignty, the Act does not permit the court to override a statute found to be incompatible with the Convention. Instead, the court has the power (s 4) to issue a declaration of incompatibility to the relevant minister, who may then at his or her discretion ask Parliament to amend the legislation. In the first year of the operation of the Act only three such declarations were issued in a total of 56 claims under the Act. For example, in *R (on the application of Pearson)* v *Secretary of State for the Home Department and Martinez; Hirst* v *Attorney-General* (2001) it was held that the Representation of the People Act 1983, which states that prisoners do not have the right to vote, was not incompatible with Article 10 of the Convention (right to freedom of expression). The Convention right is not absolute and proportionate restrictions can be imposed by the state.

However, remember that the HRA does not preclude action in the ECtHR. That is still possible if all rights of action under English law have been exhausted. Hirst exercised this right and won his case in the ECtHR (*Hirst* v *UK (No. 2)* (2005)). The ECtHR held that a universal ban on prisoner voting was a breach of the Convention because it was: 'Such a general, automatic and indiscriminate restriction on a vitally important convention right . . . It applied automatically to convicted prisoners in prison, irrespective of the length of their sentence and irrespective of the nature or gravity of their offence and their individual circumstances'. The court dismissed the UK's argument that allowing the right would 'make a mockery of the law and promote criminal behaviour' on the grounds that there was no evidence to support it and stated that UK law should be changed by August 2011. After the ECtHR decision in 2005, the UK government agreed that the law would be changed within the deadline. Consultation on this controversial issue took place, with a view to extending the right to prisoners convicted of less serious offences.

In the news

Government still reconsidering prisoner voting

Successive governments have indicated extreme reluctance about changing the current law. On a free vote in March 2010 a large majority of MPs voted against any change. The ban on the prisoner vote dates from 1870, so it is not surprising that many people in the UK are repelled by the idea of reform. However, if we look at this in a European context, we find that it is not such an alien notion. While a total ban is imposed in 13 countries including Belgium, in 30 others, prisoners may vote, though, some restrictions are imposed in some of those states.

At the time of writing it is unclear what the final outcome will be. It would be quite possible to satisfy the judgment by changing the law sufficiently to avoid a blanket ban but still prevent the great majority of prisoners from voting.

The draft Voting Eligibility (Prisoners) Bill 2012, was submitted for consideration by a cross-party parliamentary committee. It contains three alternative proposals: to leave the law unchanged or to allow prisoners serving less than six months to vote or to allow prisoners serving less than four years to vote. The Committee chose none of these but recommended in December 2013 that prisoners serving a term of one year or less should be allowed to vote. By 2015 a Bill to implement change had still not been put before Parliament.

Judicial remedies: s 8

Where a breach of the Convention is proved the court has the power to grant a number of remedies, including damages and injunctions and other orders.

The methods by which the court may determine an award for damages is well illustrated by the following case.

Direct effect: under the HRA 1998 the ECHR can be enforced in cases against a public authority in an English court.

The impact of the Act

The Act has both a **direct** and **indirect** effect on the way domestic law is interpreted and applied.

DSD and NBV v Commissioner of Police for the Metropolis (2014, EWHC)

The two applicants sought damages after obtaining a declaration under the HRA against the Police Commissioner on the grounds that his force had breached the HRA and Article 3 of the Convention by subjecting them to 'inhuman and degrading treatment.'

Both women had been raped after being drugged by a serial sex offender W and reported the crime. D was raped in 2003 and V in 2007. The police failed properly to investigate both cases. They assumed that D was lying and V's case was downgraded in priority to improve crime statistics. W was eventually arrested in 2009 after committing over 100 rapes.

Both women later brought successful civil claims against W and also received compensation from the Criminal Injuries Compensation Board.

The Court had to decide whether under the HRA s 8 and Art 5 of the ECtHR it was *'necessary'* to award damages to *'afford just satisfaction'* to the applicants.

Green J held: The fact that compensation had already been paid from other sources did not prevent a successful application. The damage caused to the parties by the police was discrete from the harm caused by the offence. Subject to proof of a link between the police failure to carry out a proper investigation of the crime and the resulting ill effects on the applicants, an award was appropriate.

When deciding the amount of damages the court had to take into account ECtHR decisions, the primary object of which was to prevent further breaches of the law, as well domestic claims. The award must reflect the degree of culpability of the defendant as well as the degree of suffering caused to the applicants. *'The police failings were not merely operational . . . they were systemic and of a deep and abiding nature. This is an aggravating factor when it comes to damages'*. They were reflective of a culture deeply embedded in the Metropolitan Police which aggravated the seriousness of its failings.

Both women suffered acute long term clinical depression as a result of the rape and the subsequent police actions. Fifty per cent of their subsequent suffering could be attributed to the police failings .It was also probable that V would not have been raped if the police had properly investigated D's complaint six years earlier.

Damages should be assessed as £22,000 for D and £19,000 for V.

Indirect effect: the HRA 1998 makes the ECHR influential on the outcome of cases not brought under the Act as the court must act compatibly with ECHR and take account of ECtHR judgments.

Direct effect

The HRA 1998 introduces an entirely new right of action for alleged breaches of Convention rights, though only against a 'public authority'. Such an action cannot be brought against a private institution or individual.

There have been some controversial cases. In *R (on the application of F and Another) v Secretary of State for the Home Department* (2010) the Supreme Court held that sex offenders should have a right to appeal against lifelong inclusion in the sex offenders register, because such registration was a disproportionate general requirement and each case should be considered separately. Generally and unsurprisingly, however, the direct impact of the Act on domestic law has not been a dramatic one. Apart from the innate conservatism of the English judiciary, Convention rights are very broadly worded, giving judges flexibility to find compatibility. Almost all Convention rights are not absolute, but instead are hedged around with qualifications. For example, the right to life (Article 2) may not be breached if a person dies while being lawfully arrested. The right to liberty (Article 5) may be limited in the interests of protecting the public against crime.

R (on the application of Laporte) v Chief Constable of Gloucestershire Constabulary (2007, HL)

Jane Laporte (and 26 other anti-war protestors) claimed that their rights to freedom of expression and freedom of assembly (ECHR, Articles 10 and 11) had been breached when the police prevented them from attending a lawful demonstration at RAF Fairford, just before the base was used to launch bombing raids on Iraq. The police stopped their coach, searched the passengers and then sealed it and escorted it back to London. The police argued that it was necessary to do so in order to prevent a breach of the peace, given the past history of some of the demonstrators and some items found on the coach (e.g. a can of spray paint). Only the three main speakers were allowed to proceed to Fairford.

Held (unanimously): the police's entirely disproportionate conduct had breached the applicants' Convention rights. They had also been unlawfully detained. At the point that the police intervened there was no reason to view them as other than *'committed and peaceful'* demonstrators. It was irrelevant that a breach of the peace might occur sometime in the future. The HRA 1998 had created a *'constitutional shift'* and created a right to peaceful protest. The right to freedom of expression was *'an essential foundation of a democratic society'* (Lord Bingham).

The court, when determining a human rights claim, has to attempt to balance the interests of the parties to ensure neither suffers an undue limitation of their Convention rights. This is sometimes described as *'proportionality'*. For example, a claim to protect a right of privacy (Article 8) must not be decided in a way that unduly curtails freedom of expression of the other party or which will unreasonably interfere with the public's right to information (Article 10). The following case provides an example of rights to family life being compromised for public benefit.

Austin v Commissioner of Police of the Metropolis (2009, HL)

Ms Austin took part in a large May Day demonstration against global capitalism in Oxford Street in London involving about 3,000 people in 2001. The police, who had not been informed that the demonstration would take place, decided that the only workable strategy to prevent injury, damage and violence was to 'kettle' [form a cordon round] the large crowd of demonstrators near Oxford Circus and then disperse them in an orderly fashion. The dispersal took seven hours due to the behaviour of a large minority of the demonstrators who became obstructive and violent. Some prised up paving stones and hurled lumps of the masonry at the police. Others obstructed arrest of violent demonstrators and refused generally to co-operate with the police.

Ms Austin claimed that by detaining her in the cordon the police had deprived her of her liberty in breach of Article 5(1) of the ECHR. Her claim was unsuccessful in the lower courts and she appealed to the House of Lords.

Held: measures by the police that impacted on an individual's liberty must be proportionate to the situation and done in good faith, in order to maintain the fundamental principle that detention must not be arbitrary. The crowd control undertaken by the police was done in the public interest with the intention of enabling orderly dispersal of the demonstrators as soon as reasonably possible. In this case the size and behaviour of the crowd had made controlled dispersal unusually difficult and slow. Consequently, the detention of the demonstrators had not amounted to a breach of the ECHR and Ms Austin's appeal must be dismissed.

The courts decide what is a proportionate response on a case-by-case basis. The outcome is dependent on the particular facts. 'Kettling' was held to be unlawful in the next case.

R (on the application of Moos and Another) v Commissioner of Police for the Metropolis (2011, QBD)

The applicants, who were demonstrating peacefully, were forcibly contained by the police. The police believed that violent unrest would be caused by the addition of some demonstrators, just dispersed from an earlier and violent demonstration a quarter of a mile away.

Held: the police had acted unlawfully under Article 5 of the ECHR. Such containment could only be justified if a breach of the peace was about to take place, which was not the case here. Despite the sustained violence at the other earlier demonstration, no breach of the peace was actually likely to happen at the time the police contained the applicants at the second demonstration.

A school may impose proportionate rules about uniform without breaching a student's human rights.

R (on the application of Begum) v Headteacher and Governors of Denbigh High School (2006, HL)

Begum's school, while accommodating Muslim dress, only permitted girls to wear the *shalwar kameez*. Begum was happy with this initially but after two years insisted on wearing the *jilbab*. For the next two years she was excluded from the school. There were other schools nearer her home which permitted the *jilbab*. She claimed that Denbigh High School had deprived her of her right to manifest her religion (Article 9) and her right to access education (Protocol 1, Article 2) of the ECHR.

Held (by majority): her right to religious expression had not been breached. The school had acted with proportionality in devising a dress code which 'respected Muslim beliefs but did so in an inclusive, unthreatening and uncompetitive way'.

Held (unanimously): she had not been deprived of access to education. Her absence from school was due to her refusal to comply with a reasonable rule and her failure to obtain a place at a school which would have accommodated her religious beliefs.

Indirect effect

As indicated above, a court as a public authority is obligated under s 6 to act compatibly with the Convention. This, combined with its duties to take ECtHR judgments into account (s 2) and to interpret statutes compatibly (s 3), means that since 2000 Convention law has been influential on the outcome of a number of cases which were not brought under the Act. In *A v B sub nom Garry Flitcroft v Mirror Group Newspapers Ltd* (2002, CA), the court refused to grant an injunction for breach of confidence to a professional footballer to prevent publication of the story of his extramarital exploits. The court in its decision balanced the claimant's right to privacy against the rights to freedom of expression and the public interest and found that these outweighed the claimant's rights. (You will find more detail on this and other similar cases in Chapter 25.)

Looking to the future

The HRA 1998 has clearly already had a significant impact on the development of the law and a human rights culture has clearly emerged. (You will find more examples of relevant human rights cases in later chapters.)

Recently there have been some controversial decisions of both the domestic courts and the ECtHR. For example, in 2012 ECtHR blocked the deportation of Abu Quatada, an international terrorist suspect from the UK to Jordan, because of the substantial risk that evidence obtained by torture would be used at his trial (*Othman (Abu Quatada) v United Kingdom* application 8139/09 (2012)). Unsurprisingly, this gave rise to a good deal of rhetoric, both in the media and in Parliament, which suggested abandoning the Convention and repealing the HRA. It is unlikely that the UK would abandon the Convention, but it can reasonably be argued that the ECHR and its enforcement mechanisms could do with an overhaul to bring them more into line with current human rights' needs. Human rights ministers from the member states of the Council of Europe issued the Interlaken Declaration in 2011, indicating commitment to reform of procedures in the ECtHR to ensure that it remained effective in the future.

In March 2012, the Commission on Human Rights set up by the Ministry of Justice in 2011 reported that seven of its nine members favoured repeal of the HRA. The Commission recommends its replacement with a Bill of Rights which would mirror the ECHR obligations and provide similar protection to the HRA, while defining some rights more clearly and redressing perceived imbalances in its application. All members agreed that the ECtHR required fundamental reform. Subsequent public consultation has taken place but no legislation has yet been tabled. The Conservative manifesto of 2015 pledged repeal of the HRA and its replacement with a Bill of Rights, but subsequent dissension in its own party ranks as well as the other parliamentary parties and pressure groups has led to withdrawal of the proposal pending further consultation. In June 2015 the government also announced that it would not currently seek to withdraw the UK from the ECHR. These reversals in policy make change unlikely in these areas in the near future.

3

How the law is made

Chapter summary

Sources of English law

EU, British Parliament and English courts.

EC institutions

The Council of the EU, the European Council, the European Commission, the European Court of Justice and the European Parliament.

European legislation

Regulations, Directives, Decisions.

British parliamentary legislation

Direct: Acts of Parliament. An Act starts life as a Bill, which must successfully pass through three readings and a committee stage in each House before receiving the Royal Assent.

Delegated: Orders in Council, statutory instruments, rules and regulations, bye-laws.

The courts

Case law: created by judges, e.g. much of contract and tort law on a case-by-case basis.

Statutory interpretation of direct and delegated legislation using literal/golden/mischief/purposive approach.

The law of precedent: judges have regard to previous decisions and must apply those which are binding.

A precedent is binding if (a) *ratio decidendi* is relevant to the current case, and (b) it comes from a higher court in the hierarchy, *or* (c) the case is being heard in the Supreme Court or Court of Appeal which follow their own decisions.

Note: Crown/county/magistrates' court decisions are not binding on other courts nor on themselves.

The Human Rights Act 1998

Direct effect: ECHR rights directly enforceable by individuals against a 'public authority'.

Indirect effect: The court must act compatibly with the Convention. Therefore, its content and case law may be influential in shaping the judge's decision in any case.

Quiz 2

1 Name the three main sources of English law.

2 Distinguish between EU Regulations and Directives.

3 Name the stages through which a Bill will pass in Parliament.

4 Name two kinds of delegated legislation.

5 Explain the difference between the literal rule and the mischief rule.

6 Explain how the *ejusdem generis* rule works.

7 When may a prec...

8 What is the difference ... of a *ratio decidendi* and an o...

9 Why might the status of a de... Judicial Committee of the Privy ... ...l be described as an anomaly in the l.../ of precedent?

10 In what circumstances may a right of action be brought under the Human Rights Act 1998?

Answers to all quizzes can be found in Appendix 2.

Take a closer look

The following cases provide important examples of how the law you have studied here has developed. They are primary sources illustrating the law in action and give you more detail about their facts, as well as helping you to understand the law and to appreciate how the judges reached their decisions.

Try looking them up in the law reports or accessing them via a database, e.g. Bailli (www.bailii.org/databases.html). LexisNexis or Westlaw may be available in your university or college library, or you may find extracts in a case book. (See Appendix 1: Additional resources.)

DSD and NBV v Commissioner of Police for the Metropolis [2014] EWHC 2493 (QB)

R (on the application of Begum) v *Denbigh High School* [2006] 2 All ER 487, HL

Royal College of Nursing v *DHSS* [1981] AC 800, HL

Sweet v *Parsley* [1969] 1 All ER 347, HL

Web activity

Please go to: https://www.liberty-human-rights.org.uk/

Click on 'Human Rights' and read about many everyday issues where Human Rights is relevant. There is a lot of interesting information on this site that you also might wish to explore.

Assignment 1

With reference to decided cases, discuss the impact of the Human Rights Act 1998 on the rights of claimants.

CHAPTER 4

Resolving legal disputes

Introduction

Legal rights are useless without an adequate means of enforcement. Similarly, legal duties need a structure within which sanctions may be imposed. This chapter explains the institutions and processes that may be relevant to the resolution of a legal dispute involving a business. It aims to give you an overview of the workings of the court system and primarily focuses on how it operates in relation to the areas of law covered in this book.

While it is important to have some idea about civil procedure, remember that the great majority of civil disputes are settled without resort to the courts at all, with private agreements being reached voluntarily between the parties, sometimes with the help of arbitration or mediation. Courts and tribunals increasingly encourage such action. Inappropriate litigation is only beneficial to lawyers' bank accounts.

Learning objectives

When you have studied this chapter you should be able to:

▶ identify the jurisdiction of each court;

▶ appreciate the different stages of civil litigation;

▶ see how the tribunal system complements and relates to the court structure;

▶ be aware of the different forms of alternative dispute resolution;

▶ distinguish between the different forms of arbitration.

The court system

The courts described below form a **hierarchy**. This means that they are positioned in a structure in which some courts are superior to others. Through the doctrine of binding precedent (explained in Chapter 3), the decisions of the superior courts are binding on the courts below.

The courts

The magistrates' court

Magistrates' courts are very busy courts in which approximately 95 per cent of all criminal offences are prosecuted. These are **summary** offences and **offences triable either way**. Summary offences are petty offences that can be tried only by the magistrates. Offences which are triable either way may be tried by either the Crown Court or the magistrates' court, usually at the choice of the defendant; they generally involve conduct that is capable of being viewed as either serious or relatively trivial, like theft or criminal damage.

All cases are usually tried by a bench of up to three **justices of the peace (JPs)**. These act voluntarily and are not legally qualified, but they are advised on points of law by the clerk of the court. Exceptionally the case may be heard before a **district judge** who will have trained as a lawyer and have relevant court experience.

Children and young people (10–17-year-olds) are tried for the majority of criminal offences in Youth Court which are not open to the public and where the procedures are less formal than the ordinary magistrates' court. A different range of sanctions apply.

The magistrates' court is the usual venue for trial of most environmental health and other regulatory offences under the Trade Descriptions Act 1968, the Consumer Protection Act 1987 and the Health and Safety at Work etc. Act 1974. Most crimes against business owners, like shoplifting and criminal damage, are usually prosecuted in the magistrates' court.

Bail and criminal legal aid applications are also heard by magistrates.

The sentencing powers of the magistrates' courts are restricted. They may impose imprisonment for up to six months and a fine of up to £5,000. A party tried for an offence carrying a potentially higher penalty may be sent to the Crown Court for sentencing.

With regard to civil and administrative jurisdiction, the Family Proceedings Court has wide jurisdiction over many aspects of domestic and matrimonial law and has significant powers under the Children Act 1989. The magistrates also have powers to license premises which sell alcohol or provide betting and gaming services and also enforce payment of council tax and business rates, and charges for gas, water and electricity.

The Crown Court

There are 77 Crown Court centres, situated mainly in county and borough towns. The Crown Court is staffed principally by High Court judges, circuit judges and recorders.

The seriousness of the offence determines the type of judge to officiate. A bench of JPs may assist a judge or recorder in appeal cases.

The Crown Court has criminal jurisdiction in the following circumstances:

Indictable offence: a criminal offence which can only be tried in the Crown Court.

1 *Trial of indictable offences.* **Indictable offences** include those offences that are so serious that they must be tried in the crown court: for example, homicide, rape and grievous bodily harm. Hybrid offences may also be tried there. Trial is by jury if the accused pleads not guilt.

2 *Sentencing cases* committed from the magistrates' court.

3 *Legal aid and bail applications.*

4 *Appeals.* The defendant found guilty in the magistrates' court may appeal against conviction or sentence to the crown court. A judge (usually a recorder) sitting with a bench of JPs hears the appeal.

The county court

There are currently 216 county courts in England and Wales, staffed by circuit judges and district judges. However, the government announced in 2015 that it planned to close 49 of these as part of a programme of financial cuts The county court has an extensive and purely civil jurisdiction, including contract, tort, recovery of land, trusts, mortgages and partnerships, contested wills, divorce, bankruptcy and company insolvency.

Since the Courts and Legal Services Act 1990 (CLSA 1990), almost any case which can be heard in the High Court can now be heard in the county court provided that it falls within specified and generous financial limits. For example, cases in tort and contract may be heard if the claimant is not suing for more than £50,000. The CLSA 1990 provisions aim to free the High Court from hearing all but the most complex, costly and specialist cases.

The following cases must generally be tried in the county court:

1 all actions worth up to £25,000;

2 any personal injury case worth under £50,000; unless its specialist nature or complexity makes trial in the High Court appropriate.

Otherwise, provided that a case falls within the prescribed financial limits, the choice of venue is determined by:

1 the amount involved;

2 whether points of law of general public interest are involved;

3 the complexity of the case;

4 the potential procedures and/or remedies: some are obtainable only from the High Court.

Cases starting in the High Court can be transferred to the county court at the request of a party or at the discretion of the judge. A successful party may not get the full costs paid if the judge believes the case should have been pursued in the county court.

4

Resolving legal disputes

The High Court

This court is staffed by High Court judges. The court's principal venue is the Royal Courts of Justice in London, but cases are also heard in provincial cities. It is divided into three divisions and primarily is concerned with the trial of civil cases outside the jurisdiction of the county court. The three divisions of the High Court are:

1 the *Queen's Bench Division*, that primarily is concerned with the trial of cases in contract and tort. It also contains the Commercial Court, which hears cases between people in business arising out of issues like imports and exports of goods, insurance, banking and agency;

2 the *Chancery Division*, which tries cases in copyright, patents and design rights, bankruptcy and the dissolution of partnerships, sale of land, trusts, mortgages and disputed wills;

3 the *Family Division*, which deals with the most complex areas of family and matrimonial law arising, for example, from contested divorce, validity of foreign marriage and divorce, legitimacy and adoption.

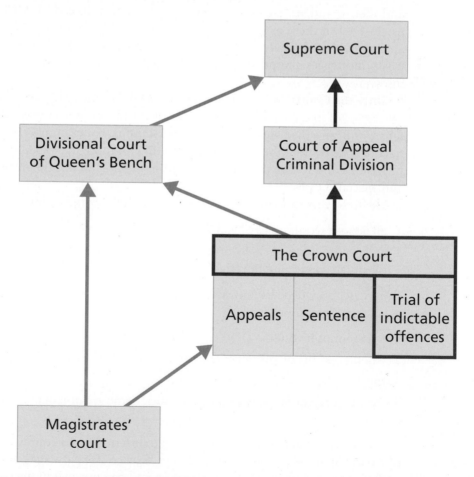

Figure 4.1 The criminal court structure

Appellate functions

Separate divisional courts hear appeals from designated inferior courts. A bench of two judges is usual.

The *Divisional Court of the Queen's Bench* hears criminal appeals from the magistrates' court by either prosecution or defence, when the interpretation of a point of law is in dispute. (Note that this is distinct from the appellate powers of the Crown Court, which hears appeals only by the defendant, where facts as well as law may also be in dispute.) It also has a supervisory jurisdiction over all inferior courts and tribunals exercised through the process of judicial review. If the Divisional Court is satisfied that a court or tribunal has exceeded its jurisdiction or has failed to conduct its proceedings impartially according to the rules of natural justice, an order may be issued overturning the outcome of those proceedings or preventing their continuance.

The *Divisional Court of the Chancery Division* hears appeals against decisions of the county court in bankruptcy cases, and in revenue law against the decisions of the Inland Revenue Commissioners.

The *Divisional Court of the Family Division* hears appeals from the magistrates' courts in domestic and matrimonial cases.

The Court of Appeal

Lord/Lady Justice of Appeal: Court of Appeal judge.

This is staffed by **Lord and Lady Justices of Appeal** and has two divisions. Cases are heard by a bench of three or five judges.

The Civil Division of the Court of Appeal has jurisdiction to hear appeals against decisions of the county court and High Court. It also hears appeals from some tribunals, including the Employment Appeal Tribunal, concerning cases originally heard at employment tribunal level.

The Criminal Division of the Court of Appeal has jurisdiction to hear appeals from Crown Court trials. (Note that the Court of Appeal cannot hear an appeal from the Crown Court where that court has itself been exercising its own appeals jurisdiction regarding cases from the magistrates' court. The only further avenue for such appeals is the Queen's Bench Divisional Court.)

The Supreme Court

In 2009 the Supreme Court replaced the House of Lords under the Constitutional Reform Act 2005 (CRA), s 23. The House of Lords (officially known as the Appellate Committee of the House of Lords to distinguish it from the parliamentary House of Lords) was the final court of appeal in England until then. The judges, then known as Law Lords or Lords of Appeal in Ordinary, were life peers entitled to sit and vote in the House of Lords. This was controversial, since it meant that they were involved in political decision-making.

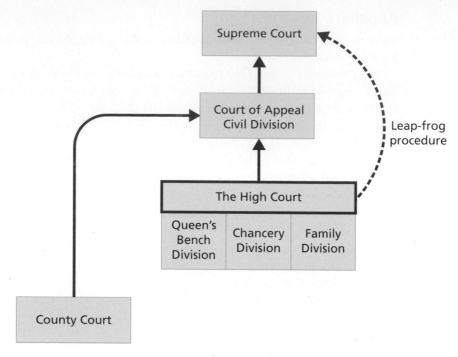

Figure 4.2 The principal civil courts and appeal routes

Justices of
the Supreme
Court:
judges in the
Supreme Court.

Law Lord/Lord
of Appeal in
Ordinary:
judges of the
House of Lords.

Leap-frog
procedure:
enables a case
tried in the High
Court to bypass
the Court of
Appeal and go
straight to the
Supreme Court
for the appeal
hearing.

The Supreme Court has the same jurisdiction as its predecessor and hears appeals from the Divisional Courts and the Court of Appeal, on points of law of public importance. The cases, which generally all concern statutory interpretation, are heard by a bench of three to seven judges known as **Justices of the Supreme Court**. The initial office holders are the **Law Lords or Lords of Appeal in Ordinary** (formerly judges of the House of Lords) who were holding office in 2009 when the Supreme Court started to sit. These no longer have the right to take any part in proceedings in the House of Lords. New Justices will be directly appointed to the Supreme Court by the Judicial Appointments Committee, which is responsible for judicial appointments in general.

Exceptionally, an appeal may be made directly from the High Court, bypassing the Court of Appeal (the **'leap-frog' procedure** introduced by the Administration of Justice Act 1969). This operates only where the point of law is already the subject of a Court of Appeal decision by which both it and the High Court are bound. This measure was introduced to overcome the restraints of the law of precedent, but is, in practice, very rarely used.

Bringing a case in the civil courts

The enforcement of legal rights is all too often perceived as a universal remedy, but there are many factors which can prevent a successful outcome. Many people who technically have a good claim in law may be unable to enforce it successfully for any of the following reasons:

(a) their opponents do not have the necessary funds to satisfy the claim;

(b) the law-breaker cannot be traced, e.g. an offending company may have gone into liquidation;

(c) the wronged party may not have the funds to pursue the claim. Litigation is a costly and protracted process, which may require expert assistance. Legal representatives do not simply send in a bill at the end of proceedings; regular payments are required pending the outcome of the case, and a party may run out of money even before the case comes to court. The scope of legal aid has been increasingly narrowed in recent years and entitlement means-tested and largely restricted to parties whose income does not exceed basic welfare benefit levels;

(d) the losing side may be responsible not only for their own legal costs, but also for those of their opponents. This may discourage pursuit of a case where the outcome is unpredictable.

The Woolf reforms 1999

In 1993, Lord Woolf (Master of the Rolls) headed an inquiry into the civil justice system prompted by concerns that its procedures were neither efficient nor effective. The report drew attention to a range of problems for the would-be litigant including the undue and often disproportionate cost of litigation, compounded by the unnecessary complexity of rules and procedures. It also expressed concerns that abuse by lawyers of the adversarial system could lead to litigation being controlled more by the lawyers rather than the parties or even the judge. Implementation of recommendations in the report in April 1999 have resulted in radical changes to civil litigation. The new Civil Procedure Rules (CPR) are drafted in plain English, with an emphasis on clarity and avoidance of legal jargon, to make them user-friendly for the unrepresented litigant and more accessible to all.

Some materials like case reports, which were published before the new rules came into effect, still use the old terminology: for example, 'plaintiff' is used instead of 'claimant'.

Settlement out of court

Litigation is time-consuming, costly and often emotionally draining for the parties. It is a step to be taken only when all alternatives have failed.

The huge majority of legal claims can be enforced without litigation, or even specialist help. Simple cases may be settled informally between the parties. A customer who is sold defective goods will usually obtain a refund from any reputable business without argument. A party who is unable to achieve a successful outcome may get a solicitor to reinforce the claim with a letter pointing out the relevant legal requirements. Sometimes the threat of litigation may produce the required result; if this fails proceedings may be started, but this does not commit either party to a court appearance. Most civil cases are settled before trial. The CPR give judges a number of powers to encourage early settlement wherever possible. For example, if a judge believes that a party has acted unreasonably in pursuing or conducting the case, penalties may be imposed as regards costs.

Payment into court and offers to settle

Payment into court: formal offer to settle made by defendant.

If proceedings have been started, the defendant may offer to make a **payment into court**. This represents the amount of compensation the defendant is prepared to pay. It is not in itself an admission of liability and the judge is not told about it prior to the conclusion of the trial. The claimant does not have to accept this offer, but may feel pressured to do so. If the case proceeds, the claimant will be liable for the defendant's costs, even if successful, if the amount of damages awarded by the court is less than the amount offered by the defendant.

Offer to settle: informal settlement out of court/ formal offer to the court by claimant.

The CPR has also introduced rights for a claimant who makes an **offer to settle** for a certain sum. If the defendant refuses the offer and the claimant then wins the case and is awarded that sum or more, the court has the discretion to increase the amount of interest payable on damages from the date of the decision by up to 10 per cent. Strategies of this kind are aimed at encouraging early settlement with a consequent saving of cost to the litigants and time for the judge.

Worth thinking about?

The great majority of potential claims are settled informally out of court. This speeds up the process, reduces stress for the litigants and saves money on legal costs. Can you see any drawbacks to the process?

Suggested solutions can be found in Appendix 2.

Civil litigation procedures

Starting a civil action

1 Letters of claim and pre-action protocols

The CPR aim to encourage the parties to clarify the issues between them before any claim is issued. The claimant must send the defendant a **letter of claim** indicating clearly their allegations and the defendants must reply with explanation of their conduct. **Pre-action protocols** requiring very detailed and specific information and documentation must be exchanged in certain types of cases, such as personal injury, clinical negligence, engineering and construction disputes, professional negligence, defamation, and housing disrepair.

2 Issue of claim

The claimant fills in the claim form with detailed particulars and submits it to the court where it is processed and served on the defendant. This is called the **issue of claim**.

3 The defendant's response

The defendant must either admit the claim or file a detailed defence within 21 days. Failure to respond may result in the claimant obtaining immediate judgment against the defendant for any sum specified in the claim.

4 The case is allocated to the relevant track

The Woolf Report stressed that the cost of and resources for litigation should be proportionate to the complexity and size of the claim. The CPR aim to achieve this by designating a case to one of three tracks with differing procedures relative to the value and difficulty of the claim.

The small claims track

Since April 2013 the **small claims track** jurisdiction covers most claims for up to £10,000 or less. The limit for personal injury claims is £5,000.

All hearings, which take place in the County Court before a district judge, are informal and the normal rules of evidence do not apply. The CPR encourages an inquisitorial approach: the judge may question witnesses and limit cross-examination. The claimant may bring a friend to support him or her. A successful party may recover the costs incurred in issuing the proceedings, travel costs and a limited contribution to any expert-witness fees and loss of earnings. Legal costs are not recoverable for any money claim. This rule aims to discourage the use of lawyers but arguably loads the dice against a consumer since a business is more likely to be represented.

It does, however, provide a relatively simple procedure which can be very helpful for consumers who wish to bring a small and simple claim without the cost of paying a solicitor. Evidence suggests that it is equally useful to businesses as a means of debt enforcement against their customers.

The fast track

Cases involving claims of £10,000–£25,000 are usually dealt with in the **fast track** in the County Court. Personal injury cases are limited to those for £10,000 or less.

The judge will give directions to the parties to clarify the issues to be tried and a trial date not later than 30 weeks ahead will be announced. A party who is not ready by that point may have problems obtaining an extension; unnecessary delay may ultimately result in costs penalties.

The trial is limited to one day's duration and limits may be imposed on how long expert-witness evidence may take.

These rules aim to ensure that time (and the litigant's money) are not wasted during the preparation or conduct of relatively small and simple cases.

The multi-track

Multi-track: civil litigation process for cases involving over £25,000.

Any case with a claim over £25,000 is allocated to the **multi-track** system in the County Court unless its complexity requires it to be tried in the High Court.

The bigger and more complex the case, the greater will be the powers of the judge to manage its progress towards trial through case management conferences involving the litigants and their legal representatives. Such case management is a strategy intended to prevent time wasting by lawyers pursuing irrelevant legal arguments and to ensure proper and full disclosure of evidence by the parties. It also enables the judge to set time limits for the achievement of any necessary processes and organise the conduct of the trial in advance.

5 The interlocutory stages

Interlocutory stage: the period between the start of civil proceedings and the start of the trial.

Interlocutory injunction: may be issued between starting proceedings and trial of a civil case.

Equitable remedy: discretionary judicial remedy granted only if the court believes the claimant is morally as well as legally entitled to it.

Freezing injunction: prevents the defendant gaining access to their assets pending trial.

The **interlocutory stages** are the periods between issue of claim and hearing when detailed preparations for the hearing are made. In multi-track cases, there are likely to be a number of case conferences called by the judge.

At this time there may also be requests for information, disclosure, and the issue of interlocutory injunctions.

Requests for information: one party may require the other to provide further clarification of the particulars of his or her claim or defence.

Disclosure: the documentary evidence on which a party intends to rely must be made available at this stage. Third parties may also be required to give access to information.

Application to the judge may be necessary to obtain compliance.

In exceptional cases a search order may be required from the court, which permits the claimant to get entry to the defendant's premises and seize evidence. An application for such an order may be made without notice to the defendant to prevent him or her from covering their tracks.

Issue of **interlocutory injunctions**: injunctions are orders from the court which may stop the defendant from doing something or require some positive act. An injunction is an **equitable remedy**, which means that a party has no right to them. An injunction is granted at the discretion of the court. The judge must be convinced that the claimant is morally entitled to the remedy and that it will not be unjust to impose it on the defendant. A **freezing injunction** may be required at the interlocutory stage to prevent the defendant from transferring assets abroad or otherwise concealing them so as to avoid compensating the claimant.

Exceptionally, an injunction may be required as a holding measure to prevent the defend-ant from causing or continuing to cause serious damage to the claimant prior to the trial.

The trial of the case

The court hears legal arguments from both parties, who will generally be represented by a barrister or a solicitor-advocate. Solicitors in general do not have the right to appear in the High Court, but under the Courts and Legal Services Act 1990 they may do so if they obtain an additional advocacy qualification by demonstrating relevant litigation experience and satisfactorily completing a training course. Witnesses may be called and questioned by both sides.

The judge who hears the case will decide which party has won and explain why that conclusion has been reached. An award of damages is the usual remedy, but, where appropriate, an injunction or any other order within the jurisdiction of the court may be issued.

Executing the judgment

Distraint order: enables goods to the value of the claimant's damages to be seized to satisfy the judgment.

Charging order: made after judgment to freeze the defendant's assets until damages paid to the claimant.

Attachment of earnings order: court order to employer to pay a specified sum direct from defendant's earnings to satisfy a judgment debt.

Third party debt order: court order enabling claimant to gain control of funds belonging to defendant but held by a third party.

A claimant who is successful at trial has won a major battle but not the war. If awarded damages, the claimant has the status of a judgment creditor, but this does not in itself compel the defendant to pay – the claimant may have to return to the court to take steps to enforce the judgment. This may be done in any of the following ways:

1 A *distraint order*. A **distraint order** entitles the claimant to seize goods to the value of the debt from the defendant's premises. Bailiffs are usually employed for this purpose, at the claimant's cost.

2 A *charging order*. A **charging order** prevents the defendant from disposing of any assets, including land, trust funds, shares and debenture stock and other financial securities, pending satisfaction of the claimant's action.

3 *Attachment of earnings*. An **attachment of earnings** order requires an employer to pay a proportion of the defendant's earnings to the claimant.

4 *Third party debt order*. A **third party debt** order enables the claimant to gain control of funds belonging to the defendant but held by a third party (usually the bank).

5 *Insolvency proceedings*. If any debt (whether resulting from litigation or not) owed to the claimant is £750 or more, the claimant may institute insolvency proceedings against the debtor. This does not guarantee payment: if there are a large number of creditors the claimant will have to join the queue, and at best may recover only a proportion of the debt.

4

Resolving legal disputes

Real life

Horace was visited at home by a double glazing salesman from Transparent Deals (TD) and, persuaded by his arguments that new patio doors would reduce the house's carbon footprint, he signed a contract for £5,000 ('A bargain price, this week only sir!'). In due course, workmen arrived and, with the help of many cups of tea and packets of biscuits provided by Horace, fitted the doors. However, despite his kind attentions the work was very poorly executed. The doors do not fit properly and there is a gap beside the frame on one side which lets warmth out and draughts in. The sliding mechanism jams, making the doors difficult to open. Horace is refusing to pay and TD is now threatening to take him to court.

There are various strategies that Horace can pursue. If TD is a member of the Direct Selling Association (DSA), it must meet certain standards of behaviour under the DSA Consumer Code, approved by the Office of Fair Trading. Horace can complain to the DSA Code Administrator. If TD is found to be in breach of the Code, the Administrator may make it refund the full cost to Horace, or replace or repair the doors without charge, or pay him compensation. The company's cavalier behaviour rather suggests that it does not belong to the DSA. What a shame that Horace did not check that before he started. His best bet now is the Small Claims Track in the county court. He should call TD's bluff and, if it does sue him, enter a counterclaim for breach of contract as his defence, or he can immediately start proceedings himself as TD is clearly in breach of contract.

Alternative dispute resolution (ADR)

Given the cost and difficulties raised by taking a case through the courts, a cheaper, happier outcome may be achieved through using an alternative method of dispute resolution. This may consist of any of the strategies set out below.

Arbitration

The parties voluntarily submit their dispute to a third party and agree to be bound by the resulting decision. Arbitration has been the most favoured method for settlement of commercial disputes for hundreds of years. Its value is recognised by the courts and it is governed by statute, which empowers arbitrators and regulates the process. More recently it has become a common method of resolving consumer disputes.

Commercial arbitration

It is common for an arbitration clause to be a term of contracts between businesses; the parties may subsequently agree to submit a dispute to arbitration. Any person acceptable to the parties may act as their arbitrator. In practice, they will tend to choose somebody with skill and experience in the relevant field. The role of arbitrator has become professionalised and the Institute of Arbitrators regulates the standards of its members.

The Arbitration Act 1996 (AA 1996) regulates to some extent the operation of arbitration procedures and the behaviour of the arbitrator. The stated purpose of the AA 1996 is to empower the parties and to increase their autonomy. It was always the case that if an arbitration agreement existed the courts would not hear the case until the arbitration procedure had taken place. Under the AA 1996, the powers of the court to intervene have been restricted further. It may determine a preliminary point of law arising in the course of proceedings. The court, on the application of a party, may revoke the arbitrator's appointment for failure to fulfil the arbitrator's duty to act with impartiality and fairness. Rights of appeal against the arbitrator's decision are limited. Appeal on a point of law underpinning the decision is possible unless the parties have previously agreed to exclude this right. It is also permitted on the grounds that the arbitrator exceeded his or her jurisdiction or committed a serious irregularity.

The Equality Act 2010 limits the ability of a party to restrict access to court action in cases concerning discrimination. Section 144(1) states:

> A term of a contract is unenforceable by a person in whose favour it would operate in so far as it purports to exclude or limit a provision of or made under this Act.

This was applied in *Clyde & Co* v *Van Winkelhof* (2011), where the court refused to stay W's proceedings for sexual discrimination even though her partnership contract imposed arbitration as the final means of resolving a dispute.

The advantages of the arbitration process are that it ensures privacy for the parties in dispute and it is more likely to ensure a friendly outcome between the parties than litigation. This may be valuable in a specialist business area where the choice of contracting parties is limited. The problem can usually be resolved relatively cheaply and speedily at a time and place convenient to both parties. Arbitrators' expertise in the business field enables them to understand the issues in dispute. There are possible disadvantages, though: arbitrators have fewer powers than the courts to obtain evidence from the parties and to expedite the proceedings; they may lack necessary legal knowledge, ultimately necessitating an appeal, which will increase the cost.

Commercial arbitration procedures are not necessarily appropriate unless the contracting parties are in a position of equal bargaining power. The Consumer Arbitration Act 1988 stipulates that an arbitration clause in a contract does not bind a consumer until a dispute arises, and only then if the consumer agrees in writing at that point. Consumers cannot be forced into arbitration.

Code arbitration

Some trade associations impose a code of conduct on their members and permit consumers to take disputes through an arbitration procedure run by the association. A well-known example is ABTA (Association of British Travel Agents). Similar codes govern dry cleaning, photographic processing, car sales and a number of other trades. eBay has a dispute resolution system which appears to be very helpful.

These codes, developed under the auspices of the Director General of Fair Trading, are aimed at the protection of consumer buyers. A fee is payable to initiate the arbitration process, but this will be refunded if the consumer wins. The trade association appoints an appropriately experienced arbitrator registered with the Institute of Arbitrators. All communication with the arbitrator is written. If the trader is at fault, the association is responsible for enforcing any award.

A consumer can take this action only if the firm involved is actually a member of the relevant trade association. It is likely to be helpful only in relatively simple cases where the facts and evidence can readily be presented in documentary form.

Ombudsmen services

The organisations responsible for the supervision of legal, banking, insurance and financial services have each appointed officials called ombudsmen who have the power to investigate and resolve problems reported to them by dissatisfied customers.

Conciliation

A conciliator aims to assist the parties to a dispute to find a resolution. The conciliator may suggest a solution, but has no power to enforce it. Parties to a dispute which has been referred to an employment tribunal are offered the services of the Advisory, Conciliation and Arbitration Service (ACAS). The case proceeds to the tribunal only if the conciliation process is refused or is unsuccessful.

Mediation

A mediator assists the parties to communicate with each other and find their own resolution to their dispute. Mediation is an increasingly popular means of sorting out property and custody issues when a relationship breaks down. Means-tested funding in such cases is provided by the Community Legal Service. Some health authorities use mediation to resolve complaints of clinical negligence. It increasingly plays a part in the pre-litigation process.

ADR is encouraged by the courts

In 1995, the Lord Chief Justice issued instructions that legal representatives must check that their clients are fully aware of the possible use of alternative means of resolving the dispute before proceeding to take a case to the High Court. The Woolf Report stressed the importance of encouraging parties to use ADR, and under the CPR judges have the power to require parties to attempt to resolve some or all the pre-trial issues of the case in this way before the case will be allowed to proceed. There is no requirement for mandatory mediation overall, although it is being encouraged.

In 2010 a telephone mediation service was introduced to assist parties to settle county court fast track cases out of court and in 2012 it resolved almost all the 15,000 cases referred to it. The service is to be expanded to accommodate all potential fast track cases. (Cm 8274 *Solving Disputes in the County Court: Responses to Consultation* 2012.) Online facilities for resolution of consumer disputes has been recommended.

In the news

Online Courts Proposal

The Susskind Report published by the Civil Justice Council in February 2015 recommends that the Courts and Tribunals Service sets up a system for online dispute resolution to deal with civil cases initially up to a value of £25,000. The scheme has the potential to be extended to some family and tribunal cases to provide a cheaper, speedier and more appropriate method of resolution than the traditional court process. This is aimed at promoting efficiency and increasing access to justice.

The Online Court would consist of three tiers. In Tier One the claimant would go through a process to enable them to evaluate their case, clarify its issues and become aware of their rights and responsibilities. Tier Two would be concerned with facilitation and involve online mediation. After studying and reviewing the relevant documents, facilitators would endeavour to help the parties to find a resolution. Telephone conferencing could be employed at this point. If success could not be achieved, Tier Three would be triggered. A judge specially trained in internet use would decide cases largely on the basis of documents sent electronically, supported by telephone conferencing.

Source: Media release Courts and Tribunals Judiciary 16/02/15.

4

Resolving legal disputes

Since 2011 parties to a divorce will generally have to go through mediation before the case will be permitted to come to court in the hope that the matter can be resolved without expensive litigation.

The EU Mediation Directive 2008/52/EC was implemented in the UK by the Cross-Border Mediation (EU Directive) Regulations 2011, which require member states to set up mediation mechanisms. The regulations will apply to cross-border disputes only.

The tribunal system

Like the courts, the tribunal system provides a means of judicial resolution to a legal dispute and hears many more cases than are processed in the courts. It determines the rights of individuals against government departments in a wide variety of cases such as tax, immigration, social security entitlement, planning and compulsory purchase, education and aspects of mental health treatment. Employment disputes between employer and employee are also heard in this way. Tribunal judges are legally qualified and are usually assisted by a panel of two lay persons with relevant specialist knowledge.

A major reform and rationalisation took place after the Tribunals, Courts and Enforcement Act 2007, which has largely unified the system and the rules which govern it. It now operates in two generic tiers. Cases are initially heard in the First Tier in a Chamber dedicated to the relevant jurisdiction, for example Finance and Tax, Health, and Education and Social Care. Appeals are heard in the Upper Tier. Further appeal to the Court of Appeal and judicial review of decisions may be possible.

Cases involving employment law and asylum and immigration rights continue to be heard by tribunals outside the generic system because of the particular nature of their jurisdiction.

From a business perspective, the employment tribunal is the most relevant part of the tribunal system. It is derives its powers from a variety of statutes including the Employment Rights Act 1996.

Its jurisdiction encompasses:

(a) disputes between employers and employees concerning unfair dismissal, redundancy and sex and race discrimination at work;

(b) appeals by employers against the imposition of improvement and prohibition orders by the Health and Safety Executive.

The judge is a lawyer sitting with two other people nominated by bodies representing employers and employees respectively and hearings are open to the public. Appeal on a point of law may be made to the Employment Appeal Tribunal, with further appeal to the Court of Appeal and beyond is possible including the European Court of Justice, as a lot of employment law is derived from the EU.

Benefits of tribunals

Tens of thousands of cases are heard by tribunals every year and the system is seen as valuable to the parties using it. The main benefits of the tribunal system as compared with the courts are perceived to be:

1 *Cheapness.* Legal representation is not essential at a tribunal and the specialist knowledge of panel members makes it unnecessary to call specialist witnesses. The parties do not generally have to travel far to the hearing.

2 *Relative informality.* Procedures are usually less formal and adversarial than those of the ordinary courts, therefore a tribunal hearing is less intimidating.

3 *Speed.* A case may take years to come to court. Cases should reach tribunals within weeks or months of proceedings being started.

4 *Flexibility.* Tribunals are not bound by their own precedents (but they are bound by relevant decisions reached by the courts).

Criticisms of tribunals

Not everyone agrees that tribunals are as effective as they should be. There are a number of criticisms that can be raised regarding the operation of the tribunal system:

1 *No access to legal aid.* There is no state-funded legal aid for most tribunal hearings, which may unfairly prejudice the chances of the claimant. At employment tribunals the employer is usually able to afford legal representation, while employees may be unrepresented unless help is provided by their trade union or other pressure group.

In social security claims, applicants have to dispute their cases with a body which has considerable experience of such hearings, and do not always receive the assistance they need from panel members. In some tribunals, e.g. The employment tribunal, the claimant has to pay a fee to bring the case.

2 *Proceedings have become legalistic*. Over time some tribunal hearings have become less flexible and more formal and consequently less user-friendly to the average claimant. Employment tribunals have been particularly criticised on this ground.

3 *Urgent cases are not resolved sufficiently quickly*. Delays are common if case-loads such as immigration appeals are very heavy.

4

Resolving legal disputes

Chapter summary

The court system

The magistrates' court

Criminal, civil and administrative jurisdiction.

Staffed by JPs, supplemented by district judges.

Crown Court

Criminal jurisdiction only: trial (indictable offences). Sentencing/appeals from magistrates' court.

Staffed by High Court judges, circuit judges, recorders, JPs.

County court

Civil jurisdiction over a wide variety of cases subject to the financial value of the claim.

Staffed by circuit and district judges.

The High Court

Three divisions (Queen's Bench, Chancery, Family) each with different jurisdiction to try civil cases outside the county court's remit.

Divisional courts: mainly appellate jurisdiction from a variety of courts and tribunals.

Staffed by High Court judges.

The Court of Appeal

The Criminal Division: appeals from the Crown Court.

The Civil Division: appeals from the county court and the High Court, Employment Appeals Tribunal.

Staffed by Lord/Lady Justices of Appeal.

The Supreme Court

Appeals from the Court of Appeal and Divisional Courts.

Staffed by Judges of the Supreme Court.

Civil claims procedure

Small claims track (maximum £10,000).

Fast track (maximum £25,000).

Multi-track (above £25,000).

Most civil cases are settled before trial.

Alternative Dispute Resolution

Arbitration: the parties agree to accept the arbitrator's decision as final. Recourse to the courts is largely ruled out. This is very popular in specialised commercial cases.

Conciliation: less formal than arbitration and access to litigation is still possible if the negotiations between the parties and led by the conciliator, break down.

Mediation: similar to conciliation but also used as a preliminary to court action.

Tribunals

Very limited specific jurisdictions in, for example, the fields of employment, and mental health.

Less formal than the courts.

Aim to produce cheaper and speedier outcomes.

Quiz 3

1 Where will the proceedings involving the following parties take place?

(a) Wackford Squeers, on a charge of manslaughter of pupils at Dotheboys Hall.

(b) Bill Sykes, who wishes to appeal against his conviction for murder.

(c) Polly Peachum, who wishes to appeal against her conviction in the magistrates' court for soliciting.

(d) Mr Micawber, from whom Uriah Heep wishes to recover a debt of £200.

(e) Mr Dombey, who is claiming £75,000 against the Great Western Railway Company for injuries caused when he fell under one of its trains.

(f) Newman Noggs, who is claiming that he was unfairly dismissed by Ralph Nickleby.

(g) Mr Dorrit, regarding repossession of his house by the Benevolent & Warmhearted Building Society.

2 What is the purpose of a freezing injunction?

3 What is the difference between arbitration, mediation and conciliation?

4 In what ways do tribunals differ from the ordinary courts?

Answers to all quizzes can be found in Appendix 2.

Web activity

Please go to: http://abta.com/about-abta

Go to 'Help and Complaints' to find out about ABTA's arbitration and mediation procedures.

Assignment 2

How far is it true to say that most cases are best settled out of court?

Discuss.

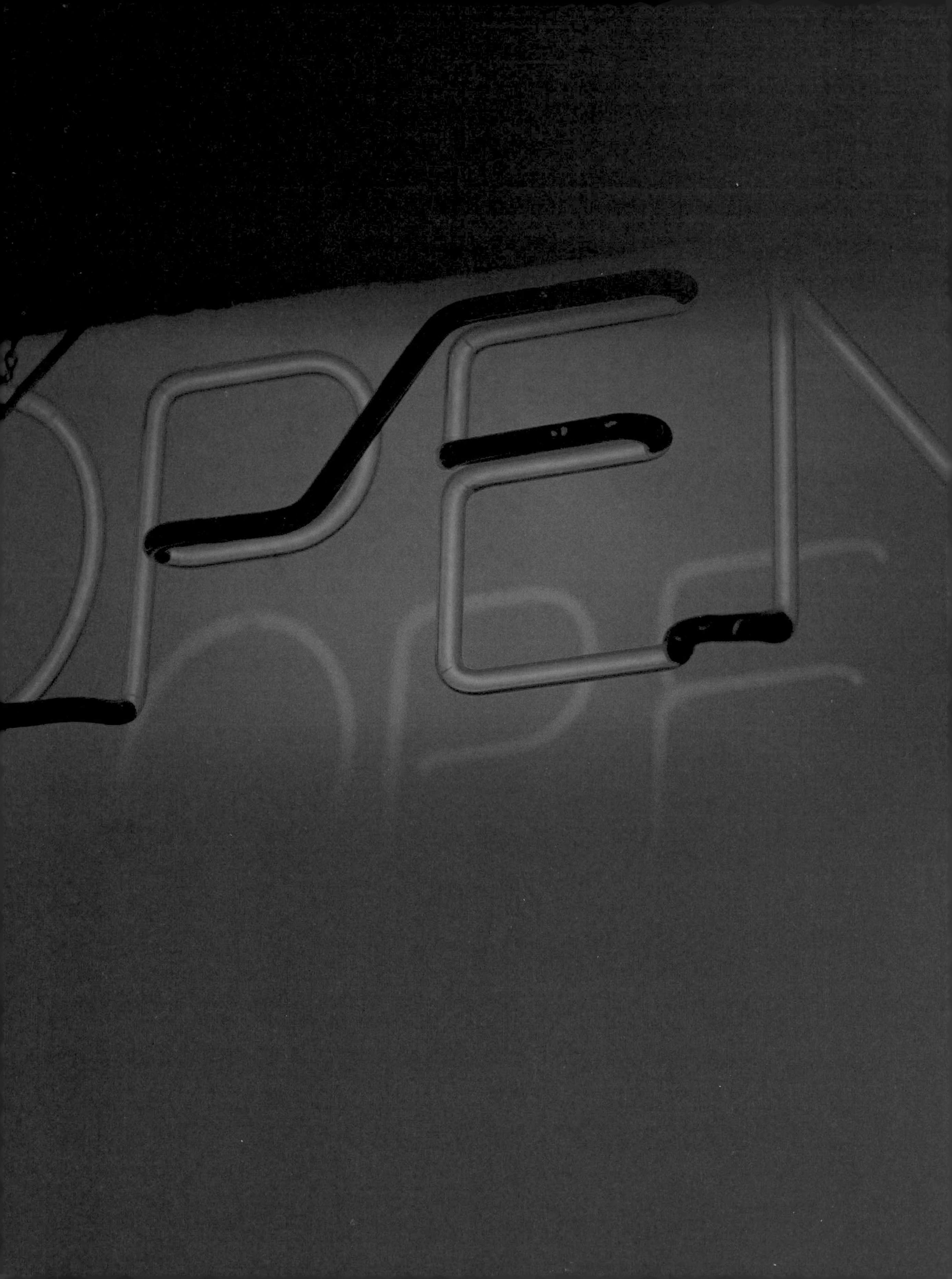

PART 2

Law of contract, agency and sale of goods

CHAPTER 5

The law of contract
Offer and acceptance

Introduction

A contract is a legally binding agreement concerning a bargain which is essentially commercial in its nature and involves the sale or hire of commodities such as goods, services or land. Such contracts are known as **simple** or **parol** contracts, since they are usually enforceable without having to be put into writing. You probably make literally hundreds of contracts every year when doing everyday things like shopping, getting your hair cut, or getting your DVD player repaired. None of the legal paraphernalia that the words 'forming a contract' may bring to mind are involved in such transactions. They are legally binding without documents, signatures or witnesses. If the goods or services provided to you are defective, you have legal rights arising from the contract you made with the shop. To enforce those rights you will, of course, need to prove the existence of the contract. The receipt is handy evidence of this. However, if you have lost this, other evidence – like a credit card docket, or a cheque stub, or the word of your Aunt Ada who was with you at the time – will be perfectly adequate.

In this chapter we shall examine how such contracts are formed. They are still governed by common law principles but statute also plays an increasingly important part. In later chapters we shall examine areas of contract law which are additionally regulated by statute: sale of goods and services, employment law, and partnerships.

Simple:
a contract that does not need to be in the form of a deed to be valid.

Parol:
see simple/parol contract (above).

> # Learning objectives
>
> When you have studied this chapter you should be able to:
>
> ▶ list the essential requirements for a binding contract;
>
> ▶ define offer and acceptance;
>
> ▶ distinguish between an invitation to treat and an offer;
>
> ▶ appreciate the importance of reasonable expectation in determining intention in offer and acceptance;
>
> ▶ demonstrate how offer and acceptance may be effectively communicated.

The essentials of a binding contract

Offer:
a full clear statement of terms on which the maker (offeror) is prepared to do business with the person(s) to whom the offer (offeree/s) is communicated.

Acceptance:
unconditional assent to the terms of an offer.

Consideration:
money/goods/ services/land representing the bargain element of the contract.

No contract can come into being unless the following features exist:

1 an **offer**;

2 an **acceptance**;

3 **consideration** (each party will contribute something of material value to the bargain);

4 **intention to create legal relations.**

Writing is not usually essential

As indicated above in the Introduction, writing is not a legal requirement for the great majority of contracts, though it may well be useful proof of the contents of a complex contract. While the law does not require a building contract to be in writing, most clients would not be very happy to have settled complicated terms by word of mouth only. Many businesses use a **standard form contract** which stipulates terms and conditions (Ts & Cs) with no room for negotiation by the other party.

Contracts which require writing

A minority of contracts *must* be written in full in order to be valid. These include contracts to sell land under the Law of Property (Miscellaneous Provisions) Act 1989, and contracts to obtain credit which are governed by the Consumer Credit Act 1974. Where

Intention to create legal relations: the parties' intention to make their agreement legally binding.

such regulation applies, the written document comprises the contract. Without the contractual document the law will treat the transaction as void (i.e. as if it does not exist), regardless of other available evidence.

Contracts which require written evidence

Under the Statute of Frauds 1677, contracts of guarantee – under which one party (the guarantor) agrees to guarantee the debt of another party for the benefit of a creditor – will be unenforceable without written evidence. This could be just an informal note containing the relevant information.

Standard form contract: comprised terms imposed by a business which are not open to negotiation.

Deeds

Some transactions will be legally valid only if put in the form of a deed, such as the conveyance of land which transfers the rights of ownership to the land and is signed by the parties in front of witnesses. This is a separate transaction from the contract of sale which only requires writing for validity. Deeds are often not concerned with bargains and may be used to make a promise of a gift legally enforceable.

The offer

Offeror: the maker of the offer.

Offeree: the recipient of the offer.

Bilateral offer: a contractual promise of performance of an act in return for the other party's promise of performance.

Unilateral offer: an offer of a promise in return for the performance of an act.

This may be defined as a clear statement of the terms on which one party (the **offeror**) is prepared to do business with another party (the **offeree**). An offer may be bilateral or unilateral.

Most offers are **bilateral**, i.e. such an offer consists of a promise made in return for a promise. In a sale of goods contract, for example, the offeror promises to take and pay for goods and the offeree promises to supply goods of an appropriate description and standard. A **unilateral offer** is a promise made in return for the completion of a specified act. An offer of a reward for the return of lost property falls into this category.

A legally binding offer will include:

1 clearly stated terms;

2 intention to do business;

3 communication of that intention.

These must all exist for a valid offer to have been made.

Clearly stated terms

A statement may be held to be too vague to comprise a valid offer.

Guthing v *Lynn* (1831)

The buyer of a horse promised to pay the seller an extra £5 'if the horse is lucky for me'. This was held to be too vague to be enforceable. No indication was given of what the promise really meant. 'Lucky' could have meant anything from the horse winning the next Epsom Derby to its refraining from biting its new owner.

In the news

'Best endeavours' clause too vague where no means of objective clarification

Dany Lions Ltd v *Bristol Cars Ltd* [2014] EWHC 817 (QB)

DL bought a rare classic car, for which he already had a customer, from BC. The contract of sale required BC to carry out renovations to the car at a cost of £153,000 which would increase its value. Soon after entering the contract BC lost the specialist workmen needed to complete the work. BC and DL entered into a settlement agreement. Clause 2 in the agreement said that DL would use its 'best endeavours' to enter into a contract for the restoration works with a named restorer [J] by a specified date. If this could not be achieved DL would be released from all its obligations under the settlement agreement and be able to claim damages for non-performance from BC. The specified date passed and DL went ahead, employed J to carry out the restoration and sued BC for breach of contract, claiming damages to cover the increased costs of the work now estimated at £249,000. BC claimed the best endeavours clause in its defence on the grounds that DL had failed to satisfy its conditions. The court had to decide whether the 'best endeavours' clause was binding on DL.

Held: BL's defence failed and it was liable for breach of contract as Clause 2 was insufficiently certain. A best endeavour agreement, even one involving securing a deal with a third party, did not necessarily prevent certainty of agreement provided its objects were sufficiently clear and there were objective criteria by which the quality of the endeavours could be assessed. In DL's case this was lacking since although the nature of the works to be completed was specified in Clause 2, no mention was made of the price which was left to be negotiated later with J. Therefore there was no way of judging whether he had agreed reasonable terms with J. Clause 2 was a mere agreement to agree. B must pay damages of £118,555 to cover the difference between the £15, 3000 they agreed in the original sale contract and the £249, 000 DL must pay J.

An apparently vague offer may be capable of clarification by reference to:

1 The parties' previous dealings and the nature of the relevant trade.

Hillas v *Arcos* (1932, HL)

A contract to supply wood for one year contained an option permitting the buyer to buy more wood the next year, but it did not specify the terms on which the supply would be made.

Held: this was a valid offer. Clarification of this rather vague option could readily be gleaned from the previous business dealings of the parties, as well as from custom and practice in the timber trade.

2 *Statutory implied terms.* For example, an offer to sell goods is valid even if no price is mentioned. Under the Sale of Goods Act 1979, s 8, if no price is stated, a reasonable price is payable.

3 *Arbitration clauses.* Sometimes the parties may purposely state terms vaguely and include provision for arbitration to settle disputes if and when they arise. This allows for later variations to take into account future needs, availability or price. Since the lack of clarity may be resolved, a binding offer exists.

Foley v *Classique Coaches* (1934, CA)

The arbitration clause in a long-term contract stated that F would supply petrol to the coach company 'at a price to be agreed in writing and from time to time'.

Held: the contract was binding as the arbitration clause would enable any lack of clarity about the price to be resolved when and if necessary.

Intention to do business

An offer represents the parties' 'last word' prior to acceptance. A statement which does not indicate commitment to be bound by its terms (if accepted) will not be interpreted as a binding offer.

Problems arise where a party, who believes that a binding offer has been made, communicates an 'acceptance'. The party then believes that a contract exists. However, if the original statement is not a binding offer, there will as yet be no contract, since a valid contract requires both binding offer and acceptance.

There are two types of pre-contractual statement which may be confused with a legally binding offer:

Invitation to treat: encouragement to make an offer, usually by advertisement of some kind.

1 **invitation to treat;**

2 negotiation.

An invitation to treat

Most advertisements for the sale of goods, land or services are not usually treated by the courts as indicating the necessary intention to form an offer. Many are just 'business puff' publicising the product or service to encourage sales by the use of catchy slogans suggesting its superiority to other similar products (e.g. 90 per cent of cats prefer Fishybits). Others may actually invite interested parties to make an offer to the advertiser, who then chooses whether or not to accept. Without acceptance, no contract exists; therefore, the offeror has no rights to the goods, etc. until this is communicated.

Catalogues, share prospectuses price lists, menus and circulars advertising so-called 'cheap offers' at local businesses are invitations to treat.

Partridge v *Crittenden* (1968)

The defendant put an advertisement in a magazine saying 'Bramble finch cocks and hens 25 shillings each'. The Wild Birds Act 1954 made it a criminal offence to offer such birds for sale and he was convicted of the offence and appealed.

Held: the defendant was found not guilty since he had not made an offer but merely encouraged others to do so. Lord Parker stated there was 'business sense' in such adverts generally being interpreted as invitations to treat.

A display of goods in a shop, with or without a price tag, is similarly merely an invitation to treat.

Fisher v *Bell* (1960)

The defendant exhibited a flick knife in his shop window and was convicted under the Restriction of Offensive Weapons Act 1959, s 1(1), for 'offering for sale' an offensive weapon.

Held: the defendant was not guilty since he had not made an offer. Goods in a shop window, even those bearing a price tag, represent an invitation to treat, not an offer. Customers make offers by saying that they are prepared to do business at the price shown. Sellers then decide if they want to accept; only if they do does any contract result.

As new methods of marketing develop the law needs to be interpreted to fit the new circumstances. Self-service shopping, which is the norm today, did not start to appear in the UK until the 1950s.

Pharmaceutical Society (GB) v *Boots Cash Chemists (Southern) Ltd* (1953, CA)

Boots introduced self-service including purchase of its patent medicines and was prosecuted by the Pharmaceutical Society under the Pharmacy and Poisons Act 1933 which made it illegal to sell certain drugs 'without supervision of a registered pharmacist'.

Held: no offence had been committed. The medicines on display were merely an invitation to treat. The customer made an offer when handing the goods to the checkout operator. A pharmacist was present at this point and could refuse the customer's offer if appropriate.

Electronic contract making became an important feature of marketing in the late twentieth century – Amazon sells a lot of copies of this book! So far, there is little case law.

As Lord Parker indicated (in *Partridge* v *Crittenden* above), there is considerable business sense in interpreting advertisements and display of goods as invitations to treat rather than offers. It is clearly in the public interest to ensure that some drugs are only sold under expert supervision or that a supermarket does not breach its licence by selling alcohol to the underage customer who presents it at the till. It is also convenient for a restaurant owner who is able to refuse to serve an abusive customer and a shopkeeper who doesn't have to demolish a complicated window display to retrieve an item which a customer demands. In this case it also protects the customer who otherwise might be committed to buying something which did not look so good when more closely inspected.

The Equality Act 2010 aims to prevent abuses of the right of a business to refuse a customer's offer where the business is acting in an illegally discriminatory manner. Similarly, misleading pricing notices may be a criminal offence under the Consumer Protection from Unfair Trading Regulations (as amended by Consumer Protection (Amendment) Regulations 2014).

Negotiation

Lengthy negotiations may lead up to the formation of a contract. Problems may occur where one party assumes that a statement represents the other party's offer and claims to have accepted it. The court will have to decide whether the alleged offeror had by that point indicated a sufficient intention to be bound. In a potentially complex contractual situation where protracted negotiations would normally be expected, a statement made early in the negotiations is unlikely to be held to be a valid offer.

Harvey v *Facey* (1893, JCPC)

The claimants were interested in buying an estate in Jamaica which the defendant had not advertised for sale. They sent a telegram asking the defendant to state the lowest price he would accept. When the defendant replied stating only 'Lowest price for Bumper Hall Pen £900', the claimants attempted to accept and sued for breach of contract when the defendant did not comply.

Held: no contract had been formed, since the statement of price was merely an indication of minimum price if the defendant ultimately decided to sell. It was at best an early step in negotiations and did not amount to a valid offer.

Gibson v *Manchester City Council* (1979, HL)

Mr Gibson requested details from the council about the proposed sale of its housing stock to existing tenants. The council replied by letter, stating that 'the council may be prepared to sell the house to you'. It included a discounted purchase price and mortgage and invited formal applications. Mr Gibson applied but after local elections the council reversed its policy and refused to sell.

Held: The council's letter was not an offer and therefore no contract had been made with Mr Gibson. His application was an offer that the council had refused. The words 'may be prepared to sell' and the request for a formal application clearly indicated that the offer was being invited from Mr Gibson.

However, it all depends on the facts; in the next case sufficient intention was found to exist:

Bigg v *Boyd Gibbons* (1971, CA)

In the course of negotiations involving a number of letters, the claimant wrote to the defendants: 'For a quick sale I would accept £20,000.' The defendant wrote back accepting and the claimant then sent another letter in reply thanking the defendant 'for accepting my offer'.

Held: a binding offer to sell for £20,000 was made in the claimant's letter. Russell LJ said:

> I cannot escape the view having read the letters that the parties would regard themselves at the end of the correspondence … as having struck a bargain for the sale and purchase of this property.

The offer must be communicated to the offeree

The offeror must know of the offer to be able legally to accept. The communication of an offer may be written or spoken, but it may often be by conduct, such as taking goods to the supermarket checkout, or putting money into a vending machine. An offer is most commonly made to an individual, but a unilateral offer may be made to the world at large. In such a case, a contract will be made with all the people who can and do fulfil the terms of the offer.

Carlill v *Carbolic Smoke Ball Co. Ltd* (1893, CA)

The defendants published an advertisement, which claimed that their product would prevent influenza, and promised that they would pay £100 to any person who, having used the product correctly, still caught influenza. The advertisement also stated that £1,000 had been placed in a separate bank account to 'show their sincerity in the matter'.

Mrs Carlill bought a smoke ball from her local chemist. When she became ill with influenza despite regularly sniffing her smoke ball as instructed, she claimed £100 from the manufacturers.

Held: the advertisement was a unilateral offer by the manufacturers to the world at large. This could be accepted by any person who knew of it and who contracted influenza after using the product as directed. The £1,000 bank deposit showed intention to enter a contract and was evidence that the advertisement was not just puffing the goods.

The offeree must, therefore, know of the offer in order legally to be able to accept it. Coincidental performance of the terms of an offer, made in ignorance of its existence, does not create a binding contract.

Bloom v *American Swiss Watch Co.* (1915)

The claimant gave evidence to the authorities which led to the arrest of some jewel thieves. He then discovered that the defendant had previously advertised a reward for such information. The defendant refused payment.

Held: the defendant was not legally obliged to pay as no contract to do so existed between the parties, since the offer of the reward had not been communicated to the claimant prior to his giving the information.

Tenders

Tender:
a competitive offer (bid) to provide goods or services.

A **tender** is a competitive offer to provide goods or services. Many businesses and other organisations will advertise to invite tenders to ensure that they get the best value for money. Some publicly funded bodies may be required to do so by law. The businesses which ultimately supplied the goods and services for the Olympic and Paralympic Games in London in 2012 were all chosen as the result of tenders to the Olympic Delivery Authority.

Although the request for tenders is an invitation to treat, it may also be an offer by the advertisers to *consider* any offer submitted to them.

Blackpool & Fylde Aero Club v *Blackpool Council* (1990, CA)

The Aero Club was invited by the council to tender for a concession to provide pleasure flights for the summer tourist trade. Although the club delivered its tender before the deadline, the council, due to an oversight, failed to clear its letter box and so the tender did not reach the appropriate committee in time to be considered.

Held: the council's request for tenders implicitly contained a unilateral offer to consider any tender submitted by the deadline. The council was therefore in breach of this contract with the Aero Club which had been deprived of its chance to be the successful bidder. Bingham LJ said:

> He [the tenderer] need not accept any tender … but whereas here the tenders are solicited from selected parties all of them known to the invitor, and where a local authority's invitation prescribes a clear, orderly and familiar procedure … the invitee is protected at least to this extent: If he submits a conforming tender before the deadline, he is entitled … as … of contractual right to be sure that his tender will after the deadline be considered … The law would I think be defective if it did not give effect to that.

The termination of offers

An offer, if not accepted, can be brought to an end in a number of different ways.

Death

If the offeree dies, the offer dies too. The death of the offeror terminates the offer if its terms require personal performance. An offer may survive if it can be performed by personal representatives.

Bradbury v *Morgan* (1862)

During his life the deceased had made a standing offer to guarantee another man's debt. The debtor failed to pay the creditor, who, not knowing of the death of the guarantor, wrote to claim his money.

Held: the guarantor's obligations could be satisfied out of his estate, because at the time he accepted the offer the creditor could not reasonably have known of the offeror's death.

Refusal and counter-offer

Counter-offer: an offer made in response to an existing offer.

If an offer is rejected it ceases to exist. If offerees then change their minds and try to accept, they will in contractual terms be making a new offer. The same result is achieved by a **counter-offer**. This is an attempt to vary the terms of the existing offer to get more favourable terms, like a price reduction.

Hyde v *Wrench* (1840)

The defendant offered to sell his farm for £1,000. The claimant at first said that he would pay only £950, but after a few days said he would pay the full price. He heard nothing from the defendant.

Held: there was no contract between the parties: the defendant had not accepted the offer from the claimant, who had destroyed the defendant's original offer by his counter-offer of a reduced price. The claimant's subsequent statement that he would pay the asking price could not revive the original offer. It was a new offer which the defendant never accepted.

If the offeree, while not accepting an offer, asks for further information, or tests out the ground to see if further negotiation is possible, this is not treated as a counter-offer; it, therefore, does not destroy the offer. Therefore, in *Stevenson* v *McLean* (1880) an offer to sell iron at a certain price was not destroyed when the offeree enquired whether delivery and payment might be made in instalments. This was not a counter-offer of different terms, merely an enquiry as to whether the terms might be varied, which did not destroy the original offer.

Lapse of time

An offer will cease to exist if not accepted within any specified time limit. Otherwise it will lapse if not accepted within a reasonable time.

Ramsgate Hotel Co. Ltd v *Montefiore* (1866)

The defendant applied to buy some shares in June but heard nothing more until November when the company informed him that the shares were his.

Held: no contract had been formed since the company's unreasonable delay in notification of the allotment of the shares had made the defendant's offer lapse and the acceptance came too late. He was not obliged to take the shares.

Revocation

Offerors are entitled to change their minds and withdraw offers at any time right up to the moment of acceptance. If, at an auction sale, you place the highest bid and the auctioneer is saying 'going, going …', you still have time to shout that you are withdrawing your offer, as it will not be accepted until the auctioneer's gavel hits the table (Sale of Goods Act 1979, s 57). However, if you do choose to do this, it might be a good idea to leave the auction room briskly.

Notice of revocation is crucial; it is not effective unless the offeree knows of it. Personal notification is usual, but is not essential as long as the offeree knew or reasonably should have known that the offer had been withdrawn.

Dickinson v *Dodds* (1876, CA)

Dodds made an offer to sell property to Dickinson, but sold it to a third party (Allan) before Dickinson effectively responded. Berry, at Dodds' request, told Dickinson of the sale and gave him a copy of Dodds' acceptance of Allan's offer.

Held: Dickinson had adequate notice of revocation. A reasonable person would have realised that, since the property had been disposed elsewhere, the offer was no longer open. James LJ said:

> It is to my mind perfectly clear that before there was any attempt at acceptance by the plaintiff, he was perfectly well aware that Dodds had changed his mind, and that he had in fact agreed to sell the property to Allan. It is impossible, therefore, to say that there was ever that existence of the same mind between the two parties which is essential in point of law to the making of an agreement.

Real life

Horace offered to sell his grand piano to his neighbour Hilda, who said she was really interested but needed to think about whether she could afford it. Later on that day Frederick, a friend of Horace, came to visit and, hearing that the piano was for sale, said he would buy it and collect it the next day. In the morning Frederick came back with the money, a van, and a burly assistant. With Horace's help, they got the piano onto a trolley and wheeled it down to the van and loaded it up. Emmeline, Horace's next-door neighbour, who is somewhat inquisitive, asked Horace what was going on and he told her. That evening Emmeline bumped into Hilda and told her what she had heard.

As *Dickinson* v *Dodds* indicates, Horace's offer to Hilda has been revoked, since *reliable* information even from a third party, not acting on the offeror's instructions, is sufficient notice.

A *promise to keep an offer open* for a certain time or to give someone 'first refusal' will not be legally binding unless the offeree gave some payment to the offeror in return for the favour. Otherwise the offeror is making only a gratuitous promise: giving something for nothing. Such a promise is not a contractual one, since it lacks consideration (see Chapter 6). In the scenario above, Horace might have lost a sale to Frederick if he had waited for Hilda to make up her mind, and then she might have come back and said she was not interested after all. The offeror is therefore free to withdraw (revoke) the promise at any time before the offer is accepted. In *Routledge* v *Grant* (1828) the defendant offered to buy the claimant's house, promising that he would keep the offer open for six weeks. It was held that he could withdraw the promise at any time before the offer was accepted, as his promise was merely gratuitous.

Option:
a promise to allow an offeree time to consider doing business on the terms of a pre-existing offer.

If the offeree does pay for the offer to be held open, a legally binding **option** is created. This means that the offeree has a contract that allows time to choose whether or not to accept the offer. This is different from putting down a deposit on goods or land. An option agreement gives you time to choose *whether* or not to buy, whereas the deposit is evidence that a contract to purchase has been made.

It would obviously be unjust to apply the ordinary rules of revocation to *unilateral offers*, for two reasons:

1 *Notice*. A unilateral offer is often made to the world at large. If the offeror decides to revoke such an offer, it would be impossible to notify everyone who saw it. Provided the offeror takes reasonable steps to give notice, this will be sufficient. Putting another advertisement in the same newspaper which carried the offer would clearly be adequate.

2 *Incomplete acceptance*. Acceptance of a unilateral offer always involves the performance of an act. If an offeree has begun but not completed the acceptance of a unilateral offer, it would be unjust to allow the offeror to revoke the offer. Therefore, revocation may not be effective if the offeree is already in the process of accepting a unilateral offer.

Errington v *Errington & Woods* (1952, CA)

A father bought a house and promised his son and daughter-in-law that it would become theirs if they paid all the instalments on the mortgage by which he had financed the purchase.

Held: although his unilateral offer would technically be accepted only when the last payment had been made, the father's promise was irrevocable as long as the payments were kept up. While the payments continued it would be unjust for the offer to be revoked.

The acceptance

The offeree, by acceptance, agrees to be bound by all the terms of the offer. To be legally binding, such acceptance must fulfil three rules:

1 it must be a 'mirror image' of the offer;

2 it must be unconditional;

3 it must be communicated to the offeror.

Acceptance must be a 'mirror image' of the offer

The offeree must be agreeing to all the terms of the offer and not trying to introduce new terms. In *Jones* v *Daniel* (1894) the offeree responded to an offer by submitting a draft contract which included some new terms. This response was held to be a counter-offer, not an acceptance.

Where two businesses are negotiating a contract, they may each wish to contract on their own standard terms (pre-set terms not open to negotiation). The offerors present their standard terms, but the offerees, instead of accepting on those terms, reply with their own set of standard terms. This is sometimes called 'the battle of the forms'.

Butler Machine Tools Ltd v *Ex-Cell-O Ltd* (1979, CA)

The claimants, on their standard terms, offered to sell machine tools to the defendants. These terms named a price but allowed the claimants to vary this on delivery. The defendants replied with their terms, which specified a fixed price and required the claimants to return an attached acknowledgement slip indicating that they were prepared to supply the defendants' order on these terms. The claimants did so, but when the goods were delivered, they tried to claim that the price could be increased.

Held: the claimants' offer had not been accepted by the defendants: their reply was a counter-offer accepted by the claimants when they returned the slip. The contract was on the defendants' terms and only the fixed price was payable.

Acceptance must be unconditional

Subject to contract: a provisional acceptance, prior to a contract being drawn up.

Conditional acceptance is not binding. An acceptance containing the words '**subject to contract**' is not generally a valid acceptance and use of this phrase is normal practice in sales of land. The parties will not be legally bound to each other until exchange of contracts takes place. This is meant to assist buyers by giving them time to carry out surveys and searches before deciding to commit themselves. It can also mean that the seller is free to sell to another buyer who is prepared to offer more money in the meantime. Such 'gazumping' may cause financial loss to the first buyer, who may have spent money on legal and survey fees and is then left without means of redress against the seller, since there is as yet no binding contract with the seller. However, the intention of the parties is paramount and exceptionally the court may decide that, despite its provisional appearance, it is outweighed by other factors and valid acceptance has taken place. In *Branco* v *Cobarro* (1947, CA) a written agreement described as 'a provisional agreement until a fully legalised contract is drawn up' was held to be a valid acceptance, since it completely reflected all the terms already agreed between the parties. In *Immingham Storage Ltd* v *Clear plc* (2011), the Court of Appeal again demonstrated that statements suggesting conditionality may be negatived by evidence of the parties' existing consensus on terms.

Immingham Storage Co. Ltd v *Clear plc* (2011, CA)

Between October and December 2009 the parties engaged in a succession of negotiations by email, letter and face-to-face concerning the availability, capacity and cost of storage facilities for a certain type of diesel fuel at Immingham's premises. Finally, in December 2009, Immingham sent an email quotation to Clear (headed 'subject to Board Approval and tank availability'). It identified Clear as buyer, the quantity of fuel to be stored and the dates during which storage was available. It stated that all other terms would be those in Immingham's general terms and conditions and that 'a formal contract will follow in due course'. Immingham's terms and conditions were attached. Clear confirmed its wish to proceed by fax. Immingham responded with an email headed 'Contract Confirmation' that started with the words 'we are delighted to accept your offer' and stated that 'a formal contract will follow in due course'. Clear later received the contract but never returned it. Clear was then unable to source the relevant fuel and Immingham claimed its charges. Clear then argued that no contract existed; the signed quote amounted only to a conditional offer because it had indicated that it was conditional on 'board approval and tank availability' and delivery of a formal contract. In addition, it claimed that Immingham's email was not a valid acceptance because it required signature of a formal contract.

Held: a contract came into existence between the parties as soon as Immingham's email validly accepted Clear's signed quotation. The signed quote was a valid offer because it included all the terms and conditions attached to it. The reference to a 'board approval' was irrelevant because these issues had already been settled. Immingham's acceptance was not invalidated by lack of a formal contract. The email as a whole evidenced full acceptance at the point it was received.

Acceptance must be communicated

The law relating to communication involves a number of different rules.

Communication is effective only if made by an authorised person

Powell v *Lee* (1908)

The claimant was notified that his job application had been successful by a member of an appointments board, which then later decided to give the job to someone else.

Held: the person who had informed the claimant had not been authorised to do so. Therefore acceptance had not been effectively communicated.

Methods of communication

Conduct

Brogden v *Metropolitan Railway Co.* (1877, HL)

Mr Brogden had supplied coal to the railway company for some time, when the company suggested that they should regularise their arrangements with a new contract. The draft contract was sent to

Brogden who added certain terms, including the name of an arbitrator. He then marked it 'approved' and sent it back to the company. He heard no more but the company continued to order coal, which Brogden supplied on the terms of the draft agreement.

Held: Brogden's amendments to the draft contract amounted to a counter-offer which had been accepted. The company's intention to assent was in itself insufficient to be acceptance. It became sufficient only once Brogden knew of it. Here the company's conduct evidenced acceptance, either when it placed the first order, or when it accepted the first delivery.

Communication is, therefore, effective only when it reaches the offeror or the offeror's place of business. Commercial practice may enable the court to interpret conduct in relation to the making of offer and acceptance. Thus, in *Confetti Records* v *Warner Music UK* (2003) the sending of an invoice together with a music track was deemed to be an offer by Confetti to sell the material to Warner to be marketed. By producing an album containing the track Warner accepted the offer.

However, only unequivocal conduct will make the acceptance binding:

Inland Revenue Commissioners v Fry (2001)

Ms Fry owed the Revenue £113,000 and sent a cheque for £10,000, with an accompanying letter stating that this was the most that she could raise and that it should be regarded as full and final settlement of the debt. The Revenue cashed the cheque on receipt and the case worker to whom the letter was forwarded subsequently phoned Ms Fry to tell her that the sum could either be treated as part payment of her debt, or she could have the money back.

Held: the Revenue had not made a valid acceptance. Cashing the cheque gave rise to no more than a rebuttable presumption of acceptance and here the presumption had clearly been rebutted by the case worker's subsequent phone call. No reasonable person would believe that banking the cheque indicated intention to be bound by the terms of the offer. The Revenue's administration system would not be likely to permit a contract, under which it gave up its rights to substantial sums of money, to be concluded in this way.

Verbal communication

Acceptance is effectively communicated only when the offeror has received notice of it. In a face-to-face situation it will usually be immediately evident if any communication problems have occurred. However, if the parties cannot see each other this may be more problematic; acceptance by *telephone* is held to be effective only on being heard by the offeror. The courts have extended this principle to *telex* transmissions. In *Entores Ltd* v *Miles Far East Corp.* (1955, CA) the Court of Appeal made it clear that acceptance by telex should be treated like acceptance by telephone: instantaneous and effective on being received.

5

The law of contract: offer and acceptance

> ### *Brinkibon Ltd* v *Stahag Stahl und Stahlwarenhandels GmbH* (1982, HL)
>
> The House of Lords suggested (*obiter dicta*) that telex messages transmitted when the receiver's office was closed would be effective only once the office had reopened.

The *Brinkibon* ruling was applied in *Mondial Shipping and Chartering BV* v *Astarte Shipping Ltd* (1995) where it was held that a telex message sent just before midnight on a Friday was communicated at 9 a.m. the following Monday when the receiver's office opened for business.

When developing such rules the courts are guided by the '**reasonable expectations of honest men**' in the context of accepted commercial practice. In *Entores* it was stressed that if it were the fault of the offeror that the message was not received (due perhaps to lack of ink in the teleprinter), the offeror would still be bound, as the offeree would reasonably expect successful receipt. This principle, generally applied by the courts, enables objective assessment of the parties' behaviour from which it can be determined whether the intention to offer or accept is adequately demonstrated.

Reasonable expectations of honest men: the objective standard by which the court decides whether a party's conduct evidences sufficient intention to be contractually bound.

Electronic communications

As yet, there do not appear to be any reported cases involving communication via fax, or answerphone. Using the reasonable expectations approach, *faxes* are likely to be treated like telex messages.

It can probably be successfully argued that messages left on *answering machines* are not communicated until, like any telephone message, the recipient actually hears them. It is, after all, immediately evident to the sender that the message is not going to be transmitted at once.

Emails have been accepted by the courts as a valid means of communication of acceptance but without any specific ruling on when communication becomes effective. In *J. Pereira Fernandes SA* v *Mehta* (2006) Judge Pelling QC in a contract of guarantee accepted without argument that email offer and acceptance is a potentially valid form of communication, but gave no indication of when communication is effective. *Immigham Storage Co. Ltd* v *Clear* (2011) (above) implies that receipt is required. It might be reasonable to argue that, once they have been sent, arrival may well be instantaneous. However, delays may occur in transmission via the server, so maybe communication should be deemed to exist once the message is capable of being downloaded to the receiver's mailbox.

Internet sales are covered, though not in detail, by the Electronic Commerce (EC Directive) Regulations 2002 (which implemented the E-Commerce Directive 2000/31/EC). Regulation 11 states that electronic orders/acknowledgements of orders 'are deemed to be received when the parties to whom they are addressed are able to access them'. This suggests that when a contract is made on the internet, the website details of goods are an invitation to treat. Presumably, the customer communicates the offer by placing the order, entering name, address and payment card details and transmitting this information to the seller with a click on the relevant button. The seller will not be deemed to have accepted until it communicates acceptance by sending a message confirming that the order has been placed successfully. This will happen only after it has successfully accessed the customer's card.

The post rule

Post rule: the default rule governing acceptance by post which is that the acceptance is binding from the moment of posting.

The **post rule** provides an exception to the usual communication rule. In the nineteenth and early twentieth centuries the normal method of communication for parties contracting at a distance from each other was the post. In the middle of the nineteenth century the postal rules were extended to cover telegrams. The rules were clarified further by *Household Insurance v Grant* (1879, CA), which held that communication of acceptance by post is effective even if a letter is delayed in the post or fails to reach the offeror, as long as this is not due to some fault of the offeree's: for example, an incorrect address.

Adams v *Lindsell* (1818)

On 2 September the defendants sent a letter of an offer to sell wool to the claimant and stated any acceptance must be made by return of post. The letter was delayed because it was wrongly addressed and did not arrive until 5 September. The claimants posted their acceptance immediately and it finally arrived on 9 September. On 8 September, the defendant, believing that the claimant was not interested, sold the wool to a third party. The claimant sued for breach of contract.

Held: The claim would succeed. The claimant had complied with the terms of the offer by posting their acceptance immediately. Once a letter of acceptance is posted, a contract comes into existence immediately. The delay in communicating the letter was entirely the fault of the defendant.

Worth thinking about?

Judges always have a reason for changing the law.

Why do you think the post rule was developed?

Suggested solutions can be found in Appendix 2.

Only postal acceptance produces an instantaneous legal effect: a postal offer or revocation is effective only on receipt.

Byrne v *Van Tienhoven* (1880)

1 October:	The defendant posted an offer from Cardiff to the claimant in New York.
8 October:	The defendant changed his mind and posted a letter of revocation.
11 October:	The defendant's offer arrived and the claimant sent a telegram of acceptance.
15 October:	The claimant affirmed his acceptance by letter.
20 October:	The letter of revocation was received by the claimant.

Held: a contract was formed on 11 October when the claimant mailed his telegram of acceptance. The revocation was not communicated to the claimant until 20 October and was, therefore, too late to be effective.

It has always been possible for an offeror to avoid the postal rules either by specifying a different means of communication, or by stating that they would not be bound until receipt of an acceptance letter. Even where an offeror specifies nothing to this effect, the courts may be prepared to imply such an intention.

Holwell Securities v *Hughes* (1974, CA)

The offeror granted an option to the offeree concerning the purchase of some land, which had to be exercised by 'notice in writing'. The claimant's letter of acceptance was posted before the deadline but failed to reach the offeror before the deadline expired, though this was not the claimant's fault.

Held: no contract resulted from the postal acceptance. The postal rule was implicitly excluded by the offeror, who, by requiring notice in writing, had indicated that for communication to be effective it must actually receive the letter of acceptance.

Today the postal rules do not play an important part in the law of contract, though they continue to feature in exam papers. Parties contracting at a distance now generally have much faster and more reliable means of communication available to them. Even where the parties choose to use the post, it is very common for offerors to state that no contract will result until they receive an acceptance.

The offeror cannot waive the communication rule

In a bilateral contract situation offerors cannot bind offerees by saying that they will assume acceptance unless the offerees tell them differently. The communication rule ensures that an offeree is not pressurised into acceptance.

Felthouse v *Bindley* **(1862)**

The claimant offered to buy a horse from his nephew, John, who was selling up all his farm stock. The claimant said that he would assume John's acceptance unless told otherwise. Intending to accept, John instructed the auctioneer to withdraw the horse from the sale, but by mistake the auctioneer sold it. The claimant sued the auctioneer in tort.

Held: the claimant's action failed because he was unable to prove that he was the horse's owner. Since John had not communicated his intention to accept to the claimant, there was no contract under which ownership of the horse could pass. The auctioneer had not disposed of the claimant's property. When the sale took place the horse still belonged to John.

In a unilateral contract acceptance and performance constitute the same act, so no prior communication of acceptance is practicable. If you see a notice offering a reward for the return of lost property, you will be able to accept only if you find it and actually return it, thereby performing the act for which the reward was promised. You cannot be refused it because you have not given advance notice.

The offeror may expressly require a particular method of communication

The court will usually be prepared to treat any reasonable method of communication as effective. Where no mode is specifically requested, the mode of offer and the nature of the subject matter of the contract may indicate suitable methods of response. For example, a telephone offer of perishable goods would necessitate a swift means of communicating acceptance.

pter summary

Formation of a simple contract requires the following factors to be present:

Agreement (offer and acceptance).

Bargain (consideration).

Intention to create legal relations.

Writing not essential unless required by statute.

Offer

The statement of *final* terms on which the offeror is prepared to contract which becomes effective once received by the offeree.

An offer may be bilateral (a promise in return for a promise) or *unilateral* (a promise in return for an act).

An invitation to treat or merely negotiating statement is not an offer because it invites an offer or further negotiation and does not indicate finality or intention to be bound.

An offer may be revoked up until the time of acceptance.

An offer will lapse unless accepted within a stipulated or reasonable time.

Acceptance

Acceptance is only binding in law if it is firm and completely reflects the offer terms. Any attempt to vary the terms may amount to a counter-offer.

It must be communicated. This usually requires receipt by the offeror, but a letter of acceptance is binding once posted unless the offeror specifies otherwise.

Determining the legal existence of offer and acceptance: the court interprets the behaviour of the parties objectively in accordance with 'the expectations of reasonable men'.

Quiz 4

1 Does an offer exist in the following circumstances?

(a) Joshua puts a teddy bear wearing a price ticket in his shop window.

(b) Ruth distributes flyers stating 'Cheap Offer: 10% off the cost of all our pizzas'.

(c) Mary advertises a reward of £50 for the return of her lost bracelet.

(d) Martha returns Mary's bracelet and then discovers that a reward was offered.

(e) Peter offered to sell his car to Esther for £3,000; Esther told him she would pay only £2,500.

(f) Elizabeth offered to sell her fridge-freezer to Paul for £100. He asked her to give him three days to decide. The next day she sold the freezer to Jacob.

2 Has a valid acceptance resulted in the following situations?

(a) John offers to sell potatoes to Thomas, who replies that he will take them if he can raise the money.

(b) Eve offers to sell apples to Matthew and tells him that she will assume that he wants to buy them unless he tells her to the contrary by 10 o'clock on Saturday morning. The deadline has now passed but Matthew has not been in touch.

(c) Luke sent a letter to Michael offering to sell an antique clock. Michael replies accepting, but his letter is lost in the post.

(d) Susanna offered by telephone to rewire Antony's house. He accepted, but Susanna did not hear because the line went dead.

Answers to all quizzes can be found in Appendix 2.

Take a closer look

The following cases provide important examples of how the law you have studied in this chapter has developed. They are primary sources illustrating the law in action and give you more detail about their facts, as well as helping you to understand the law and to appreciate how the judges reached their decisions.

Try looking them up in the law reports or accessing them via a database, e.g. Bailli (www.bailii.org/databases.html). LexisNexis or Westlaw may be available in your university or college library, or you may find extracts in a case book. (See Appendix 1: Additional resources.)

Carlill v Carbolic Smoke Ball Co. Ltd [1893] 1 QB 256, CA

Blackpool & Fylde Aero Club v Blackpool Council [1990] 3 All ER 25, CA

Entores Ltd v Miles Far East Corporation [1955] 2 All ER 493, CA

Immingham Storage Co. Ltd v Clear plc [2011] EWCA Civ 89; 135 Con LR 224

5 The law of contract: offer and acceptance

Web activity

Please go to: www.carbolicsmokeball.co.uk

Read the law report, see a full colour reproduction of the famous advertisement with testimonials and find out what a smokeball actually looked like. You will also find a photograph of Miss Carlill aged 87 looking hale and hearty.

Assignment 3

Iris made an offer to sell her piano to Diana for £500 on Monday. Diana replied: 'I will buy it if I can raise the money.' Iris promised that she would not sell to anyone else before Saturday, and added that Diana could collect the piano any time before noon on Saturday. On Wednesday, Diana phoned and left a message with Iris's daughter, Athena, saying that she had got the money and would come to collect the piano on Saturday morning. Athena forgot to pass on the message. On Thursday, Iris was visited by Juno who said that she would pay £600 for the piano.

Iris accepted this offer. Later that day Iris posted a letter to Diana telling her that she could not have the piano. Mercury, the postman, delivered it to the wrong address and Diana, who never received the letter, appeared with a hired van to collect the piano at 10 o'clock on Saturday morning.

Advise Iris of her legal position. (Some hints on answering problem questions, including an analysis of the above assignment, can be found in Chapter 1.)

CHAPTER 6

The law of contract
Consideration, intention and privity

Introduction

Essentially, the law of consideration is about price: money or money's worth. Contracts are commercial agreements: they are about striking bargains, or achieving what is sometimes called '**mutuality**'. Both parties stand to gain materially from the transaction: each receives a '**consideration**'. Where one party agrees to do something for the other with nothing promised in return, that party is said to be making a '**naked**' or '**gratuitous**' promise. In effect it is a promise of a gift. A legally binding contract cannot result from such a promise, only a moral obligation. It can only be made enforceable by putting it in the form of a deed.

It is quite possible to find agreements in which the elements of offer, acceptance and consideration can be identified, but the agreement will not be binding as a contract unless that is deemed to be the parties' intention. When they entered into the agreement, they may not have intended that failure to perform the agreement would make them liable to legal sanctions for breach of contract.

A contract may be made for the benefit of a third party who does not contribute consideration but the common law rule of **privity of contract** generally prevented him or her from enforcing it. This is now mitigated by the Contracts (Rights of Third Parties) Act 1999.

Mutuality: both parties support their promises by consideration.

Consideration: money/goods/services/land representing the bargain element of the contract.

Naked promise: see gratuitous promise below.

Gratuitous promise: a promise which is not supported by consideration.

Privity of contract: exclusivity of contractual rights and duties to parties who contribute consideration.

> # Learning objectives
>
> When you have studied this chapter you should be able to:
>
> ► define consideration;
>
> ► recognise the circumstances when valid consideration exists;
>
> ► appreciate the exceptions to the rules governing valid consideration;
>
> ► describe the operation of the promissory estoppel doctrine;
>
> ► appreciate the characteristics of agreements which demonstrate intention to create legal relations;
>
> ► explain how the Contracts (Rights of Third Parties) Act 1999 has impacted on the doctrine of privity of contract.

Consideration

Consideration has been defined by the courts in different ways. In *Currie* v *Misa* (1875) it was held to constitute a benefit to one party or a detriment to the other. Generally, it is easy to analyse contracts on this basis. When you buy a DVD recorder from a shop, the benefit you receive is the DVD recorder, and the detriment is the money you pay the shop. The shop clearly enjoys a corresponding benefit, and suffers a corresponding detriment in taking your money and parting with the DVD recorder.

In *Dunlop* v *Selfridge* (1915, HL), the House of Lords defined consideration in terms of the price by which one party bought the other party's act or promise. This is also clearly reflected in the example of the sale of the DVD recorder.

Executory consideration: a contractual promise which has not yet been performed.

Executed consideration: a contractual promise which has been performed.

Executory and executed consideration

Executory consideration

A binding contract may be formed by the exchange of promises to be carried out at a later date. If you order goods which are to be paid for on delivery, a binding contract results on your order being accepted. Failure to deliver the goods to you would be a breach of contract. The consideration in such a contract consists of the mutual promises and is described as 'executory' because the promises have not yet been **executed** (performed).

Executed consideration

Sometimes no contractual obligation to pay arises unless or until another party has executed their consideration. For example, if someone advertises a reward for the safe return of a lost cat, that person is making a unilateral promise to pay money that will become binding on the performance (execution) of an act (the return of the cat). The consideration provided by the person who returns the cat is called 'executed consideration'.

The rules governing consideration

Consideration must not be past

The act claimed to represent consideration for another party's promise to pay must not precede that promise, or it will be treated as past consideration and the promise will be merely gratuitous.

Real life

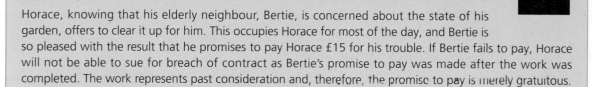

Horace, knowing that his elderly neighbour, Bertie, is concerned about the state of his garden, offers to clear it up for him. This occupies Horace for most of the day, and Bertie is so pleased with the result that he promises to pay Horace £15 for his trouble. If Bertie fails to pay, Horace will not be able to sue for breach of contract as Bertie's promise to pay was made after the work was completed. The work represents past consideration and, therefore, the promise to pay is merely gratuitous.

To be contractually binding, it must be shown that a promise to pay preceded the act so that the promise and act form one undivided transaction. The principle is clearly illustrated in the following case:

Re McArdle (1951, CA)

A house was left by Mr McArdle to his wife for life. On her death it was to be sold and the proceeds divided equally between the children of the marriage. The wife of one of the children paid for home improvements at a cost of £488. When the work had been done all the children agreed that she should recover this sum from the proceeds of the eventual sale. After Mrs McArdle died the validity of this agreement was disputed.

Held: no valid contract existed since the home improvements were past consideration; they had been carried out before any promise to pay had been made.

There is an exception to this rule when a subsequent promise is enforceable. Valid consideration may be held to exist in the absence of an express prior promise to pay provided that:

1 the act was done in response to a specific request; and

2 the situation was one where payment would normally be expected.

Re Stewart v *Casey (Casey's Patents)* (1892, CA)

An employee contributed many hours of his own time to the development of an invention for his employers at their request. When the work was completed, the employers promised that they would pay him a share of the profits once the invention was patented.

Held: the employers were bound by the promise as the employee had done the work at their request, and the nature of their relationship implied that future payment would be made.

The subsequent explicit promise to pay in such situations is seen as an affirmation of an implied promise which accompanied the request that the work be carried out.

Consideration must move from the promisee

This rule prevents a party from enforcing a contract unless he or she has contributed consideration. However, a number of exceptions exist under common law and statute and further reform has resulted from the Contracts (Rights of Third Parties) Act 1999 (see below).

Consideration must be sufficient

Consideration must be of material value, capable of assessment in financial terms. Usually the financial nature of the consideration is obvious where goods, land or money is involved. Any legal right has a financial value. Settling a case out of court involves a contract under which one party agrees not to exercise their legal right to sue the other, provided that the other pays an agreed sum of compensation. The consideration for the promise of compensation is the promise not to sue. In *Alliance Bank* v *Broome* (1864) a bank was held to have provided consideration, for the defendant's promise to give security for a loan, by promising not to take action to recover it.

White v *Bluett* (1853)

A son whose father had cut him out of his will agreed not to bore his father by nagging him to make a new will in his favour. In return his father agreed to release him from a debt. After his father's death the executors sued the son for payment and the son claimed that the debt had been discharged by his agreement with his father.

Held: the father was not bound by his promise as the son had not provided valid consideration. He had no right to dictate how his father disposed of his property, so he had not given up anything of material value by stopping nagging his father.

Note that consideration *may be sufficient without being adequate*. Provided the alleged consideration is of financial value, it is irrelevant that it is not an adequate return. The courts are not interested in whether the parties have made a *good* bargain, but only in whether they have made a *bargain* at all. Therefore, proof of financial value, however minute, will be enough to make consideration sufficient.

Thomas v Thomas (1842)

A widow was promised a house in return for ground rent and promising to keep the property in good repair.

Held: an annual rent of £1 was held to be sufficient consideration for the promise.

Advertising campaigns sometimes offer to supply goods in return for wrappers, packet tops or vouchers cut from relevant product wrapping. If you comply with what is asked, then a binding contract results and you are entitled to the tea towel, cuddly toy or other delight being offered.

Chappell v Nestlé & Co. Ltd (1959, HL)

Nestlé ran an offer to promote a particular chocolate bar. Anybody who sent three of the relevant wrappers plus one shilling and sixpence (75 pence in today's money) was entitled to a record of a current pop hit 'Rocking Shoes'. Nestlé threw away the wrappers on receipt.

Chappell, which disputed the amount of copyright compensation, sued Nestlé and the court had to decide whether the wrappers amounted to a portion of the consideration.

Held: Nestlé would derive a clear economic benefit from any increase in sales resulting from the promotion, so it was irrelevant that the wrappers would be thrown away on arrival.

Sufficiency usually involves taking on some *new obligation* in return for the other party's promise of payment. Performing an existing legal duty does not generally amount to sufficient consideration.

Collins v Godefroy (1831)

The claimant was a key witness at a trial and was under a court order to attend. Failure to do so would have made him guilty of the crime of contempt of court. The defendant was a party to the proceedings; because the claimant's attendance was important to him, he promised to pay the claimant if he would attend.

Held: the defendant's promise of payment was not contractually binding. The claimant had not provided sufficient consideration merely by promising to perform his existing legal duty.

In a case like this the claimant is effectively promising the defendant that if the claimant pays him money he will not commit a criminal offence, and such agreements are treated as being against *public policy* (not in the public interest).

6

The law of contract: consideration, intention and privity

Similarly, where two parties have made a contract, a subsequent promise of additional payment to encourage performance is not a binding contractual promise. The promisee is already contractually bound to perform and is therefore providing no fresh consideration.

Stilk v *Myrick* (1809)

Two sailors deserted from a ship in the course of a voyage. The captain promised the remainder of the crew that he would pay a bonus to each man if they got the ship home to England from Scandinavia.

Held: this promise was not binding. Crew members were required by their contracts to cope with the normal difficulties of a voyage, which in those days included crew shortages of this kind. Therefore, there was insufficient consideration to make the captain's promise enforceable.

Economic duress: an attempt to obtain favourable contract terms by threatening financial loss to a contracting party.

The court's unwillingness to enforce promises of this kind generally results from a concern that the promisee has exerted **economic duress** – blackmailed the promisor into offering extra payment. (This topic is explained in Chapter 9.)

The court may take a more generous attitude if satisfied that the public interest is not adversely affected and that enforcing the promise would produce the fairest outcome. The court may justify such a decision in one of three ways:

1 by finding that the promisee has exceeded the scope of his or her legal duty. The excess represents the consideration; or

2 by finding that the promisee, in carrying out the legal duty, has actually conferred a new benefit on the promisor; or

3 by deciding that the act of the promisor enabled the promisee to *avoid* some material *disadvantage*.

Hartley v *Ponsonby* (1857)

The facts of this case are similar to those in *Stilk* v *Myrick*, but here the depletion of the crew and the length of the journey were so great that the crew's existing contract of employment was discharged.

Held: by getting the ship home, the crew effectively were taking on a new set of duties and thus providing sufficient consideration for the captain's promise of more pay.

Glasbrook Bros v *Glamorgan County Council* (1925, HL)

The defendant mine owners, fearing vandalism of their premises during an industrial dispute, promised that if the police authority provided a full-time guard, they would make a donation to a police charity.

Held: this promise was binding, as the police could have fulfilled their legal duty by periodic inspection of the premises: the full-time guard exceeded this and was therefore sufficient consideration.

Williams v *Roffey Bros* (1990, CA)

Roffey was a builder who had a contract to refurbish a building for a housing association. This contract contained a delay clause under which Roffey was required to pay substantial sums if the work was not finished on time. Roffey sub-contracted carpentry work to Williams, who later ran into financial difficulties and told Roffey that because of this he would be unable to continue. Roffey promised him payment of extra money to complete the contract on time. He then refused to honour this undertaking arguing that Williams was merely doing what he had originally contracted to do.

Held: Roffey's promise was binding, since by securing the completion of the contract he was obtaining a benefit, or at least avoiding a burden. He avoided having to pay the delay costs to the housing association. He had freely entered into the agreement and not been forced by economic duress.

In making this decision the Court of Appeal was breaking new ground judicially, but the ruling reflects current commercial practice. It was applied in *Opel GmbH and Renault SA* v *Mitras Automotive* (2008), where it was held that the termination agreement imposed by the defendants was supported by consideration, as it enabled the claimants to avoid breaching contracts with their clients. However, the contract was voidable for economic duress. (See page 189 for full facts.)

Note that *Stilk* v *Myrick* is not overruled by *Williams* v *Roffey Bros*. There are clear distinguishing features. It must be decided on the facts of a case which decision will apply.

Worth thinking about?

In what ways can *Williams* v *Roffey* be distinguished from *Stilk* v *Myrick*?

Suggested solutions can be found in Appendix 2.

The *Williams* v *Roffey* principle was limited and clarified by the Court of Appeal in the following case:

Re Selectmove (1995, CA)

Selectmove owed arrears of tax to the Inland Revenue which threatened to start liquidation proceedings. Selectmove negotiated with a tax inspector and stated that it would pay all future tax as and when it fell due and that it would pay off all arrears of tax at £1,000 a month. The tax inspector said that if Selectmove heard nothing more it could assume that this plan was agreeable to the Revenue. Later, the Revenue then started liquidation proceedings.

Selectmove claimed that the Revenue was bound by the tax inspector's agreement since, under the *Williams* v *Roffey* principle, it obtained a benefit or at least avoided a disbenefit. If the company went into liquidation the Revenue might not acquire full repayment of the tax arrears and would not get the benefit of future tax payments.

Held: promising to carry out an existing duty can only be binding under *Williams* v *Roffey* if the duty is to perform *an act*, not just to *pay money*. The rule in *Pinnel's* case (below) applies to part payment of debt.

Part payment of debt is not sufficient consideration

> ### The rule in *Pinnel's Case* (1602)
> A promise by a creditor to accept less than the full sum owed does not discharge the debtor from the legal obligation to pay the balance.

The rule in *Pinnel*'s case is illustrated by the following example:

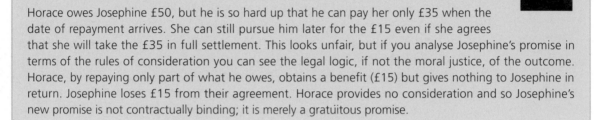

Real life

Horace owes Josephine £50, but he is so hard up that he can pay her only £35 when the date of repayment arrives. She can still pursue him later for the £15 even if she agrees that she will take the £35 in full settlement. This looks unfair, but if you analyse Josephine's promise in terms of the rules of consideration you can see the legal logic, if not the moral justice, of the outcome. Horace, by repaying only part of what he owes, obtains a benefit (£15) but gives nothing to Josephine in return. Josephine loses £15 from their agreement. Horace provides no consideration and so Josephine's new promise is not contractually binding; it is merely a gratuitous promise.

There are some exceptions to this rule. The debt will be discharged by part payment if the creditor requests:

1 part payment at an earlier date; or
2 part payment at a different place; or
3 some goods or other material benefit to accompany the part payment.

In these situations the debtor is providing some consideration by doing something different at the creditor's request. For example:

Real life

Horace did building work at James's delicatessen for £1,000. When payment was due James was unable to pay in full, so Horace agreed to take £900 plus £100's worth of smoked salmon for his parents' forthcoming silver wedding anniversary celebration.

Part payment by a third party in return for a promise from the creditor not to pursue the original debtor for the balance also discharges the whole debt. An agreement (**composition**) between creditors has a similar effect. It is common business practice for the multiple creditors of a debtor to agree that they will each accept a proportionate repayment of their debts. An individual creditor cannot renege on this contract to pursue the balance of his or her debt as this would be a fraud on the other creditors.

A form of such an agreement, commonly known as an Individual Voluntary Arrangement (IVA) was introduced and is regulated by the Insolvency Act 1986. IVAs are brokered by finance businesses for a commission and allow debtors to repay a proportion of their debt to their creditors over a specified period which is usually five years. In recent years the number of people dangerously in debt has grown and IVAs have become very popular as an alternative to bankruptcy. (See 'In the news' below.)

Composition (with creditors): a legally binding agreement between creditors that they will each take only a proportion of what the debtor owes, in full settlement of the entire debt.

In the news

IVAs: numbers continue to rise in 2014

Insolvency Service statistics indicate the great popularity of IVAs and the huge growth in use since their introduction in 1987, when there were under 5,000. Between 1990 and 2003 there were under 10,000 every year. Numbers then gradually increased and 2010–12 numbers hovered around the 50,000 mark. Statistics for 2014 indicate that the number of IVA arrangements rose yet again to 52,190, an all-time high. This means that 53 per cent of all personal individual insolvencies in 2014 resulted in IVAs compared with the 2005 figure of 30 per cent

Setting up these arrangements very quickly became an industry, with many firms charging substantial commission and some failing to advise clients appropriately, since IVAs are not suitable for everybody. To prevent mis-selling The Office of Fair Trading set guidelines for advertising in 2007 and required providers to conform within four weeks. The Insolvency Service run by BIS (Department for Business, Innovation and Skills) has issued protocols since 2008 to promote good practice in consumer IVAs. These provide a simple and straightforward framework for setting up the transaction. The current version was introduced in 2012. Advice is available from organisations like the Citizens' Advice Bureau (CAB). Stepchange (the debt advice charity) provides its own IVA.

Sources: www.bis.gov.uk/insolvency; www.citizensadvice.org.uk/; www.stepchange.org/.

The cases of *Re Selectmove* (1995) (above) and *Re C (A Debtor)* (1994), indicate that the Court of Appeal is not prepared to allow the principle in *Williams* v *Roffey* to validate agreements to pay *less* than the agreed sum, rather than *more*. This would otherwise undermine the rule in *Pinnel*'s case.

Promissory estoppel (*High Trees* doctrine): an equitable defence which a party may use when a contract has been gratuitously varied for their benefit and the other party seeks to enforce it in its original form.

Promissory estoppel

Promissory estoppel is an equitable defence which may be relevant in part-payment situations. Under this principle, parties who gratuitously promise that they will not enforce existing contractual rights may lose their entitlement to do so if it would be unfair to allow them to go back on their promise; they are prevented (*estopped*) from breaking the promise. This defence was developed in the following case:

The law of contract: consideration, intention and privity

6

Central London Property Trust v *High Trees House* (1947)

The defendants owned a block of flats on land leased to them by the claimants. By September 1939, many flats had become vacant due to outbreak of war. Consequently, the defendants were having difficulties paying their ground rent. The claimants agreed that they would accept reduced payments. The defendants continued to pay the reduced rent even when the flats refilled and the war was over.

The claimants brought a test case claiming arrears of rent for the last two quarters of 1945 (by which time the war had ended).

Held: the claimants were found to be entitled to the arrears they claimed, but it was also held (*obiter dictum*) that had they claimed for arrears prior to the end of the war this would have been refused. It would be unfair to allow them to go back on their promise on which the defendants had naturally relied. The claimants' gratuitous promise operated to suspend their rights to full payment while the extenuating circumstances in which the promise had been made continued to operate.

This *obiter dictum* (persuasive ruling) from a then youthful Mr Justice Denning has been applied by the House of Lords. In *Tool Metal Manufacturing Co. Ltd* v *Tungsten Ltd* (1955) a gratuitous promise, to suspend rights to royalty payments on a patent during the war, was held to be a good defence to a subsequent claim for such payments.

However, although the doctrine of promissory estoppel has been much discussed by the Court of Appeal and the House of Lords in subsequent cases, it has been used very little and its scope is far from clear. Two elements are certain:

1 *It can operate only as a defence*. Denning LJ clarified this aspect of the doctrine in *Combe* v *Combe* (CA, 1951). Describing it as a 'shield and not a sword', he emphasised that the doctrine 'should not be stretched too far' and the principle 'did not create new causes of action where none had existed before' and that 'the doctrine of consideration is too firmly fixed to be overthrown by a side wind.'

   Therefore, if we apply this reasoning to *High Trees*, it is clear that the defendants could not have sued on the claimants' promise, but it would have been a good defence against the claimants if they had tried to enforce their original contract rights for the period in which they had been suspended.

2 *It is an equitable principle*. The court will not grant an equitable remedy unless it will produce a just result for both parties; parties seeking such a remedy must show that they have behaved morally as well as legally.

D & C Builders v *Rees* (1965, CA)

Mrs Rees persuaded the builders, whom she knew to be in financial difficulties, to accept payment of £300 in full settlement of a debt of almost £483, by telling them that they would otherwise get nothing.

Held: it would not be equitable to allow their promise to be used as a defence against them, given that Mrs Rees had effectively '*held the builders to ransom*' (Denning LJ) forcing them to accept the smaller sum.

Intention to create legal relations

In determining whether the parties intend their agreement to be legally binding, the courts are guided by two presumptions concerning the parties' **intention to create legal relations**:

1 parties to a domestic or social agreement do not intend to be legally bound;

2 parties to a business agreement intend to be legally bound.

These are presumptions only and can be rebutted (disproved) by sufficient evidence to the contrary.

Domestic and social agreements

The courts believe that family members and friends do not generally intend agreements, made merely for their mutual convenience, to be legally enforceable. Property rights between family members are generally adequately covered by other areas of the law. Unless there is clear evidence of what is at heart a commercial transaction – for example, the sale of a car between family members – an intention to be contractually bound will not be presumed.

Balfour v *Balfour* (1919, CA)

Held: no intention to create legal relations existed in an agreement under which a husband working abroad promised to pay maintenance to his wife in England.

The courts take a different view if the couple does not intend to continue in the marriage. In *Merritt* v *Merritt* (1970, CA) a contractual relationship was held to arise from a post-separation maintenance agreement.

Car pool agreements may involve the necessary intention:

Albert v *Motor Insurers Bureau* (1971, HL)

Held: if lifts are provided on a regular and systematic basis under which drivers anticipate payment, an intention to create a legally binding relationship is present.

The relative financial risk to one party and the reliance by that party on the other party's promise may be relevant.

6

The law of contract: consideration, intention and privity

Parker v *Clark* (1960)

The Parkers (niece and nephew to the Clarks) agreed to sell their house and move in with the Clarks. The Parkers received a letter from Mr Clark confirming that, in return for moving in, sharing household expenses and taking on some household tasks, for the rest of both the Clark's lives, the house would become theirs under Mr Clark's will.

Sadly, the arrangement broke down and the Parkers, who were told to leave, sued for breach of contract.

Held: sufficient intention to be legally bound was evidenced by the clear terms of the agreement and because Mr Clark had changed his will. The Parkers had relied upon it to their considerable financial detriment having given their daughter their house sale proceeds to buy a flat.

Even a 'fun' transaction may implicitly contain a more formal intention.

Simpkins v *Pays* (1955, CA)

The claimant lodged in the defendant's boarding house. Every week she, the defendant and the defendant's granddaughter entered a fashion competition in a Sunday newspaper. They took it in turns to pay the entry costs and postage and agreed that any winnings should be divided equally. One week their entry, sent in the defendant's name, won £750 but she refused to pay the claimant her share. The claimant sued in breach of contract and the defendant argued that no legally binding relationship had been intended in the transaction.

Held: the claimant should succeed since the parties demonstrated sufficient intention to be legally bound. This was more than just a friendly agreement. It was a joint enterprise to which each of the parties contributed financially in the expectation of sharing prize money.

A clearly defined agreement must exist before evidence of intention to be bound can be deduced.

Wilson and Another v *Burnett* (2007, CA)

The claimants organised a girls' night out to the local bingo hall with the defendant, a workmate. The defendant won substantial prizes totalling £101,354. The claimants alleged that at the start of the evening they had all agreed to share equally any prize over £10. The defendant disputed this. At the trial Judge Nelligan said:

> I accept the defendant's evidence that there was chat or talk about sharing winnings which went no further than discussion or chat, and did not cross and cannot be inferred to have crossed that line which exists between talk and 'meaning business', or an intention to create a legal relationship, that is to share the prize money.

He therefore held that the claimants were not entitled to share the money. The claimants appealed.

Held: Judge Nelligan had been justified in coming to his decision. In agreements between friends it was presumed that there was no intention to be legally bound, though every case must be examined on its facts. Although there had been discussion about sharing winnings, there was insufficient evidence of any clear agreement sufficient to prove the existence of such intention, so the claimants lost their case.

It is easy to see clear differences between the facts in the two cases above. In *Simpkins* v *Pays* the parties had regularly entered the competition together following the same process each time and each party contributed to it and had a stake in the outcome. In *Wilson* v *Burnett* the parties were engaged in a one-off outing and the evidence of any potential agreement was conflicting.

> **Exam tip**
>
> If the question describes parties in a problem as friends or family members, this may be to nudge you into mentioning the issue of intention to create legal relations.

Business agreements

In the world of business, the presumption that agreements are intended to have legal consequences means that a very clear indication of lack of intention to create legal relations is necessary to rebut the presumption that a legally binding relationship was intended.

Rose & Frank Co. v *J. R. Crompton & Bros* (1925, HL)

The claimant was a US company, selling carbon paper, and it agreed to permit the defendant, an English company in the same line of business, to market its product in the USA. The wording of the agreement stated that it was not 'a formal legal agreement and shall not be subject to legal jurisdiction in the law courts either of the United States or England, but it is only a definite expression and record of the purpose and intention of the parties concerned to which they each honourably pledge themselves'.

The defendant subsequently breached the agreement and claimed that it did not amount to a binding contract.

Held: this clause was effective to exclude intention to be legally bound as it was clear and specific.

Next time you see an advertisement for a competition, check the small print and you will usually find that it contains similar words. In *Jones* v *Vernons Pools* (1938) it was held that no legally binding contract was created between punter and pools company: the entry coupon stated clearly that the relationship between the parties was 'binding in honour only'.

Comfort letters

In business it is not uncommon for a parent company to reassure a financial institution of the creditworthiness of a subsidiary company by issuing a 'letter of comfort'. If the subsidiary fails to repay any resulting loan, the lender may try to sue the parent company to recover the money. Despite the highly commercial context, such letters are not necessarily legally binding and the context of preceding negotiations and the wording is crucial.

Kleinwort Benson v *Malaysia Mining Corporation Bhd* (1989, CA)

A comfort letter issued by Malaysia Mining in support of its subsidiary, MMC Metals Ltd, stated that: 'It is our policy to ensure that the business [of MMC] is at all times in a position to meet its liabilities to you.'

Held: this was merely a statement of current intention and of Malaysia Mining's policy. It was not intended to have a legally binding effect and did not amount to any guarantee of the future reliability of MMC.

Privity of contract

Promisor:
a recipient of a promise.

Promisee:
a party making a promise.

Sometimes a contractual situation may arise where one party (**promisor**) agrees with another (the **promisee**) to provide a benefit for a third party. From your study of consideration (earlier in this chapter), you may remember that the common law rule is that parties who have not contributed consideration to a contract cannot sue on it if it is breached. This is because they are not full parties to the contract: in the rather archaic language still used by lawyers, they are not *privy to the contract*, or there is no *privity of contract* between the parties. Thus, the beneficiary cannot sue if the contract is breached.

Tweddle v *Atkinson* (1861)

William Tweddle was engaged to marry Miss Guy. The fathers of the happy couple contracted that they would each put up a sum of money when the marriage took place, but Mr Guy died before making payment.

Held: William had no right to sue Mr Guy's estate for the money since he had provided no consideration for the promise and was merely a beneficiary of the contract. As a mere beneficiary, William was not *privy to the contract*: he was not truly a party to it because he was not contributing to the consideration.

Similarly, the burdens of a contract cannot be enforced against a party to whom no consideration has been promised.

> ### *Dunlop Rubber Co. Ltd* v *Selfridge* (1915, HL)
>
> Dunlop supplied tyres at a discount (less than list price) to Dew & Co., who agreed not to resell below list price to trade buyers unless those buyers also agreed not to resell below list price. Dew supplied Selfridge, who breached the resale price agreement. Dunlop tried to take action against Selfridge.
>
> **Held:** Dunlop could not sue Selfridge, as there was no privity of contract between them: Dunlop had given no consideration to Selfridge in return for the promise to stick to the resale price. (Any action could only be taken against Selfridge by Dew for breach of the contract between them.)

Exceptions to the rule of privity

To prevent injustice, a number of exceptions to the rule have been acknowledged to enable beneficiaries to enforce their rights.

1 *Agency.* Where agents make contracts on behalf of their principals with third parties, the principals may sue or be sued on those contracts as if they had made them themselves. (See Chapter 11.)

2 *Third-party insurance.* A third party may claim under an insurance policy made for their benefit, even though that party did not pay the premiums (for example: life assurance and third-party motor insurance).

3 *Assignment of contractual rights.* The benefits (but not the burdens) of a contract may be assigned to a third party, who may then sue on the contract (for example: selling debts). The original debtor may be sued by the new creditor to whom the rights to collect the debt have been assigned. The duty to perform a contract cannot be assigned.

4 *Trusts.* This is an equitable concept by which one person transfers property to a second person (the trustee), who holds it for the benefit of others (beneficiaries). The party who created the trust, which is often done by a will, lays down the rules under which it is to be administered. If these are not complied with, the beneficiaries have the right to ask the court to enforce the trust for their benefit.

5 *Collateral contracts.* The performance of one contract between A and B may indirectly bring another into being between A and C.

6 *Contracts for the benefit of a group.* Where a contract to supply a service is made in one person's name but is intended to benefit a group of people, the members of the group have no rights to sue at common law if the contract is breached; there is no privity of contract between them and the supplier of the service. The court, however, may take some of their losses into account when awarding damages to the buyer.

Shanklin Pier Ltd v *Detel Products Ltd* (1954)

Detel advised Shanklin Pier Ltd that their paint was suitable for maritime use and would last for at least seven years. Shanklin Pier Ltd contracted with a decorating firm to paint the pier; a term of the contract required the decorators to buy Detel's paint for the purpose. The paint began to peel off within three months.

Held: Shanklin Pier Ltd could successfully sue Detel Products on a collateral contract which was linked to the main contract between Shanklin Pier Ltd and the decorating firm. Detel had made promises about the quality of their paint and Shanklin Pier had provided consideration for this promise by requiring their decorators to use it.

Jackson v *Horizon Holidays Ltd* (1975, CA)

Horizon provided such a poor level of service that the Jackson family holiday was ruined.

Held: Mr Jackson, who had made the contract, was the only party who could sue but the damages he was awarded took into account the loss to the whole family resulting from Horizon's failure to deliver a holiday of the promised quality.

Statutory reform of the privity rule

In 1996, the Law Commission (Report No. 242) stated that reform was needed since the law at that time:

(a) prejudiced third parties who may have relied on contracts which they had no power to enforce;

(b) caused problems in commercial life;

(c) was out of step with other EU members and much of the common law world, including New Zealand and the USA.

As a result, reforming legislation was introduced.

Contracts (Rights of Third Parties) Act 1999

Section 1 gives a third party the right directly to enforce any contract which expressly permits this or where the contract is intended to benefit them. This gives the third party the same remedies as any other party to a breach of contract action. They must be expressly identified in the contract by name or class or description, but need not be in existence when the contract is made. Thus, a contract to provide an ongoing benefit to 'all my children' could benefit any children born after formation of the contract.

Section 2 further protects third parties by preventing cancellation or variation of the contract without their permission unless the contract *expressly* provides for this. Generally, a third party's rights cannot be withdrawn or varied without their consent if: they have communicated agreement by words or conduct to the terms, or the promisor is aware that they have relied on the terms, or the promisor should have reasonably foreseen that they would rely on the term and they have in fact done so. In exceptional circumstances (e.g. mental incapacity of the third party) the court may dispense with the right of consent.

Section 5 protects the promisor from double liability. If the promisor fails to perform the duty owed to the third party, they will not be liable to the third party for any losses that the promisee has already recovered from the promisor. This prevents the third party from recovering twice for the same losses. Third-party rights cannot be enforced in some contract situations. Section 6 specifies some exceptions: for example, a third party cannot enforce any term against an employee in an employment contract; in a contract for carriage of goods, a third party has no enforceable rights except for the protection of any exclusion or limitation clause in the contract.

Note that the 1999 Act does not abolish the privity doctrine: it just introduces a new right. Section 7 specifies that existing third-party rights and remedies remain unchanged.

Chapter summary

Consideration

The bargain element that distinguishes a contract from any other sort of agreement legally binding or otherwise.

Definition: material benefit gained/detriment arising from performance of a contract.

Price paid for the other party's promise or act. Benefit/detriment.

The rules of consideration

It must not be past: not precede the promise to pay.

It must be sufficient: represent some detriment/benefit though not necessarily an adequate price.

Generally, only a party who provides consideration may enforce the contract (see Privity, below).

Part payment of a debt does not generally discharge it (*Pinnel's* case).

Promissory estoppel may provide a defence for a defendant sued for breach of contract, if he or she can prove that the claimant had previously gratuitously varied the contract in the defendant's favour so that it would be unjust to let them go back on their word.

Intention to create legal relations

The parties to a contract must intend it to be legally binding or it will not be enforceable in the courts. Two rebuttable presumptions operate here.

An agreement between friends or family members is presumed not to reflect that intention, while business agreements are.

Privity of contract

Generally, the doctrine of privity of contract prevents anyone except a party who contributes to the bargain from enforcing it.

The Contracts (Rights of Third Parties) Act 1999 enables a contractual beneficiary to sue for breach of a contract that was clearly made for their benefit, even though they have not provided any consideration.

Quiz 5

1 Are the following promises legally binding or merely gratuitous?

   (a) Red returned Brown's lost tortoise. Brown promised him £5.

   (b) Green agreed to sell his vintage sports car to Black for 10p.

   (c) Scarlet promised her employee, Orange, that she would give him a £10 bonus if he arrived at work on time for a week.

   (d) Blue was owed £50 by Yellow, but agreed to take £45 in full settlement if Yellow made the repayment a week early.

   (e) Pink agreed that his tenant, Turquoise, might pay a reduced rent while he was out of work.

2 White told his tailor to make a wedding suit for White's nephew, Grey, who chose the style and material. The cost was to be charged to White's account. When the suit was finished it did not fit Grey, who had to hire one. Has Grey any rights against the tailor?

Answers to all quizzes can be found in Appendix 2.

Take a closer look

The following cases provide important examples of how the law you have studied in this chapter has developed. They are primary sources illustrating the law in action and give you more detail about their facts, as well as helping you to understand the law and to appreciate how the judges reached their decisions.

Try looking them up in the law reports or accessing them via a database, e.g. Bailii (www.bailii.org/databases.html). LexisNexis or Westlaw may be available in your university or college library, or you may find extracts in a case book. (See Appendix 1: Additional resources.)

Re McArdle [1951] Ch 669

Williams v *Roffey Bros* [1990] 1 All ER 512, CA

Simpkins v *Pays* [1955] 3 All ER 10, CA

Jackson v *Horizon Holidays* [1975] 3 All ER 92, CA

Web activity

Please go to: www.stepchange.org/

Click on IVAs to find out more about how these work and their pros and cons.

Assignment 4

(a) Is it true to say that the doctrine of privity of contract is redundant since the Contracts (Rights of Third Parties) Act 1999?

(b) Arthur rents a house to his friend Brian for £400 a month in January. In May, hearing that Brian is in financial difficulty, Arthur offers to reduce the rent to £250 'until things pick up for you again'. In October, Cathy, Brian's wife, is left £20,000 by her uncle. In December, Arthur finds out about this windfall and asks for full rent from October onwards. Advise Arthur.

CHAPTER 7

The terms of the contract at common law

Introduction

As you will be aware (from your study of Chapter 5), a contract is only formed when a bundle of promises (clearly defined terms) is offered by one party and accepted by the other. The size of the bundle is determined by the nature and complexity of the contract. A contract to get your hair cut is obviously a much simpler transaction than one to build a housing estate. However, both will include some explicitly stated **express terms**, like the cost of the haircut or the number of houses to be built, and the parties will usually also be bound by some **implied terms** that they have not expressly agreed, but which by law are standard to the type of the contract. So you may assume that the hairdresser will cut your hair with reasonable competence whether they have promised this or not.

Not all contract terms are necessarily of the same importance. Some terms (**conditions**) are crucial to the contract; others (**warranties**) are more trivial, and therefore different legal consequences flow from breach of them. In a construction contract the number of buildings is much more important than some aspects of the finish to those buildings like taps or door furniture. Sometimes the importance of a term is disputed; then the court has to decide into which category such an **innominate term** fits.

When making a contract either as a business or as a consumer you need to keep a sharp eye open for **exclusion (or exemption) clauses**, which may enable the other party to avoid liability for a breach of contract. You may already have noticed some of these notices clearly displayed by the coat pegs in a

---

Express term: a contractual term specifically stated to be part of the contract.

Implied term: a term which was not specified in the contract, but may be implied into it by statute or common law.

Condition: a major contractual term crucial to its existence. If breached, the innocent party may refuse further performance and sue for breach.

Warranty: a minor contractual term, breach of which entitles the innocent party to damages.

Innominate term: a term capable of giving rise to a variety of breaches of different degrees of seriousness.

Exclusion or exemption clause: a contractual term which attempts to limit or exempt a party's contract/tort liability against another. Sometimes called an exemption clause.

...ser's or restaurant, stating that the management will not be liable for theft ...omers' property. These may be sufficient to prevent you making a successful ...f your coat is stolen.

...s chapter is concerned with the common law approach to terms, but since the ...eenth century statute has also assumed an increasingly important role in relation ...ome areas of contract law, like employment and the sale and supply of goods and services. (We shall examine the role of statute in Chapter 8.)

Learning objectives

When you have studied this chapter you should be able to:

▶ appreciate the difference between express and implied terms;

▶ distinguish between conditions, warranties and innominate terms;

▶ explain the purpose of exclusion clauses and the common law rules governing them;

▶ be aware of the role of the EU and Parliament in the composition of the contract

Express and implied terms

The terms of a contract fall into three categories: conditions, warranties and innominate terms (explained below). These terms may be expressed or implied. Express terms are specifically communicated by the offeror. Other terms may be implied by statute, custom or the courts.

The sources of implied terms

Terms implied at common law

The court may be prepared to imply a term into commonly occurring contracts, such as employment (see Chapter 16) and landlord and tenant, to protect against exploitation of the more vulnerable party.

Liverpool City Council v *Irwin* (1977, AC and HL)

The lifts and rubbish chutes and lighting in the stairs in a block of flats owned by the council were frequently vandalised with resulting inconvenience to the tenants, who withheld rent as a protest. The tenancy agreement imposed duties on tenants, including paying rent, but did not oblige the council to maintain the general facilities in the building.

Held (by the House of Lords): since proper access to the building was not possible without maintenance of these facilities, a term should be implied in any tenancy agreement requiring the landlord to take reasonable care in maintaining such facilities. However, as there was no actual breach of duty here, the tenants were not entitled to withhold payment.

Business efficacy

Business efficacy: the obvious common sense but unspoken intention of the contracting parties.

The court is not generally sympathetic to parties who claim rights under a contract that were not expressly promised to them. However, the courts have implied terms perceived as representing the will of the parties assessed objectively. A term may be implied to give 'business efficacy' to the contract and make full sense of it. The court will do this if the contract lacks a very obvious term. For example, if you asked the dairy to deliver you 'two pints of milk', it is unlikely that you would feel the need to specify that the milk must be in a container rather than left in a puddle on your doorstep.

The Moorcock (1889, CA)

The claimant hired docking space at the defendant's wharf and suffered losses when his ship was damaged when it grounded at low tide.

Held: The claimant was entitled to assume that the state of the river bed adjacent to the dock was safe for his ship and this should be implied by the contract.

This strategy prevents a party from avoiding contractual liability on a technicality and gives effect to the obvious common sense but unspoken intention of the parties.

Judges are increasingly extending this purposive approach to interpretation of ambiguous express terms.

Pink Floyd Music v *EMI Records* (2010, CA)

Held: The Court of Appeal held by majority that a term prohibiting EMI from selling 'albums', in any form other than as delivered, included sale of their contents separately as downloads or ring tones. It made 'commercial common sense' (Neuberger LJ) to enable Pink Floyd to control the integrity of their albums as delivered and how their contents was marketed in digital form.

The Court of Appeal took a similar approach more recently in *Thorney Park Golf Ltd* v *Myers Catering Ltd*.

In the news

Court of Appeal seeks purpose behind unclear contract wording

Thorney Park Golf Ltd v *Myers Catering Ltd* (2015, CA)

Myers Catering had a franchise to supply catering services to a golf club for a fixed term of three years, subject to termination with notice. The club was sold on to Thorney Park. The new owners terminated that agreement and the parties made a new agreement. Clause 4 stated that 'In order for this contract to be reasonable for both parties to develop and invest in a viable business development plan an initial term of three years (with the fee reviewed annually) must be agreed'. The agreement also stated that it was terminable with four months' notice.

A year later Thorney Park sought to terminate the contract. Myers claimed that this was a breach of contract given that the contract was for a fixed term and could only be terminated with four months' notice at the end of three years. Thorney Park claimed that clause 4 meant that it could be terminated at any time with appropriate notice.

The Court of Appeal held unanimously that Myers' interpretation was preferable. The Court must determine the parties' intention by an objective assessment of the evidence taking into account that it had been drafted by lay people and might lack precision. The reference in clause 4 to the issue of reasonableness and time needed for investment and development was important evidence. To allow early termination would be likely to defeat that requirement. It was also striking that this reasonableness provision was expressly drafted into the agreement with Thorney when the previous one had only provided for termination by either side with notice. The parties clearly intended a change from the previous terms.

Worth thinking about?

Can you think of any other scenario when the court might imply a term to give business sense to a contract?

Suggested solutions can be found in Appendix 2.

Trade custom and practice

In some trades it is customary for certain practices to prevail in performance of a contract, or for risks to be allocated between the parties in a particular way.

> ### *Hutton* v *Warren* (1836)
>
> *The claimant was given notice to quit his agricultural tenancy. Local custom obliged him to continue planting crops during the notice period, although he was unable to harvest them before he left.*
>
> **Held:** The local custom gave the tenant a reciprocal right to recoup a reasonable sum to cover the subsequent expense. This right became an implied term of the contract, so the claimant could recover his losses.

A party is generally entitled specifically to exclude the effect of any implied term unless prevented by statute from doing so. (See exclusion of liability below at page 130.)

Statute

Parliament may provide that terms be implied in certain types of contract. For example, the Sale of Goods Act 1979 (as amended by the Sale and Supply of Goods Act 1994) is one of the most important sources of implied terms for most businesses. It includes special safeguards for the buyer by implying certain terms concerning the standard and quality of goods in most sale contracts. The seller is in breach if the goods do not meet these standards, regardless of whether the seller gave any undertakings expressly to the buyer. Greater protection for consumer buyers has been a feature of recent developments in this area, which is heavily influenced by EU legislation, e.g. the Consumer Rights Act 2015. (We shall examine this legislation in Chapter 8.)

The relative importance of contractual terms

The terms of a contract are not necessarily equally important. Breach of contract, therefore, gives rise to different rights according to the importance of the breached term. Generally, terms can be classified as conditions or warranties. Whether terms are to be classified as conditions or warranties is determined by the parties' apparent intentions when they made the contract. An apparently trivial matter like a sea view from the hotel bedroom may be elevated to the status of a condition of the contract if its necessity is stressed before acceptance takes place.

Conditions

Conditions are the most important terms which form the main structure of the contract. For example, when you are booking hotel accommodation, the dates of your stay and the type of room (single/double) are some of the most crucial requirements. If particular details are crucial to one party, this must be pointed out to the other party before the formation of the contract is completed. If you are booking a double room, this may result in your being given single or double beds unless you stipulate which you prefer.

Breach of a condition gives the injured party the right to treat itself as free of any further contractual duties and to claim compensation.

Warranties

Warranties are more minor terms; they are ancillary to the contract rather than crucial to it. For example, when you are booking hotel accommodation, the promise of tea- and coffee-making facilities and colour TV will not be vital to the performance of the contract. Their absence does not stop you from getting most of the enjoyment that you expect from the holiday.

Breach of a warranty does not entitle the injured party to refuse to perform its side of the contract. That party is entitled only to compensation for consequential loss, i.e. loss resulting from the breach.

The next two cases illustrate the distinctions between these two types of term.

Poussard v *Spiers & Pond* (1876)

An actress was employed for a season, but was delayed by illness from taking up her role until a week after the opening night.

Held: her employers were entitled to terminate the contract: her presence on the opening night was crucial to the contract.

Bettini v *Gye* (1876)

A *singer, engaged* for a season, failed to turn up for the first three of the six prescribed rehearsal days.

Held: given the length of the contract and because no performances were missed this amounted only to a minor breach; the employer was not entitled to repudiate.

Innominate terms

Not all terms are clearly and immediately identifiable as conditions or warranties. Some, described by the courts as 'innominate', are worded broadly to cover a variety of possible breaches, some more serious than others. The court then has to decide whether a particular breach is to be treated as one of condition or warranty.

Hong Kong Fir Shipping Co. Ltd v *Kawasaki Kisen Kaisha* (1962, CA)

*A contract stated that a ship would be 'in every way fitted for cargo service'. This te*rm was capable of including many types of breach, from a large hole in the hull to a malfunctioning toaster in the canteen. Due to the incompetent engine room crew and a malfunctioning engine, the ship broke down and 20 weeks' *use of the ship was lost from* a two-year charterparty (hire contract). The defendants who had hired the ship abandoned the contract and the claimant owners sued them for breach.

Held: the breach of the term relating to the ship*'s fitness was not sufficiently serious to permit the* defendants to terminate the contract. The importance of the term must be judged in relation to the actual damage resulting from it. The damage caused did not strike at the root of the contract (the ship was still available for more than 18 months of the hire period), and therefore no breach equivalent to a breach of condition had occurred.

Diplock LJ stated that the judge's task in cases of this kind was 'to look at the events which had occurred as a result of the breach at the time which the charterers purported to rescind the charterparty and to decide whether the occurrence deprived the charterers of substantially the whole benefit which it was the intention of the parties as expressed in the charterparty that the charterers should obtain' (from the performance of the contract).

Hong Kong Fir was a controversial decision since it was subsequently argued that the so-called 'damage test', would promote uncertainty, since parties to a contract would not be aware of the importance of a term until it was breached.

It was applied again in:

Cehave NV v *Bremer Handelsgesellschaft (The Hansa Nord)* (1975, CA)

A contract stated that a cargo of citrus pellets for animal feed would be shipped 'in good condition'. On arrival some of the cargo from one hold was damaged. The buyers rejected the whole cargo, then later purchased it at a lower price and used it for its original purpose.

Held: the term was innominate and since the damage did not destroy the main purpose of the contract the buyers had no right to reject the goods.

The *Cehave* decision was clearly a just one in the circumstances since the buyers still used the cargo for its original purpose and it would have been unjust to allow them to make a profit at the other party's expense from a trivial fault.

However, the Court of Appeal indicated clearly that the damage test was a last resort where no other clear indicator existed. It set out the following criteria to interpretation of the status of an innominate term:

1 The express intention of the parties is paramount: if the contract specifies that a particular breach will entitle a party to opt out of the contract that is conclusive.

2 The use of the words 'condition' and 'warranty' to describe a term is of evidential value only – it is not conclusive in itself.

7

The terms of the contract at common law

3 If a party has a statutory right to terminate the contract if a term is breached, the term is a condition (for example, Sale of Goods Act implied conditions).

4 Consistently established commercial practice will determine the status of a term.

5 Finally if none of the above provides assistance the damage test may be used. The innocent party may repudiate their obligations only if the damage resulting from the breach is so extensive that it substantially deprives them of the benefit of the contract.

The next three cases illustrate the operation of the second criteria:

Lombard North Central plc v *Butterworth* (1987, CA)

A contract for the lease of a computer stated that prompt payment of instalments was of the essence of the contract and that failure to comply would entitle the hire company to terminate the agreement. The defendant paid the third, fourth, and fifth instalments late and the sixth became six weeks overdue. At this point the claimant repudiated the agreement and sued for damages for breach of contract.

Held: late payment in such circumstances would not normally be grounds for repudiation of the contract, but here the term had been elevated to the status of a condition, because the supplier had specifically made the time factor crucial. The supplier was entitled to repudiate even if payment was minimally late.

Mustill LJ stated:

> A stipulation that time is of the essence, in relation to a particular contractual term, denotes that timely performance is a condition of the contract. The consequence is that delay in performance is treated as going to the root of the contract, without regard to the magnitude of the risk.

Schuler AG v *Wickman Machine Tool Sales* (1974, HL)

Wickman was given sole selling rights for Schuler's products for four-and-a-half years. A term of the contract stated that it was 'a condition of the contract' that Wickman would send its representative weekly to solicit orders from the six largest UK manufacturers.

Held (by majority): this term was not a condition in the sense that a single breach, however trivial, would entitle the innocent party to terminate the contract.

The reasonableness or otherwise of treating a term as a condition was crucial to deciding whether the parties intended breach of the term to give rise to repudiation rights.

Lord Reid said: We are seeking to discover intention as disclosed by the contract as a whole. Use of the word 'condition' is an indication – even a strong indication – of such an intention but is by no means conclusive.

Valilas v *Janusaj* (2014, CA)

A dentist rented premises and agreed with his landlord that the monthly rental would be based on his NHS earnings calculated with reference to the specified number of treatments that he was required to carry out every year. Rent was to consist of half the sum paid to the dentist monthly in advance by the NHS. The NHS contract required the dentist to make proportionate refunds if he failed to carry out the annual minimum number. The landlord agreed to repay the dentist half of any such refund.

The contract worked well initially but later the relationship soured. The dentist found that he was unable to fulfil the statutory number of treatments. He did not believe that the landlord would perform his duty to make refunds if the contract ended and so told him that in future he would pay only half the agreed rental every month, but would be entirely responsible for paying any rebate to the NHS at the end of the year. The landlord claimed that this was a breach of contract and that he was entitled to repudiate it.

The Court of Appeal held (affirming the decision of the County Court): the landlord was not entitled to repudiate the contract for this breach because timely rental payment was not stipulated in the contract and therefore time was not of the essence. The payment obligation was not a condition but merely an innominate term which only gave the right to repudiate if breach went to the root of the contract and effectively deprived the landlord of the main benefit of the contract. Although the dentist was in breach the landlord was still in effect getting the same rent; therefore the landlord had no right to repudiate.

Customary business practice (criteria 4) determined the outcome of the next case.

The Mihalis Angelos (1970, CA)

The Court of Appeal held that an 'expected readiness to load' term in a **charterparty** was, as a matter of commercial practice, always to be treated as having the force of a condition, provided that the party in breach had given the undertaking untruthfully, or without reasonable grounds for believing that it could be fulfilled.

Charterparty: a contract to hire a fully crewed ship.

Criteria 5 [the damage test] was applied in the next case and as in *Cehave* enabled the seller to avoid an unjust disadvantage.

Reardon Smith Line v *Hansen-Tangen* (1976, HL)

At the point the buyer entered a shipbuilding contract there was a boom in trade. At the point when the ship was ready for delivery, however, a recession had occurred and the vessel was now surplus to his requirements. The vessel built fulfilled all its contractual specifications except that it was built at a different shipyard from that named in the contract and he claimed he was entitled to reject it because of this breach.

Held: the breach was of an innominate term; no damage resulted so there was no right to repudiate.

The court, when applying these criteria, seeks to do justice between the parties, as well as act in the public interest. If you take these considerations into account it may help to make these cases easier to grasp. Charterparty rules form part of the law which under-pins an important part of the national economy. It has been formed from the custom and usage of international traders with whom good business relationships are crucial. In Mihalis Angelis Edmund-Davies LJ said: 'It would be regrettable to … disturb an established practice.' In both the *Cehave* and *Reardon Smith* cases, the damage test was employed to prevent the buyer from unfairly avoiding contractual responsibility on a technicality and obtaining an unjust financial advantage.

Limitation and exclusion of liability

Many contracts include a term by which one party seeks to limit financial claims against it in the event of loss or damage to the other party, or to exclude itself from legal liability altogether. For example, by a **limitation clause** a holiday firm's contract may restrict customers' claims in the event of delay, postponement and cancellation of flights to specified sums for meals and overnight accommodation. When you pay to use a car park, it is usual for the contract to include an **exclusion clause** stating that the proprietors have no legal liability for damage to or theft of or from your vehicle.

Such limitation of or exclusion from liability may be a perfectly reasonable business practice, but is subject to control, both by the courts and statute, to prevent abuses. Without such regulation a business could avoid liability for flagrant negligence, or for gross and irresponsible breach of contract.

(Please note that to make reading and writing less cumbersome a reference to 'exclusion clauses' in this book generally covers both exclusion and limitation clauses.)

Before any exclusion clause can be effective it must satisfy two criteria at common law:

1 it must be incorporated with advance notice within the contract;
2 it must be clear and unambiguous.

Incorporation

In order for any term to be incorporated in the contract (form part of it), the party to be bound by it must have sufficient notice of it. Two factors are crucial to the issue of notice:

1 timing;
2 sufficiency.

Timing of notice

Notice of exclusion of liability must be given to the other party prior to that party's acceptance.

Limitation clause:
a contractual term which seeks to restrict the amount of damages payable to the innocent party in the event of a civil action.

Exclusion Clause:
seeks to prevent any legal liability for breach of contract.

Notice may consist of a written sign of some kind displayed at the place of business, or in a contractual document. Its content should be clearly evident to customers before they commit themselves to the contract.

Here are three case examples of ineffective notice:

Olley v *Marlborough Court Hotel* (1949, CA)

A notice in Mrs Olley's bedroom stated that the hotel proprietor would not be liable for theft of guests' property. Later jewellery and furs were stolen from her room.

Held: the contract between Mrs Olley and the hotel had been concluded at the reception desk when Mrs Olley booked in, before she read the notice, which consequently did not form part of the contract. The hotel was therefore not exempt from liability for the theft.

Thornton v *Shoe Lane Parking* (1971, CA)

A notice inside a car park stated that the proprietors would not be liable for injuries to customers. This was also printed on the ticket dispensed from the automatic barrier at the car park entrance.

Held: the exemption clause did not form part of the contract: by driving alongside the machine at the car park entrance from which the ticket was dispensed, the claimant had already communicated acceptance of the defendant's offer to supply parking space

Chapelton v *Barry UDC* (1940, CA)

The claimant, who wished to hire a deckchair at the beach, took one from a pile beside which there was a notice. This stated that payment of the specified hire charge should be made to the attendant. When he paid, the claimant was given a ticket that stated that the council would not be liable for accidents arising from use of the chairs. Later the claimant was injured when the chair collapsed because it had been negligently maintained.

Held: the ticket was not a contractual document but merely a receipt, which the claimant did not receive until after he had accepted the offer by taking the chair from the pile.

Previous business dealings may evidence effective notice if the court is satisfied that these have occurred regularly on the same terms, over a reasonable length of time.

Kendall v *Lillico* (1968, HL)

The parties had contracted 100 times in the previous three years on consistent terms for delivery of goods including a sales note which contained an exemption clause. The next delivery was defective, but was not accompanied by the sales note and the buyer claimed that the seller was not protected by the exemption clause.

7

The terms of the contract at common law

Held: the buyer had adequate notice, since the notification had been consistently supplied through-out the long course of previous dealings.

However, such an implication is unlikely to be made in a consumer contract.

McCutcheon v David McBrayne Ltd (1964, HL)

The claimant had shipped his car on a number of occasions on the defendant's ferry. Sometimes he had been asked to sign a risk note with a clause exempting the ferry company from liability for damage to goods. On one occasion, when a note had not been supplied, the ferry sank due to the defendant's negligence and the claimant's car was lost.

Held: the exclusion clause did not protect the defendant; the claimant had not had notice of the exemption. The previous dealings between the parties had not been sufficiently consistent, as risk notes had not been supplied regularly.

Sufficiency

Generally, a clause will not be binding unless the offeror has taken reasonable steps to draw it to the customer's attention.

The more onerous the term, the greater is the degree of notice required. Exclusion clauses contained in the body of a document should be printed in clear type, which may need to be underlined or otherwise highlighted.

The next case does not involve an exemption clause, but the principle is relevant to any contractual term.

Interfoto Picture Library Ltd v Stiletto Productions (1988, CA)

In a contract for hire of photographic transparencies there was a clause imposing a lateness penalty of £5 per transparency per day. It was contained in the delivery note which comprised the contract.

Held: this was not binding as the supplier had not done enough to draw the attention of the hirer to this onerous clause. A special cover note was needed, or at least bold type on the delivery note.

Signature implies receipt of notice

Customers have constructive notice of the contents of any contractual document which they sign; this means that they are deemed to have notice of its contents, whether they have read it or not. There is no obligation to alert the signer to the presence of an exclusion clause.

L'Estrange v Graucob (1934)

The claimant signed a 'sales agreement' for a cigarette vending machine without bothering to read it but was held nonetheless to be bound by an exemption clause contained in it.

It is useless for customers to claim that they misunderstood the effect of the clause, unless the seller helped to cause the misunderstanding.

Curtis v *Chemical Cleaning & Dyeing Co.* (1951, CA)

The claimant took her wedding dress to be cleaned and was asked to sign a note exempting the cleaners from liability for damage to the dress. She queried this, but signed it when told not to worry as it was there only to protect the company if beads or sequins were damaged. The dress was returned to her badly stained. She sued for breach of contract and the defendant cited the exemption clause in its defence.

Held: the defendant was liable. The exemption clause was not effective as the customer had been misled about its scope.

Contra proferentem rule: any ambiguity of a contract term is resolved against the party who would most benefit from it.

An exclusion clause is not effective if it is ambiguous

Where its wording is unclear, the court may apply the *contra proferentem* **rule** to restrict the effects of an exclusion clause. The clause is construed *contra* (against) *proferentem* (the party who offered it); the meaning least favourable to the offeror is therefore adopted.

Andrews v *Singer* (1934)

A contract expressly stated that new cars would be supplied. An exemption clause stated that the supplier would not be liable for breach of any condition or warranty implied by statute. When the cars were delivered one was secondhand.

Held: the buyer could reject the secondhand car: breach of an express term of the contract had occurred. The exemption clause referred only to implied terms.

Liability for fundamental breach

Fundamental breach: so serious a breach of a condition, that it completely defeats the entire object of the contract.

Where a breach of contract is so serious that it defeats the whole purpose of the contract (**fundamental breach**), the courts may still be prepared to allow an exclusion clause to protect the party in breach. The nature of the contract and the type of breach will be evidence of what the parties are deemed to have intended. For example, in a travel contract the provider promises to take the customer to a particular destination at a particular time; such contracts usually include a clause to limit or completely exclude the liability of the provider in the event of cancellation of services in bad weather. Failure to transport the customer on time is not the fault of the provider in such circumstances, though it may defeat the customer's purposes completely. Such exclusions are likely to be treated as effective. The customer is deemed to have intended to accept the risk.

Issues of insurance are also relevant, and an exclusion clause will protect a provider where the court believes that insurance responsibilities were intended to remain with the other party.

Photo Production Ltd v *Securicor Transport Ltd* (1980, HL)

While on duty at the claimant's premises, Securicor's employee intentionally started a fire. The contract stated that there would be no liability for such damage unless Securicor was negligent; the claimant did not allege negligence. It was clearly a fundamental breach: Securicor was the cause of the destruction of the property which it had promised to keep safe. The only issue was whether the exemption clause was effective.

Held: the clause protected Securicor from liability for fundamental breach; the parties had bargained on equal terms that periodical visits should be made by a patrolman for a modest charge (26p) per visit. It was reasonable to leave the risk for fire damage with the claimant, who would be the most appropriate party to insure against such damage.

The 'Real life' example below should help your further understanding of how the common law rules apply in an everyday situation.

Real life

Horace goes shopping by car to the Buymore-Stuff shopping centre. A notice near the entrance to the underground car park states:

Parking: £1.70 per hour. Please pay at machines inside car park and display ticket on your vehicle windscreen. Buymore-Stuff will not be liable for death or injury to any person using these premises, nor for any damage to any vehicle or other property however caused.

After displaying his ticket, he shuts the car door with a loud bang, which triggers a fall of masonry from the badly maintained roof above. This damages the car and a piece of masonry crushes his foot.

If the notice is clearly displayed so that people can see it before they are committed to entering the car park, the exclusion clause forms part of Horace's contract with Buymore. (See Thornton v Shoe Lane Parking, above.) However, Buymore may not be relieved of liability. If the roof fall is caused by Buymore's negligence in failing adequately to maintain its premises, then, applying the *contra proferentem* rule, a court would be likely to hold that since the wording of the clause does not precisely specify exclusion from negligence liability, this is not covered. So Horace should get compensation for harm to himself and the car.

The outcome would be the same if Horace brought his claim under the Consumer Rights Act 2015. (See Chapter 8.)

To be effective any exclusion clause must also comply with the Unfair Contract Terms Act 1977 or the Consumer Rights Act 2015 (both of which are fully covered in Chapter 8). This means that a party may be able to defeat an exclusion clause using both common law and statutory provisions.

Chapter summary

A contract is composed of promises called 'terms'. These may be express or implied.

Classification of contract terms

Conditions.

Warranties.

Innominate terms.

Exclusion clauses

Use is controlled by the common law and statute.

Common law controls of exclusion clauses

Incorporation of the terms requires timely and sufficient notice unless a party signs the contract.

The *contra proferentem* rule protects a vulnerable party from being disadvantaged by ambiguous language.

Quiz 6

1 Distinguish between conditions and warranties.

2 What is an innominate term?

3 How do the courts determine the status of an innominate term?

4 What is the difference between a limitation clause and an exclusion clause?

5 Are exclusion clauses incorporated in a contract when notified in the following ways:

(a) in a notice on the counter of a shop?

(b) in a signed document?

(c) in a hotel bedroom?

(d) in a receipt?

6 What is the *contra proferentem* rule?

Answers to all quizzes can be found in Appendix 2.

Take a closer look

The following cases provide important examples of how the law you have studied in this chapter has developed. They are primary sources illustrating the law in action and give you more detail about their facts, as well as helping you to understand the law and to appreciate how the judges reached their decisions.

Try looking them up in the law reports or accessing them via a database, e.g. Bailli (www.bailii.org/databases.html). LexisNexis or Westlaw may be available in your university or college library, or you may find extracts in a case book. (See Appendix 1: Additional resources.)

Interfoto Picture Library Ltd v *Stiletto Productions* [1988] 1 All ER 348, CA

Lombard North Central plc v *Butterworth* [1987] QB 527, CA

Valilas v *Janusaj* [2014] EWCA Civ 436

Thorney Park Golf Ltd v *Myers Catering Ltd* [2015] EWCA Civ 19

Web activity

Remember it is not just consumers who have legal problems. In business to business transactions the use of exclusion clauses is very common. Find out about what information Citizen's Advice provides for businesses.

Please go to: www.adviceguide.org.uk/england/

Click 'Search' and type 'legal advice for businesses' then scroll down to 'consumer protection for businesses'.

Assignment 5

Widgets plc entered into a three-year contract with Crankit plc under which Crankit agreed to service Widgets' production line machinery. Widgets signed a document headed 'Service Agreement' consisting of 150 terms, including the following:

10. It shall be a condition of the contract that Crankit will attend in response to any call-out request by Widgets within 24 hours.

36. Crankit will not be responsible to Widgets for any defect in quality of any spare parts supplied by Crankit when servicing customers' machinery.

142. Crankit reserves the right to terminate the contract immediately if Widget delays in paying or fails to pay the agreed monthly retainer fee or any part thereof on the agreed date.

Advise the parties how these terms will affect the outcome of a claim in the following circumstances:

(a) When carrying out the first annual service, Crankit fits a new fuel pump. This malfunctions 48 hours later, causing an explosion which completely destroys the factory.

(b) Twenty months into the contract, Crankit is called upon by Widgets, which reports that a major mechanical failure has brought its production line to a halt. Crankit replies that due to a lack of staff, it will be unable to attend for three days. Next day, Widgets tells Crankit that it is opting out of the contract as immediate servicing is obtainable from Best and Sons Ltd.

(c) Twelve months into the contract Widgets changes its banking arrangements and due to a mistake in the transfer arrangements the new bank only pays Crankit half its monthly retainer on the next due date. Crankit immediately cancels the contract.

7

The terms of the contract at common law

CHAPTER 8

Statutory terms in contracts for sale of goods and services

Introduction

How many contracts to buy goods have you made in the last week? Huge numbers of contracts involve such sales; they are essential to healthy national and international trade.

This chapter is concerned with elements of the role of statutory legislation in the regulation of contracts for the sale of goods and related business transactions. The first Sale of Goods Act in 1893 was primarily concerned with the needs of commercial buyers and sellers; the *caveat emptor* principle (buyer beware) was highly influential, so the parties were treated very much on equal bargaining terms and free to negotiate. In the latter half of the twentieth century Parliament acknowledged that many buyers did not enjoy unlimited freedom to bargain. With the end of post-war austerity there was a much greater range of goods available in the domestic and leisure markets and the consumer (customer buying for personal use) was particularly vulnerable to exploitation especially with regard to quality and safety issues. As a result the Sale of Goods Act 1979 (SGA 1979) (later amended by the Sale and Supply of Goods Act 1994) ensured that certain terms must be implied in sales contracts to extend protection for buyers. It also enhanced the buyer's rights to reject defective goods.

The Unfair Contract Terms Act 1977 (UCTA 1977) introduced the first statutory regulation of exclusion clauses for all buyers. Greater protection followed for consumers in the Unfair Terms in Consumer Contract Regulations 1999. By 2013 consumer contracts were regulated by a rather confusing web of different statutes and various sets of regulations reflecting EU impact.

▶

In consequence Parliament announced a Consumer Rights Bill in 2013, the aim of which was to simplify and enhance the position of consumers by consolidation of all the existing legislation and introduction of further protection. The Consumer Rights Act 2015 was passed and came into operation that year.

Part 1 of this chapter is concerned with sales contracts between businesses. We shall examine statutorily implied terms and the buyer's right to reject under the SGA 1979 (as amended) and related legislation. The statutory regulation of exclusion clauses in UCTA 1977 contracts between businesses involving goods concludes this section of this chapter.

Part 2 focuses on similar issues in sales contracts between a consumer buyer and a business seller which are governed by the Consumer Rights Act 2015 (CRA 2015).

Learning objectives

When you have studied this chapter you should be able to:

▶ distinguish between different types of sales contracts and the legislation governing them;

▶ appreciate the difference between a business and a consumer buyer;

▶ understand how the provisions of the SGA 1979 and related statutes protect the buyer;

▶ get an overview of consumer buyer protection before 2015;

▶ explain the rights of the consumer in contracts regulated by the CRA 2015.

Part 1: Commercial sales contracts

By commercial sales we mean those contracts made between parties who run businesses as opposed to those made by a business seller with someone buying for their own domestic use. Businesses enjoy less protection and choices if the contract runs into difficulties since the law perceives them as trading with each other on more equal terms than in consumer contracts.

Sales of goods between a non-business seller and a consumer buyer remain regulated by the SGA 1979 and are not within the scope of the CRA 2015.

A number of different types of selling are potentially involved in commercial sales contracts and are governed by different statutes. For example a clothing manufacturer will make contracts with other businesses to buy materials and sell on the finished stock (SGA 1979). It will need to make a contract for goods and services if it is buying new machinery from a company which is also installing it on site (Supply of Goods & Services Act 1982 [SOGAT 1982]). This Act will also apply in the case of a construction company needing to hire heavy plant like cranes. Businesses sometimes buy goods on hire purchase, in which case the Supply of Goods Implied Terms Act 1973 (SGIT 1973) will apply to the goods aspect of the contract. In these statutes certain terms are implied in the relevant contracts which give a good degree of protection to the buyer. They also govern the right of the buyer to repudiate the contract. The SGA 1979 is the key statute with related legislation largely mirroring its terms concerning buyer rights. The key elements of this legislation are explored below.

The terms implied by the Sale of Goods Act 1979

A sale of goods contract is defined as 'a contract by which the seller transfers or agrees to transfer the property in goods to the buyer for a money consideration called the price' (s 2(1)).

Under ss 12–15 of the SGA 1979, a seller automatically assumes certain obligations to the buyer as a result of what are stated to be 'conditions' which are automatically implied in every such contract. The buyer may therefore assume that:

1 the seller has lawful authority to transfer ownership of the goods (s 12);
2 the goods will match their description (s 13);
3 the goods will be of satisfactory quality (s 14(2));
4 the goods will be suitable for any purpose specified by the buyer (s 14(3));
5 the goods will match any sample shown to the buyer prior to the contract being made (s 15).

These terms apply to all sales of new or secondhand goods, apart from terms 3 and 4 which apply only to sellers who are acting in the course of a business.

Breach by the seller of any of these terms puts the buyer in a strong position because:

1 *These terms all impose strict liability on the seller.* The seller is liable for breach of contract without the buyer having to prove that the seller is at fault. Indeed, it is irrelevant for the seller to prove that it is blameless and that it was not aware of the alleged defect in the goods. The seller will still be liable.
2 *All of these terms are defined by the Act as being conditions of the contract.* Breach of a condition enables victims to refuse further performance of their contractual obligations and enables them to recover any money or other property which they have tendered. (See Chapter 7.)

These implied terms are now examined in more detail.

Title: s 12

Title: ownership.

In a contract of sale, the seller implicitly promises that he or she has the right to sell the goods (to transfer **title** in them to the buyer) or, in an agreement to sell, the seller implicitly promises that he or she will have such a right at the time when the property is to pass. The seller can fulfil this promise only if he or she has ownership (title) himself or herself, or is acting with the real owner's permission, at the time of transfer.

Rowland v *Divall* (1923, CA)

The defendant had bought in good faith a car which had in fact been stolen. The thief could not pass good title, and neither could the defendant when he sold the car on to the claimant. After the claimant had used it for four months, the real owner turned up and took the car back.

Held: the claimant was entitled to recover the full purchase price from the defendant. No discount was allowed against his four months' use, as he had never received what he had contracted to buy — full ownership of the car.

Description: s 13

Almost all goods are sold by description, and the seller is in breach of contract if this is inaccurate.

The form of the description

The description may be given by word of mouth ('these boots are waterproof'), or by a written notice put in place by the seller ('silk shirts'). The seller is also responsible for any descriptions which the seller personally did not attach to the goods but which came from a manufacturer or other source: for example, labels attached to the goods or wording on the packaging ('produce of Spain', 'machine washable').

In practice, the huge majority of sales involve the use of some kind of description. In a self-service situation, where the goods are picked out by the customers, the customers rely on the label on the tin to tell them whether they are buying baked beans or sweetcorn. Some selling situations (like catalogue or mail order sales) are entirely reliant on descriptions of goods which the buyer will not see before making the contract.

Sales by sample and description

Where the sale is by sample as well as by description, the seller will be in breach of s 13 even though the goods match the sample, if they do not match the description. Many selling situations involve sample and description. You may examine a carpet sample, but gain knowledge of its composition only from an accompanying notice. If this information is incorrect, a breach of contract exists even though in all other respects the carpet meets the statutory requirements.

The relationship of description to quality

The seller's obligations concerning quality and description may overlap. Stating the age of a car can be said to involve a description and also a reference to its quality; the two factors are inextricably interlinked. This may be advantageous to the buyer, as s 13 obliges all sellers to be accurate in their descriptions, whether or not they are selling by way of business.

Description may be a completely separate issue from quality. Goods can be rejected on the ground of incorrect description even though they are not defective in any other way.

Arcos v *Ronaasen* (1933)

An order was placed to buy wooden staves, described by the seller as 'half an inch thick'. When delivered, the width of the staves varied from between half an inch to nine-sixteenths of an inch.

Held: the goods could be rejected as they did not match their description.

Liability depends upon reliance

If the buyer did not know of the description or did not rely upon it (having checked it with a third party), the sale is not by description. Examination of the goods does not automatically preclude reliance by the customer. The average customer does not have sufficient knowledge to spot that the description is inaccurate. In *Beale* v *Taylor* the fact that the buyer had examined the car prior to purchase did not prevent his being held to have relied on the seller's description of it. However, if a buyer with expert knowledge buys from a non-expert seller, that buyer is not likely to be held to have relied on the seller's description. The customs of the trade may be relevant here. Note the comment of Nourse LJ in *Harlingdon & Leinster Enterprises* below.

Harlingdon & Leinster Enterprises v *Christopher Hull Fine Arts* (1990, CA)

An art dealer who, to the buyer's knowledge, was not an expert on German impressionist painting, offered to sell two paintings which he claimed were by a famous German impressionist. After inspecting the pictures, the seller bought them. The description later turned out to be incorrect.

Held: the buyer had relied on his own skill and judgement when deciding to buy, so sale was not by description.

8

Statutory terms in contracts for sale of goods and services

Nourse LJ commented:

Many dealers [in the art market] habitually deal with each other on the principle *caveat emptor*. For my part, being confident that that principle would receive general acceptance amongst dealers, I would say that the astuteness of lawyers ought to be directed towards facilitating, rather than impeding, the efficient working of the market. The court ought to be exceedingly wary in giving a seller's attribution any contractual effect.

The goods must be of satisfactory quality: s 14(2)

Satisfactory quality: meets the reasonable expectation of a person buying the particular goods.

Where goods are sold in the course of business, there is an implied condition that the goods are of **satisfactory quality**.

The meaning of 'satisfactory quality'

The goods must meet the standard which a reasonable person would regard as satisfactory, taking into account all 'relevant circumstances', including price and any description attached to the goods (s 14(2A)). The court objectively assesses the quality of the goods with reference to the expectations of the average buyer. Section 14(2B) gives examples of some factors which might be 'relevant circumstances':

- whether the goods are fit for the purposes for which such goods are normally used;
- appearance and finish;
- freedom from defects;
- safety and durability.

Trac Time Control Ltd v *Moss Plastic Parts Ltd and Others* (2005)

The defendant supplied what he described as high-quality polycarbonate mouldings to the claimant light manufacturer. Floodlights with housings made using the materials were returned to the claimant by dissatisfied customers who claimed that the housings had broken because they were brittle. The claimant sued the defendant for breach of contract.

Held: the defendant was liable as the goods did not match their description under SGA 1979, s 13 and neither were they of satisfactory quality under s 14(2) nor fit for their purpose under s 14(3).

How liability arises under s 14(2)

Goods which are physically dangerous, or which do not work at all, are clearly not of satisfactory quality, whether they are expensive or cheap, reduced in a sale, new or secondhand. A buyer of secondhand goods may, however, be expected to put up with some defects in finish or performance. Even with new goods, you are entitled only to get what you pay for. The finish and durability of a cheap item will not be the same as that to be expected at the luxury end of the market.

The buyer merely has to prove that the defect exists, not how it happened nor that the seller was in any way at fault. Section 14(2) protects the buyer against inherent defects of quality, therefore no proof of reliance on the seller's judgement is required. If the seller is found liable, he or she can recover his or her losses from the party who supplied the goods.

Liability may arise from goods that are of satisfactory quality in themselves but are contaminated by foreign bodies, since these impurities prevent normal use. In *Chaproniere* v *Mason* (1905), a bun made of otherwise normal ingredients contained a stone and was held not to be of appropriate quality.

Wilson v *Rickett Cockerell Ltd* (1954)

A delivery of coal included fragments of detonators. This resulted in an explosion when the coal was burnt, which caused serious structural damage to the buyer's premises.

Held: the coal was not of satisfactory quality, being inseparably contaminated with the explosives.

The goods include their *packaging* and *instructions*. Defects in these may render the goods defective or dangerous. Liability may arise even if the packaging remains the property of the seller. Therefore, in *Geddling* v *Marsh* (1920), the seller of mineral water was liable for failing to supply goods of satisfactory quality when the returnable bottle, in which the water was supplied, exploded and hurt the buyer.

The limits to liability under s 14(2)

Section 14 applies only where the sale arises *in the course of business*, not where sale is by a private seller.

The seller is not liable if *the buyer knows about the defects* (s 14(2C)). Such pre-sale notice may be acquired in two ways:

1 *Notice of the defects may be given by the seller*. Such notice must explicitly describe the defects. For example, a notice might be displayed on a washing machine saying 'instruction manual missing' or 'dents in casing at rear'. The notice only covers those defects. If the motor turned out to be faulty, the seller would be liable for breach of s 14 even if the fault were traced to the accident that caused the dents.

2 *Inspection by the buyer*. Buyers are not generally under any obligation to inspect the goods, but if they do, they cannot claim that the seller is liable for any defects that should have been reasonably evident, given the level of inspection to which they subjected the goods. Thus, a superficial inspection can reveal only superficial defects, but latent defects will not generally be revealed even by thorough inspection. The buyer's level of skill and expertise is relevant: a lay car buyer looking at a car engine would not be expected to spot the clues that would alert a professional dealer.

If the buyer *fails to follow the instructions supplied* with the goods, the seller is not liable for any resulting damage. The seller will also not be liable for damage caused by the buyer's *mistreatment* of the goods.

Aswan Engineering Establishment Co. Ltd v *Lupdine Ltd* (1987, CA)

The sellers supplied waterproofing material in plastic pails. These collapsed spilling their contents, having been stacked by the buyer in piles six pails high in bright sunshine and temperatures up to 150° F for several days.

Held: the sellers were not in breach of their duty. The packaging was appropriate for normal storage practices.

The buyer is expected to take any precautions that would normally be employed when using the relevant type of goods. Therefore damage arising from failing to follow good industrial practice or even plain common sense is unlikely to give rise to seller liability.

The goods must be suitable for their purpose: s 14(3)

Where goods are sold in the course of business, they must be reasonably suitable for any purpose for which such goods are normally sold. They must also fulfil any special purpose that the seller claims for them, provided that the buyer reasonably placed reliance on the seller's skill.

The buyer will only succeed with a claim if it can be shown that the buyer placed reliance on the seller. Such reliance may be implicit or explicit.

Implicit reliance

Such reliance occurs where the buyer neither knowledgeably inspects the goods to check their suitability, nor asks any questions about them. The condition will be breached if the goods turn out to be unsuitable for the usual purposes of such goods, or for any particular uses specified by the buyer. A Supermarket buying food designed for humans can assume that it is suitable for human consumption. Similarly, if it buys a shampoo, the label of which says that it is suitable for use on small children, it can assume that this is safe for them. If the buyer does not specify particular needs, the seller is not liable if the particular needs of the buyer exceed what is normally required.

Explicit reliance

The buyer may question the seller about what the goods may be used for, or ask the seller to recommend the goods which will best suit the buyer's purposes. If you visit a sports shop and ask to buy a watch suitable for use when diving, what you are sold should not leak or respond unfavourably to changes in water pressure.

Real life

Horace runs a shop called Happy Camper Supplies. He recently bought some stock from a wholesaler including anoraks all labelled 'waterproof'. He also bought some tents which the wholesaler describes as 'simple to erect' and 'ideal for the first time camper'. Horace decides to use one as part of his own sales display but after half an hour of bitter struggle eventually gives up the attempt. He then discovers that a crucial piece of information is missing from the instruction leaflet.

Two days later a customer brings back one of the anoraks complaining that after one outing a seam has split letting in water and demanding her money back.

The wholesaler is in breach of the SGA 1979, s 13 as clearly neither the anorak nor the tent live up to their description. They also do not fulfil s 14 since the anorak ripped after minimal use indicating that it is clearly neither of satisfactory quality nor fit for its purpose and the misleading instructions for the tent mean that it does not meet the reasonable expectations of the novice camper.

The goods must correspond with their sample: s 15

Many types of goods are sold by sample, including carpets, wallpaper, perfume and some types of make-up and toiletries. It is an implied condition in a contract for sale by sample that:

1 *The bulk will correspond with the sample in quality.* The buyer will have to show that any defect complained of in the bulk of the goods was not present in the sample.

2 *The goods will be free from any defect rendering them unsatisfactory which would not be apparent on reasonable examination of the sample.* Therefore, buyers cannot reject the goods for defects that they should have spotted in the sample, but can reject if other defects are present.

Godley v Perry (1960)

A shopkeeper was able to show that he had tested a sample catapult for strength by pulling back the elastic.

Held: this was sufficient to check that the sample was not defective.

Generally, a sale by sample will also be a sale by description, so these requirements need to be studied in conjunction with those concerning s 13 (above).

The right to reject the goods: s 35

Breach of any of the above terms is a breach of condition, which means that buyers are entitled to reject the goods wholly or partially and recover the price from the seller, unless the defect is a trivial one. Buyers have a limited time to exercise this right. If they delay too long, they will be deemed to have accepted the goods regardless of defects.

In that situation they will be entitled to be compensated for the defects, but cannot reject the goods. Once acceptance has taken place, the breach becomes one of warranty rather than of condition.

The courts have often held that acceptance has resulted from the buyer using the goods for anything more than a very short time and/or retaining and continuing to use the goods after having complained about them, or agreeing to them being repaired.

The issue of repair is often contentious. It may cause inconvenience to the buyer, who is temporarily deprived of the use of the goods: sometimes a whole saga of delay and incompetence starts to unfold. At this point the buyer may find out that he or she need not have agreed to the repair in the first place and seeks to reject the goods. To safeguard the buyer in such situations a 1994 amendment to the SGA 1979 states that a buyer is not to be assumed to have accepted the goods merely by agreeing to their being repaired (s 35(6)). This may increase the opportunities for a buyer to reject the goods.

The House of Lords recently held in *J & H Ritchie Ltd* v *Lloyd Ltd* (2007) (below) that when goods are returned to a buyer for inspection with a view to repair, this constitutes a separate agreement from the contract of sale itself. It puts the seller under an implied duty to inform the buyer of the nature of the defect so that the seller can then decide whether or not to repudiate the sale of goods contract.

J & H Ritchie Ltd v *Lloyd Ltd* (2007, HL)

The claimant farming contractor bought a seed drill and harrow from the defendant. As soon as it was used, the claimant noticed that it vibrated very loudly, and he operated it only for a short time before reporting the matter to the defendant. The defendant agreed to remove the equipment for inspection, with a view to possibly repairing it. In due course, it was returned, having been repaired to what the defendant described as 'factory gate specification' but without any explanation about what had caused the defect. When pressed, the defendant refused to explain what the problem had been, but the claimant found out informally, from a mechanic, that bearings had been missing. The claimant then rejected the goods because of concerns that this fault might have caused damage to other parts of the equipment and compromised the manufacturer's guarantee.

Held: the claimant was entitled to reject the goods. It was implied in the agreement to repair that the defendant would inform the claimant about the cause of the problem and that the claimant would retain his right to reject until he had the necessary information to make a '*properly informed choice*' (Lord Hope) as to whether he wanted to keep the goods or not.

Lord Brown commented:

> Even though the harrow after repair was … in as good as new condition, the seller's failure to follow the procedure implicitly agreed justified the buyer in refusing to accept the goods sold. The buyer was still prepared to accept the goods, if the seller at its expense obtained a clean engineer's report, but the seller refused to do this either. The buyer was in this situation justified on 26 May 1999 in rejecting the goods.

Other key statutes which regulate contracts involving goods

Not all contracts involving goods come within the SGA 1979. The following types of contract all involve goods but are regulated by other statutes giving similar protection to buyers.

The Supply of Goods and Services Act 1982 (SOGAT 1982)

The following terms, which are designated as *conditions* under SOGAT, are implied in a contract of hire, goods and services, and barter contracts:

- title;
- description;
- satisfactory quality and suitability for purpose;
- sample.

The buyer has the same rights to reject the goods where a breach of the above terms occurs as a buyer in a sale of goods contract.

The following terms are also implied in all contracts involving a supply of services:

- the work will be performed with all reasonable care and skill
- the work will be carried out within a reasonable time;
- the price charged will be reasonable.

Under SOGAT 1982 these are *terms* only: they are not designated as conditions or warranties. Their status depends on what, if anything, was agreed in the contract. Sometimes the amount of damage caused by the breach will be used as evidence of their importance. They are a good example of *innominate terms*. (See Chapter 7.)

The buyer/hirer/barter party has similar rights to terminate the contract as the buyer in a sale of goods contract.

Sale of goods and services contracts

Goods and services contract: the sale of the goods is incidental but necessary to the performance of a service.

In a **goods and services contract** the sale of goods is incidental to the provision of a service. For example, having double glazing installed, or getting new brake pads fitted to your car. Such contracts are regulated by the Supply of Goods and Services Act 1982. Contracts to hire goods also come within this statute.

Contracts for the supply of services alone do not come within the Act. In *Trebor Bassett Holidays and Cadbury UK Partnership* v *ADT Fire & Security* (2012) the Court of Appeal held that a contract for design and supply of a fire suppressant system was not a contract for sale of goods and services but merely one for the supply of services and so did not contain an implied term regarding satisfactory quality.

Hire contracts

Hire contract: entitles the hirer to possession of the goods for the hire period but not title.

Hire contracts are regulated by the Supply of Goods and Services Act 1982. The hirer is entitled to possession, but not ownership, of the relevant goods for the agreed period.

In the news

Baxter v *Barnes* (2015)

The claimant was an arborist who hired a mobile elevated platform for use while pruning a tree on uneven sloping ground from the defendant who was a tree surgeon. As the ground was soft the defendant supplied plastic bearing plates for the feet of the platform to prevent them sinking in. The claimant was seriously injured when it toppled sideways and he fell. One of the platform feet had apparently slipped off the plate rendering the platform unstable.

Held: The claimant's injuries were a result of the goods not being of satisfactory quality in breach of the Supply of Goods and Services Act 1982. There was nothing wrong with the platform as such but the bearing plates were unsuitable for their purpose as they needed to be attached to the feet in order to make them stable and this rendered the goods defective.

Contracts to barter

Bartering: exchanging goods or services for other goods and services.

In a **bartering** situation the parties exchange goods or services; even if goods are involved, it is not a sale of goods contract as no money changes hands. A part-exchange contract is generally treated as a sale of goods contract under which the buyer is given the option to tender goods in part satisfaction of the contract price.

A 'free' gift linked to a sale contract

Such transactions are probably regulated by the Supply of Goods and Services Act 1982 since this covers contracts not regulated elsewhere under which title to goods will pass.

Worth thinking about?

It is a common sales tactic to offer the customer something 'free' as in 'buy one get one free' promotions. What is the contractual position if the shop tries to charge you for both?

Suggested solutions can be found in Appendix 2.

The Supply of Goods (Implied Terms) Act 1973

Hire-purchase contracts

The goods aspect of such contracts is regulated by ss 8–11 which state the same implied terms concerning title, description, quality and fitness for purpose and sample as in a sale of goods contract. Under a **hire-purchase contract**, the person

Hire-purchase contract: the hirer gains immediate possession of goods with the option to take ownership when all price instalments are paid.

supplied with the goods is, in the eyes of the law, the hirer not the buyer. The contract initially gives the hirer possession of the goods only. The hirer may choose to buy the goods when all the instalments have been paid. If they do so they then become the owner.

Unfair Contract Terms Act 1977

The scope of the Act

The Unfair Contract Terms Act 1977 (UCTA 1977) applies almost exclusively to contracts giving rise to *business liability* (s 1(3)). Thus, it is primarily concerned with sellers or suppliers who seek to limit or exclude liability incurred in the course of business. Private sellers or suppliers are generally not restricted in the use of exclusion clauses. (See s 6, below.)

Certain types of contract are *expressly excluded*: for example, contracts of insurance and contracts for the sale or lease of land.

Although the title of the Act refers to 'contract terms', the Act also regulates noncontractual notices which attempt to restrict liability for negligence. For example, a notice, outside premises, stating that people enter at their own risk may be ineffective because of UCTA 1977.

The substance of the Act

Negligence liability (s 2)

Under s 2(1), liability cannot be excluded if death or personal injury is caused by negligence. Damage to property through negligence is addressed by s 2(2). Under that provision, negligence liability may be excluded if this is *reasonable* in the circumstances. Note that under s 7(2) of the Contracts (Rights of Third Parties) Act 1999 (see Chapter 6) the reasonableness defence is not effective against a claim by a third party beneficiary.

Standard terms: contract terms on which a business always trades and which are not open to negotiation.

Consumer: this generally means a buyer who purchases goods/services etc. for personal use, but UCTA 1977 includes companies contracting for accessories for their business unrelated to its main business purpose.

Breach of contract (s 3)

Liability for breach of contract may not be excluded where a party enters into a contract made on the other party's **standard terms** (when no negotiation will have been possible), or where the party deals as a consumer, unless the exclusion is *reasonable*. UCTA 1977 gives guidance on how the term 'reasonable' is to be interpreted and this is explained later in the chapter.

Breach of implied terms in contracts for sale/hire purchase/supply/hire of goods (ss 6–7)

A commercial seller is restricted in imposing exclusion of the conditions relating to title, description, suitability and sample implied under the Sale of Goods Act 1979 and related legislation. **Consumers** enjoyed special protection in a commercial contract and none of these conditions could be effectively excluded against them.

8

Statutory terms in contracts for sale of goods and services

A commercial buyer has never enjoyed such comprehensive protection. The condition regarding title (under ss 6–7) can never be excluded; the others may be excluded if the clause is 'reasonable' in any contract with a non-consumer buyer.

Note that a *private seller* is free to exclude liability for breach of any of the relevant terms above in a sale of goods or hire-purchase contract (s 6(4)). This only covers the terms regarding title, description and sample, since the term regarding satisfactory quality is implied only in contracts where the seller/supplier is a business.

What is 'reasonable' for the purposes of UCTA 1977?

Section 11 of UCTA 1977 provides guidance as to what is 'reasonable' for the purposes of the Act:

1 a contract term will satisfy the requirement of reasonableness if it is fair and reasonable with regard to all the circumstances which should have been considered by the parties when they entered the contract (s 11(1));

2 if the claim relates to a non-contractual notice, reasonableness is judged with reference to all the circumstances prevailing when the damage was caused (s 11(3)).

Schedule 2 to the Act offers further guidelines:

1 *Imbalance of bargaining power*. The parties to a contract may not enjoy equal bargaining power. In a standard terms contract, one party is presented with a set of terms and given no opportunity to negotiate existing terms or add others. The buyer of goods or services may be heavily reliant on the technical knowledge and expertise of the seller, and that ignorance produces power imbalance.

2 *Inducements and choices*. If a customer is given an unfair inducement to accept the exclusion clause, this may make it unreasonable. If that party could have made a similar contract with another party without being subject to such a term, this may make the exemption reasonable.

3 *Prior knowledge*. If the customer should reasonably have been aware of the existence and extent of the term, taking into account previous dealings between the parties and trade custom, it may be reasonable to impose the exclusion.

4 *Special requirements*. If the goods were made or adapted to meet the customer's special requirements, an exemption may be binding.

The courts have also taken other factors into account, including the issue of insurance and whether the customer should have taken independent advice.

The following cases illustrate the approach of the courts to the interpretation of reasonableness.

Smith v *Eric Bush* (1989, HL)

The claimant bought a house in reliance on a surveyor's report, prepared on the instructions of the building society. The report stated that it was issued without any guarantee of accuracy or acceptance of any legal liability. The surveyor negligently overlooked some serious defects which led to the chimney collapsing into Mrs Smith's bedroom, and resulted in a large bill for structural repairs.

Held: the exclusion of liability was not effective as it was unreasonable:

1 *The parties did not have equal bargaining power*. Mrs Smith could not be expected to know whether or not the surveyor's report was correct, because of her lack of special knowledge.

2 *The financial resources of the claimant*. It was not reasonable to expect Mrs Smith to go to the expense of getting a second opinion. She was a first-time buyer of a modest property and, like most such purchasers, pushed to her financial limits.

3 *The surveyor had failed in a simple task*. Any reasonably competent surveyor ought to have spotted the defects.

4 *Insurance cover*. This was readily available at modest cost to the surveyor, while the purchaser was unlikely to enjoy such protection.

Green v Cade Bros (1978)

A standard terms contract, which complied with the requirements of the National Association of Seed Potato Merchants, restricted the right of rejection of seed potatoes to three days from delivery; any compensation was limited to the return of the contract price. The stock supplied to the buyer was infected by a virus which was not detectable until the growing process had started.

Held: the three-day time limit was not reasonable given the type of damage suffered. The limit on compensation was reasonable: it was usual in the trade, the parties enjoyed equal bargaining power, and the buyer had received no inducement to accept the limitation. The buyer could have bought guaranteed seed potatoes for a higher price.

George Mitchell v Finney Lock Seeds Ltd (1983) HL

The claimant ordered cabbage seed from the defendant which did not match its description. It was also inferior in quality. The claimant lost his entire crop, sustaining a £61,000 loss. The contract limited liability for breach to replacement of the goods or a refund of the price.

Held: this was not reasonable because:

1 the breach arose from the seller's negligence;

2 the seller could have insured against crop failure at a modest cost;

3 in the past the seller had settled claims in excess of the limitation sum – this indicated that the seller did not always consider the clause fair and reasonable.

St Albans City & District Council v International Computers Ltd (1996) CA

Computer software, supplied and installed by the defendant company to provide a database facility for the local authority, was defective. It caused errors in the estimation of the number of eligible poll-tax payers, and as a result the local authority lost substantial funds. A limitation clause in the contract restricted the defendant's liability to £100,000.

8

Statutory terms in contracts for sale of goods and services

Held: the limitation clause was unreasonable because:

1 the defendant was a multinational company with substantial resources;

2 the defendant carried product liability insurance of £50 million and the limitation of liability was too small relative to the possible risk and the loss actually suffered;

3 the claimant's specialist needs greatly limited its choice of providers;

4 it was fairer to put the risk on the defendant who stood to make a profit on the contract. If the risk lay with the local authority, its taxpayers would be unjustly burdened by the loss.

As should be evident from the above examples, the facts of each case are crucial to its outcome. The issues of the knowledge and resources of both parties are crucial to determining bargaining power. Issues of policy may also play a part. For example, compare the *St Albans* case, where, in effect, losses would have fallen on council taxpayers, with the *Watford Electronics* case (below), where the claimant was a private company and bespoke software was involved.

Watford Electronics v *Sanderson* (2001 CA)

A specially designed computer software package was provided by the defendant under a contract that excluded liability for indirect and consequential losses and limited any general liability to the value of the contract price (£104,600). Due to defects in the software the claimant suffered £4.5 million losses from lost profits, replacement of the system and increased working costs.

Held: each clause was reasonable, as the clauses were negotiated between parties of appropriate experience representing equally substantial companies. There was equal bargaining power between the parties.

Chadwick LJ commented:

> Where experienced businessmen representing substantial companies negotiate an agreement, they may be taken to have had regard to matters known to them. They should be taken to be the best judge of whether the terms of the agreement are reasonable. The court should not assume that either is likely to commit his company to an agreement which he thinks is unfair or which he thinks included unreasonable terms. Unless satisfied that one party has in effect taken unfair advantage of the other or that a term is so unreasonable that it cannot properly have been understood or considered the court should not interfere.

The issue of one party seeking to use a clause to take unfair advantage is illustrated by *Overseas Medical Supplies* v *Orient* (1999) where an exclusion clause stating that the defendant would not be liable for loss of goods in transit was held to be unreasonable given that another term in the contract required the defendant to insure the goods, which had not been done. The existence of an alternative remedy may make what would appear to be an unreasonable term acceptable.

Regus v *Epcot Solutions (2008 CA)*

Regus (R) were IT trainers who rented accommodation for their courses from Epcot (E). The air conditioning system broke down, making work conditions on the premises very difficult for R's employees and customers. E failed to rectify the situation after a number of requests by R who then refused to pay the rent. E sued R for breach of contract and R counterclaimed for their losses. E claimed that it was protected by a clause 23(3) which stated that it would not be liable 'in any circumstances' for any loss of business or profits, third-party claims and any consequential loss. Clause 23(4) stated that in any event R's losses would be limited to 125 per cent of the fees or £50,000 whichever was higher.

R successfully claimed in breach of contract in the High Court which held that clause 23 was unreasonable under UCTA, s 3 because it deprived R of any remedy at all and covered intentional acts because it was to operate 'in any circumstances'.

E appealed.

Held (dismissing the appeal): clause 23 was not unreasonable because it did not leave R without a remedy as it was still entitled to claim for diminution in value of the services provided. 'In any circumstances' could not be construed as excluding liability for fraud/wilful/reckless/malicious damage. However, this argument was irrelevant since E had not refused to repair the air conditioning from a wish to harm R's customers but from a desire to save money.

It was not unreasonable for E to restrict liability for breach of contract. There was no inequality of bargaining power between the parties and E had made it clear that customers should make their own insurance arrangements to protect themselves against business losses.

Part 2: Consumer sales

The word 'consumer' in this context refers to somebody purchasing goods intended primarily for their own personal as opposed to business use. Such buyers have been afforded increasing special legal protection since the 1970s. This area of the law has grown haphazardly and piecemeal in a complex web of statutory amendment and sets of regulations which have often been prompted by EC legislation.

Simplification and some enhancement to take into account modern marketing methods were necessary and this led to the introduction of the Consumer Rights Bill in 2013 which is now enacted as the CRA 2015.

An overview of consumer sales protection before the CRA 2015

The Sale of Goods Act 1979 and related legislation

The Implied Terms

Consumers enjoyed the protection of all the implied terms explained above but with certain enhancements.

Satisfactory quality

After amendment in 2003 to reflect the Sale and Supply of Goods to Consumers Regulations 2002, 'satisfactory quality' was extended to covers 'public statements' by the manufacturer relating to 'specific characteristics of the goods' like advertising, labelling and any other sales information accompanying the goods. The seller could only avoid liability for a misleading statement if he could prove that he did not know or was not reasonably aware of the statement, or, before the relevant contract was made, the seller had publicly corrected or withdrawn the statement.

The right to reject goods

The consumer was entitled to reject goods with trivial defects while the commercial buyer could not and the courts were sometimes prepared to be more flexible concerning time limits in a consumer sale.

Repair and replacement

The consumer buyer had the right to demand repair or replacement of goods that did not conform to the contract at the time of delivery.

Exclusion of liability and the Unfair Contract Terms Act 1977

UCTA 1977 gave the same protection against exclusion for liability for negligence to all parties but some additional protection to consumers concerning the implied terms in contracts involving sale and supply of goods.

Sections 6–7 prevented exclusion of liability for breach of any of the implied terms in in the SGA 1979 and related legislation in any contract for sale of goods and hire made by a business with a consumer. A was defined as someone not contracting in the course of a business (UCTA 1977, s 12) and this was interpreted generously.

Thus, in *R & B Customs Brokers Co Ltd* v *United Dominions Trust* (1988, CA) 'consumer' was held to include anyone obtaining goods for use in their business, as long as these they were not integral to the course of the business, or regularly bought for incidental purposes. A contract to buy a car for private and business use made by a company owned by a husband and wife was therefore deemed to be made by a consumer. This reasoning was affirmed by the Court of Appeal in *Feldaroll Foundry plc* v *Hermes Leasing (London) Ltd* (2004) on the grounds that it furthered the intention of UCTA, which was to safeguard a buyer's protection under the terms implied under relevant sale and supply legislation.

The Unfair Terms in Consumer Contracts Regulations 1999 (UTCCR 1999)

These regulations implemented EC Directive 91/13/EC and replaced the 1994 regulations of the same name. They only protected *consumers* who entered a contract deemed to be unfair according to criteria laid down in the regulations. Such a term was voidable by consumers, i.e. they were not bound by it unless they chose to comply, but the rest of the contract remained binding.

The substance of the regulations

Consumers were defined as human beings (as opposed to a company) making contracts for non-business purposes (with a seller or supplier) in the course of its business. If the contract was written the seller or supplier had to use clear, intelligible language. Any ambiguity is resolved in favour of the consumer.

Unfairness of a term

A term was unfair if it failed to fulfil the requirements of good faith and this caused a significant imbalance in the parties' contractual relationship, prejudicial to the consumer's interests. In assessing whether the seller or supplier acted in good faith, the court had to have regard to all the circumstances relevant to formation of the contract.

The effect of an unfair term

The consumer was not bound by an unfair term and the rest of the contract remained effective if it was still effective without the problem term.

The regulations contained an illustrative but not comprehensive list of potentially unfair terms.

It was up to the consumer to prove that the term was unfair, taking into account the nature of the subject matter of the contract, the legal and commercial context in which the contract was made and the reasonable expectations of both parties; all the circumstances surrounding the contract are relevant to determining any imbalance.

Enforcement of the regulations

The regulations could be used by consumers directly to enforce their contractual rights. The Office of Fair Trading (OFT) also had a crucial investigatory role (performed since 2014 by the Competition and Markets Authority (CMA)) requiring it to investigate complaints from consumers and trading standards departments about allegedly unfair terms. If the complaint was upheld the CMA could take legal action to require the offending business to change or withdraw the term. Successful interventions include *Office of Fair Trading* v *Foxtons* (2009) where the Court of Appeal held that an injunction should be granted to prevent the enforcement of unfair terms in an estate agent's contract and also *Office of Fair Trading* v *Ashbourne Management Services Ltd and Others* (2011) which concerned gym contracts.

The Consumer Rights Act 2015 repealed these regulations entirely and largely replicates their substance.

The Consumer Contracts (Information, Cancellation and Additional Charges) Regulations 2013

These regulations which came into operation in 2014 largely implemented the Consumer Rights Directive (2011/83/EU) and increased the duties of the seller in consumer sales.

8

Statutory terms in contracts for sale of goods and services

Greater provision of accurate pre-contract information about the goods and the contract terms to the buyer was required in all contracts.

Stricter controls were introduced in distance contracts (those not made by a consumer actually on the seller's premises) to ensure transparency of pricing and to prevent imposition of hidden extra charges. For example, the seller in an online contract is prohibited from using ticked boxes in an order form to make you buy additional items like cancellation insurance.

Cancellation rights in all distance contracts were extended to 14 days.

Other measures covered by the regulations introduce new rights concerning the purchase of digital content in either tangible form such as DVDs and CDS, or in downloadable form such as ring tones, games, music and video. In all contracts the seller must give specific information about how the materials function: for example the scope of their regional operation and compatibility with certain other devices must be clearly stated. The buyer loses their right to a 14-day cancellation period once they have downloaded the goods.

These regulations run in tandem with the CRA 2015 which does not amend or repeal them but includes some of the same rights and implements some other aspects of the directive.

The Consumer Rights Act 2015

This legislation radically alters the consumer rights landscape. As explained above it consolidates all the special protection for consumers in the Sale of Goods Act 1979, UCTA 1977, UTCCR 1999 and some other related statutes and regulations involving provision of goods and services. It also introduces some new rights.

CRA Part 1: Consumer contracts for goods, services and digital content

This part of the Act applies to all contracts between a trader and a consumer which involve supply of goods, services and digital content. Therefore it affords protection to the consumer in contracts for the sale of goods, goods and services, hire and hire purchase and any other contract involving the transfer of goods. Such contracts may be written or oral.

Section 2 definitions of certain key terms

Trader: a person who is 'acting for purposes relating to that person's trade, business, craft or profession'.

Consumer: 'an individual acting for purposes that are wholly or mainly outside that individual's trade, business, craft or profession'. In the event of dispute it is up to the trader to prove that the buyer is not a consumer.

A person buying secondhand goods at *an auction sale which they had the option to attend* is not a consumer for the purposes of the Act.

Goods: covers not only all tangible moveable items but also gas, electricity and water.
Digital content: any data in digital form.

The consumer's rights in all contracts for supply of goods

Pre-contractual information about the goods and the content of the contract is to be treated as part of the terms of the contract. This includes details about the seller as well as information about the goods, price and delivery (s 12).

Every contract involving supply of goods is to be treated as containing the following terms:

- s 9 – goods will be of satisfactory quality;
- s 10 – goods will be suitable for their particular purpose;
- s 11 – goods will match their description;
- s 13 – goods must correspond to sample;
- s 17 – the trader has the legal right to transfer the contract goods which means that the trader must have the right to transfer possession of goods in a hire contract and the right to transfer ownership (title) in a sales contract.

These all carry the same meanings as those used in the interpretation of terms in consumer contracts under the SGA and related statutes.

New rights are also introduced:

- Section 14 – goods must match any model previously shown to the consumer or examined by them.
- Section 15 – where the contract requires the trader to install the goods they will not conform to the contract if they are installed incorrectly by the trader or their agent. Therefore if you have asked for installation of your new washing machine and it fails to work because of defective fitting you are entitled to reject it even though the machine itself is without fault.

    The goods will 'not conform to contract' if any of the above terms are not fulfilled and the contract will be breached.

- Section 16 – any goods which include any digital material will not conform to the contract if the digital content does not conform. If you have bought a computer with programmes installed on it which do not work you may have rights to reject the computer. This section does not apply to contracts purely for the sale of digital content which are covered by a discrete part of the Act (see below).

Rights to reject the goods

Where the goods do not conform to the contract by breaching the requirements of the implied terms or containing incorrect or misleading pre-contract information the consumer has three choices:

1 a 'short term' right to reject the goods within 30 days of delivery (s 22);
2 a timely and effective repair or replacement of the goods (s 23);
3 a 'final right' to reject the goods after one attempt to repair them which fails or which is not carried out within a reasonable time (s 24).

This should help to clarify the position of the consumer where goods turn out to be defective. The 30-day limit seems reasonably generous and gives a welcome certainty previously lacking, as illustrated by the plight of the unfortunate claimant in the *Bernstein* case:

> ## *Bernstein* v *Pamson* (1987)
>
> After 21 days and with only 140 miles on the clock, the engine of the claimant's brand-new Nissan seized up on the motorway, due to sealant coagulating in the cooling system.
>
> **Held:** the engine was clearly not of appropriate quality and the claimant was entitled to damages. However, he had lost his right to reject the car since a reasonable time had elapsed since taking delivery. The judge held that a reasonable time meant long enough to give the car a reasonable road test, not necessarily long enough to discover latent defects.

Before the Act agreeing to a repair would sometimes trigger a saga of unsuccessful attempts to correct the defect before the trader would, if you were lucky, agree to your rejection of the goods. In *Rogers* v *Parish* (1987) it was held that a top of the market Range Rover could be rejected after seven months, with a 5,000 mileage, since it had been a martyr to endless mechanical problems from the moment of delivery, and had spent much of its life in the garage while many unsuccessful repairs were attempted.

The consumer's exercise of either right to reject brings the contract to an end (s 20). All moneys or any other property that was tendered to the trader must be returned within 14 days from the trader's acceptance of the consumer's choice. No refund fees can be claimed nor deductions made by the trader.

Section 23 requires that any repair or replacement must be completed within a reasonable time and without significant inconvenience to the consumer. The trader must bear the cost unless this is impossible or disproportionate in which case the consumer can exercise their rejection rights or seek a price reduction.

No liability exclusions

The trader cannot exclude, limit or undermine its liability for any of the above terms in contracts involving sale of goods (s 31).

Contracts to supply digital content

This covers data in any digital form so includes everything from CDs and DVDs to apps and ringtones. It covers any digital content supplied free with other goods or with other digital content for which a price was paid.

Terms as to pre-contractual information, quality (s 34), purpose (s 35), description (s 36), pre-contract information (s 37) and the trader's right to supply (s 41) automatically form part of the contract and the goods will not conform to the contract if they are breached. In addition s 46 states that if the goods cause damage to a device belonging to the consumer and this would not have occurred if the trader had acted with reasonable care and skill the consumer is entitled to exercise their rights to reject or accept a repair. If, for example, you bought a computer program and due to some fault by the trader it was contaminated by a virus you would have a remedy as a result of this provision.

Rights of the consumer if the digital content does not conform to the contract

Free replacement or repair

As with any other defective goods under the Act this must be done within a reasonable time and the seller may refuse if the cost is disproportionate or it is impossible to repair or replace the item (s 43).

In that situation the consumer may ask for a partial reduction or refund (ss 44–45) which is payable within 14 days of the trader agreeing that the consumer is entitled. A refund may only be a partial price reduction if only part of the digital content supplied is defective. However, apart from that the seller must not make deductions or impose extra costs.

Repeat performance

The consumer may ask for repeat download if performance was defective. The trader must carry this out within a reasonable time and without causing undue inconvenience unless it is impossible (s 45).

Compensation

If the goods cause damage to a device or other digital content belonging to the consumer the trader may be required to repair the other goods or pay compensation for the damage (s 46).

Note that the Act does not give a consumer in such contracts any rights to reject the goods. Limited and sufficient rights are given by the Consumer Contracts (Information, Cancellation and Additional Charges) Regulations 2013 (see above, page 157).

Exclusion of liability in digital content contracts

The trader is not permitted to exclude liability for defective goods in respect of satisfactory quality (s 35), description (s 36), right to supply (s 41) or damage to the consumer's device or other digital property if the contract involves digital content (s 46).

Contracts to supply services

This part of the CRA applies to any contract under which a service is to be performed whether or not goods are also supplied as part of it. It is largely a consolidation of the previous legislation, but, as with all consumer contracts regulated by the Act, includes the additional requirement that pre-contractual information becomes a term of the contract (s 50). Other sections stipulate:

● the service must be carried out with all reasonable care and skill (s 49);

● a reasonable price is payable (s 51);

● performance must take place within a reasonable time (s 52).

8

Statutory terms in contracts for sale of goods and services

Remedies for defective performance

A repeat performance may be requested if the initial performance is defective (s 55), which must be carried out within a reasonable time and avoid inconvenience to the customer as far as practicable.

A reduction or refund (s 56) may be payable to the consumer where repeat performance is not appropriate because it is impossible, or (s 55) the trader has failed in its obligation to carry out the repeat performance requested.

'Reasonable' as in other contracts regulated by the Act means that the service and price meet the expectations of the average consumer taking into account all the particular circumstances pertinent to the contract.

Exclusion of liability (s 57)

The seller is not permitted to exclude liability for:

● the duty to use reasonable care and skill (s 49); or

● pre-contractual information (s 50); or

● reasonable price (s 51); or

● carrying out the service within a reasonable time (s 52).

General contractual remedies

The CRA makes clear that, in addition to the remedies which it prescribes, a party is still free to pursue an action for damages or seek a decree of specific performance or injunction for breach of any contract covered by the Act.

CRA Part 2: Unfair terms

This part of the Act is relevant to all terms of all contracts between a trader and consumer. It repeals and largely replicates the UTCCR 1999 and those parts of UCTA 1977 which provided consumer protection and which are repealed by the Act. It allows the consumer to avoid the effect of such terms if they are found to be unfair as defined by the Act (s 61). It also covers any notice given or displayed by the trader which relates to rights and obligations owed to the consumer by the trader, or by which the trader tries to exclude or limit liability to any consumer.

Good faith: general honest dealing. Under the CRA 2015 a term's failure to evidence this makes that term voidable.

Significant imbalance: a lack of equal bargaining power, which may evidence unfairness.

Meaning of unfair

Section 62 defines unfair as being 'contrary to the requirement of **good faith**' and causing 'a **significant imbalance** in the parties' rights and obligations … to the detriment of the consumer'. The nature of the contract, its subject matter and all the surrounding circumstances must be taken into account in determining whether this has occurred. No unfair term or notice is binding on a consumer.

This is the same rather nebulous definition used in the UTCCR 1999. The Courts have given some help with interpretation of this which is still relevant. For example, in *Director General of Fair Trading* v *First National Bank* 2001 Lord Bingham said that good faith was reflected by 'good standards of morality and commercial practice' and would be evidenced by 'fair and open dealing'. Just because a term is not beneficial to the consumer and may come, as their Lordships commented, as 'a nasty surprise' does not necessarily indicate unfairness or breach of good faith.

Written terms must be expressed in plain and intelligible language (s 68) The concept of good faith requires fair dealing and equality between the parties. Transparency of the terms of the contract is therefore crucial. If the meaning is unclear the court will choose the interpretation most favourable to the consumer.

Examples of unfair terms

There is a long list of examples of terms that may be judged unfair in Schedule 2 of the Act. For example, a term which permits a trader to hold on to a deposit if the trader pulls out of the contract before performance, or one which imposes a penalty sum on a consumer who pulls out.

Core terms:
relate to subject matter or price and are not subject to a fairness test under the CRA 2015.

Core terms of the contract cannot generally be assessed for fairness. These include the main subject matter and the price as long as they are legible, transparent and sufficiently prominently presented in any documentation (s 64). However, if they appear in the list of potentially unfair examples in Schedule 2 then they do come within this section's scope.

The courts have tended to give a restrictive interpretation to what comes within the scope of 'price or remuneration' to prevent consumer protection from being undermined. This was stressed by the House of Lords in *Director General of Fair Trading v First National Bank*, which held that the disputed term which related to payment of interest was not excluded from the court's jurisdiction.

This approach was followed in *Bairstow Eves London Central Ltd v Smith* (2004), where an escalating commission rate charged by an estate agent was deemed not to come within the core terms exclusion.

However, the Supreme Court took a tougher line with regard to overdraft charges in *Office of Fair Trading v Abbey National plc and Others* (2009, SC). After lengthy litigation the Supreme Court decided that charges imposed on customers going overdrawn without an arranged overdraft came within the core terms of the contract, provided that this was clearly and intelligibly notified to the customer prior to acceptance.

Negligence liability for personal injury cannot be excluded (s 65)

This applies to notices like 'Persons entering these premises do so at their own risk' or any contractual term directly or indirectly attempting to avoid liability in any degree for death or other personal injury. Therefore liability for harm negligently caused by the trader not just to the buyer but to any visitor to the premises cannot be excluded.

This does not apply to insurance contracts or to situations where the trader is not issuing the notice as part of their trade or profession (s 66). This covers situations where, for example, a farmer allows a village fete to take place in their field.

8

Statutory terms in contracts for sale of goods and services

The consequences of an unfair term (s 67)

Any term or notice which is deemed to be unfair is not binding on a consumer who therefore may avoid the effect of that term but the rest of the contract continues to be effective.

CRA Part 3: Enforcement

The consumer is entitled to take action personally if rights are breached, but as under UTCCR 1999 some public authorities and industry watchdogs are designated in the CRA Schedule 3 as **regulators**. These include the Competition and Markets Authority (CMA) the Financial Conduct Authority (FCA), the Gas and Electricity Markets Authority (GEMA), the Office for Rail Regulation (ORR) and the Consumers Association (CA).

Schedule 3 gives regulators powers to investigate and resolve complaints within their jurisdiction. This includes the power to seek an injunction if necessary to prevent continued use by any trader of any term or notice attempting to restrict liability for breach of any contract regulated by the Act or any term or notice seeking to exclude liability for death or personal injury or any other term judged to be unfair.

Regulator: a body authorised by the CRA to investigate complaints about breaches of the Act and to seek remedies

Chapter summary

Contracts concerning goods made between businesses and those between a business and a consumer are governed by different statutes and regulations which give extra protection to the consumer buyer.

Regulation of inter-business contracts

The Sale of Goods Act 1979.

The Sale of Goods and Services Act 1982 (includes hire contracts).

The Supply of Goods (Implied terms) Act 1973 (includes goods supplied under hire-purchase).

Implied conditions of contracts regulated by these statutes

Title will validly pass.

Goods match description.

Goods of satisfactory quality.

Goods suitable for purpose.

These statutes also give rights to rejection, replacement or repair of goods supplied in breach of these terms and all other common law remedies such as damages.

Exclusion clauses

Inter-business contracts are governed by UCTA 1977 which limits the extent to which liability can be excluded in contract and tort.

Consumer buyers rights (primarily protected by the Consumer Rights Act 2015)

Pre-contractual statements become terms of the contract.

Protection is introduced for contracts for sale of digital content.

All the implied terms above are automatically included in a contract concerning goods between a consumer buyer and business seller but with enhancements to ensure added protection.

Rights to reject are also enhanced to permit rejection of goods generally within 30 days of acceptance, but longer where the buyer requests a repair which is not successful.

Negligence liability causing death or physical injury cannot be excluded.

Any other exclusion clauses or terms found to be unfair terms because they breach good faith are voidable by the consumer.

The CMA and certain other bodies have powers to enforce the Act.

Quiz 7

1 What terms are implied in a contract under the Sale of Goods Act 1979?

2 When does a business buyer have the right to reject goods bought under a contract with another business seller?

3 In what circumstances may a business seller exclude liability for negligence?

4 What legislation currently protects consumer rights in contracts concerning computer games?

5 Rosanna had a new washing machine installed in her home 14 days ago but today it ceased to work. Explain her rights.

6 Ali entered a two-year phone contract with Concoms plc. From the outset signal levels have been very limited: he has been with no or very little connectivity for days at a time. After three months of fruitless complaints he wants to terminate the contract. Concoms say he is liable to a contractual penalty of one year's full rental. What can he do?

Answers to all quizzes can be found in Appendix 2.

Take a closer look

The following cases provide important examples of how the law you have studied in this chapter has developed. They are primary sources illustrating the law in action and give you more detail about their facts, as well as helping you to understand the law and to appreciate how the judges reached their decisions.

Try looking them up in the law reports or accessing them via a database, e.g. Bailli (www.bailii.org/databases.html). LexisNexis or Westlaw may be available in your university or college library, or you may find extracts in a case book. (See Appendix 1: Additional resources.)

Aswan Engineering Establishment Co. Ltd v Lupdine Ltd [1987] 1 All ER 135, CA

Baxter v Barnes 2015 EWHC

Watford Electronics v Sanderson [2001] 1 All ER (Comm) 696, CA

J & H Ritchie Ltd v Lloyd Ltd (2007, HL)

Director General of Fair Trading v First National Bank (2001) 1All ER 97 HL

Web activity

Find out about what information Citizen's Advice provides for consumers.

Please go to: www.adviceguide.org.uk/england/

Assignment 6

In practice the Consumer Rights Act 2015 is unlikely to confer many benefits on a consumer buyer that they could not access under previous legislation. Discuss.

8

Statutory terms in contracts for sale of goods and services

CHAPTER 9

Defects in the contract

Misrepresentation, mistake, duress and undue influence

Introduction

Although on the face of things a contract has been formed, it may contain elements that make it defective. These may be caused by a number of factors varying from active dishonesty or negligence, through to honest mistake. They have differing legal consequences; some, while upsetting to a party, will not affect the validity of the contract at all. Others may render a contract voidable or exceptionally, void. It is important to grasp the difference between these concepts.

1 *A voidable contract:* here the parties have successfully made a contract but it contains a defect (often, though not always, caused by one of the parties) that enables the injured party to pull out of or avoid the contract. Usually the court will order the return of any property that was transferred. This chapter examines misrepresentation, duress and undue influence, all of which may make a contract voidable.

2 *A void contract:* although the parties believe they made a contract, the defect is so serious that in the eyes of the law no contract ever came into existence. Even if both parties wish to enforce the contract, this is not possible. If property has changed hands, ownership is not usually transferred and the property may be recovered. In this chapter the law of mistake provides an example of how a void contract may arise. As you will see, in practice it is very rare for the court to decide that a contract is void. In law, as in life, we often have to live with our mistakes.

▶

Learning objectives

When you have studied this chapter you should be able to:

▶ explain the difference between the legal consequences for parties to a void and a voidable contract;

▶ identify the different forms of misrepresentation and the remedies applicable to each;

▶ understand the concept of operative mistake;

▶ recognise the circumstances where operative mistake occurs;

▶ be aware of the forms which duress may take;

▶ appreciate how duress differs from undue influence.

Misrepresentation

During pre-contractual negotiations, statements (representations) may be made which induce a party to enter the contract. Such statements may, for example, be made by sales staff by word of mouth, or be included in catalogues or brochures. If untrue, they are called misrepresentations. A remedy in **misrepresentation** is available to the innocent party whether or not the statement became a term of the contract. If it is a term, an action for breach of contract provides alternative remedies.

Misrepresentation makes the contract **voidable**. The **misrepresentee** (the party to whom the statement was made) is entitled to avoid the contract or to persist with it.

An actionable misrepresentation is:

1 An untrue statement of fact, which

2 is a material inducement to enter the contract.

These principles have legal implications which it is important to grasp.

Misrepresentation:
an untrue statement and a material inducement to a party to enter a contract.

Voidable contract:
a contract exists but the innocent party may refuse to perform it.

Misrepresentee:
person to whom a misrepresentation is made.

Statement of fact

This can be written, spoken or pictorial, and may also arise from other conduct. Here are a few brief examples.

Gordon v *Selico* (1986)

Held: the seller of premises who deliberately concealed dry rot was guilty of misrepresentation to the buyer. In effect he was saying that the premises were sound.

Goulding J said:

> I believe it to be the law that conduct alone can constitute a fraudulent misrepresentation . . . The concealment of dry rot . . . was a knowingly false representation by Mr Azzam that Flat C did not suffer from dry rot, which was intended to deceive purchasers and did deceive the plaintiffs to their detriment.

A statement of fact does not include *statements of opinion*.

Bisset v *Wilkinson* (1927)

The vendor sold land to the buyer, having told the buyer that, if properly worked, he estimated the land would carry 2,000 sheep. In fact, it was capable of supporting many fewer.

Held: the vendor had not made a misrepresentation. Since he had never used his land for sheep farming, he was not making a statement of fact merely stating an honest opinion when he told the buyer how many sheep he believed the land would support.

However, statements of opinion may be treated as statements of fact if the maker, with knowledge of the underlying circumstances, could not reasonably have held the opinion.

Smith v *Land & House Property Corp.* (1884)

A vendor of a house described its tenant, Frederick Fleek, as a 'most desirable tenant', knowing that Fleek was in arrears with rental payments.

Held: the vendor was liable for fraudulent misrepresentation, as he was clearly lying. It was obvious to the vendor that Fleek was far from desirable as a tenant.

Statements of intention may be treated as statements of fact if at the time of making the statement the maker had no such intention.

Edgington v *Fitzmaurice* (1885)

A company prospectus said that the proceeds from the sale of debentures were to be used to improve buildings and extend the business; in fact the directors intended to use the money to pay off pressing company debts.

Held: a misrepresentation had been committed. Bowen LJ said: *The state of a man's mind is just as much a fact as the state of his digestion . . . A misrepresentation as to the state of his mind is therefore a statement of fact.*

9

Defects in the contract

More recent cases indicate a willingness by the courts to treat an estimation of future performance as a statement of fact, where it was reasonable for the other party to rely on it.

Esso Petroleum v Mardon (1976, CA)

A sales forecast for a filling station, given by Esso's experienced manager to a prospective tenant of the garage, turned out to be radically incorrect.

Held: Esso was liable for misrepresentation as a person as skilled as the manager should be able to be relied upon to give a reasonably accurate forecast.

Misrepresentor: person who makes a misrepresentation.

Statements of law are not usually regarded as statements of fact. Everybody is supposed to know the law and therefore to be aware when it is incorrectly stated. However, a statement relating to existing civil law rights of the **misrepresentor** concerning the subject matter of the contract is likely to be treated as a statement of fact.

Lawrence v Lexcourt Holdings Ltd (1978)

The vendor's statement that 'existing planning permission covers use of this building as an office' was held to be a statement of fact.

Although there is a duty to answer questions truthfully, *failure to volunteer information* is generally not misrepresentation, even if the representee is clearly under a misapprehension.

Smith v Hughes (1871)

A race horse trainer assumed that he was buying old oats, when actually they were new, but he did not ask the seller their age.

Held: no misrepresentation had occurred. The seller had said nothing about the age of the oats and it was irrelevant that he was aware of the importance of this to the buyer.

Liability for failure to disclose information may arise, however, in any of the following circumstances:

1 *Half-truths.* A statement may be true as it stands, but still mislead because it is incomplete.

Nottingham Patent Brick & Tile Co. Ltd v Butler (1886)

A solicitor who, without checking, told the buyer of some land that he 'did not know' of any restrictive covenants affecting it, was liable for misrepresentation.

Similarly, misrepresentation was held to have occurred in *Dimmock* v *Hallett* (1866), where the seller described the land as occupied by certain named tenants, but did not also tell the buyer that they had given notice.

2 Circumstances change between making the statement and acceptance.

With v *O'Flanagan* (1936, CA)

A doctor, who was selling his practice, gave the buyer correct information about its value. However, before the buyer notified acceptance the value had considerably diminished, as many patients went elsewhere when the doctor became ill.

Held: his failure to notify the buyer of the drop in value amounted to a misrepresentation as his original statement was no longer true and the buyer should have been notified of this.

Fiduciary relationship: a legal relationship with a very high degree of trust by one party in another's expertise, knowledge etc., giving that other party the capacity to influence their decisions.

3 A *fiduciary relationship exists between the parties*. A **fiduciary relationship**, involving a high degree of trust between the parties, exists, for example, between partners, and between solicitor and client. It is also relevant to insurance contracts, which are voidable unless full disclosure is made of all material facts, meaning those 'which would influence the judgment of a prudent insurer' (Marine Insurance Act 1906). For example, in a contract for carriage of goods by sea, the fact that goods are to be transported on deck, not in the hold, would be material *(Hood* v *West End Motor Car Packing* (1917)).

It is irrelevant that the failure to disclose was not careless or intended to deceive. Some people have found that they were deprived of insurance cover because they quite innocently failed to reveal that their cars had modified features (e.g. alloy wheels and sun roof) that were not standard to a particular model.

The statement acted as a material inducement

The misrepresentation must be a sufficiently important influence on the misrepresentee. It must be enough to incline a reasonable person to enter the contract, but it need not be the only reason for them doing so.

Vahey v *Kenyon* (2013, CA)

Mr Vahey was negotiating buying land from Mr Kenyon and asked him about its flooding history, because it was near a flood plain. Mr Kenyon said that, despite local flooding 30 years previously, his land had not been affected. Later, when the house was found to be damp, Mr Kenyon admitted, after further questioning, that the stream which flowed through the grounds occasionally burst its banks but had never flooded the house. The sale went ahead subject to a £10,000 discount. Soon after completion the property was flooded and Mr Vahey discovered that the garage and house had been flooded some years before, during Mr Kenyon's occupancy.

9

Defects in the contract

Held: the contract was voidable for fraudulent misrepresentation. It was clear from his enquiries that the issue of flooding concerned Mr Vahey and that the reassurances from Mr Kenyon had been material in getting him to enter the contract otherwise he would have sought to negotiate a higher discount.

Evidence that a misrepresentee was prepared to take unreasonable risks in pursuit of large profits may incline the court to discount the weight of the misrepresentor's statement. In *Hurst & Others* v *Hone & Others* (2010) a well-known former footballer was persuaded by the defendants' fraudulent statements suggesting huge financial gain in return for a substantial loan to further a building project in Spain. He lost all his money but it was held that the misrepresentations had not materially induced him. The prospect of quick and substantial profits had encouraged him to participate in the deal and he had been prepared to ignore third party advice about the risks.

Where the misrepresentor has technical knowledge the court is inclined in favour of a consumer who trusts in that, especially where third party advice is unlikely to be sought. See *Webster & Others* v *Liddington & Others* (2014, CA) (see 'In the news below').

In the news

Webster & Others v *Liddington & Others* [2014] CA

The claimants were all women who had been treated with a skin-rejuvenating product by the defendants who were clinics using a particular manufactured product.

Prior to buying the treatment, the claimants had all been given information brochures by the clinic they were contracting with. Some brochures had been produced by the manufacturer, others composed by the clinic based on the manufacturer's information. These all stressed the efficacy of the product due to its natural purity and claimed that, unlike Botox and similar treatments, it did not import foreign matter into the patient and that it contained only the patient's skin. The product was an injectate based on a small sample of the patients' skin which was sent by the clinic to the manufacturer. Bovine products were used in the process of creating the injectate; traces of these products sometimes remained, which in 3–10 per cent of cases could cause an allergic reaction. None of this information appeared in the brochures.

The claimants sued the clinics in misrepresentation. None had suffered ill effects but all wanted damages for having been sold an adulterated product of a different quality from what they had been led to believe.

Held: The defendants were guilty of misrepresentation since they were liable for the contents of all the brochures which they had distributed and thereby implied were an accurate, safe, reliable information source for patients. The patients were consumers who trusted in the superior specialist knowledge of the clinicians. The defendants had not issued any disclaimer for inaccuracies in the brochures. The misrepresentation about the content of the injectate was material. Had the patients known about the bovine product content and the medical risk they might well have decided against buying the treatment.

The misrepresentee must both *know* of the statement and *rely* on it.

Re Northumberland & Durham District Banking Co., ex parte Bigge (1858)

A contract with a shareholder was not voidable: he was unable to prove that when he bought the shares he had already seen reports which had been issued about the company which later proved to be false.

Attwood v Small (1838)

The seller of a mine misrepresented its capacity. However, the contract was not voidable because the buyer had not relied on the seller's statement, but had commissioned his own survey which also turned out to be inaccurate.

The misrepresentee is entitled to take the statement at face value and has no obligation to check the truth of the statement, even if the misrepresentor offers the opportunity to do so.

Redgrave v Hurd (1881)

A solicitor who was selling his practice gave information about its income and told the buyer that he could check the figures against relevant documentary evidence. The buyer did not choose to do so, and it was held that this did not prevent the contract from being voidable.

Exclusion of liability for misrepresentation

The Misrepresentation Act 1967, s 3, as amended by the Unfair Contract Terms Act 1977, permits exclusion or limitation of liability for misrepresentation so far as is reasonable in a contract between business parties. Reasonableness must be proved by the party who seeks to enforce the exemption. The Consumer Rights Act 2015 has further amended s 3 so that it does not apply to a term in any consumer contract covered by the CRA 2015.

The remedies for misrepresentation

Fraudulent misrepresentation: an untrue statement made intending to deceive or recklessly not caring whether it is true or false.

The remedies available to the misrepresentee depend on the perceived state of mind of the misrepresentor at the point at which the statement was made. A misrepresentation may be made fraudulently, carelessly or wholly innocently.

Fraudulent misrepresentation

Misrepresentation is **fraudulent** if the misrepresentor knows that the statement is untrue, or makes the statement recklessly, not caring whether it is true or false.

Rescission: an equitable remedy requiring a party to a voidable contract to give back money/property to the other party who has avoided the contract.

The misrepresentee may sue in the tort of deceit and obtain damages and/or **rescission** of the contract. Rescission is an equitable remedy issued at the discretion of the court; it seeks to return the parties to their pre-contractual position. This enables the misrepresentee to recover any money paid to the fraudulent party.

In practice, successful deceit actions are quite rare, though fraudulent misrepresentation is common. It happens, for example, every time somebody obtains goods with a stolen credit card, thus fraudulently representing themselves as the card holder. In situations like these the misrepresentors quickly disappear and action against them is not possible. If action is taken, the burden of proof of intention is a very heavy one for the claimant to discharge.

Careless misrepresentation

Under s 2(1) of the Misrepresentation Act 1967, a representor who induces the claimant to enter into a contract, by a statement which the representor did not reasonably believe, may be liable in damages. Rescission may also be granted. It is up to the representor to prove reasonable belief in the statement.

Howard Marine & Dredging Co. Ltd v *Ogden & Sons Ltd* (1978, CA)

The defendant was informed that barges chartered from the claimant had a certain capacity. The claimant's manager made this statement on the basis of insurance documentation. In fact, this was incorrect, as reference to the ship's papers would have shown. (Ship's papers are a sort of birth certificate issued with a new vessel at sale and held by the current owner.)

Held: the claimant was liable under s 2(1). The claimant had not discharged its burden of proof that it had reasonable belief: in such an important matter reference to a primary source of information was necessary.

Careless misrepresentation: an untrue statement made without reasonable belief in its truth.

Section 2(1) thus provides a remedy for **careless misrepresentation**. Also, since a potentially fraudulent misrepresentor cannot be said to have had a reasonable belief in the truth of the statement, the victim may claim under s 2(1) instead of pursuing an action in deceit. This relieves the claimant of the burden of proof but gives access to an identical remedy. In *Doyle* v *Olby* (*Ironmongers*) (1969, CA) it was held that, since deceit is an intentional tort, the defendant was liable for all the direct consequences of its behaviour. In *Royscot Trust Ltd* v *Rogerson* (1991) the Court of Appeal decided that damages under s 2(1) should be calculated in the same way as damages for fraud. This sometimes means that a party may recover a more generous measure of damages than if calculated according to contract principles that attempt to put the claimant in the position he or she would have enjoyed if the contract had been properly performed.

The victim of careless misrepresentation may also have a remedy in negligence under the rule in *Hedley Byrne* v *Heller* (which is explained in Chapter 14). This is helpful where parties have been misled and suffer loss, but then find out that the statement is incorrect before they enter the contract. It may also be used by someone who

Parity with remedies for breach

Before the 1967 Act, the victim of a misrepresentation was always able to avoid the contract regardless of the seriousness of the effect on it of the misrepresentation. This produced the anomalous result that the victim of a misrepresentation might be in a better position than a victim of a breach, who could only treat the contract as voidable if a condition was breached rather than a minor term. Section 2(2) enables the court to withhold rescission for non-fraudulent misrepresentation and award damages instead, thus solving this problem.

Mistake

Although it is common for a party to make a contract under a misapprehension, it is unusual for the resulting contract to be void. Such a contract may be voidable for misrepresentation; remedies for breach of contract may also be available.

Real life

Horace was buying a new house and after a lengthy search thought that at last he had found the place of his dreams, a pretty Victorian terraced house in a quiet street, with roses growing round the front door. Cuthbert the vendor was delighted to accept Horace's offer, as he had had a long difficult relationship with his next door neighbours, Baggy and Snitch, who were often very noisy in the evenings and who had started actively to harass Cuthbert after he had written to report them to the Council. A sale of land contract requires the vendor to complete a Sellers' Property Information Form. Cuthbert, desperate to escape, answered 'no' to the question about whether he had had any disputes with, or had made any complaints to/about his neighbours, or had sent any letters that might affect the property. The sale was duly completed but Horace is now enduring substantial noise nuisance from his neighbours who threatened him when he politely requested them to keep it down a bit.

Horace can rescind this contract for fraudulent misrepresentation and claim damages. We may have some sympathy with Cuthbert, but he clearly was lying. In less clear-cut circumstances Horace would be better off suing under the Misrepresentation Act 1967, s 2(1) which requires the misrepresentor to prove reasonable belief in their statement.

An operative mistake makes the contract void

Exceptionally, a mistake will be so fundamental that the contract will be rendered **void**. Such a mistake is said in law to be **operative** because it strikes at the root of the contract, effectively preventing any true agreement. In practice this is very rare.

Mistakes as to *quality* do not make the contract void. A mistake as to the *attributes* of the subject matter of the contract or of a party to it is never an operative mistake, even if the other party induces the mistake (misrepresentation), or fails to correct

> **Void contract:** no contract exists in the eyes of the law.

Operative mistake: one which makes a contract void because it prevents true agreement between the parties.

the mistaken party's false impression. If you ask to buy a food processor from a shop, under the mistaken belief that it has a juice-making facility, your mistake does not make the contract void. If the shop assistant told you that a juice maker was included, the contract is voidable for misrepresentation. If you were not actively misled, the contract is binding. The shop may be prepared to let you exchange the goods, or even give you a refund, but there is no legal obligation on it to do so.

Here are some cases of mistakes as to quality that have come before the courts.

Bell v Lever Bros (1932, HL)

Bell and Snelling, directors of a subsidiary company of Lever Bros and, without its knowledge, fraudulently used their position to speculate to make secret profits. Later, when leaving the company they negotiated a generous severance package. Lever Bros sought to recover this when they discovered the fraud, arguing that this contract was void because of a common mistake as to entitlement to the money. It did not know at the time of payment that they had committed fraud and the evidence was that Bell and Snelling had forgotten about it.

Held: the contract was valid as the mistake was merely as to the quality of the employment contract which could have been terminated summarily on grounds of fraud, with no compensation payable.

Lord Atkin said that a mistake as to quality by both parties will never make a contract void unless it 'is to the existence of some quality which makes the thing without the quality essentially different from the thing it was believed to be'.

It is quite hard to imagine circumstances which would satisfy the Atkin criteria. The courts have stuck firmly to his line ever since.

In contracts for the sale of land, the courts were sometimes prepared to treat a contract as voidable under equitable principles. Rescission was sometimes granted if both parties made the same mistake. This was possible only if it produced the most just result. Similarly, the court would not allow a party to obtain a decree of specific performance, if this would permit a party to exploit a mistake unfairly. This equitable doctrine was abolished by the Court of Appeal in *Great Peace Shipping* v *Tsavliris (International) Ltd* (2002). (Full information about equitable remedies can be found at the end of Chapter 11.)

Operative mistake may occur in the following circumstances.

Common mistake: both parties make the same mistake.

Common mistake concerning the existence of the subject matter

In **common mistake** both parties reasonably but wrongly believe that the subject matter exists at the time they make the contract.

Couturier v Hastie (1856, HL)

The parties made a contract for the sale of a cargo of corn which was being conveyed on named ship from a foreign port. Unknown to either party, the corn had already been disposed of by the carrier because it had started to ferment and become a risk to the safety of the ship.

Held: there was no possibility of a contract coming into being if the specific goods did not exist at the point when the parties reached agreement. It was impossible to buy that cargo any longer.

The contract may be void even if the subject matter never existed as long as it was reasonable for the parties to believe that it did.

Associated Japanese Bank (International) v Credit du Nord (1989)

The claimant bank contracted to buy £1 million-worth of computers from a rogue (Bennet) and lease them back to him, with a guarantee from the defendant bank to cover his repayment. The computers were the security for the guarantee but never actually existed. Bennet went bankrupt and the claimant tried to enforce the guarantee.

Held: the contract was void for common mistake from the outset, since the computers did not exist and never had existed, although this was unknown to the parties to the case. Existence of the security for the loan had been crucial to the contract. Without that promise the defendant would never have agreed to the guarantee.

Leaseback contracts of this kind are a very common commercial transaction, with goods passing unseen to the lessee (the party who bought them and is now renting them back from the other party). Provided there is nothing to alert the lessor (the buyer of the goods to be leased) to the integrity of the other party, they are not expected to check that the relevant goods exist.

However, the contract will not be void if one party has responsibility to check that the subject matter exists.

McRae v Commonwealth Disposals (1951)

The parties entered a contract under which the defendant gave the claimant rights to salvage a wrecked ship and its cargo of oil, which the defendant said would be found on a reef at a given map reference. After much costly searching by the claimant, the wreck could not be found at that site.

Held: the defendant was liable for breach of contract since it had been careless in promising the existence of the wreck.

Worth thinking about?

What is the legal situation if the parties make a contract about property, which is currently in existence but ceases to be before the contract is performed?

Suggested solutions can be found in Appendix 2.

Mutual mistake concerning the identity of the subject matter

Mutual mistake: both parties each make a different mistake.

In **mutual mistake** both parties operate under different misapprehensions and are at cross-purposes. This objectively assessed is seen as preventing any real consensus and is not due to the fault of either party. Such cases are rare, but occasionally the long arm of coincidence strikes.

Raffles v *Wichelhaus* (1864)

Two ships called *Peerless* were both carrying cotton from Bombay. The parties contracted for the sale of such a cargo. The buyer believed that he was buying one consignment while the seller was disposing of the other.

Held: this mistake prevented any agreement coming into being and therefore the contract was void. No true agreement existed between them since they were entirely at cross purposes about what was being bought and sold.

Unilateral mistake

Unilateral mistake: one contracting party is mistaken.

In **unilateral mistake** only one party makes a mistake. Such mistakes are very common, but usually they only make a contract at best voidable or even leave it unaffected.

A unilateral mistake can only make the contract void if:

1 One party enters a contract crucially mistaken and would not have made the contract if they had known the truth.

2 The other party should reasonably have known of the mistake.

3 The mistaken party is not at fault.

There are two types of such mistakes: identity of a party or of a term of the contract.

Unilateral mistake by one party regarding the identity of the other

Although mistaken identity is very common, it is very unlikely to make a contract void, particularly if the parties have contracted face to face.

Voidable title: provisional ownership of goods lost by the misrepresentor if the misrepresentee avoids the contract before a bona fide third party buys them.

Mistaken identity usually arises from a fraudulent misrepresentation, which enables a fraudster (commonly called 'a rogue' in law books) to take possession of the victim's property. The resulting contract, between claimant and rogue, is voidable for misrepresentation. Ownership of the goods passes to the rogue, under what is called a **voidable title**. Unless the claimant takes steps to avoid the contract made with the rogue *before* the goods are sold on, the party who buys the goods from the rogue becomes the legal owner. Since the victim of the fraud cannot usually contact the rogue directly, giving information about the swindle to the police has been held to be sufficient to avoid the contract (*Car & Universal Finance* v *Caldwell* (1964)).

In practice, the victim is usually unable to avoid the contract with the rogue before the goods are sold on, so an innocent third party becomes owner of the goods.

The only hope for the victim is to persuade the court that the contract is void for mistake, since this would mean that the goods have not become the property of the party who bought from the rogue and could be recovered. The problem for the court is how best to do justice between two innocent parties – the rogue's victim (the claimant) and the person who bought the goods from the rogue in good faith (the defendant). Generally, the courts are more likely to sympathise with the defendant, unless the claimant is able to prove that it was entirely reasonable for the claimant to be duped by a virtually foolproof deception by the rogue. The rationale for this approach is that it is fair that the original seller carries the risk of the buyer not being creditworthy, by letting the buyer remove the goods.

A contract will not be void for mistaken identity unless the claimant can prove the following:

1 *The claimant intended to deal with some person other than the contracting party*. The claimant must be mistaken not merely as to the attributes (quality) of the other party, but also as to that party's actual identity. Therefore, the claimant's case will collapse unless he or she can prove that there are *two persons* – one with whom he or she contracted and one with whom he or she intended to contract.

King's Norton Metal Co. v *Edridge, Merrett & Co.* (1897)

A rogue represented himself to the claimant company as the agent of a successful business enterprise which did not actually exist. The claimant entered into a postal contract which was held not to be void since the claimant clearly intended to make a contract with somebody and the only entity with whom this was possible was the rogue.

Compare:

Cundy v *Lindsay* (1878, HL)

A rogue, Blenkarn, represented himself as Blenkiron & Co., a reputable company already known to the claimant and trading from an address in the street where the rogue had set up his premises. He ordered, by post, linen handkerchiefs from the claimants, never paid for them and sold them on to a third party whom the claimants sued.

Held: the contract between the claimant and Blenkarn was void, as the claimants reasonably believed that they were dealing with another party than the rogue. This meant that the claimant could recover the goods which had been sold on to the defendant.

1 *The other party was aware of the claimant's mistake*. This is not generally a problem, since usually the other party is bent upon deception.

2 *The issue of identity must have been crucial when the contract was made*. The claimant will have to satisfy the court that at the point the contract was made he or she intended to contract only with the person whom the rogue claimed to be. In *Cundy* v *Lindsay*, which was a postal contract, the court was prepared to accept this. In later

cases, the courts have adopted a different approach where the contract is made face to face and have placed a heavy burden of proof on the claimant, who must show that it was reasonable to place reliance on the rogue's representations. Otherwise, it is presumed that the claimant intended to contract with the person before them and the contract will not be deemed void for mistake, but will merely be voidable for misrepresentation.

The conduct of the parties is judged objectively to determine whether the claimant has acted reasonably.

Phillips v *Brooks* (1919)

The claimant jeweller contracted to sell a ring to a rogue who claimed to be Sir George Bullough. He then pawned the ring with the defendant and the claimant sued to recover it.

Held: the claimant could not recover the jewellery since the contract he had made with the rogue was not void. The issue of identity was clearly not crucial to the claimant who had merely checked the name and address in a street directory and was satisfied by such flimsy evidence which did not demonstrate any real link between the rogue and the person he claimed to be. It proved nothing more than that a Sir George Bullough did live at a particular address.

The Court of Appeal reached an apparently conflicting decision in:

Ingram v *Little* (1960, CA)

A rogue offered to buy a car from three elderly sisters. They initially refused to take a cheque so the rogue claimed to be P.G.M. Hutchinson and said he was a successful businessman. He also supplied an address. While two of the sisters kept the rogue talking, the third went to the post office and checked the particulars in the telephone directory and found that the name and address given by the rogue were correct. This, of course, proved nothing except that the rogue knew Hutchinson's name and address, but the sisters agreed to sell. The cheque was not honoured and the rogue sold the car to the defendant, a car dealer.

Held (by majority): the contract was void and therefore the car was recoverable from the defendant. The test was whether the rogue should reasonably have believed at the time of entering the contract that the offer from the seller was to the person they represented themselves as being. The sisters had intended to deal only with Hutchinson, as was evidenced by their initial refusal to accept the cheque until they had checked the phone book. Every case in these circumstances must be determined on its facts and *Phillips* v *Brooks* could be distinguished as the jeweller had agreed to sell before he checked the street directory.

While it is difficult to see any material difference between the facts of the two cases above, the decision in *Ingram* v *Little* may be justified as reflecting the customary approach of protecting the more vulnerable party at the expense of the business party. Remember it was a dealer who bought the car from the rogue.

Lewis v *Averay* (1971, CA)

The claimant (Mr Lewis) sold his car to a rogue, who had claimed to be Richard Green, a film actor well known for portraying Robin Hood in a popular TV series. Before the sale was agreed, the rogue showed the claimant a chequebook in the name of R.A. Green, and a pass to Pinewood Studios. The pass bore an official stamp, the name Richard Green and the rogue's photograph. The rogue then sold the car to the defendant (Mr Averay) and the claimant sought to get it back.

Held: his claim must fail. The contract with the rogue was not void and therefore the defendant purchaser of the car had acquired ownership. The claimant had not proved that it was crucial to him to contract with the rogue as he accepted less than convincing evidence of the rogue's identity. All it showed was that the rogue's name was probably Richard Green and that he worked at Pinewood. 'Green' is a common name and there are many jobs at film studios which do not involve leading acting roles.

Lord Denning MR said:

> Mr Lewis made a contract with the very man, the rogue, who came to the flat. We say he 'made a contract' because . . . we do not look into his intentions or into his mind to know what he was thinking, or into the mind of the rogue. We look to the outward appearances. It was still a contract though voidable for fraud . . . under which this property passed to the rogue and in due course to Mr Averay before the contract was avoided. Though I very much regret that either of these two good and reliable men should suffer, in my judgement it is Mr Lewis who should do so.

The court (by majority) refused to apply *Ingram* v *Little* and instead applied the *Phillips* v *Brooks* decision. *Ingram* v *Little* was perceived as anomalous as the facts of all three cases were indistinguishable.

In the next case the Court of Appeal refused to follow this decision, distinguishing it on its facts.

Shogun Finance Ltd v *Hudson* (2002, CA)

A rogue, who represented himself as Mr Patel, using a driving licence stolen from Mr Patel as evidence, obtained a car on hire purchase from the claimant finance company, which had made very limited identity checks on the electoral register and county court judgment records. He later sold it to Hudson. The finance company succeeded in its claim to recover the car from Hudson as the contract between it and the rogue was deemed void.

Held (by majority):

1 Identity was a crucial issue for the finance company. In these circumstances the rogue would reasonably believe that the offer was being made not to him personally but to Mr Patel.

2 This was not a face-to-face contract as the car dealer was not acting as agent of the finance company when dealing with the rogue. Therefore, the presumption that the claimant intended to deal with the person before him did not apply.

All the judges hearing this case commented on the confusing state of the law in this area and the need for statutory reform to enable a clear and fair system of loss distribution in such cases. Hudson appealed to the House of Lords.

Shogun Finance Ltd v *Hudson* (2004, HL)

The House of Lords (by majority) affirmed the Court of Appeal's decision.

Held: no hire-purchase contract had been created between the finance company and the rogue, but a contract had been concluded with Mr Patel, who was clearly identified in the agreement in accordance with the way prescribed by the finance company. Mr Patel was the only person the company had been willing to do business with. The delivery of the car to the rogue by the dealer did not create any contract with the rogue.

It was not appropriate to depart from the House of Lords' previous decision in *Cundy* v *Lindsay*, since it made good sense to maintain the presumption, in face-to-face contracts only, that the seller intended to contract with the person before them.

The determination of the courts to protect Shogun Finance in this case may seem surprising. This sort of fraud is widespread and it could be argued that hire-purchase companies should be encouraged to take greater precautions to prevent it regardless of how the contract is made. The evidence it relied upon, in reality, only told the company that Mr Patel had a current driving licence, was on the electoral register and had no unsatisfied court judgments against him. None of it proved that the rogue was Mr Patel.

Unilateral mistake regarding the terms of the contract

Parties will not usually be able to treat a contract as void by claiming that they were mistaken about the terms on which the contract was based. Exceptionally, the contract will be treated as void if the error would have been clearly evident to the other party, who will not be allowed to rely on it.

Hartog v *Colin & Shields* (1939)

A written contract to sell hare skins stated that the price would be calculated by the pound. It should have stated that the goods would be sold by the piece. This had been agreed orally between the parties and reflected the customs of the trade.

Held: the buyer was not entitled to take unfair advantage of what he must have realised, with his experience of the trade, was a clerical error in the written contract which must be treated as void.

Only a very obvious mistake will invalidate the contract.

> ### *Wood* v *Scarth* (1858)
>
> The defendant's written offer to let premises did not include a premium, and the claimant was not informed of such a requirement when he concluded the contract with the defendant's agent.
>
> **Held:** the contract was not invalidated by this mistake, since the claimant could not reasonably have been expected to have anticipated that a premium would be payable.

The equitable remedy of rectification

If a contract is found to be void for operative mistake the court will require any money or property which has changed hands to be returned: as no contract exists in law, title does not pass.

Rectification: an equitable remedy to amend a document to reflect the parties' true intention.

However, the court may be prepared to order a decree of **rectification** to amend a written contract which contains a unilateral mistake relating to its terms. It will only be granted if there is clear evidence that, as it stands, it does not represent the intention of the parties and that injustice would result from enforcement of the written document in its existing form.

Documents signed by mistake

The courts are generally very unsympathetic to people who try to avoid the effect of a mistakenly signed document. It is usually binding, unless misrepresentation or undue influence makes it voidable. Exceptionally, a plea of *non est factum* (this is not my deed) may be applicable.

Non est factum: 'This is not my deed.' May be pleaded by a party who has mistakenly signed a contract for a radically different purpose than he or she was led to believe.

The House of Lords has specified certain proof points for this plea, which if satisfied will result in the mistakenly signed document being void. Signers must prove that:

1 the document signed is radically different in its effect from what they believed they were signing;

2 the signers were not careless. The standard of care exercised by a signer is judged subjectively, taking into account age and physical and mental capabilities.

> ### *Gallie* v *Lee (Saunders* v *Anglia Building Society)* (1970, HL)
>
> Mrs Gallie, who was 78, had poor sight and had mislaid her spectacles, signed a document without reading it. She assumed it to be a deed of gift assigning her house to her nephew, Wally. She had previously agreed to give him the house so that he could raise money on it for a business venture, provided that she would be able to continue living there. In fact, the document presented to her for signature by Lee, Wally's friend and business colleague, actually assigned the house to Lee for £3,000. He never paid Mrs Gallie the money, but mortgaged the house to the building society. He then failed to make any repayments and so the building society attempted to repossess the house. By the time the case reached the House of Lords, Mrs Gallie was dead and the parties to the case were her executor and the building society.

Held: the plea of *non est factum* failed.

1 The document was not sufficiently different in purpose from what Mrs Gallie believed she was signing: it transferred the ownership of the house, which was what she intended. It was irrelevant that it transferred the house to a different person, by sale not gift.

2 Mrs Gallie had not taken sufficient care before signing. She should at least have checked the contents of the document by asking someone to summarise it for her if she was not able to read it for herself.

The courts have shown great reluctance to allow a plea of *non est factum* to succeed in most of the cases where it has been raised. The fact that Mrs Gallie was clearly vulnerable to the wiles of her nephew and his mate seems to have cut no ice with the court. Initially the contract would have been voidable for misrepresentation or undue influence (see below) but by the time the building society foreclosed it was too late.

Duress and undue influence

The essence of a contract is that it is a voluntary agreement. Evidence that a party entered a contract under compulsion may make it voidable.

Duress

Duress:
physical threat to force a party to enter a contract.

Duress is a common law doctrine, under which threats or use of violence to force a party to make a contract may make it voidable. In practice, physical duress is very rare, though exceptions do exist. In *Barton* v *Armstrong* (1975, PC) the claimant, who had been subjected to a campaign of physical threats to persuade him to part with a valuable shareholding, was able to avoid the resulting contract.

Traditionally, the doctrine of duress encompassed only threats and violence against the person, but the courts, in the latter half of the twentieth century, extended the doctrine to cover economic duress. Such duress usually consists of threats by one party not to perform the contract with the other party unless the terms of the contract are varied in favour of the coercive party. In the past, the courts have tended to treat such variations as void in law because of an absence of consideration, but increasingly they are tending to hold them voidable because of economic duress. In *Opel GmbH and Renault SA* v *Mitras Automotive* (2008) (facts below) the judge (Donaldson QC) described it as *'a more refined control mechanism'.*

In *Pao On* v *Lau Yiu Long* (1979) Lord Scarman held that the following criteria are relevant to deciding whether the contract is voidable:

1 The extent of the pressure employed. This must exceed the acceptable levels of pressure normally to be expected in commercial dealings.

2 The level of protest evidenced by the aggrieved party.

3 Whether the aggrieved party had any real choice about complying with the other party's threats.

4 Whether independent advice was available to the aggrieved party.

The cases below illustrate how much must be at stake for a claim of economic duress to succeed.

Atlas Express Ltd v *Kafco Importers & Distributors* (1989)

The claimant had contracted to transport goods for the defendant at a certain price calculated (by the claimant) on the basis of an estimated size of load. The first load was actually much smaller than was economic. The claimant then said that they would not make any further trips unless the price was renegotiated with a raised minimum cost per load. The defendants felt obliged to accept this as there was not time to find another carrier; they were also heavily dependent on a current order to Woolworths, where the next delivery was to be made.

Held: where a party is forced to renegotiate terms to its disadvantage and is left without bargaining power with no alternative but to accept the new terms offered, economic duress has occurred. Kafco's business would have been in danger of collapse if it was unable to supply its main customer.

A greatly disproportionate rise in cost may be convincing evidence of duress.

Opel GmbH and Renault SA v *Mitras Automotive* (2008)

The claimants, Opel and Renault, had contracted for some time with the defendant Mitras (M) for the supply of bumper mountings for vans. Eventually, they repudiated the contract with six months' notice because of changes in design to their vans. Mitras responded with a 'termination agreement' demanding several hundreds of thousand pounds 'in recompense' for losing the contract and increased costs of production. The claimants were placed in a very difficult position as they only had supplies sufficient for 24 hours of production, and M was refusing further delivery. They reluctantly agreed to M's terms and paid but subsequently claimed that this leaving agreement was not binding as it was made under economic duress.

Held: economic duress invalidated the agreement, making it voidable. The defendants had applied illegitimate pressure to the claimants by threatening to breach the supply contract, as the claimants would have suffered huge losses if production had ceased and consequently they were placed in a no-choice position. No alternative supplier was immediately available. The agreement was voidable and the claimants could recover the money they had paid.

Serious loss of business reputation is also influential.

Kolmar Group AG v *Traxpo Enterprises PVT Ltd* (2010)

The claimant, Kolmar, agreed to buy a specified amount of ethanol at a specified price from the defendant, Traxpo. Time of delivery was crucial, as Kolmar intended to sell the ethanol to a very important client in urgent need. Later, Traxpo told Kolmar that it could only deliver a smaller amount than specified and at a higher price. Kolmar went ahead with the purchase, as he felt he had no choice, but later sued for the difference in price.

Held (Clarke J): Traxpo had placed Kolmar under economic duress by subjecting him to illegitimate pressure and placing him in a take it or leave it position which it had no alternative but to accept in order to supply its client: 'and, if it failed to do so, would not merely suffer a severe loss of reputation with a client of great potential importance but would in all probability be exposed to very large claims'.

Kolmar was entitled to damages to cover the increased price.

Undue influence: inequitable influence making a contract voidable.

Undue influence

Undue influence is an equitable doctrine, applicable where one party abuses his or her personal influence or authority over another to make that other party enter a transaction. If the influence is effective, the transaction is voidable.

Williams v *Bayley* (1866, HL)

A father was told by his bank that his son would be prosecuted, unless he (the father) paid back money that the son had fraudulently obtained from the bank by forging his father's signature.

Held: the resulting contract was voidable against the bank by the father because he had not entered into it freely.

Avon Finance v *Bridger* (1985, CA)

An elderly couple were buying a retirement home; their son was making the financial arrangements and was providing part of the money. To do this, he obtained a loan from the claimant, but did not tell his parents, who signed a legal charge as security, that it related to their home. The son then failed to keep up the repayments and the claimant took action to possess the house.

Held: the security agreement was voidable for undue influence by the son, which was attributable to the claimant. The son was in effect acting as the claimant's agent. The claimant should have been aware that the son would exercise influence over his parents, who had not received independent advice.

Where there is *no fiduciary relationship* between the parties the burden of proof of undue influence is on the complainant. He or she will have to satisfy the court that, but for the influence to which he or she had been subjected, he or she would not have entered the transaction. Proof that the complainant had no independent advice before entering the transaction may be evidence that he or she did not act with free will.

Where a *fiduciary relationship* exists between the parties, undue influence is presumed, provided that the complainant can prove that the resulting transaction was disadvantageous to him or her. The transaction will be voidable unless the other party can prove that the complainant was not prevented from exercising freedom of will. Evidence that the complainant had access to independent advice will be proof of this.

A fiduciary relationship is deemed in law to exist automatically in some situations. These include:

1 doctor and patient;
2 solicitor and client;
3 principal and agent.

However, the court may be prepared to acknowledge that particular circumstances give rise to a fiduciary relationship in the case before it. In *Re Craig* (1971) a secretary companion, who persuaded her frail and elderly employer to make gifts to her from the bulk of his savings, was held to be in a fiduciary relationship to him. He was both physically and emotionally dependent on her. She had to repay the money to his estate. In the next case the amount of control taken by the defendant over an elderly man's business affairs was sufficient to create a fiduciary relationship.

Goldsworthy v Brickell (1987, CA)

The claimant, who was elderly, owned a large and valuable farm which had become very run down. He came to rely heavily on the defendant (his neighbour) for advice. Within a few months the defendant was effectively managing the farm. The claimant then gave the defendant a tenancy of the farm on terms very favourable to the defendant, but took no independent advice.

Held: the tenancy was voidable because undue influence was presumed. A fiduciary relationship was held to exist because of the very close working relationship of the parties in which the defendant clearly dominated the claimant.

In general, the courts have not often been persuaded to find a fiduciary relationship to exist between husband and wife, even if the relevant transaction was for the benefit of the husband.

Barclays Bank v O'Brien (1993, HL)

The facts of this case are set out below. The House of Lords indicated that a more generous approach may be appropriate where a wife stands **surety** for a husband's debts:

1 The informal nature of business dealings between spouses raises a substantial risk that the husband might fail accurately to inform his wife of the extent of the liability she is undertaking.

2 Many wives place trust and confidence in their husband's judgement in financial matters.

3 Similar principles would apply to transactions between cohabitees where there is an emotional bond, whether heterosexual or homosexual.

Surety: a person who provides security to a creditor for a loan.

Occasional exceptions are made but no fiduciary relationship is usually acknowledged to exist between a bank and its customers. The bank does not even have a duty to ensure that a customer takes independent advice prior to entering into a transaction with it. However, failure to do so may prevent the bank from enforcing a contract in its favour, if it is perceived as having constructive notice of undue influence or misrepresentation which led the customer into the transaction. Such notice may be given by the nature and substance of the agreement and the relationship between the customer and any other party involved in or benefiting from the transaction.

Barclays Bank v *O'Brien* (1993, HL)

Mr O'Brien persuaded his wife to sign a mortgage on the jointly owned matrimonial home, as security for the overdraft for her husband's company in which she had no interest. He told her that the overdraft was limited to £60,000 for a period of three weeks. In fact, it was unlimited in both respects. When it rose to £154,000, the bank sought to enforce the mortgage. The branch where Mrs O'Brien had entered the transaction had failed to carry out instructions from head office to make sure that both parties were fully aware of the nature of the transaction and to recommend independent advice.

Held: if the circumstances surrounding the transaction should have put the bank on notice that a wife had been subject to undue influence or misrepresentation, she could avoid the transaction, unless the bank had warned her in confidence of the need to take independent advice. Mrs O'Brien was entitled to avoid the transaction as the bank had been put on notice of her husband's likely misbehaviour and had not taken adequate steps to safeguard her.

Later cases indicate that it is hard to persuade the court that the bank did have constructive knowledge unless the circumstances are exceptional.

Credit Lyonnais v *Burch* (1997)

The defendant was a junior employee in a small company and a family friend of the owner, who was also her boss. She was persuaded by him to take out a second mortgage on her flat and to give the bank an unlimited guarantee of the company's debts, to enable the company to increase its overdraft from £25,000 to £270,000. Neither he nor the bank ever revealed to her the heavy state of indebtedness of the company. The bank urged her to take legal advice before signing the relevant documents but when she refused, in a letter clearly written in consultation with her employer, it allowed her to enter what it knew to be a precarious contract.

Held: that the bank had constructive notice of the influence her employer was capable of exercising over her and of the lack of legal advice and, therefore, could not enforce the mortgage and guarantee against her.

In the majority of cases the court has held that the bank does not have constructive notice once the vulnerable party has been advised to take independent advice. The courts have usually interpreted the concept of independent and adequate advice in favour of the bank. However, in the *Etridge* case (below) the House of Lords has restated and clarified some of the issues and has revived a little of the spirit of the *O'Brien* decision. Nevertheless, there are still concerns about whether the surety is sufficiently protected with regard to the issue of independent legal advice. As the law now stands, the surety's only remedy in most cases may be an action in negligence against the solicitor, rather than being able to avoid the transaction with the bank.

Royal Bank of Scotland v *Etridge (No. 2)* (2001, HL)

Held:

(a) The bank is automatically put on notice when the surety is not acting in the course of business.

(b) The bank must reasonably ensure that the surety has understood the consequences of what he or she is signing, has been warned of the risks in non-technical language and has freely chosen to sign. However, the bank need not personally meet with the surety. Confirmation from the solicitor advising the surety will normally be sufficient.

(c) Independent advice may be supplied to the surety by the borrower's solicitor. That solicitor must determine whether there is any conflict of interest which indicates that the surety should be separately advised.

Once the bank was informed that the surety had been advised, the bank could assume that the advice had been delivered competently.

The limits of rescission

The only remedy for undue influence is *rescission*. This is an equitable remedy and, therefore, available only at the discretion of the judge. The right to avoid the transaction may be lost in the following circumstances:

1 *Affirmation*. The complainant performs the contract with no complaint once freed from the other party's domination.

2 *Delay*. In *Allcard* v *Skinner* (1887) the claimant joined a religious order and made large gifts to it. She stayed in the order for eight years and then left. Six years later she tried unsuccessfully to recover the money despite evidence of undue influence.

3 *A third party has acquired bona fide rights over the contract property*. If property was transferred under a contract voidable for undue influence and sold on before the complainant had time to avoid the contract, the right to rescind is lost.

Chapter summary

Misrepresentation

An untrue statement of fact, made by the misrepresentor, which induces the misrepresentee to enter the contract and makes the contract voidable. A misrepresentation may be fraudulent or innocent.

Fraudulent misrepresentation: made intentionally/recklessly.

Innocent misrepresentation: misrepresentation made carelessly without reasonable belief or wholly innocently with reasonable belief.

Remedies for misrepresentation

Fraudulent: action in deceit, rescission and damages.

Careless: action under Misrepresentation Act 1967, s 2(1). Burden of proof of reasonable belief is on defendant. Rescission and damages.

Wholly innocent: action under Misrepresentation Act 1967, s 2(2). Rescission is the usual remedy but damages may be substituted if rescission is not justified by the nature of the misrepresentation.

Mistake

An operative mistake makes a contract void.

Mistake may be operative in the following circumstances:

Common mistake about the existence of the subject matter.

Mutual mistake about the existence of the subject matter.

Unilateral mistake about the identity of a contracting party.

Unilateral mistake about a term of the contract.

Remedies

The court requires any property or money which has changed hands between the parties to be returned. Rectification may keep a contract alive if there is unilateral mistake regarding its terms.

Duress

Forcing a party to enter a contract by physical threats to their person or by threatening their business interests may make the contract voidable.

Undue influence

A contract resulting from more subtle forms of illicit persuasion than duress may be voidable.

Presumed undue influence: exists if the parties are in a fiduciary relationship and the resulting contract is disadvantageous to the less powerful party.

Actual undue influence: exists if the parties are not in a fiduciary relationship but one party can prove unfair exercise of power by the other party to get them to enter into a contract.

Remedy

Rescission.

Quiz 8

1 What effect does a successful claim of (a) mis-representation, (b) mistake, (c) duress, (d) undue influence and (e) *non est factum*, have on a contract?

2 On what grounds may the following contracts arguably be defective?

(a) Crockford sold his house to Wisden, having placed a large and heavy bookcase to conceal subsidence cracks in the wall.

(b) Kelly contracted to sell Bradshaw 1 tonne of jelly babies, which both parties believed to be in a warehouse in Scunthorpe. Earlier the same day, a massive fire had destroyed the contents of the warehouse.

(c) Chambers wrongfully told Webster that he was Pears, the famous flute player. As a result, Webster agreed to sell him his antique flute.

(d) Whittaker, who is frail, elderly and heavily dependent on his son, Moore, sold Moore valuable shares for a fraction of their market price, because Moore threatened that otherwise he would go and live abroad.

Answers to all quizzes can be found in Appendix 2.

Take a closer look

The following cases provide important examples of how the law you have studied in this chapter has developed. They are primary sources illustrating the law in action and give you more detail about their facts, as well as helping you to understand the law and to appreciate how the judges reached their decisions.

Try looking them up in the law reports or accessing them via a database, e.g. Bailli (www.bailii.org/databases.html). LexisNexis or Westlaw may be available in your university or college library, or you may find extracts in a case book. (See Appendix 1: Additional resources.)

9

Defects in the contract

Esso Petroleum v *Mardon* [1976] 2 All ER 5, CA

William Sindall plc v *Cambridgeshire County Council* [1994] 1 WLR 1016, CA

Shogun Finance Ltd v *Hudson* [2004] 1 All ER 215, HL

Credit Lyonnais v *Burch* [1997] 1 All ER 144, CA

Web activity

Please go to: http://www3.hants.gov.uk/tradingstandards/tradingstandards-consumer.htm

Click on 'Scams Alerts'. Have a look at some of the scams on offer and see if any involve misrepresentation or undue influence or unfair contract terms like those in this chapter.

Assignment 7

(a) Explain the remedies for misrepresentation.

(b) James sold his car privately by cheque to a rogue who represented himself as Robert Gould, whose chequebook and banker's card the rogue had recently stolen. For additional proof of identity the rogue showed James a travel pass in Robert's name on to which the rogue had put his own photograph. The rogue then sold the car on to a second-hand car dealer called Harry. The cheque bounced when James presented it and he has traced the car to Harry's showroom.

Advise James.

Would it make any difference to your answer if James had become suspicious shortly after selling the car and had notified the police?

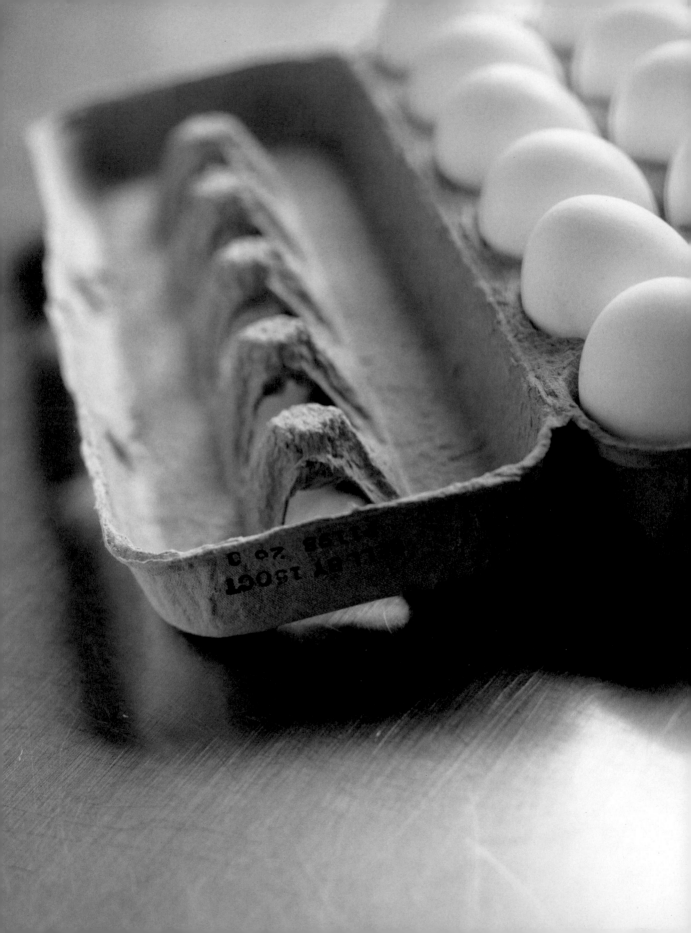

CHAPTER 10

More defects
Illegality and incapacity

Introduction

In this chapter we examine some more contractual defects: illegality and incapacity.

In the law of contract, the word 'illegal' has a wider meaning than that understood by lay people. It includes not only contracts which are actually *prohibited* by law, but also contracts to achieve a *purpose which is against the law*, as well as contracts seen to be against the public interest but which do not actually break the law. A contract found to be illegal is void.

In general, any person is legally *capable* of making a contract and, therefore, may sue or be sued on any contract to which he or she is a party. However, some types of person have *limited contractual* capacity and will not necessarily be bound by all the contracts that they make. This chapter examines the rules concerning two categories of people whose capacity is limited to protect them against exploitation – minors and mentally impaired persons.

Learning objectives

When you have studied this chapter you should be able to:

▶ appreciate the scope of the concept of illegality of contracts;

▶ recognise the circumstances in which making a contract is illegal;

▶ grasp the difference between contracts which are illegal and those which are merely void;

▶ understand when a contract in restraint of trade is enforceable;

▶ explain what kinds of contracts are enforceable against minors and mentally impaired people.

Illegality

Illegal contract: includes contracts which are not prohibited by law but which are against the public interest.

The rules governing **illegal contracts** are found in statute and common law.

Contracts illegal by statute

These are numerous and include the following:

1 The Competition Act 1998 prohibits a variety of contracts which restrict, distort or prevent competition such as price-fixing agreements.

2 The Gaming Act 1845 makes gaming and wagering contracts void. While not prohibiting gambling as such, it effectively prevents a party to such a contract from having any rights to pursue gambling debts through the courts.

Contracts illegal at common law

The court determines the existence and extent of the illegality by reference to public interest considerations, sometimes described as 'the public policy'. Contracts invalidated for public policy reasons fall into two categories: illegal and merely void. An illegal contract is one where the parties agree to do something which is directly or indirectly against the law. One which is merely void is one with a purpose perceived as undesirable and therefore against the public interest.

The following types of contract are illegal.

A contract to commit a crime, a tort or a fraud

> #### *Everet v Williams* (1725)
>
> Two highwaymen agreed to rob a stagecoach and share the proceeds. One held up the coach at gunpoint while the other collected all the valuables from the unhappy passengers. They were successful in carrying out their plan, but the one who had grabbed the valuables refused to part with any of them so the other one sued him in contract.
>
> **Held:** since the contract was to commit a crime, it was illegal and void.

A contract which is damaging to the country's foreign relations

Regazzoni v *Sethia* (1957, HL)

India's export regulations prohibited exports from India to South Africa. To avoid the prohibition, the claimant and defendant agreed to export the goods initially to Italy. From there they would be sent on to South Africa. The buyer sued for breach of contract when the seller failed to deliver.

Held: the buyer's claim must fail because the contract was illegal. Its performance would breach the law of India and was likely to endanger its friendly relationship with Great Britain.

A contract for a sexually immoral purpose

Pearce v *Brooks* (1866)

The claimant coach builders supplied a carriage to the defendant, knowing that she would use it to ply her trade as a prostitute.

Held: the contract was illegal. The coach builders could neither recover payment from the defendant nor repossess the carriage. They had effectively aided and abetted soliciting.

These days such a contract might not be treated so severely. The court operates according to current moral standards and tries to avoid unjust enrichment.

Armhouse Lee Ltd v *Chappell* (1996)

The defendant refused to pay the claimant for advertising the defendant's sex chat phone lines.

Held: the contract was legally binding. It was not a criminal or civil offence to place such adverts. There was no evidence that 'any generally accepted moral code condemned these sex lines'.

A contract which prejudices the administration of justice

Keir v *Leeman* (1809)

After a riot, criminal proceedings instigated by the claimant against the defendant were compromised when the defendant promised £50 to the claimant in return.

Held: this contract was illegal and void because it undermined the administration of justice and the claimant was not entitled to the money.

However, you may remember that civil cases may be legally compromised through an out of court settlement and arbitration agreements are actively encouraged by the law (see Chapter 4).

A contract to defraud the Revenue

Miller v *Karlinski* (1945)

The defendant employer agreed to pay a salary of £10 to the claimant and told him that he could claim expenses in which he could include the amount he should have paid in tax on the salary. The employer then failed to pay and the defendant sued for breach of contract. He claimed 10 weeks' salary and just over £21 expenses.

Held: the contract was void for illegality: it was clearly intended to evade paying tax. Over three-quarters of the expenses claimed represented what the claimant should have paid in income tax.

A contract endangering public safety

Contracts most often invalidated for this reason have been those made in wartime with an enemy alien. It is important to distinguish contracts made during wartime from those made before a war broke out. In the latter case the contract though valid when made will be discharged once the war starts (see Chapter 11).

Contracts promoting corruption in public life

Sales of honours or public office are good examples.

Parkinson v *College of Ambulance* (1925)

The defendant charity persuaded the claimant to make it a donation of £3,000 on the understanding that the charity would ensure that he got a knighthood, but then failed to deliver on its promise. The claimant sued for breach of contract.

Held: this was an illegal contract because it tended to promote corruption and the claimant could not recover the money.

Contracts prejudicial to marriage

A contract to restrict marriage such as one requiring a person not to marry at all or to marry a particular person or a member of a group is void, but other contracts which used to be deemed illegal reason may now be regarded differently.

A marriage brokerage contract (where a fee is paid to the person who arranged the marriage) was held to be void in *Herman* v *Charlesworth* (1925). A contract made prior to marriage which stated financial arrangements in the event of separation was also held to be illegal in *Cartwright* v *Cartwright* (1853).

However, attitudes have changed and subject to certain conditions both types of arrangement may now have some legal effect. Contracts with dating agencies are now enforceable. The growth of pre-nuptial agreements has led the courts to give them considerable influence in deciding how matrimonial property should be distributed, although they have stopped short of declaring them enforceable contracts.

Radmacher v *Granatino* (2010, SC)

The Supreme Court held that pre-nuptial agreements should be given full evidential weight by the court when determining the parties' financial post-divorce arrangements, provided there is no evidence of misrepresentation or undue influence.

The consequences of an illegal contract

The general principle is that illegality taints the whole contract, rendering it void. A party may find him or herself indirectly penalised for having made the contract. For example, if a party was aware of the illegal purpose before entering the contract, he or she will not generally be able to recover any property which has changed hands. This can be seen as a deterrent to discourage parties from making such contracts and may result in the instigator of the contract profiting from it. Unjust enrichment is, however, offensive to the courts and they may seek ways to prevent this.

The court may be influenced by the public interest aspects of the case and be more lenient in what it perceives as less serious involvement by one party. For example, a party who withdraws from the contract before it is carried out may recover (*Kearley* v *Thompson* (1890)).

Sometimes the court will waive the illegality to protect the more vulnerable party against exploitation.

Kiriri Cotton Co. Ltd v *Dewani* (1960, CA)

A tenant was allowed to recover the cost of an illegal premium a landlord had demanded before granting a tenancy because the statute which banned the premium was intended to protect the tenant against just such exploitation.

A party may be able to enforce a legal right to property independent of the contract.

Tinsley v *Milligan* (1993, HL)

The House of Lords permitted a party to a contract based on fraud to retain her share of a house.

Held: she had an equitable interest in the property which arose from all the work she had done towards the repair and upkeep of the premises.

If a party withdraws from the contract before performance they may be treated more leniently by the courts. Historically this only covered cases where the party pulled out because they thought better of their dishonest behaviour but proof of such regret is no longer necessary (*Tribe* v *Tribe* (1996)). Recently, in *Patel* v *Mirza* (2014), this was extended to a situation where the contract had become frustrated (impossible to perform due to circumstances outside the parties' control).

In the news

Patel v *Mirza* (2014, EWCA)

M was involved in the foreign exchange business and told P and their mutual friend G that they could use his betting account to bet on the changes in price of RBS shares. P paid him £620,000 to place bets because M told him that he had contacts in the bank able to give insider information about share value, once the government issued a statement about the size of the investment it would make in the bank. The contract was illegal because it involved insider dealing which amounts to conspiracy to commit a criminal offence.

Ultimately the plan fell through because the government statement was never made and so the bets were not placed. M then mistakenly paid P's money to G instead of P and P claimed it back from M.

The High Court held that a party who withdraws from an illegal contract before it is discharged may be said to have 'repented in time' and may then recover money paid to the other party. However, P's claim must fail because he had not withdrawn from the illegal contract before it was frustrated by the non-appearance of the anticipated information on which the bet was to rely.

The Court of Appeal by majority reversed the High Court decision and held: that P could recover his money from M. Recent case law (*Tribe* v *Tribe* (1996)) indicated that withdrawal from an illegal contract prior to performance could permit recovery without proof of repentance from the claimant. It was impossible to judge whether a party's repentance was genuine and was a purely subjective assessment. It would therefore be an illogical distinction to hold that recovery should be refused if the claimant had not withdrawn but the contract had become frustrated.

Contracts which are merely void

Such contracts do not involve law breaking but are perceived to be against the public interest since they are perceived as encouraging undesirable activities. The parties will not be penalised by the courts for making them. The contract will be enforceable as far as it is not void and property which has changed hands is always recoverable. The most important type of contract in this category is one said to be in restraint of trade.

Restraint of trade: restriction on freedom to work for/do business where/with whom you choose.

Contracts in restraint of trade

Restraint of trade is commonly a feature of the following agreements:

1 *Contracts of employment.* Employees may be required to give undertakings not to reveal trade secrets or to compete with their employers on leaving their service.

2 *Contracts for the sale of a business.* Where a business is sold as a going concern, the seller may undertake not to set up in competition with the buyer.

3 *Solus agreements.* A seller of a particular product may agree to deal with only one supplier in return for a discount or some other financial benefit (a **solus agreement**). This is very common in contracts for the supply of petrol. The owner of a filling station obtains a discount price, or financial assistance from the supplier to develop a site, in return for a promise to sell only that supplier's brand.

> **Solus agreement:** contract under which one party agrees to deal with only one supplier, etc.

The use of such restraints is generally regarded as not being in the public interest, because they tend to hamper competition and freedom of movement of labour. All such restraints are said to be prima facie void – i.e. they will initially be treated as against the public interest – but will be enforced if proved reasonable. This means that the court will not give a remedy (like an injunction) to help a party enforce the restraint, unless there is evidence that in the particular circumstances the restraint is reasonable.

Three questions are relevant to determining reasonableness:

1 Is the business interest one which can legally be protected? Such interests are limited to trade secrets and influential relationships in employment contracts. If the contract concerns the sale of a business, the goodwill may be protected.

2 How long is the restraint intended to last?

3 How wide a geographical area is covered by the restraint?

Provided that a legally recognised business interest is found to exist, the issues of time and geographical area are determined in the light of the particular facts of the case. The courts have exceptionally upheld lifelong or worldwide restraints. In practice, however, most restraints operate only within a very limited time and area.

Restraints in employment contracts

An employer may in a contract of employment seek to impose restrictions on employees who have moved to a new employer.

With regard to *trade secrets*, an employer may restrain employees with access to unique information concerning the manufacturing process or composition of goods from revealing this information to others or using it for their own purposes.

Forster & Sons Ltd v *Suggett* (1918)

The employee had access to secret bottle-glass manufacturing processes invented by his employer.

Held: it was reasonable to restrict the employee from being involved in such a trade for five years after he stopped working for the employer, anywhere in the UK.

10

More defects: illegality and incapacity

Business connections created by an employee through close relationships forged with customers during the relevant employment may also be protected. This is to prevent an ex-employee from poaching customers.

Fitch v *Dewes* (1921, HL)

Held: a solicitor's managing clerk could reasonably be restrained from working as a solicitor for the rest of his life, within a seven-mile radius of Tamworth town hall, as he had dealt confidentially with many clients within his employer's practice. They might follow him if he were allowed to practise locally.

Employees who have learnt skills and obtained business knowledge from their employment cannot be legally prevented from using these skills elsewhere, unless trade secrets were imparted or close relationships with customers resulted.

Morris v *Saxelby* (1916, HL)

Held: a draughtsman and engineer could not be restrained from working in the crane components manufacturing business. Knowledge about the way in which his ex-employers organised a similar business was not an interest which could be protected.

Eastham v *Newcastle United Football Club* (1963)

Football Association rules stated that players who left a club at the end of a contract could be placed on a retainer list. This prevented them from seeking employment with any other club in the UK or abroad, for as long as their ex-club paid them 'a reasonable wage'.

Held: this rule was not binding since no legitimate trade interest was protected by it.

Faccenda Chicken Ltd v *Fowler* (1986, CA)

The claimants sold frozen chickens door to door. Mr Fowler was their sales manager but had no direct contact with customers. He left Faccenda's employment and set up a similar business in the area, using his ex-employers' customer lists. Eight of the claimants' other employees left to work for him.

Held: Fowler could not be restrained from this activity: the information he had used was not a trade secret and he was not breaching his ex-employers' confidence by using it. He was at liberty to offer jobs to any person that he thought suitable.

The issue of reasonableness must be determined in the way most likely to produce a fair outcome for both parties. In each of the three cases above, the employer was merely trying to prevent legitimate competition by an ex-employee. This would have unduly restricted the employee selling his labour, or setting up in business elsewhere.

Real life

Horace trained as a graphic designer, but left the industry and for the past five years has worked as a personal trainer at the FitQuick Gym in Oldcastle. His friend Sidney owns a company running a chain of fitness clubs with branches in nearby towns and has just opened a new one in Oldcastle. He offers Horace a job as promoter and publicity manager.

Horace's contract of employment with FitQuick states that he cannot work as a personal trainer or in any related job connected with the fitness industry in Oldcastle, or within 30 miles of it for one year after leaving FitQuick's employment.

As Horace will have built up a personal relationship with clients at FitQuick, it is reasonable for it to protect this business interest, and seeking to prevent him from working as a personal trainer for one year within Oldcastle itself is not an excessive time or too wide a locality. However, trying to prevent Horace from working as a personal trainer outside the town, or taking a job in the fitness business not involving a close personal relationship with clients, may well be deemed unreasonable. It rather depends on how far away the nearest gym in Sidney's chain is located and whether his new job would permit him to exploit his relationship with his old clients.

The courts recognise that employees do not usually share equal bargaining power with their employers. The wording of a contract is therefore strictly interpreted to prevent unreasonable restraints upon employees, particularly if their youth and inexperience make them prey to exploitation.

Proactive Sports Management Ltd v *Wayne Rooney and Others* (2010)

Proactive claimed that Rooney was in breach of a contract which entitled it to 20 per cent of all profits from the exploitation of R's image for eight years. Rooney had entered the contract with Proactive at the age of 17 and neither he nor his parents appeared to have been legally advised during the process.

Held (Judge Hegarty QC):

The contract between Proactive and Rooney was in restraint of trade and unenforceable because it was unreasonable in its duration, area and scope.

As it stood, the restraint would last about half of his footballing career, as he would be 25 when the contract term finally expired. It gave worldwide exclusive control to Proactive, and imposed significant restrictions on Rooney's freedom to exploit his talents in any way he chose. He had agreed 'not, without Proactive's prior consent, to negotiate or enter into contracts with any other firms or agents or representatives or persons or any other businesses which might reasonably be regarded as competitors of Proactive or might wish to exploit his intellectual property rights.'

The court, however, must balance the parties' interests and do not allow one party to twist the meaning of the restriction to construct an unreasonable meaning.

PSG Franchising Ltd v Lydia Darby (2012)

The claimant sought an injunction against the defendants, claiming that they were in breach of a restraint clause in a franchise agreement concerning the provision of property search services.

The restriction, lasting one year from termination of their franchise, prevented them from selling such services or being interested in any company providing similar services 'within the territory' which covered Milton Keynes and its adjacent postcodes. The defendants argued that this was unreasonable in scope as it would prevent them from providing any such services *anywhere* to those that PSG supplied within the Milton Keynes district.

Held: an injunction would be granted to the claimants as the restriction was reasonable: it only restricted the defendants from doing similar business within the Milton Keynes area.

Where ambiguity arose from contract wording, the court must adopt the meaning that any reasonable person, knowing the background to the transaction, would take from the words in question. Its aim should be to interpret the words to limit the restriction to protect legitimate business interests.

The court may not always take the literal meaning of the words if this would allow an employee to abuse the employer's legitimate interests. Instead, a purposive approach may be adopted. The contract is interpreted in the way which prevents the employee from avoiding a reasonable degree of restraint.

Home Counties Dairies v Skilton (1970)

Skilton's employment contract required him not to sell milk or dairy products to any person whom he had served during his time with the dairy, for one year after leaving the dairy's employment.

Held: the object of the clause was to prevent the dairy's loss of customers from Skilton's old milk round, not to prevent him from taking up work, for example, in a grocery shop selling butter and cheese. It was therefore valid in so far as it prevented him from poaching his ex-employer's customers when working as a milkman.

Littlewoods Organisation v Harris (1978, CA)

The claimant, who had planned the contents of Littlewoods' mail order catalogue for the next year, left to work for Littlewoods' main competitor, Universal Stores. His contract with Littlewoods stated that he must not work for Universal Stores for one year after leaving Littlewoods.

Held: this very generally drafted restraint, if interpreted literally, would prevent Harris working in any capacity for Universal Stores. It must be interpreted with implied reference to Harris's very high degree of access to crucial trading information in the mail order market sector. Once this was taken into account, the clause became reasonable as it protected Littlewoods' secret information.

Restraint on the seller of a business

Buyers of the goodwill of a business may protect themselves against loss of customers by restraining the sellers from setting up in a similar business too close and too soon. The only business interest that can be protected here is the existing custom enjoyed by sellers: they can be restrained only from running a business of *exactly the same kind* as they are selling.

BRC Engineering v Schelff (1921)

Schelff sold his business, which was concerned with the sale of loop concrete road reinforcements. The contract of sale contained a clause that attempted to restrain him from being involved in the sale or manufacture of *any type* of concrete reinforcement.

Held: the only business interest that could validly be protected here concerned the sale of loop reinforcements. Any wider restraint was unreasonable as it related to business interests that were not being sold.

Nordenfelt v Maxim Nordenfelt Guns & Ammunition Co. Ltd (1894)

Nordenfelt sold his arms manufacturing business to the Maxim Nordenfelt Co. The contract restrained him from being involved, for 25 years, in any way with the armaments trade. No geographical limit was mentioned.

Held: given the wide scope of the business (a large variety of armaments were manufactured by Nordenfelt) and the very small number of customers involved (state governments), this was held to be a reasonable restraint.

Solus agreements

These most commonly arise in contracts between petroleum companies and retail petrol outlets.

Esso Petroleum v *Harper's Garage (Stourport) Ltd* (1968, HL)

Two solus agreements were made between Harper's and Esso: agreement 1, which was to last four-and-a-half years, was made in return for a price discount on the petrol; agreement 2, which was to last 21 years, was made in return for a mortgage loan of £7,000 from Esso secured on the filling station and which was repayable over that period.

Held: agreement 1 was binding as it was entirely reasonable. Agreement 2 was held to be unreasonable in relation to its time span. It was longer than necessary to allow Esso to protect their business interest in maintaining stable levels of distribution. It was irrelevant that it had been agreed in relation to a mortgage.

Notice that in the above case Harper's already occupied the land at the point that they took the mortgage. They were giving up their freedom to trade from there with whomever they chose. The restraint rules do not apply where a party agrees to a restraint *as a condition* of being given possession of land.

Cleveland Petroleum v *Dartstone Ltd* (1969, CA)

The defendants took a lease of a garage from Cleveland. The lease stated that they could sell only Cleveland's petrol for the duration of the lease.

Held: it was not an unreasonable restraint of trade, since the defendants had not previously been in occupation of the land and had taken on the tenancy with full knowledge of the restriction.

The same principle applies to tied pubs.

The consequences of a void restraint

The fact that a restraint is void does not prevent the rest of the contract from being valid. A party can sue successfully for breach of a contract of employment or sale of a business, as long as the alleged breach does not relate to the void restraint.

The court may be able to sever (cut out) the unreasonable part of a restraint. The remainder of the restraint can then be enforced.

Goldsoll v *Goldman* (1915, CA)

The defendant sold an imitation jewellery business situated in London. Much of the business was conducted through mail order in the UK. In the contract of sale he undertook that he would not for two years be involved in the sale of real or imitation jewellery in any part of the UK, France, the USA, Russia, or within 25 miles of Berlin or Vienna.

> **Held:** this was clearly too wide to be reasonable as regards:
>
> 1 *business interest*: the claimant was buying an imitation jewellery business only, and could restrict the defendant's trading only in that respect;
>
> 2 *the geographical area covered by the restraint*: this was wider than reasonably necessary to protect a business interest where sales had previously been limited to the UK.
>
> The reference to real jewellery must be severed, as must the geographical references, apart from the UK.

Severance means what it says – cutting out; the court does not take it upon itself to rewrite a restraint to make it reasonable.

Even if severance is not applicable, the purposive approach adopted by the courts in cases like *Home Counties Dairies* v *Skilton* (described above) may enable a widely drafted restraint to be interpreted reasonably.

Contractual incapacity

Minors

Minor: person under the age of 18.

Minors (people under the age of 18) are legally capable of making most kinds of contracts and may take steps to enforce them against the other party. The law protects minors by restricting the extent to which their contracts may be enforced against them. Some – like a contract to lend money to a minor – are never enforceable by the creditor; others are binding only to a limited extent.

Contracts capable of binding a minor

Necessaries: goods/services proved to be appropriate to the minor's needs.

Contracts to purchase **necessaries** are capable of binding a minor. 'Necessaries' are defined by s 3 of the Sale of Goods Act 1979, as 'goods suitable to the condition in life of the minor . . . and to his actual requirements at the time of sale and delivery'.

There are two issues here:

1 Are the goods capable of being necessaries? The lifestyle and social standing of the minor may be relevant.

> ### *Peters* v *Fleming* (1840)
>
> **Held:** a watch chain was capable of being a necessary to the defendant undergraduate and his social standing made it reasonable for it to be a gold one.

2 Were the goods necessary to the minor's requirements at the time of sale and delivery?

Nash v *Inman* (1908)

The claimant supplied clothing to the defendant minor, a Cambridge undergraduate. The clothing included 11 fancy waistcoats.

Held: as the defendant was already amply supplied with clothing appropriate to his station in life the clothing purchased could not amount to necessaries and the action must fail.

The concept of necessaries also, by analogy, covers services. All the following are capable of being necessaries: food, clothing, lodgings, transport to work, legal advice, education.

A minor's liability in a contract for necessaries is limited to payment of a *reasonable* price. The minor is not necessarily bound by the price specified in the contract. Sale of Goods Act 1979 s3 states that a 'reasonable price' is payable for goods 'sold and delivered'. The court may require the minor to pay less than the price agreed with the seller. The words 'sold and delivered' suggest that the minor has a duty to pay only when delivery of the goods has been made.

A *harsh or onerous contract* will not be enforced at all.

Fawcett v *Smethurst* (1914)

A contract for hire of a car made the minor liable for any damage sustained to it whether caused by the minor or not.

Held: although this contract was for necessaries, it was void as it put an unreasonably heavy burden on the minor.

Beneficial contracts of employment are also capable of binding a minor. These include training and apprenticeship contracts, but not trading contracts. The contract is binding on the minor if overall it is for the minor's benefit, but not if it is unduly burdensome.

De Francesco v *Barnum* (1890)

Under a dancing-apprenticeship contract, a girl of 14 promised that she would not marry during the apprenticeship, or accept any engagements, without her master's permission. He was under no obligation to find her engagements, or to pay her if she was unemployed. When employed her pay was very poor (9d per night) even by then existing standards. She refused to go on working under these conditions and he sued her for breach of contract.

Held: the contract was void; it was onerous and unfair to the minor who was at the total disposal of the claimant.

Voidable contracts include a number of different types of contracts that create continuing obligations. Tenancy agreements, partnership agreements and contracts for the purchase of shares are examples. A minor can opt out of such a contract at any time before majority, or within a reasonable time after, but is liable for any obligations (rent, calls on shares) which accrued before then.

Proform Sports Management Ltd v *Pro-Active Sports Management Ltd* (2007)

Wayne Rooney, who was under contract to Everton, entered into a 'representation agreement' with the claimants giving them the right, for a certain period of time, to represent him in any transfer negotiations into which he might enter. During the agreement's currency, Rooney was approached by the defendant company which persuaded him to enter an exclusive transfer agreement. The claimant sued the defendant arguing that the defendant had induced Rooney to break his contract with the claimant.

Held: no breach of contract had occurred. The representation agreement amounted to a voidable contract only. It was insufficiently analogous to a contract for necessary services, apprenticeship or education to be binding on a minor and Rooney was entitled to avoid it at any time.

Judge Hodge said: *Players' representatives do not undertake matters that are essential to the player's training or his livelihood. They do not enable the minor to earn a living or to advance his skills as a professional footballer.*

Contracts which are not enforceable against a minor

Unenforceable contract: contract to loan money/supply non-necessary goods to a minor cannot be enforced *against them*. The minor has the right to sue.

All contracts which do not fit into the categories discussed above are not binding on minors. The commonest **unenforceable contracts** are for loans of money or the sale of non-necessary goods and services.

Historically, parties who did business with minors did so at their peril, and often found themselves out of pocket. Today they may be able to obtain payment or recover goods under the Minors' Contracts Act 1987, which aims to redress the sometimes excessive immunity enjoyed by minors:

1 *Guarantee of minors' debts.* Under s 2 of the Act, contracts by a third party to guarantee payments by minors under contracts not enforceable against them are binding on the third party.

Restitution: an equitable remedy requiring a party to hand back specific property to another party.

2 *Restitution orders against minors.* This is an equitable remedy available at the court's discretion whereby a minor may be required to return to the other party any property acquired under the contract (Minors' Contracts Act 1987, s 3). This remedy was available prior to 1987 and was sometimes granted in cases of fraud, where minors obtained property under a contract by lying about their age. The court may also order minors to hand over the proceeds of sale of any goods supplied to them (*Stocks* v *Wilson* (1913)). It does not generally enable a creditor to recover a money loan, since the actual coins or notes supplied are no longer recoverable from the minor, having been spent (*Leslie* v *Sheill* (1914)).

3 *Ratification of debts contracted during minority.* Section 1 of the 1987 Act provides that if, on attaining majority, persons ratify debts transacted in their minority, this ratification (confirmation) is binding on them.

Worth thinking about?

How does the law treat contracts supplying mobile phone services to minors?

Suggested solutions can be found in Appendix 2.

Ratification of debt: the binding acknowledgement on reaching majority, of the obligation to pay a debt contracted while a minor.

Mentally impaired persons

The contractual capacity of a person who is mentally impaired is limited in two situations:

1 *Where the other party knew of the impairment.* If the other party to the contract knew or reasonably should have known of a party's mental impairment, the contract is voidable by the impaired party, i.e. the impaired party can choose to opt out of it. If the other party was not aware of the impairment, the contract is valid and enforceable.

2 *Contracts for necessaries.* Under s 3 of the Sale of Goods Act 1979, a mentally impaired person is obliged to pay a reasonable price for necessaries when they are supplied by a seller who is aware of that person's mental state. The court will not interfere with the price if the seller was not aware of the buyer's mental state.

Chapter summary

Illegality of contracts

A contract may be void for illegality because:

It is prohibited by statute.

It is against public policy because its purpose is to break the law.

Consequences: such contracts are absolutely void – property may not be recovered.

Other contracts are merely void because they do not involve law breaking but are against the public interest.

For example: contracts in restraint of trade because they potentially inhibit competition.

Consequences: valid if it can be shown that the restraint is reasonably necessary:

(a) to protect a business interest;

(b) and does not cover too wide a geographical locality;

(c) and does not last too long.

A *purposive approach* is used to interpret the words of the restraint.

Severance of unreasonable aspects of the contract is also possible.

Capacity to contract

The law protects some vulnerable classes of person by limiting the types of contracts which fully bind them.

Minors

Binding on a minor

Contracts for necessary goods/services.

Beneficial contracts of employment.

Voidable by a minor

Contracts creating some continuing interest or obligation are voidable at the minor's option.

Unenforceable against a minor

All other contracts (including contracts to loan money) are unenforceable against the minor.

Mentally impaired persons

Bound to pay a reasonable price for necessaries even if the seller is aware of the incapacity.

All other contracts are voidable by them if the other party should have been aware of the incapacity.

Quiz 9

1 How does illegality affect the validity of a contract?

2 Why may the following contracts be illegal?

  (a) a contract to rob a bank;

  (b) a contract to make a pornographic film;

  (c) a contract by an English firm to supply arms to terrorists in the US.

3 Are the following contracts enforceable against Algernon who is 17?

  (a) to buy a suit to wear at job interviews;

  (b) to buy 50 Christmas cakes which he intends to distribute to local old people's homes;

  (c) to work for Busby Ltd as a packer in their dispatch department;

  (d) to borrow £50 pounds from Jemima.

Answers to all quizzes can be found in Appendix 2.

Take a closer look

The following cases provide important examples of how the law you have studied in this chapter has developed. They are primary sources illustrating the law in action and give you more detail about their facts, as well as helping you to understand the law and to appreciate how the judges reached their decisions.

Try looking them up in the law reports or accessing them via a database, e.g. Bailli (www.bailii.org/databases.html). LexisNexis or Westlaw may be available in your university or college library, or you may find extracts in a case book. (See Appendix 1: Additional resources.)

Regazzoni v *Sethia* [1957] 3 All ER 286, HL

Eastham v *Newcastle United Football Club* [1963] 3 All ER 139

Littlewoods Organisation Ltd v *Harris* [1978] 1 All ER 1026, CA

Home Counties Dairies v *Skilton* [1970] 1 All ER 1227

Web activity

Please go to: http://www.adviceguide.org.uk/england.htm

Search for 'who can make a consumer contract' to find out more day to day issues concerning contractual capacity.

Assignment 8

Boffin is employed by Sweeties Ltd and has learnt secret toffee-making processes exclusively used by Sweeties in the UK. His contract states that if he leaves Sweeties he must not be involved in the manufacture of toffee or any other confectionery in the UK or the US for one year.

1 Is this restraint lawful?

2 If unlawful, is it capable of being made lawful?

10

More defects: illegality and incapacity

CHAPTER 11

Discharge of the contract and remedies for breach

Introduction

You have now almost completed your study of the law of contract. In this chapter we examine how contractual obligations come to an end. When you make a contract you would normally expect the obligation to end with its full performance: you pay the contract price and the other party provides the service you requested. However, life is not always quite so simple. What happens if performance is interrupted in some way or only partial performance takes place? Will that be sufficient to get you both off the contractual hook?

Maybe you change your minds and agree not to perform the contract or want to vary it in some way, how do you ensure this agreement is binding?

Sometimes things go badly wrong. What is the legal position if you have booked a photographer to take pictures at your wedding and on the day he is too ill to attend, or alternatively, in excellent health, does attend with results that are a testimony only to his incompetence instead of being a wonderful record of your special day?
This chapter examines how the law resolves issues like these.

Learning objectives

When you have studied this chapter you should be able to:

▶ list the ways in which a contract may be discharged;

▶ appreciate the concept of complete performance and the exceptions to it;

▶ describe how a contract may be discharged by agreement;

> ▶ give examples of when a contract may be frustrated;
> ▶ explain the rights of the parties to a frustrated contract;
> ▶ grasp when a breach is capable of discharging the contract;
> ▶ apply the remoteness of damage rules;
> ▶ distinguish between the different types of damages available for breach of contract;
> ▶ be aware of when the court may impose an equitable remedy for breach of contract.

Discharge of contracts

Discharge by performance

The general rule: a contract is discharged only by complete performance; all the obligations in the contract must have been carried out. A party's failure to perform may make him or her vulnerable to an action for breach of contract by the other party, who may also be entitled to withhold payment. Although it may generally be fair to hold someone to the letter of a bargain, this rule is capable of producing some unjust results.

Cutter v *Powell* (1795)

The defendant, Captain Powell, engaged Lieutenant Cutter as part of his crew for a voyage from Jamaica to Liverpool. The contract stated that payment was due only on completion of the voyage, but the Lieutenant died 19 days before the ship reached Liverpool.

Held: his widow, who sued on behalf of his estate, could not claim any part of his salary since payment of it was not due until the voyage had been completed when the entire obligation would have been discharged.

Exceptions have been developed to prevent injustice.

Entire contract: contract consists of one obligation only and no payment is due unless/until that obligation is fully performed.

1 Divisible contracts

The contract made by Lieutenant Cutter was an **entire contract**; he was obliged to perform one whole obligation in order to be able to claim payment – complete the voyage from Jamaica to Liverpool. The outcome for Mrs Cutter would have been happier if this obligation had been **divisible** – broken down into smaller units (for example, weeks), on completion of each of which payment of a proportion of his wages would have been due. She would then have been able to claim for three weeks' wages.

Ritchie v *Atkinson* (1808)

A contract stated that goods would be shipped at a cost of £5 per tonne. When only part of the agreed cargo was transported, the owners claimed that they were not bound to pay.

Held: since the obligation was divisible, payment was owing for each tonne of the cargo which had been carried.

Contracts of employment are divisible, with payment due on a weekly or monthly basis. Building contracts are another example: specified sums become payable on completion of performance of specified portions of the work.

Divisible contract: the contract consists of a number of distinct obligations and payment must be made for as many as are properly performed.

2 One party prevents the other from completing performance

Grand opportunities for fraud would occur if a party could claim that they were not bound to pay contract prices when they themselves had prevented the other party from completing the necessary work. To prevent such injustice, the party who prevents performance is deemed to be in breach, which releases the other party from the obligation to tender complete performance.

Planché v *Colburn* (1831)

The claimant entered into a contract to write a book for the defendant publisher and was to be paid £100 when the book was completed. He had researched and written part of the book when the defendant told him that it would not be required.

Held: he was entitled to a sum to represent the value of the work he had done towards completion of the contract.

---

3 Acceptance of part performance

Part performance: incomplete performance which may discharge the contract if accepted.

Where the contract is entire, part performance does not discharge a party's obligation. However, **part performance**, if voluntarily accepted by the party to whom it is offered, does release the other party from the remainder of the obligtion. The accepting party must then pay an appropriate price. The accepting party must have a genuine choice to accept or reject the part performance. A buyer can refuse to take delivery of a consignment of goods, but may have no real choice in a contract to supply goods and services if materials have become part of their own property.

Sumpter v Hedges (1898)

The claimant contracted to build a barn for the defendant, but then abandoned the project when it was only half completed.

Held: no payment was due since the defendant, who had completed the barn himself, had no choice but to accept part performance and make the building safe by finishing the work. The defendant did have to pay for materials which the claimant had left behind and which the defendant had chosen to use to complete the building.

4 Substantial performance

Substantial performance: Almost complete performance which must be accepted.

Provided a party has received **substantial performance** (the bulk of what was agreed) payment is due, even if final performance deviates marginally from the letter of the contract. The payer is then entitled to a discount to cover the minor failure to perform. The court has to decide whether the performance is sufficiently substantial to discharge the obligations. Compare the following two decisions.

Bolton v Mahadeva (1972)

Held: a contract to install a central heating system was not substantially completed: fumes escaped into the house, which was also substantially less warm than was promised as a condition of the contract.

Hoenig v Isaacs (1952)

Held: a contract to decorate and furnish a flat had been substantially performed since the defects (repairs to a bookcase and replacement of a wardrobe door) were superficial and easily remedied. The total cost of the contract was £750 and the cost of the defects £55.

Note that none of these exceptions would have helped in the *Cutter* v *Powell* case:

- Lieutenant Cutter's contract was an *entire* obligation; payment was made on the basis of completion of the whole voyage, not on a weekly or daily basis;
- the captain did not *prevent completion* of the contract: fate intervened;
- the captain had no choice but to accept part performance;
- performance was not *substantial*; Cutter had not performed more than about two-thirds of what was required of him.

Today a remedy would be provided under the Law Reform (Frustrated Contracts) Act 1943 (see below).

Discharge by agreement

Having formed a contract, the parties to it may agree not to go through with it. This agreement (which is in effect a secondary contract) will be binding as long as the necessary requirements of a valid contract are satisfied. The issue most likely to be problematic is consideration.

Bilateral discharge

Where the first contract is still wholly or partially executory (neither party has performed all his or her obligations), consideration will consist of each party's promise not to insist on the other party's performance of those obligations. Each party is giving up legal rights under the first contract.

Unilateral discharge: accord and satisfaction

Accord and satisfaction: a legally binding agreement to discharge an existing contract.

Where one party has completely performed his or her obligations under the original contract and the other party wants to be released from their obligations, a promise by the first party to allow this is binding only if the other party promises some material benefit (consideration) in return. Such a transaction is described as **accord and satisfaction**. A promise, to pay a sum of money, or to provide some other consideration in return for the other party giving up his or her rights, will immediately discharge the contract.

Discharge by frustration

Frustration: impossibility of contract performance occurs subsequently to formation but before performance.

If, between formation and performance of the contract, events outside the parties' control render further performance impossible or futile, the contract may be discharged by **frustration**. The party claiming that the contract has been frustrated must satisfy the court that the supervening events have radically changed the nature of the contractual obligation. This doctrine was developed in the nineteenth century to prevent injustice where a party is prevented from carrying out a contract through no fault of his or her own.

Frustration may discharge the contract in the following situations:

1 destruction or unavailability of the subject matter;
2 the death or illness of one of the parties;
3 supervening illegality;
4 government intervention;
5 the event on which the contract is based fails to occur;
6 delay in performance.

1 Destruction or unavailability of the subject matter

> ### *Taylor* v *Caldwell* (1863)
>
> **Held:** a contract to let a music hall was found to be frustrated when the hall was destroyed by an arsonist.

Gamerco SA v ICM/Fair Warning (Agency) Ltd (1995)

Held: a contract under which the Guns N' Roses band was going to perform was frustrated when the stadium where the concert was supposed to take place became unsafe and it was impossible to find another suitable venue in time.

2 Death or illness of one of the contracting parties

This affects contracts involving a service which can be performed only by the relevant party. Illness does not necessarily frustrate the contract. The average employment contract is not frustrated by an employee having a week off with influenza Relevant factors to consider include the length of the illness relative to the length of the contract and whether the essential nature of the contract is threatened by the loss of performance. A seven-year contract with an actor in *The Mousetrap* will not be frustrated by one night's laryngitis, but this would prove fatal to a contract for a one-night performance by a famous soprano at the Royal Opera House.

Condor v The Barron Knights (1966)

Condor, drummer with the Barron Knights pop group, became ill with nervous strain. His doctor said that he should perform no more than four nights a week.

Held: the contract was frustrated, since such limited performance was incompatible with the nature of the work. In the music business, performance dates might not arise at regular intervals. It might involve performance seven nights a week at busy periods.

The law relating to disability discrimination now prevents an employer from sheltering behind the doctrine of frustration to avoid observing the rights of an employee who acquires a disability. (See *Warner* v *Armfield Retail & Leisure Ltd* (2014) below.)

In the news

Warner v Armfield Retail & Leisure EAT (2014, ICR)
Mr Warner had worked for some years as a carpenter for Armfield. He then suffered a minor stroke which made him unable to use his left hand or pick up heavy objects. He received discretionary sick pay from Armfield for several months, until his entitlement ran out. Armfield then sent him his P45 and dismissed him, arguing that the contract was frustrated because he could no longer perform his job. Mr Warner argued that Armfield had discriminated against him by failing to perform its duty to investigate whether reasonable adjustments could be made to enable him to return to work. The employment tribunal

agreed with the employer that the contract was frustrated because there were no reasonable adjustments that could have been made in the circumstances and dismissed the case. The EAT affirmed the employment tribunal's decision. The contract was frustrated by the claimant's disability: there was nothing the employer could reasonably have done to get Mr Warner back to work even if it had carried out an investigation into possible adjustments. The doctrine of frustration could never discharge the contract where disability discrimination was relevant unless reasonable adjustment was not practicable.

A contract with a sole trader may be frustrated through their illness if their input is sufficiently crucial.

Atwal v *Rochester* (2010)

Mr Rochester, a sole trader, became very ill with heart disease while carrying out a building contract for Mr and Mrs Atwal. After bypass surgery he was advised by his doctor to give up work. The Atwals had to get their work completed by another builder at a greatly increased price which they tried to recover by claiming that Mr Rochester had wrongfully repudiated the contract.

Held: the contract was frustrated not breached. It was in effect a personal service contract. He had no members of staff who could carry out the work on his behalf. He did much of the work personally, assisted by casual labourers and sub-contracted out the specialist work.

3 Supervening illegality

A contract which is completely legal when formed may become illegal by a change in the law occurring before performance. A contract with a foreign national will be made illegal if Britain subsequently declares war against that person's country, since performance would in effect have involved trading with the enemy. Therefore, in *Fibrosa Spolka Akcyjna* v *Fairbairn Lawson Combe Barbour Ltd* (1943, HL) a contract by a British firm to sell machinery to a Polish firm was frustrated when Germany, with whom Britain was at war, annexed Poland in 1939.

4 Government intervention

This has often arisen in wartime due to the internment or conscription of personnel and requisitioning of property. In *Morgan* v *Manser* (1947) the conscription in wartime of a comedian frustrated his contract. At the point when he received his call-up papers there was no indication of how long hostilities would last.

Other exercise of power by government agencies may have the same effect. In *Shepherd* v *Jerrom* (1987) the imposition of a prison sentence was held to frustrate a contract of apprenticeship. Compulsory purchase of land may invalidate a contract of sale.

11

Discharge of the contract and remedies for breach

5 The event on which the contract is based fails to occur

Here the letter of the contract can usually still be performed, but performance has become futile and in no way reflects the object which the parties intended to achieve.

Krell v *Henry* (1903)

Held: a contract for the one-day hire of a room for the purpose of viewing Edward VII's coronation procession was frustrated when the coronation was postponed due to the King's illness. While it would have been possible for the hirer and his party to have sat and watched the traffic on the booked date, this clearly was not what the parties had intended.

If part of the purpose of the contract can still be achieved, however, the contract will not be frustrated.

Herne Bay Steam Boat Co. v *Hutton* (1903)

Hutton hired a boat to take a party of guests to view the fleet and watch the naval review on Edward VII's coronation day but due to the postponement of the coronation the review was also cancelled.

Held: the contract was not frustrated since it was for two purposes only one of which had failed to happen. The fleet could still be toured.

6 Delayed performance

Delay, caused by some supervening event which suspends or unreasonably delays performance of a contract, may lead to frustration of the contract, if it makes the outcome radically different from what the parties originally planned. See *Davis Contractors* v *Fareham District Council* (1956, HL), *Metropolitan Water Board* v *Dick Kerr & Co.* (1918) and *Gryf-Lowczowski* v *Hinchingbrooke Healthcare NHS Trust* (2006) below.

The limitations of the frustration rule

The courts do not willingly free parties from their contractual obligations. An event which should have been foreseeable when the contract was made will not frustrate the contract unless its occurrence was outside the parties' control. Even then the court may still take the view that this eventuality (e.g. bad weather) should have been covered by the contract. It is also irrelevant that subsequent events have caused mere inconvenience or delay, or made the performance of the contract more expensive, or less profitable, than was planned. In *Tsakiroglou & Co.* v *Noblee Thorl GmbH* (1961, HL) it was held that closure of the Suez Canal did not frustrate a shipping contract although it added to the length, and therefore to the cost, of the journey.

Davis Contractors v Fareham District Council (1956, HL)

Davis had contracted to build houses for the council and had specified a fixed price. Due to bad weather, lack of materials and reduced manpower because of post-war shortages, the contract took much longer to complete than the builders had expected and was much more costly.

Held: frustration had not occurred. Inconvenience and expense were not sufficient: frustration occurs only where the end result of the contract is radically different from what the parties intended. (If the contract had been frustrated, the council would have had to pay a price truly in line with the cost to the builder. (Remedies for frustration are explained later in the chapter.)

Amalgamated Investment & Property Co. Ltd v John Walker & Sons (1977)

Held: applying *Davis* (above), a contract to buy a property with a view to development was not frustrated by the building later being listed by the local authority because of its architectural interest, which in effect prevented any real development taking place. The listing did not prevent the contract being carried out. Listing was an inherent risk that would certainly drastically reduce the price but there was no express or implied term in the contract that the property would continue to be capable of development. The listing therefore did not make the contract radically different.

The above case illustrates particularly well how the court is unsympathetic to the plight of an experienced business, which in effect gambles and loses on a risky contractual deal. The nature of the premises meant that listing was a considerable probability, and the buyer had asked the vendor whether it knew of any plan by the local authority to do so. The buyer still chose to go ahead, clearly aware that it was a risky enterprise. It was fair to treat the buyer as having accepted the inherent risk.

Force majeure clauses

Force majeure clause: a contract term which states the rights of the parties in the event of specified problems.

An effective *force majeure clause* may prevent a contract being frustrated. It determines the rights of the parties in the event of specified circumstances outside their control. A *force majeure* clause can be useful in two ways:

1 To exempt a party from, or limit its liability for, breach of contract to cover situations where failure to perform arises from circumstances which are unlikely to be treated as frustrating the contract. Hazards which commonly prevent performance are deemed by the courts to be foreseeable and therefore incapable of frustrating the contract. For example, bad weather is a common cause of delay in the performance of transport, travel and construction contracts. They may also be interrupted by trade union action, or through outbreak of civil or national hostilities. (Remember that exemption and limitation provisions are subject to the controls which you studied in Chapters 7 and 8.)

2   To avoid the contract being discharged by events which would normally frustrate it. This will be effective only if the court is satisfied that the parties really intended to keep the contract alive in the circumstances which are now threatening its existence.

Metropolitan Water Board v *Dick Kerr & Co.* (1918)

A contract made in July 1914 for the construction of a reservoir within six years contained a provision that the time limit could be extended in the event of delay arising from difficulties, delays or impediments, however caused. On the outbreak of war the following September, the work was halted by government order.

Held: the clause did not prevent the contract being frustrated, since the delay occasioned by interruption of the work appeared likely to be much more lengthy than the parties could have contemplated when they made the contract.

Self-induced frustration

The courts are not sympathetic to a party who causes the allegedly frustrating event.

Maritime National Fish Ltd v *Ocean Trawlers Ltd* (1935)

The defendants hired a trawler equipped with an otter trawl which required a licence. The defendants applied for five licences, to cover their own ships and the hired ship, but only four were granted. The defendants, therefore, used these to license their own ships. They claimed that the lack of a licence for the claimant's ship frustrated the contract of hire by making its performance illegal.

Held: the contract was not frustrated as the defendants had chosen which ships to license and could have licensed the hired ship instead of one of their own.

The difference between frustration and mistake

It is important to note the difference between a contract which is void for mistake and one which is frustrated due to destruction of the subject matter. The distinguishing feature is one of time (as you can see from the 'Real life' example outlined below).

(For operative mistake, see Chapter 9.)

Real life

Horace works as a sales representative for Stephen's Toys Ltd. He contracts to sell a consignment of teddy bears to Matilda. He believes that they are safely stored in a warehouse at Stephen's factory but unknown to both parties the warehouse has just caught fire after being struck by lightning and the goods ceased to exist before Horace made his offer. Here no contract ever came into existence. It was void from the outset for operative mistake, as it was based on non-existent subject matter. It was impossible for a contract to result.

If destruction of the teddies had occurred after Matilda had accepted Horace's offer, the contract would be frustrated, since it was formed with reference to goods which existed at the time the contract was made, but destroyed before it was performed.

The consequences of the contract being frustrated

When a contract is discharged by frustration, it ceases to exist from that moment on. Rights that have already arisen with regard to a party remain that party's property, but the party loses any rights which are due to arise later. This means that a party who has received property is entitled to retain it; a party with no entitlement to claim payment before the contract was frustrated loses its right to do so under the contract. Prior to 1943 such loss was said to 'lie where it fell' at the time when the contract was frustrated. There was no means by which a party could recover prepaid money, or payment for services rendered in preparation for performance of the contract.

Appleby v *Myers* (1867)

The claimants contracted to install machinery on the defendant's premises. Payment was to be made on completion of the work. The defendant's premises were destroyed by fire prior to completion. It was held that the claimants were unable to recover any of the cost of their labour and materials.

The injustice of this principle was reduced by the decision in *Fibrosa*:

Fibrosa Spolka Akcyjna v *Fairbairn Lawson Combe Barbour Ltd* (1943, HL)

(The facts in this case are set out above, page 225.)

Held: since consideration had completely failed and the Polish firm should recover the £1,000 which it had already advanced and was not liable for the remaining £600 advance payment since it had received no benefit whatever from the contract.

While the common law still determines the situations where frustration may occur, the rights of the parties to a frustrated contract are now regulated by statute.

The Law Reform (Frustrated Contracts) Act 1943

Payer's right to recover prepaid sums (s 1(2))

All prepaid sums are returnable to the payer once the contract has been frustrated and any sum already due ceases to be payable.

Payee's right to recover expenses (s 1(2))

A proviso protects the payee. If the payee has incurred expenses in performance of the contract before the frustrating event they may, at the discretion of the court, retain or claim up to the maximum of any prepaid or prepayable sum to cover those expenses, if with regard to all the circumstances it is fair and just to do so.

Gamerco SA v ICM/Fair Warning (Agency) Ltd (1995)

(The facts in this case are set out above.)

The defendant had been paid $412,000 in advance while the claimant promoters had incurred approximately $450,000 expenses. The defendant's expenses were assumed to be about $50,000.

Held (by Garland J, somewhat controversially): given the extent of the claimant's expenses and the absence of any real evidence of those of the defendant, the defendant must repay the whole $412,000.

Note the limits to the protection of this proviso in s 1(2): if the work done by the payee exceeds the prepaid/prepayable sum the difference cannot be claimed. However, its effect may be to make the payer part with money without seeing any benefit.

Payee's right to cost of a valuable benefit (s 1(3))

A party who, prior to the frustrating event, has conferred a valuable benefit on the other (apart from the payment of money) may claim its value, if it is just to do so. This right exists as an alternative to, or in addition to, the rights conferred under s 1(2). Unfortunately, the 1943 Act does not define what is meant by a 'valuable benefit'. Some guidance was given in the next case, which also illustrates how a just sum should be calculated.

BP Exploration Co. v Hunt (1982, HL)

Hunt owned an oil concession in Libya. His contract was with BP, under which it was to explore the concession to see if it was commercially viable and, if so, to develop it. This would be done at BP's risk and cost. If oil were found in commercial quantities, BP would be repaid out of Hunt's share. A substantial oil field was developed and went into production, but the contract was frustrated when the Libyan government withdrew the concession. BP claimed that the oil Hunt had received was a valuable benefit.

Held: the Act must be interpreted purposively to prevent either party obtaining an unfair financial advantage.

The valuable benefit was the end product of the service as opposed to the service itself. Hunt had been given his share of the oil and, therefore, received a valuable benefit from BP's performance of contractual services.

The value of the benefit must be determined at the moment the contract was frustrated. This represented the upper limit of any award. The value of Hunt's share of the oil so far was $85 million, but this must be reduced to take into account gains made by BP so far and the terms of the contract.

The just sum to be awarded to BP was $35 million, since it had already recovered $62 million of its $85 million development costs but had also paid Hunt $10 million. The fact that BP bore the main risks attached to the contract was also relevant to determining this sum.

The next case clearly illustrates the operation of s 1(3) and the nature of a valuable benefit.

Atwal v *Rochester* (2010)

(The facts in this case are set out above.)

The total cost of building work prior to frustration of the contract by his illness was £89,450, some of which had been paid. The part-completed building work was clearly of financial value representing a 'valuable benefit' under s 1(3) and he was entitled to £13,550 for it.

The Act, therefore, always protects a payee who has asked for some prepayment. The payee will be covered, whether or not he or she has actually provided any valuable benefit. However, if the payee has (perhaps unwisely) not stipulated any advance payment, the Act will assist only if the payer has received a valuable benefit. Therefore, if *Appleby* v *Myers* (1867) (see above) was being decided today, the outcome would be the same unless the builder had obtained some payment up front.

It is instructive to see how the doctrine of frustration would affect the outcome of *Cutter* v *Powell*, which was explained at the beginning of this chapter. Today, Lieutenant Cutter's contract would be frustrated by his death. By serving on the ship, he would have provided a valuable benefit to his employer prior to his death; so now a proportion of his wages would be recoverable by his widow.

Discharge by breach

Not every breach of contract is capable of resulting in its discharge. The distinction between conditions and warranties (which you studied in Chapter 7) is important here:

1 *Breach of warranty*. The innocent party has the right to claim damages if he or she has suffered any actionable damage or loss. The breach is not capable of bringing the contract to an end.

2 *Breach of condition*. Where a term has the status of a condition and, therefore, is crucial to the contract, the innocent party is entitled to **repudiate** (refuse further performance of his or her obligations); he or she may recover any property transferred under the contract and obtain damages. Notice that the innocent party, in theory at least, has a choice. An innocent party can free himself or herself from his or her obligations if he or she wishes, or may attempt to hold the other party to the bargain. In many cases no real choice exists, as the breach will be so ruinous to the contract that the injured party will be only too glad to be able to avoid his or her obligations. A breach of condition may consist of a refusal to perform, or arise from performance which is so inadequate that the innocent party is effectively deprived of the bargain. It may occur before or at the date of performance.

Repudiate: refuse to recognise or perform an obligation.

Anticipatory breach

Anticipatory breach: notice that a contract will not be performed once performance is due.

So-called **anticipatory breach** of a contract occurs where one party indicates, before the time for performance is due, that he or she repudiates the contract. This may consist of either a total refusal to perform or a statement that performance will be different from that set out in the contract. Once this occurs the innocent party may repudiate his or her side of the contract and sue for damages.

Hochster v *De La Tour* (1853)

The parties made a contract in April, under which the defendant agreed that the claimant should act as his courier on a foreign tour, due to begin on 1 June. On 11 May, the defendant informed the claimant that his services would not be required.

Held: the claimant could sue for damages immediately: he did not have to wait for the performance date.

Refusal of performance must be clear and unambiguous to amount to repudiatory breach.

Dalkia Utilities Services plc v *Caltech International Ltd* (2006)

In 1995 Dalkia entered a contract to provide energy services for 15 years, payable by monthly instalments. The contract gave Dalkia the right to terminate the contract and claim a termination fee if Caltech committed a material breach.

Caltech was late paying some instalments between 2000 and 2003, and in June 2003 Caltech warned Dalkia that Caltech was experiencing financial difficulties and was considering sale of the business or putting it into administration. By 1 August, three months' instalments were owing and Caltech told Dalkia that it did not have the means to pay and was facing insolvency. It asked for a moratorium and suggested a scheme for repayment. Within days Dalkia served a demand for the arrears and issued a termination notice as prescribed by the contract. Caltech then paid the arrears.

Held: the contract was not discharged. Caltech's statement on 1 August was not sufficient to amount to refusal of further performance. While clearly Caltech had breached the contract it had not repudiated it. Caltech had not refused payment permanently nor shown any intention to deprive Dalkia of the substantial benefit of the contract. Caltech had 'sailed close to the wind' in its reference to insolvency but regarded this 'no doubt as lever in the negotiations'. It had given 'a mixed message' lacking 'the necessary clarity to constitute repudiation'.

Obiter dictum: even if Caltech had committed a repudiatory breach, Dalkia had not evidenced acceptance of it but arguably had chosen to affirm the contract by using the termination clause instead of pursuing the normal remedies for breach.

Victims of an anticipatory breach therefore, are entitled to repudiate their contractual obligations only if the other party has already indicated his or her own repudiation.

The innocent party must then give notice of intention to repudiate. This may be implied from the conduct of the parties and/or commercial practice.

Vitol Sa v Norelf (1996, HL)

The buyer of a cargo wrongly repudiated the contract because of unfounded fears about delay in loading and notified the seller, by telex, of what he was doing. The seller took no further action to perform the contract and, therefore, did not send the buyer the bill of lading which would, in this sort of contract, normally be sent once the cargo was loaded.

Held: the absence of the bill of lading should have made the buyer aware of the seller's intentions. The seller's behaviour in the context of trade practice 'clearly and unequivocally' evidenced intention to treat the contractual obligations as discharged by the buyer's breach.

Formal communication of notice is not necessary and may be effective even if it comes from an unauthorised third party. The issue is whether a reasonable person would have believed that the innocent party was opting out of further performance.

Note that the Court of Appeal in *Stocznia Gdanska SA v Latvian Shipping Co. (No. 3)* (2002) has stated that affirmation is not irrevocable.

When the nature of breach is such that performance may still be possible, a party, who affirms but later gets tired of waiting, may then repudiate.

If the innocent party chooses to wait for the performance date in the hope that the other party will, after all, perform, three consequences may follow:

Mitigate: reduce the loss arising from a breach of contract.

1 The innocent party may have no duty to **mitigate** any loss before the date when the other party's obligations become due. The innocent party's duty to take reasonable steps to avoid adding to the loss arising from the breach may not arise until he or she acknowledges the breach or until the date of performance, whichever comes first. The innocent party may continue with his or her performance, where this can be done without the co-operation of the other party, and claim his or her full costs.

White & Carter (Councils) Ltd v McGregor (1962, HL)

Mr McGregor, who owned a garage, was persuaded to advertise it through White's advertising plates, which the company contracted to display on council litter bins for three years. McGregor's obligation to pay arose only once the plates were installed. He attempted to cancel the contract the same day that he had made it, but the company refused to accept his repudiation.

Held: the company, having performed its obligations, was able to claim the full sum. As the company had not chosen to repudiate the contract, no duty to mitigate arose, i.e. the company was under no obligation to look for another advertiser so as to avoid losing money.

The facts of the above case were exceptional since performance was completely within White & Carter's control and the product was only of any use to McGregor. The House of Lords (*obiter dictum*) stated that such a claim should not be successful unless the innocent party had a legitimate interest in keeping the contract alive.

Clea Shipping Corpn v Bulk Oil International (1984)

Twelve months into a 24-month charter the ship went out of commission after a breakdown and the charterers immediately repudiated the contract. Nonetheless, the owners carried out extensive repairs and kept the ship manned and ready for the remainder of the charter period and took no steps to find another hirer.

Held: the owners should have mitigated their loss by seeking another charterer. They had no legitimate interest in behaving as they had rather than just claiming damages for the wrongful repudiation.

However, the facts of the case determine whether a legitimate interest should be acknowledged. In *Isabella Ship Owners* v *Shagang Shipping Co Ltd* (2012) below where the High Court came to the contrary decision in what superficially seems to be a very similar case.

Isabellaship Owner v Shagang Shipping Co. Ltd (2012)

Shagang terminated a 61-month charter 94 days before the finish date and argued that the owners should have mitigated their loss instead of refusing to accept repudiation.

Held: the owners had a legitimate interest in keeping the contract alive, as there was nothing perverse or unreasonable about their decision in the circumstances. Market conditions and the short time left in the charter period made it very unlikely that another hirer could be found.

Spot the differences: in *Clea Shipping* the ship breakdown, which was the owner's risk in this sort of charter, was the initial cause of all the problems and prompted the repudiation. In *Isabella Shipping* the repudiation was spontaneous, instigated by the hirers, and there was only three months of a much longer charter left to run and real problems in finding new charterers.

2 The contract remains alive for the benefit of both parties. The innocent party is not discharged from his or her duties under the contract until he or she repudiates the contract. If he or she does not repudiate, but fails to perform obligations as they fall due, the innocent party could be liable for breach.

3 If the contract is frustrated before the performance date, the innocent party loses any rights to sue for breach.

> ### *Avery* v *Bowden* (1855)
>
> The claimant hired a ship to the defendant at a port in Russia. Before the hire date the defendant told the claimant that he would not be able to fulfil the contract, but the claimant chose to wait to see if he would change his mind. The Crimean War then broke out.
>
> **Held:** the outbreak of war frustrated the contract and the claimant no longer had any right to sue. The contract from which his rights had been derived had ceased to exist.

Actual breach

Actual breach: failure to perform at all or properly once performance is due.

Actual breach occurs when performance is due, or in the course of performance. It takes one of two forms: a failure to tender any form of performance, or performance which is so inadequate that it largely destroys the purpose of the contract. An example of the latter occurred in December 1994, when passengers on the QE2 were transported to New York while the ship was still in the process of refitting; the ship resembled a construction site rather than a luxury liner. Although the passengers were delivered to their destination on the correct date, the conditions under which they had travelled were so appalling that their contractual expectations were largely defeated. There is little doubt that a court would treat such poor performance as amounting to a breach of condition. A very high standard of comfort, with access to the facilities to be expected on such a trip, is central to such a contract. Cunard immediately offered all the passengers a full refund of their fares.

Remedies for breach of contract

The most common remedy for breach is damages, but an equitable remedy is sometimes appropriate.

Damages

The purpose of damages is to compensate the injured party for loss or damage arising from the breach. The court awards a sum that is aimed at putting the injured party in the financial position that he or she would have enjoyed if the contract had been performed. The court must assess the damage alleged to result from the breach and decide whether any of it is too remote. It may not be justifiable to blame defendants for all the results of their actions, which may be knock-on effects of the breach. Having decided how much of the damage is attributable to the defendant, the court must decide on the quantum of damage, i.e. determine how much money the damage is worth. *Milner and Milner* v *Carnival* (2010) (see below, page 241) provides a good example of how this is done.

Hadley v *Baxendale* (1854)

The defendant contracted to carry the claimant's mill shaft from Gloucester to London, where it was to be used as a pattern to construct a new one. Due to the fault of the defendant, there was a considerable delay in the return of the shaft. The claimant claimed damages for his lost profits due to the mill being out of action.

Held: the defendant was not liable for this loss because it was too remote. There was nothing to alert him to the problem, since the claimant had not indicated that failure to return the shaft within the promised time limit would produce this result.

Usual damage: *(Hadley v Baxendale)* damage normally expected to arise from a breach.

Non-usual damage: *(Hadley v Baxendale)* damage which is too remote unless the defendant should have known of special circumstances which made it likely.

In *Hadley* v *Baxendale*, the court distinguished between the two types of damage that might follow a breach: usual and non-usual damage.

1 *Usual damage.* **Usual damage** is the damage that anybody might reasonably anticipate would arise from a contract of the relevant kind. For example, breakage is an obvious hazard in a contract to transport china.

2 *Non-usual damage.* **Non-usual damage** arises because of particular circumstances which will not necessarily be known to the other party, unless these are drawn explicitly or impliedly to that party's attention before the contract is made. For example, in a contract to transport china, failure to disclose that the delivery time is crucial to a highly profitable sale would prevent a claim for more than normal profits in the event of a late delivery.

The following cases illustrate how these principles may be applied.

Victoria Laundry v *Newman Industries Ltd* (1949, CA)

Victoria Laundry, wishing to extend its business, asked the defendant to deliver a boiler by a stated date in June. Delivery did not take place until November, due to damage caused by the defendant. Due to this delay, the claimant was unable to take on some particularly lucrative dyeing contracts. The defendant knew that expansion of the business would be delayed if the boiler was not promptly delivered.

Held: the defendant was liable for the profits that would have resulted from the use of the boiler between June and November. However, the defendant knew nothing about the dyeing contracts, so it was not liable for those losses.

Koufos v *Czarnikow Ltd (The Heron II)* (1969, HL)

The defendants contracted to carry a cargo of sugar for the claimants. They knew that the claimants were sugar merchants and that there was a sugar market at the destination port. Due to delay caused by the defendants, the sugar was sold at a loss.

Held: the claimants were entitled to recover their lost profits because of the defendants' knowledge of the nature and purpose of the contract. This should have alerted them to the consequences of delay.

The remoteness rule in contract is more stringent than the reasonable foreseeability test in tort, because of the parties' relationship to each other. (See *Transfield Shipping* v *Mercator Shipping* below.) When negotiating a contract, the parties have the opportunity to discuss risk allocation and may refuse to do business if this cannot be resolved satisfactorily.

Transfield Shipping Inc v *Mercator Shipping Inc* (2008, HL)

T chartered a ship from M. It was agreed that it would be returned by 4 May 2004. M entered into another charter with a third party running from 8 May 2004. However, due to delays on the voyage T did not return the ship until 11 May 2004. The new charterers agreed to take the ship, but at the new market price which was lower than when they had initially entered the contract.

M claimed damages of the difference in market price for the whole of the new charter period, while T maintained that it should only be liable pro rata for the number of days delay before it had returned the ship. The issue was initially determined by arbitrators who supported M's claim on the grounds that the loss should have been reasonably foreseeable to T. T appealed.

Held: T was only liable for the three days' loss. The remaining loss was too remote.

Reasonable forseeability alone was too crude a test to apply to remoteness of damage in contract. Under the rule in *Hadley* v *Baxendale* as affirmed by the House of Lords in the *Heron II*, the issue must be determined not by probability but also by what the contracting parties presumably had in mind with regard to the nature and object of their transaction when they entered into it.

Lord Hope said:

> In this case it was within the parties' contemplation that an injury which would arise generally from late delivery would be loss of use at the market rate, as compared with the charter rate . . . This is something that everybody who deals in the market knows about and can be expected to take into account. But the charterers could not be expected to know how, if there was a subsequent fixture, the owners would deal with any new charterers. This was something over which they had no control and, at the time of entering into the contract, was completely unpredictable.

Quantum of damages

Quantum of damages: the amount of money necessary to compensate for the damage caused.

When establishing the **quantum of damages** (the financial value of the claimant's loss) the court is governed by a number of criteria:

1 the loss must be financially quantifiable;

2 agreed damages will not be altered, but penalty sums will not be enforced;

3 the injured party has a duty to mitigate any loss;

4 contributory negligence may reduce the amount of damages.

1 Quantifiable loss

Quantifiable damage: loss or harm capable in law of being compensated by money.

It must be possible to assess the loss to the injured party in financial terms (**quantifiable damage**). This is easy where goods are damaged, since the costs of repair or replacement are easily verified. The measure of damages for breach of a building contract is normally the cost of reinstatement (correcting the defect) rather than the diminution in value of the end product, but this is subject to exceptions in the interest of producing a just result.

Ruxley Electronics & Construction Ltd v *Forsyth* (1995)

A contract to build a garden swimming pool specified that it would be 7 foot 6 inches at its deepest part, but on completion it was found to be 9 inches shallower there and 18 inches shallower at the point where diving would take place.

Held: reinstatement damages were unreasonable here as they would be 'out of all proportion to the benefit to be obtained'. Ruxley was entitled to £2,500 for loss of amenity.

Claims for loss of profit are common in contract. Under s 50 of the Sale of Goods Act 1979, a buyer who refuses to take delivery of goods may be liable to the seller for any loss on the resale of the goods due to fluctuation of the market price.

Reliance loss: the amount lost by the claimant preparing to perform their side of the contract prior to the defendant's breach.

A party may also recover **reliance losses**: expenses incurred while preparing to perform a contract which never takes place due to the breach of the other party. So in *Anglia TV* v *Reed* (1971) Robert Reed, who unlawfully repudiated a contract to appear in a film, was held liable for the costs Anglia TV had incurred in preparing for the production.

Other damages are less easily quantifiable. Where a party suffers personal injuries, his or her resulting financial losses may also often be calculated with reasonable accuracy. There are, though, some rather arbitrary rules that exist to enable the court to compensate for non-financial losses like pain and suffering.

Until recently, the courts were reluctant to award damages for mental distress, hurt feelings and disappointment. In *Addis* v *Gramophone* (1909, HL) it was held that damages were not available to compensate for the claimant's hurt feelings and distress at being wrongfully dismissed, nor for the fact that the mode of his dismissal made it difficult for him to obtain future employment.

Stigma damages: Damages for the claimant's loss of reputation caused by the defendant's misconduct

This principle was for many years deemed to apply to all contracts but a number of distinctions and exceptions have gradually developed.

Damages may be awarded for loss of reputation. The House of Lords recently developed the concept of **stigma damages**.

Malik v *Bank of Credit & Commerce International* (1998, HL)

The defendant bank went into liquidation after its dishonesty and corrupt dealings emerged. The claimant, an ex-employee, was awarded damages for the losses he incurred, caused by a continuing difficulty in securing employment, because of the misdeeds of his previous employer.

Held: *Addis* did not apply here. This was not a distress claim. Malik's claim could succeed on the grounds that the bank was in breach of the employment contract. Employer and employee have a mutual duty of trust and confidence. Failing to conduct business honestly was a breach of this. (See Chapter 18.)

The basic principle of *Addis* continues to be upheld by the court and damages for distress arising from the *manner* of dismissal are not recoverable.

Johnson v *Unisys* (2001, HL)

The claimant suffered a nervous breakdown after being summarily dismissed by the defendant and he was unable to get a new job. He was awarded the statutory maximum (just under £12,000) under the statutory scheme for unfair dismissal at the employment tribunal.

He argued that he also had a claim for breach of contract at common law and claimed £400,000 in lost earnings on the grounds that the manner of his dismissal was a breach of the employer's duty of trust and confidence.

Held (by majority): the duty of trust and confidence did not relate to the termination of the contract. The needs of the claimant concerning dismissal were already covered by the statutory scheme and the claimant could not avoid the statutory limit to compensation by bringing a common law action.

In *Edwards* v *Chesterfield Royal Hospital NHS Foundation Trust* (2011) the Supreme Court affirmed this principle. However, the House of Lords decided that, if the breach of duty arises while the contract is still running, a right of action at common law may exist.

Eastwood and Another v *Magnox Plc and McCabe* v *Cornwall County Council* (2004, HL)

In *Eastwood* two employees claimed that before they were unfairly dismissed, their employer had conducted a campaign to demoralise and undermine them, which caused them psychiatric illness. The employee in *McCabe* claimed that he had suffered psychiatric illness because his employer failed to carry out a proper investigation into the allegations against him and had not conducted the disciplinary proceedings appropriately.

Held: the employees had a right to sue for the breach of contract caused by the behaviour of the employers and which had preceded the unfair dismissal.

The claimants in the above case had two causes of action: one for breach of contract at common law in the court and a statutory one for unfair dismissal in the employment tribunal. The House of Lords pointed out that, if they brought both types of action, any overlapping heads of damage could not be recovered twice. (For more information about statutory unfair dismissal rights, see Chapter 18.)

Breach of an advertising contract may result in an award of damages for lost reputation, since the contract is intended to enhance reputation not to detract from it. In *Aerial Advertising Co.* v *Batchelors Peas* (1938) the defendant had contracted to advertise the claimant's product by flying an aircraft with a suitably worded banner over a number of locations. In breach of the contract, the defendant flew the aircraft over Salford during the two-minute silence on Remembrance Day. People were so scandalised by this disrespectful behaviour that Batchelors suffered a boycott of their product and damages were awarded for the damage to their reputation.

On the same principle, distress losses are recoverable in contracts with consumers, provided that the purpose of the contract is to provide pleasure or peace of mind or freedom from distress, but where the breach has in fact caused any of these to be lost.

Jarvis v *Swans Tours* (1973, CA)

When he bought a skiing holiday package, Mr Jarvis was promised a house party atmosphere with full bar facilities, a welcome party, afternoon tea and cakes, and a yodeller evening. There were only 13 guests in the first week. During the second week Mr Jarvis was the only guest. The yodeller turned up in working clothes rather than national dress, and sang only a few songs. The afternoon tea consisted of crisps and dry nut cakes. The bar was open on one evening only and the skiing facilities were very poor.

Held: Mr Jarvis was held to be entitled to damages both for his disappointment at the absence of all the promised facilities which were central to the contract's performance, and the full cost of his holiday, a total of £125.

Heywood v *Wellers* (1976)

The claimant contracted with the defendant solicitor to obtain an injunction to prevent her ex-boyfriend from harassing her. Due to the solicitor's negligence the procedure failed and she continued to be molested. Damages were awarded for her distress since the entire purpose of the contract was to prevent this occurring.

Even where the court is not prepared to categorise a contract as one for peace of mind, it may award damages for distress directly resulting from physical inconvenience caused by the breach. In *Perry* v *Sidney Phillips* (1982, CA) the defendant, who was under contract to the Perrys to survey premises they wished to buy, overlooked roofing faults and a defective septic tank. Once they moved in the need for repairs became evident, especially as the smell from the septic tank was causing nuisance to the neighbours.

The court refused to categorise an ordinary surveyor's contract as one for peace of mind and freedom from distress. However, damages were awarded for the distress arising from the physical inconvenience of the execution of the repairs.

Cases since the late 1990s generally indicate greater readiness by the courts to recognise peace of mind obligations in contracts. In *Farley* v *Skinner (No. 2)*, below, the House of Lords held that the particular circumstances of the contract should determine whether it placed such obligations on the surveyor.

Farley v *Skinner (No. 2)* (2001, HL)

The claimant specifically requested the defendant surveyor to advise whether the property he was interested in buying was badly affected by aircraft noise from Gatwick airport.

Held: the claimant was entitled to £10,000 since the surveyor's favourable report proved grossly inaccurate. It was sufficient that a major or important part of the contract was to give peace of mind, pleasure or relaxation, for recovery of such damages to be permissible.

The Court of Appeal (*Milner & Milner* v *Carnival, t/a Cunard* (2010)) has clearly indicated the limitations on such damages in consumer contracts.

Milner and Milner v *Carnival plc t/a Cunard* (2010)

Mr and Mrs Milner, the claimants, booked what was described by Cunard as a glamorous world maiden-cruise and a 'legendary experience exceeding expectations'. Sadly, due to structural problems with the ship, their cabin was very noisy and uncomfortable and they abandoned the cruise at Hawaii.

At appeal the amount of damages for distress and inconvenience was reduced by more than half to approximately £4,000 each.

Held (Ward LJ):

Physical inconvenience and discomfort is necessarily ephemeral. Disappointment, distress, annoyance and frustration are likewise the feelings one experiences at the time and which last painfully for some time thereafter. But one is not disabled, the psyche is not injured and one gets on with life.

The courts have resisted attempts to extend peace of mind damages into contracts between two businesses.

Hayes v *James & Charles Dodd* (1990, CA)

The defendant solicitors failed to warn a commercial client of acute access problems to land that the client was buying.

Held: damages were not payable for the mental distress caused.

2 Liquidated damages and penalties

Liquidated damages: pre-estimated damages for breach agreed when the contract is made.

Penalty: a contractual sanction intended to enforce performance.

It is quite common for a contract to specify that, in the event of a breach, a sum of agreed or **liquidated damages** will be payable. If the court is satisfied that this sum represents a genuine attempt by the parties to determine a reasonable pre-estimate of the loss likely to result from such a breach, that sum will be awarded whether or not it represents an appropriate level of compensation. If the sum is not adequate, the injured party cannot claim more, since it contractually agreed to accept it. If it is more than necessary, the injured party does not have to return the difference. However, the court is not prepared to enforce a sum that is held to represent a **penalty**, i.e. a punishment to be suffered by the guilty party if it fails to perform its obligations, rather than an appropriate level of compensation. The object of awarding damages in contract is to compensate an injured party, not intimidate the other party into performance. If the court decides that the sum represents a penalty, this will be disregarded; instead a sum will be awarded which is representative of the injured party's actual loss. In the following case, Lord Dunedin proposed the following tests to distinguish between liquidated damages and penalties:

1 the words used to describe the sum are evidence of what the parties intended but are not conclusive;

2 the sum should be treated as a penalty, if grossly disproportionate to the greatest damage likely to result from the breach;

3 where the breach consists of a failure to pay money, the prescribed sum is a penalty if it exceeds the sum payable;

4 where one sum is payable in the event of the commission of any of a number of different breaches, some of which are trifling and some of which are more serious, it is probably a penalty;

5 even if accurate pre-estimation is almost impossible, this does not prevent a sum from being treated as liquidated damages, as long as it represents a genuine attempt to make a reasonably accurate assessment.

Dunlop Pneumatic Tyre Co. Ltd v *New Garage & Motor Co. Ltd* (1915, HL)

Dunlop had a clause in its contract of sale which attempted to impose a minimum price restraint on resale of its tyres by New Garage. It stated that breach of this term would make New Garage liable to pay '£5 by way of liquidated damages for every tyre, cover or tube'.

Held: this sum was liquidated damages. It was impossible to forecast precisely the damage resulting from each sale in breach of the agreement and there was no reason to suspect that this was not a genuine bargain to assess damages. (Application of criterion 5 above.)

Since £5 was quite a substantial sum in 1915, this seems a rather surprising decision. Perhaps the House of Lords felt such a restraint was appropriate to the development of a completely new area of the market, the future of which was unpredictable at the point when the contract was formed.

The following cases illustrate how the courts apply the criteria in the *Dunlop* case.

Jeancharm v *Barnet Football Club* (2003, CA)

Jeancharm contracted to supply football kit to the club. A term in the contract stated that in the event of late payment the club should pay interest at 5 per cent per week (equivalent to 260 per cent per year). In the event of late delivery, Jeancharm promised to pay 20p per garment per day.

Held: the 260 per cent interest was an unrealistic sum to pay for Jeancharm's administrative costs, and the term must be treated as a penalty clause which was therefore unenforceable. It was totally disproportionate in comparison to the greatest loss that Jeancharm was likely to suffer.

Tullet Prebon Group v *Ghaleb El Hajjali* (2008, QB)

E, the defendant, was a specialist broker who, after taking legal advice, entered an employment contract with T. This stated that if he failed to take up the job he would be liable for liquidated damages equal to at least 50 per cent of his net annual salary. His solicitor drew this clause specifically to his attention prior to signing. E having accepted, later told T, the claimant, that he wasn't interested in the job after all. I attempted unsuccessfully to find a replacement and claimed liquidated damages for breach of contract from E who refused to pay the money arguing that it was a penalty sum.

Held: E was crucial to the performance of a particular function or project. By failing to take up the job he made T suffer loss. T had made all reasonable efforts to mitigate its loss. The liquidated damages clause was not a penalty clause since it was not a disproportionate sum in the circumstances. E had entered the contract after legal advice and with full notice of the term so the parties enjoyed equal bargaining power.

Azimut-Benetti SpA v *Healey* (2010) makes it clear that in a commercial contract where the parties are on equal terms the relevant payment should be treated as liquidated damages: 'The evidence clearly shows that the purpose of the clause was not a deterrent, and that it was commercially justifiable as providing a balance between the parties upon unlawful termination by the builder' (per Blair J).

3 The duty to mitigate

The injured party cannot claim the cost of damage which it could reasonably have avoided. It is up to the party in breach to prove that the damage was avoidable.

Brace v *Calder* (1895)

A clerk with a fixed contract of employment with the defendant's partnership lost his job when the partnership was dissolved when one of the partners left. The partnership was immediately reformed by the remaining partners who had offered the clerk a job on his old contractual terms. He refused and sued to claim the wages which would have been payable had his contract run for its remaining two years.

Held: the clerk was not entitled to damages since he had been given a perfect opportunity to mitigate his loss completely and had failed in his duty to do so.

However, only reasonable steps need be taken to fulfil the mitigation duty. In *Pilkington* v *Wood* (1953) it was held that it was unreasonable to expect the claimant to take legal action against the seller of land to correct a defect in title, which the defendant solicitor had negligently failed to notice when acting for the claimant during the purchase of the land. In *Milner and Milner* v *Carnival, t/a Cunard* (2010) (see the facts above) the Court of Appeal held that the claimants acted unreasonably in refusing the defendant's offer of alternative accommodation on the ship, abandoning their cruise and incurring the unnecessary expense of the flight home.

4 Contributory negligence

It is possible that this may reduce the amount of damages awarded by the court. The Law Reform (Contributory Negligence) Act 1945, which regulates this defence in the law of tort, does not refer to contract liability. It is arguable whether in its current form it can legitimately be extended to cover contractual situations. The courts have been prepared to reduce damages where claimants' own lack of care has aggravated their loss. This appears to have been restricted to cases where a defendant is in breach of an obligation to act with reasonable care and skill which would entitle the claimant to sue in tort or contract. In 1993, the Law Commission recommended a new statute explicitly extending the defence to claims arising from any breach of a contractual duty to act with reasonable care and skill. So far Parliament has not implemented this recommendation.

Equitable remedies

A dominant characteristic of such remedies is that they are discretionary. The court has a choice whether or not to award them, unlike damages, which must be awarded if a party proves its case. A party may be refused access to an equitable remedy unless the court believes that it is just to both parties. The party claiming the remedy must show that:

1 damages would not be an adequate remedy;

2 he or she acted completely honestly: dishonest, though legal, behaviour will defeat a claim.

For example, the seller of a house has no legal duty to declare its defects unless asked. If, however, a seller knowingly failed to disclose such defects, a decree of specific performance would not be awarded against a buyer who discovered the defects later and refused to perform his or her contractual obligations.

Imposition of the equitable remedy must not be unnecessarily oppressive to the other party.

The victim of a breach of contract may exceptionally be awarded one of the following remedies.

1 Rescission

The court sets the contract aside and restores the parties to their pre-contractual positions. Note that the courts are more generous to a breach victim than to a party who claims rescission on other grounds, like misrepresentation. Rescission may be granted in a breach action even though the party at fault cannot be restored to his or her pre-contractual position: for example, where the victim of the breach has consumed the goods.

2 Specific performance

Specific performance: an equitable remedy which orders a party in breach to perform their contractual obligation.

The court orders a party to perform his or her contractual obligations. **Specific performance** is rarely granted except in relation to contracts for the sale of land. It will never be granted to enforce a contract of employment since it would be an unreasonable restriction of personal liberty to enforce performance of such a contract. It is also unlikely that the outcome of such enforced performance would be satisfactory. A sale of goods contract concerning a unique item, like a rare antique or a work of art, might attract the remedy. Generally, damages are regarded as adequate, as the buyer can obtain similar goods elsewhere. In *Cohen* v *Roche* (1927) a contract to sell a set of Hepplewhite chairs was held not to be specifically enforceable since the chairs were regarded as 'ordinary articles of commerce'.

Specific performance is unlikely to be granted to enforce a continuing obligation which requires continuing supervision. So in *Ryan* v *Mutual Tontine Association* (1893) specific performance was held not to be appropriate to enforce a requirement in a lease relating to the provision of a janitor in full-time attendance at a block of flats.

However, the need for limited supervision will not deter the court from issuing the order to carry out work. In *Rainbow Estates Ltd* v *Tokenhold* (1998) specific performance was granted to a landlord to make a tenant carry out repairs as required by the lease. It was held that the schedule of work was sufficiently clear and specific to make it readily capable of enforcement. Once complete, no further supervision would be required.

Specific performance has been used to enforce a debt owed by a third party to the estate of a deceased person.

Beswick v *Beswick* (1968)

Peter and John Beswick made a contract, under which John promised Peter that he would pay an annuity to Peter's wife after Peter's death. John failed to perform this obligation and Peter's widow sued him for breach of contract.

Held: as she was not privy to the contract between Peter and John, she had no rights to claim on her own behalf. However, she could succeed in her claim as the administratrix of her husband's estate which entitled her to pursue the action on behalf of her husband's estate. As the estate itself had suffered no loss through the breach, any damages would be nominal, so in the interests of justice, specific performance of the contract should be ordered to prevent John from getting away with the breach.

Worth thinking about?

Beswick v *Beswick* is a good example of the court using an equitable remedy to avoid the unjust result which would arise from strict application of the law. What statute could Mrs Beswick use to enforce payment if she was bringing this case today?

Suggested solutions can be found in Appendix 2.

As indicated above, an equitable remedy will not be granted unless it will do justice to both parties in all the circumstances of the case. Therefore the court may, in its discretion, refuse to enforce a contract where this would cause unreasonable hardship to the party who is refusing to perform. Thus, in *Patel* v *Ali* (1984) Mrs Ali contracted to sell her house, but almost immediately she suffered considerable domestic trauma including the death of one of her children. She no longer wanted to move, as she spoke little English and had friends and neighbours nearby whom she relied upon for help. Specific performance was refused.

Hardship can also be relevant to commercial contracts.

Co-operative Insurance Society v *Argyll Stores (Holdings) Ltd* (1997, HL)

The defendant opened a supermarket in a shopping centre owned by the claimant. The 35-year lease contained a covenant by the defendants that during the currency of the lease the store would be kept open for trade during normal retail hours. Six years into the lease the defendant closed the store and the claimant requested specific performance. Damages were not an adequate remedy as it was virtually impossible to quantify them accurately for the remaining 29 years of the lease.

Held: the contract would not be enforced as it would be unjust to force someone to run an unprofitable business, and also supervision of performance was impracticable in the circumstances.

3 Injunction

Injunction:
an equitable
remedy which
orders a person
to do or refrain
from doing
something.

An **injunction** is a commonly requested remedy for breach of restraint of trade contracts (see Chapter 10). It will not generally be granted to force one party to employ or work for another, as this would amount to enforcing a contract of employment indirectly. In *Page One Records* v *Britton* (1968) it was held that an injunction would not be granted to restrain The Troggs (a pop group) from employing a new manager, since this would force them to go on employing the claimant. But compare *Page One Records* v *Britton* with the following case.

> ### *Warner Bros* v *Nelson* (1936)
>
> The film star, Bette Davis (Nelson), breached her contract, under which she had agreed not to act on stage or screen for anybody except Warner Bros for one year, by agreeing to make a film with a UK company.
>
> **Held:** an injunction would be granted to restrain Bette Davis from making films for the rival company. The contract restrained her from acting for anyone other than Warner, but did not prevent her from earning her living in other ways. The injunction did not force her to perform the contract if she was prepared to earn her living in a less profitable way.

Very exceptionally, a court may use an injunction actually to compel performance of a contract where this is in the interests of justice. In *Gryf-Lowczowski* v *Hinchingbrooke Healthcare* (2006) Mr Justice Grey clearly felt that an injunction was necessary to assist the claimant to obtain a fair outcome in a situation where his employers had treated him very inappropriately.

11

Discharge of the contract and remedies for breach

Chapter summary

Discharge of contracts

Performance: must generally be complete.

Exceptions: contract divisible, acceptance of part performance, prevention of performance, substantial performance.

Agreement: mutuality essential.

Frustration: performance becomes impossible or futile due to circumstances beyond the control of either of the parties and not due to their fault.

The Law Reform (Frustrated Contracts) Act 1943 determines how far the parties may recover any resulting financial losses.

Breach of a condition gives the innocent party the option of avoiding the contract and suing immediately or awaiting performance date.

Remedies

Damages: the innocent party may claim damages for any quantifiable loss or harm resulting but not too remote from a breach of condition or warranty.

Remoteness of damage: *Hadley* v *Baxendale* (1854) states that damage may be too remote if it is 'non-usual' (not a normally anticipated consequence of breach in the particular contract situation).

Quantum of damages: the amount necessary to put the claimant in his or her pre-contractual position. Covers lost profits, reliance losses, tangible damage to person/property and exceptionally intangible damage such as loss of reputation, or pleasure or peace of mind.

Equitable remedies

Awarded in exceptional cases at the court's discretion:

● rescission;
● injunction;
● specific performance.

Quiz 10

1 Is Flannel discharged from his contractual obligations in the following circumstances?

   (a) He delivers 50 kilos of turnips to Denim who had ordered 70 kilos, and:

      (i) the turnips were costed at 50 pence per kilo, or

      (ii) the turnips were costed at £250 for 70 kilos, but Denim agrees to take the smaller order.

   (b) He contracts to decorate Wool's house. When the work is half complete, Wool refuses to let him in.

2 On 1 May, Chambray contracted to hire his vintage Rolls-Royce to Linen on 30 May. On 15 May, Chambray tells Linen that he is not prepared to supply the car on the due date. Linen says he will wait and see if Chambray will change his mind. On 29 May, Chambray's chauffeur writes off the car. What is the legal position? What difference would it make to your answer if the accident had already happened at the point Chambray and Linen made the contract?

3 Distinguish between the concepts of remoteness and quantum of damage.

4 When may the court refuse to award a decree of specific performance?

Answers to all quizzes can be found in Appendix 2.

Take a closer look

The following cases provide important examples of how the law you have studied in this chapter has developed. They are primary sources illustrating the law in action and give you more detail about their facts, as well as helping you to understand the law and to appreciate how the judges reached their decisions.

Try looking them up in the law reports or accessing them via a database, e.g. Bailii (www.bailii.org/databases.html). LexisNexis or Westlaw may be available in your university or college library, or you may find extracts in a case book. (See Appendix 1: Additional resources.)

Davis Contractors Ltd v *Fareham UDC* [1956] 2 All ER 145, HL

Koufos v *Czarnikow Ltd (The Heron II)* [1969] 1 AC 350, HL

Jarvis v *Swan Tours* [1973] 3 WLR 954, CA

Milner and Milner v *Carnival plc, t/a Cunard* [2010] EWCA Civ 389; [2010] 3 All ER 701

Web activity

You may have noticed that a number of cases in this chapter concern builders.

Please go to: http://www.adviceguide.org.uk/england/consumer_e/consumer_builders_and_home_improvements_e.htm

and find out practical steps that can be taken in the event of a problems arising from contracts of this kind.

11

Discharge of the contract and remedies for breach

Assignment 9

Janet and Arthur engaged Cuthbert to carry out extensive repairs to the electrics in their house. Cuthbert promised that the work would be finished in four weeks. To avoid the disruption, Janet and Arthur and their son George (aged nine months) moved to a hotel. A month later, the work was still not complete, but they could no longer afford to stay in the hotel and had to return home. The work was not finished for another two weeks. They had to buy a camping stove, lamps and bottled gas and pay for a laundry service. Janet became ill with stress and they were left £600 out of pocket.

Advise Cuthbert.

Would it make any difference to your advice if new safety regulations were implemented after the contract was made, which required Cuthbert to install additional fail-safe devices, and it was this extra work that made the contract run past the deadline?

CHAPTER 12

The law of agency

Introduction

You will already be aware of a number of situations where an agent may be employed – when you want to buy a house you may employ an estate agent; perhaps you have obtained insurance through an insurance broker, or bought shares through a stockbroker. An employer may choose to obtain staff through an employment agency. In many sale of goods situations, agents may be employed by sellers or buyers to obtain customers or to arrange transport for international trading deals. In all these situations an agent is employed because of their expertise in the relevant business area.

However, an agent is not necessarily a professional, engaged for commercial purposes. An agency relationship may arise, for example, where a person agrees to handle the affairs of a friend who is currently unable to act personally, because of being abroad or in ill health.

An agency relationship may therefore arise in any situation where one party (the principal) authorises another person (the agent) to act on his or her behalf. Any contract made by the agent on the principal's behalf is binding by or against the third party with whom the agent negotiated. The agent may also be liable to the principal if the agent acted negligently or in breach of any contract of agency.

Learning objectives

When you have studied this chapter you should be able to:

▶ describe how an agency relationship may be created;

▶ explain the rights and duties of the agent and the principal;

▶ distinguish between the ways by which the agency relationship may be terminated;

▶ appreciate the nature of some particular types of agency relationships.

The creation of agency

Agent:
a person with
the authority
to carry out
business on
behalf of
another person.

The authority of the **agent** is the keystone of the agency relationship. Provided an agent has legal authority to do business on the principal's behalf, any resulting contract is binding by and against the **principal**.

The agent must make the principal a party to a contract it makes with a third party or no agency relationship exists. Even if one party exercises some control over another and receives a benefit from the contracts which the other party makes, this may not be sufficient evidence of authority to give rise to an agency relationship.

Spearmint Rhino Ventures UK Ltd v *Revenue and Customs Commissioners* (2007)

Lap dancers worked on a self-employed basis in Spearmint Rhino Clubs to dance and provide entertainment for customers. They had to do a minimum number of shifts per week and were paid a fee per shift plus a fee for every 'sit down' (a period of 'dancing and companionship' in a private room). In return, Spearmint provided the necessary facilities, security, advertising and administration.

The Revenue claimed that lap dancers were Spearmint's agents and, therefore, it should pay VAT on the services they provided to customers.

Held: VAT was not payable as no agency relationship existed between the club and the dancers. Their agreement with Spearmint was a licence, from which Spearmint derived some benefits, to allow them to ply their trade on club premises. In no way did it give a dancer any authority to act on Spearmint's behalf. She decided which and how many customers she would entertain individually and kept the resulting fees and gratuities. The fact that a fee was payable to Spearmint per 'sit down' did not mean that the 'sit down' was organised on behalf of Spearmint. A dancer worked only on her own behalf.

Worth thinking about?

Spearmint Rhino Clubs pay lap dancers to work in their clubs. If they failed to pay, could the lap dancers sue in breach of contract for their earnings?

Suggested solutions can be found in Appendix 2.

Principal: person for whom an agent acts. May be disclosed or undisclosed.

Legal authority to do business on the principal's behalf normally arises from agreement between the parties, but exceptions exist in the interests of commercial efficiency. The relationship may be deemed to exist to avoid injustice to a third party or the agent. Sometimes a principal can create authority retrospectively to allow it to take advantage of an unauthorised transaction.

Agency by agreement between the parties

An agency relationship is most commonly created by an agreement between the parties under which the agent is given *actual authority* by the principal. The agency agreement may be made in the following ways:

Power of attorney: authority created by deed enabling agent to manage affairs for a principal who is currently incapable of doing so because of ill health, for example.

1 *Formally by deed*. This gives a **power of attorney** to the agent. This is essential where an agent is appointed to act on behalf of a person who has become incapable of managing his or her own affairs. More detail on this topic appears at the end of the chapter.

2 *Informally by written or spoken agreement*. No particular written formalities are generally required: it is possible to appoint an agent by word of mouth. The parties may choose to evidence the agreement in writing, but this does not necessarily include all the terms binding the parties. In *Chaudhry* v *Prabhakar* (1988, CA) an agreement between friends, under which one who claimed knowledge of cars agreed to find a suitable secondhand model for the other, was held to have created an agency relationship.

3 *By implication*. The relationship of the parties may give rise to an implied agency agreement. This commonly arises from the employer and employee relationship. It may also exist between a cohabiting husband and wife since the wife has implied authority from her husband to pledge his credit (run up bills) to satisfy household requirements. However, despite some recent progress towards equality between the sexes, the husband cannot do the same.

The agency agreement may exist without any contractual relationship between principal and agent. An agency may be purely gratuitous, with the agent receiving no payment for his or her services. If a colleague asks you to buy a lunchtime sandwich for her, in law she is appointing you as her agent, but neither of you will anticipate that payment will be made for performance of the service. However, if you are trying to sell your house through an estate agent, a contract exists between you. Under its terms, the

12

The law of agency

agent is entitled to payment of commission from you if a sale takes place with a buyer introduced by the agent.

Where the agency is created by agreement the agent has actual authority. Actual authority is divided into two kinds: express and implied.

1 *Express*. The power is derived from the principal's explicit directions.

2 *Implied*. The principal is unlikely to spell out every detail of what is required. The principal is, however, deemed to have impliedly given the agent authority to accomplish anything necessarily incidental to the performance of the principal's directions.

The extent of implied authority is indicated by all the circumstances in which the agency arose, such as the relationship between the parties, the usual authority of the agent in the relevant area of business and the nature of the principal's orders. For example, if you ask an estate agent to find you a buyer, you give the agent actual authority to do so. You also impliedly authorise the agent to photograph your house and use this for advertisement purposes. In *Real and Personal Advance* v *Palemphin* (1893), the matron of a hospital was held to have implied authority to contract in her employer's name to buy essential supplies for the hospital.

In the news

Ramsay v *Love* (2015)

Gordon Ramsay the celebrity chef claimed that he was not bound by a personal guarantee because it had been given by Mr Hutcheson, the chief executive of his company and his father-in-law, without authority.

Gary Love, a property developer bought some premises to convert into a small hotel and restaurant. Hutcheson entered into a contract on behalf of Ramsay's company to buy these premises provided that the finished work met his approval. The defendant asked for a personal guarantee from Ramsay which Mr Hutcheson provided using an electronic writing machine to reproduce Gordon Ramsay's signature. Later Hutcheson repudiated the contract as he found the work unsatisfactory. The developer claimed on the guarantee. Ramsay sought a declaration from the court that he had not given authority for the guarantee.

Held: the evidence showed that Hutcheson had a wide remit to enter into a variety of commercial contracts on Ramsay's behalf. Ramsay's own testimony showed that he had complete trust in Hutcheson and openly admitted that he relied upon him because of his own lack of business acumen. In the past, Hutcheson had signed many legal documents with the electronic machine with Ramsay's knowledge. Personal guarantees were common practice in deals of this kind. Ramsay had given a number in the past sometimes when not even expressly asked.

Morgan J said:
> I find that when Mr Hutcheson committed Mr Ramsay to the guarantee in the lease of the premises, Mr Hutcheson was acting within the wide general authority conferred on him by Mr Ramsay at all times . . . I also find, in particular, that in Mr Ramsay's own words . . . that authority extended to Mr Hutcheson offering, on behalf of Mr Ramsay, Mr Ramsay's guarantee in relation to a lease when the business required it.

Agency by estoppel

Estopped: prevented in law from denying the existence of a right of another person.

Apparent authority: the agent has no real authority but it appears that they do, because of failure by the principal to give notice that it has ended or to correct the impression that it exists.

Ostensible authority: see apparent authority.

In certain circumstances a third party may presume that a person ~~is~~ an agent even if this is not so. If the principal's behaviour reason~~ably gives~~ this impression, the third party may enforce a resulting contract ag~~ainst him.~~ Provided there was nothing to alert the third party to the true fa~~cts, the principal is~~ **estopped** (prevented) from denying that the relationship exists. The agent in such circumstances has **apparent** or **ostensible authority**.

Apparent authority may exist in the following situations:

1. An agency relationship has ceased to exist but the principal has failed to give notice of this to third parties.

2. No agency relationship has ever existed, but the 'principal' allows a third party to believe the 'agent' was acting on the principal's behalf.

3. An agency relationship exists and the principal allows a third party to believe that the agent's authority is greater than it is. As long as the agent's behaviour seems to comply with relevant business practice, apparent authority generally exists unless the principal does something to rebut this presumption.

Barrett v *Deere* (1828, HL)

The defendant went to the claimant's counting house to pay a debt and handed his payment over to a rogue, who was in the claimant creditor's counting house and appeared to be responsible for transacting business there.

Held: this was sufficient to discharge the debt. It was reasonable for the debtor to believe that the rogue was the creditor's agent and had the creditor's authority, since the creditor had the right to control all transactions taking place on the premises.

Common knowledge in the business world may be sufficient to provide reasonable belief.

Racing UK Ltd v *Doncaster Racecourse Ltd and Doncaster Borough Council* (2005)

The Chief Executive (CE) of Doncaster Racecourse Ltd signed, 'as duly authorised representative', an agreement granting TV rights to Racing UK Ltd. It was claimed by Racing UK and the racecourse that this contract bound the council. The council claimed that it was not bound as the CE did not have any authority to act as its agent.

Held (by the Court of Appeal): since it was common knowledge in the racing world that the council owned the racecourse and in the business world that the owner of a course held the television rights, the CE had ostensible authority to enter the contract on behalf of the council. Therefore, the contract was binding on the council.

A company's lawyers may be justified in believing that an executive director has authority to instruct them.

Newcastle International Airport Ltd v Eversheds LLP (2012)

The Airport (N) claimed that Eversheds (E) had been negligent in accepting instructions from D, an executive director on N's remuneration committee, which awarded payment of very significantly increased bonuses to executive directors as part of a new refinancing agreement. In fact, committee members had only agreed in principle to a bonus distinct from the refinancing agreement. E argued that it had not been negligent as D had apparent authority to give these instructions.

N argued that E knew that the remuneration committee's function was to obtain the best possible terms for the airport and that D had a conflict of interest. Therefore, E should have checked with the chair of the committee before going ahead.

Held: E had not been negligent. D had apparent authority because:

1 The chair had apparently deliberately chosen to leave communication to D and the other executive directors had not questioned the proposals. It was common practice for remuneration committees to instruct solicitors through their executive directors. E had advised D on what the effects of the drafted changes meant believing that, he would pass this on to the committee. R had signed off the draft agreement when E sent it to her. There was nothing more that E could have done to fulfil its duty of care to N.

2 It was very important for solicitors to be able to place reliance on the apparent authority of a company's agent unless it was unreasonable or irrational not to do so. No evidence that D was acting without authority was in any way apparent here.

Sometimes the agent's behaviour should put the third party on notice that no authority exists.

Quinn v CC Automotive Group (t/a Carcraft) (2010, CA)

On 5 July 2005 Mr Quinn consulted Mr Khan, who was employed by the defendant, Carcraft, in Leeds, about the sale of his silver Jaguar in part exchange for a new red one to drive to his daughter's wedding on 22 July 2005. As no red Jaguar was available, he agreed to buy a blue one, with finance arranged through Carcraft, who agreed to pay off the money still owed on the silver car. Shortly afterwards, Mr Khan phoned him and said that he had located a red Jaguar in Bury and showed Mr Quinn the car via the internet. He agreed to buy it. Shortly afterwards, Mr Khan told Mr Quinn that the finance company required an additional £700. When Mr Quinn said he could only afford £400, Mr Khan agreed to accept it, with the balance to be paid subsequently. Two days before the wedding, they met at a service station between Bury and Leeds and exchanged cars. Mr Quinn paid £400 in cash and signed documents to cancel the old contract and agree to the purchase the new one.

Mr Khan sold the silver Jaguar to a *bona fide* purchaser in a private deal and pocketed the money. Mr Quinn cancelled the finance agreement on his silver Jaguar and the finance company sued him for the outstanding payment of £15,000. The red Jaguar had never been part of the Carcraft's stock and its provenance was uncertain.

Mr Quinn sued Carcraft, arguing that it was vicariously liable for Mr Khan, who had acted as its agent with apparent authority to make the deal.

Held: Carcraft was vicariously liable for Mr Quinn's loss. Mr Quinn honestly trusted in Mr Khan's authority, thinking he was being particularly helpful in getting the car in time for the wedding.

Gross LJ stated:

> the . . . factors relied upon by the defendant as putting Mr Quinn on inquiry, are to be considered in context and without the benefit of hindsight . . . The transaction was within the class of acts – and squarely so – that a car salesman . . . is usually authorised to do.

Agency arising from necessity

An agency relationship may arise in an emergency situation, where one party spontaneously takes steps to preserve somebody else's property interests. This enables that party to avoid liability for the reasonable costs of the intervention on the owner's behalf.

Agency of necessity may arise if *all* the following conditions are satisfied:

> **Agency of necessity:** agency created by an emergency requiring the agent to take reasonable steps to preserve the principal's property.

1 while one party has possession of another party's goods an emergency occurs; and

2 this forces that party to take action regarding the goods *for the benefit of their owner*; and

3 it is impossible to communicate with the owner first.

Such an agent has authority to take such reasonable and prudent steps as are necessary in the best interests of the owner of the property.

Sachs v *Miklos* (1948)

The defendant gratuitously stored the claimant's furniture. During the war he wanted the space it was occupying, but was unable to contact the claimant. He sold the goods.

Held: no agency of necessity arose here because there was *no emergency* justifying the sale and the claimant was acting for *his own benefit*. Therefore, the defendant was liable to the claimant in the tort of conversion (unlawful disposal of the claimant's goods).

In the past, such agency often arose in situations where carriers were forced to make decisions to pay for the food and accommodation for livestock (*Great Northern Railway* v *Swaffield* (1874)) or to dispose of perishable goods. Such circumstances are unlikely to occur today, given that generally it is possible for a carrier to communicate directly with the owner and obtain emergency instructions.

If agency of necessity exists:

1 the agent may claim expenses;

2 the agent has a defence if sued for trespass for disposing of the goods;

3 a third party who has acquired goods from such an agent gets good title to the goods.

Agency by ratification

Even if a party had no authority or exceeded the given authority to act for another when making the contract, authority can be given subsequently if the other party wants to adopt the transaction. This **ratification** creates antecedent authority for the agent: the law treats the agent as having had authority from the outset.

For ratification to be valid the following requirements must be fulfilled:

Ratification: acknowledgement that a prior obligation is binding.

1 the agent must expressly or impliedly indicate that it is acting as someone's agent;

2 the principal must both exist and have the capacity to make the contract when it was made (promoters of a company making pre-incorporation contracts are not acting as company agents as the company as yet has no legal existence (see Chapter 19);

3 ratification must be within a reasonable time;

4 ratification must be complete: the principal must agree to all, not part, of the contract with full knowledge of what is involved;

5 notice of ratification must be communicated: this may be done by conduct, such as retaining goods which have been delivered.

The consequences of ratification are as follows:

1 the agent is freed from any liability for acting without authority;

2 the agent is entitled to remuneration from the principal where appropriate;

3 a third party obtains title to any property which has been transferred under the contract;

4 a contract made by the agent on the principal's behalf is retrospectively binding on the principal.

The disclosed and undisclosed principal

Disclosed principal

When agents enter into contracts on behalf of principals, they usually name the principals or at least indicate that they are acting as agents. Here the principal is said to be disclosed even if not actually named.

In general, the disclosed principal is liable on any resulting contract and the agent is not. Exceptions may arise where words, conduct or surrounding circumstances indicate that the agent and principal are jointly liable, or that the agent is to remain solely liable. Thus, if an agent signs a deed without indicating that he or she is signing as an agent, he or she will be personally liable.

Undisclosed principal

Sometimes the agent behaves as if no principal is involved, although in fact one is; here the principal is undisclosed. The contract will be binding by and against the principal if:

1   the agent was acting under the principal's actual authority at the time the contract was made;

2   the terms of the contract do not preclude the existence of the principal.

In *Humble* v *Hunter* (1848) an agent signed a charterparty so that he appeared to be sole owner of the ship involved. It was held that the principal could not enforce the contract. However, if the third party can show that it intended to do business only with the agent personally, the principal cannot enforce the contract against the third party. In *Collins* v *Associated Greyhound Race Courses Ltd* (1930) a contract to underwrite a share issue involved exclusive reliance on the agent's business reputation and integrity. The principal was held to be excluded.

The rights and duties of the agent

Rights

Payment

The agent does not have an automatic legal right to payment. Such a right exists only where the agency agreement indicates such an intention. If the agency is gratuitous, no payment is intended. Even if the agency is contractual, payment is due only if the terms of the contract governing payment are fulfilled. Payment may be conditional on a particular result being achieved.

G.T. Hodges & Sons v *Hackbridge Residential Hotel* (1939)

The owner of a hotel asked an estate agent to find a buyer. A representative from the War Office was introduced by the agent and began negotiations which then lapsed. Some months later the War Office announced that it would compulsorily purchase the hotel.

Held: this compulsory sale did not entitle the agent to their commission, as this was not the sort of sale contemplated by the parties when the owner put his property in the agent's hands.

Where the agency is contractual, the agent may sue for breach if the principal fails to make appropriate payment. The agent may also be entitled to exercise a lien (legal right to retain) over any property still in his or her possession that was purchased for the principal and for which the agent has not yet been paid.

Indemnity: payment to make good expenses/ losses incurred by one party while acting for the benefit of another.

Indemnity

Whether the agency is gratuitous or contractual, an agent is entitled to **indemnity** and therefore may recover any expenses incurred or losses suffered, if these are sufficiently incidental to the agent's authorised conduct.

Anglo Overseas Transport Ltd v *Titan Industrial Corpn* (1959)

An agent was engaged to make arrangements for shipping of the principal's goods. The principal was late in delivering the goods to the port which, by the customs of the trade, made the agent liable for losses incurred by the ship owner.

Held: the principal must indemnify the agent for its loss.

A gratuitous agent may request the court to order the principal to pay restitution.

Duties

The agent is in a fiduciary relationship with the principal: he or she enjoys the trust and confidence of the principal, and consequently has a number of legal duties which must be performed whether the agency is contractual or gratuitous.

Performance

An agent must carry out the principal's orders within the limits of the agent's authority. Generally, the agent is required to perform the duties personally and without delegation because of the agent's confidential relationship with the principal. Delegation may be permissible, however, if the principal consents, or if delegation is in keeping with trade practice. For example, if a case is being handled by country solicitors but it is to be heard in London, it is normal for some tasks to be delegated to a London firm. It may also be allowed if the delegated tasks require no exercise of special skill or discretion by the agent. Thus solicitors may delegate claim-form-serving duties to their clerks.

Reasonable skill

Agents must perform their duties with reasonable care and skill and may be liable in breach of contract, or negligence, if they fail to do so.

An agent with trade or professional skills is expected to act with the level of skill reasonably to be expected of a person from such a trade or profession.

Where a contract of agency exists, failure to perform duties appropriately will be a breach of contract.

Chaudhry v *Prabhakar* (1988, CA)

The defendant was a friend of the claimant and claimed to be knowledgeable about cars. He was asked by the claimant to find a car for her that had not been involved in an accident. He found what he claimed was a suitable vehicle, although he noticed that the bonnet had probably been replaced and that it came from a garage which did crash repairs. Within a few months it turned out to be unroadworthy because of previous crash damage.

Held: the defendant was liable to the claimant in negligence as he had not exercised the level of care and skill to be expected from somebody with the level of expertise he had claimed to possess and on which the claimant had reasonably relied.

Arensen v *Casson Beckman Rutley & Co.* (1977)

A professional share valuer placed too low a valuation on his principal's shares.

Held: he was liable for breach of his duty to act with the degree of skill to be expected from a person with his level of professional experience.

Accountability

The agent must account for any profits resulting from the exercise of authority and transfer to the principal any monies or financial benefits derived from performance of the agent's duties. This duty is closely related to the agent's duty to avoid conflict of interest.

Real life

Horace's great uncle William wants to sell his antique pocket watch and asks Horace to find a suitable buyer. He tells Horace that he wants at least £1,000 for it. Horace takes the watch to an antique market where Cedric, a stall holder, offers him £1,200 pounds. Ernest, another stall holder butts in at this point and says he will pay £1,400 and give Horace a bonus of £50 for taking his offer. Horace sells to Ernest but he should tell his uncle about the £50 when he hands over the proceeds of the sale as the £50 is an advantage which he obtained while acting as his uncle's agent and he must account for all profits. Maybe his uncle will let him hang on to the extra £50 but in law it is his property.

Avoidance of conflict of interest

The agent must ensure that the principal's interests take priority over the agent's, and must not exploit the relationship for the agent's own profit.

An agent who takes a bribe is in flagrant breach of the duty to avoid a conflict of interest. If an agent accepts payment from a third party in return for making a contract with that party in the principal's name, the contract is voidable for fraud. The principal is entitled to dismiss the agent without payment, and recover the amount of the bribe. The principal may also repudiate the contract with the third party and claim damages for any loss which has resulted from the contract being made.

Armstrong v *Jackson* (1917)

A principal instructed his agent to buy shares in a particular company. Unknown to the principal, the agent owned some shares in the company and sold these to the principal instead of obtaining them elsewhere.

Held: the agent had failed to avoid a conflict of interest and must pay the principal the profit obtained on the sale.

The rights and duties of the principal

In relation to the agent

The principal's rights and duties largely mirror the duties and rights of the agent. Therefore, the principal is entitled to the benefits to be derived from the agent's performance of his or her fiduciary duties. In return the principal must make any necessary payment to the agent.

In relation to third parties

Contractual duties

Any contract made by the agent with a third party is binding on the principal provided that it was made within the limits of the agent's apparent authority. The principal is therefore liable for any misrepresentation or breach of contract, even though this was caused by the agent.

Tort liability

A principal may be vicariously liable for any torts committed by the agent closely connected with the exercise of the agent's apparent authority.

Quinn v *CC Automotive Group (t/a Carcraft)* (2010) provides a good example of vicarious liability.

The Commercial Agents (Council Directive) Regulations 1993 (as amended)

The common law rights and duties between agent and principal have been put on a statutory footing, but only in commercial agencies for the sale of goods. The regulations amended by the Commercial Agents (Council Directive) (Amendment) Regulations 1998 give the parties additional protection, including a right to a written contract and to a minimum period of notice if the agency contract is to be terminated. The agent is given rights to commission. This must be paid within specified time limits. The agent is entitled to check the principal's books to ensure that he or she has been paid at the correct rate.

Termination of agency

The agency relationship may come to an end either:

1 by operation of law; or
2 by the acts of the parties.

By operation of law
Death

Since the relationship of principal and agent is a confidential one, the death of either party brings the agency to an end.

Mental incapacity

If a person's mental condition precludes him or her from having a reasonable level of understanding, he or she will be treated as no longer having the ability to be a party to a contract. If either party to an agency agreement becomes mentally incapable, this usually terminates the relationship. However, where the agent has been granted an irrevocable or lasting power of attorney, a principal's mental incapacity does not discharge the agency. (See below.)

Bankruptcy

The bankruptcy of either party terminates the agency, since the bankrupt's property passes into the control of the trustee in bankruptcy to enable payment of creditors.

Frustration of the agency agreement

Any event rendering further performance of an agency contract illegal, impossible or futile will terminate the agency. (See Chapter 11.)

By the acts of the parties

Performance

Once the object of any short-term agency has been achieved, the agency ends.

Agreement or revocation

Both parties may agree to terminate the relationship. One party may revoke the agreement regardless of the other party's wish to continue. If the agency is contractual, this revocation may be a breach of contract entitling the other party to claim damages. No notice period is required, except where principal and agent are also in an employer–employee relationship.

Exceptionally, an agency cannot be revoked. An irrevocable agency exists in the following circumstances:

1 *The agent's authority is linked to the agent's own interest.* The purpose of this agency is to provide security for some pre-existing interest which the agent has with the principal. The agency cannot be revoked until the interest (usually the principal's debt with the agent) is discharged. For example, a debtor who currently is unable to repay a creditor may authorise the creditor to liquidate some of the debtor's assets in order to raise the funds to repay the debt. Such an agency will be terminated by operation of law, however, if the principal subsequently becomes bankrupt or insane, unless the agent has obtained an irrevocable power of attorney.

2 *The agent has been granted an irrevocable power of attorney.* Under the Powers of Attorney Act 1971, s 4, an **irrevocable power of attorney** may be granted by the principal (donor of the power) to the agent (donee), which prevents an agency relationship from being terminated by the death, incapacity or bankruptcy of the principal. Similarly, if the principal is a corporate body the agency will survive its dissolution or winding up. An irrevocable power of attorney will be granted only to a donee who can prove that it is necessary to assist the donee to preserve a pre-existing interest in the principal's property. An irrevocable power of attorney exists for the benefit of the agent and must be distinguished from a lasting power of attorney.

3 *The agent has been granted a lasting power of attorney.* The Mental Capacity Act 2005 (MCA), s 9 allows a donor to grant a **lasting power of attorney** (LPA). Since 2007, this replaces the previous system of enduring power of attorney. LPAs provide greater protection for the donor. For example, an LPA is only effective if registered with the Office of the Public Guardian and must contain the name of a person to be notified and asked for their permission before the power is invoked.

An LPA has a broader scope than an enduring power of attorney since it enables the donee to make decisions, not only about managing the donor's property, but also regarding his or her personal welfare: for example, deciding whether/what medical treatment is to be undertaken. Under the MCA, s 11 the donee has no authority to act unless the donor is deemed to lack the capacity to make the relevant decision as defined by s 2. This states: 'a person lacks capacity in relation to a matter if at the

Irrevocable power of attorney: to protect the agent's interest in the principal's property; it cannot be revoked by the principal/their incapacity/death/bankruptcy.

Lasting power of attorney: enables the agent to make decisions about an incapacitated principal's welfare as well as managing their property.

material time he is unable to make a decision for himself in relation to the matter because of an impairment of, or a disturbance in the functioning of the mind or brain'. This may be a permanent or temporary state of affairs.

Some common types of specialist agents

Estate agents

Estate agents act for the seller of a property; their function is to find a buyer. They are regulated by the Estate Agents Act 1979, which requires estate agents to be insured against the loss of any deposits which they may be required to handle. They must also inform the seller of their commission charges before agreeing to act for them. Commission is payable only if a sale takes place to a purchaser whom they have introduced. Further controls were introduced under the Consumers, Estate Agents and Redress Act 2007, which required estate agents to register with an Estate Agents Redress Scheme. This enables complaints against them to be investigated by the Property Ombudsman. Registration imposes a range of duties on estate agents including transparency of terms and conditions of business including payment of fees in addition to the other legal duties of agents as described in this chapter. Since 2014 lettings agents have also been required by law to sign up to a government recognised redress scheme (the Redress Schemes for Lettings Agency Work and Property Management Work (Requirement to Belong to a Scheme etc) (England) Order 2014). This handles complaints by both tenants and landlords about lettings and management agents. The Consumer Rights Act 2015, s 83 requires letting agents to display fees clearly to their clients.

Auctioneers

The auctioneer initially acts as the agent of the seller, with the authority to sell to the highest bidder unless any reserve price is not reached. Once a sale has taken place the auctioneer becomes the agent of the buyer too.

An auctioneer is not authorised to transact a sale by credit. The buyer must pay immediately after the sale has taken place, although a cheque is acceptable instead of cash.

Brokers

Broker:
an intermediary who introduces parties to enable them to do business.

There are a number of different types of **brokers**, all of whom act primarily as intermediaries between two parties, one of whom has something to sell – like stocks and shares, insurance or commodities – which the other party is interested in buying. The broker effects the introduction and may assist in the formation of the contract in return for a commission. Unlike factors (below), brokers do not generally have physical possession of the property which is being sold. Brokers' authority may be defined by customs relating to their particular trade.

Factors

Factor:
a 'mercantile agent' who sells goods on behalf of a customer and also lends money on the security of goods pledged with him or her.

The Factors Act 1889, s 1, defines a **factor** as 'a mercantile agent having in the customary course of his business as such agent authority either to sell goods or to consign goods for the purpose of sale or to buy goods or to raise money on the security of goods'. A factor, therefore, not only has apparent authority to sell goods – which any agent may have apparent authority to do – he or she also has apparent authority to pledge goods or the documents of title to goods. Such pledges are very commonly used to raise money on imports of commodities like cocoa or wheat.

A factor is given physical control of the goods. The sale or other disposition of the goods within the factor's apparent authority to a purchaser acting in good faith is binding on the owner, even if the factor has disregarded orders and exceeded their actual authority.

Chapter summary

Creation of agency agreement:

By deed (power of attorney); or

in writing; or

by word of mouth.

The authority of the agent is usually:

Actual: express/implied and derived from the agreement.

Exceptionally agency arises without actual authority:

By estoppel: if the principal allows a person to behave like their agent that person has apparent/ostensible authority.

From necessity: where one party in control of another's property has to take steps to protect it in an emergency.

By ratification: a party subsequently ratifies a contract made by another for their benefit.

Duties of the agent

The agency relationship is fiduciary: the agent must account for any profits arising from his or her work for the principal and avoid any conflict of interest.

He or she must carry out their work with reasonable care and skill.

Duties of the principal

To the agent: perform reciprocal fiduciary duty.

Pay agreed remuneration.

Indemnify expenses.

Principal's liability to third parties:

Liable to perform authorised contracts.

Vicariously liable for the agent's torts.

Termination of the agency relationship

Operation of law: incapacity/death, bankruptcy, or frustration of the agency agreement.

Act of the parties: performance, agreement or revocation.

Enduring/irrevocable/lasting power of attorney may prevent termination.

Quiz 11

1 Under what types of authority do the following agents act?

 (a) North, who was asked by South to take South's DVD player to be repaired.

 (b) East, who was asked to drive West's car to the airport to collect West's business client and had to buy petrol as the tank was almost empty.

2 Port, while in Starboard's employment, had collected stationery supplies from Compass once a week. He is sacked by Starboard, but the following week collects the supplies from Compass, who has not been told that Port has been sacked. Port makes off with the stationery. Is Starboard bound to pay?

3 When is a third party not bound by a contract with an undisclosed principal?

4 When is an agent entitled to delegate performance duties?

5 When will mental incapacity not bring the agency relationship to an end?

Answers to all quizzes can be found in Appendix 2.

Take a closer look

The following cases provide important examples of how the law you have studied in this chapter has developed. They are primary sources illustrating the law in action and give you more detail about their facts, as well as helping you to understand the law and to appreciate how the judges reached their decisions.

Try looking them up in the law reports or accessing them via a database, e.g. Bailli (www.bailii.org/databases.html). LexisNexis or Westlaw may be available in your university or college library, or you may find extracts in a case book. (See Appendix 1: Additional resources.)

Anglo Overseas Transport Ltd v *Titan Industrial Corpn* [1959] 2 Lloyd's Rep 152

Arensen v *Casson Beckman Rutley & Co.* [1977] AC 747

Quinn v *CC Automotive Group (t/a Carcraft)* [2010] EWCA Civ 1412

Sachs v *Miklos* [1948] 1 All ER 67

Web activity

Please go to: www.gov.uk/government/publications/register-a-lasting-power-of-attorney to find out more about this process.

Assignment 10

(a) 'If an agent is clothed with ostensible authority, no private instructions prevent his acts within the scope of that authority from binding his principal.' Discuss and illustrate this proposition.

(b) Patricia was part of a group that went on a two-year trip to search for lost tribes in the Amazon jungle. She left her cat, Tabitha, with her friend Brian and asked him to take good care of her and not to let her out in case she got lost. Six months after Patricia left, Tabitha managed to escape from Brian's house and was run over by a car and badly injured. Brian immediately took her to the vet who said that it would cost £4,000 to treat her. If treated, she stood a very good chance of full recovery, but the only other option was to put her to sleep.

Advise Brian on his legal responsibilities as Patricia's agent.

12

The law of agency

PART 3

The law of tort

CHAPTER 13

Tort liability for defective goods

Introduction

In this chapter we start to examine the law of tort, which is concerned with breaches of civil law that cause personal injuries, damage and interference to property and other sorts of personal loss. This, like the law of contract, is a crucial area of law for businesses which may be liable, not only to customers in a contractual relationship with them, but to a wide variety of other people affected much more tenuously by their business practices, products, the state of their premises and the conduct of their staff.

This chapter looks at liability in tort for defective products. To take a very simple example: a colleague buys sausage rolls from the bakers down the road from where you work to share with you at lunchtime. This kind gesture backfires, since they are contaminated with salmonella. As a result of eating your share you become very ill for three weeks, are unable to work and lose the commission you would normally make. Do you, as the consumer of the offending object, have a claim in law? You can't claim in contract since that area of law protects only the buyer of the defective goods. Other people harmed by the goods cannot generally sue in contract because of the lack of privity (a contractual relationship) between themselves and the seller.

However, you may sue in tort, since you are protected by the law of negligence, and selling contaminated food seems to indicate failure to observe hygienic processes in the bakery. You also have a claim under the Consumer Protection Act 1987 (CPA 1987), as the food is clearly defective. Which is the most effective claim for you?

You will be able to find the answers in this chapter.

Learning objectives

After studying this topic you should be able to:

▶ appreciate the relationship of the law of contract to tort liability for defective products;

▶ understand the scope of duty of care in negligence relating to defective products;

▶ grasp the difference between consequential and pure economic loss;

▶ know and be able to apply the main principles of the CPA 1987;

▶ distinguish between the circumstances where liability in negligence and/or the CPA 1987 may arise.

Negligence liability

The tort of negligence gives rights to persons who have suffered damage to themselves or to their property, against a party who has failed to take reasonable care for those persons' safety. Negligence is the commonest tort claim and is relevant to the whole gamut of accidental injury situations: for example, road accidents, illness and injuries caused by workplace conditions and harm arising through medical treatment. It also plays an important part in product liability: a person who suffers damage because of defects in a product, caused by the carelessness of the manufacturer or other party responsible for the state of the goods, may have a right to sue in negligence.

To be successful in a claim of negligence, the claimant must prove that:

Duty of care: a person undertaking an activity or course of behaviour owes a duty not to harm any person reasonably expected to be caused loss/ damage as a result.

1 the defendant owed the claimant a **duty of care**; and

2 the defendant failed to perform that duty; and

3 as a result, the claimant suffered damage.

1 The duty of care

The claimant must be able to show that he or she is someone who, in the circumstances, the defendant should have had in mind when embarking on the course of conduct which led to the alleged damage. This concept was established by the House of Lords in the following key case.

Donoghue v *Stevenson* (1932, HL)

Mrs Donoghue and a friend stopped for refreshment at a café one hot afternoon. The friend purchased from the proprietor some ginger beer manufactured by the defendant. This was supplied in stone bottles which were opened at the table. Having happily consumed a glassful, Mrs Donoghue tipped the bottle to make sure nothing was left; to her horror what appeared to be the decomposing remains of a snail slithered into her glass. She consequently became ill with gastro-enteritis and sued Stevenson (the manufacturer) in negligence.

Held (by a majority): the manufacturer did owe Mrs Donoghue a duty of care. As she was the user of its product, she was somebody who reasonably foreseeably would be affected by the way the manufacturer processed its product.

Lord Atkin stated:

> A manufacturer of products, which he sells in such a form as to show that he intends them to reach the ultimate consumer in the form in which they left him, with no reasonable possibility of intermediate examination and with the knowledge that the absence of reasonable care in the preparation or putting up of the products will result in an injury to the consumer's life or property, owes a duty of care to the consumer to take reasonable care.

In these consumer conscious days it comes as a surprise that prior to the decision in *Donoghue* v *Stevenson* a person in Mrs Donoghue's position had no rights in tort. Defective goods only gave rise to contract liability. Mrs Donoghue's friend could have sued but only to recover the cost of the drink, apart from that she had suffered no damage or loss and she could not claim reparation on behalf of Mrs Donoghue. Before 1932, liability in negligence for defective goods was restricted to harm caused by those products which were dangerous in themselves, such as guns or explosives. *Donoghue* v *Stevenson* established a general principle of product liability in negligence known sometimes as the '**neighbour principle**'. This is because Lord Atkin said that a duty was owed only to one's neighbour, which in law means: 'persons who are so closely and directly affected by my act that I ought reasonably to have them in my mind as being so affected when I am directing my mind to the acts or omissions called into question'

Neighbour principle: formulated in Donoghue v Stevenson by Lord Atkin indicating that the defendant only owes a duty of care to persons with sufficient proximity to him or her.

The scope and influence of Lord Atkin's judgment

Lord Atkin's judgment has had a huge impact on the civil law. The 'neighbour principle' has enabled successive judges to use it as a springboard for the development of negligence in *all* its forms, far removed from product liability. To understand its influence, it is necessary to analyse some of the terms used by Lord Atkin and see how they have been interpreted in later case law.

Manufacturer

The duty was soon extended from the maker of goods to those delivering services such as fitting and installing or repairing goods (see *Stennet* v *Hancock* (1939) below), and defendants with responsibility to check the goods prior to sale. Today it covers the whole range of products and service industries. (This aspect of duty is covered in greater depth in Chapter 14.)

Product

Case law illustrates that liability in negligence covers a huge variety of products in normal daily use for example, cars (*Herschtal* v *Stewart & Ardern Ltd* (1940)), computer software (*St Albans City Council* v *International Computers* (1996)), and includes some less likely items such as tombstones (*Brown* v *Cotterill* (1934)), and itchy underpants (*Grant* v *Australian Knitting Mills* (1936)).

Lord Atkin referred to the *'preparation or putting up of the products'* so the duty of care extends to the packaging and any instructions accompanying the product. The goods may be perfectly safe in themselves but become dangerous because inappropriately packaged, or because they do not carry correct instructions or a warning (e.g. medicines, weed-killer).

The ultimate consumer

Ultimate consumer: any person directly or indirectly harmed by a defective product or service.

Mrs Donoghue is the perfect example of an **ultimate consumer** – the actual user of the defective goods who is harmed by the defects, but who is not necessarily the buyer.

'Consumer' in this context has a very wide meaning, which extends beyond mere users of the goods or service. A consumer may be defined as someone reasonably likely to be affected by the goods in question. Consumers will be owed a duty, since the supplier should have taken their needs into account.

Barnett v *Packer* (1940)

A shop assistant laying out chocolates for display was injured by a wire protruding from one of them.

Held: the manufacturer owed a duty of care to the shop assistant, as well as to people who ate the goods, as anybody handling the chocolates could have suffered injury from this foreign body.

Even a bystander with no relationship to a party to the original transaction may come within the neighbour principle.

Stennett v *Hancock* (1939)

The claimant, a pedestrian, suffered a leg injury when he was hit by part of a wheel which came off a passing lorry.

Held: the garage which had recently negligently fitted the wheel owed a duty to the claimant, since it was reasonably foreseeable that any road user in the vicinity of the lorry could be harmed if a wheel became detached.

The limits of the duty of care

> ### *Marc Rich & Co. AG* v *Bishop Rock Marine* (1995, HL)
>
> The House of Lords held that, when deciding whether a duty of care exists in any negligence action, the court must take into account whether the following criteria are satisfied:
>
> 1 reasonable foreseeability;
>
> 2 proximity;
>
> 3 public interest taking into account fairness, justice and reasonableness.

These factors are interlinked and interdependent.

Reasonable foreseeability

Reasonable foreseeability: limits the scope of duty of care as this is owed only when it is reasonable to anticipate damage to the claimant.

No duty of care will exist unless it is **reasonably foreseeable** that the particular claimant was vulnerable to the risk created by the defendant. For example, in *Stennett* v *Hancock* (above) it was reasonably foreseeable that, if the lorry wheel was not securely fitted, an accident endangering any pedestrian in the vicinity might result.

Proximity

Proximity: a sufficiently close relationship must exist between claimant and defendant at the time the dangerous behaviour occurred for a duty of care to exist.

There must be a close enough relationship of **proximity** between the defendant's acts and the claimant at the time of the wrong complained of. Lord Atkin (*Donoghue* v *Stevenson*) stated that proximity was not restricted to 'mere physical proximity, but [should] be used . . . to extend to such close and direct relations that the act complained of directly affects a person whom the person bound to take care would know would be directly affected by his careless act'. The claimants in *Barnett* v *Packer* and *Stennett* v *Hancock* (above) provide good examples of such proximity. They both lacked close physical proximity but nonetheless stood to suffer from the negligence of the defendant.

In the following circumstances such *proximity* is lacking.

1 *The goods are no longer under the defendant's control.* The defendant ceases to have control if, prior to use, the goods have been tampered with or examined by a third party or claimant, in such a way as would probably cause or reveal a defect. Remember that in *Donoghue* v *Stevenson* the ginger beer was supplied to Mrs Donoghue in an opaque bottle which was opened in Mrs Donoghue's presence. There was no possibility that its unwanted inhabitant could have got there through the intervention of a third party. The bottle arrived at the table in the same state as when it left the manufacturer. The stone bottle prevented the hazard from being evident until its contents were removed.

2 *Too much time has elapsed since the product left the defendant.* Whether the goods have been used or not, it would be unfair to place the manufacturer under a duty for an indefinite time.

> ### *Evans* v *Triplex Safety Glass* (1936)
>
> Mr Evans bought a new Vauxhall car fitted by the manufacturer with a windscreen made of toughened safety glass manufactured by Triplex. One year later, he and his family were injured during a car journey when the windscreen shattered.
>
> **Held:** Triplex did not owe Evans a duty of care because:
>
> - any weakness in the glass might have been caused by Vauxhall when fitting the windscreen;
> - a defect might have been detectable on inspection by Vauxhall prior to fitting;
> - too much time had elapsed between the product leaving their control and the accident – the glass could have been weakened in use.

3 *The claimant has failed to take reasonable precautions prior to or when using the product.* A claimant must be able to show that the product has been used appropriately, in accordance with instructions.

Public interest

Public interest/policy: benefit of people in general. Influential on the court's decision to permit/refute a duty of care.

This criterion covers a wide range of circumstances involving what may be described as policy or **public interest** issues. A duty of care will not be acknowledged unless it is fair, just and reasonable to the parties but also not damaging to the interests of the public at large, however beneficial it might be to the individual claimant.

The court may refuse to develop the scope of negligence to provide a right of action already covered by an existing area of the law, or to develop the law so as to discourage people from taking reasonable precautions, such as insurance, to protect their own interests.

A duty may be developed because it will actively promote the *public interest*.

In *Donoghue* v *Stevenson*, public health considerations made it desirable to impose a duty, as well as the fact that Mrs Donoghue had no other legal rights to pursue. It was fair to put the loss on the manufacturer who stood to profit in general from his product.

In the news

No duty of care in negligence

OPO v *MLA* (2014, EWCA Civ)

The claimant OPO sought an interim injunction to prevent publication of a book in order to protect his young stepson. The book which was dedicated to the stepson was written by his biological father, a very successful performance artist. The book in part described the author's traumatic time at school where he suffered a lengthy period of sexual abuse leading to mental illness and self-harm.

The stepson suffered from Asperger's syndrome and related learning difficulties and the claimant argued that if he discovered the details of his father's past it was likely to cause him great emotional distress.

This argument was supported by psychiatric reports which stated that discovering this information would *'exert a catastrophic effect on [his] self-esteem and . . . cause him enduring psychological harm'*. However, the boy could gain knowledge of the book's contents without accessing a copy because of his access to the internet. A biography of his father was already available on Wikipedia and would be updated after publication of the book.

The injunction was sought on a number of grounds including negligence. It was defeated completely in the High Court and an appeal followed.

The Court of Appeal held: there was no duty of care in negligence in this case. A parent's duty towards their children is effectively the same as any other person's and is confined to situations where the parent is responsible for the supervision of the physical safety of their children. The High Court was correct in stating 'there is no authority for a general common law duty of parents, enforceable by injunction or compensatable in damages, to protect their children from emotional or psychological injury'.

It was not fair, just or reasonable to impose a duty which 'would encompass a whole range of commonplace activities in which a parent is involved in caring for his child' (Arden LJ).

[Note the use of initials: this is to ensure confidentiality which was deemed necessary to protect the child.]

Pure economic loss rarely gives rise to a duty of care

Pure economic loss:
loss of money alone, not arising from personal injury to the claimant or damage to other property.

The courts have not usually regarded it as just and reasonable to impose a duty of care where the defect results in **pure economic loss**. Such loss, which is derived from the goods being defective rather than dangerous, merely causes the claimant to be out of pocket. The courts treat such losses as contractual only as they relate only to the *quality* of the goods rather than any actively dangerous fault, which causes damage. However, this limitation is not helpful to a party who did not buy the goods from the defendant in the first place.

Real life

Horace was given an electric blanket for Christmas by his Aunt Betty, who bought it from Flash Electricals plc. The blanket was manufactured by Cosiwarm Ltd. Due to a production defect, it set fire to his bedroom on Christmas night with resulting damage to carpets and furniture. Horace was made ill due to smoke inhalation. He is entitled to claim damages from Cosiwarm Ltd which made the blanket for:

1 the pain and suffering caused by the smoke inhalation;

2 loss of earnings while he recuperated and the cost of replacing furnishings and decorating his bedroom

These are the knock-on costs from the damage caused by the defendant's negligence and are described as *consequential economic loss*.

Horace would not be entitled to recover the cost of replacing the defective electric blanket, which is categorised as *pure* economic loss; *the defect* does not of itself give rise to liability of the manufacturer in negligence. It is *the physical damage to person or other property* which imposes the duty. The lack of *quality* in the goods does not in itself give rise to negligence liability.

This difference between pure and **consequential economic loss** is also illustrated by the following case.

Muirhead v *Industrial Tank Specialities Ltd* (1986)

The claimant, who ran a lobster farm, was supplied with oxygen pumps manufactured by the defendant through a contract with a third party. The pumps proved to be incompatible with the English electricity system and kept cutting out. The claimant's lobsters died and he was unable to restock for a substantial period of time while he attempted to work out what was wrong.

Held: the claimant was entitled to recover the consequential cost of restocking the lobsters and for the loss of profits on those that died. He was not entitled to recover for profits lost during the time that lobster production was suspended, or the cost of replacing the pumps, since these were pure economic losses only.

Exceptionally, the claimant may be able to claim for pure economic loss if it can be shown that the claimant obtained the goods after having personally and directly consulted the manufacturers and placed reliance on their expertise. This creates a high degree of proximity between the parties, which is deemed to make it fair, just and reasonable to impose the duty.

Junior Books v *Veitchi* (1982, HL)

Junior Books made a contract for the construction of a warehouse. They told the building contractor that they wanted flooring to be supplied by the defendant, who was consequently a nominated sub-contractor. The flooring was so defective that the warehouse was unusable until the floor was replaced causing considerable expense.

Junior Books had no claim in contract as, by nominating Veitchi, Junior Books had relieved the building contractor of responsibility for the appointment, and no contract had been formed between Junior Books and Veitchi. Consequently, Junior Books claimed in negligence.

Held: the claimant's reliance on the defendant's expertise was sufficient to bring the parties into close proximity, and so a duty of care existed for the pure economic loss.

Consequential economic loss: financial loss resulting from injury to the claimant and/or damage to some property other than the defective product.

Veitchi was not applicable in the *Muirhead* case as Muirhead had not nominated the manufacturer to his supplier. The court usually takes the view that a contract between the claimant and supplier provides the appropriate route to compensation. The supplier should have been able to negotiate terms to give himself or herself adequate protection, or, if this is not workable, to insure against possible pure economic losses, such as business interruption. (The issue of duty of care for pure economic loss is explored further in Chapter 14.)

2 The claimant must prove breach of duty

It is not enough for the claimant to prove that the defendant owed them a duty of care. The claimant must prove that by objective standards the defendant failed to take reasonable care, i.e. did not provide a reasonable level of protection against reasonably foreseeable accidents. This includes taking into account the particular needs of a target group and giving adequate warning or instructions about the use of the product. For example, a soft-toy manufacturer must consider that baby and toddler users of its teddy bears may literally try to consume them. Thus, it must ensure that non-toxic materials are used and that the bears' eyes and noses are very firmly attached. (In the next chapter we will examine breach of duty in more detail and with regard to negligent service delivery.)

3 The claimant must prove consequential damage

Strict liability: exceptionally (as in claims under the CPA 1987) the claimant can succeed merely on proof that the tortious behaviour occurred and that damage resulted.

The claimant must also prove that it was the defendant's breach of duty which actually caused the damage suffered. In the story of Horace and the electric blanket outlined earlier, Horace would not be successful, despite proof of a defect in the blanket making it a fire risk, if there was evidence that the fire was actually caused by defective wiring in Horace's house.

Defendants are not necessarily liable for all the consequences of their behaviour: some may be deemed *too remote* from their original act. In negligence a defendant is generally liable for all reasonably foreseeable damage, but not for highly improbable or fluke results.

(The issues of breach and consequential damage are explored in greater depth in Chapter 14.)

The Consumer Protection Act 1987 (Part I)

The Consumer Protection Act 1987 Part 1 (CPA 1987), which was enacted to implement the EC Product Liability Directive (85/374/EC), has introduced a measure of **strict liability** for defective products into English law.

The difference between fault and strict liability

Fault liability: most tort actions require the claimant to prove that the defendant was at fault, i.e. acted intentionally, carelessly or without reasonable foresight.

Most torts, including negligence, are based on **fault liability**. The claimant has to prove not only that the defendant's behaviour broke the law and caused damage, but also that the defendant either intended to cause harm to the claimant, or was blameworthy in overlooking the risk to the claimant.

Strict liability is exceptional in tort. Where it exists the claimant is relieved of the need to prove any intent or carelessness on the part of the defendant; the claimant merely has to prove the causal link between the defendant's tortious behaviour and the damage suffered. This may increase the claimant's chances of a successful claim, as proof of failure to take care is often problematic.

Cases involving injuries caused by the side-effects of drugs like Thalidomide, which caused serious injuries to many unborn foetuses during the 1960s, raised public perception of the problems caused by fault liability and encouraged recommendations for reform from the Pearson Commission of 1978, as well as from judges and pressure groups. Successive governments ignored these recommendations, and change came only after intervention by the EC prompted the enactment of the CPA 1987.

As cases emerged some commentators perceived that the way in which the law was being interpreted seemed to provide no more protection for claimants than an action in negligence. This was a concern since the Product Liability Directive had indicated that its purpose was to enable claimants to avoid the need to prove fault by the defendant, thus overcoming one of the main obstacles to a successful claim. The Act (s 1) stated that it was intended to comply with the directive. The lack of successful claims prompted intervention from the EU.

European Commission v *UK* (1997, ECJ)

The Commission claimed that the UK was failing in its obligations to implement the purpose of the directive with respect to the concept of a defective product and the scope of the state of the art defence. This controversially protects a manufacturer who proves that current technical knowledge did not indicate any fault in the product.

Held: it was essential that the Act be construed in accordance with the purpose of the directive and that the directive must prevail in the event of conflict.

In the next case the judge constantly referred to the directive for assistance when interpreting the meaning of 'defective' and the scope of the state of the art defence.

A and Others v *National Blood Authority* (2001)

The claimants contracted Hepatitis C after being given transfusions of contaminated blood products supplied by the defendant.

Held: the product was defective under the Act. The claimants did not have to prove fault or negligence, merely that the product did not meet the reasonable expectations of the public to be safe for any foreseeable use. A reasonable person would expect that blood used for transfusion would not be infected.

Both the Act and the directive required the court to take into account 'all the circumstances attendant upon the reasonable person's expectations of safety'. These did not include the questions of whether the defendant could have avoided the danger, nor whether this would have been impracticable, costly or difficult.

The state of the art defence should be narrowly interpreted in order to avoid defeating the purpose of the directive. It only protects the defendant against unknown risks in the context of the most advanced available knowledge which should have been accessible to them when marketing the product.

The main provisions of Part I of the Consumer Protection Act 1987

Who may sue? s 2(1)

Any person suffering damage giving rise to liability under the Act to their person or property and resulting from defective goods has a right to claim.

Methods of supply: s 46

The goods may have been supplied by way of sale, barter, hire, prize or gift provided that the supplier was acting in the course of business.

Potential defendants: s 2

Section 2(1) provides that 'where any damage is caused wholly or partly by a defect in a product', the following persons shall be liable:

Producer: manufacturer/ processor.

1 *The producer*. This includes the manufacturer and persons responsible for winning or abstracting a product, for example, mineral water or electricity.

2 *The self-branding supplier or marker* 'who, by putting his name on the product or using a trade mark or other distinguishing mark in relation to the product has held himself out as the producer of the product'.

   So where goods are marketed under an 'own brand' label (like many supermarket goods), the business whose name appears on the label is likely to be treated as the producer. If the label indicates that the goods were manufactured by another producer ('produced for Sainsburys by X plc'), it may be arguable that the supplier is not the producer as they are not 'holding themselves out as the producer'.

Importer: first party to import the product into an EU country from a non-EU country.

3 *The importer*. The party who initially imported the product into the EU may be liable. (This is not necessarily the party responsible for the goods entering the UK.)

4 *The supplier*. Suppliers are liable only if they fail, on request from the injured party, to identify the manufacturer, producer or importer.

The meaning of 'product': s 1

Product: covers a wide variety of goods, including agricultural produce, utilities like water and gas, and even blood.

'**Product**' includes packaging and instructions and potentially covers a huge variety of manufactured and other goods and utilities.

1 *Manufactured products*. This includes components of another product. Although buildings are not goods, building components which become fixtures to the land like window frames or girders are 'products' under the Act.

2 *'Substances won or abstracted'*. This includes things like electricity and water.

3 Things which owe their 'essential characteristics' to an 'industrial or other process'. In *A and Others* v *National Blood Authority* (2001) blood and blood products supplied by the defendant were 'products' within the meaning of s 1 because they had

been subject to an industrial process. Anti-coagulants are mixed with blood on collection and it may be subject to other processes before storage.

4 Agricultural products like growing crops and game, which were not originally included have been covered since 2000 when the Act was amended by the Consumer Protection Act 1987 (Product Liability) (Modification) Order 2000 to implement Directive 99/34/EC.

It is unclear how far goods conveying information such as books and computer programmes are covered by the Act. It is possible for information transmitted in this form to cause harm through its defects. A book on fungi might incorrectly describe a species as edible, with disastrous consequences. There is medical evidence which suggests that some computer games may trigger fits and migraine. Unless and until such matters are conclusively determined by the courts, this will remain an uncertain area.

Causation and liability: s 2

The claimant must prove that the defect was the cause of the damage claimed. Since liability is strict the claimant does not have to prove that the defendant was careless, merely that the product comes within the statutory meaning of defective.

Defective means dangerous: s 3

The CPA is not concerned with the *quality* of the product but with its *safety*. Therefore, a product is not **defective** under the Act unless it is unsafe: there is no liability unless it actually causes damage to the consumer or the consumer's other property. The Act specifies the following factors to be relevant to determining safety:

Defective: goods dangerous physically to person/property.

1 *The packaging and any warnings or instructions*. A medicine may be perfectly safe in and of itself, but rendered dangerous because it lacks clear instructions or a warning that it is unsuitable for people with certain medical conditions.

2 *The normal uses of the product*. The needs of the relevant class of consumer must be taken into account in deciding whether the manufacturer has rendered the product safe. Toys marketed for use by small children require different safety standards, in relation to things like sharp edges, non-toxic materials and the size of removable parts, than goods for the entertainment of adults. If the consumer is harmed by use of the product for purposes which are not normal, liability does not arise. By indicating the purpose of a product and the age group for which it is intended, the manufacturer may limit the 'normal use' of the product.

3 *The time when the product was issued*. This is relevant to issues like shelf life, or situations where the product met appropriate standards of safety when issued but current research now indicates that those standards were not high enough.

The standard of safety under the Act is that which people 'generally are entitled to expect' which is actually set by the court rather than necessarily reflecting public expectation, which may be regarded as unreasonably high. The next two cases aptly illustrate this point.

Bogle and Others v McDonald's Restaurants Ltd (2002)

This case concerned a number of child litigants who had sustained scalding injuries after tea and coffee purchased from McDonald's had been spilt on them. Many of the injuries were serious involving severe pain and the need for skin grafts. However, in no case was the spillage directly caused by McDonald's staff but resulted from other restaurant users, or the claimant dropping or knocking over the drink.

The claimants argued that the hot drinks, a product of McDonald's, were defective because of the temperature at which they had been served and the mode of delivery, including the nature of the cups, lack of appropriate staff training and failure to give warning of the likelihood of scalding.

Held (Field J): McDonald's had not supplied a defective product under the CPA because:

1 Staff obtained very thorough training, with supervision in their first six months of training and regular assessment after that. This training included ensuring that tops were firmly attached to cups before handing them over to customers and giving a tactful warning about the danger of spillage where appropriate. The drinks were served at a temperature which customers would expect. Buyers of tea and coffee were usually people old enough to appreciate such risks and take precautions against them.

2 The cup design did not encourage spillage. A standard cup would only tip over at an angle of 20 degrees and a large one at 18 degrees. With the lid on, the contents would not spill if knocked over or dropped. Even if the lid was removed (to add sugar, for example), it was still effective when replaced.

3 'Persons generally expect tea or coffee purchased to be consumed on the premises to be hot. Many prefer to consume a hot drink from an unlidded cup rather than through a spout in the lid. Persons generally know that if a hot drink is spilt onto someone, a serious scalding injury can result. They accordingly know that care must be taken to avoid such spills, especially if they are with young children. Given that the staff were trained to cap the drinks securely and given the capabilities of the cups and lids used, I am satisfied that the safety of the hot drinks served by McDonald's was such as persons generally are entitled to expect.'

Tesco Stores Ltd and Another v Pollard (2006, CA)

The claimant, aged 13 months, was injured by consuming some dishwasher powder after he had managed to remove the 'child-proof' cap from the container, which did not meet the relevant British standard.

Held: Tesco was not in breach of the CPA, since the reasonable expectation test was satisfied since the bottle was harder to open than one with an ordinary screw top. It could reasonably be expected to defeat the attentions of so young a child who was unlikely to be unsupervised for long enough to get it open.

13

Tort liability for defective goods

Some products do have inherent risks attached to their use which cannot be entirely prevented, like power tools. Other products would require disproportionate expenditure to eliminate or reduce risk which would make them over expensive. Risk/benefit analysis is necessary in such cases to determine a reasonable standard.

Abouzaid v *Mothercare (UK) Ltd* (2000, CA)

The claimant, who was 12 years old, was blinded in one eye while attempting to attach the defendant's product (a Cosytoes sleeping bag) to his little brother's push chair. An elastic fastening strap sprang from his hand and the attached buckle struck his eye.

Held: the product was defective under s 3, since the reasonable expectations of the public that the product was safe to use were not satisfied, given the vulnerability of the eye and potential seriousness of such injuries. There was a risk attached to use of the product but no warning was given to the user to enable them to avoid the risk.

Defences

Under s 4 of the Act, the defendant will have a defence if able to show the following:

1 The goods comply with EC or UK safety standards and the defect is attributable to compliance with those standards.

2 The goods became defective after they were supplied. The defendant is liable only if the defect is present when the goods are put in circulation. If it arises later due to use or abuse by the consumer or a third party, the defendant is not liable because they did not cause the defect.

This may be a problematic area of proof for the claimant.

Piper v *JRI (Manufacturing) Ltd* (2006)

Mr Piper had a total hip replacement using a prosthesis made by JRI. Not long after it had been implanted it sheared in two and had to be removed and replaced, causing him increased loss of mobility, as well as the additional pain and suffering of undergoing more surgery.

He claimed that the prosthesis was defective under the CPA 1987. JRI argued that they were protected by s 4 as Mr Piper could not prove that a defect was present at the point the goods were released from the factory. They argued that the defect was more likely to have been caused when the prosthesis was implanted.

Held: Mr Piper's claim must fail as he was not able to prove that the defect arose from the production process. Defects arising during manufacture which might have weakened the prosthesis would most probably have been picked up by the scanning process used by the defendant to check the goods.

This may place a very heavy burden of proof on the claimant and endangers the principle of strict liability. It comes very close to requiring proof of negligence.

Worth thinking about?

Who else might Mr Piper consider claiming from?

Which tort would his claim be based on?

What problems might he have in proving the case?

Suggested solutions can be found in Appendix 2.

13

Tort liability for defective goods

The Court of Appeal gave some assistance to claimants in *Ide* v *ATB Sales* (2008) (below) by stressing that as the claim was made under the CPA there was no need to prove the nature of the defect, only that a defect was present and that the damage arose from that, and not some other competing cause. It was up to the judge to analyse the evidence and determine which, on the balance of probability, was the more likely cause.

Ide v *ATB Sales* (2008, EWCA)

The claimant was injured when the handles of his mountain bike snapped as he was riding over the South Downs. He claimed that this was due to a manufacturing defect and the defendant's expert witness argued that the snapping happened after he fell and was caused by the bike hitting either the ground or his body. The claimant was an experienced rider, the bike had been properly maintained and metallurgy tests indicated how the snapping could have arisen. The judge assessed the evidence and held that the more probable cause was an inherent defect.

The Court of Appeal affirmed the judge's decision saying that his reasoning regarding assessment of the evidence was entirely appropriate.

This was applied in *Hufford* v *Samsung Electronics (UK) Ltd* (2014) where the court held that the evidence that a fire arose from a defect in a freezer was a more probable cause than that claimed by the defendant, that it was caused by an improperly extinguished cigarette. The claimant was a smoker but always did so outside the house because of his parents' objections.

3 The 'state of the art/developments risk' defence. This is a special defence under the Act which potentially undermines the strict liability element. The defendant will not be liable if it can be shown that when the product was released the defendant had done all that was required to fulfil safety standards in accordance with current research and technological expertise, and in consequence the defect was not discoverable.

This defence is meant to be a safeguard for manufacturers of new products. It is argued that without it manufacturers fearful of litigation might restrict important new product development of great potential benefit to the public. However, this remains a controversial subject. The directive does not prohibit such defences and the approach of other EU countries varies. Prior to the Act, both the Law Commission (Law Com. 82) and the Pearson Commission rejected exemption from liability on the grounds of development risk. It is highly arguable that a drug like Thalidomide could slip through the liability net through the use of this defence. No such defence is available under the law of contract and it can be argued that with appropriate insurance a manufacturer can protect itself against liability. The need to interpret the defence in accordance with a purposeful application of the directive was stressed in *A* v *National Blood Authority* (2001) (above).

4 The defendant did not at any time supply the product to another in the course of business.

Contributory negligence and consent are also relevant. (These are examined at the end of Chapter 15.)

Actionable damage: s 5

This covers death, personal injuries and damage to property (including land) which the claimant is *not* using for business purposes. A claim for property damage must be for at least £275; there is no upper limit.

Since pure economic loss is not recoverable, the cost of replacing or repairing the defective item cannot be claimed. The same principles apply here as in negligence.

Time limits

Under the Limitation Act 1980, s 11A, claimants must take action within three years of the date when they first became aware of the damage, the defect, and the identity of the defendant. There is a final cut-off date of 10 years from the date on which the product was supplied to the claimant and no action can be started after that time.

Liability for defective products is summarised in Figure 13.1.

Real life

Horace was injured and suffered damage to his property when an electric blanket, manufactured by Cosiwarm and which was a present from his Aunt Betty, caught fire on its first use. As well as a claim in negligence, Horace also has a claim under the CPA 1987, as his losses certainly exceed the £275 minimum.

Cosiwarm, the manufacturer, is liable as producer under the CPA 1987 if the blanket is proven to be defective. Even if Cosiwarm is not clearly identifiable as producer of the blanket, it may still be best to claim under the CPA, as this may give Horace more flexibility in his choice of defendant.

Flash Electricals, from which Aunt Betty bought the blanket, would be the 'marker', if the blanket was marketed as Flash's own brand. If there is no label saying who the producer is, Flash may still be personally liable as 'supplier' unless it identifies the producer. Even if Flash merely imported the blanket, it could still be sued as 'importer' if it obtained the goods directly from any country outside the EU.

As long as he can prove that the electric blanket was defective and actually caused the fire, he will be successful and will not have to prove failure to take reasonable care as the CPA 1987 imposes strict liability.

Area of law	Contract	Tort	Tort
	Sale of Goods Act 1979 (SGA 1979) Supply of Goods and Services Act 1982 (SGA 1982)	Negligence	Consumer Protection Act 1987
Who can sue?	Buyer only	Injured party (ultimate consumer)	Injured party
Who can be sued?	Seller	Manufacturer of goods Servicer of goods Supplier – if duty to inspect	Producer of product Manufacturer Own-brand labeller Importer Supplier
What must be proved?	Goods – breach of SGA 1979, ss 13, 14, 15 Goods and services – breach of CPA 1987, ss 4, 5 Goods – like SGA 1979 SGSA 1982 Services – lack of reasonable care and skill, reasonable timeliness, reasonable charging	(i) Duty of care (ii) Breach of duty (iii) Consequent damage	(i) Product defective and unsafe (ii) Damage suffered as a result
Damage compensated	Any loss or damage to buyer as long as not too remote, including purchase price	Any loss or damage to injured party as long as not too remote; excluding purchase price and other pure economic loss	Death/personal injury Damage to land, goods (over £275)
Liability	Goods – strict Services – fault Civil only	Fault Civil only	Strict Criminal liability also possible under CPA 1987, Part II

Figure 13.1 Liability for defective products

The impact of the Consumer Protection Act 1987

After a disappointing start, judicial interpretation in the light of the original directive, has provided a more level playing field for the consumer who is the party which the directive was aiming to assist. It can also be seen as a sensible loss distribution system since the losses of the claimant are made the responsibility of the manufacturer that sought to make a profit from its product. The manufacturer is not unreasonably burdened as the losses are insurable and that cost is passed on to the consumers.

13

Tort liability for defective goods

Chapter summary

A person harmed by a defective product may claim in:

(a) *breach of contract* against the seller (provided claimant purchased the goods); or

(b) *tort* (negligence/CPA 1987, Part 1).

Negligence

Defendant: the manufacturer.

Claimant must prove: duty (owed by manufacturer to ultimate consumer of the goods), breach (failure to take reasonable care), resulting damage.

Liability: based on fault: proof of failure to take reasonable care.

Compensation covers personal injury and all consequential economic loss. Generally, pure economic loss cannot be recovered.

The CPA

Claimant: any person harmed by the product.

Defendant: producer/'own brand' provider/supplier/importer.

Liability: strict. Claimant must prove that the product is dangerous (does not conform to reasonable public expectation of safety) and caused the relevant damage.

Claims are limited to those over £275. Pure economic loss is never recoverable.

Quiz 12

1 What must a claimant in an action for negligence prove?

2 In an action for negligence, what factors are important to proof of duty of care?

3 What circumstances may bring a duty of care for defective goods to an end?

4 Basil buys a pork pie from Tarragon Stores. The pie was manufactured by Marjoram Foods.

Basil shares the pie with Rosemary and they both become ill. What are the civil law rights of Basil and Rosemary?

5 What are the main differences between liability for negligence and liability under the Consumer Protection Act 1987?

Answers to all quizzes can be found in Appendix 2.

Take a closer look

The following cases provide important examples of how the law you have studied in this chapter has developed. They are primary sources illustrating the law in action and give you more detail about their facts, as well as helping you to understand the law and to appreciate how the judges reached their decisions.

Try looking them up in the law reports or accessing them via a database, e.g. Bailli (www.bailii.org/databases.html). LexisNexis or Westlaw may be available in your university or college library, or you may find extracts in a case book. (See Appendix 1: Additional resources.)

Donoghue v *Stevenson* [1932] AC 562, HL

Junior Books v *Veitchi* [1983] 2 All ER 301, HL

A v *National Blood Authority* [2001] 3 All ER 289

Network Rail Infrastructure Ltd v *Conarken Group Ltd and Another* [2010] EWHC 1852; [2010] TCC 132

Web activity

Please go to: http://en.wikipedia.org/wiki/Donoghue_v_Stevenson

Scroll down to find links to a full law report, and explore the site to uncover some interesting background information to the case.

Assignment 11

Florence visits a supermarket with her daughter Daisy, aged eight. A promotion for Funny Mug face paints is taking place and children are being offered a free make-over. Florence lets Daisy take part. Florence buys some frozen puff pastry and a bag of mixed salad leaves that bears a notice saying 'Wash thoroughly before consumption'. Then she visits the deli counter to buy some ham for Edwina, her elderly next-door neighbour. When she gets home an hour later she immediately delivers the ham to Edwina and puts the puff pastry in her freezer in accordance with the instructions on the packet. She uses the leaves to make a salad for tea for herself and her husband, Gordon.

That evening, Florence and her husband, Gordon, become ill from bacteria in the salad.

Next day, Daisy develops an allergic rash, which her doctor says is caused by the face paints.

Later in the week, Edwina contracts salmonella poisoning which is traced to the ham.

A month later, Florence retrieves the puff pastry from the freezer and defrosts it. When she rolls it out, she discovers that it smells strongly of petrol and is therefore unusable.

Discuss the remedies available to Daisy, Edwina, Florence and Gordon.

CHAPTER 14

Tort liability for defective services

Introduction

This chapter is divided into two parts. The first part is concerned with duty of care in negligence for defective services and includes analysis of some other problematic duty of care situations outside the traditional scope of negligence liability. The second part is concerned with breach of duty and causation.

As indicated in the previous chapter, under *Donoghue* v *Stevenson* principles, any third party reasonably likely to be affected by the workmanship of a service provider is clearly owed a duty of care in negligence if he or she directly suffers personal injury or damage to property. A central heating engineer, therefore, will owe a duty to people in a building who suffer carbon-monoxide poisoning from the system which the engineer negligently installed.

Sometimes there may be a large pool of potential claimants. The garage which services your car owes a duty of care to carry out the work safely not only to you, but to your passengers as well as other road users and pedestrians in the vicinity of your vehicle when it is in use. However, the law is unwilling to make defendants vulnerable to every possible claim of damage resulting from their negligent behaviour. Liability in negligence is greatly restricted by the courts in some situations. The problem of recovering pure economic loss was mentioned in the preceding chapter. There are also a number of other problematic duty situations relevant relating to negligent statements, shock-induced injuries, liability for damage caused by third parties and the exercise of statutory discretion by public authorities such as local councils and the police.

Proof of duty alone does not guarantee a successful claim. If you bring a negligence action, you must also prove that the defendant breached the duty by failing to take reasonable care and that you suffered damage as a result, which is not too remote.

Learning objectives

After studying this chapter you should be able to:

▶ recognise the relationship from which a duty of care for pure economic loss may arise;

▶ decide when a duty of care arises for negligent statements;

▶ appreciate the scope of nervous shock liability;

▶ describe when a duty exists for omissions and third-party acts;

▶ understand when a public authority may be liable in negligence when exercising statutory discretion;

▶ explain the circumstances when a breach of duty of care may occur;

▶ distinguish between causation in fact and in law;

▶ be able to apply the rules of remoteness of damage.

Part 1: problematic duty situations

As will be seen in this chapter, the tort of negligence has traditionally covered claims for death, personal injury and damage to property. In claims of this sort the existence of duty of care is not in doubt. In *Caparo* v *Dickman* (1990, HL) Lord Oliver said: 'the existence of a nexus of duty between the careless defendant and the injured plaintiff can rarely give rise to any difficulty', and in *Sandhar* v *Department of Transport* (2004) May LJ affirmed this: 'Personal or physical injury directly inflicted is the first building block of negligence . . . it will almost always be a component of breach of duty of care owed by the person inflicting the injury to the person or owner of the material object injured.'

However, although the law of negligence today embraces liability for less traditionally recognised types of damage and their cause, the courts are wary of imposing liability in these less traditional areas. The criteria relevant to existence of duty (reasonable foreseeability, proximity, justice and reason) may be stringently applied. In order to limit the scope of duty to make it just and reasonable, the court may take a very restricted view of what is reasonably foreseeable and require proof of a very close relationship of proximity. Policy issues (whether it is just and reasonable to impose a duty) often underpin such judgments even if not expressly mentioned by the judge.

Pure economic loss

Negligence liability does not usually arise from the poor *quality* of a service, but from the *physical damage* to people and property caused by it. Any purely financial loss arising from defective performance is not generally recoverable, as indicated by the decisions in *Spartan Steel Alloys* v *Martin* (1972, CA) and *Murphy* v *Brentwood Council* (1990, HL) (below).

Distinguishing between consequential and pure economic loss

Students initially studying this area often find it difficult to tell consequential from pure economic loss. Judges usually just talk about 'economic loss' without clearly indicating what sort they mean and leave you to work it out from the context. It may help you to think about this in terms of the cost of the damage to the claimant and their goods caused by the defendant's product or service (consequential economic loss) as opposed to a loss of money alone, which is often related to future and possibly notional income (pure economic loss).

Pure economic loss caused by negligent acts

The next case clearly evidences the courts' reluctance to allow negligence claims for pure economic losses.

Pride & Partners v *Institute for Animal Health* (2009)

Held: the defendants were liable for the consequential financial losses to farmers whose stock were culled as a result of a foot and mouth disease outbreak, which was caused by the virus escaping from the Institute. However, claims by other farmers who suffered purely financial losses due to the movement restriction orders, such as reduced milk production and extra feeding costs, were struck out. Tugendhat J acknowledged that claims for lost market value, caused by stock losing condition due to delayed sales, were potentially consequential losses, but would still not succeed because they were only an indirect consequence of the defendants' negligence.

The next case provides a helpful example of how to distinguish between the two different types of economic loss and illustrates some of the many ways used by judges to avoid liability in this area.

Spartan Steel Alloys v *Martin Ltd* (1972, CA)

Early one morning the negligent operation of a power shovel outside the claimant's steelworks resulted in a power cut which put its furnace out of action for the rest of that day. The metal, which had been in the furnace when the power was cut off, was spoilt and no further consignments could be processed that day.

Held: the claimant was entitled to damages for the cost of the spoilt metal and for the profit which would normally have been made on its sale in good condition as this was a directly consequential loss. However, the claim for the lost profits on the melts which could not be processed that day must fail, as it was purely economic loss and did not result from any damage to the claimant's property.

Lord Denning said: 'at bottom I think the question of recovering economic loss is one of policy. Whenever the courts draw a line to mark out the bounds of duty, they do it as a matter of policy so as to limit the liability of the defendant.'

Lord Denning held that no duty of care existed concerning the unprocessed melts because:

1 It would be unfair to impose a duty on the defendants since statutory providers of electricity and other utilities enjoy exemption from liability for pure economic loss arising from interruption of supply.

2 Such interruption is well known and commonplace. Most people temporarily deprived of electricity supply 'do not go running round to their solicitor. 'They may insure against possible losses or install a back-up generator as a precaution 'or make up the economic loss by doing more work the next day. This is a healthy attitude which the law should encourage'.

3 A huge number of claims would arise if a duty existed in this situation 'some might be genuine, but many might be inflated or even false . . . it would be well-nigh impossible to check the claims'.

4 It would place an unreasonable burden on the contractor. 'The risk of economic loss should be suffered by the community who suffer the losses, usually many but comparatively small losses rather than . . . on the contractor on whom the total of them . . . might be very heavy.'

5 'The law provides for deserving cases', i.e. those where physical damage results to the claimant or material property.

Should the claimant have been insured?

While you may sympathise with the claimant in *Spartan Steel*, it is important to understand that in many cases of pure economic loss insurance plays a part, as Lord Denning indicates. Business interruption insurance is readily available to the likes of Spartan Steel. No doubt Martin carried insurance too, but the court tends to take the view that the claimant should carry the risk in situations where it expects them to be insured, to prevent too great a burden being placed on the defendant. Something else to bear in mind is that prior to litigation the claimant will often have made a successful claim on their own insurance and then their insurers take the case in the insured's name to recover what was paid out. The court is unlikely to feel that it is fair to allow the insurers to recoup a loss that may well have been more than covered by insurance premiums.

Murphy v *Brentwood Council* (1990, HL)

The claimant's newly built house subsided when the foundations turned out to be defective. As a result, he had to sell the house for £35,000 less than its proper market value. He claimed that the local authority building inspection department had been negligent in its checks on the foundations.

Held: the house was defective, but no personal injuries had been caused to Mr Murphy and none of his property had been damaged. Therefore, the local authority did not owe a duty of care to the claimant, since his only loss was purely economic: only the diminution on the value of the house was affected.

There was insufficient proximity between the parties, since it was not reasonably foreseeable to the council that Mr Murphy would place reliance on its checks which were carried out in order to comply with the building regulations to safeguard public health rather than protect the financial position of future home owners. No liability in tort would rest on a builder for damage to someone like Mr Murphy who had no contractual relationship or other sufficiently proximate relationship and it would be unfair to impose liability on the council which was less directly involved. It also was not just and reasonable to burden local taxpayers with homeowners' financial losses in such circumstances. Lord Oliver said: 'I am not sure that I see why the burden should fall on the community at large rather than be covered by private insurance.'

Again, in *Murphy* the issue of policy is extremely influential and the issue of personal insurance is relevant to determining what is fair, just and reasonable. Many of us would rather see our council tax being used on public services rather than assisting individual home owners. However, as consumer groups afterwards pointed out, normal buildings insurance does not cover structural problems which arise from defective materials or workmanship, but only those caused by natural phenomena like drought or geological features.

Is there an alternative remedy?

The court may be unwilling to expand the boundaries of negligence liability if the claimant could have pursued compensation by another established route.

Home owners may be able to sue under the Defective Premises Act 1972 (DPA). Section 1(1) imposes a duty on 'any person taking on work in connection with the provision of a dwelling . . . to see that the work is done in a workmanlike . . . or professional manner . . . so that the dwelling will be fit for human habitation when completed'. This covers pure economic loss but was no help to Mr Murphy as his claim arose after the six-year limitation period had elapsed.

Property bought subject to a transferable guarantee from the builder who constructed or substantially renovated it is also protected. Such compensation schemes provide more generous terms than the DPA. Claims can be made by the buyer and subsequent purchasers for the lifetime of the guarantee, so no contractual relationship with the builder is required.

A high degree of proximity between the parties is crucial in pre-economic loss claims

In *White* v *Jones* (1995, HL) (below) the claimants were successful in their pursuit of a lost inheritance as the House of Lords acknowledged that there was a very close relationship between them and the defendant.

White v *Jones* (1995, HL)

An elderly man, after a quarrel with his two daughters, cut them out of his will. Three months later he forgave them and informed his solicitor that he wished to make a new will under which the daughters were each to be given a legacy of £9,000. Two months after giving his instructions he died, before the solicitor completed the necessary work. Due to this negligent delay, the daughters did not receive their inheritance. They successfully sued the solicitor.

Held: the solicitor was brought into a special relationship of close proximity with the sisters. By agreeing to draft the will, he was deemed voluntarily to have accepted the responsibility for ensuring the creation of a valid will. It was reasonably foreseeable that any potential beneficiary would suffer pure economic loss if the will was invalid.

Note the different but equally valid criteria applied by the House of Lords for determining proximity in these cases:

- *Murphy* v *Brentwood Council*: reasonable reliance by the claimant;
- *White* v *Jones*: voluntary assumption of responsibility by the *defendant*.

The *White* v *Jones* approach is more realistic, where the defendant is asked by a third party to do something which affects the well-being of a claimant, who is unaware of the request and so cannot realistically be said to be placing reliance on the defendant.

In some cases both factors may be present (see, for example, Hedley Byrne v Heller, below).

West Bromwich Albion FC v *El-Safty* (below) indicates that a special relationship requires clear evidence that the defendant actually assumed responsibility for very specific consequences to make it reasonably foreseeable that the claimant is likely to rely upon it.

West Bromwich Albion Football Club Ltd v *El-Safty* (2007)

Michael Appleton damaged his knee during a training session with the claimant club. His contract required him to be treated by one of the medical advisers employed by the club's insurance scheme. The defendant was a service provider to the insurers and his fees in respect of the treatment were settled by that company. The defendant negligently recommended reconstructive surgery and as a result Appleton became unable to play professional football. Had the appropriate conservative treatment been carried out, he would have been match fit within four months.

As a result, the club claimed that they had lost millions for the loss of Appleton's services, including the expense of finding a replacement and covering the costs of his lost salary.

Held: the defendant did not owe a duty of care to the claimant for these losses. He was paid under the insurance scheme to treat WBA's players, not to advise it about its players' treatment or its financial affairs. No special relationship existed between the claimant and defendant as the defendant had not assumed responsibility to the claimant for this type of loss. Also it was not fair, just and equitable to impose a duty in these circumstances.

Negligent statements

In principle, there is no difference between liability arising from negligent statements and from negligent acts. A party may suffer physical damage by reliance on incorrect advice just as he or she may be injured by other negligent conduct.

T v *Surrey County Council* (1994)

T was injured by the actions of a child-minder whom the defendant council had negligently recommended to his mother.

Held: the council owed a duty of care to T. By advising his mother, the council had been brought into close relationship to T, and it was reasonably foreseeable that he would be affected by the quality of the advice acted upon by his mother.

Special relationship: essential to liability for pure economic loss claims in negligence The claimant reasonably places a high degree of reliance on the defendant's knowledge or expertise.

In practice, the duty is generally limited because a negligent statement has the potential to have more far-reaching effects than a negligent act. One snail-infested bottle of ginger beer will poison only one or two people, but a negligent statement may affect thousands and its effects may be long-lasting. The courts are not willing to make the defendant liable to potential claims from a large and unidentifiable class of persons, for an indefinable period of time.

Duty of care for negligent statement covers both pure and consequential economic loss

The duty arises from the claimant's close relationship to or reliance on the defendant. In *Hedley Byrne* (below) the relationship was described variously as a '**special relationship**', or '**quasi-fiduciary**' in character and 'akin to contract'.

Hedley Byrne v *Heller* (1963, HL)

A firm called Easipower entered into a contract with the claimant, an advertising agency, to book advertising on TV and the national newspapers on terms which made the claimant personally liable for the cost if their client defaulted. Satisfied by an initial reference from Easipowers's bank the claimant went ahead. Three months later it sought further reassurance asking whether Easipower could be relied on 'to the extent of £100,000 per annum'. The bank replied repeating its initial statement that it believed Easipower 'to be respectably constituted and good for its normal business engagements', but adding 'your figures are larger than we would normally expect to see'. The reference was headed 'Confidential. For your private use and without responsibility on the part of this bank or its officials.' Reliant on this, the claimant continued to work for Easipower, but lost over £17,000 when it went into liquidation. The claimant sued the defendant bank for giving negligent advice.

Held: the defendant did not owe a duty of care to the claimant because of the disclaimer. However, in the absence of an effective disclaimer, a duty not to make a careless statement which causes pure economic loss might exist, provided that a special relationship of close proximity 'akin to contract' existed between the parties.

Quasi-fiduciary: describes a relationship involving a high degree of trust, though not a fiduciary relationship as such.

The criteria determining existence of a 'special relationship'

This relationship which is essential to success in *all* pure economic loss claims in negligence must satisfy certain criteria.

Proximity

The parties must have been brought sufficiently into a close relationship of proximity with each other. A high degree of trust will be involved. This relationship may arise in a number of ways:

1 *The statement may be made directly to the claimant by the defendant.*

This is illustrated by the facts of *Hedley Byrne* v *Heller*.

2 *The statement may be made to a third party who passes it on to the claimant.*

Smith v *Eric S. Bush* (1989, HL)

The defendant surveyors' valuation report prepared for a building society was shown with their knowledge to the claimant buyer. In reliance on this Ms Smith bought the property.

Held: the defendant owed a duty of care to the claimant since she could reasonably be expected to rely on the advice.

(For more detail see Chaper 7.)

3 *The statement may be made to a third party who relies upon it thus causing consequent loss to the claimant.*

Spring v *Guardian Assurance* (1994, HL)

The claimant had worked for the defendant insurance company but was made redundant. He applied for a job with Scottish Amicable. LAUTRO (the regulatory organisation for insurance companies) requires a reference from a previous employer for applicants to such jobs. The reference was described by the trial judge as 'so strikingly bad as to amount to . . . the kiss of death to his career in insurance. Scottish Amicable wanted no truck with the man it described.' This slur on his character was completely unwarranted so the claimant sued the defendant in negligence in preparation of the reference.

Held (by majority): the defendant owed a duty of care to the claimant under the *Hedley Byrne* principle. It had special knowledge of the claimant's character, skill and diligence evidenced by the way he had worked while employed by it. The defendant had assumed responsibility to the claimant by giving the reference to Scottish Amicable and the claimant had relied upon it to compose the reference with reasonable care and skill.

Reasonable reliance and assumption of responsibility

It must have been reasonable for the claimant to rely on the statement and thus reasonably foreseeable to the defendant that reliance would be placed. The defendant will then be taken to have responsibility.

These factors usually form two sides of the same coin, but note *White* v *Jones* (above), which indicates that the circumstances may be such that the defendant will be assumed to have taken responsibility even though the claimant may not at that time have placed reliance upon it.

In *Hedley Byrne v Heller* (1963), the House of Lords indicated criteria helpful to establishing when reliance can reasonably be placed.

1 *The defendant's ability to give reliable advice.* Specialist knowledge, professional qualifications or other expertise are all relevant.

2 *The circumstances in which the advice was given.* Specialist advice cannot reasonably be relied on when given off the cuff, or on a purely social occasion. Even if given in a business context, it may not be reasonable to rely on it if it is given without proper checks on relevant data.

3 *Disclaimer or condition.* If the defendant indicates expressly or impliedly that the advice should not be relied upon, this may make the claimant's reliance unreasonable and, therefore, not reasonably foreseeable. In *Hedley Byrne* v *Heller* a **disclaimer** by the bank was a factor preventing imposition of a duty of care. Today the Unfair Contract Terms Act 1977, s 2(1) makes it impossible to exclude liability for negligence for death or personal injuries so specific disclaimer is not necessarily effective protection for the defendant. However, liability for negligence may be excluded for other damage or loss if reasonable (UCTA, s 2(2)). (See Chapter 8.)

> **Disclaimer:** a statement by which a party seeks to avoid liability for the consequences of negligent advice or behaviour.

Even if no disclaimer is given, any doubt raised by the way the advice is worded – for example, statements like 'as far as I know', or 'if performance reflects last year', or 'without checking my figures', or 'you might want a second opinion' – may make it unreasonable for the claimant to rely upon the defendant.

Restriction of the *Hedley Byrne* principle

In *Hedley Byrne* and the other cases we have so far examined, the only person likely to be harmed was the claimant him or herself. In *Caparo* v *Dickman* (1990) **(facts below)** the court was confronted for the first time by a statement issued to the public. This necessitated restriction of the *Hedley Byrne* principle to prevent a defendant from being potentially liable to a large and unascertainable group of people. The House of Lords held that no duty of care arises unless the following conditions are satisfied:

1 when the advice was given the defendant must reasonably have anticipated what it would be used for (e.g. *Caparo Industries plc* v *Dickman* (1990, HL);

2 the defendant must reasonably have known the destination of that advice – a specific (not necessarily named) individual, or a member of a clearly ascertainable group (e.g. *Caparo Industries plc* v *Dickman* (1990, HL));

3 the defendant must reasonably have anticipated that the advice would be acted upon without the claimant seeking further clarification or independent advice (e.g *James McNaughten Paper Group Ltd* v *Hicks Anderson & Co.* (1991, CA).

It must be just and reasonable to impose a duty

You may find some apparently conflicting case decisions in this area. This is because the courts may interpret the concepts of proximity and foreseeability more strictly in some cases than others in order to prevent the duty of care from developing in ways that are perceived not to be in the public interest. While glad to assist a vulnerable consumer like Ms Smith (see above) without many financial resources, the courts do not wish to encourage a lack of responsibility in economically powerful parties with access to independent advice, particularly those pursuing a speculative deal with high stakes, as in *Caparo* v *Dickman* (1990) (see below).

Similarly, remember that if alternative legal remedies are available, a right of action in negligence may be perceived to be redundant, even though the other remedies may not be applicable to the particular claimant due to the particular circumstances of the case.

The following cases illustrate the operation of some of the Caparo criteria.

Caparo Industries plc v *Dickman* (1990, HL)

The claimant company owned shares in Fidelity plc. The defendants were the accountancy firm which had audited the annual accounts. These negligently stated that Fidelity had profits of £1.3 million; it had actually made a loss of over £465,000. The claimant increased its shareholding and later made a successful takeover bid. It then discovered that its acquisition was much less valuable than it had been led to believe by the accounts.

Held: no duty of care was owed to the claimant. The purpose for which the information was given was crucial here. The accounts were to enable shareholders to decide how to vote at the annual general meeting, not to give them personal investment advice.

If a duty was imposed, it would protect not only the shareholders but potential buyers on the open market, thus creating potential liability to a diffuse group of people which would not be appropriate.

James McNaughten Paper Group Ltd v *Hicks Anderson & Co.* (1991, CA)

No duty was owed by accountants to a company director for whom they prepared draft accounts for consideration prior to a takeover bid.

Held: the defendant was not liable because it was not reasonably foreseeable that the claimant would rely on the draft accounts, particularly as he had access to expert advice to evaluate them. The defendant was also aware that the accounts had been swiftly compiled in draft form, providing a guide to the company's financial health rather than a definitive statement.

Compare the two decisions above with the following:

Morgan Crucible Co. plc v Hill Samuel Bank (1991, CA)

The claimants' takeover bid was made in reliance on a profit forecast issued to them by the defendant company. The defendant accountants and bank stated that this had been made in accordance with the company's accounting procedures, after full and careful enquiry.

Held: the defendants were liable. They had intended the claimants to rely on the information when making the bid, which they had done. The claimants' reliance was reasonable since, although they had independent advice, much of the information was available only to the defendants and could not be independently verified.

See also *Smith* v *Eric S. Bush* (1989) (described in Chapter 7).

Most of the reported cases on negligent statement concern pure economic loss; the next one concerns a personal injuries claim.

T v Surrey County Council (1994)

T was a small baby. His mother consulted the council to check on the suitability of a registered child-minder. The council failed to tell T's mother that previously a young baby had been brain-damaged while in the minder's care and, although there was no conclusive evidence against her, it had been suggested that she should in future only look after children over two years old. T subsequently suffered severe brain damage when shaken violently by the child-minder.

Held: the council owed a duty of care to T since it had given advice directly relevant to his safety and thus created a relationship of sufficient proximity. The council should reasonably have foreseen that the advice, which came from one of their professional officers with special knowledge, would be relied upon. If incorrect, it would clearly jeopardise T's safety.

Although the judge in the above case said that a *Hedley Byrne* relationship existed in this case, where physical rather than pure economic loss has occurred it is sufficient that a straight-forward analysis of *Donoghue* v *Stevenson* principles is applied. In *Clay* v *Crump* (1963) the defendant architect was held liable to workers on a demolition site injured after a wall, which he had negligently stated was stable, collapsed on to them. It was held that it was reasonably foreseeable to the defendant that the workmen would be endangered if his advice was incorrect.

Interesting and as yet unsolved questions of liability are raised by specialist information on financial and legal issues broadcast to the public on radio and TV programmes and published in some periodicals. There are also books which claim to help you to do your own conveyancing, or to make a will. Here the large class of potential claimants which exists might make the courts unwilling to entertain claims. On the other hand, such publications often encourage reliance on the given information by offering help and suggesting that this will be provided by experts. The more focused

14

Tort liability for defective services

such information is (e.g. one-to-one on a radio phone-in), the greater the likelihood of a duty arising unless an appropriate and effective disclaimer is given.

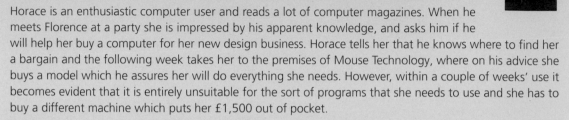

Real life

Horace is an enthusiastic computer user and reads a lot of computer magazines. When he meets Florence at a party she is impressed by his apparent knowledge, and asks him if he will help her buy a computer for her new design business. Horace tells her that he knows where to find her a bargain and the following week takes her to the premises of Mouse Technology, where on his advice she buys a model which he assures her will do everything she needs. However, within a couple of weeks' use it becomes evident that it is entirely unsuitable for the sort of programs that she needs to use and she has to buy a different machine which puts her £1,500 out of pocket.

Horace may unwittingly have made himself liable to Florence by taking her under his wing. Although he is not an expert in the relevant technology, he has held himself out as having that knowledge and a Hedley Byrne relationship has been held to exist in non-business relationships. In *Chaudhry v Prabhakar* (1988) amateur advice on buying a secondhand car gave rise to liability. However, unlike Ms Chaudhry, Florence was present when the computer was purchased and could have checked the advice with a shop assistant, so her reliance on Horace might well not be regarded as reasonable.

Nervous shock (psychiatric harm)

Nervous shock: psychiatric or physical harm caused by the shock of being involved in or witnessing an accident caused by the defendant's negligence.

Primary victim: nervous shock victim directly endangered by the defendant's negligence.

A duty of care readily exists where the claimant has suffered physical injury from the defendant's careless behaviour. It may be harder to establish a duty of care when the claimant suffers illness induced by acute shock or distress caused by the defendant. Damages are *not* recoverable for the *actual shock or distress*, but liability may arise from the *medically recognisable* illness or condition triggered by it. Such illness could be physical, like a heart attack, but most recent claims concern psychiatric conditions like post-traumatic stress syndrome.

In *Page* v *Smith* (see below) the House of Lords held that the rules determining duty of care for **nervous shock** are different according to whether the claimant is categorised as a **primary** or a **secondary victim** of the accident caused by the defendant. Primary victims were defined as those directly involved in the accident, who, as a result, have been physically hurt or reasonably put in fear for their own safety.

Dulieu v *White* (1901)

The defendant negligently failed to control his horse and cart, which demolished the wall of the pub where the claimant was working as a barmaid. She managed to shelter from the shower of masonry and was not directly hurt. Later, however, she suffered a miscarriage from the shock.

Held: the defendant was liable because it was reasonably foreseeable that the claimant would suffer shock from fear for her own physical safety in the dangerous situation created by the defendant's negligence.

Secondary victims: a claimant in a nervous shock claim who sustains damage as a result of directly witnessing the accident caused by the defendant's negligence.

Secondary victims are not so closely involved since they merely witness the accident or are involved in the aftermath but not endangered by it. Stricter rules are therefore necessary to limit the duty to them, as large numbers might claim and it would not be fair, just and reasonable to make the defendant responsible for them all.

Primary victims

Since the defendant has caused a dangerous situation to arise, the duty is largely based on basic negligence principles. A duty of care arises because there is reasonable foreseeability of some physical or psychiatric injury to the claimant.

Page v *Smith* (1995, HL)

The defendant's negligent driving caused his car to collide with that of the claimant. Minor damage resulted to the vehicles but the claimant appeared unhurt. Shortly afterwards, however, he suffered a recurrence of ME (myalgic encephalomyelitis, then perceived as a psychiatric condition) from which he had enjoyed a lengthy remission.

Held: the defendant owed the same duty of care to the claimant as he would to any other fellow road user, since it was reasonably foreseeable that he might suffer personal injuries if the defendant drove negligently. It was not necessary for the claimant to prove that psychiatric damage might result. The distinction between physical and psychiatric injury was irrelevant in these circumstances.

The House of Lords indicated the limits of *Page* v *Smith* in *Johnston* v *NEI International* (2007, HL) which comprised four claims by various employees who had developed pleural plaques as a result of exposure to asbestos by their employers. Prior to this decision, claims for pleural plaques were potentially successful.

Johnston and Others v *NEI International* (2007, HL)

The claimants were all diagnosed with pleural plaques (hardening of lung tissue), which while harmless in themselves indicate exposure to asbestos. Diagnosis occurred years after the employer's negligent behaviour. Fear that they might develop asbestosis resulted in Mr Johnston and two others suffering anxiety and distress and one (Mr Grieves) developing clinical depression and irritable bowel syndrome.

Held: all the claims failed.

1 Mr Johnston and the two other claimants, who argued that the defendants were liable for the pleural plaques and their consequent anxiety and distress, failed because legal liability requires some actual injury recognised by law. The plaques were just a simple physical change, not the cause of illness. They were harmless in themselves and neither they nor the fear of future illness amounted to actionable damage. Even when combined, they did not amount to actionable harm.

2 Mr Grieves' claim failed because it was not reasonably foreseeable that a person of reasonable fortitude would develop a medically recognised disease as a result of the fear of future illness.

His other argument that he was a primary victim and therefore owed a duty because physical harm, i.e. asbestosis, was a reasonably foreseeable result of asbestos exposure, also failed because the principle in *Page* v *Smith* was limited to injury resulting directly and immediately from the negligence of the defendant where the claimant's injury was 'an immediate response to a sudden and alarming incident of which the plaintiff had no opportunity to prepare himself' (Lord Hope). Twenty years had passed between exposure to the asbestos and the diagnosis of pleural plaques and, therefore, there was no causative link between them.

The *Johnston* decision was controversial. The insurers who had previously had to pay out for these claims were delighted but potential future claimants and their supporters loudly protested. The Scottish government promptly legislated and passed the Damages (Asbestos-Related Conditions) (Scotland) Act 2009, which in effect reversed the *Johnston* decision in Scotland from the date of the judgment. The Northern Irish Assembly passed a similar Bill in 2011.

In 2010 the government announced that pleural plaques would not give rise to legal liability in England and Wales because the plaques did not in themselves cause illness.

Involuntary participants

> **Involuntary participants:** a primary nervous shock victim, who, though blameless, feels implicated in an accident caused by the defendant's negligence.

The claimant, an **involuntary participant**, is made to feel responsible for the accident although it is the defendant's conduct which is the real cause, may also be treated as a primary victim.

Dooley v *Cammell Laird* (1951)

The claimant was operating a crane which had been negligently maintained by his employer. The crane cable snapped and he saw the heavy crate attached to it hurtle into the hold. His shock at the anticipated fate of his workmates (who miraculously escaped injury) induced an acute nervous breakdown.

Held: the employer was liable since the claimant's response was prompted by his feelings that he had helped to cause the accident, and fear for his colleagues was reasonably foreseeable.

It is not easy to persuade the court that sufficient foreseeability exists in this area. In *Monk* v *Harrington Ltd and Others* (2008) (see below), Mr Monk's genuine belief that he was responsible for the accident, which had aggravated his trauma, was not justified in the circumstances and he lost his claim because it was held that it was not reasonably foreseeable that anyone in his situation would suffer psychiatric injury.

Rescuers

Until the House of Lords' decision in *White* v *Chief Constable of South Yorkshire* (below) rescuers were automatically deemed to be primary victims, provided they had a sufficient degree of involvement in the accident. The rationale of this principle was that it was in the public interest to encourage people to act humanely in an emergency.

Chadwick v British Rail (1967)

The claimant became acutely clinically depressed after spending a gruelling night giving first aid and comfort to severely injured and dying victims within the compacted wreckage of a horrific train crash.

Held: it was reasonably foreseeable that volunteers would render assistance and might suffer psychiatric injury as a result and, therefore, a duty of care was owed to the claimant.

The duty of care to rescuers was restricted by the House of Lords in *White* v *Chief Constable of South Yorkshire,* which held that a duty of care to rescuers exists only if the rescuer was actually in danger or reasonably believed that they were.

White v Chief Constable of South Yorkshire (1999, HL)

At Hillsborough football stadium 95 people were killed and hundreds injured in the crush resulting from the failure of senior police officers adequately to control admission to the stadium. The claimants, who were junior police officers, claimed for post-traumatic stress syndrome resulting from the harrowing scenes in which they had been heavily involved for many hours as rescuers.

Held: these claims must fail, since the claimants had not been exposed to or put in fear of danger and therefore no duty of care was owed to the claimants by their employers.

This decision can be justified on policy (public interest) grounds. The House of Lords was concerned to limit the increasing number of claims for compensation from members of the emergency services whose employment as a matter of course involves potential exposure to harrowing, though not necessarily dangerous, situations. The cost of settling such claims could, if not checked, undermine the provision of the services themselves and put an unreasonable burden on the taxpayer. However, someone like Mr Chadwick might not win his case today unless the court was prepared to acknowledge sufficient danger or reasonable fear. This point is well illustrated by the next case.

Monk v Harrington Ltd and Others (2008)

During the building of Wembley stadium an accident was caused by the negligence of the defendant construction firm. Two of Mr Monk's workmates fell 60 feet when a platform collapsed. One died shortly afterwards and the other broke a leg. M tried to help both men. Subsequently, as a result of what he had seen, he began to suffer from post-traumatic stress disorder and depression.

Held: when M rendered assistance, it was unlikely that he believed himself to be in danger and there were no reasonable grounds for his subsequent belief that he had caused the accident. Therefore, he was not a primary victim and no duty of care was owed to him.

This case illustrates the problems caused by the limitation of the rescuer category. By so doing, their Lordships have effectively barred the courts from assisting other litigants in areas where policy might well suggest that liability should be imposed. The construction industry, although better regulated than it used to be, is still well known for a poor accident record. While it is questionable that imposing liability necessarily drives up safety standards, at least deserving claimants like Mr Monk would be entitled to compensation for the loss of their livelihood as result of their acting humanely.

Negligent statements and nervous shock

Sudden and immediate attack: the nature of the trauma which may give rise to nervous shock liability.

Close bond of love and affection: the required relationship between claimant and accident victim in nervous shock claims.

Liability may arise from statements as well as acts. There is a duty of care to deliver bad news with sufficient sensitivity to prevent reasonably foreseeable psychiatric damage (*AB* v *Tameside & Glossop Health Authority* (1997)). Similarly, there is a duty to deliver news accurately. In *Allin* v *City & Hackney Health Authority* (1996), it was held that the defendant was liable for nervous shock suffered by the claimant when she received the sensitively delivered but *inaccurate* news that her baby was dead. Where negligent statements are involved duty may be based more on a *Hedley Byrne* relationship than the normal rules relating to nervous shock.

Liability to primary victims may be costly for service providers. This is evidenced by the Kings Cross fire, where London Transport was liable for multiple successful claims, including fire-fighters. A mass claim was brought by traumatised victims and relatives of the 193 people who drowned when the *Herald of Free Enterprise* ferry to Zeebrugge capsized in 1987. The sinking of *The Marchioness* pleasure boat on the Thames in 1989, with 51 dead, is another case in point.

Secondary victims

These merely witness the accident or, if involved, are not in danger or reasonable fear of it. The next case was the first secondary victim claim and laid down most of the basic principles governing such claims today.

Hambrook v *Stokes* (1925, CA)

A mother saw the defendant's driverless lorry careering down the hill in the direction of her two daughters who had just disappeared round the corner of the road. Although she did not see the accident, she heard the impact when the vehicle crashed through a wall after mounting the pavement close to her daughters. Miraculously, the girls were unhurt, but their mother suffered a fatal heart attack due to the shock resulting from fear for her children's safety.

Held: the defendant was liable. A duty of care was owed to a person who suffered nervous shock from directly witnessing an accident caused by the defendant's negligence, where such trauma was *reasonably foreseeable in a person of reasonable fortitude. The shock might result from the claimant witnessing the build-up to the accident and/or the immediate aftermath, but without seeing the accident itself.* The shock must be a product of what the claimant actually witnessed *with their own senses*, not what was reported to them by a third party.

In a later case, the House of Lords further developed the law, stressing the need for proximity of the claimant both in place and time to the accident and imposed limits on the concept of immediate aftermath.

McLoughlin v *O'Brian* (1982, HL)

The claimant suffered acute depression and personality change resulting from the shock of witnessing serious injuries caused to her husband and children by the defendant's negligent driving.

Held: her claim was successful. Although she was not present when the accident occurred, the harrowing scenes she witnessed at the casualty department an hour afterwards were horrific enough to make her sufficiently proximate, and her response reasonably foreseeable.

In *Alcock* v *Wright* the House of Lords rationalised the criteria determining duty of care to secondary victims.

Alcock v *Wright* (1991, HL)

The 16 claimants had loved ones who had perished in the horrific occurrences at the Hillsborough stadium **(see Web activity below)**. None was successful because they did not fulfil the necessary criteria laid down by the House of Lords, which restrict the concepts of reasonable foreseeability and proximity applicable in such circumstances.

Held: claimants must be able to prove the following:

(a) They have suffered some medically recognised illness or condition as a result of a '**sudden and immediate attack**' upon their senses. This excludes claimants who do not suffer a quick and sudden trauma, but whose illness is caused by a build-up of stress and fear.

(b) It was reasonably foreseeable that they would react in this way: there must be a '**close bond of love and affection**' between them and the accident victim. This is presumed only between spouses and parents and children; all other claimants must prove that the bond exists in the relevant circumstances. (Not all the Alcock claimants could satisfy this test.)

(c) Their reaction was that of a reasonably brave person given the level of trauma that they witnessed.

(d) *They were* **sufficiently proximate** *to the accident.* Proximity is measured both in terms of time and space. The claimant must usually be present at the scene when the accident occurs, although seeing the build-up to it and/or the immediate aftermath may be sufficient. The claimant must have witnessed the accident directly with his or her own senses and not have had the scene interpreted for him or her by a third party. (This ruled out some of the *Alcock* claimants, who had seen events unfold through a simultaneous TV broadcast, or who had identified a body at the mortuary eight hours after the accident.)

Worth thinking about?

Why do you think the House of Lords in Alcock (above) insisted that secondary victims must witness the accident directly and ruled that TV transmitted pictures did not count?

Suggested solutions can be found in Appendix 2.

The *Alcock* criteria make a very useful checklist for you to refer to, particularly when answering problem questions on this topic. Their application is usefully illustrated by the next two cases.

Taylorson v *Shieldness Products* (1994, CA)

The claimants were the parents of a 14-year-old boy who died three days after being crushed by a lorry driven by the defendant's negligent employee. The parents, who did not witness the accident, only briefly glimpsed their son after initial treatment when he was transferred to a second hospital. They were not present while he was being treated. The father visited on the night of the accident but the mother did not see him until the next day. They both remained with him for the next two days while he was on a life support system. They claimed that they suffered clinical depression as a result of the experience.

Held: no duty of care existed, as there was insufficient proximity of the parents in time and space to the accident. It was also probable that the damage to the claimants was more the result of grief than shock.

The only successful reported claim from a Hillsborough victim was that of John McCarthy (*McCarthy* v *Chief Constable of South Yorkshire* (1996)), who received over £200,000 damages for his ongoing post-traumatic stress. His half-brother, Ian, died from asphyxiation in one of the grandstands. John satisfied the *Alcock* criteria as he was at the ground though in a different stand with a view of the events as they unfolded. He was therefore deemed to be sufficiently proximate, and the close nature of his relationship to Ian evidenced a close bond of affection.

In practice, very few claims by secondary victims have succeeded.

Palmer v *Tees Health Authority* (1999, CA)

The claimant's daughter was abducted and murdered by a psychiatric patient. The claimant suffered acute post-traumatic stress disorder and alleged that the defendant authority were negligent in failing to diagnose that the patient was a risk to children. She claimed that within 15 minutes of discovering that her daughter had disappeared she was told that she had been abducted and this produced an immediate shock to her nervous system. When the child's body was discovered three days later, the claimant was within the vicinity of the patient's house but was not allowed to see her daughter's body at that point. She claimed that the psychiatric illness was caused by her presence at the scene and the immediate aftermath of the abduction and the search for and discovery of the body, which she later identified.

Held: her claim must fail on two counts:

(a) she had not witnessed the abduction, nor the murder, nor the discovery of the body, nor was she involved in the immediate aftermath, so she was not sufficiently proximate;

(b) what she had witnessed and experienced did not amount to a sudden and shocking event within the scope of *Alcock*.

Her situation was similar to that of unsuccessful Hillsborough claimants who went through a period of acute anxiety before their worst fears were realised. Her imagination of what had happened was not the same as 'the sudden appreciation by sight or sound of the horrifying event'.

However, the Court of Appeal has been prepared to interpret the *Alcock* principles more generously to deal with extreme circumstances.

North Glamorgan NHS Trust v *Walters* (2002, CA)

Due to the negligence of the Health Trust, the claimant's son died of liver failure. During the 36 hours leading up to his death, the claimant witnessed a number of traumatic events after the child had been admitted to the hospital, starting with her waking to find her son having a violent epileptic fit and vomiting blood all over his cot and ending when he died in her arms when life support was eventually terminated. She was given conflicting information about the likely outcome for her son. In effect, she was on an emotional roller coaster throughout: '*her hopes were lifted and then dashed and finally destroyed*' (Ward LJ). As a result, she suffered a pathological grief reaction.

Held: these circumstances must be treated as one entire 'horrifying' event and, therefore, the *Alcock* criteria were satisfied and a duty of care was owed to her.

A close link between the alleged traumatic event and the original accident is crucial to establish liability where a succession of events has led to the trauma. The *Walters* case was later distinguished on its facts in *Taylor* v *Novo UK* (2013).

Taylor v *A. Novo UK Ltd* (2013, CA)

The claimant's daughter suffered severe injuries when, due to her employer's negligence, a stack of shelving fell on her. Initially she was making a good recovery, but three weeks later she died as a result of thrombosis and an embolism caused by a blood clot. The claimant was present at the death and suffered severe traumatic stress.

Held: the defendant was not liable because the claimant could not prove sufficient proximity. Witnessing the death was the immediate trigger for the claimant's trauma rather than the previous accident. In the interests of policy the accident and the death could not be treated as one event. Otherwise a claim might be successfully brought if death occurred years after the accident, while a claim by someone coming upon an accident scene shortly after the accident could not recover. 'The idea that Ms Taylor could recover in the first situation but not in the others would strike the ordinary reasonable person as unreasonable and indeed incomprehensible. In this area of the law, the perception of the ordinary reasonable person matters.' (Lord Dyson Master of the Rolls)

This is a complex and controversial area of the law of negligence. The rules often seem arbitrary and may sometimes produce apparently unjust results. In 1998 a Law Commission Report (No. 249, *Liability for Psychiatric Damage*) was published which proposed statutory reform of the duty of care regarding secondary victims to replace the *Alcock* rule. The Report included the following recommendations:

(a) *The class of persons presumed to have a close bond of love and affection should be extended* to include siblings and cohabitees of at least two years' standing (including same-sex partners).

(b) *The claimant's illness need not be caused by a sudden shock* but might arise from a build-up of anxiety and stress over a period of time.

(c) *The claimant's proximity to the accident or its aftermath should be irrelevant.*

(d) *If physical injury were reasonably foreseeable, there would be liability* even if only psychiatric injury resulted.

So far, none of these proposals has been implemented by Parliament.

Omissions to act and liability for damage caused by third parties

Omissions

The law of tort is concerned with compensating acts by a defendant that have actively damaged the claimant (*misfeasance*), rather than with the defendant's failure to act for the claimant's benefit (*nonfeasance*). Consequently, it is rare for a duty of care to result from an omission to act. In *Stovin* v *Wise* (1996) Lord Goff said:

> There are sound reasons why omissions require different treatment from positive conduct. It is one thing for the law to say that a person who undertakes some activity shall take reasonable care not to cause damage to others. It is another thing for the law to require that a person who is doing nothing in particular shall take steps to prevent another from suffering harm.

He went on to say that there are political, moral and economic reasons for this approach. Imposing liability would unduly restrict personal freedom. There is no moral justification in making one person bear the economic burden of compensating a claimant when he or she may be one of a number who might morally be expected to intervene.

> Liability to pay compensation for loss caused by negligent conduct acts as a deterrent . . . But there is no similar justification to require a person who is not doing anything [wrong] to spend money on behalf of someone else.

As Lord Goff indicates, it is important to distinguish between moral and legal duties as the two do not necessarily overlap. For example, you would not be liable in negligence or any other tort if you failed to stop a blind person from walking into a road in front of an oncoming bus, if you had no previous legal responsibility for their safety.

'False omissions' may give rise to a duty of care

There are situations where a failure to act does give rise to a duty, though if we examine them closely, we see that the omission was not an isolated failure to act but was part of a chain of events already giving rise to liability or that the claimant was in a dependent relationship with the defendant. In both these situations a duty of care already exists between the parties. For example, you will be liable for harm to any pedestrian you knock down with your car, if the accident happened because you omitted to use your brakes, or to keep a proper lookout. If you choose to help a blind person across the road, you will by intervening create a duty of care and may be liable to that person if you bungle the rescue operation. Similarly, a school teacher may be liable for failing to stop a pupil from climbing into the bear pit on a visit to the zoo, as might a doctor who harms patients by failing to warn them that the drug prescribed cannot be safely combined with certain foods.

Acts of third parties

There is a presumption in law that we are all responsible for our own behaviour, therefore, it is rare to find cases where one party is liable for the tort of a third party (apart from circumstances giving rise to vicarious liability (see Chapter 15).

This is an area of liability which may impact on a business where the claimant is adversely affected by third party activity on premises controlled by the defendant.

Smith v *Littlewoods Organisation* (1987, HL)

Littlewoods bought a disused cinema with a view to opening one of its stores on the land. While the cinema was being demolished, at a time while no contractor or Littlewoods employees were present, vandals entered the premises and started a fire. This spread to Smith's adjoining premises. Smith alleged that Littlewoods were in breach of a duty to prevent this damage, by making the premises secure against trespassers. Both parties agreed that only a twenty-four-hour guard could have prevented entry by trespassers.

Held: although occupiers of premises have a duty to take reasonable care that their premises are not a source of danger to neighbouring landowners, Littlewoods did not owe a duty of care as there were no special circumstances indicating that such vandalism was reasonably foreseeable.

Lord Griffiths stated:

> I do not say that there will never be circumstances in which the law will require an occupier to take special precautions against such a contingency, but they would have to be extreme indeed . . . there was nothing inherently dangerous . . . stored on the premises, nor can I regard a cinema stripped of its equipment as likely to be any more alluring to vandals than any other recently vacated building in the centre of a town. No message was received . . . from the local police, fire brigade or any neighbour that vandals were creating a danger on any premises.

To require a 24-hour guard would be 'an intolerable burden' in the circumstances.

The *Littlewoods* case is a good example of the court taking a restricted view of what is reasonably foreseeable. Vandalism is a well-known problem in urban areas. However, in cases involving property damage the court expects a claimant to be insured, so it is usually unsympathetic to claims for negligent omissions and third party damage.

The aim of this policy is to encourage property owners to be prudent and to prevent insurance companies from fronting a successful action to recover their losses.

Occupiers do not generally have a duty to secure their premises in order to safeguard neighbouring premises unless alerted by evidence that they represent a risk. If the defendant's premises have previously been subject to trespass and vandalism, this would be more likely to make the court take the view that the damage to the claimant was reasonably foreseeable.

A *duty* may arise in the following circumstances:

1 The defendant had a responsibility to control the third party's behaviour because of a pre-existing relationship with the party. Businesses will be keen to avoid liability in cases such as:

Home Office v *Dorset Yacht Co. Ltd* (1970, HL)

The Home Office was held liable when the claimant's yacht was damaged by improperly supervised Borstal trainees who had escaped from a nearby work camp.

2 The defendant's pre-existing relationship to the claimant makes the defendant responsible for preventing the damage.

Stansbie v *Troman* (1948, CA)

Stansbie was a decorator who was left in sole charge of Mrs Troman's house. He left it unlocked when going out to buy wallpaper and was held liable for the loss arising from the burglary which took place in his absence.

Public authorities and statutory discretion

Public service providers, such as the fire brigade, the police and local authorities, operate in the context of statutory duties and powers. Such duties are mandatory but often widely drafted, leaving a large element of discretion to the authority about how it is implemented. For example, a local authority must provide full-time education for children in its catchment area, but how it does so is left largely to its discretion. The authority decides, for example, whether single-sex education shall be an option and determines the selection methods, if any, for transfer to secondary schools. Some local authorities provide special schools for pupils with some acute physical disabilities and learning difficulties, while others choose to place such students in mainstream schools. Such choices are made with regard to the perceived needs of the particular community and may be limited by budgetary concerns.

The statutory duty exists to benefit the public at large through the provision of services relevant to local needs. The courts have traditionally been unwilling to permit a duty of care in negligence to be owed by a public authority to individual members of

> **Statutory discretion:** flexibility in implementation of a statutory duty derived from the wording of the relevant Act of Parliament.

the public who claim to be harmed by the way the authority has used its **statutory discretion** in performing its public duties. Usually, such claims arise where an omission to exercise the power is allegedly the cause of the damage or where a third party is actually responsible for the harm. These factors combined with the desire of the courts not to fetter discretion derived from Parliament makes them particularly reluctant to impose a duty of care. Policy plays a very important role in such circumstances.

The fire brigade and ambulance services owe a limited duty

Capital and Counties Bank plc v *Hampshire Fire Brigade* (1997, CA)

Here the brigade fought a fire on the claimant's premises but left having turned off sprinklers in the roof area, which was still smouldering. Later it reignited and the building was destroyed.

Held: a fire brigade was under no duty at civil law to attend a fire. Duty of care was to be limited to situations where acts of the fire brigade directly worsened the claimant's problems. The defendant fire brigade was liable, as its intervention had increased the damage to the claimant.

Remember that the court's decision in cases like this will be influenced by the expectation that the claimant will have insurance against fire damage. Maybe if a case concerning death or physical injury occurs we may see a different approach.

Ambulance services, because their remit involves giving assistance to people requiring medical care, owe a duty to provide a timely service once a caller has been told that an ambulance will be dispatched.

Kent v *Griffiths and Others (No. 3)* (2001, CA)

The claimant had an acute asthma attack and suffered severe brain damage when delay caused by negligence by the ambulance service prevented her from receiving timely treatment.

Held: provided an ambulance was available and a caller was told that it would be sent, it should attend within a reasonable time. The ambulance service was part of the health service. It was therefore appropriate to regard it as providing services of the same kind as those provided by hospital services rather than being equivalent to those of the fire brigade and police.

The police

While the police authority will be liable in the same way as any other employer for negligent driving by its officers or failure to protect a person in custody from coming to harm, the court has refused to hear cases where the police were apparently negligent in preventing crimes from occurring. It was perceived that this would unduly restrict discretion in an area where much flexibility was needed and could lead to defensive behaviour by the police that would be prejudicial to the public.

Osman v Ferguson (1993, CA)

A schoolmaster who became obsessed with a pupil, harassed him and his family, carried out acts of vandalism against their property and tried to ram their car while it was being driven. The police were informed and interviewed the man but did not take steps to arrest him. He continued his campaign of harassment which culminated in his shooting both father and son, killing the former and injuring the latter. An action in negligence was taken against the police.

Held: the action must be struck out. Arguably, there was sufficient proximity between the police and the victims of the shooting to give rise to a special relationship. However, it was not fair, just and reasonable to impose a duty of care by the police to the victims of crime. It would not improve standards and could dangerously divert police resources from the general investigation and suppression of crime necessary to protect the public.

This case seemed to indicate that the police enjoyed complete immunity from litigation concerning policing discretion.

The courts have been compelled to take a less prescriptive approach since *Osman v UK* (1999), where the European Court of Human Rights held that giving the police immunity was in effect a breach of Article 6 of the ECHR (right to a fair trial). The House of Lords (*Barrett v Enfield Borough Council* (1999)) subsequently held that any claim where immunity of any public authority is in question must be tried to determine whether a duty of care exists. This, of course, does not mean that a duty will necessarily be held to exist, but it gives the claimant the opportunity to have his or her own case considered, thus enabling his or her right to a fair trial.

Given the House of Lords' decision (below), it seems almost impossible to persuade the court that a duty of care in negligence or liability by the police for breach of Article 2 of the ECHR exists.

Chief Constable Hertfordshire v Van Colle and Smith v Chief Constable of Sussex (2008, HL)

These two cases involved claims against the police for failing to intervene to protect a party in danger of alleged violent attack. The first case concerned X, a witness who was murdered days before he was due to give evidence at a trial for theft by a party later convicted for his murder. In evidence, it was alleged that X had been subjected to a number of threats and intimidation by Y which the police had known about.

Smith repeatedly told the police that A (his former partner) had threatened to kill him and provided sufficient evidence to justify his arrest. For example, he had received over 130 text messages from A. Some contained very explicit threats such as: 'U are dead'; 'Look out for yourself psycho is coming'; 'I am looking to kill you and no compromises'; 'I was in the Bulldog last night with a carving knife. It's a shame I missed you'. However, the police chose to ignore Mr Smith's complaints. Eventually, A attacked him with a claw hammer causing serious injury. X's representative claimed breach of the ECHR, Article 2 (right to life) and Mr Smith claimed in negligence.

Held: both appeals must be dismissed.

X's claim: under *Osman* v *UK* the test of liability stipulated that the court should not acknowledge a breach unless 'at the time' the police should have known of a 'real and immediate risk to life of an identified individual from criminal acts of a third party'.

Y was a seriously 'disturbed and unpredictable individual'. Therefore, it could not be said that the police by involving X as a witness and making him a member of a special class separate from the public at large, should have anticipated that Y was a sufficient risk to X's safety. The *Osman* test did not impose an invariable standard and the particular facts were relevant to determining whether or not it was satisfied.

Mr Smith's claim (Lord Bingham dissenting): under the rule in *Hill* v *Chief Constable West Yorkshire* (1989, HL) the police owed no common law duty of care to protect individuals from attacks by criminals, unless there were very special circumstances justifying departure from the principle which protected the public interest. A specific and evident threat would have to exist for the police to owe a duty. It had not existed here.

The Supreme Court affirmed this principle in *Michael* v *Chief Constable of South Wales* (2015).

In the news

Michael v *Chief Constable of South Wales* (2015, SC 2)

The police received a call for help from Ms Michael after she had been attacked by her ex-partner. He had briefly left the premises threatening to return at once to kill her. Fifteen minutes later she called again and was heard screaming. Eight minutes later the police arrived to find her dead. Police records showed a history of violent attacks on her by her partner. A claim in negligence was made against the police on behalf of her estate.

Held (by a majority of five to two): no duty of care was owed by the police to an individual member of the public even where that individual had given credible evidence of imminent physical danger. No special exception should be created to cover crimes of violence. There was insufficient proximity between police and victim to permit a duty unless the police gave a very specific representation to them that they would assist. The call handler saying that the information would be sent to the police was insufficient to amount to this.

Apart from the potential restriction on police discretion the cost of imposing liability on the police was not justifiable.

While this can look unjust, bear in mind that the victims of such crimes as these do have alternative means of dispute resolution, such as the Criminal Injuries Compensation Board, formal complaint systems or under the Human Rights Act. See *DSD and NBV* v *Commissioner of Police for the Metropolis* (2014, EWHC) where the court awarded a considerable sum of damages against the defendant police force for failing to prevent the claimants being attacked by a serial rapist (see Chapter 3 for a detailed account).

Education and social services

The courts in the past generally refused to allow claims to proceed in negligence against a local authority's education and social services departments, on the ground that this would fetter executive discretion in the use of resources, and interfere with social policy. In *X* v *Bedfordshire County Council* (1995) the House of Lords struck out two claims concerning allegedly negligent decisions by local authorities in failing to take children into care. It was held that no duty of care existed in such cases or social services departments would be unduly constrained. They might be inclined to act defensively and unnecessarily take children into care.

As indicated above, this attitude has had to change since the ECtHR decision in *Osman*. This was evidenced by the House of Lords decision in (*Barrett* v *Enfield Borough Council* (1999) (above)).

A case of failing to take a child into care may now succeed (*Pierce* v *Doncaster Metropolitan Borough Council* (2008, CA)). However, a claim by a parent that their child was wrongly taken into care is still unlikely to be successful. In *Lawrence* v *Pembrokeshire County Council* (2007, CA) the claimant's children were mistakenly put on the at-risk register when Ms Lawrence was wrongfully suspected of abusing them. Her action was struck out since no duty of care was deemed to exist. The claimant appealed, arguing that application of Article 8 (right to family life) of the ECHR in domestic law since implementation of the HRA 1998, should result in an incremental change in the law of negligence. The Court of Appeal held that the House of Lords (*D* v *East Berkshire Community Health NHS Trust and Others* (2005)) had already decided (albeit prior to implementation of the HRA) that no duty of care in negligence was owed to parents wrongly suspected of abuse provided the local authority had acted in good faith. An extension in the scope of duty of care would be a step too far. There was a lack of proximity between Ms Lawrence and the council. It would also militate against the public interest, which required that a child protection authority should be able to exercise its discretion freely during the investigation and prevention of abusive behaviour, without being inhibited by threat of potential litigation.

In such cases, alternative remedies are often available. Ms Lawrence had already received compensation after an ombudsman investigation and an action under the HRA was also possible.

The impact of the Human Rights Act 1998

Since 2000, an action under the Human Rights Act 1998 for breach of the Convention is now possible in cases against a public authority. This may well be more appropriate than an action in negligence and more likely to be successful, where the claim involves omission to act, failure to prevent damage by a third party or negligent exercise of a statutory discretion. In *Z and A* v *UK* (2002) the claimants (two of the child claimants involved in *X* v *Bedfordshire County Council* (1995)) successfully claimed that the council had breached its duty under Article 3 (the right not to be subjected to inhuman or degrading treatment) by failing to protect them from prolonged and serious ill-treatment and abuse. Article 8 (right to respect for family life) was breached in respect of another child who was wrongly taken into care. Her mother also succeeded with an Article 8 claim. Such claims can now be brought in the English courts, which must have regard to decisions of the European Court of Human Rights. (See Chapter 3.)

In conclusion: duty criteria are guidance only

From your study of all the various problematic duty situations examined in this chapter, you will now be aware that judges determining the existence of duty of care often refer to such criteria as reasonable foreseeability, proximity and justice and reason (policy). Students often ask their lecturers to tell them what exactly these words mean in the hope that this will provide a magic key to unlock a secret door to understanding. Be warned that this is a fruitless quest. Such words cannot be defined as legal terms and in themselves, do not provide certain answers to the question of whether a duty of care exists in a particular case. The context in which they are applied, i.e. the circumstances of the particular case, heavily influences their definition and limits, so that apparently conflicting decisions are made. As May LJ said in *Merret* v *Bubb* (2001): it would be 'reaching for the moon . . . to expect to accommodate every circumstance which may arise within a single short abstract formulation'.

It may help you to keep in mind that the courts take an *incremental* approach to the development of duty of care, particularly in the controversial areas of duty examined above. Therefore, any change is likely to be a small step at a time rather than a leap into the dark,

A duty is unlikely to be acknowledged for any case which:

- is *not* concerned with *physical damage directly caused* to the claimant or their property;
- involves loss insurable by the claimant;
- could be remedied by a claim in a different area of the law;
- opens up claims to an indefinable class;
- is perceived as being against the public interest in any other respect.

Part 2: breach of duty

It is up to the claimant to prove that the defendant failed to take reasonable care in performing the duty of care. What is reasonable is measured objectively against the standards of the so-called '**reasonable man**' in the circumstances of the particular case. Certain criteria exist to guide the court.

The likelihood of an accident happening

The greater the likelihood of an accident the more care the defendant may need to take. The court will need to be satisfied that the incidence of risk was reasonably reduced. It need not be completely removed for the standard to be met.

Reasonable man: the standard by which reasonable care is judged. This is said to reflect the behaviour of the average person in the given circumstances.

Bolton v *Stone* (1951)

The claimant was injured by a cricket ball hit from the cricket club grounds controlled by the defendant. The boundary fence was 17 feet high and the ball had travelled over 80 yards from the wicket. There was evidence to show that such a hit was a very rare occurrence.

Held: the defendant was not liable as reasonable care had been taken to reduce the chances of such an occurrence, given the height of the fence and the distance from the wicket and the previous history of balls rarely escaping from the ground.

However, a similar accident occurring in different circumstances gave rise to liability for the defendant since the chances of an accident were very likely.

Hilder v *Associated Portland Cement* (1961)

Children were often known to play football on some land belonging to the defendant company which was close to a road and bordered by a wall less than three feet high. A motorcyclist was killed when a ball was kicked into the road.

Held: the defendant was liable since it had not taken reasonable care to reduce the chances of a very likely accident. It had neither prevented the children from playing on its land nor provided a boundary fence sufficient to prevent footballs escaping into the highway.

The extent of the potential harm

The greater the extent of the likely damage the more the defendant is expected to do to reduce its risk.

Paris v *Stepney Council* (1951)

The claimant was employed in a manual job by the defendant company. He had only one eye and was then blinded in his good eye in an accident at work.

Held: the defendant had failed to act with reasonable care by failing to supply goggles to the claimant. It was irrelevant that the work he was doing would not necessitate use of goggles by a normally sighted person. The consequence of injury to his eyes was much more serious than to other employees.

The practicability of taking precautions: risk–benefit analysis

The court when determining reasonable care seeks to impose a standard of care that gives reasonable protection to the claimant while not unduly burdening the defendant. This may be described as a **risk–benefit analysis**. A risk-free environment can never be fully guaranteed.

Withers v *Perry Chain Ltd* (1961)

The claimant, who was employed in a factory where contact with grease was involved at every stage of the production process, became allergic to grease and developed a skin condition. Her employer moved her to the most grease-free job that fitted her capabilities but the allergy persisted.

Held: the defendant company had done everything that it could reasonably be expected to do to prevent harm to the claimant and was therefore not in breach of its duty and Ms Withers' claim must accordingly fail.

Latimer v *AEC* (1953)

A factory floor was slippery after a flash flood. The defendant spread sawdust over most of the walkways in the factory and issued warnings to employees. The claimant, who was injured when he slipped in an area which had not been saw-dusted because it was less often used, argued that the building should have been closed until it had dried out.

Held: the extent of the risk and likely injury did not justify this extreme response. The precautions taken were all that was practicable in the circumstances.

Risk–benefit analysis: a balancing exercise to determine the required level of care relating to an activity to determine what precautions are necessary, without unreasonably inhibiting its beneficial effects.

The defendant's resources and the nature and size of business may be relevant factors for the court to take into account. However, the greater the risk and extent of damage the less relevant the cost factor to the defendant. This is an area of the common law where standards have been influenced by statutory developments in health and safety regulation (see Chapter 16). This commonly requires prior risk assessment for certain activities. Evidence that this process was sufficiently comprehensive and resulted in relevant precautions is often sufficient to discharge the duty of care. Risk assessment is accepted practice even where it is not statutorily required.

Wilson v *Haden* (2013)

The defendant ran an adventure centre. The claimant scoutmaster was injured by falling from a slippery fireman's pole on an obstacle course in wet weather.

Held: the defendant was negligent. Failure by staff to take proper account of the centre's risk assessment process and to give proper instructions to visitors was a breach of duty.

Skilful claimants

If a claimant has a skill which should make him or her aware of an inherent danger, the defendant will not be expected to take steps to protect him or her from it.

Roles v *Nathan* (1963)

Two sweeps died when they were overcome by fumes while attempting to seal a hole in a flue while the boiler on the defendant's premises was still alight.

Held: the defendant was not negligent. The sweeps were experienced tradesmen and knew that the boiler should have been extinguished before work was started. It was not up to the defendant to put it out or issue warnings.

The qualifications claimed by the defendant

Defendants will be held liable if they fail to act with the reasonable degree of care and skill to be expected from a person with the qualifications which the defendants claim to have – *Bolam* v *Friern Hospital Management Committee* (1957) (see below).

Phillips v *William Whitely* (1938)

The defendant jeweller who pierced the claimant's ears was not liable for the abscess which resulted.

Held: the defendant was not negligent. He had acted in accordance with the level of care and skill to be expected from a person with his training. The standards of a surgeon could not be expected of him.

Only the level of qualification is relevant. Lack of experience is not taken into consideration: the same standards are expected of a newly qualified professional or craftsperson as of one with considerable experience. In *Wilsher* v *Essex Area Health Authority* (1986) the Court of Appeal held that it was irrelevant that the doctor who treated the claimant was newly qualified and had been working excessively long hours when she treated the claimant (for facts see below).

This extends to learner drivers, who are required to demonstrate the same standard of care as those who have passed a driving test (see *Nettleship* v *Weston* (1971, CA)). This is to prevent insurance companies avoiding liability to third parties.

A defendant claiming no special training or skill is expected to take such care as can reasonably be expected in the circumstances. In *Perry* v *Harris* (2008) the Court of Appeal held that the defendant was not liable for the injuries sustained by a child hurt when using a bouncy castle at a children's birthday party. She had acted as a responsible adult in her supervision of the children at the time and constant supervision was not required as serious injury was not reasonably foreseeable. Similarly, the standard required of an amateur carpenter's repairs is not as high as that required of a professional tradesperson (*Wells* v *Cooper* (1958, CA)).

Children are expected to exercise a level of skill commensurate with their age. In *Orchard* v *Lee* (2009), the Court of Appeal decided that a 13-year-old boy, who seriously injured a dinner lady on colliding with her in the playground when he was playing tag, had not breached his duty of care. A reasonable 13-year-old would not have reasonably foreseen that such harm would be likely to result from his conduct.

Good practice

Conformity with accepted and current good practice may be indicative of reasonable care. Thus, in *Thompson* v *Smiths Ship Repairers Ltd* (1984) the defendant employer's failure to provide ear protectors was held not to amount to a failure to take reasonable care until they had been alerted to the necessity by government circular.

There may be more than one type of good practice: both claimant and defendant may produce expert witnesses with conflicting views. The judge does not have the relevant professional skill to decide whose procedure was correct. The claimant must prove that on the balance of probability the defendant was in breach. If there is proof that what the defendant did would also have been done by another similar professional in compliance with good practice then the claimant fails.

Bolam v *Friern Hospital Management Committee* (1957, CA)

The claimant, who suffered a fractured pelvis when undergoing electro-convulsive therapy, brought expert evidence that his limbs should have been restrained during treatment.

Held: on the balance of probability there was no proof of a failure to take reasonable care. The hospital was able to prove that its practice of cushioning limbs was equally well accepted in respected medical circles.

The House of Lords approved the *Bolam* principle in *Bolitho* v *City and Hackney Area Health Authority* (1997), but stressed that it is not enough to show that other professionals subscribe to the practice: an expert witness must be able to justify its use in the circumstances of the particular case, having weighed up its risks and benefits.

Unhappy outcomes

In *Bolam* v *Friern Hospital Management Committee* Lord Justice Denning neatly summarised the nature of reasonable care when he said 'the doctor does not promise to cure the patient nor the lawyer to win the case'. All reasonable care may be taken but the claimant may still suffer damage. Proof of damage to the claimant or even proof of a mistake by the defendant does not necessarily prove that the defendant has failed to take reasonable care.

Luxmoore May v *Messenger May Bakers* (1990, CA)

The defendant auctioneers claimed to be expert picture valuers. They failed to judge correctly the potential of two paintings owned by the claimant, who consequently obtained only a tiny fraction of their true value when they were sold.

Held: the claimants had failed to prove that the defendants acted without reasonable care. Evidence from the defendant indicated that a competent valuer could have made the same mistake.

Encoding the standard of care

The Compensation Act 2006

Section 1 states that when a court is deciding whether a defendant has taken reasonable care it may:

have regard to whether a requirement to take those steps might –

(a) prevent a desirable activity from being undertaken at all, to a particular extent or in a particular way, or

(b) discourage persons from undertaking functions in connection with a desirable activity.

From what you have read earlier, you will see that this statute merely reflects current judicial practice, so may appear to be a redundant piece of legislation. Parliament's intention was presumably to improve awareness of this aspect of the law and to attempt to ensure that normal activities are not inhibited by fear of litigation and excessively risk-averse behaviour. There does appear to be an increase in such restrictions of late usually as a result of defensive behaviour by public authorities and businesses rather than by the courts. These encourage the popular belief that life should be risk free, and that, since any and every accident is preventable somebody must be legally liable.

Reflecting this legislation, the Health & Safety Executive published (August 2006) proposals for a code of principles for risk management which states that, while the safety of workers and members of the public should be properly protected, sensible risk management is not about 'creating a totally risk free society' or 'stopping important recreational and learning activities' or 'scaring people by exaggerating or publicising trivial risks'.

This view has been reinforced by the courts on a number of occasions. In *Sutton* v *Syston Rugby Football Club Ltd* (2011) (see below) Longmore LJ said:

It is important that neither the game's professional organisation nor the law should lay down standards that are too difficult for ordinary coaches and match organisers to meet. Games of rugby are, after all, no more than games and, as such are obviously desirable activities within the meaning of s 1 of the Compensation Act 2006.

The Social Action, Responsibility and Heroism Act 2015 is another statute many lawyers think that we could manage without. It was prompted in part by a report on volunteering (*Helping Out: A national survey of volunteering and charitable giving*, September 2007) which found that the perception of the danger of personal liability and risk discouraged some people from participating. It requires the court in a case of negligence or breach of statutory duty to have regard to whether the defendant was engaged in activity beneficial to the public (s 2) or was attempting to protect 'the safety or interests of others' (s 3) when deciding whether reasonable care was taken. You will be aware already from what you have read earlier in this chapter that existing case law shows that the courts do not expect the same standard of care from a lay person as from a professional (*Perry* v *Harris* (2008) *Wells* v *Cooper* (1958)). Where acts of heroism are concerned any person who intervenes in a manner reasonably commensurate with the urgency of the situation and to their own abilities is unlikely to find themselves liable for any injury they cause. In *Watt* v *Hertfordshire County Council* (1954, CA) Denning LJ said:

> It is well settled that in measuring due care one must balance the risk against the measures necessary to eliminate the risk . . . One must balance the risk against the end to be achieved. The saving of life or limb justifies taking considerable risk.

It should also be noted that the common law protects volunteers if they are injured as a result of their philanthropic behaviour through the negligence of others. They are entitled to the same safety precautions as anyone else involved in the organisation relative to their needs and experience. Anyone who goes to the rescue of another person in a dangerous situation in a reasonable manner will, if harmed, have a remedy against any person who caused the original accident negligently. (See Chapter 15.)

Proving consequent damage

The claimant must prove the link between the defendant's failure to take reasonable care and the damage which the claimant has suffered. Two elements are involved: the claimant must first prove that but for the defendant's behaviour the damage would not have occurred (*causation in fact*) and secondly that the damage is a reasonably foreseeable result (*causation in law*).

1 Causation in fact: the 'but for' rule

'But for' principle: damage to the claimant must be a result of the defendant's breach.

The defendant's failure to take care must be the material cause of the damage. A claimant must show that he or she would not have been injured **but for** the defendant's act or failure to act.

Barnett v *Chelsea & Kensington Hospital Management Committee* (1969)

A man died from arsenic poisoning which the hospital negligently failed to detect.

Held: the hospital was not liable, as according to expert evidence he would still have died even if the hospital had diagnosed the problem and treated him appropriately.

McWilliams v *Arrol* (1962)

The claimant's husband fell from a roof that he was repairing; he had not been wearing a safety belt. There was evidence that, although belts were normally available, on the day of the accident, the shed where they were stored was locked. The claimant argued that if the belts had been available her husband would not have fallen.

Held: she must lose her case since the defendant employer was able to prove that her husband did not usually bother to wear a belt.

Here is a more recent case:

Sutton v *Syston Rugby Football Club Ltd* (2011, CA)

Mr Sutton was injured during rugby training when he fell on a broken cricket marker near the pitch boundary while attempting to score a try. He claimed that club's negligence in failing to carry out a proper pitch inspection had caused the accident.

Held: failure to inspect was a breach of duty, but the Club was not liable because there was no causative link between the failure to inspect and Mr Sutton's injuries. The evidence indicated that, even if a reasonably careful inspection had been carried out, it would probably not have revealed the stump of broken marker, which was largely concealed by the grass.

Multiple causes

The 'but for' principle works well as long as there is only one likely cause of the damage. Where there are multiple causes, the claimant may be unable to prove on the balance of probability that it was the defendant's behaviour which was a material cause of the accident.

Wilsher v *Essex Area Health Authority* (1988, HL)

Failure by the hospital to give the claimant, a premature baby, the correct oxygen mixture was alleged to be the cause of his becoming visually impaired.

Held: the claimant could not succeed since the 'but for' test had not been satisfied, as he was suffering from a number of other conditions, any of which could have caused the same damage. It had not been proved on the balance of probability that the oxygen mixture was a material cause.

In a previous case the House of Lords had adopted a different approach.

McGhee v *National Coal Board* (1972, HL)

The claimant worked in very hot and dirty conditions in a brick kiln. No showers were provided and he could not get clean until he had cycled home from work. He contracted dermatitis. He could not prove on the balance of probability that showering before leaving work would have prevented the dermatitis.

Held: the NCB was liable as the medical evidence indicated that lack of showers greatly increased his chances of developing the condition.

In *Wilsher* v *Essex Area Health Authority* the House of Lords described the *McGhee* approach as 'robust and pragmatic': correct on its facts but not a principle of law. This cast doubt on the standing of *McGhee*, and produced a puzzling distinction for many students.

However, in 2002 the House of Lords clarified the law. Its decision and the cases and legislation which followed it had a big impact both on relevant businesses and their insurers.

Fairchild v *Glenhaven Funeral Services* (2002, HL)

The claimants in this case all contracted mesothelioma (a form of invariably fatal cancer) after being exposed to asbestos fibres at work. There was clear evidence of flagrant breach of safety standards by all the employers. Causation was problematic, however, as all the claimants had been employed by more than one employer. Each employee could only have contracted the disease during one period of employment, and it was impossible for them to prove which one was the source of the disease.

Held (unanimously): given the impossibility of proof, the claimants should succeed. It was fair and just to use the less stringent *McGhee* rule here, as by breaching safety standards all the employers had materially increased the claimants' chances of contracting the condition. The facts could clearly be distinguished from those in *Wilsher* where a number of possible causes, apart from the oxygen, could have led to the claimant's disability. In *Fairchild*, asbestos was the only possible cause. The House of Lords in *Wilsher* was incorrect in failing to acknowledge *McGhee* as establishing a new principle of law.

The defendants were jointly and severally liable. Therefore, the claimants were entitled to full compensation from the employer who was being sued, since that employer could seek contribution from any other employer who had exposed the claimant to the risk.

The *Fairchild* decision is important as it firmly establishes the *McGhee* approach as a principle of law. It is also a good example of a public interest or 'policy' decision. Had the employers escaped liability, others might be encouraged to ignore safety standards in similar situations, secure in the knowledge that the causative link could not be established. Insurers, too, would have unjustly profited.

14

Tort liability for defective services

Four years later in *Barker* v *Corus UK Ltd*, *Murray* v *British Shipbuilders Ltd*, *Patterson* v *Smiths Docks Ltd* (2006, HL) a differently constituted House of Lords decided three cases in which the facts were subtly different from Fairchild. This resulted in the principle in Fairchild being both expanded in one respect and restricted controversially in another.

The expansion

Mr Barker had been exposed to the risk of mesothelioma not only by his employers but also during a period of self-employment, but this was held to be irrelevant to his employers' liability. It was held that, provided there was evidence of negligence by the defendant which materially increased the risk of contracting mesothelioma, it was irrelevant that the claimant had also been exposed to the risk from another source. It was irrelevant that that other exposure might have been caused by tortious or non-tortious behaviour or some natural cause.

The restriction

In *Barker*, etc. the House of Lords by majority held that joint and several liability could only be imposed if the defendants had actually *caused the claimants to contract* the disease. It also held that only a minority of the House of Lords in *Fairchild* had actually decided that the defendants had done so. The majority (three out of five) had merely held that the defendant had exposed the claimants to the *risk of contracting* the disease. Therefore, their Lordships restated the decision in *Fairchild* holding that each defendant could only be held liable severally (only for the damage it had personally caused) and so would pay compensation proportionately to the period of time the claimant had been employed by them. This impacted unfavourably on the current claimants as all previous employers bar the current defendants were insolvent and, as mentioned above, Mr Barker had been self-employed for a time.

This was a very controversial decision as regards the several liability issue. Lord Hoffmann said that it would 'smooth the roughness of the justice which a rule of joint and several liability creates'. It certainly pleased the defendant insurers. However, it may be argued that it roughened the justice for the claimants and their dependants, as Lord Rodger clearly indicated in his dissenting judgment where he called upon Parliament to come to their assistance. Richard Leyton (president of the Association of Personal Injury Lawyers) declared that it was 'an insult to the victims' families' and Parliament was quick to intervene to remove the *Barker* restriction.

The Compensation Act 2006, s 3

Section 3 in effect imposes joint and several liability for negligence and breach of statutory duty arising from the circumstances of exposure covered by the *Fairchild* and *Barker* decisions but s 3(5) expands this to cover liability for failure to protect from exposure.

The Act received Royal Assent in July 2006 and s 3 has retrospective effect, which means that all future cases must be decided in accordance with it, even if the damage occurred before the section came into force. It also means that the outcomes of some past claims may need to be varied.

This was a very welcome parliamentary intervention for those of us who agree with the House of Lords in *Fairchild*, that perfect justice cannot be obtained in this problematic causation situation and that any injustice should be borne by a party who is culpably in breach of their duty of care, rather than their innocent victims.

We must not disregard the *Fairchild* and Barker cases in future. Section 3 clearly reflects them pretty precisely as regards exposure issues and the causation principle. Parliament has in effect made that part of those decisions statutory, so they will still be as relevant in future cases to courts interpreting and applying s 3. In *Sienkiewicz v Greif (UK) Ltd* and *Knowsley Metropolitan Borough Council v Willmore* (2011) the Supreme Court directly applied its previous decision. It held that both single or multiple defendants were liable if the claimant proved under the *Fairchild* causation rule that the defendant's breach of duty had been a material cause of the claimant's illness. Section 3's reference to 'material' was intended to rule out insignificant risks but not to require proof that the defendant had doubled the risk of exposure to the claimant.

Lost chances

The more liberal approach to causation in *Fairchild* has not been extended to claims for a lost chance. Although damages may be award for such losses the claimant must as usual in civil cases, establish that the defendant was on the balance of probabilities the material cause of the loss.

In *Hotson v East Berkshire Health Authority* (1987) the claimant fractured his hip and the hospital negligently failed to spot that he had associated nerve damage which resulted in long-term damage to his hip joint, severely reducing his mobility. He claimed that he had been deprived of his mobility by the hospital's failure to treat the condition. He lost his claim because he was unable to prove that but for the defendant's negligence he would have been cured, since expert evidence showed that treatment was only successful in 25 per cent of cases. Therefore, he could not prove that on the balance of probability he would have regained full mobility, because he was unable to prove that treatment was successful in at least 51 per cent of cases. This principle was affirmed by the House of Lords in 2005 in *Gregg v Scott*. Due to the defendant's negligence, Mr Gregg's cancer was diagnosed late, reducing his chance of a cure to 25 per cent. Prompt diagnosis would have increased this chance to 46 per cent. His claim failed since even swift intervention would not on the balance of probability have resulted in his cure.

This principle was applied in a similar case more recently:

JD v Mather (2012)

Due to the defendant doctor's failure to diagnose the claimant's cancer, there was a seven months delay before a different doctor correctly identified it. By then it had spread and by the time the case reached trial the claimant was not expected to live much longer.

Held: the defendant was liable for reducing the claimant's life expectation.

Expert predictive evidence indicated that, on the balance of probability, prompt diagnosis would not have enabled a cure but would probably have slowed down the progress of the disease and increased life expectation by three years.

2 Causation in law (remoteness of damage)

The damage must not be too remote. The defendant is not held legally responsible for all the results of the breach.

The law treats intentional and unintentional torts differently as regards determining remoteness. We are presumed to intend all the direct consequences of our intentional acts, so in a tort like trespass the defendant will be liable for all the direct consequences regardless of whether they could reasonably have been foreseen (*Re Polemis* (1921, CA)). However, it was decided in *The Wagon Mound* (1961) (below) that damage caused to the claimant by a non-intentional tort like negligence or nuisance must be of a reasonably foreseeable type.

Overseas Tankships & Engineering v *Morts Dock & Engineering Ltd (The Wagon Mound (No. 1))* (1961, PC)

Fire damage was caused to the claimant's dock when a spark from a welding torch being used on the claimant's dock ignited oil which the defendants had negligently discharged into the harbour.

Held: the chance of fire breaking out in such circumstances was not reasonably foreseeable by the defendants who were therefore not liable.

In *Corr* v *IBC Vehicles Ltd* (2008) the House of Lords held Mr Corr's employer (IBC) liable for his death. The acute clinical depression arising from the disfigurement and post-traumatic stress resulting from the negligence of his employers made it reasonably foreseeable that he would commit suicide.

Provided that the *type of damage* is reasonably foreseeable, the defendant will be liable. It is irrelevant that the defendant might not have been able to foresee its cause or its severity.

Hughes v *Lord Advocate* (1963, HL)

The defendant telephone engineers left an inspection hole for the night, covered only by a tent and surrounded by lighted paraffin lamps. The child claimant was severely burned when he fell down the hole carrying a lamp which exploded as it hit the ground, producing a fireball.

Held: the defendants were held liable as it was reasonably foreseeable that a child would be attracted by the lamps and might be burned when playing with them. It was irrelevant that the explosion and the severity of the burn damage were not reasonably foreseeable.

Their Lordships reaffirmed this principle in the following case:

Jolley v *London Borough of Sutton* (2000, HL)

The defendant council failed to remove an abandoned boat from its land. The claimant (aged 14) was seriously injured when it fell on him after he had jacked it up to try to repair it.

Held: the council was liable, as the precise circumstances causing the accident did not have to be foreseeable. The boat was a safety hazard and likely to attract children.

Intervening acts

Intervening acts: events aggravating the claimant's damage which occur between the defendant's act and resulting damage.

Sometimes subsequent behaviour of the claimant or a third party may lead to an aggravation of the damage set in train by the defendant. The question for the court to decide is whether that **intervening act** breaks the chain of causation and thus prevents the defendant from being liable for the resulting damage. However, if the act is reasonably foreseeable and/or the defendant has a duty to prevent it then liability remains with the defendant, as the damage is not too remote.

McKew v *Holland & Cubitts Ltd* (1969, HL)

The defendant negligently injured the claimant's leg. As a consequence, it would quite often give way. In full knowledge of this, the claimant attempted to descend a steep stairway without using the hand rail. His leg gave way and he fell down the stairs, sustaining further injuries.

Held: the defendant was not liable for the injuries sustained in the fall; the claimant's descent of the stairs was an intervening act which was not reasonably foreseeable to the defendant. It was unreasonable of the claimant to behave as he had.

A different result was reached in *Wieland* (below) due to the claimant being unaware of the full effects of her previous accident.

Wieland v *Cyril Lord Carpets* (1969)

Due to negligence of the defendant, the claimant suffered injuries. She was sent to hospital and was fitted with a surgical collar. This impeded her head movement and, consequently, use of her bifocal spectacles. The next day when she was returning home from a check-up at the hospital, she felt so unwell that she called in at the defendant's showrooms, where her nephew worked, to get him to take her home. Unable to see properly, she fell down some steps and hurt herself.

Held: the defendant was liable for all the claimant's injuries since its negligence had left her unable to cope with the normal necessities of life. Descending the stairs was not unreasonable and did not break the chain of causation. She had not had time to adjust to the effects of her treatment and was still suffering from some residual shock at the time of the second accident.

When a third party is involved, the issue of whether the defendant had a duty to control them or to prevent such acts is relevant to determining liability.

Reeves v *Commissioner of Police for the Metropolis* (1999, HL)

Reeves committed suicide while in police custody. He was known at the time to be in a mentally unstable condition.

Held: the police were liable for his death as it was their negligence, in failing to supervise him appropriately, which enabled him to end his life. His intervening act was both reasonably foreseeable and the very thing that they were meant to prevent.

The 'eggshell skull' rule

'Eggshell skull' rule: exception to remoteness rule, which makes the defendant liable for unforeseeable damage to a claimant arising from a pre-existing medical condition or weakness.

The **'eggshell skull' rule** is an exception to the *Wagon Mound* principle. If the claimant has some particular weakness that makes him or her susceptible to a type of harm which is not reasonably foreseeable, the defendant will nevertheless be liable.

Smith v *Leech Brain & Co. Ltd* (1962)

Due to the defendants' negligence, an employee suffered a minor burn to his lip which would normally have caused only superficial damage. However, pre-cancerous cells in his lip which might otherwise have remained dormant were activated and he died. It was held that the defendants were liable for their employee's death although such serious damage was not foreseeable.

In *Page* v *Smith* (1995) the House of Lords held that the eggshell skull principle applied to both mental and physical conditions. The principle has also been held to apply to a claimant whose financial situation makes him or her more vulnerable to the damage caused by the defendant.

Mattocks v *Mann* (1993)

The claimant's car was damaged by the negligence of the defendant. When it had been repaired, there was a delay before she could recover it, as the garage refused to part with it until the insurance company came up with the money. The claimant did not have the funds to pay the bill herself.

Held: the defendant (in reality, his insurers) was liable for the cost of her hiring a car until she could recover her own.

Chapter summary

Problematic duties of care

The requirements for proof of duty of care in these problematic areas are rigorous and based on a high degree of foreseeability and proximity and public interest.

Pure economic loss

A special relationship of close proximity between the parties is essential, involving reliance by the claimant on the defendant's expertise and/or assumption of responsibility by the defendant. A disclaimer or conditional undertaking by the defendant prevents creation of the relationship.

Liability may result from negligent advice as well as other negligent behaviour.

Nervous shock

Shock causing physical/psychiatric injury which must be medically recognised.

Primary victims: if duty for physical harm exists it includes nervous shock.

Secondary victims: for a duty to exist the claimant must satisfy the *Alcock* criteria:

(a) sudden shock causing medically recognised condition;

(b) reasonable foreseeability of this reaction;

(c) claimant's reaction that of a reasonably brave person;

(d) claimant close to the accident in time and space.

Omissions/third-party acts

The defendant must generally owe a duty of care to the claimant/have a duty to control the third party.

Public authority exercise of statutory discretion

Duty of care is very rarely upheld.

Limited duty: fire and ambulance services.

Human rights action may be more viable.

Breach of duty of care

The claimant must prove that the defendant failed to take reasonable care taking into account:

(a) seriousness of the risk arising from the defendant's conduct;

(b) the extent of the reasonably foreseeable damage to the claimant;

(c) any relevant skill of the claimant; and

(d) the skill/qualifications of the defendant.

Causation: the link between the breach and the damage to the claimant must exist:

(a) *in fact:* the damage must be the result of the breach ('but for' test);

(b) *in law:* the damage must not be too remote from the breach of duty.

Test for remoteness: damage must be of a reasonably foreseeable kind in unintentional torts like negligence and nuisance.

Intervening acts make damage too remote unless they were reasonably foreseeable to the defendant.

Quiz 13

1 May a duty of care exist in the following circumstances?

  (a) To Ruby, who was wrongly advised by Turquoise on the value of her antique clock?

  (b) To Sapphire, by Beryl Electrical Appliances, the manufacturer of an electric kettle which was given to her for Christmas and which did not work?

  (c) To Emerald, who witnesses a horrific accident caused by Diamond in which Emerald's daughter Crystal was killed?

  (d) To Amber, who suffered theft from her premises; the thieves gained access to her premises through a hole in the next-door fence which belongs to Garnet?

2 What is the relevant standard of care against which the defendant will be judged in a negligence action?

3 What is the eggshell skull rule?

Answers to all quizzes can be found in Appendix 2.

Take a closer look

The following cases provide important examples of how the law you have studied in this chapter has developed. They are primary sources illustrating the law in action and give you more detail about their facts, as well as helping you to understand the law and to appreciate how the judges reached their decisions.

Try looking up the law report or accessing it via a database, e.g. Bailli (www.bailii.org/databases.html). LexisNexis or Westlaw may be available in your university or college library, or you may find extracts in a case book. (See Appendix 1: Additional resources.)

Hedley Byrne v *Heller* [1963] 2 All ER 575, HL

Alcock v *Wright* [1991] 4 All ER 907, HL

Fairchild v *Glenhaven Funeral Services* [2002] 3 All ER 305, HL

Overseas Tankships & Engineering v *Morts Dock & Engineering Ltd (The Wagon Mound) (No. 1)* [1961] 1 All ER 404

Web activity

Please go to: www.bbc.co.uk

Type 'Hillsborough Disaster' into the search facility. You will find some interesting materials on the background to the case and subsequent official inquiries.

Assignment 12

Alice bought a small bakery business. It was surveyed by George, for Happy Homes Building Society, which provided Alice with the mortgage. Alice paid Happy Homes for a summary report from George. This stated that there were no major structural problems and that the premises were worth the asking price. It concluded: 'This report is for valuation purposes only and will not give rise to any legal liability.'

Alice contracted with Industrial Kitchen Fitters Ltd (IKF) to refit the kitchen. They installed a new oven manufactured by Cinders plc.

On moving in, Alice discovered severe and large-scale dry rot when she fell through a storeroom floor and broke her leg. Her injuries and the eradication of the dry rot delayed the opening of the premises for several months.

A week after the business eventually opened, the new oven malfunctioned. As a result, a wedding cake was badly burnt, leading to a claim for damages for breach of contract against Alice, by the bride's father.

IKF have gone out of business.

Advise Alice of the possible liability in negligence of George and Cinders.

CHAPTER 15

Tort liability for premises

Introduction

This chapter explains the duties imposed by the law of tort on occupiers in relation to the maintenance and use of their premises. As an occupier, you have a duty to maintain the premises safely for the benefit of third parties on or outside the premises. You must also ensure that the use of premises does not cause unreasonable inconvenience to other people.

If you run a business this is particularly important, as your premises are likely to be visited more often than residential premises and may actually be open for public access.

A business must take account of the safety of staff, customers and other business visitors. It must also consider the neighbours and the wider public and take reasonable steps to prevent any business activity from causing harm, disruption or unreasonable disturbance to them.

If a legal action is brought against a business it will not be found liable if it can show a good defence. However, it is no defence to argue that it was an employee who committed the tort, as the business is generally vicariously liable.

An overview of the general defences in tort and the doctrine of vicarious liability conclude the tort section of this book.

Learning objectives

After studying this chapter you should be able to:

▶ appreciate the different ways in which an occupier may be liable for damage caused by the state of his or her premises or activities taking place there;

▶ distinguish between the effect of the Occupiers' Liability Act 1957 and the Occupiers' Liability Act 1984;

▶ recognise the situations where liability for public and private nuisance will arise;

▶ describe the circumstances where the defences to liability may exist;

▶ apply the doctrine of vicarious liability to hypothetical situations.

The occupier's liability to people on the premises

Negligent activities

Occupiers who carry out *activities* on their land without taking reasonable care may be liable to a third party under the general principles of negligence which you studied in the previous two chapters. If the harm is caused by the structural condition of the premises then liability may exist under the Occupiers' Liability Acts of 1957 and 1984. If caused by some activity on the premises the more appropriate claim is negligence.

Ogwo v *Taylor* (1987, HL)

The defendant negligently set the roof space on fire while using a blowtorch to burn off paint from weatherboarding on his house. The claimant, a fire-fighter, was injured in the ensuing conflagration.

Held: negligence was a more appropriate cause of action than the Occupiers' Liability Act 1957, given that the fire was triggered by the defendant's negligent use of the blow torch, rather than the condition of the premises. The defendant was liable as the claimant's injuries were a reasonably foreseeable consequence of the defendant's negligent behaviour.

Dangerous premises

Occupier (OLA 1957/1984): the person who is in control of the premises at the relevant time.

Occupiers have a legal duty to maintain the structure of their premises in a reasonably safe condition. If, for example, you run a hotel, you must take care to avoid harm to your guests from over-polished floors, low beams or slippery tiles. This part of the law is covered by statute.

The Occupiers' Liability Act 1957

Visitor: a person entering premises with the permission of the occupier under the OLA 1957.

The 1957 Act (OLA 1957) covers the liability of an **occupier** to what the Act calls '**visitors**', i.e. those people who are on the premises with the occupier's consent –family members, employees, customers, the window cleaner and the meter reader are obvious examples. However, under s 2(6) any person exercising a right conferred by law is also covered. This includes the police and fire fighters and anybody entering premises that are open to the public.

Maloney v *Torfaen CBC* (2005, CA)

M, who was drunk, was returning home in the dark. When taking a short cut from the road to his house he fell down a steep grassy slope onto the concrete floor of a subway, sustaining injuries.

Held: the defendant was not in breach of the OLA 1957, since M was not a visitor; the grassy slope was intended purely to be landscaping, not access, and so there was no implied permission to be on it.

Who is the occupier?

In *Wheat* v *Lacon* (1966) the occupier was defined as the person *in control of the premises* at the time of the accident. If you abandon your premises during radical refurbishment, the builder, shop fitter or plumber who is the cause of the hazard will be liable to the injured person rather than you. There may be more than one occupier at a time. In *Wheat* v *Lacon* the licensee and brewery owner of a pub were both held to be the occupiers of a pub since, under the lease, the brewery was responsible for repairs and thus controlled the state of the premises, while the licensee should have alerted the landlord to what was required.

What are premises?

Premises: under the OLA 1957 any fixed or moveable structure, widely construed by the courts.

Premises are widely defined by the Act and cover not only buildings and open spaces but also 'any fixed or moveable structure', and include 'any vessel, vehicle or aircraft' (s 1(3)). This has been held to include a wide variety of things, including scaffolding (*Kearney* v *Eric Waller* (1966)) and a large excavating machine (*Bunker* v *Charles Brand* (1969)).

The extent of the occupier's duty

The occupier must take reasonable care to ensure that the visitor is reasonably safe for the purposes for which the visitor is on the land (s 2(2)). There is no duty to eliminate all the risks attached to the visit. The occupier can reasonably assume that the average able-bodied adult will be aware of hazards which are normally found on the relevant premises and will take care to avoid them. So an hotel owner who fails to ensure that an upstairs window has restricted opening has not breached his duty to an adult who leans out so far that he falls from it (*Lewis v Six Counties* (2005, CA)).

Notice that the occupier's duty is limited to taking reasonable care to ensure reasonable safety and only for the purposes of that visit. The occupier's consent to a visitor's presence is limited by the purpose of the visit. If a visitor strays into a part of the premises where he or she is not reasonably expected and suffers injury, the occupier is unlikely to be liable under the 1957 Act as the visitor has exceeded the scope of his or her permission to be on the premises. There may be liability instead under the Occupiers' Liability Act 1984, which covers duty of care to entrants to premises without the occupier's permission (see *Tomlinson v Congleton Borough Council* (2003)) (see below).

The standard of care

As in negligence, there exists a duty to take *reasonable* care. The occupier is not liable just because the accident happens; the injured visitor will have to prove that the occupier failed to take reasonably adequate precautions to prevent it. What is reasonable is determined with reference to all the circumstances.

Cunningham v Reading Football Club (1991)

Due to the club's failure to maintain its terraces, loose lumps of masonry provided handy missiles for the use of football hooligans. As a result the claimant, a policeman on duty at the ground, was injured and sued the club.

Held: the club was in breach of its duty. It was reasonably foreseeable that troublesome elements which were known to cause problems at matches would use the masonry for illicit purposes.

The type of hazard, the nature of the premises and the needs of the visitor are all relevant. Each case has to be decided on its own facts.

Murphy v Bradford Metropolitan Council (1991)

A school keeper had twice cleared snow from a notoriously slippery path before 8.30 a.m. on the morning when the claimant was injured by a fall.

Held: reasonable care had not been taken: the nature of the path, the numbers of people using it and the severity of the weather demanded the use of grit, not just regular clearance.

Hufton v Somerset County Council (2011, CA)

The claimant student was seriously injured after slipping in a small patch of rain at an entrance to the school assembly hall. It was the practice on rainy days for signs to be displayed at the entrance to the council's school buildings requiring pupils to take a detour and not enter the school assembly hall directly from the playground. There was absorbent rubber matting at the entrance to the hall.

Held: the defendant was not liable. The school's risk assessment of this issue was appropriate and had been properly implemented. If rain started during a break there would reasonably be a short delay before the detour notices were displayed and during this time some students might already have entered the hall with wet feet.

Written warnings are not effective for those who cannot reasonably be expected to read or understand them: for example, children or the visually impaired.

A warning is not required where the hazard should have been obvious to the user.

Trustees of Portsmouth Youth Activities Committee v Poppleton (2008, CA)

P (an adult) was injured while using a climbing wall at the appellant's indoor premises. The floor was covered with thick matting. Rules forbidding jumping were displayed outside the climbing room. P attempted to jump off the climbing wall to a buttress on the opposite wall, but fell and became paralysed from the head down as a result. He argued that he believed that the matting would protect him if he fell and that he should personally have been told of the danger.

Held: no breach of duty had occurred. The risk of falling was entirely evident. No reasonable person could imagine that matting, even in large quantities, could protect against injury from an awkward fall.

Actionable damage

Damage to the person or to goods may give rise to liability under the 1957 Act.

Excluding liability

It is possible to exclude liability for breach of the duty imposed by the 1957 Act (s 2(1)), subject to the Unfair Contract Terms Act 1977 and the Consumer Rights Act 2015. Business liability cannot be excluded if the visitor dies or suffers personal injuries from the occupier's failure to take reasonable care.

Liability for damage to property may be excluded if this is judged to be reasonable in the circumstances: for example, if the damage is caused by a third party who is not subject to the occupier's control.

15

Tort liability for premises

Real life

Horace recently moved house. The path leading to the front door is slippery in wet weather. The other day after a heavy shower, Bernard, who was delivering advertising flyers for the local pizza parlour, slipped and fell straining his back. He has not been able to work since. As an occupier, Horace has a duty under the OLA 1957 for Bernard's reasonable safety, unless he has a notice on his gate saying 'No Junk Mail'. An occupier impliedly consents to people entering the premises to deliver items unless notice to the contrary is clearly given. He may be in breach of his duty if he should have taken precautions to reduce or remove the risk. He might genuinely not know that it exists if it is only apparent in wet weather and maybe it had not rained since he moved in. If he should have known, a suitably clear notice ('Take care slippery path!') would probably be sufficient at least as an interim measure.

However if Horace displayed a notice saying 'No Junk Mail' on the front gate, Bernard becomes a trespasser by entering,

Under the OLA 1984, Bernard has no claim unless he can prove that Horace owes him a duty. If there has previously been sufficient rain to alert Horace to the problem, he may owe a duty as the problem with the path is one which could quite easily be rectified. Horace might argue that the notice refusing junk mail means that he need not anticipate people delivering it, but this will not be any use if he knows that the notice has already been ignored by other people. If a duty does exist, it could be discharged by displaying a suitable warning notice.

The Occupiers' Liability Act 1984

This Act regulates the duty of an occupier of premises to people who do not have permission from the occupier to be on the premises. The Act embraces not only trespassers but other entrants such as visitors to national parks or people exercising a 'right to roam' under the Countryside and Rights of Way Act 2000. Not surprisingly, the occupier owes only a very limited duty of care. It would not be in the public interest to encourage a burglar to claim damages after falling down the stairs of the house which he was rifling. However, more innocent parties, straying onto premises containing highly dangerous plant or machinery, clearly deserve some protection. This is illustrated by the following case, which preceded the 1984 Act but was based on similar principles.

British Railways Board v Herrington (1972, HL)

The claimant, a child of six, was injured when he strayed onto the railway from a public park through broken fencing belonging to the railway, whose drivers previously had reported trespassers on the line.

Held: the Board was liable for the child trespasser's injuries since it knew of the possibility of trespassers and could have avoided the risk at 'small trouble and expense' (i.e. by mending the fence).

When is the duty owed?

Under s 1(3) of the 1984 Act, the following criteria must all be satisfied:

1 the occupier must have reasonable knowledge of the danger;

2 the occupier must know or reasonably suspect that potential entrants, etc. are in the vicinity of the premises or are reasonably likely to come into the vicinity;

3 the risk is one against which, in all the circumstances, it is reasonable for the occupier to offer some protection.

The courts will take account of the resources of the occupier relative to the likelihood of entrants and the extent of the danger. A lake in a remote hill area presents much less of a danger than an electrified railway running through a heavily populated locality. The following two cases will indicate possible approaches to determining whether the criteria in s 1(3) have been satisfied.

Maloney v *Torfaen CBC* (2005, CA)

(For facts see above, page 341.)

Held: the defendant did not owe a duty under the OLA 1984 as the danger, which was heightened by the claimant being drunk and the accompanying darkness, was not so obvious that the defendant should reasonably have known of it. Further, the presence of the claimant on the slope could not reasonably be anticipated. A safe path nearby led directly to the claimant's premises.

Keown v *Coventry Healthcare NHS Trust* (2006, CA)

K, aged 13, fell when climbing the underside of a fire escape on premises owned by the hospital and used by the public as a cut through.

Held: the defendant was not liable. No duty of care was owed to K, as the danger did not arise out of the state of the premises. K was injured as a result of what K chose to do on the premises rather than the condition of the premises.

Premises not dangerous to an adult might present a hazard to a child and it was a matter of fact or degree whether or not they did. It was not necessarily appropriate, however, to ignore a child's choice to indulge in dangerous behaviour just because he was a child.

In *Keown* the court may have been influenced by the fact that the claimant had strayed from a public access area on to the fire escape. Making the latter inaccessible to trespassers might have created a worse risk to people in the building in the event of fire.

The extent of the duty

The occupier's duty under the 1984 Act is limited to taking such care as is reasonable to see that the entrant *does not suffer injury* from the relevant danger (s 1(4)). It is

15

Tort liability for premises

interesting to compare this with the *positive* duty owed to the lawful entrant under the 1957 Act whereby the occupier must ensure that visitors are *reasonably safe*. The occupier's responsibility to the entrant is a *negative* one: to take reasonable steps to prevent harm.

Performing the duty

Such a minimal duty can be performed by taking reasonable steps to keep people out. A sufficiently explicit warning clearly displayed will generally be deemed enough for adults, while properly maintained boundary fencing should be a sufficient deterrent to children.

The following case illustrates how these principles are applied.

Ratcliff v *Harper Adams Agricultural College* (1999, CA)

The claimant was a student at the college. One night he entered the grounds of the college pool by climbing over a seven-foot wall. He was paralysed when he broke his neck after diving into the pool where the water was too shallow.

Held: the college was not liable. Even if it should have been aware that students trespassed in this manner, it was not in breach of its duty. Their duty did not extend to warning adult trespassers against evident risks, or to lighting the premises at night to make them safe for trespassers.

The House of Lords took a similarly robust approach in the following case.

Tomlinson v *Congleton Borough Council* (2003, HL)

Mr Tomlinson dived into shallow water in a lake in a public park. He was paralysed when he struck his head on a rocky outcrop. The lake was a flooded quarry and signs beside it clearly prohibited swimming and warned that it was dangerous.

Held: no duty was owed. Since the claimant must have known of the risk of striking his head on the lake bottom before he dived, there was no duty to warn of risks that were obvious and against which the defendant could not reasonably be expected to offer some protection.

It would be unreasonable to impose a duty on public authorities to protect people from self-inflicted injuries that resulted from taking risks voluntarily in the face of obvious dangers.

Actionable damage

Liability under the 1984 Act is restricted to death and personal injuries only (s 2(9)).

Duties of an occupier to people outside the premises

An occupier owes a variety of duties in tort to people who are not actually on the premises. Where physical damage to people or their property occurs which is caused by an adjoining occupier's failure to take reasonable care, action may be taken in negligence.

A heavier burden of liability, based purely on the reasonable foreseeability of damage, is imposed through the law of nuisance. This imposes liability not only for tangible harm, but also for unreasonable levels of inconvenience arising from the occupier's use of premises. The law of nuisance is composed of two separate torts (private and public nuisance) which have some characteristics in common.

Private nuisance

Occupier (private nuisance): the owner/tenant of the premises affected by the nuisance.

This protects an **occupier** of land against unreasonable interference with the enjoyment of his or her premises caused by the state of a nearby occupier's land or activities taking place on it. A nuisance is usually caused unintentionally, indirectly and as a by-product of an on-going state of affairs on the defendant's land.

Proof of liability

The claimant must prove, first, that the defendant has caused *damage*. This includes:

1 *Damage to the structure of the claimant's premises.*

2 *Damage to goods on the claimant's land.* In British *Celanese* v *Hunt* (1969, CA) metal foil stored on the defendant's premises blew onto power cables causing a cut in the electricity supply to the claimant's factories. The defendant was liable for damage to machinery and components.

Liability for personal injury may also arise, though this is only actionable if the injury was caused by the defendant's negligent or intentional conduct. Private nuisance protects interests in land, rather than personal injuries.

Amenity damage: nuisance liability may arise as a result of intangible interference with enjoyment of the premises, such as noise or smell.

3 *Amenity damage.* Liability may arise for **amenity damage** where the defendant's behaviour has unreasonably reduced the comfort and convenience of use of the claimant's premises. This may accompany, or exist independently of, property damage and can cover a wide range of annoying activities, commonly including noise, smells, smoke and vibrations. In *Halsey* v *Esso* Petroleum (1961) Esso were held liable for a variety of nuisances emanating from their processing plant. Pungent and nauseating smells invaded the claimant's premises and at night noise from the boilers made the claimant's doors and windows vibrate, preventing sleep. All day the passage of heavy lorries caused a high level of noise.

Davey v Harrow Corporation (1957, CA)

Mr Davey sued Harrow Corporation for subsidence damage caused to his house by trees growing on the corporation's land.

Held: the council was liable as it had unreasonably interfered with the claimant's land by allowing the encroachment of the tree roots onto the claimant's land.

In a private nuisance claim, the claimant must show that the defendant's activities caused *an unreasonable level of interference*. It is usually sufficient to prove some tangible damage.

St Helen's Smelting Co. v Tipping (1865, HL)

Fumes from the defendant's chemical works damaged the claimant's trees.

Held: this damage indicated an unreasonable interference with the claimant's enjoyment of his land. It was irrelevant that the defendant's activities were not out of keeping with the locality.

However, where amenity damage only is claimed, it is harder to prove unreasonable interference. Most of us would claim to suffer disturbance from our neighbours' activities; few of us, however, would be able to persuade the court that the level of interference was unreasonable. The law aims to maintain a fair balance of interest between parties and requires a certain amount of give and take. While your shop is being refitted your next-door neighbour may be somewhat inconvenienced by noise or dust, but, provided you are doing what you reasonably can to keep it under control, you are within your legal rights. In six months' time, when your neighbour is having major work done, you will be expected to show a similar understanding.

Each case is decided on its own facts, but any of the following criteria may be relevant:

1 *Locality.* In *Sturges v Bridgeman* (1879), Thesiger J declared: '*What would be a nuisance in Belgrave Square would not necessarily be so in Bermondsey.*' No doubt Mr Justice Thesiger was glad to live nearer Belgrave Square than Bermondsey, but you can see the common sense of his pronouncement. If you live in an industrial and commercial area with a high density of population, the level of peace and quiet is bound to be reduced. Similarly, agricultural activity is to be expected in a rural area and some level of related smell or noise must be endured. Note, however, that locality is relevant only in a claim restricted to amenity damage. It is not appropriate where some tangible loss has been caused to the claimant (see *St Helen's Smelting Co. v Tipping*).

Planning permission is no defence to nuisance. In *Wheeler v Saunders* (1996) the defendant had been granted planning permission to expand his pig farm. This resulted in a pervasive unpleasant and intense smell in the neighbourhood. The Court of Appeal held that the planning permission only allowed the building and operation of the farm, not the creation of the nuisance. If you can persuade the court that the planning permission was so radical that, in effect, it authorised a change in the nature of the locality, this may be a justification for resulting disruption. In *Gillingham Borough Council* v *Medway Chatham Dock Ltd* (1993) the Dock Company was granted planning permission to operate around the clock. What had been a largely quiet and residential area became busy, noisy and dirty due to the constant passage of heavy lorries to and from the dock, but the claimants lost their case because it was held that the planning permission had changed the character of the area and the issue of reasonableness must be judged by reference to this new character. However, this will only apply in exceptional cases because the court is generally unwilling to acknowledge a character change.

Watson and Others v *Croft Promo-Sport Ltd* (2009, CA)

The defendants were granted planning permission to run motorcycle racing on a former airfield, in an essentially rural location. The claimants, whose houses were 300 metres from the race track, complained of the noise.

Held: the grant of planning permission does not automatically affect third-party rights to quiet enjoyment of land. Here it had in no way changed the nature of the locality and the level of the defendant's activity was unreasonable. Therefore an injunction would be issued limiting use to 40 days per year.

The Supreme Court produced a useful checklist of factors for the court to take into account concerning the relevance of planning permission to the creation of nuisance in *Coventry and Others* v *Laurence* (2014) (see 'In the news' below). It indicates something of a shift in judicial approach by indicating that while planning permission may be highly relevant it is only one piece of the evidence under consideration and is not conclusive in and of itself.

In the news

Coventry and others v *Lawrence* [2014] SC

For over 13 years the defendants had operated motor racing activities on their premises in rural Suffolk with planning permission which limited time and frequency of use. These restrictions were observed by the defendants. Subsequently the claimants moved into a house about half a kilometre from the stadium and claimed that they had been unaware of the activities taking place there before moving in. They sued the defendants for noise nuisance and were successful in the High Court which granted damages with the option of applying for an injunction. On appeal this judgment was overturned. The claimants then appealed to the Supreme Court which re-instated the High Court decision and held the defendants liable.

Held: The planning permission only justified the defendants' activity in so far as it did not amount to a nuisance. Planning permission does not automatically permit creation of nuisance.

A planning authority should not be able to deprive an occupier of their rights to object to what would otherwise amount to a nuisance without providing compensation, when nothing in the relevant legislation suggested this possibility.

A planning decision in and of itself did not determine the civil law rights of the occupier.

The evidence before the planning authority did not dictate the outcome to the court but was merely for the court's consideration. Each case regardless of the size of the development, or a change in the nature of the locality, turns on its facts and is open to the judge's discretion.

2 *The timing, level, duration and frequency of the nuisance.* Night-time noise is more likely to be actionable than noise during the day. See, for example, *Leeman v Montague* (1936) on the nocturnal crowing of cockerels. The more substantial the inconvenience to the claimant the less important is lengthy duration or frequency. The court may be prepared to allow the activity to continue subject to reduction of such factors to a reasonable level (see *Watson and Others v Croft Promo-Sport Ltd* (2009, CA) (above)).

3 *The practicability of preventing the nuisance.* In *Andreae v Selfridge* (1938) the defendant was held liable in nuisance through failure to prove that it had taken reasonable steps to reduce the noise and dust arising from building operations. The law acknowledges that some annoyance to the claimant may be an inevitable consequence of the defendant's activity. A defendant who can prove that they have taken all reasonable precautions to avoid causing annoyance is rarely liable for intangible, as opposed to tangible, damage.

Moy v *Stoop* (1909)

The claimant complained about the noise of children crying in the defendant's day nursery next door.

Held: the noise was an unavoidable consequence of the defendant's activity. It was not caused by neglect by the defendant of the children's welfare, and therefore the defendant was not liable.

4 *The defendant's motive.* Most nuisance is caused by unthinking behaviour, but occasionally the defendant may actually be trying to cause distress to the claimant. If the claimant can prove such motivation, this may cast new light on the defendant's behaviour, rendering potentially reasonable behaviour unreasonable.

Hollywood Silver Fox Farm v *Emmett* (1936)

Believing that the presence of the claimant's farm was inhibiting the sale of building plots on his own land, the defendant carried out intensive shooting operations on his land throughout the silver fox breeding season. He knew that this would disturb the animals and discourage successful breeding and thus cause damage to the claimant's business.

Held: the defendant was liable since his malicious intentions made his behaviour unreasonable.

5 *The claimant's sensitivity.* The claimant will have to prove that the level of nuisance is higher than that which the average person could reasonably be expected to endure. A sensitive claimant cannot impose a heavier duty on the defendant to accommodate his unusual need. However, if the level of interference would be unreasonable to the average claimant, the defendant will be liable to one who is sensitive, provided the damage is reasonably foreseeable.

Robinson v *Kilvert* (1889)

The defendant installed a boiler in his basement. This caused a rise in temperature and a drop in humidity in the claimant's adjoining basement. Most people would have been pleased, but the claimant complained because the previous conditions were essential for the storage of paper which became damaged by the warmer and drier air.

Held: the defendant's behaviour was not a nuisance as warming the premises did not amount to unreasonable behaviour. The claimant's damage arose from the peculiar sensitivity of his goods.

But compare this superficially similar case which produced a contrary result.

McKinnon Industries Ltd v *Walker* (1951)

The escape of noxious fumes from the defendant's premises caused damage to the claimant's orchids.

Held: the defendant was liable as any plants would have suffered similarly, not just exotic blooms.

6 *Public benefit.* This will be taken into account to some extent in assessing competing interests and reasonableness. The fact that planning permission exists for the particular land use may be relevant here. However, if the defendant's behaviour is found to be unreasonable, the fact that it is of public benefit does not prevent liability, though it may affect the nature of the remedy.

Dennis v *Ministry of Defence* (2003)

RAF low-flying training activity caused noise of great severity and frequency over the claimant's estate.

Held: the disturbance amounted to unreasonable interference. However, it was in the public interest that such training flights should continue, so damages must suffice in lieu of an injunction.

Reasonable foreseeability

The burden of proof is easier for the claimant to discharge in nuisance than in negligence, since in nuisance the claimant does not need to prove that the defendant failed to take reasonable care. The claimant needs show only that the type of damage caused was a *reasonably foreseeable consequence to a person in the defendant's position*. The state of the defendant's knowledge is crucial.

Defendants will naturally be expected to anticipate the consequences of their own actions. Where the nuisance arises from a state of affairs created by a third party like a previous occupant or a trespasser, a defendant will not be liable unless they should reasonably have known about this and of the risk to the claimant.

Sedleigh-Denfield v *O'Callaghan* (1940, HL)

A ditch ran across the boundary of the defendant's property. The local authority installed a culvert (drainage pipe) in the ditch near the point where the ditch left the defendant's land. The end of the pipe extended into the defendant's property and a grid should have been placed at the other end of the pipe. The workman, however, left it on top of the pipe where it was completely useless. The defendant had not given permission to the local authority which was therefore trespassing when it entered his land. The defendant was aware that there was a danger of flooding if debris blocked the pipe. Usually, the defendant kept the pipe clear, but once this job was overlooked, rubbish built up and caused a flood on the claimant's property during heavy rain.

Held: the defendant was liable in private nuisance as it had failed to take reasonably practicable steps to remove a known hazard from the land. It would have been very easy to put the grid into place and the flood would not have occurred.

The courts have extended this principle to cover entirely naturally occurring events.

Leakey v *The National Trust* (1980, CA)

The claimant owned a house at the foot of a steep hill in the care of the National Trust. The claimant alerted the Trust to evidence of minor landslips which had occurred due to drought. A major slippage then occurred and large quantities of debris landed in the claimant's garden.

Held: as the Trust knew of the risk of such damage, it would be liable as it had failed to take reasonable steps to prevent landslips.

Who may sue in private nuisance?

Private nuisance protects the right to peaceable enjoyment of land and has traditionally been seen in law as the exclusive right of the owner-occupier, or tenant, since it pertains to the capital or amenity value of the land. Other residents do not have the right to sue in private nuisance.

Malone v *Laskey* (1907)

The claimant and her husband lived in premises owned by the defendant, her husband's employer, but without a tenancy. The claimant was hit on the head by a lavatory cistern which became detached from its fixings due to the vibration of machinery on adjoining premises, and she claimed against the defendant in private nuisance.

Held: her claim could not succeed, because she was 'a mere licensee' and had no proprietary rights over the premises.

The principle was upheld by the House of Lords in *Hunter* v *Canary Wharf* (1997), which disapproved the Court of Appeal's decision in *Khorasandjian* v *Bush* (1993) to extend the right to sue to members of the occupier's family.

Who may be sued?

The current occupier is the most usual defendant, but the party who caused the nuisance (for example, a previous occupant) may be sued. A landlord who lets premises knowing that their use will create a nuisance is also liable. Thus, in *Tetley* v *Chitty* (1986) a landlord, who had let some premises for development as a go-karting track, was liable for the resulting noise nuisance.

However, to be actionable the nuisance must be an inevitable result of the letting and must relate to the land use by the tenant.

Hussain and Livingstone v *Lancaster City Council* (1999, CA)

The claimants were victims of a sustained campaign of racial harassment by a number of people including the defendant's tenants. The council had statutory powers under the Housing Act 1985 to evict tenants and other occupants causing nuisance or annoyance to neighbours.

Held: the defendant was not liable in nuisance. This was restricted to the use of land by the defendant which interfered with the claimants' land. The harassment complained of fell outside the tort of nuisance; the campaign was not the result of the letting.

The defence of prescription

Prescription: the right to continue to commit a nuisance which has already persisted for 20 years.

Defendants will not be liable if they can prove that they have been causing the nuisance for *20 years* without anybody taking action against them. It is not enough to show that an activity has been carried on for that length of time; the court will have to be satisfied that it caused a nuisance to the claimant or his predecessors for the whole of that time for **prescription** to be a defence.

Sturges v *Bridgeman* (1879)

A confectioner had a workshop in premises adjacent to the claimant dentist. Noisy equipment in the workshop had been in use for over 20 years, but caused no problems until the dentist built a new consulting room in his garden, near the boundary wall where the noise was highly audible. He sued the confectioner.

Held: the defendant was liable in private nuisance since the noise level was unreasonable. Prescription was not an appropriate defence as it was the activity rather than the nuisance which had continued for 20 years. It was irrelevant that the claimant had moved into the noisier environment.

Public nuisance

The scope of liability

The tort of public nuisance resembles private nuisance as it may arise from similar situations, including the escape of noise, smells, dust and vibration. However, the scope of public nuisance is wider, covering any activity that unreasonably interferes with the comfort and convenience of the public. This includes the obstruction of highways or waterways. Behaviour giving rise to a public nuisance always involves criminal behaviour. Today there are a large number of statutory criminal offences to protect public health, covering pollution of all kinds and regulating businesses involved in the preparation and marketing of food. Until the twentieth century, these activities were prosecuted under the umbrella of public nuisance. Civil action may also be taken.

Potential defendants

Action may be taken against the person who created the nuisance, or the current occupier of land from which a nuisance emanates.

Potential claimants

Tort action may be taken to protect the public at large and an injunction may be sought, by the Attorney-General or by a local authority. Individuals are entitled to take action only where they have suffered special damage greater than that suffered by the public at large.

Notice that, unlike private nuisance, claimants are not required to have any occupational rights to the land where they suffer damage, to entitle them to sue. Sufficient geographical proximity to the nuisance is all that is required.

Mint v *Good* (1950, CA)

A garden wall belonging to the defendant collapsed onto the pavement and injured the claimant.

Held: the claimant should succeed in his claim. Blockage of the pavement was a public nuisance: any members of the public passing by would be inconvenienced. The claimant who was injured clearly physically suffered special harm.

Proof of liability

To establish public nuisance, the following points must be satisfied:

1 *The nuisance must be capable of affecting 'the public'.* The nuisance must potentially affect too many people to make it reasonable to expect any one person to take action to stop it.

Corby Group Litigation v *Corby District Council* (2009)

The 18 young claimants in this case were all born with limb deformities between 1986 and 1999 to mothers who lived in, or regularly visited, Corby while pregnant. They claimed that the council was liable for the birth defects that they had suffered resulting from their mothers' ingestion or inhalation of toxic substances released by the council's reclamation of land, which had previously been occupied by a vast steelworks.

Held: subject to proof of causation by each individual claimant, the council was liable in public nuisance, negligence and breach of the Environmental Protection Act 1990 from 1985–1997. It had not taken reasonable care to prevent reasonably foreseeable airborne exposure of the claimants' mothers to a variety of dangerous toxins, including cadmium, chromium and dioxins. These had been present in the dust and mud disturbed at the sites that were being reclaimed and were spread by wind across the locality or along local roads when materials were being moved by lorry. The statistically significant size of the cluster of birth defects, in children born between 1989 and 1998 in the defendant locality, supported this conclusion.

2 *The level of inconvenience must be unreasonable.* Similar criteria are relevant here as apply to private nuisance.

3 *Damage must result.* This includes physical damage to the person, land or goods, as well as amenity damage. Pure economic loss may also be actionable. Thus, in *Lyons & Co.* v *Gulliver* (1914) the defendants were held liable for causing loss of custom to the claimant's tea shop, access to which was blocked by long queues outside the defendants' theatre.

4 *The damage must be reasonably foreseeable to the defendant.* As in private nuisance, the claimant is not required to prove any failure to take reasonable care. Defendants may avoid liability by showing that they took all reasonably practicable precautions to prevent reasonably foreseeable damage. A very high standard is required where the nuisance occurs on the highway.

Dollman v *Hillman* (1941)

The claimant was awarded damages for injuries caused by slipping on a piece of fat, which had been dropped on the pavement outside the defendant's butcher's shop.

The rule in *Rylands* v *Fletcher*

This principle is derived from the case of *Rylands* v *Fletcher* (1865) concerning a mill owner who employed contractors to construct a reservoir on his land. In the course of the construction disused mine shafts were uncovered and negligently sealed. When the reservoir was filled, water leaked through the shafts and flooded an adjoining mine owned by the claimant, causing considerable loss and business interruption. It was held that the defendant was *strictly liable* for this damage, because 'a person who for his own purposes, brings onto his land and collects or keeps there anything likely to do mischief if it escapes, must keep it in at his peril and if he does not do so is prima facie liable for all the damage which is the natural consequence of its escape' (Blackburn J). This was affirmed on appeal by the House of Lords, with qualification that the defendant's use of land must be *'non-natural'*.

The proof points of the rule

1 *'Things' within the rule*. Potentially this covers anything likely to do harm on escape. Something perfectly safe if contained can do much damage if it escapes. There are innumerable examples, e.g. gas (*Batcheller* v *Tunbridge Wells Gas Company* (1901)), electricity (*National Telephone Co* v *Baker* (1893)), as well as some rather bizarre cases such as *Hale* v *Jennings* (1938): escaping chair-o-plane demolishing an adjacent shooting gallery at a fair, and *Crowhurst* v *Amersham Burial Board* (1878): yew branches falling from the defendant's graveyard and poisoning the claimant's cattle in the field next door.

2 *Accumulation*. The defendant must have brought the thing onto the land; it must not have got there in the course of nature.

3 *Non-natural use of land*. This has gradually been defined more and more strictly by the courts. As early as 1913 it was held that it must be more than unusual: 'it must be some special use bringing with it increased danger to others and must not be the ordinary use of land or such a use as is proper for the general benefit of the community' (Lord Moulton in *Rickards* v *Lothian* (1913)). In *Read* v *Lyons* (1947) which concerned storage of explosives at a munitions factory in wartime, Lord Porter held that 'all the circumstances of time and place and the practices of mankind must be taken into consideration, so that what might be regarded as dangerous and non-natural may vary according to the circumstances'. Unsurprisingly, *Rylands* v *Fletcher* liability was not held to exist. In *Transco plc* v *Stockport Corporation* (2003) Lord Nicholls held the defendant's use of land must be *'extraordinary and exceptional'* to give rise to liability, and Lord Hoffmann suggested that only those risks against which it would be unreasonable to expect the claimant to be insured against should be covered.

4 *Escape*. The thing must escape from a place occupied by the defendant to a place outside their occupation and control. The defendant need have no proprietary interest over land from which escape takes place; it is their *control* of the thing which is crucial. Escape may be onto the highway, so the claimant also need not have a proprietary interest in land.

At first, *Rylands* v *Fletcher* was treated by the courts as a new legal principle governing a vaguely defined category of what at the time were regarded as exceptional and dangerous activities. Large numbers of cases concerned escapes from industrial installations. In the nineteenth and early twentieth centuries these were more prevalent and successful litigation commonplace, so initially there were many successful claims. Today, we would regard such use of land as commonplace and such activities as generally safe.

The strict liability principle has been judicially undermined and liability today is based on reasonable foreseeability as it is in nuisance (*Cambridge Water Co* v *Eastern Counties Leather* (1994)). A whole range of defences has also developed, such as statutory authority which gives protection to some public bodies from liability, provided no negligence is involved. Claimants who succeed do so because they can prove nuisance or negligence and today *Rylands* v *Fletcher* is generally regarded merely as '*a sub-species of nuisance*' (Lord Bingham in *Transco plc* v *Stockport Metropolitan Council* (2003)). Some judges have suggested that it should be abolished altogether, but the House of Lords in the *Cambridge Water* and *Transco* cases did not approve of such a move. It was acknowledged as a viable cause of action in *Colour Quest and Others* v *Total Downstream UK plc and Others* (2009), though as negligence liability existed, strict liability was not in issue.

Colour Quest Ltd v *Total Downstream UK plc and Others* (2009)

In December 2005 a huge explosion and resulting fire occurred at an oil storage facility in Hertfordshire controlled by Total UK. Staff at the facility failed to notice that a gauge had stuck, causing a tank to overfill. The back-up switch also failed and the facility was flooded with oil. The vapour ignited and there was a massive explosion (2.4 on the Richter scale and audible across the English Channel). Forty people were injured and the blast destroyed oil storage facilities belonging to other parties on the site, as well as considerably damaging businesses and property within a radius of seven miles.

Held: Total UK was liable in negligence to Colour Quest for its failure to employ appropriate procedures to prevent tank overflow, despite the fact that this was a recurring problem. It was liable in *Rylands* v *Fletcher* to persons who had suffered damage outside the site and in nuisance to those on and outside the site. Total is expected to have to pay £750 million in damages to the other oil companies on the site and hundreds of local businesses and householders.

Remedies

In claims in public and private nuisance and *Rylands* v *Fletcher*, the remedies are damages and/or an injunction.

The impact of the Human Rights Act 1998

The courts have acknowledged the relevance of the Human Rights Act 1998 in some nuisance cases.

> ## *McKenna* v *British Aluminium Ltd* (2002)
>
> The claimants were all children from over 30 families who claimed nuisance by British Aluminium in permitting a factory to emit fumes and noise which had caused them mental distress and physical harm. They argued that this breached their rights under Article 8 (right to respect for privacy and family life) and under Protocol 1, Article 1 (right to peaceful enjoyment of possessions) of the ECHR.
>
> British Aluminium argued that the claims should be struck out as none of the children had the necessary proprietary interest in the land to enable them to sue in nuisance.
>
> **Held:** the action should not be struck out since there were strong arguments supporting the claim. Potentially the law of nuisance was in conflict with the Convention rights and arguably needed to be developed compatibly. Otherwise, a person living in his home where enjoyment of property was interfered with would be unable to protect his Convention rights unless he also had proprietary rights. The matter could only be decided at trial.

Note that the *McKenna* case does not in itself change the law of nuisance. That could only happen after a full trial decision, which might well result in appeal to the House of Lords. No such proceedings seem to have taken place. However, this case does indicate the potential for development in the light of the Human Rights Act 1998.

In *Dennis* v *Ministry of Defence* (2003) (see above) the judge held that a declaration that the Ministry of Defence had breached Article 8 and Protocol 1 would have been in order, had the nuisance action not provided an appropriate remedy.

An action under the Human Rights Act 1998, therefore, may provide an alternative where a public authority is the defendant. Had the Hussains (*Hussain and Livingstone* v *Lancaster City Council* (1999, CA) (see above) been able to sue the council for breach of Article 8, they might well have been successful, but sadly their claim arose before the Act was implemented.

Defences in tort

Even if a claimant can satisfy the court that the defendant's conduct does amount to a tort, the defendant may be able to prove that there are mitigating circumstances which remove, or at least reduce, liability. The following defences may be relevant to any of the torts covered in this book.

1 Consent

If the claimant expressly or impliedly consented to the defendant's behaviour, the defendant is not liable. The claimant must make the decision with full knowledge of the likely outcome and be free to make a choice.

Legal area	1957 Act	1984 Act	Public nuisance	Private nuisance
Potential defendant	Person(s) in control of premises	Person(s) in control of premises	Owner/tenant/creator of nuisance	Owner/tenant/creator of nuisance
Potential claimant	Lawful entrants	Trespassers	Any member of public suffering special damage	Occupiers of adjacent premises
Where damage occurred	On defendant's premises	On defendant's premises	Anywhere inside or outside defendant's premises	On premises occupied by claimant
Type of damage	Personal injuries, damage to goods	Personal injuries only	Personal injuries, damage to property, interference with enjoyment of premises	Damage to property, interference with enjoyment of premises, possibly personal injuries
Cause of damage	State of premises	State of premises	State of premises and activities taking place there or obstructing highway	State of premises and activities taking place there
Nature of liability	Failure to take resonable care of visitor's safety	Failure to take resonable care to avoid causing injury to trespassers	Failure reasonably to foresee damage to claimant	Failure reasonably to foresee damage to claimant

Figure 15.1 The occupier's civil legal liability for premises

> ### *Smith* v *Baker* (1891, HL)
>
> The claimant quarryman was injured by rocks falling from overhead machinery. He had protested about the danger, but continued to work after being ordered to do so and being told that he could leave if he was unhappy with his working conditions.
>
> **Held:** the claimant had not consented to the risk of injury as, although he knew of the danger, he had never freely consented to the risk. He had no real choice in the matter.

Rescue cases

If the claimant is injured rescuing somebody from a hazard created by the negligence of the defendant, the claimant only consents to the risk, if:

1 *They had no legal or moral duty to intervene.* The nature of the claimant's job may impose a legal duty to assist in an emergency: firefighters and the police are obvious

examples; a schoolteacher supervising children on an outing would also qualify as they have a legal duty to act as a responsible parent to their pupils. Most people seeing a third party in danger could be said to be under a moral duty to take *some* action.

2 *Their method of intervention was unreasonable in the circumstances.* The greater the danger and the more able the rescuer, the more reasonable it will be to take risks. Nobody expects a non-swimmer to plunge into deep water to rescue someone in distress, as one potential drowning may turn into two certain ones. However, a non-swimmer may have a moral duty at least to throw a lifebelt and summon assistance.

Compare the next two cases to see the difference between reasonable and unreasonable risk.

Haynes v *Harwood* (1935, CA)

A policeman was injured when attempting to stop bolting horses which were pulling a van in a busy street.

Held: the defendant was liable for the policeman's injuries; the policeman had not consented to the risk as he had a legal duty to prevent danger to the public and his intervention was a natural and foreseeable result of the defendant's negligence in failing to secure the horses.

Would-be heroics must be justified in the circumstances or will be treated as reckless.

Sylvester v *Chapman* (1935)

The claimant, while visiting a travelling menagerie, attempted to extinguish a cigarette end that he noticed was smouldering near straw bales beside a leopard's cage. To do so he climbed a safety barrier. The leopard, displeased by the disturbance, reached out between the bars of the cage and clawed him.

Held: the claimant had consented to the risk. While he had a moral duty to alert the staff to the fire risk, by putting himself unnecessarily in danger he had acted unreasonably.

Consent to negligence

It is not generally in the public interest to allow defendants to avoid liability for their careless behaviour. Where claimants have clearly acted recklessly, though, without regard for their own safety, or have willingly participated in the defendant's careless behaviour, the defendant may be provided with a defence.

ICI v *Shatwell* (1964, HL)

The claimant shot firer was injured when helping to carry out a controlled explosion. The claimant was experienced in the work and had encouraged the team leader to use inappropriate equipment.

Held: the claimant had consented to the risk of injury by acting recklessly in regard to his own safety.

> ### *Ratcliff* v *Harper Adams College* (1999, CA)
>
> A student, who was paralysed after breaking his neck when trespassing in his college swimming pool outside opening hours, was deemed to have consented to the risk of diving into shallow water.

2 Contributory negligence

Under the Law Reform (Contributory Negligence) Act 1945, the court may reduce the damages payable by the defendant if the claimant has failed to take reasonable care for *their own safety* and so aggravated the damage suffered. In cases where failure to wear a seat belt has aggravated injuries to a claimant it is usual to reduce damages by 25 per cent (*Froom* v *Butcher* (1975, CA)). The defence may succeed where their argument of consent fails and is applicable to any tort not based on intentional behaviour, e.g. deceit.

Here are two illustrative cases.

> ### *Sayers* v *Harlow Urban District Council* (1958, CA)
>
> The claimant visited the defendant's public lavatory and was trapped when the lock jammed. After trying to attract attention for 15 minutes, she attempted to climb out over the partition. Unfortunately, she fell when the toilet roll, which she was using as a foothold, rotated and threw her to the floor.
>
> **Held:** the claimant's escape attempt was reasonable; she had not consented to the risk of injury. Her choice of foothold, however, involved an unreasonable risk, so the damages payable by the defendant would be reduced by one-quarter.

> ### *Stone* v *Taffe* (1974, CA)
>
> The claimant's husband was killed when, after a party hosted by the Royal and Antediluvian Order of Buffaloes, he catapulted himself down the unlit staircase in the defendant's pub. The claimant's wife and a friend who had preceded him had completed the descent safely.
>
> **Held:** damages should be reduced by 50 per cent to take account of the lack of care taken by the deceased for his own safety.

The defence applies to cases of industrial disease if the claimant's own behaviour has made him more open to the risk.

> ### *Badger* v *Ministry of Defence* (2006)
>
> Mr Badger died from cancer mainly caused by the negligence of the defendant in exposing him to asbestos, but B also was a long-term smoker which was a contributory factor.

Held: his damages must be reduced by 25 per cent to reflect his contributory negligence for his death since, by the 1970s (when health warnings already appeared on cigarette packets), he was medically advised to give up smoking and received further warnings from doctors in 1991, 1992 and 1995, but still did not comply.

It may also apply where the claimant harms themselves intentionally. In *Reeves* v *Metropolitan Police Commissioner* (2000), the police were liable for negligently allowing a suicide to occur but damages claimed by the deceased's next of kin were reduced by 50 per cent.

3 Statutory authority

Public authorities are empowered by statute to carry out specific duties and powers and while this is no defence to negligence or breach of statutory duty, the statute may provide a defence to nuisance or *Rylands* v *Fletcher* liability, e.g. the Civil Aviation Act 1993, s 76 states no action may be brought in nuisance in relation to low flying aircraft, as long as this is reasonable in relation to weather conditions and all the other circumstances of the flight.

A defence of statutory authority may be challenged under the Human Rights Act 1998 on the grounds that the provision is incompatible with the ECHR with a further claim to the European Court of Human Rights if the action fails in the domestic courts.

Vicarious liability

Vicarious liability: liability for the tort of another person.

Employee: Part/full-time waged/salaried worker whose job description is defined by a contract of service.

Contract of service: a contract between employer and employee.

Usually we are liable only for our own torts, but in certain situations we may be sued for the torts of others for whom we are said to be *vicariously* liable. **Vicarious liability** most commonly arises in relation to employers, with regard to the behaviour of their employees, but it also extends to the agency relationship.

The difference between employees and independent contractors

An employer may be liable for the torts of its own **employees** but not usually for those of independent contractors. It is therefore important to be able to distinguish the two.

When you run a business you will employ your own staff but may need to bring in others to carry out some essential services. For example, if you run a shop you may employ sales assistants, while window cleaning is done by an outside firm. You are vicariously liable for any torts committed by the shop assistants because of the employer–employee relationship arising from the **contract of service**. Such a relationship does

Independent contractor: self-employed person providing services to a business/individual.

Contract for services: a contract between a party and an independent contractor.

not exist between you and the window cleaner, who is your **independent contractor** and works for you under a **contract for services**. The window cleaner is an accessory to your business rather than integrated within it.

This distinction may be difficult to see in big workplaces, where services like catering and cleaning may be contracted out to other firms. The distinction between the staff of the contractor and the 'real employees' is not immediately apparent; so determining those employees for whose actions the owner of the workplace is vicariously liable may be problematic. The terms of the contract provide crucial evidence of the intention of the parties. Where work is contracted out, the contractor generally remains the employer of the relevant employee. A party who provides plant, tools and materials and undertakes financial risks in carrying out a job will be deemed to be an independent contractor, even though the employer may exercise considerable control over the contractor's business enterprise.

Ready Mixed Concrete v Ministry of Pensions and National Insurance (1968)

Drivers employed by Ready Mixed Concrete had to buy their own vehicles from a supplier nominated by Ready Mixed and paint them in Ready Mixed's livery. They could not use the vehicles for their own purposes, and had to make them available whenever required by Ready Mixed, with a substitute driver if necessary.

Held: the drivers were independent contractors. Despite the high degree of control by Ready Mixed, the financial stake that they acquired by the purchase of their own vehicles and the fact that they could get a substitute driver to perform their contractual duties indicated that the parties intended the contract to be for services.

The Court may be prepared to impose vicarious liability on the grounds that a relationship analogous to employment exists between an employer and a party acting under their directions.

Cox v Ministry of Justice (2014, EWCA)

The claimant C was on the catering staff of a prison assisted by prisoners who were paid nominally for their work. A prisoner injured C by accidentally dropping a loaded sack onto her back when she was kneeling down to clean up a spillage.

C's original claim that the defendant was vicariously liable failed because the prisoner was not employed by the defendant. C appealed.

The Court of Appeal held: the defendant was vicariously liable because the relationship between the prisoner and the Ministry of Justice was akin to the employment relationship. The law relating to vicarious liability had developed incrementally and there were sufficiently similar circumstances in those decisions to justify a finding of liability in this case. It was fair, just and reasonable to impose liability. The prisoner was carrying out work for the benefit of the defendant saving it the expense of paying the full market rate. There was no reason why the defendant should not carry the financial burden resulting from this as well as the benefits.

The extent of the vicarious liability

As long as the activity which gave rise to the tort was sufficiently closely connected with carrying out designated contractual duties, the employer is liable, even if the employee was negligent or disobeying orders concerning the execution of those duties. This may seem hard on the employer, but the law takes the view that employers are obliged to supervise their workforce properly.

Bayley v *Manchester, Sheffield and Lincolnshire Railway* (1873)

Mistakenly believing that Mr Bayley had boarded the wrong train, the defendant's porter hauled him from it when it had begun to move away, causing him injuries.

Held: the porter had been carrying out his duties, although in a bungling and incompetent manner, and the railway company was vicariously liable.

Century Insurance v *Northern Irish Road Transport Board* (1949, HL)

While discharging petrol from a tanker the defendant's employee was smoking. This was forbidden under work rules. An explosion causing serious damage resulted.

Held: the defendant employer was vicariously liable. The employee was carrying out his duties in an unauthorised way.

If, however, the employee's behaviour is not sufficiently coincidental to his job, the employer is not vicariously liable. In *Beard* v *London Omnibus Co.* (1900) the company was not liable for injuries caused to Mr Beard when a bus conductor tried his hand at reversing the bus at the terminus, since he was not employed to drive the bus.

Warren v *Henlys Garage Ltd* (1948)

A pump attendant challenged Mr Warren, believing that he intended to drive off without paying for his petrol. Mr Warren then said he would report him to the manager for insolence; the attendant, in response, hit him on the chin.

Held: the employer was not vicariously liable; the attendant had not been acting to protect his employer's interest when he hit Mr Warren, but to avenge himself and therefore was acting outside the scope of his employment.

Similarly in *Mohammud* v *Morrisons Supermarkets plc* (2015) the Court of Appeal held that a lack of close connection between a supermarket assistant's duties and an unprovoked abusive attack on a customer prevented the supermarket from being vicariously liable to the customer.

The application of the doctrine of vicarious liability is increasingly dictated by policy. Where the court believes that the employer should be publicly accountable it will be generous when interpreting the issue of close connection, even where on the face of things the employee has acted only to further his own interests. This is well illustrated by the next case.

Lister v *Hesley Hall* (2001, HL)

A warden of a care home sexually abused boys for whom he was responsible.

Held: the employer was vicariously liable because there was a very close connection between the acts of abuse by the warden and the work he was employed to do. By abusing the boys he was failing in the very obligation he had contracted to fulfil which was ensuring the care and safety of the children.

Sufficiently close connection in such cases may occur outside residential care.

Maga v *Trustees of the Birmingham Archdiocese* (2010, CA)

The claimant appealed against a High Court decision that the defendant Archdiocese was not vicariously liable for sexual abuse of the claimant by one of its priests.

The claimant was befriended and groomed by the defendant's priest when he was about 12 years old. Initially, the priest got into conversation with the claimant in the street when he was admiring the priest's car. The priest gradually befriended him, encouraging the boy to do odd jobs for him and to come to parish youth discos. The relationship became abusive when he took him back to the presbytery after the boy had stayed behind to help clear up after a disco.

Held: the defendant was vicariously liable since the abusive acts were within the course of the priest's employment, being closely linked to his official responsibilities.

The defendant's priest had been given special responsibility for youth work and was performing this duty when he befriended M. It enabled him to develop a relationship with the boy by encouraging him on to church premises to take part in organised church functions and had the opportunity to escalate the relationship to an abusive one.

A contract may specifically forbid certain wilful behaviour and indicate that the employer is vicariously liable for such occurrences even though there may be an element of personal revenge. In *Gravil* v *Carroll and Redruth Rugby Club* (2008, CA), G claimed damages against the rugby club in trespass to the person after he sustained a broken cheekbone from a punch by C as a scrum broke up when the whistle had blown for close of play. The Court of Appeal held that the rugby club was liable for C's behaviour: it was sufficiently closely connected to his employment since incidents of this kind were commonplace in such circumstances and the terms of his contract made it clear that such behaviour was not authorised.

The House of Lords has affirmed that an employer may be liable for an employee's breach of statutory duty as well as common law torts. In *Majrowski* v *Guy's & St Thomas' NHS Trust* (2006, HL), the trust was vicariously liable for the employee's breach of the Protection from Harassment Act 1997.

Worth thinking about?

How does the doctrine of vicarious liability benefit the claimant?

Suggested solutions can be found in Appendix 2.

Liability for independent contractors: non-delegable duties

Although a person who employs an independent contractor is never *vicariously* liable for the contractor's torts, there are circumstances where the employer may be held *personally* liable for damage resulting from the contractor's work. Such liability arises where a non-delegable legal duty is imposed on the employer because they have particular responsibility, which cannot be transferred to anybody else. In practice the courts are very reluctant to acknowledge such a duty. It was traditionally limited to the following circumstances:

1 *Public nuisance affecting the highway*. For example if scaffolding used by building contractors working on your premises causes an obstruction, you will be personally liable.

2 *Injury to a servant*. Employers have a non-delegable duty to provide a safe working environment for their servants (employees, etc.) and will be personally liable for injuries caused by contractors' work. (This is covered in more detail in Chapter 16.)

3 *Hospitals have a non-delegable duty to ensure that proper care is taken of patients* (*A* v *Ministry of Defence* (2004)) and so will be personally liable for the torts caused by medical staff of all kinds even if no contract of service exists to give rise to vicarious liability.

However in *Woodland* v *Essex County Council* (2013) the Supreme Court introduced a new category covering situations where a vulnerable claimant, in the custody of the defendant, is adversely injured by the negligence of a third party over whom the claimant has no control, who was performing a task ordered by the defendant, in circumstances where the defendant is deemed to have assumed responsibility for that vulnerable person. The Supreme Court gave examples of persons likely to be regarded as vulnerable including: patients, children, care home residents and prisoners.

Woodland v *Essex County Council* (2013)

Annie Woodland aged 10, a pupil in a school controlled by Essex County Council, suffered serious brain damage as a result of nearly drowning during a swimming lesson at Basildon pool supervised by a swimming teacher and lifeguards who were independent contractors. She included Essex County Council in her claim for negligence because she argued that the school had a non-delegable duty making it responsible for the damage caused by the negligent behaviour of the swimming teacher and lifeguards working at Basildon Council's pool under the management of Harlow Council. Essex argued that a school did not owe a non-delegable duty to its pupils and claimed that this part of the claim should be struck-out before the case was heard.

The Court of Appeal held that a non-delegable duty did not exist in this case and the claimant appealed to the Supreme Court which overturned the Court of Appeal decision.

Held: the Council did owe a delegated duty of care to the claimant. It had a duty to ensure that swimming lessons, which were part of the school curriculum, were carried out with all reasonable skill. It had delegated responsibility for the supervision and teaching of those lessons to Harlow Council and the swimming teacher. The alleged negligence occurred during the performance of the actual function for which the school had assumed responsibility and which it had delegated. Therefore if there was negligence in performance the school and vicariously Essex Council remained liable for it.

The *Woodland* principle was applied in the case of *GB* v *Home Office* (2015) where the High Court held that the claimant, a detainee in an immigration removal centre, was a vulnerable person in Home Office custody. The Home Office owed her a non-delegable duty for any negligence in her compulsory medical care provided by a local medical practice authorised by the Home Office.

Chapter summary

Tort liability and premises

Negligence: damage to a person or their property caused by some activity taking place on the defendant's premises.

Occupiers' Liability Acts of 1957 and 1984: defective structure or condition of the defendant's premises, which adversely affects 'visitors' (OLA 1957) and trespassers (OLA 1984).

Public and private nuisance: covers interference emanating from the defendant's premises and interfering unreasonably with the right of peaceful enjoyment of occupiers of nearby premises/highway.

Please see Figure 15.1 (above) for a detailed summary of the scope of the OLA 1957 and 1984 and public and private nuisance.

Defences

Consent: express/implied consent by the claimant to the defendant's behaviour may be an effective defence.

Contributory negligence: damages may be reduced proportionately in relation to the claimant's failure to take care for their own safety.

Vicarious liability

An employer is liable for the torts of those working for him or her under a contract of service, provided that the tortious behaviour of the employee is sufficiently closely connected to the employee's work.

Personal liability for independent contractors

Exists if the employer owes a non-delegable duty to the claimant.

Quiz 14

1 What is the likely tort liability of Red Leicester in the following circumstances?

(a) Mrs Double Gloucester is hit by a can of paint dropped from the top of a ladder into the street by Cheddar, who was up the ladder painting Red's shop front.

(b) Stilton slipped on a spillage while climbing the stairs in the shop. A notice at the bottom of the stairs said 'Take care: wet floor, please use other stairs'.

(c) Lymeswold, aged seven, went through a door in the shop marked 'Private' and cut himself on some broken glass in a storeroom.

(d) Sage Derby, Red's next-door neighbour, has discovered wet rot in his premises caused by condensation from an unlined boiler flue on Red's premises.

2 What defence may be open to Cheshire, whose car collided with Wensleydale who was riding his motor bike and not wearing a crash helmet?

3 What is the difference between an employer's liability for the torts of employees and for those of independent contractors?

Answers to all quizzes can be found in Appendix 2.

15

Tort liability for premises

Take a closer look

The following cases provide important examples of how the law you have studied in this chapter has developed. They are primary sources illustrating the law in action and give you more detail about their facts, as well as helping you to understand the law and to appreciate how the judges reached their decisions.

Try looking them up in the law reports or accessing them via a database, e.g. Bailli (www.bailii.org/databases.html). LexisNexis or Westlaw may be available in your university or college library, or you may find extracts in a case book. (See Appendix 1: Additional resources.)

Ogwo v *Taylor* [1987] AC 431

Ratcliff v *Harper Adams Agricultural College* [1999] 1 WLR 670

Hunter v *Canary Wharf* [1997] 2 All ER 426

Lister v *Hesley Hall Ltd* [2001] 2 All ER 769

Web activity

Please go to: www.river-swimming.co.uk/occu.htm

See some interesting comment on *Tomlinson* v *Congleton Borough Council* (2003, HL) (see above) and some other occupiers' liability cases concerning outdoor activity.

Assignment 13

Healing plc recently opened an anti-stress clinic on the edge of the village of Much-Dozing-in-the-Dell. Farmer Oswald's arable farm is immediately adjacent to the clinic's premises, which includes a swimming pool. For three weeks during the summer, Grinders Farming Contractors Ltd are employed by Oswald to bring in the harvest. The work involves daily use of huge machines. The noise of the machinery upsets the clinic's patients, many of whom cancel expensive courses of treatment. The dust and dirt from the harvesting process forms a thick film on the swimming pool making it unusable, and clogs the filter causing it to break down and require expensive repairs. Ned, one of Grinders' employees, drops a cigarette end which starts a fire in the field. It spreads into the clinic's grounds and destroys a summer house.

Advise Healing plc about its possible rights in tort.

PART 4

Elements of employment law

CHAPTER 16

Rights at work
The contract of employment and health and safety at work

Introduction

The operation of employment law is very important to you, whether you run your own business or are employed in one, as it provides the basic structure of the employer and employee relationship from the time an employee is interviewed for a job until the time they leave. Although the common law of contract is still highly relevant to employment law, statutory regulation since the 1970s did much to promote a more equal balance of power between employer and employee. Employers lost their traditional freedoms to select, hire and fire staff at will and to contract purely on their own terms. Employees were given a greater variety of remedies. The current government sees a need to push the pendulum in the opposite direction as part of its 'red tape challenge'. This is aimed at reducing regulations on employers which it perceives as restricting business development, growth and productivity. Legislation implementing some of these proposals will be covered later in this section of the book.

The employer and employee relationship is based on the contract of employment. In this chapter we focus on how this contract of employment is formed and the terms which the law requires it to contain to protect both parties.

Unfortunately, many accidents occur in workplaces, so what happens if you get hurt or become ill due to workplace conditions? In this chapter we also examine employers' liability in tort and criminal law for the health and safety of their employees.

Learning objectives

When you have studied this chapter you should be able to:

▶ distinguish between an employee and an independent contractor;

▶ be aware of the main terms in an employment contract;

▶ understand the common law contractual duties of employer/employee;

▶ grasp the extent of the employer's civil liability for industrial illness and injury;

▶ appreciate the role of the Health and Safety at Work etc. Act in promoting the welfare of employees.

The employment contract: a contract of service

Workers, employees and independent contractors

Worker: works under a contract of service but with fewer rights than an employee

A business may be served both by its own or **workers** and **employees** under a **contract of service** and by **independent contractors** under a **contract for services**.

The employer is responsible for paying National Insurance contributions and sick pay (to employees only) and for deduction of income tax.

Employee: individual worker with a contract of service with the party he or she works for.

Workers

Workers are generally employed on a casual and agency basis. Their contract of service does not entitle them to sick pay, holiday pay and certain other benefits and they may not claim unfair dismissal.

Contract of service: contract between an employer and employee.

Employees

An employee's contract of service entitles them to the full range of existing employment rights including sick and holiday pay and the right to claim for unfair dismissal and redundancy.

Independent contractor: business/ individual providing services under contract to another business/ individual.

Shareholder employees

Contract for services: contract between an independent contractor and another party.

The Growth and Infrastructure Act 2013 introduced this new category of employees. This intervention is intended to give small, rapidly growing companies more flexibility, by enabling them to dismiss staff more readily. Such employees choose to forgo their rights to claim unfair dismissal (except when related to discrimination or redundancy payments) in return for an allotment of shares, but otherwise generally enjoy much of the same rights as other employees including holiday and sick pay.

In October 2014 the Department for Business, Innovation and Skills (BIS) announced a wide-ranging review aimed at clarifying and enhancing rights for workers. It said that there appeared to be widespread confusion among both workers and employers about the extent of workers' as opposed to employees' rights. If BIS achieve this it will no doubt be an excellent thing not only for workers and employers but for all students, lecturers and writers who have been struggling with these anomalies for some time!

Please note that in this chapter a reference to employees includes workers unless the contrary is stated.

Independent contractors

An independent contractor may be a company or partnership with its own staff or a single self-employed person providing services to an employer on or off site. An employer is not vicariously liable for illegal behaviour by an independent contractor (see Chapter 15) and the contractor does not enjoy the same rights as an employee.

Modern workplace practice has made the distinctions between employee and contractor less evident. Increasingly, large firms have taken to contracting out a variety of services like catering. The contractor's staff may work on site for similar hours to other staff and may even be required to wear a uniform in the business livery. Litigation to determine the status of the parties and their resulting rights and liabilities is common.

Factors which may help the court to determine status

1 *The contract:* the court uses a purposive approach to ascertain the intention of the parties. Calling a party 'self-employed' does not always make them an independent contractor in law.

2 *Financial risk and capital outlay:* Who pays? Does the employer provide all necessary equipment? An employee is generally entitled to payment and equipment from the employer.

3 *Delegation or personal performance?* A contractor is often free to delegate while an employee must perform in person.

Community Dental Services v *Sultan Darmon* (2010)

The claimant dentist was held not to be an employee as he was not working under a contract of employment under the ERA 1996, s 230(1), nor was he a worker under s 230(2) because his contract with Community Dental Services allowed him to appoint a locum to do his work if necessary. Under s 230(3), a contract under which an employee or worker is employed will always require personal performance of all contractual duties.

The requirement of personal performance was the decisive feature of the next case and produced a contrary result.

Pimlico Plumbers v *Smith* (2014, EAT)

The EAT held: Mr. Smith was not an employee of Pimlico Plumbers, but he was a worker rather than an independent contractor.

Mr Smith's contract with Pimlico required him to wear the company uniform and use a van with the Pimlico logo. He was also required to deal with all his own tax and insurance issues as well as providing his own tools. Although he was required to do a minimum number of hours per week he could chose when to work and could reject a job at will. Pimlico was under no obligation to provide him with work.

Despite his high degree of autonomy and the burden of financial risk this was a contract to provide service in person since the contract did not grant any substitution rights. He was therefore a worker rather than an independent contractor since the latter always has an unfettered right to employ a substitute.

4 *Control:* the extent to which the employer controls working hours and directs a party in the manner of discharge of their duties may help to indicate status.

The next case unsurprisingly attracted a lot of cover in the popular press. It is also a good illustration of how the court approaches cases of this kind.

Stringfellow Restaurants Ltd v *Quashie* (2012, CA)

Ms Quashie worked as a lap-dancer in one of the defendant's clubs. She claimed unfair dismissal when the defendant dispensed with her services after suspicion was raised that she was involved with drugs on the premises.

Held: Ms Quashie was not entitled to claim. She did not have a contract of employment with the defendant because:

1 The club did not pay her. She negotiated her own fees for private dances with customers and these were remitted to her by the club minus agreed deductions. She was required to provide her own dance outfits as deemed suitable by the employer.

2 Her contract, which stated that she was self-employed, did not entitle her to sick or holiday pay and she paid her own tax.

3 The control element was insufficient to make her an employee. Although she was required to work one shift at weekends she could otherwise choose when and how many hours a week she would work. She could take such leave as she wished by prior written notice.

The form of the contract of service

The validity of a contract is not dependent on its form. It can arise quite informally by word of mouth; writing is not essential to the existence of the contract. However, s 1 of the Employment Rights Act 1996 (ERA 1996) obliges an employer to provide an employee with a *written statement* of the key terms of the employee's contract within two months of starting work. This statement must include:

1 the parties' names and addresses;

2 the date when the employee started the job;

3 the date on which the employee's continuous employment began. This may not be the same as 2 above if, for example, the employee was already employed by the same employer but in a different post. The length of continuous employment is crucial to rights relating to unfair dismissal and redundancy, which are discussed below but which are not relevant to workers;

4 a note of any disciplinary and grievance procedures;

5 full particulars of:

   (a) pay entitlement;

   (b) hours of work;

   (c) any holiday entitlement and pay;

   (d) any sick leave and pay entitlement;

   (e) any pension rights (unless these are controlled by a statute which itself ensures notification);

   (f) length of notice required to be given to and by the employee;

   (g) the title of the employee's job and a brief description of what it involves;

   (h) if the job is not intended to continue indefinitely, the period for which it is expected to last, or the date it is intended to end if it is for a fixed term;

   (i) the place(s) where the employee will be required to work (employees required to work outside the UK for more than one month must be told how long this will be for, what currency they will be paid in, any entitlement to additional benefits and any terms relating to their return to the UK);

   (j) any collective agreement directly affecting the job.

Failure to provide this statement does not invalidate the contract. It is merely intended to provide employees with sufficient written evidence of some of the conditions under which they are employed to enable them to enforce their statutory rights. The statement does not represent all the terms of the contract, which are described below.

Sources of the terms of the employment contract

The terms of the contract will not generally be found in one written document since they may be both express and implied and may be traced to a number of sources.

Express terms are stated in any written contract of employment, but are also to be found in the written statutory information described above. They may also consist of promises made by word of mouth prior to acceptance.

16

Rights at work: the contract of employment and health and safety at work

The court may imply a term from any of the following sources:

Custom and practice: business behaviour accepted locally/ nationally/in the particular industry.

Collective agreement: made with an employer, by a trade union on behalf of its members.

- **custom and practice;**
- works and staff rules;
- **collective agreements;**
- statute;
- common law rights and duties of employers and employees;
- business efficacy (see Chapter 7).

Custom and practice

Relevant business practices acceptable nationally, locally or in the particular trade or workplace may be implied as terms of the contract. To be enforceable they must be reasonable, certain and not contrary to law. For example, in Lancashire, weaving factories employers customarily made deductions from pay for poor work. This was held to be a term of the contract (*Sagar* v *H. Ridehalgh & Son Ltd* (1930, CA)).

This source of terms has diminished in importance with the increased formalisation of the employment contract. In the event of conflict with the written contractual terms, the written terms prevail.

Works and staff rules

While not necessarily terms of the contract, failure to obey works and staff rules is likely to be treated as evidence of failure to obey reasonable orders. If the rule does not have the status of a contractual term this is advantageous to the employer, since a rule may be introduced and varied at will without the consent which would be required from the employee to make a contractual term or variation binding. Policy considerations may influence judicial decisions on such issues.

Collective agreements

The terms of a collective agreement between union and employer may expressly or impliedly form part of a contract of employment. With the decrease of union recognition in recent years, only a small minority of workers' contracts is likely to be influenced by such agreements.

Statute

Legislation increasingly restricts the freedom of employers to impose the terms of their choice on employees. For example, the Working Time Regulations 1998 (implementing the Working Time Directive) impose limits on the hours which an employee can be asked to work and include requirements for minimum rest breaks and annual paid holidays.

Terms implied at common law

The common law implies certain terms into contracts of employment which impose duties on both employer and employee. For example, the common law requires employees:

1 to do their job with reasonable care and skill;
2 to obey all reasonable orders;
3 to act in good faith towards the employer.

Each of these duties is implied in the contract. They are discussed in detail below.

The common law duties of the employee

The duty to work with reasonable care and skill

Essentially this means that an employee must not be negligent. What is a reasonable standard depends on the status of the employee within the organisation and the level of qualification, skill and experience held by the employee. Grossly negligent performance may entitle an employer summarily to dismiss the employee.

The duty to obey reasonable orders

An order is usually treated as reasonable as long as it does not require the employee to do something outside their job description, since under the terms of the contract the employee has expressly or impliedly agreed to do anything necessarily incidental to performing the job. In *UK Atomic Energy Authority* v *Claydon* (1974) the employment contract stated that Claydon could be asked to work in any base in the UK It was held that by refusing a transfer he had failed to obey a reasonable order.

An order is not reasonable if its performance is likely to endanger the personal safety or liberty of the employee. The employee must be able to show that *imminent* danger will result from carrying out the order. Compare the following two cases.

Ottoman Bank v *Chakarian* (1930)

The defendant was an Armenian refugee who had escaped from Turkey where he was under sentence of death.

Held: in the circumstances it was not reasonable to expect him to accept a posting in Turkey.

Walmesley v *UDEC* (1972)

Walmesley was ordered to accept a transfer to Ireland, which he refused because he was frightened of being harmed by the IRA.

Held: he was acting in breach of his contract since he was unable to prove any imminent and specific threat of harm.

An employee cannot be ordered to break the law.

Morrish v *Henlys (Folkestone) Ltd* (1973)

An employee who had refused to falsify the company's accounts was held not to be acting in breach of contract.

In determining what is reasonable, current standards of good industrial relations practice are taken into account.

An employee cannot choose how far to perform an employer's reasonable orders. Some forms of industrial action, short of going on strike, may entitle the employer to dock pay for part performance. The employees must receive prior notification of the employer's refusal to accept part performance. In *Wiluszynski* v *London Borough of Tower Hamlets* (1988, CA) it was held that council employees who refused to answer councillors' enquiries could legally be deprived of all their earnings for the five weeks that this action continued, even though they were carrying out all other aspects of their work. The employees had received specific and prior notice of the consequences of their action.

The duty to act in good faith

Employees must act with complete honesty towards their employers when carrying out their contractual duties. The motivation of employees is irrelevant to their liability.

Dalton v *Burtons Gold Medal Biscuit Co. Ltd* (1974)

Dalton falsified a clocking-in card to benefit another employee.

Held: he had breached his duty of good faith by cheating his employer. It was irrelevant that he obtained no personal benefit from the dishonest action.

The duty to act in good faith may be divided into three separate obligations:

1 *Not to act in conflict with the employer's interests.* Employees must not compete with the employer's business, even if they do so in their spare time. If the contract requires the employee to work for the employer exclusively, doing any paid work for another person is a breach of duty.

2 *Not to reveal confidential information.* The employee must not reveal confidential information about the employer's profits, customers, work systems, products or services. This duty remains enforceable, though to a more limited extent, even after an employee has left the employer's service. (There is detailed information about breach of confidence by employees in Chapter 25.)

3 *To account for all profits.* Taking bribes is obviously a gross breach of duty, but this duty may be breached by an employee who makes any unauthorised profit from the job.

Employees, therefore, are not entitled to any secret commission. Tips may be retained in jobs where these are seen as part of payment, as in the restaurant trade.

The common law duties of the employer

It is implied in the contract of employment that the employer will:

1 pay the employee as agreed by the contract;

2 not undermine the trust and confidence of the employee;

3 provide the employee with safe working conditions.

The duty to pay the employee

Minimum wage: statutory entitlement under the Minimum Wage Act 1999. Subject to updating by the DTI.

Most employees (not just those with a contract of service) are entitled to a **minimum wage**, under the Minimum Wage Act 1998. Some people are not entitled under the Act, for example the self-employed, volunteers, students doing work as part of an undergraduate or post-graduate course and workers on certain government training schemes.

The hourly rates, revised every October, are at the time of writing: £6.70 for workers aged 21 and over. Workers aged between 18 and 21 are paid a development rate of £5.30; 16–17-year-olds are entitled to £3.87 and apprentices of any age get £3.30. Since October 2009 it has been illegal for an employer to use tips paid through payroll to make up the minimum wage.

In the news

Companies named and shamed for not paying minimum wage

In March 2015 the Department for Business, Innovation and Skills (BIS) issued its latest name and shame list of 48 companies which had been found, after full investigation by Her Majesty's Revenue and Customs (HMRC) to have flouted the minimum wage regulations. The businesses represented a wide spectrum of commerce but the traditionally poorly paid areas like retail and the care and leisure industries predominated. For example, Foot Locker London had failed to pay £16,718.25 to 601 workers and French Connection London owed £16,436.05 to 367 workers. The then Business minister Jo Swenson said: 'There's no excuse for companies that don't pay staff the wages they're entitled to – whether by wilfully breaking the law, or making irresponsible mistakes.'

The name and shame system was introduced in 2011 to deter employers from flouting their legal responsibilities on fair pay. Lists are published by BIS throughout the year. As well as being named, an employer may also be fined. Originally this was limited to a one off fine of up to £20,000 but the Small Business, Enterprise and Employment Act (SBEEA) 2015, s152 amends the Minimum Wage Act 1998 to make the fine payable per employee, so the bigger the employer the greater the penalty for flouting the law.

Source: BIS press release 24/03/15, https://www.gov.uk/government/news/new-national-minimum-wage-offenders-named-and-shamed

The employer has no right to make pay deductions unless, like income tax or National Insurance contributions, these are authorised by statute or agreed in writing with the employee. In practice, the contract of employment often provides for employer's deductions, and the employee thus waives the protection of the common law in this respect.

The obligation to pay the employee exists *whether or not the employer has provided work*. In general, there is no duty to provide work but, if the nature of the work means that the employee is likely to obtain a benefit other than payment from doing the work, the employer may be under a duty to provide work. For example, actors and other performers require the publicity that performance brings. Similarly, apprentices are entitled to the opportunity to practise the skills they have contracted to learn.

Zero hours contracts may enable an employer to avoid their obligation to pay for hours where no work was provided. It all depends on how the contract is structured; they vary greatly in their terms but do not create mutuality of obligation as they may require an employee to work on demand within the terms of the contract while not requiring an employer to pay if no work is provided. This is clearly contentious as at worst it fails to provide the employee with any financial security. Some employees find them a convenient means of fitting part-time working round caring or study commitments. Employers like them because of the flexibility it gives them to draw on a pool of labour according to need. Originally the use of such contracts was largely restricted to businesses with fluctuating seasonal demand, but by 2013 they had become much more widespread and a number of high-profile businesses now use them, including Cineworld, Sports Direct, the Tate Gallery and Buckingham Palace. They have been taken up by the NHS and a number of local authorities.

The Office for National Statistics reported in 2014 that there were approximately 670,000 people on such contracts: an increase of 11,000 from the previous year. The controversy surrounding the use of such contracts led BIS to hold an enquiry and reform was recommended to redress the imbalance of power. The SBEEA 2015, s153 bans exclusivity clauses in zero hours contracts. This means that an employer cannot tie an employee into a contract which prevents that employee from concurrently entering a contract with another employer.

Not to undermine the trust and confidence of the employee

In *Malik* v *BCCI* (1998) Lord Steyn held that the employer shall not, 'without reasonable and proper cause, conduct itself in a manner calculated or likely to destroy or seriously damage the relationship of confidence and trust between employer and employee.'

This is aimed at preventing the employer from indulging in unreasonable and abusive conduct towards the employee; and is reciprocal to the employee's duty to act in good faith. A wide variety of behaviour can give rise to a breach of this duty: for example, failing to provide extra support to staff at busy times (*White* v *London Transport Executive* (1982)), criticising a supervisor in front of employees who worked under him (*Associated Tyre Specialists* v *Waterhouse* (1976)), failure to protect an employee against harassment (*Bracebridge Engineering Ltd* v *Darby* (1990)).

Isle of Wight Tourist Board v *Coombes* (1976)

A manager, within earshot of the claimant who was his personal secretary, said to another employee: 'She is always an intolerable bitch on Monday mornings.' He did not attempt to apologise.

Held: his behaviour shattered a close and confidential working relationship thus undermining the employee's trust and confidence.

In *RDF Media Group plc* v *Alan Clements* (2007) Livesey QC held that while a press article vilifying the claimant (even if truthful) did amount to a breach of his employer's duty, deliberations by the board of directors discussing his character in very negative terms did not, because: 'the Board of Directors is the controlling mind of the Company and representations between individuals on the Board are merely equivalent to the Company thinking aloud to itself. It is not yet the law that an employer is prohibited from thinking even negative and unworthy thoughts about an employee on his payroll.'

Breach of this duty may be grounds for a claim that the employee has been *constructively* dismissed. If the employer's conduct is sufficiently serious, the employee is entitled to leave without notice. However, the duty is a mutual one, so if the employee himself acted in breach of this duty prior to the alleged breach by the employer, he will not succeed in his claim. In *RDF Media Group plc* Clements lost his case for constructive dismissal since by taking a job with a competitor in breach of his contract with RDF he had already breached his own duty of loyalty and fidelity to RDF. His own breach had prompted the behaviour he complained of.

To provide safe working conditions

Employers must take all reasonable care to provide safe working conditions for their employees. Liability for breach of this duty is also imposed through the law of tort, both at common law and statute. In practice, actions for personal injury to employees are brought by an action in tort rather than for breach of contract. In the following section this is explained in that context.

The law of tort: employers' civil liability for industrial injuries

Two possible rights of action in tort may be open to an employee injured at work:

1 an action for breach of the employer's common law duty of care;
2 an action for breach of statutory duty.

16

Rights at work: the contract of employment and health and safety at work

Employers' common law liability

This is a **non-delegable duty**. This means that an employer cannot avoid liability merely by showing that a hazard has been created by a third party. The responsibility to maintain safety remains with the employer. Therefore, if independent contractors cause a spillage on which a member of the employer's staff slips and breaks a leg, the employer may be liable. The employee will have to prove that in the given circumstances, in a properly managed workplace, the employer would have ensured that the spillage was cleared up. Liability, therefore, is not strict, but requires an employer to take reasonable care to avoid reasonably foreseeable harm, as in a negligence action.

The common law duty comprises three interlinked obligations:

1 to provide competent staff;
2 to provide safe premises, plant and equipment;
3 to provide a safe system of work.

Competent staff

The employer must take reasonable care to ensure that its staff is competent to do their work so that they are not a danger to their fellow employees. Reasonable care must be taken in the selection, training, supervision and discipline of the workforce. The duty includes preventing hazards arising from activities that are not necessarily closely connected to the job in hand.

Hudson v *Ridge Manufacturing Co. Ltd* (1957)

An employee, who had previously been reprimanded more than once for skylarking, injured a fellow employee when playing a practical joke.

Held: the employer was liable since it had been alerted to the fact that the employee was a potential danger by his previous behaviour and should have taken adequate steps to control him.

Safe premises, plant and equipment

This includes providing appropriate tools, machinery and materials maintained to an adequate standard. The premises must also be reasonably safe. In *Pagano* v *HGS* (1976) an employer which failed to maintain its vehicles in a safe condition, despite having been alerted to the problem by complaints from its workforce, was held liable for breach of duty.

Under the Employers' Liability (Defective Equipment) Act 1969, if equipment is defective due to the fault of a third party such as a manufacturer or repairer, the employer may be held liable even though it is not personally to blame and could not have known of the defect. The courts interpret 'equipment' purposively so any item or materials that employees are required to handle while carrying out their duties is usually covered. In *Knowles* v *Liverpool CC* (1993) a paving stone which shattered during installation was deemed to be work equipment.

A safe system of work

This encompasses a huge variety of activities. It includes providing protective clothing with instructions about its use, setting up safe working procedures and appropriate training, ensuring sufficient washing and first aid facilities, and appropriate use of warning signs.

Pennington v Surrey County Council and Surrey Fire & Rescue Services (2006, CA)

The claimant fire-fighter was injured when his finger got caught in the moving part of a power ram which he was using to assist in a motor accident rescue operation. He had not been trained to use such a heavy ram although he was used to operating a lighter model.

Held: the employer was in breach of his duty to the claimant by allowing him to use equipment that he had not been trained to use, in a stressful situation. This was not a safe system of work.

An employer's liability may arise from a mixture of breaches of these three interdependent duties. For example, a computer operator claiming repetitive strain injury might be able to prove (i) lack of proper equipment (the seating and desk not being at an appropriate height), and (ii) failure to maintain a safe system of work (if employees are required to use keyboards for lengthy periods without a proper break).

Real life

Horace works as an administrative officer for Smallville Borough Council. Recently he had a bad day at the office. On his way to a meeting with his boss, he tripped over some large packages left in a dark corner of a corridor by Cedric, a new employee. His hand was badly sprained and it was four weeks before he could use it fully.

The council appears potentially to be in breach of all three aspects of its duty as employer.

First, Cedric does not appear to have been trained to an appropriate level of competence. If the corridor is so dark that obstructions are not readily spotted this amounts to failure to provide safe plant or equipment. Finally, leaving obstructions in a passage way may be evidence of failure to impose a safe system of work. Similarly, if the passage was dark because the lighting had not been appropriately checked for faults, this would also point to lack of a safe system of work.

Stress-related illness

Historically, claims against employers have been for physical injuries, but recently cases have come before the courts in which employers have been found liable for stress-related illness.

Walker v *Northumberland County Council* (1995)

The employers, who knew that Mr Walker had already suffered psychiatric illness due to stress at work, increased his workload. This caused the illness to recur so badly that he had to take early retirement. The judge, who awarded substantial damages, said that there was no difference in principle between mental and physical injury in the context of the employer's duty to provide reasonably safe working conditions.

Increasing numbers of similar claims have come before the courts since the decision in *Walker.*

In *Hatton* v *Sutherland* (2002) the Court of Appeal laid down guidelines which stressed the need to avoid imposing too great a burden on employers:

- No occupation should be regarded as intrinsically dangerous to mental health.
- The employer should be alerted to the risk to an employee when a reasonable employer would foresee that risk.
- Injury to health (not just emotional stress) must be reasonably foreseeable.
- It is reasonable for the employer to assume that the employee could cope with the level of stress normally associated with the job. Often it will be up to the employee to bring the issue to the employer's attention rather than suffering in silence.
- A breach of duty must be judged by the normal criteria: the magnitude of the risk, the gravity of harm and the practicability of taking precautions.
- If the only way to resolve the risk is to dismiss the employee, the employer will not be in breach if the employee is allowed to continue working.
- The duty can often be performed by the offer of counselling or other treatment.
- The issue of causation is often problematic for employees given that stress-related illness can come from a number of sources, not just the working environment.

Application of these principles by the House of Lords is illustrated by the following case:

Barber v *Somerset County Council* (2004, HL)

In 1995, restructuring took place at the school where Mr Barber worked and he was obliged to take on extra duties to enable him to continue at his current salary. In May 1996 he took three weeks' certificated sick leave due to anxiety and depression. When he returned to work, he met with the school's senior management team, which was unsupportive and did nothing to help him. Over the next three months, Mr Barber visited his GP on a number of occasions with stress-related issues and eventually left the school in November 1996 after losing control and shaking a pupil.

Held: the employer had a duty to take some action to assist the claimant, from the time it was put on notice of his condition. This occurred when he had met with senior staff. The employer had breached its duty by failing to make enquiries into his position to discover what could be done to support him.

It was irrelevant that all the staff were stressed and overworked because of the severe problems currently facing the school.

The employer had breached its duty by falling below the standard to be expected of a reasonable and prudent employer, and had not taken positive precautions to safeguard the safety of its employees, in the light of what it knew or ought reasonably to have known.

In *Yapp* v *Foreign & Colonial Office* (2015, CA) the Court of Appeal held that stress-related illness would generally be regarded as too remote a category of damage unless the claimant had evidenced signs of it previously to their claim or where the conduct of the employer was so extreme as to be likely to have such an effect on a person of reasonable robustness.

Civil liability for breach of statutory duty

Any criminal or administrative legislation, which does not expressly give rights to take action in tort for damages, may be treated by the courts as capable of doing so. This means that an employee who is the victim of an industrial accident or illness may be able to sue the employer for breach of a duty imposed on the employer by legislation designed primarily to impose public rather than civil law duties on an employer. The claimant will have to prove the following:

1 *The legislation gives the right to sue for damages*. The legislation may make this explicit one way or the other. Section 47 of the Health and Safety at Work, etc. Act 1974 clearly rules out an action for damages for breach of the employer's *general duty*; no action is possible here. However, s 47(2) states that action is possible for breach of any regulations made under the authority of the Act unless expressly excluded. Many successful actions imposing strict liability resulted from breaches of duties imposed by the Factories Act 1961 and subsequent related legislation. Breach and subsequent damage required proof, but not any fault by the employer. In recent years many of these duties have been replaced by regulations governing most aspects of workplace safety and derived from implementation of a whole raft of EC directives, for example the Management of Health and Safety at Work Regulations 1999. These have often proved a fertile ground for claims by injured employees and was resented by employers.

The Enterprise and Regulatory Reform Act 2013 (E&RRA) amended s 47(2) to prevent liability unless the employee can prove that the employer was negligent, unless the relevant legislation specifies otherwise. The government claimed that this removed an unjust burden from employers. Parties representing employees argue that this will lower health and safety standards and prevent just claims. It is likely that this will in practice only affect claims against private sector employees; EU directives concerning health and safety legislation incorporated into English law still have a direct effect on the state and thus its public authorities. Therefore public service employees may be able to sue their employer for strict liability in circumstances where those in the private sector cannot.

2 *The employee is part of the class of persons protected by the legislation.* Sometimes legislation is very limited in its application. For example, breach of a regulation to protect a machine operator might not protect a different type of employee. In *Knapp* v *The Railway Executive* (1949) a train driver injured in an accident caused by failure to close level-crossing gates, was held not to be protected by legislation intended to protect members of the public.

3 *The defendant is in breach of the duty.* The extent of the duty is specified by the statute. It may be advantageous to sue under statute if the burden of proof is placed on the employer to show that he or she discharged the duty. The employee must prove fault by the employer must be proved unless the statute specifies otherwise.

Chipchase v *British Titan Products* (1956)

Building safety regulations required the provision of platforms of at least 34 inches wide when work was being conducted six-and-a-half feet above ground level. The claimant, who was working at a height of six feet, was injured when he fell from a platform which was only nine inches wide.

Held: he had no right to claim for breach of the regulations since he had been working six inches below the regulated height when the accident happened.

Provided the conditions above are fulfilled, the court is often prepared to interpret unspecific statutory terms purposively as a matter of policy and justice. In the next case it seems common sense that an employer should be responsible for its employee's safety while she was taking an appropriate route out of the building in which she worked and over which her employer had at least some control of health and safety.

Reid v *PRP Architects* (2007, CA)

Precious Reid was injured at the end of the working day, due to poor maintenance of a lift which she was using to vacate the multi-occupancy office building where her employer, PRP, was based, and which was in the common part of the building.

She argued that PRP was in breach of the Provision and Use of Work Equipment Regulations 1998, reg 5(1), which requires an employer to ensure work equipment is efficiently maintained and in good repair. Work equipment is defined (reg 3(2)) as 'any machinery, appliance, apparatus, tool or installation for work (whether exclusively or not)'.

Held: PRP was liable because a lift was capable of coming within the meaning of an 'installation' which was being used for work under the regulations. On the facts of this case, it was not appropriate to draw a line on the employer's liability at the point an employee left its offices to take the lift. It provided the main route out of the building.

Similarly, in *Spencer-Franks* v *Kellogg Brown & Root Ltd* (2008, HL) the claimant was injured when repairing a door closer in an oilrig control room. The House of Lords held that if an item was used at work it was work equipment and everyone using the control room door used it for the purpose of their work. The regulations (and the directive on which they were based) in no way suggested that repairing should be interpreted narrowly or deprived of its ordinary meaning. Here, the ordinary meaning was that the door closer was work equipment. The employer's argument that the door closer was part of the premises, was not workable. The fact that Mr Spencer had been repairing the door at the time of his accident meant that he still was using the necessary component in order to do his job.

Worth thinking about?

What other civil action was open to Precious Reid? (See *PRP Architects* v *Reid* (2006).)

Suggested solutions can be found in Appendix 2.

Criminal law regulation of safety in the workplace

Since the Factories Act 1802, the welfare of employees has increasingly been regulated by statute as well as by the common law. In recent years the UK's membership of the EC has led to an increase in development of the law in this area.

The Health and Safety at Work, etc. Act 1974 was intended to implement a general policy of integrated statutory control of health and safety in the workplace. Powers are delegated under the Act to enable the Department of Employment (now the Department of Work and Pensions (DWP)) to make regulations covering specific areas of workplace safety. The Act was an important development in three respects:

1 it imposed general duties on both employers and employees to maintain health and safety;

2 it created the Health and Safety Executive, with powers to enforce the legislation;

3 it gave wide powers to the Department of Employment to make detailed legally binding regulations to cover particular hazards.

The employer's and employee's statutory duties

The employer's general duty to employees: s 2

Employers have a duty 'to ensure as far as is reasonably practicable the health, safety and welfare of all their employees'. (This means only those under a contract of service to an employer.) Employers are not made strictly liable by the 1974 Act. They are responsible only if they have failed to take *reasonably practicable* precautions. This has been criticised for its vagueness. It is very similar to the common law duty of reasonable care, but the reference to practicability indicates that the resources of employers may be relevant in judging how much can be expected of them.

The scope of the duty is spelt out in s 2 and encompasses particular areas of employer responsibility that closely mirror the employer's common law duty in tort.

The employee's duty: s 7

Employees are also placed under a two-part duty:

1 to take reasonable care for their own health and safety and for that of others likely to be affected by their acts and omissions at work;

2 to cooperate with the employer as far as is necessary to enable it to carry out its legal responsibilities.

The employer's duty to persons other than employees: s 3

Section 3 places the employer under a duty to conduct its business as far as practicable in a way that does not endanger persons other than employees who might be affected by it. This includes independent contractors, as well as visitors to the premises. Section 3 imposes a similar duty on self-employed persons. The s 3 duty is a negative requirement not to expose them to risks, compared with the positive duty in s 2 'to ensure as far as practicable'.

Health and safety policies: s 2

The 1974 Act seeks to ensure that employees are involved in and kept informed about health and safety provision in their workplace. An employer with a workforce of five or more must have a written health and safety policy and ensure that this is kept up to date and brought to the attention of the employees. A workplace safety committee must assist in the process. The employer must consult health and safety representatives from trade unions if required by BIS regulations.

The powers of the Health and Safety Executive (HSE)

HSE inspectors are given wide powers to enter and investigate workplaces and to enforce sanctions under the 1974 Act; and this has been widened by other subsequent legislation, for example, the Management of Health and Safety at Work Regulations 1999.

The HSE has the following powers:

Prosecution of any offence specified in the Act

Offences may arise not only from breach of duty, but also from obstruction of the inspectors.

The Health and Safety (Offences) Act 2008, which came into force in January 2009 empowers the magistrates' court to impose a fine of up to £20,000 and a prison sentence of up to 12 months. The Crown Court already had the power to impose an unlimited fine, but since January 2009 it may impose a prison sentence of up to two years. Certain offences which previously could only be tried in the magistrates' court become triable in either the Crown Court or magistrates' court, which increases the possibility of a heavier penalty for more offences.

Improvement notices: s 21

If in an inspector's view the statute is being breached and this state of affairs is likely to continue, the inspector may issue a notice requiring the contravention to be corrected within specified time limits. Compliance may be enforced by prosecution if necessary.

Prohibition notices: s 23

If the inspector believes that the way the business is being conducted is likely to result in serious personal injury, a prohibition notice may be issued. This prohibits continuance of the relevant activity until the situation is resolved. These notices have to set out clearly the nature of the problem and may include advice about how it can be remedied. Section 24 gives rights to appeal against an order to an employment tribunal.

Ministerial regulations

The 1974 Act empowers the Department of Employment (now BIS) to make specific regulations to ensure performance of duties under the Act. Progress was initially slow in this area, but the need to comply with EC directives issued between 1989 and 1991 forced the Department to issue the Management of Health and Safety at Work Regulations 1992. These came into force progressively between 1993 and 1997 and replace most of the provisions of statutes like the Factories Acts and the Offices, Shops and Railway Premises Act 1963. These regulations expand the scope of obligations imposed on employers by the Health and Safety at Work etc., Act 1974, since they incorporate aspects of EC law not envisaged by the 1974 Act.

Chapter summary

A business is served both by employees and independent contractors and has different contractual relationships with each.

The *contract of service* governs the relationship of employer and employee. It is valid without writing but ERA 1996 requires an employer to provide each employee with a written statement of the key terms.

It contains express and implied terms which may be derived from:

(a) custom and practice;

(b) works/staff rules;

(c) collective agreements;

(d) statute and common law.

Common law duties of employee:

(a) reasonable care and skill to fulfil all reasonable orders;

(b) good faith (confidentiality, account for profits, no conflict of interest).

Common law duties of employer:

(a) payment;

(b) trust and confidence;

(c) safe working conditions.

Employer's liability for injuries at work

Civil liability: common law duty

The employer has a non-delegable duty to take reasonable care to provide reasonably safe working conditions including:

(a) competent staff;

(b) safe plant and equipment;

(c) safe systems of work.

Breach of statutory duty

An employee may also sue an employer for failing to perform a statutory duty provided:

(a) Parliament intended a civil remedy to be possible (can the statute be interpreted like this?);

(b) the employee is a member of the class protected by the statute;

(c) the employer has breached the statute;

(d) damage has resulted from the breach.

Criminal liability

May arise under a variety of regulations and the HSWA 1974.

The HSE is empowered to enter premises, issue improvement orders and prosecute employers.

Quiz 15

1 What are the main differences in the legal obligations of an employer to an employee and to an independent contractor?

2 Angelica is employed by Juniper plc as personal assistant to the managing director. What contractual duties may Angelica have breached in the following circumstances?

(a) She takes an evening job with Coltsfoot Ltd.

(b) When serving refreshments at a meeting at Juniper plc, she drops a full coffee pot into the lap of Lupin, the chairman of the board.

(c) After the meeting, Hawksbeard, a visiting consultant, who had enjoyed Lupin's discomfiture, gives Angelica a £10 tip.

3 Heather, who is employed by Rush, was run over on work premises by a forklift truck driven by Bogbean. Her injuries were aggravated by difficulties in locating the first aid kit. What are Rush's liabilities?

4 What powers are available to HSE inspectors who discover that a health and safety offence has been committed?

Answers to all quizzes can be found in Appendix 2.

Take a closer look

The following cases provide important examples of how the law you have studied in this chapter has developed. They are primary sources illustrating the law in action and give you more detail about their facts, as well as helping you to understand the law and to appreciate how the judges reached their decisions.

Try looking them up in the law reports or accessing them via a database, e.g. Bailli (www.bailii.org/databases.html). LexisNexis or Westlaw may be available in your university or college library, or you may find extracts in a case book. (See Appendix 1: Additional resources.)

Hudson v *Ridge Manufacturing Co. Ltd* [1957] 2 QB 348

RDF Media Group plc v *Alan Clements* [2007] EWHC 2892 (QB); [2008] IRLR 207

Reid v *PRP Architects* [2006] EWCA Civ 1119; [2007] ICR 78

Spencer-Franks v *Kellogg Brown & Root Ltd* [2008] UKHL 46; [2008] ICR 863

Web activity

Please go to: www.hse.gov.uk and click on 'news' and check out 'health and safety myths' to see some of the dafter ideas falsely attributed to health and safety requirements

Assignment 14

Evaluate the ways in which the law regulates employers with regard to the health and safety of their employees.

CHAPTER 17

Rights at work
Protection against discrimination

Introduction

The Equality Act (EA 2010) has brought the law relating to illegal discrimination within the compass of one statute, and aims to create a harmonised body of law from the patchwork of previous legislation, which developed in a piecemeal fashion from the middle of the twentieth century. It covers all aspects of discrimination law, including education and services, but this chapter focuses on discrimination at work only.

The Act repeals, re-states and to some extent simplifies the provisions of the previous legislation in this area and creates some new obligations for employers. The law generally remains the same in substance, so existing case law must therefore be regarded as valid unless the Act or subsequent litigation indicates to the contrary. Any statutory references in this chapter are to the EA 2010 unless stated otherwise.

Learning objectives

When you have studied this chapter you should be able to:

▶ appreciate the scope of legal protection under the EA 2010;

▶ understand what is encompassed by the 'protected characteristics';

▶ define the nature of behaviour prohibited under the Act;

▶ grasp the difference between direct and indirect discrimination;

▶ give examples of 'occupational qualifications';

▶ describe the functions of the Commission for Equality and Human Rights.

The Equality Act 2010: the core provisions

In this part of the chapter we will examine the operation of the central provisions of the EA 2010, which tell us who is covered by its provisions and the nature of conduct made illegal by it and relevant to all claims under it.

The protected characteristics: s 4

Protected characteristic: designation of a person or group protected against unfavourable treatment under the EA 2010.

This section lists the areas of discrimination protection covered by the Act which are described as '**protected characteristics**'. They are: age, disability, gender re-assignment, marriage and civil partnership, pregnancy and maternity, race, religion and belief, sex and sexual orientation.

Prohibited conduct

This is behaviour which is illegal under the Act: direct and indirect discrimination, harassment and victimisation.

Direct discrimination: s 13

Section 13 states that 'a person (A) discriminates against another (B) if, because of a protected characteristic, A treats B less favourably than A treats or would treat others'.

It occurs where A treats B less favourably because of B's protected characteristic than he would treat others without that characteristic. The definition includes *discrimination by association* (treating one person unfavourably because of their association with another) or *perception* (treating someone unfavourably because of an incorrect and maybe stereotypical belief about their attributes, abilities, beliefs, etc).

This largely mirrors previous equality legislation, although before the Act associative discrimination could not be claimed in cases involving age, disability, gender re-assignment or sexual discrimination. Perceptive discrimination did not apply to disability, gender re-assignment and sexual discrimination claims.

Direct discrimination: openly treating an employee less favourably than others because of protected characteristic.

There is no defence to **direct discrimination** except on the grounds of occupational requirement.

Combined discrimination: s 14

This occurs 'if, because of a combination of two relevant protected characteristics, A treats B less favourably than A treats or would treat a person who does not share either of those characteristics'. For example, a person might allege that they were discriminated against simultaneously because of their race and disability. However, the Chancellor of the Exchequer announced in the Budget in March 2011 that this section would not be implemented on the grounds of cost to, and over-regulation of, employers.

Indirect discrimination: s 19

This arises if 'if A applies to B a provision, criterion or practice which is discriminatory in relation to a relevant protected characteristic of B's'.

In other words, this would put B at a disadvantage compared with others who do not share the protected characteristic. For example, a minimum height restriction as a criterion for a job may be judged as indirectly discriminatory on the grounds of sex, as men are on average taller than women and so would put a large number of women at a disadvantage. The defence of justification applies when the employer can show that the practice is a proportional response to a legitimate aim in the particular circumstances (s 19(2)(d)).

While this section clearly reflects the previous legislation, it extends protection to disabled and transgender people.

Comparators: s 23

Liability in all cases of direct or indirect discrimination is determined by comparing the defendant's treatment of the claimant with that of an actual or hypothetical person who does not share their protected characteristics. So an employer will, for instance, be liable if they treat a person with a disability in a way that puts them at a disadvantage compared with an able-bodied person doing similar work.

Irrelevance of alleged discriminator's characteristics: s 24

The fact that A, who has allegedly discriminated against B, has the same protected characteristic as B is irrelevant to determining liability. So, for example, a woman may be liable for acting in a discriminatory way to another woman.

Occupational requirement: Schedule 9, s 1

Discrimination may be legal if the defendant can show that the nature of the job makes it essential to restrict employment to people of a certain characteristic. For example, it would be reasonable on the grounds of authenticity to advertise waiting jobs in a Chinese restaurant to people of Chinese ethnicity. This is the only defence available against a claim of direct discrimination.

Other prohibited conduct

All the following behaviour was illegal under the previous legislation but is newly defined in the Act.

Harassment: s 26

There are three types:

1 unwanted conduct related to the claimant's gender which has the intention or effect of violating their dignity or *'creating an intimidating, hostile, degrading, humiliating or offensive environment'*;

2 unwanted conduct of a sexual nature that has the same intention or effect as in 1 above;

3 less favourable treatment or **harassment** on the grounds of sexual or gender assignment. A provision imposing liability on the employer for harassment by a third party was later repealed by the Employment and Regulatory Reform Act 2013.

> Harassment: verbal/non-verbal behaviour which creates an intimidating/ hostile/degrading/ offensive environment and is intended/ has the effect of violating a person's dignity.

Victimisation: s 27

This protects anyone who has asserted their rights under the EA or someone supporting them from subsequent unfavourable treatment by their employer. There is no need to find a comparator to determine liability but the victim must have suffered some detriment.

Vicarious liability: s 109

As you may remember (from your studies of Chapter 15), an employer may be vicariously liable for the torts of their employees working under a contract of service or an agent with the authority of the principal. This common law principle was replicated in the previous equality legislation and repeated in the EA and extended to cover any breach of the Act.

It is no defence that the employer or principal did not know about the behaviour (s 109(3)), although the employer will not be liable if they took 'all reasonable steps' to prevent it. In such circumstances a claimant may sue the offending claimant directly (s 110).

Potential claimants and defendants

The employment provisions of the Act generally cover anybody in or seeking work, not necessarily under a contract of service. It therefore not only covers employees in the strict sense but also job applicants, the self-employed with a contract for services, workers, and also for example agents, agency workers, apprentices, partners or prospective partners, barristers' pupils, people in work experience placements and police personnel. Members of the armed forces are included but enjoy only limited protection. It does not cover volunteers (*X* v *Mid Sussex Citizens Advice Bureau* (2013, SC)).

In this chapter, for ease of expression, all potential claimants will generally be referred to as 'employees'. Similarly, those for whom they are working will be referred to as 'employers'. An employee who commits a breach of duty under the Act is personally liable and therefore may also be a defendant (s 110).

The operation of the Equality Act 2010

This part of the chapter explains the protected characteristics in more detail and illustrates the way the Equality Act is likely to operate in practice with reference to case law and examples. You may wish to refer to the definitions of prohibited behaviour and other concepts explained above, since, to avoid repetition, these are not spelt out in relation to each protected characteristic. You may assume that they apply unless the contrary is stated.

Age

Until the Employment Equality (Age) Regulations 2006 (implementing the Equal Treatment Amendment Directive (2002/73/EC)) came into force on 1 October 2006, age discrimination was legal under English law. In its core principles explained above, the EA 2010 largely replicates the protection given by the regulations but protects people of any age, while the regulations gave protection to people up to 65 years old only.

The definition of the protected characteristic of age: s 5

Where the Act refers to the protected characteristic of age, it means a person in a particular age group. Such a group includes people of the same age and people of a particular range of ages. When people fall in the same age group they share the protected characteristic of age. E.g. 18-year-olds or 50-year-olds are two different age groups but an over-60s age group includes anybody of 60 upwards.

The comparator (s 23) in age discrimination cases would be someone from a different age group from the claimant who is treated more favourably for that reason.

Prohibited behaviour

Direct discrimination and indirect discrimination: ss 13 and 19

The next case is a good example of indirect discrimination.

Baker v *National Air Services Ltd* (2009)

The defendant employer refused to allow Mr Baker, aged 50, to train as an air traffic controller. It claimed that the age limit of 35 was a legitimate and proportionate aim, because of safety concerns and the need for applicants to be in the job sufficiently long to justify the cost of training.

Held: the defendant was guilty of indirect discrimination: the defendant's aim was legitimate but not proportionate. It reflected 'the received wisdom that air traffic controllers must start young and older individuals will not be suitable'. The existing safety precautions were sufficient in themselves, as they ensured scrutiny of all employees' health at all times and further restriction was superfluous. Such an arbitrary universal age ban was unreasonable: it would unnecessarily prejudice older applicants.

The introduction of the Employment Equality (Age) Regulations 2006 was largely prompted by concerns about discrimination against older people. However, one of the first cases brought under the regulations concerned a young woman.

Thomas v *Eight Members Club and Killip* (2007)

Megan Thomas, aged 19, was sacked from her job as membership secretary of an exclusive City club after four months. The managers told her that she was too young to deal appropriately with the club's clientele. The tribunal held that she was the victim of direct discrimination and awarded her a compensation for hurt feelings, which was all that was required, as she had mitigated her loss by immediately obtaining better paid employment with a City firm.

Canadian Imperial Bank of Commerce v *Beck* (2010)

Achim Beck was 42 when his employers claimed that they were making him redundant from his job as marketing director and then replaced him with someone of 38.

The Employment Appeal Tribunal affirmed that Mr Beck had been dismissed on account of his age because of proof of instructions from the employer to an employment agency stating that it wanted to head-hunt 'a younger entrepreneurial profile'. This raised sufficient evidence of age discrimination to shift the burden of proof to the bank, which had not proved that the question of age was sufficiently significant. Indeed, the bank's evidence did not appear genuine, but more a rationalisation after the event. Mr Beck had suffered both direct and indirect discrimination.

Occupational qualification: Schedule 9(1)

It may be a good defence to an employer if they can prove that it is appropriate to appoint someone in a particular age group, for example in a dramatic production, because it is essential to the integrity of the production.

Retirement age

The Employment Equality Age Regulations prevented compulsory retirement at 65 (men) or 60 (women) stating that this was the default retirement age (DRA). People wishing to continue working after that could *request* their employer for an extension.

An ongoing government review concluded in 2010 that the DRA should be abolished for both men and women. This coincided with government plans to raise the age of entitlement to the state retirement pension. The Employment Equality (Repeal of Retirement Age Provisions) Regulations 2011 were subsequently passed, which abolished the DRA from April 2011, and EA 2010 was amended to mirror this change.

Although there is no longer a default retirement age an employer may be entitled to impose retirement, as long as this requirement is a 'proportionate means of achieving a legitimate aim' under the EA, s 13(2). Some guidance in determining this provision in such cases was provided by the Supreme Court in 2012.

> ### *Selsdon* v *Clarkson Wright* (2012, SC)
>
> The Supreme Court held that the following criteria must be taken into account:
>
> 1 *Social policy*. It may be reasonable for an employer to impose a retirement age in the interest of 'inter-generational fairness'. This means ensuring a wide age range of employees with equal opportunity of promotion and advancement within the business. It also enables the employer to retain able, younger staff members who otherwise might be tempted to seek better opportunities elsewhere. Only broad social policy considerations are relevant to deciding whether direct discrimination on the basis of age is justified under s 13(2). Particular concerns of the employer such as saving money or upping competition are not relevant (although they may be in cases of indirect discrimination under s 19(2)).
> 2 *Dignity of the employee*. Imposition of a retirement age may enable an employer to ease out older workers who have become incompetent or who are under-achieving. This is preferable to a formal dismissal which might result in litigation.

You will notice that the Supreme Court's criteria are by their nature rather wide and woolly. The facts of each individual case will be crucial.

Harassment and victimisation: ss 26, 27 and 40

Employees with the protected characteristic of age now enjoy full protection against harassment and victimisation.

Disability

Disability: physical/mental impairment having substantial long-term adverse effect on a person's ability to do his or her job.

The **Disability** Discrimination Act 1995 (DDA), with amendments, governed the rights to equal treatment of people with disabilities prior to 2010. Protection has been clarified and increased by the EA 2010.

The protected characteristic of disability

This is defined by s 6(1) of EA 2010, which states:

1 A person (P) has a disability if:
   (a) P has a physical or mental impairment, and
   (b) the impairment has a substantial and long-term adverse effect on P's ability to carry out normal day-to-day activities.

This rather superficial definition is clarified by Schedule 1 to the EA 2010 and largely replicates the DDA definition. However, the EA does not require proof that the impairment affects a specific capacity, such as hearing, mobility or eyesight, which should make it easier for claimants to prove that their disability is covered by the Act.

What is 'impairment'?

Guidance issued by the Department of Work and Pensions (DWP) indicates that the words 'physical or mental impairment' should be given their usual meaning. Previous litigation is also relevant to deciding this. Therefore, to give rise to liability, the impairment must be medically recognised and relate, for example, to mobility, manual dexterity, eyesight, hearing, memory, concentration or comprehension. Progressive conditions are also included (e.g., multiple sclerosis, HIV/AIDS). Severe disfigurement such as birthmarks, scars, skin diseases may be a disability. Some previous case examples include asthma (*Cox* v *Post Office* (1997)); soft tissue injuries (*O'Neill* v *Symm & Co. Ltd* 1998)) acute abdominal pain (*Howden* v *Capital Copiers* (1998)) recurrent infections (*Sussex Partnership NHS Foundation Trust* v *Norris* (2012)). Mental impairment includes clinical depression, bi-polar disease and learning difficulties.

No case concerning obesity has yet come before the UK courts but in 2014 the ECJ held that discrimination on that ground is not necessarily unlawful (*Kaltoft* v *Billund* (2014, ECJ)). It could be unlawful if the obesity gives rise to long-lasting physical or psychological impairment which hinders 'the full and effective participation of the person concerned in professional life on an equal basis with other workers'.

Certain conditions, such as addiction to alcohol, nicotine and other similar substances are not covered, although it is possible to claim if such a condition triggers a statutory impairment. In *Power* v *Panasonic* (2002), the EAT held that because the claimant had clinical depression, it was irrelevant whether she was depressed because she was an alcoholic or had become an alcoholic because she was depressed.

The effect of the impairment must be 'substantial', which means that a person's ability to carry out ordinary daily tasks must be considerably inhibited compared with people without the impairment. So, for example, the DWP guidance suggests that the length of time taken to complete the task, the means necessary to achieve it and its cumulative effect on the claimant are relevant. For example, someone with asthma could successfully claim that its effect was substantial if it took them longer to climb a flight of stairs than an able-bodied colleague who did not have to pause to catch their breath every few steps and use their inhaler to recover from severe breathlessness once they had got to the top. Recurrence is also a relevant issue.

How long is 'long term'?

Schedule 1, para 9 says that the disability should have lasted, or be expected to last, for at least 12 months.

Prohibited conduct

Direct discrimination

The EA 2010 core provisions concerning direct discrimination (s 13), which includes discrimination by perception and by association, are basically similar in scope to those in the DDA and give rise to liability if their effect is to treat a disabled person less favourably than someone who is able-bodied.

In this context, discrimination by perception relates to general incorrect assumptions about the nature of the relevant disability. It would include, for example, refusing to shortlist a severely visually impaired person for a job involving computers, in the belief that this disability would automatically render the applicant incapable of using them.

A new development under the EA 2010 is the inclusion of discrimination by association. This occurs where an able-bodied person claims that they have suffered discrimination because of their connection to someone with a disability. This corrects the problem that arose in *Coleman* v *Attridge Law* (2008), where Ms Coleman claimed that she had been discriminated against on the grounds of her son's disability, because her employers refused her the flexible working hours that she needed in order to cope both with her job and her responsibilities as his carer. She won her case only when, in compliance with the judgment of the ECJ, the Employment Appeals Tribunal found in her favour by interpreting the DDA in accordance with the relevant EC directive.

Under s 13(3) it is not illegal to treat a disabled person *more* favourably than able-bodied colleagues.

The occupational requirement defence: Schedule 9(1)

This may be a defence to direct discrimination. For example, a flawless complexion may reasonably be required to advertise facial cosmetics, so a person with a severe facial disfigurement might reasonably be rejected for that job.

Consequential unfavourable treatment: s 15

This is a new provision, relevant only to people with a disability. It makes it illegal knowingly to treat a person unfavourably because of anything arising *as a consequence of that person's disability*, provided this is not a *proportionate means of achieving a legitimate aim*. A person is treated unfavourably if put at a disadvantage. For example, a person being treated for cancer might need to take more sick leave than other, fitter, colleagues. It would be discriminatory to dismiss her for that reason because it is a result of her disability.

Indirect discrimination

The EA 2010 (s 19(3)) extends this to cover people with disabilities.

It occurs if an unjustifiable 'provision, criterion or practice', applied to everyone, particularly disadvantages people who share the disabled person's disability compared to others who do not. Proving that the discriminatory behaviour is a proportionate means of achieving a legitimate aim is a good defence. Thus, prescribing rigorous physical fitness criteria for fire-fighters may be justifiable.

Comparator: an actual or hypothetical person with whom the claimant is compared who does not share their protected characteristic.

Comparators: s 23

To determine whether a claimant has been unfairly treated, a comparison exercise must be carried out to decide whether another person without the claimant's impairment but with the same abilities or skills would have been treated in the same way.

Note that no **comparator** is needed when determining consequential discrimination (s 15).

The duty to make reasonable adjustments: s 20

This requires the employer to ensure that a person with a disability is not put at a 'substantial disadvantage' compared with able-bodied employees. The duty can be divided into three areas:

(a) *Adjustments to working arrangements.* For example, allowing an employee caring for a person with a disability to work flexible hours.

(b) *Making physical alterations to the premises.* It might be appropriate to install a ramp for a wheelchair user.

(c) *Provision of aids to facilitate carrying out employment duties.*

Tarling v *Wisdom Toothbrushes* (1997)

Ms Tarling had a club foot, which made it difficult for her to stand for long periods. This impaired her work performance, which led to her dismissal.

Held: her dismissal was discriminatory and due to the failure of the employer to make reasonable adjustments. Her employer knew that a special chair was available, on four weeks' free trial at a subsidised cost which reduced the price to £200, but took no steps to obtain one.

Failure to make reasonable adjustments amounts to discrimination: s 21

What is reasonable is dependent on the circumstances and any changes must be proportional not only to the needs of the employee but also to the employer. The size and nature of the business and its premises must be taken into account and expense is a factor to be considered, though not necessarily decisive. The Code of Practice issued by the DWP suggests that the cost of appointing and training a new employee may be an appropriate indication of the cost of the adjustment. Issues of health and safety are also relevant.

Occasionally there may be nothing an employer can reasonably do to enable an employee to work. In *Dyer v London Ambulance NHS Trust* (2014, EAT) the claimant, who worked in a large control room with numerous staff, often visited by members of the public, became acutely allergic to aerosol sprays and perfume. The employer notified staff repeatedly about the need to avoid use of these but the order did not have the necessary effect and the claimant suffered five attacks of anaphylactic shock, requiring hospitalisation. The fifth attack was almost fatal. At this point the employer dismissed the claimant on the grounds of incapability. She claimed discrimination. The EAT held that no discrimination had occurred as there was nothing more her employers could reasonably do to accommodate her disability.

Enquiries about disability and health: s 60

This is a new provision. Previously, an employer was able legally to ask such questions prior to, or at, a job interview, but not to discriminate against an applicant in response to their answer. This new provision is intended to add transparency to the recruitment process and prevent information about health and ability from acting as a disincentive to the employer at this stage. Under s 60, an employer generally must *not* ask a job applicant about their health or disability prior to offering them a job.

Such questions can only be asked:

(a) to find out whether the applicant would be able to participate in an assessment to test their suitability for the job;

(b) to make reasonable adjustments to enable the disabled person to take part in the recruitment process;

(c) to find out whether a job applicant would be able to cope with functions intrinsic to the job, with any reasonable adjustments;

(d) to monitor diversity in the appointments process;

(e) to support positive action in employment for disabled people; and

(f) to assist an employer where there is a genuine occupational requirement for the person to be disabled.

While on the face of it this appears to be an improvement on the DDA provisions, you may wonder whether the information given under the exception rule may not sometimes lead to a biased response.

Gender re-assignment

The protected characteristic of gender re-assignment (s 7) includes both male to female and female to male transsexuals and is continuous from the time they decide that they wish to change gender and live as a member of the opposite sex, whether or not they are undergoing or have undergone medical treatment. This increases the previous rights under the Sex Discrimination Act 1975 (as amended by the Sex Discrimination (Gender Re-assignment) Regulations 2007), which only protected a transsexual person who was undergoing or had previously undergone relevant medical treatment. Now the process of moving from one gender to another is perceived as personal rather than medical. There is no obligation to tell an employer of the status but it may be appropriate to ensure that arrangements are made to avoid unfavourable treatment.

Prohibited behaviour

In addition to the usual protection against direct discrimination under s 13, protection against indirect discrimination (s 19) has been extended to transgender people.

They are also protected by s 16, which states that it is discrimination to treat someone absent from work due to gender assignment treatment less favourably than anyone else taking sick leave.

Transsexuals also now enjoy full protection against harassment and victimisation.

Occupational requirement defence

Under Schedule 9, para 1(3), if an employer can show that *not* being a transsexual is an occupational qualification for a job, less favourable treatment may be justified as long as the employer proves that this is a proportionate and justifiable means of pursuing a legitimate aim. For example, a pre-operative male to female transsexual man could legitimately be refused employment as a female model for nude life-drawing classes.

The Gender Recognition Act 2004

This enables transsexuals to apply at least two years after transition for a gender recognition certificate that gives them full legal recognition of their change of gender. They may also obtain a new birth certificate reflecting the change. Generally a birth certificate is sufficient for most employment purposes. An employer should not legitimately need to require sight of a gender recognition certificate more than once. Additional requests may amount to harassment.

Marriage and civil partnership

The protected characteristic

Any person who is currently married or is currently in a civil partnership has this protected characteristic (s 8) and is entitled not to be treated unfavourably because of it.

Dunn v *Institute of Cemetery and Crematorium Management* (2011, EAT)

Ms D claimed marital discrimination in breach of the Sex Discrimination Act 1975, s 3 (now EA, s 8) on the grounds that she had been treated unfavourably by the defendant employer because she was married to Mr Dunn, who was also in dispute with the defendant, before her own difficulties at work had begun.

Held: she had the right to claim. Correct interpretation of the law (in accordance with the ECHR Articles 8, 12, and 14) covered situations where discrimination had arisen, not just because the claimant was married, but because of whom she was married to.

Marriage includes any form of marriage regarded as legal under UK law.

Prohibited behaviour

Indirect discrimination is prohibited, but people with this protected characteristic only have a claim for basic direct discrimination, not for discrimination by perception and association. They are protected against victimisation but not harassment.

However, members of a civil partnership could claim harassment on the grounds of their protected characteristic of sexual orientation.

Occupational qualification defence

Occupational qualification: essential personal requirement for a job which may permit employer to discriminate against those employees who lack it.

Under Schedule 9, para 1(3), if an employer can show that *not* being married or not being in a civil partnership is an **occupational qualification** for a job, less favourable treatment may be justified as long as the employer proves that this is a proportionate and justifiable means of pursuing a legitimate aim.

Pregnancy and maternity

Pregnancy and maternity is listed in s 4 with the other protected characteristics.

Anti-discrimination rights in this area remain virtually the same as they were before the Act, under the Sex Discrimination Act 1975 and related legislation. These rights are derived from EU law, which includes the Pregnant Workers Directive (92/85/EEC) and the amended Equal Treatment Directive (2006/54/EC).

A woman enjoys a protected status in relation to unfavourable treatment at work during pregnancy and for a limited time afterwards. This gives her special protection while pregnant or on maternity leave, in addition to that covered by other relevant aspects of the protected characteristics.

Prohibited behaviour

The 'protected period'

Protected period: period of protection for a woman while pregnant or on maternity leave.

Unfavourable treatment of a woman because of her pregnancy, or because of illness resulting from or relating to her being on maternity leave is illegal if it takes place during '**the protected period**' (s 18(2)). Such treatment includes dismissal (*Webb* v *EMO Cargo (No. 2)* (1995)), demotion and refusal of training opportunities.

The protected period starts when a woman becomes pregnant and continues until the end of her maternity leave, or when she returns to work if that happens sooner (s 18(6)). During this time liability is strict, the employer's motivation or intention is irrelevant and a comparator is not necessary to determine liability.

Once the protected period is over any further claim of unfavourable treatment is treated as one of gender discrimination, unless it arises from a decision made during the protected period (s 18(5)).

Direct and indirect discrimination: ss 13 and 19

A woman with this protected characteristic may claim direct or indirect discrimination under s 18, but not discrimination by perception or association.

17

Rights at work: protection against discrimination

413

Note, however, that any employee who is treated less favourably through associating with a pregnant woman, or a woman who has recently given birth, may claim for sex discrimination. This would protect, for example, a member of the woman's family who provides care to the woman after the birth.

Victimisation

Section 18(4) covers victimisation during the protected period arising from unfavourable treatment caused by her exercising her rights to maternity leave.

Harassment

There is no specific protection against harassment for women with this protected characteristic but the sex discrimination provisions of the Act (see) are relevant.

Race

The EA 2010 largely replicates the Race Relations Act (as amended) in prohibiting discrimination on the grounds of race.

The protected characteristic: s 9

Race includes (s 9(1)):

- colour;
- nationality;
- ethnic or national origins.

A person with this protected characteristic will be a member of a racial group (s 9(2)). A racial group may consist of two or more distinct racial groups (s 9(4)).

The interpretation of these terms

Nationality

Nationality indicates a person's legal relationship to the state in which they were born or became a citizen through naturalisation. It determines their voting rights and rights to access state provided services. It is also relevant to determining duty to perform military service.

Ethnic or national origins

Ethnicity is interpreted more widely than race.

> ### *Mandla* v *Dowell Lee* (1983, HL)
>
> **Held:** an ethnic group existed if it was regarded by its members and by outsiders as a clearly distinguishable community with its own cultural traditions and a long-shared history. Other relevant factors were said to include a common geographical origin, or language, religion, or literature.
>
> Therefore, Sikhs constituted a distinct ethnic group. School rules forbidding Sikh boys from wearing turbans and requiring their hair to be cut to a specified length indirectly discriminated against them.

In *Commission for Racial Equality* v *Dutton* (1989, CA) the Court of Appeal applied the *Mandla* decision and held that 'gypsies' (we would call them 'Roma' today) constituted an ethnic group that had not merged wholly with the general population, although it was no longer derived from a common racial stock.

Other legally recognised ethnic groups include Jews, and Scottish and Irish Travellers.

National origin must be distinguished from nationality. You cannot change your national origin but you might take on a new nationality. For example, a person born in Turkey is of Turkish national origin, but might immigrate to the UK, become naturalised and thus acquire British nationality.

National origins have both historical and geographical identifiable elements, which indicate that a nation currently exists or previously existed. For example, the English and the Scots have separate national origins because Scotland was originally a separate nation.

Racial group

All racial groups are protected against unfavourable treatment under the Act.

A racial group is made up of people who have colour or nationality, or their ethnic or national origins in common. A person may be a member of more than one racial group, for example black, with British nationality of Indian national origin and a Jew.

17

Rights at work: protection against discrimination

In the news

Legislation to prohibit caste discrimination expected in 2015

Caste discrimination is not specifically prohibited by the EA 2010 but it is possible to interpret s 9 to include caste in some circumstances. In *Chandok & another* v *Tirkey* (2014, EAT) the claimant, a nanny, sued her employers claiming they had mistreated her because of her caste. The Employment Appeal Tribunal held that while caste is not currently a protected characteristic in its own right, discrimination is illegal where caste is determined through birth or where it involves an identifiable ethnic identity.

Shortly before the *Chandok* v *Tirkey* decision, s 9 was amended by the Enterprise and Regulatory Reform Act 2013. This states that the government 'must by order amend Section 9 [of the Act] so as to provide for caste to be an aspect of race'. The government published a timetable in 2013 scheduling consultation in 2014 with legislation to follow in 2015 but no legislation had yet been tabled by January 2016.

As the intention of the Act is primarily intended to protect racial minorities, the courts may need to interpret it purposively.

Redfearn v *Serco Ltd* (2006, CA)

R was dismissed by the defendant bus company when it discovered that he was a member of the British Nationalist Party and a local councillor. The defendant argued that he was a risk to health and safety, as it was feared that Asians, who made up the majority of the customers and staff, might react violently to him. He had not worked for the defendant long enough to enable him to bring a case of unfair dismissal so he attempted to claim discrimination on 'racial grounds' under s 1(1)(a) of the RRA 1976.

Held: R had not been discriminated against on racial grounds (because he was white) but because of his particular views, which were shared by a tiny proportion of the white population.

However, Mr Redfearn later made a successful claim to the European Court of Human Rights (*Redfearn* v *Serco* Ltd (2012)), which held that his rights to freedom of assembly and association had been violated and that a legal system that allowed dismissal merely because of political belief was defective. A change in the law was necessary to enable implementation of this decision. As a result, the government amended ERA 1996 s 108 to provide that an employer may be liable for unfair dismissal of an employee, regardless of the length of time they have been employed, if the principal reason for the dismissal was political belief. The employer will be liable unless it proves that its procedures and reasons for the dismissal were fair. This does not make dismissal for political belief automatically unfair, nor does it mean that dismissal on these grounds is categorised as discrimination.

Worth thinking about?

A claim under the Race Relations Act was always going to be a longshot for Mr Redfearn. It was many years before his claim in the European Court of Human Rights was resolved. What other legal claims, not available in 2006, might Mr Redfearn pursue today? What are his chances of success?

Suggested solutions can be found in Appendix 2.

Prohibited conduct

This means treating a person less favourably because of their colour, nationality, ethnic or national origins than others without the protected characteristic of race.

Direct discrimination: s 13

This includes discrimination by association and perception. Special protection includes prohibition of deliberate segregation (s 13(5)) of either an individual or racial group. This is automatically illegal and no comparator is required.

Occupational qualification is a defence: Schedule 9, para 1

An employer has the right to make a specific racial characteristic a requirement of employment provided it fulfils a legitimate aim and is a proportional requirement of the job. It may be relevant to jobs involving the provision of welfare services to a specific racial group, where applicants may be required to be members of that group themselves.

Indirect discrimination: s 19(1)(b)

This occurs when a 'provision, criteria or practice' is imposed which discriminates against people with the protected characteristic of race because they cannot comply with it, to their personal detriment. This is clearly illustrated by the next case.

> ### *Mandla* v *Dowell Lee* (1983, HL)
>
> **Held:** school rules forbidding Sikh boys from wearing turbans and requiring their hair to be cut to a specified length indirectly discriminated against them on the grounds of their ethnic origins.

The 'proportionate means' defence

If the condition can be shown to be a 'proportionate means of achieving a legitimate aim', indirect discrimination may be justifiable (s 19(2)(d)). In *Panesaar* v *Nestlé* (1980) a rule forbidding long beards and hair in the defendant's factory, while indirectly discriminating against Sikhs, was nonetheless justifiable on hygiene grounds. This decision would be differently decided today on the grounds that while the aim (preserving high standards of hygiene) is legitimate, the means to achieve it is disproportionate. Suitable head and face covering would readily solve the problem and are commonplace in the food industry.

Vicarious liability: s 109

In *Jones* v *Tower Boot Co. Ltd* (1997, CA) the claimant was subjected to verbal and physical racial abuse in his workplace from other employees. His employer was vicariously liable. However, an employer may be vicariously liable for torts caused by employees even if not personally at fault.

Real life

Nigel Flash has just been made chief executive at Smallville Borough Council, which is Horace's employer. Nigel, keen to make his mark, has made a variety of organisational changes, including a new dress code. This bans women from wearing trousers to work. Horace, as union representative for his department, has been approached by two female employees adversely affected by this rule. Ravinder, a Sikh, who works as a telephonist complains that her line manager won't let her wear the *shalwar kameez* because it includes trousers. Her religion requires her to cover her legs and the *shalwar kameez* is required dress in her community. Alice works in the stores department and has always worn smart trousers to work. She finds this convenient given the nature of her job, which involves actively handling stores and transporting them round the building. Since she has complied with the code, her colleague Percy has made a number of comments about her legs, and the other day was peering up her skirt while she was up a step ladder.

Horace takes up both these issues with the human resources department. He argues that the dress code indirectly discriminates against Ravinder on both racial and religious grounds. That seems a sound claim. Imposing a rule of this kind is justifiable only if it is a proportionate response by an employer, whereas this seems to be a rigid rule imposed for no good reason except uniformity.

Horace claims on behalf of Alice that the dress code directly discriminates against women and treats her less favourably than male colleagues. Current case law suggests that this would be successful. In *Owen* v *Professional Golf Association* (2000) the employment tribunal held that instructing a female employee to return home and change from a smart trouser suit into a skirt was sex discrimination.

Percy's behaviour is sexual harassment and Smallville will be liable if steps are not taken to resolve the situation.

Religion or belief

Protection against discrimination in this area has existed since 2003, when Employment Equality (Religion or Belief) Regulations 2003 were introduced to implement the Equal Treatment Directive of 2000. The EA largely replicates the regulations.

The protected characteristic of religion or belief: s 10

The definition reflects Article 9 of the ECHR (freedom of thought, conscience and religion).

Religion

This is defined in the Act as including lack of religion (s 10(1)). It includes all religions, and any religious or philosophical belief, including atheism and agnosticism. Denominations or sects of religions like Baptists or Sephardic Jews are also protected. While it includes religions that are not mainstream, a religion must have a clearly defined belief system and structure. The EAT (*Greater Manchester Police Authority* v *Power* (2010)) recognised that spiritualism was a religious belief, pointing out that the Spiritualist Church was the eighth largest worshipping group in Great Britain.

Belief

Both religious and non-religious belief comes within this definition. A belief does not have to involve faith or worship but must fulfil certain broad criteria. In *Grainger plc and Others* v *Nicholson* (2010) Burton J helpfully described belief:

> It must be a belief as to a weighty and substantial aspect of human life and behaviour. It must attain a certain level of cogency, seriousness, cohesion and importance. It must be worthy of respect in a democratic society, be not incompatible with human dignity and not conflict with the fundamental rights of others.

He refused to strike out Mr Grainger's claim that he had suffered discrimination at work because of his belief in climate change. Belief in the sanctity of life and that foxhunting should be consequently be banned was held to be a protected belief in *Hashman* v *Milton Park (Dorset) Ltd* (2011); however, the belief that a poppy should be worn as a mark of respect for military war dead was not (*Lisk* v *Shield Guardian Co. Ltd* (2011)).

Prohibited behaviour

When the protected characteristic is religion or belief, it is illegal for one person to treat a person with this characteristic less favourably than they would, or do, treat others without that protected characteristic.

Direct and indirect discrimination: ss 13 and 19

Unfavourable treatment arising from direct or indirect discrimination including discrimination by perception or association is actionable. Indirect discrimination may be justifiable if the employer can show that it is proportionate and necessary to fulfil a legitimate aim. Cases have often arisen on grounds of rules regarding uniform or dress requirements, which may amount to unfavourable treatment by preventing a person from manifesting their religion. The next case is a good example of how such cases are determined and how discrimination can be justified.

Azmi v *Kirklees Metropolitan Borough Council* (2007, EAT)

Ms Azmi was suspended from her job as a teaching assistant when she persisted in wearing a full veil, despite instructions not to do so.

She claimed that the council had directly and indirectly discriminated against her, as her religion required her to wear a veil while the class teacher, who was male, was in the room.

17

Rights at work: protection against discrimination

The council denied the claim arguing (from observing her at work) that the veil which covered her face and mouth interfered with her ability to communicate properly with the children and interfered with their learning to read.

Held: no direct discrimination had occurred. She had not been treated any differently, on the grounds of her religious belief, than any woman employee, Muslim or otherwise, who covered her face for non-religious reasons. They would have been subject to the same rule. No indirect discrimination had occurred. While the council's dress policy contained a provision which some Muslim women might not be able to fulfil, it did not target the veil but acknowledged that the policy had an impact in that area and that every case would be dealt with on its merits. The policy was neutral or at least applicable to non-Muslims. The council had acted with proportionality in order to achieve a legitimate end (the children's learning).

In *Eweida* v *British Airways* (2010) the Court of Appeal held that Ms Eweida, a devout Christian who usually wore a crucifix, had not suffered indirect discrimination due to BA's uniform rules, which forbid wearing any jewellery round the neck. The intention of the provision against indirect discrimination was to offer protection to a group of people rather than one person alone. There was no evidence that other Christians were adversely affected by the policy. However, the court stated that, had indirect discrimination been determined, BA could not have justified it as a proportionate restriction. Subsequently, BA revised its uniform policy to accommodate wearing religious symbols. Ms Eweida appealed successfully to the European Court of Human Rights. (See 'In the news' below.)

In the news

Eweida and others v *UK* (2013, ECtHR)

Held: freedom of religion is a crucial right in any democratic society, but in determining whether the right has been infringed restrictions may be justified where its exercise unduly impinges on the rights of other people. An appropriate balance must be established between the extent of duty of the employer to protect the rights of others and the rights of the applicant to practise their religion.

BA had breached Ms Eweida's rights to freedom of religion under Article 9. A fair balance had not been struck between BA's legitimate aim to project a corporate image by its uniforms and Ms Eweida's right to manifest her belief. Other employees were allowed to wear religious specific clothing such as hijabs and turbans with no deleterious effect on the company image. Clearly the restriction on Christian symbols had not been sufficiently important to BA, particularly given that the dress code had later been amended to permit them.

Ms Chaplin, another party in the above case, lost her claim. She was a nurse and health and safety concerns had motivated her employers' ban on jewellery of any kind for employees performing clinical duties. The European Court of Human Rights court held that asking her to remove her cross was a proportionate response by her managers, who were in a better position to make safety judgements and therefore her case must fail.

These cases illustrate that while the right to hold to a religion or belief is in itself absolute, the right to manifest that belief is a qualified one.

Sometimes a conflict may arise between the needs of people with different protected characteristics. In *Eweida and Others* v *UK* (2013) (above), two of the unsuccessful parties, Ms Ladele and Mr Macfarlane, had lost their jobs because they believed that their Christian beliefs did not allow them to condone homosexuality. Ms Ladele, an employee of Islington Council, had refused to perform civil partnerships and Mr Macfarlane, employed by Relate, had refused to counsel lesbian and gay couples. It was held that their Convention rights had not been breached because their employers' equal opportunity policies were designed to protect the rights of both employees and their clientele, including same-sex couples whose rights were also protected by the Convention. Previous decisions of the ECHR indicated that adverse treatment on the grounds of sexual orientation could only be permissible when serious justification could be proved. Same-sex couples should be treated equally with mixed-sex couples regarding the protection and legal recognition of their relationship.

Occupational requirement

Special dispensation is granted by the Act in relation to organised religions and certain institutions with a religious ethos.

Organised religions

Schedule 9, para 2 enables an employer which is an organised religion to require its ministers and holders of key posts to be of a specified gender and sexual orientation. Transgender people and lesbian, gays and bisexuals may be legally excluded. Marital status may also be specified to exclude people who are divorcees, if their spouse is still alive.

For example, the Church of England can legally refuse to employ a priest who is lesbian or gay. The Roman Catholic Church can require its priests to be unmarried and not divorced.

Such a requirement can only be imposed by a recognised religion to comply with religious doctrine and to avoid conflict with the majority of the religion's followers.

It is construed narrowly and only applies to posts which involve direct ministry carrying out religious services and related pastoral care.

Employers with a religious ethos

Under Schedule 9, para 3, an employer with an ethos based on a recognised religion or belief is also entitled to protect its key posts with the occupational requirement. Ethos may be defined as the reflection of the religion or belief evidenced by the culture and philosophy of the relevant institution as derived from its constitution and functions.

This, for example, covers church schools, higher educational institutions training people for the priesthood and other organisations reflecting a particular religion or belief in the nature of their work, like the Humanist Society.

Sex

Before the EA 2010, the Sex Discrimination Act 1975 (as amended) was the relevant legislation in this area. Its coverage included marriage, pregnancy and maternity and transgender discrimination. Under the EA, sex discrimination becomes discrete.

Although the SDA was enacted primarily to combat sexual discrimination against women, men are given equal rights under its terms. In some years men brought more successful cases than women. The EA closely mirrors the SDA regarding sexual discrimination with a few enhancements.

The protected characteristic of sex: s 11

This includes male and female persons of any age. In relation to a group of people it refers to men/boys or women/girls.

The EA 2010 makes it illegal to discriminate directly or indirectly against persons on the grounds of their sex. Treating men and women differently does not amount to illegal discrimination unless it results in members of one sex being treated less favourably than the other.

The sex equality clause: s 66

This is intended to ensure that the terms in an employment contract are not more or less favourable to an employee on the grounds of their gender. All contracts with employees must include such a clause or such a term will automatically be implied. It requires that a term in the employment contract which is less favourable than that of a comparator of the opposite sex doing the same or similar work must be altered to reflect the term in the comparator's contract. Similarly, if the comparator's contract includes a favourable term which is not in the employee's contract, such a term must be implied in the employee's contract of employment. Proof of a material difference may be a justification.

Prohibited behaviour

Direct discrimination: s 13

Direct (overt) discrimination occurs if a person is treated on the grounds of her sex less favourably than a person of the opposite sex. Reserving a job for male candidates only is an obvious example. In *Batisha* v *Say* (1977), a woman who applied for a job as a cave guide was turned down on the ground that it was 'a man's job'. In *Moyhing* v *Barts and London NHS Trust* (2006), the EAT deemed a policy requiring a male nurse to be chaperoned while undertaking intimate examinations of women, to be directly discriminatory to male nurses. No such requirement applied to the intimate examination of male patients by female nurses.

Direct discrimination includes associative and perceptive discrimination.

Qualities like physical strength and stamina must not be treated as sex specific. A woman cannot automatically be excluded from consideration for a job because it involves heavy lifting. Some women are stronger than some men, even if in general men are stronger than women.

Occupational qualification: Schedule 9, para 1

This defence may protect an employer who can prove that the essential nature of the job requires a specific gender.

A job may be reserved for a man or a woman specifically if this is essential for physiological reasons, such as striptease artists. Issues of privacy and decency may also be legitimate concerns, for example when staffing single-sex hospitals and prisons. It might be also legitimate to discriminate in appointments to residential jobs if appropriate separate sleeping or sanitary facilities cannot reasonably be provided.

Etam plc v *Rowan* (1996, EAT)

Held: being female was not essential for a shop assistant selling women's clothes. A male applicant could fulfil the bulk of the job. A female staff member could supervise changing rooms without any inconvenience to the employer or embarrassment to women customers.

Indirect discrimination: covert discrimination. Selection criteria, policies, benefits, rules or conditions, that are applicable to the whole workforce, but discriminatory to members of a relevant characteristic.

Indirect discrimination: s 19

Indirect discrimination or covert discrimination occurs when an employer imposes on an employee an apparently neutral 'provision, criterion or practice' which puts an employee at a disadvantage when compared to employees of the opposite sex and which the employer cannot show to be a 'proportionate response to a legitimate aim'.

Home Office v *Holmes* (1984)

Held: a requirement that employees worked full-time, not part-time, was indirectly discriminatory against women. Their opportunities to go out to work full-time were more likely to be limited by childcare responsibilities than men's. The nature of the job did not justify the full-time requirement.

Harassments: ss 26 and 40

Specific protection is provided against sexual harassment (s 26(2)).

Porcelli v *Strathclyde Regional Council* (1986)

Ms Porcelli worked as a technician in a laboratory with two male colleagues who mounted a campaign of sexual insults and physical intimidation to try to make her leave.

Held: she was the victim of discrimination, since the behaviour of her colleagues was 'a particular kind of weapon which . . . would not have been used against an equally disliked man'.

Equal pay

This has always been a particularly contentious area of sex discrimination against women. Historically, women's work has been undervalued, with low rates of pay in those areas of employment most often filled by women, like cleaning, nursing, catering and shop work. Where men have been employed alongside women, they have often been paid at a higher rate than women doing similar, or even identical, work. Legislation aimed at correcting this discrepancy was first introduced by the Equal Pay Act 1970, which was amended in 1983 under the Equal Pay (Amendment) Regulations to comply with the Equal Pay Directive (75/117/EEC) to cover work of equal value. Sadly, despite the legislation, women were still on average earning nearly 16 per cent less than men in 2014 according to statistics compiled by the TUC. Women bosses came off even worse; according to figures published the same year by the Chartered Institute of Management they received 35 per cent less than their male equivalent.

The EA 2010 largely replicates the previous legislation but with some minor expansion of protection. The **equality clause** (s 66) (see above) has particular relevance to equal pay issues, as it requires an entitlement to equal pay to be implied in a contract of employment that does not make it specific. Occupational pension entitlement is also included for the first time under the EA 2010 (s 67).

The equal pay provisions cover not only wages and salaries but also all monetary benefits such as paid holiday leave, sick pay and overtime. Non-monetary benefits, like access to social and sporting facilities, are also covered.

Equality clause: implied term in an employment contract to ensure parties are treated equally favourably.

Like work: work rated as equivalent to that of a comparator under a job evaluation scheme.

Equivalent work: work of the same or similar nature.

Work of equal value: work that is different in its general characteristics from that of a comparator but has the same monetary worth.

Equal work: s 65

A woman is entitled to claim equal pay and other contract terms with a male comparator who is doing:

- 'like work', which means that the job is the same or largely similar; or
- 'work rated as equivalent', which means that although different in its nature it has been rated as similar under a job evaluation scheme; or
- 'work of equal value', which means that although the job is a different one, it should be viewed as of similar value with regard to such elements as the level of skill, decision-making or management responsibility it requires.

The court is required under EU law to interpret these provisions purposively.

Let us now look at them in a little more detail to see how they are likely to work in practice.

'Like work'

The woman must show that her work is identical or broadly similar to a male comparator looking at the job as a whole and considering any particular skill or responsibility that goes with it. Provided she can do this, she will succeed in her claim unless the employer can prove a material difference; for example, the qualification or training involved to do the job, the anti-social hours when it is performed; or that the physical *effort* required to perform it could be of practical importance.

A cosmetic difference, such as giving the man's job a superior title, does not fool the court.

Capper Pass v *Lawton* (1977)

Held: a woman employed to cook meals for the directors' dining room was doing essentially similar work to the assistant chefs in the canteen. The only differences were that the canteen chefs cooked more meals for greater numbers, were supervised and worked for four hours more every week than she did.

Heavy work may justify higher pay.

Noble v *David Gold & Sons (Holdings) Ltd* (1980)

Male warehouse workers were paid more than women working alongside them.

Held: this was justified by the fact that the men loaded and unloaded goods while the women's work was lighter and involved sorting, labelling and packaging goods.

Notional responsibilities that are not actually performed will not be treated as a material difference.

Shields v *Coomes (Holdings) Ltd* (1978)

It was claimed by the employer that a male counter assistant at a betting shop was paid more than a female counter assistant because he was there for security purposes.

Held: she was entitled to equal pay since the employer was unable to prove that the male assistant had received any security training, or that he had ever had to deal with troublemakers; there was no material difference between his function and the woman's.

Equivalent work

A woman is entitled to claim breach of the equality clause if her employer has a valid job evaluation scheme in operation, under which the woman's job is graded at the same level as a man's but he is paid more, or if the woman's job would have been graded at a higher level under the scheme if the evaluation had not been made according to different values for men and women. The same criteria must be applied to both men and women and the scheme must be drawn up in such a way as to avoid sex discrimination.

This provides a means whereby jobs may be systematically assessed to find their relative value. It rates the jobs on a points scheme using criteria such as level of responsibility, skill, effort and decision-making focusing on the jobs in their entirety, so comparison of very different types of job is possible.

Job evaluation schemes are not compulsory and, due to the relatively small number in operation, claims in this area are uncommon.

'Equal value'

To determine the value of the work, the demands of the relevant jobs must be assessed and compared by the tribunal. It must take into account the skill, knowledge, trade or professional qualification, physical and mental effort, and levels of responsibility and decision-making.

Hayward v *Cammell Laird Shipbuilders* (1988, HL)

Held: the work of a cook in the works canteen was of equal value to that of other skilled workers such as joiners, painters and insulation engineers. Therefore she was entitled to the same basic pay as they were. It was irrelevant that her entitlement to sickness benefits, holiday leave and meals entitlement were superior to other skilled workers.

This provision means that a wide range of jobs is comparable. A skilled manual job may be of the same or greater value than one involving an administrative role.

Comparators

The comparator must be, or have been, employed at the claimant's workplace or at another workplace associated directly or indirectly with the woman's employer.

The claimant has the choice of the comparator. This was originally determined by the House of Lords in *Pickstone* v *Freemans plc* (1988) as being necessary to prevent an employer from putting a 'token male' into the same line of work as the woman and paying him at the same rate. She may choose more than one comparator. Sometimes this may be essential to success if it is necessary to compare a number of terms in her contract that may not relate to the terms of service of just one comparator. The comparator need not be employed contemporaneously with the claimant (s 64(2)). This reflects the Court of Appeal's decision in *Macarthys* v *Smith* (1981) and prevents an employer from replacing a male employee with a woman on a lower rate of pay.

Hypothetical comparators

This provides new protection where no comparator may be found. For example, if an employer tells a woman that he would pay her more if she were male, but there are no comparable jobs in her own or an associated workplace, she can claim sex discrimination and use a hypothetical comparator (s 71).

Occupational pensions

Neither the EPA 1970 nor the SDA 1975 applied to pensions, but EC law led to anti-discrimination legislation:

Barber v *Guardian Royal Insurance* (1990, ECJ)

Held: it was contrary to Article 141 of the Treaty of Rome for a man who had been made compulsorily redundant to be entitled only to a deferred pension, if a woman of the same age and in the same position would be entitled to claim her pension immediately.

The Pensions Act 1995, ss 62–66 required equal treatment regarding pensionable service for all persons retiring since 17 May 1990.

The sex equality rule (s 67(1) EA 2010) now aims to enable men and women to obtain equal treatment both in terms of access to and benefits from an occupational pension. Section 61 requires a non-discrimination rule to be implied into every occupational pension scheme and prohibits 'a responsible person' from discriminating against or victimising or harassing anyone who wants to join the scheme or is a member of it.

Material difference

Under (s 69), an employer who can prove that the reason for a pay differential between men and women is 'a material factor', will not be liable. A material factor will be one that is genuine, relevant and significant and does not constitute direct sex discrimination. If it gives rise to indirect sex discrimination it will only be a valid defence if it is a proportionate means of securing a justifiable aim. Effectively, the employer is saying that the difference in pay between men and women is coincidental and that it is provably linked to material differences between the two parties other than their sex. Such differences have been held to include levels of qualification, length of service, place of work and anti-social hours of work. Organisational and economic factors may also justify a pay differential, but it is a question of fact for the court to decide in each case.

Staff shortages were held to represent a genuine material difference in the next case:

Rainey v *Greater Glasgow Health Board* (1987, HL)

The Board set up a prosthesis service within the NHS. Some prosthetists were recruited from the NHS sector and were paid at its current rate, but this was insufficient to recruit the numbers required and so a further 20 (all male) were recruited from the private sector and paid at a higher rate to reflect their previous, more favourable, salary. Ms Rainey, an NHS recruit, claimed that this was discriminatory.

Held: this pay differential was justifiable on the grounds of market forces.

The market forces argument is only relevant while the particular circumstances prevail. Once they ease, equal pay must be paid (*Benveniste* v *University of Southampton* (1989)).

Economic conditions were held not to be relevant in the following case:

North Yorkshire County Council v *Ratcliffe* (1995, HL)

Held: paying dinner ladies less than men judged to be doing work of equal value could not be justified on the ground that it was done to enable the employers to make the winning bid in compulsory competitive tender negotiations. This was 'the very kind of discrimination which the Act sought to remove'.

In *Blackburn and Another* v *Chief Constable of West Midlands Police* (2008) the Court of Appeal held that working night shifts was a material factor. Therefore, paying male police officers an enhanced rate for these shifts did not illegally discriminate against female officers who had opted out of night work because of childcare commitments. It could be objectively justified since it fulfilled the legitimate aim of rewarding people for working anti-social hours.

Equal pay during pregnancy and maternity

A woman should not be subject to inferior pay and conditions during pregnancy or while on maternity leave and a maternity clause is implied in her contract to that effect. No comparator is needed to determine such issues (s 73).

During her leave her normal pay arrangements will be suspended but she will obtain maternity pay if entitled under her terms of service. However, she is still entitled to any bonus or pay rise awarded while she is on leave if she would be entitled to it at work (s 74).

If she is a member of an occupational pension scheme, an implied maternity clause protects her against loss of pension rights while she is away from work on *paid* maternity leave (s 75(1)–(6) and (9)).

Pay transparency

In the interest of promoting equality, the Act aims to ensure that employers make pay structures clear and understandable to all employees and trades unions.

Some employers promote secrecy by including a gagging clause in employment contracts to prevent employees discussing and comparing salaries, which may enable continuance of hidden inequalities of pay. Such a clause is unenforceable under s 77 if it stops a person from making a 'relevant pay disclosure' or seeking disclosure from a current or previous colleague.

A disclosure is 'relevant' under the Act (s 77(3)) if it is about pay and aims to find out whether discriminatory practice is involved on the basis of any protected characteristic. An employer seeking to penalise an employee for making or seeking disclosure may be guilty of victimisation.

Section 78 gave the government power to make larger employers publish information indicating whether there are differences in pay scales between the men and women they employ but these powers were never used. However, things are set to change since the SBEEA 2015, s 178 requires the Secretary of State 'as soon as possible and no later than 12 months after the passing of this Act, [to] make regulations under section 78 of the Equality Act 2010 (gender pay gap information) for the purpose of requiring the publication of information showing whether there are differences in the pay of males and females'. This will apply to all employers with a workforce of 250 or more.

Enforcing an equal pay claim

A woman is entitled to information from her employer if she believes she is receiving unequal pay and failure to provide a clear response within eight weeks entitles an employment tribunal to infer that inequality exists (s 138(4) and (5)).

However, before taking the matter to the tribunal, the woman should attempt informal resolution and if this fails present a formal written grievance in line with the ACAS code. ACAS can also provide a conciliator.

The employment tribunal has special procedures for dealing with equal pay cases. If a claim is successful, the tribunal may issue a declaration setting out the woman's pay entitlement and if appropriate order payment of damages to cover arrears of pay and other lost benefits (s 132). Damages are not awarded for hurt feelings in an equal pay claim.

Publication of pay information by employers

Regulations may be issued by the DWP requiring employers of 250 people or more to publish information about pay structures (s 78). The government announced in 2011 that no such regulations would be issued for at least two or three years.

Sexual orientation

Introduction

Until 2003, an employee enjoyed little legal protection against discrimination on the grounds of sexual orientation. Human rights legislation provided some redress. The European Convention on Human Rights (Articles 8, 13 and 14, which prohibit discrimination) does not refer expressly to sexual orientation but can be interpreted purposively. The implementation of the Convention in the English courts by the Human Rights Act 1998 enabled further developments of English law in this area.

The ECHR, in *Smith and Grady* v *UK* (1998), held that the ban on lesbians and gay men in the armed forces violated their rights under Article 8 (the right to privacy and family life) and Article 13 (the right to an effective domestic remedy). This eventually led to a radical change in policy by the Ministry of Defence, which lifted the ban in 2005.

EC law eventually prompted change under the Equal Treatment Directive 2000, which was implemented by the Employment Equality (Sexual Orientation) Regulations 2003.

These regulations made it unlawful to discriminate against any employee by treating them less favourably on account of their sexual orientation. It thus became illegal to discriminate against a heterosexual, lesbian, gay man or bisexual because of their sexuality.

The EA largely replicates the rights under the regulations but has enhanced rights against harassment and victimisation

The protected characteristic: s 12

Sexual orientation means a person's sexual orientation towards—

(a) persons of the same sex,

(b) persons of the opposite sex, or

(c) persons of either sex.

It therefore includes lesbians, gay men, heterosexuals and bisexuals.

Prohibited behaviour

Treating a person unfavourably because of sexual orientation is illegal under the Act.

Comparators

This should be someone in similar circumstances but who does not share the same characteristic. However, comparing a person who is a civil partner with one who is married is not a sufficient material difference (s 23(3)).

Direct and indirect discrimination: ss 13 and 19

As mentioned above, direct discrimination includes perceptive and associative discrimination and discrimination by association. Negative stereotyping of lesbians and gay men readily gives rise to unfavourable treatment.

Occupational qualification

Under Schedule 9, para 3, this is a defence to direct discrimination on the grounds of sexual orientation if it fulfils a legitimate aim and is carried out in proportionate manner. A support group for young lesbian and gay people might be justified in advertising for an advice worker as a position open to gay and lesbian candidates only on the grounds that its clients would be more prepared to approach someone of their own sexual orientation and shared experience.

Harassment: ss 26 and 40

People with this protected characteristic may claim harassment both by an employer (s 26) and third parties (s 40).

A heterosexual person may be harassed with homophobic 'banter' even though his colleagues do not actually believe him to be gay. In the case of *English v Thomas Sanderson* (2008), Collins LJ held on a preliminary issue:

> If one were to ask the question whether the repeated and offensive use of the word 'faggot' in the circumstances of this case was conduct 'on grounds of sexual orientation' the answer should be in the affirmative irrespective of the actual sexual orientation of the claimant or the perception of his sexual orientation by his tormentors. If the conduct is 'on grounds of sexual orientation' it is plainly irrelevant whether the claimant is actually of a particular sexual orientation.

Note, however, that Mr Sanderson's case ultimately failed when it came to trial because, although he had been made the subject of homosexual banter, harassment had not occurred, as he was found not to have been offended by the behaviour. As Mr Sanderson joined in the banter and remained good friends with his tormentors, no harassment occurred. The EAT upheld this decision (*Thomas Sanderson Blinds Ltd* v *English* (2011)).

Vicarious liability

An employer with knowledge of illegal behaviour by employees will continue to be vicariously liable if it takes insufficient steps to prevent the illegal behaviour continuing (s 109(4)).

Martin v *Parkham Foods* (2006)

In May 2005, abusive and homophobic graffiti naming Mr Martin appeared on the toilet wall at his workplace. He complained to the human resources department and a very limited cleaning operation took place which merely obliterated his name. Notices were put up telling staff not to deface the building, but homophobia was not mentioned.

In October 2005, his name reappeared on the graffiti. He complained again but was told that there was little that could be done to discover the culprit. He then wrote a formal complaint letter and Parkham suspended him to allow an investigation to take place.

In December 2005, while suspended, Mr Martin resigned and claimed harassment, direct discrimination and constructive dismissal.

Held: Parkham was vicariously liable for the harassment and had directly discriminated against Mr Martin.

It had not taken all reasonable steps to prevent the recurrence of the homophobic behaviour, which should have been addressed by appropriate training, team briefings or notes in pay-slips to make it crystal clear to all employees that homophobic behaviour would not be tolerated.

The grievance had not been diligently investigated and the failure to apologise to him was also culpable.

His suspension, given the connotations it carried, was inappropriate. All of these factors led to a breach of Mr Martin's trust and confidence and meant that he had been constructively dismissed.

Enforcing anti-discrimination legislation

A complainant may apply to take the matter before an employment tribunal. An application must usually be made within three months of the alleged behaviour. Initially, grievance and possibly conciliation procedures are implemented, but if these fail the case will be heard by the tribunal.

The promotion of equality

The Act seeks to do more than right individual complaints of discrimination. It seeks to promote equality in general.

The public sector equality duty: s 149

This duty was implemented in April 2011.

Public Bodies listed in Schedule 19 to the Act have a three-part duty to:

(a) eliminate discrimination, harassment, victimisation and any other conduct that is prohibited by or under this Act;

(b) advance equality of opportunity between persons who share a relevant protected characteristic and persons who do not share it;

(c) foster good relations between persons who share a relevant protected characteristic and persons who do not share it.

Duty (a) applies to all protected characteristics but (b) and (c) are not relevant to marriage and civil partnership.

Schedule 19 indicates that s 149 covers ministers of the Crown, most government departments and local authorities. Other bodies which are not public bodies but exercise some public duties are subject to the requirement of s 149 with regard to their public duties.

The Equality and Human Rights Commission has the power to issue compliance notices and take whatever steps are necessary within its powers to ensure performance of the duty.

Specific equality duties

Under s 153, a minister has the power to issue by regulation specific equality duties 'for the purpose of enabling the better performance by the authority of the duty imposed by section 149(1)'. The government is consulting on this issue and so far no regulations have been created.

The socio-economic duty: s 1

The Act places public sector employers such as local authorities, health and primary care trusts and police forces under a legal duty to consider the impact their strategic decisions will have on individuals who are from disadvantaged backgrounds. However, the government has scrapped this provision.

Positive action: s 159

An employer may appoint or promote a candidate with a protected characteristic where people with that particular protected characteristic are underrepresented in the workforce. This can only be done where the relevant candidates are equally qualified: each case must be considered on its merit.

This section does not permit an employer to have a policy of appointing people with a specific protected characteristic in preference to others without it.

17

Rights at work: protection against discrimination

The Equality and Human Rights Commission

Equality and
Human Rights
Commission:
body responsible
for monitoring the
operation of anti-
discrimination law
in the UK.

The **Equality and Human Rights Commission** (EHRC) was created under the Equality Act 2006, s 1. From October 2007, it replaced the Equal Opportunities Commission, the Commission for Racial Equality and the Disability Rights Commission, which had been responsible for overseeing the working of the legislation relevant to sexual, racial and disability legislation respectively. The EHRC took over their functions, but with additional powers enabling it to exercise a unifying role in monitoring anti-discrimination legislation as a whole. It is also responsible for the promotion of a culture of equality and human rights.

The core functions of the Commission

The Commission's core functions are currently:

1 Promoting and encouraging awareness and good practice in equality and diversity.

2 Promoting understanding of rights under the legislation through provision of easily accessible advice and information.

3 Enforcing rights under the legislation through individual case work support.

4 Working towards eliminating unlawful discrimination and harassment through promotion of awareness and provision of advice and through strategic enforcement, including the use of investigations and enquiries.

5 Promoting awareness, understanding and protection of human rights by initiating good practice in public authorities, in order to improve compliance with the Human Rights Act 1998.

6 Promoting good relations between the different groups covered by the equality laws and between them and society at large.

Future reform

The government announced in 2011 that, as part of its policy concerning 'quangos', it intends to reform the Commission to clarify its brief, cut non-core functions, create greater transparency in its operations and ensure that it provides better value for money. In 2013 the Commission's budget was slashed by over two thirds and its staff reduced by over a half. In future the government believes that it should not be a campaigning body and instead concentrate on making recommendations on the basis of facts. The Enterprise and Regulatory Reform Act 2013 (E&RRA) has left the Commission's main functions intact. However, some peripheral powers such as the duty to monitor continuing progress towards equality and the power to impose conciliation procedures have been axed.

Chapter summary

The scope of the Equality Act 2010

The Act protects individuals against unfavourable treatment with reference to eight protected characteristics: age, disability, gender re-assignment, marriage and civil partnership, pregnancy and maternity, race, religion and belief, sex and sexual orientation.

Structure

The Act states the forms of relevant prohibited behaviour:

(a) direct/indirect discrimination (occupational qualifications may provide a defence; the legitimate aims defence is relevant only to indirect discrimination);

(b) harassment;

(c) victimisation.

An employer may also be vicariously liable for discriminatory behaviour of employees.

The Act imposes particular duties regarding people with certain specific protected characteristics. For example, it requires reasonable adjustments to be made for people with disabilities.

Positive discrimination is permitted to a limited extent.

Defences to liability are included. The defence of 'occupational requirement' applies in positive discrimination claims. It is a defence to indirect discrimination to show that it is a proportional means of attaining a legitimate aim.

Promotion of equality

Public service bodies are under a general duty to enhance and promote equality (s 149).

Section 159 permits limited positive action by employers making appointments to posts.

The Equality and Human Rights Commission

The Commission is responsible for the promotion of equality, by monitoring the operation of the EA 2010, assisting individuals in making claims, carrying out investigations and making recommendations for improvement.

17

Rights at work: protection against discrimination

Quiz 16

1 (a) Ms Antelope, who is employed as a cleaner by Cheetah plc, is paid less than the male packers.

   (b) Mr Buck was refused a job at the Warren Family Planning Clinic because he is male.

2 What legal rights may they have?

3 What is the difference between direct and indirect discrimination?

4 When may it be legal to advertise a job as being open only to members of a particular ethnic group?

5 While Ms Rabbit was on maternity leave she didn't get a bonus paid to all other employees on her grade. Her friend Ms Hare approached their boss, Mr Fox, and pointed out that Ms Rabbit was entitled to the money under the Equality Act 2010. Two weeks later, Mr Fox made her redundant. Advise Ms Hare and Ms Rabbit.

Answers to all quizzes can be found in Appendix 2.

Take a closer look

The following cases provide important examples of how the law you have studied in this chapter has developed. They are primary sources illustrating the law in action and give you more detail about their facts, as well as helping you to understand the law and to appreciate how the judges reached their decisions.

Try looking them up in the law reports or accessing them via a database, e.g. Bailli (www.bailii.org/databases.html). LexisNexis or Westlaw may be available in your university or college library, or you may find extracts in a case book. (See Appendix 1: Additional resources.)

Azmi v *Kirklees Metropolitan Borough Council* (2007) ICR 1154, EAT

O'Neil v *Symm & Co.* [1998] IRLR 232, EAT

Rainey v *Greater Glasgow Health Board* [1987] AC 224, HL

Eweida and Others v *UK* [2013] ECHR 37

Web activity

Please go to: www.acas.org.uk/

Click on 'Advice A-Z' then under E find 'Equality', and explore the wide range of resources on offer.

Assignment 15

Trumpet Ltd provides public relations and publicity services. Madeline has been working for the company as a receptionist for seven years. Recently she was severely injured in a road accident unconnected with her job and is now confined to a wheelchair. Trumpet has given her notice saying that it cannot guarantee her safe evacuation from the building in the event of fire and that the toilet arrangements are not safely accessible to wheelchair users.

Raj, recently recruited to the company, receives an anonymous message through the internal mail saying 'Why don't you get a job nearer home?' and others follow containing website addresses for airlines doing bargain flights to Pakistan. He reports the matter to his manager, Gladys, who says he should ignore it and, anyway, there is nothing she can do about it.

Jane has worked in public relations for several years. She recently applied to Trumpet for a job and in her application was able to demonstrate conformity with all the essential and desirable requirements in the job description. At her interview, when asked to give examples of successful projects, she describes a publicity campaign that she ran for 'Outcome', a lesbian and gay organisation. She does not get the job and afterwards finds out that it has been given to another applicant less well qualified than she. She queries this with Trumpet's human resources manager who tells her: 'We were not convinced that your professional experience fits the needs of our client group.'

Advise Madeline, Raj and Jane.

17

Rights at work: protection against discrimination

CHAPTER 18

Rights at work
Protection against dismissal and redundancy

Introduction

Generally, it is the employee who discharges their employment contract by giving in their notice and moving on to a new job. Sadly, sometimes things do not go smoothly and it is the employer who takes the initiative. In this chapter we will examine how this may occur and the remedies that an employee may obtain if the employer has broken the law protecting the employee's rights.

There are three ways in which the employer may illegally bring an employment contract to an end:

- *Wrongful dismissal.* At common law an employee dismissed without appropriate notice may sue in the civil courts for breach of contract at common law.
- *Unfair dismissal.* Provided that the required notice is given, dismissal is lawful at common law, but nonetheless may be unfair as an employee is potentially vulnerable to dismissal at the whim of the employer. Since 1971, statutory rights have existed which protect employees found to have been dismissed unfairly. An employee may be entitled to bring a claim before an employment tribunal, whether dismissed with notice or not. Unless the employer can prove that it was fair to dismiss the employee (because of incompetence, for example), he or she may have to pay compensation to the employee who might, in exceptional cases, be reinstated.
- *Redundancy.* An employer may need to reduce the size of the workforce, but an employee consequently made redundant has a right to be treated fairly in the process and may have a statutory entitlement to compensation.

These concepts are explained in detail below.

Wrongful dismissal

Wrongful dismissal: breach of contract by the employer.

Summary dismissal: employee is dismissed without notice.

Wrongful dismissal is a breach of contract action which may be brought by an employee if the contract of employment is terminated by the employer without the appropriate notice, or, in the case of a fixed-term contract, if termination is enforced before the contract's completion date.

Summary dismissal (without notice) may be justified only if the employer can prove that the employee was guilty of gross misconduct. This usually involves theft, fraud, violence or drunkenness, reckless behaviour or wilful refusal to obey a reasonable order.

Minimum notice periods

Under the Employment Rights Act 1996 (ERA 1996) the following notice periods apply unless a longer period is specified in the contract (s 86):

● up to one month in employment: no notice;

● one month to two years' employment: one week's notice;

● two to 10 years' employment: one week's notice for every completed year;

● over 10 years' employment: 12 weeks' notice.

Remedies for wrongful dismissal

An employee is entitled to sue for breach of contract in the courts to recover any lost earnings payable during the notice period, as well as any commissions and gratuities that the employee would normally have acquired. An apprentice is entitled to be compensated for loss of prospects. An employee may also obtain compensation for benefits lost where the wrongful dismissal prevented the employee from completing the necessary period of continuous employment to entitle the employee to pursue a claim for unfair dismissal.

Alternatively, action may be brought in the employment tribunal, though here the damages are limited by ERA 1996. Claims before the tribunal are usually time barred after three months from termination of the contract, while a limitation period of six years applies to court claims. (See also remedies for breach of contract in Chapter 9.)

Unfair dismissal

This area of the law, which has been subject to constant change since its inception, is currently largely governed by the ERA 1996 (as amended). Some important changes have recently been introduced through the Enterprise and Regulatory Reform Act 2013. All statutory references in this chapter refer to ERA unless otherwise specified.

Any employee entitled to sue for wrongful dismissal may also be entitled to bring a claim for unfair dismissal to an employment tribunal. However, an employee who has not been dismissed wrongfully may qualify to claim for **unfair dismissal**. Employers, therefore, are no longer necessarily free to dispense with an employee's services unless they can satisfy the tribunal that they acted fairly and with reasonable cause within the legislative criteria

Certain types of employee are not eligible to claim unfair dismissal: for example, shareholder employees.

Unfair dismissal: dismissal which cannot be justified as fair by the employer.

Eligibility to claim

Claims must be brought within *three months* of the termination of the contract. The following criteria must be satisfied:

1 continuous employment;
2 the employee must prove the fact of the dismissal;
3 the employer must prove the dismissal was fair.

The employee must have been continuously employed for at least two years

This applies to both full and part-time employees. The number of hours worked per week is irrelevant.

Employment remains continuous despite certain interruptions:

- sickness;
- pregnancy and maternity leave;
- temporary lay-offs;

- holidays;
- change of job with the employer or its associate;
- takeover by a new employer.

The Unfair Dismissal and Statement of Reasons for Dismissal (Variation of Qualifying Period) Order 2012 raised the **continuous employment** requirement from one to two years. This was part of the implementation of government policy aimed at cutting red tape for employers by simplifying the dismissal process and reducing the number of potential cases brought to the employment tribunal. A change can be introduced by order of the Secretary of State under the ERA, s 209.

Continuous employment: minimum of two years working for the same employer which qualifies an employee to claim unfair dismissal at the employment tribunal.

Employees must prove that they have been dismissed

Dismissal may be actual, constructive or deemed.

Actual dismissal: employer tells employee that he or she is dismissed.

- **Actual dismissal.** The employer clearly indicates an intention to dispense with the employee's services.
- **Constructive dismissal.** The employee resigns claiming that the employer's behaviour made it impossible for the employee to stay. Breach of the employer's duty not to undermine the trust and confidence of the employee is often the ground for such a claim. A number of such cases have arisen from an employer's failure to prevent sexual harassment and bullying. *Martin* v *Parkham Foods* (2006, EAT) is a good example of this (see above, page 432).

Constructive dismissal: employee feels forced into resignation by employer's behaviour.

- **Deemed dismissal.** An employee who has been on maternity leave but has given appropriate notice that she wishes to return to work is deemed to be dismissed if the employer refuses to let her resume her job.

Deemed dismissal: an employer who refuses to permit an employee to resume her job after maternity leave is deemed to have dismissed her.

In the following circumstances dismissal does *not* occur:

1 *The employee fails to return to work after leave of absence has expired.* This may deprive an employee of the right to return but it is not a dismissal.
2 *Completion of purpose of employment.* Employees will not be able to claim that they were dismissed if they were appointed to complete a specific project. Once this is done, their employment ceases. This is common in seafaring and fishing contracts.
3 *Resignation.* Provided that the employee neither resigned voluntarily, nor was forced into doing so (see constructive dismissal, above).

The burden of disproving unfairness lies with the employer

The employer must prove:

(a) grounds for the dismissal;
(b) that in the circumstances it is fair.

Grounds for dismissal

Section 98 of the ERA 1996 lays down five grounds, any of which may justify dismissal:

1 lack of appropriate qualifications/capability to do the job;
2 the employee's conduct;
3 the employee was redundant: the job had ceased to exist;
4 continuance of employment would result in illegality;
5 any other substantial reason.

There are numerous cases to illustrate the application of these criteria, including the following examples. Each case is judged on its particular facts.

Lack of qualification or capability

The missing qualification must be essential to the proper performance of the current job.

Litster v Thom & Sons Ltd (1975)

Litster was given a job on condition that he obtained an HGV licence. However, he failed the test and was transferred to a fitter's post. Later he was given notice.

Held: he had been unfairly dismissed. The lack of a licence had not prevented him from serving his employer. (Presumably, if he had been sacked immediately on failing the driving test that might have been justifiable.)

Negligence

Negligence may justify dismissal. One isolated act of negligence is unlikely to be sufficient grounds for dismissal unless it is gross negligence and/or endangers the life and limb of third parties.

Taylor v Alidair (1978)

An airline pilot who once landed a plane in such a careless manner as seriously to disturb his passengers and crew was subsequently dismissed.

Held: this was not unfair because very high standards of safety needed to be maintained given the high risks attaching even to a momentary lapse in skill by a pilot.

Employer's fault

Dismissal is not deemed fair if the employee's lack of capability can be attributed to the fault of the employer. In *Davison* v *Kent Meters* (1975) a production line worker was held to have been unfairly dismissed for wrongly assembling several hundred components since she had been neither properly trained nor supervised.

18

Rights at work: protection against dismissal and redundancy

Long-term sickness

Long-term sickness may make dismissal fair if it places an unreasonable burden on the employer. The employer must prove that they made proper enquiries, including (where appropriate) with the employee's medical adviser. The employer must show that used all practicable means to avoid dismissal such as offering reduced hours or different duties to accommodate the employee's needs or the employee may have the right to claim discrimination on grounds of disability.

Misconduct

Misconduct covers a multitude of obvious evils, including lying, fighting, theft, and dangerous and careless behaviour, but a wider range of behaviour may constitute grounds for fair dismissal. Employees who are guilty of rudeness to superiors, drinking on duty, or who refuse to cooperate with management instructions may also be fairly dismissed. The crucial factor is that the misconduct must be incidental to the job that the employee was employed to do.

Thomson v Alloa Motor Co. (1983)

A petrol pump attendant was dismissed after she managed to demolish one of the pumps by carelessly driving her car into it.

Held: this was held to be unfair dismissal as her dubious driving skill was not relevant to how she did her job.

In *Community Integrated Care Ltd* v *De Smith* (2008), the EAT held that Ms De Smith's dismissal for swearing at a resident of the care home where she worked was fair. Such behaviour was defined as gross misconduct under the employee rules at the home, which gave fair warning of the consequences of breach.

Conduct which occurs in the employee's spare time may be incidental to employment if it reflects adversely on the employee's suitability for the job or reasonably reduces the employer's confidence in the employee.

Moore v C & A Modes (1981)

Ms Moore worked as shop assistant for C & A. She was caught shoplifting in another shop.

Held: this was fair dismissal. Her conduct clearly reflected adversely on her integrity and made it reasonable for the employer to suspect that she might help herself to the firm's property.

It is generally a mistake to sleep with your employer's spouse.

Whitlow v *Alkanet Construction* (1987)

Whitlow was asked by a senior executive to do some work at his house, where he departed from management instructions by starting an affair with the executive's wife.

Held: he was fairly dismissed since he was in breach of his duty of good faith.

Dismissal for misconduct was held to be fair in all the following cases: *Atkin* v *Enfield Hospital Management Committee* (1975): failure to wear appropriate clothing; *Boychuk* v *Symons Holdings* (1977): wearing provocative badges in breach of instructions and several warnings; *Newman* v *Alarm Co. Ltd* (1976): conducting a sexual relationship in the company's time; *Parsons* v *McLoughlin* (1981): fighting; *Minter* v *Wellingborough Foundries* (1981): refusing to attend a training course.

Modern technology and social media provide new opportunities for misbehaviour. Posts which are likely to be damaging to the employer's business by bringing it into disrepute may well justify dismissal. Facebook was the first to feature in litigation after an employee published scurrilous comments about a fellow worker.

Teggart v *Teletech UK Ltd* (2012)

Mr T stated on his Facebook page that a fellow female colleague had slept with most of the other Teletech staff. When she objected and tried to get the comment removed, he posted a comment suggesting that she indulged in bestiality. Teletech sacked him for gross misconduct in that he had brought the company into disrepute and harassed a fellow employee.

Held: he had been fairly dismissed for harassing a colleague. However, there was no evidence to suggest that the postings had brought the company into disrepute.

The Employment Appeals Tribunal held that abusive tweets were potentially grounds for dismissal in *Games Retail Limited* v *Laws* (2014).

Breaching the workplace smoking policy may also be sufficient to justify dismissal.

In the news

Using E-cigarettes at work may get you the sack

Use of E-cigarettes at work may be grounds for dismissal an employment tribunal has held in *Insley* v *Accent Catering* (2014).

Ms Insley, who worked as a catering assistant at a school, was threatened with disciplinary proceedings to decide if her use of an E-cigarette in the playground in view of the pupils was sufficient grounds for dismissal.

18

Rights at work: protection against dismissal and redundancy

She resigned before the hearing and claimed constructive dismissal. The tribunal held that she had not been constructively dismissed as the employer was reasonable in seeking to conduct a hearing. However, if she had been dismissed that would have been unfair since the employer's non-smoking policy did not specifically cover E-cigarettes.

ACAS provides some useful guidance to employers on the best way to draft policies in relation to both smoking and the use of social media

Worth thinking about?

What behaviour in relation to the use of social media do you think would be likely to justify dismissal?

Suggested solutions can be found in Appendix 2.

Facebook and YouTube are admissible as evidence of misconduct.

Gill v SAS Ground Services UK Ltd (2009, ET)

Mrs Gill was on sick leave after minor surgery and took the opportunity to attend London Fashion Week. She posted on Facebook that she had been 'auditioning 300 models' and had choreographed a fashion show, while footage on YouTube showed her on the catwalk, presenting a bouquet to the event organiser.

Held: she had been fairly dismissed as her presence at the event had been much more than purely social.

Redundancy

This topic is dealt with in depth later in this chapter.

Statutory restriction

This is where the employer claims that the employee can no longer be legally employed, or can no longer legally perform the job. Disqualification from driving is an obvious example, provided that driving is central to the job description. Dismissal is not automatically fair in such circumstances. The nature of the job, the length of disqualification, the type of criminal offence from which it arose and the possibility of redeployment must all be considered.

Mathieson v Noble (1972)

A travelling salesman who lost his driving licence arranged to pay for a driver out of his own pocket, but his employer dismissed him.

Held: he should not have been dismissed unless or until it was evident that this arrangement was unworkable.

Retirement

There is no longer a specific retirement age. An employer may be able to show that imposing one is justifiable in particular circumstances under equality legislation (see Chapter 17).

Some other substantial reason

A variety of circumstances which do not fit into any of the above categories may make dismissal reasonable. In *Gorfin* v *Distressed Gentlefolks' Aid Association* (1973) it was held that dismissal of an employee to resolve a personality clash may be reasonable to restore harmony to the workplace, when all other reasonable steps to resolve the situation have failed.

Farr v *Hoveringham Gravels Ltd* (1972)

A term in Farr's contract required him to live within reasonable travelling distance of his workplace, as he was sometimes needed to cope with emergencies outside working hours.

Held: it was fair for his employer to dismiss him after he had moved house to an address 44 miles away.

- *Long-term sickness* may amount to a 'substantial' reason to justify dismissal, though the employer must show that it has made all reasonable efforts to accommodate the employee. (See also disability discrimination, Chapter 17.)
- *Economic reasons* may also be treated as 'substantial', provided that the employer can show that these are based on good business practice. Employment tribunals seem readily convinced by such arguments. Employees who leave in protest at attempts to impose detrimental changes to their contracts may well fail in a claim that they have been constructively and unfairly dismissed. If, for instance, the employer can show that the new terms will result in cost saving, necessary to the continuance of the business and maintenance of most of the existing workforce, these are likely to be treated as substantial reasons.

St John of God (Care Services) Ltd v *Brooks* (1992, EAT)

A hospital, after large cuts in government funding, offered its staff new contracts which reduced pay and overtime and removed paid holiday entitlement.

Held: the employer had proved substantial reasons for its decision, which must be examined with reference to all the relevant circumstances and not just to its impact on the employees.

Fairness of dismissal

It is not enough for the employer to prove that there were adequate grounds for dismissal. The appropriate procedures must also be followed.

Polkey v *A.E. Dayton Services Ltd* (1987, HL)

An employee claimed unfair dismissal on the grounds of redundancy because the employer had failed to carry out the required consultation procedure. The employer argued that this was irrelevant, as redundancy was inevitable regardless of consultation.

Held: the dismissal was unfair purely because the proper procedure had not been carried out, though where the procedure would have made no difference the amount of damages may be reduced.

Section 98(4) states that fairness is judged by deciding whether in all the circumstances of the case the employer acted reasonably. This 'shall be determined according to equity and the merits of the case'. It is not enough for the employer to prove that the employee received contractual notice and that one of the relevant criteria is satisfied. Good industrial practice demands that dismissal (except for gross misconduct, justifying summary dismissal) must not come out of the blue.

To justify the dismissal, the employer must prove that he or she dealt with the problem in a reasonable way in the particular circumstances. If the employee was dismissed after disciplinary proceedings, the employment tribunal should take into account whether the employer has complied with the ACAS Code of Practice on Disciplinary Practice and Procedures in Employment. This requires appropriate grievance procedures which may help to prevent situations escalating to the point where disciplinary proceeding may result.

Requirements of the grievance procedure

The grievance procedure requires that the employer must:

- notify the employer of the nature of the grievance;
- hold a meeting with the employee within a reasonable time;
- allow the employee to be accompanied to the meeting by a representative (e.g. union representative or lawyer);
- decide what action is appropriate;
- allow the employee to take the matter further if resolution cannot be achieved.

Unreasonable failure by the employer to comply with the Code gives the tribunal the discretion to increase damages in a successful case by up to 25 per cent.

Disciplinary proceedings

The Code requires these to be timely and fairly constituted to prevent bias. The employee must be permitted to bring a colleague or trades union representative.

Dismissal should be the last resort and the employee must be given every opportunity to change. Spoken or written warnings should be given. Where appropriate the employer should provide training, support and supervision. In some cases the employer should explore the possibility of redeployment.

Appeals

The Code requires appropriate appeal procedures. After any dismissal the employee is automatically entitled to an appeal hearing in person. Appeals in writing are not sufficient. Failure to follow these procedures entitles the employee to claim unfair dismissal and, if this claim is successful, his or her damages may be increased by up to 25 per cent.

Dismissal is automatically unfair in certain specified circumstances

The following employees are entitled to take their cases to the tribunal without having to satisfy the continuous employment requirement:

- ERA 1996, s 99 (as amended by the Employment Relations Act 1999): women dismissed in connection with the exercise of maternity rights. This right covers *any person* exercising rights to parental leave to take time off for domestic incidents;
- ERA 1996, s 100: health and safety representatives;
- ERA 1996, ss 102 and 105: trustees of occupational pension schemes;
- ERA 1996, s 103: employees representing the workforce in redundancy consultations;
- ERA 1996, ss 103A and 105A (as amended by the Public Interest Disclosure Act 1998 and the ERRA 2013) protects employees dismissed for 'whistle blowing' provided the disclosure was made in the public interest to the appropriate person,
- ERA 1996, s 104: employees who have taken legal action against their employer to enforce statutory rights;
- ERA 1996, s 105: employees who have been made redundant;
- ERA 1996 s 108(4) as amended by E&RRA: political opinion or affiliation;
- Trade Union and Labour Relations (Consolidation) Act 1992 (TULR(C)A 1992), s 152: trade union membership or activity. This protection is extended by s 14 of and Schedule 5 to the Employment Relations Act 1999 (adding s 238A to TULR(C)A 1992) to include protection for employees participating in official industrial action;
- Employment Relations Act 1999, s 12: employees accompanying workers to a disciplinary hearing.

Real life

Horace, trade union representative for his section at Smallville Borough Council, receives an email from Clarence, a housing officer who is currently on leave. Clarence explains that he is about to resign as he has been unhappy at work ever since Arnold became his line manager. He says Arnold has been endlessly and unjustifiably critical of his work, made him alter his leave plans to attend a tenants' conference, has been unsupportive when Clarence sought his help in dealing with difficult and abusive tenants and reprimanded him for incompetence in front of a queue of people at the enquiry desk.

This all suggests that Clarence may have a good case for constructive dismissal if he does leave. He would be able to cite these incidents as evidence that Smallville is in breach of its duty of trust and confidence to him. Horace should suggest that he attempts to resolve the matter through Smallville's grievance procedure. However, if he does choose to resign he must make sure that he repeats all the information that he gave Horace in his letter of resignation to indicate his grievance. Otherwise, he would be in danger of having his case struck out.

Redundancy

A redundant employee may have the right to make one or both of the following claims:

Redundancy: an employee's job ceases to exist because the employer restructures/ changes business practices/ceases to carry on business/or closes location where employee works.

1 *Redundancy payment.* While it is legitimate to reduce the size of a workforce, thus rendering some employees surplus to requirements, those employees may have statutory entitlement to compensation for losing their jobs (a **redundancy payment**).

2 *Unfair dismissal.* Employees who can prove that the method by which they were selected for redundancy did not meet the standards of good industrial practice, may additionally have a claim for unfair dismissal which might result in a compensatory award or an order for their reinstatement.

Redundancy payment

Eligibility

In order to be able to claim compensation the claimant must be able to prove the following:

1 Two year's continuous service with the relevant employer.

2 *Relevant employee status.* Certain categories of employees excluded from claiming unfair dismissal are also excluded from statutory redundancy protection.

3 *Dismissal.* To be able to claim, employees must be able to prove that they have been actively or constructively dismissed within the meaning of ERA 1996, s 136. Dismissal includes the expiration of a short-term contract where renewal is not offered. An employee is also dismissed if the employer dies, or if the employer is a partnership or company which is dissolved or wound up. An employee who leaves voluntarily, having been warned of the threat of redundancy, is not dismissed.

4 *Redundancy has caused the dismissal.* Under ERA 1996, s 139 redundancy may occur where:

   (a) the employer ceases to carry on business or ceases to carry on business at the location where the employee worked; or

   (b) the employer restructures the business or changes production methods so that fewer employees are needed.

(An employee may also be redundant if dismissed by the employer who intends to take any of the above actions.)

Change of workplace location

Where the employee's contract contains a term that the employee may be required to work at any place of business the employer directs, the employee is not made redundant by being moved. If no term exists, it is a question of fact whether or not redundancy has occurred. Distance is often a material fact in deciding this. Where compliance with the employer's order would force the employee to move house or undertake a much longer journey to work than before, the employee will be able to claim to have been constructively dismissed in circumstances which make the employee redundant. Compare the following two cases.

O'Brien v *Associated Fire Alarms* (1969)

Reduction in the amount of business available in Liverpool resulted in the employer offering O'Brien a transfer to its Barrow-in-Furness branch. When he turned the offer down he was dismissed.

Held: he had been made redundant. Taking it up would have increased his journey to work very considerably.

Managers (Holborn) Ltd v *Hohne* (1977)

Held: an employee dismissed when he refused a transfer from an office in Holborn to one in Regent Street (a short tube ride) had not been made redundant.

Offers of suitable alternative employment

Employees offered suitable redeployment cannot, if dismissed, claim that they have been made redundant (ERA 1996, s 138(1)). What is 'suitable' is a question of fact to be determined by the tribunal in each case. Factors like travelling distances, domestic problems and lack of appropriate educational facilities for the employee's children may it was all have to be taken into account. In *Devon Primary Care Trust* v *Readman* (2013, CA) held that when deciding if a refusal is reasonable the court must apply a two-pronged test. First, the court must determine whether judged objectively the employer's offer was reasonable. Secondly, a subjective test is used to decide whether the employee's refusal is unreasonable given their particular circumstances.

While an employer must show reasonable sensitivity and regard for the individual employee, there are limits. In *Fuller* v *Stephanie Bowman Ltd* (1977) a secretary working at her employer's Mayfair branch was held to have acted unreasonably when she refused to transfer to a Soho office because it was situated over a sex shop.

Under ERA 1996, s 138(2) an employee who takes up an alternative post has at least four weeks to decide if it is workable. If the employee gives up within the time limit, any rights to redundancy pay are not prejudiced.

Time limitation on redundancy claims

Employees must start their claims within six months of the date when a short-term contract expired or when their notice period expired. Late claims may be admitted by the tribunal if this is judged to be just and equitable.

Financial entitlement

This is calculated with reference to the age of the employee and the length of service up to a maximum of 20 years:

- 18–21: half a week's pay per year of service;
- 22–40: one week's pay per year of service;
- 41–64: one-and-a-half weeks' pay per year of service.

A week's pay is currently subject to an upper limit of £475, but there is, of course, nothing to stop an employer from voluntarily exceeding this. The Secretary of State is empowered to vary this sum (s 227) and under the Employment Relations Act 1999 does so with reference to the Retail Price Index.

Unfair dismissal arising from redundancy

An employee who has been made redundant may have an additional claim for unfair dismissal (s 98). To avoid liability, the employer must show that he or she acted reasonably in selecting the employee for redundancy. Criteria determining selection should include safeguards against bias. The employee must have been given proper warning, adequate consultation must have taken place, and proper consideration must have been given to the provision of alternative employment. (The relevant awards of compensation are described below.)

What is reasonable is judged with reference to the size and resources of the employer's business. A successful claimant is entitled to the same levels of compensation as any other unfairly dismissed employee.

Transfer of undertakings

Transfer of undertakings: a new employer takes over an existing business.

In the event of a new employer taking over an existing business entity (a **transfer of undertaking**) current employees have enjoyed protection of their job security and existing conditions of service since 1981 when, prompted by the Acquired Rights Directive 1977 (ARD), the Transfer of Undertakings (Protection of Employment) Regulations 1981 (TUPE 1981) were introduced. These were replaced by the Transfer of Undertakings (Protection of Employment) Regulations 2006 (TUPE 2006). The rights and obligations of the previous regulations remain in place, but the 2006 regulations clarify and update them to reflect case law developments and increase the rights of employees and the duties of employers. The Collective Redundancies and

Transfer of Undertakings (Protection of Employment) (Amendment) Regulations 2014 in turn amend and update the 2006 Regulations but do not replace them.

The regulations apply to a 'relevant transfer'.

In *Holis Metal Industries* v *GMB* (2007) part of a British-owned curtain making business, was transferred to an Israeli firm which refused to take on any of the current workforce. The EAT refused to strike out the GMB's claim and held that potentially TUPE may apply to transfers to business outside the UK HHJ Ansell said:

> I am persuaded that the wording of both the ARD and Regulation 3 is precise in setting the application of the regulation to transfers of undertakings situated immediate before the transfer in the UK Set against the purpose of protecting the rights of workers in the event of change of employer it seems to me that a purposeful approach requires that those employees should be protected even if the transfer is to be across borders outside the EU.

The meaning of 'relevant transfer'

Relevant transfer includes:

- transfer of a business, undertaking or part of one to another employer as a going concern (e.g. a company takeover or merger); or
- a 'service provision change', e.g. contracting out of services or re-tendering or bringing the work in-house.

The 2014 regulations require the activities carried out by the transferee employer to be 'substantially the same' as before the transfer. This provides clarity and brings the definition in line with case law which has developed in the intervening years.

A business transfer only takes place when the identity of the employer of a discrete group of employees changes. Certain types of transfer are, however, specifically excluded, such as transfer by share takeover, where the employer (the company) remains unchanged despite a change of shareholders.

The meaning of 'undertaking'

This has been interpreted widely by the courts and covers non-commercial operations as well as ordinary businesses, for instance, contracting out of public services by competitive tendering, or charities. No one factor is crucial to this definition and the ECJ has warned against the application of technical rules in this context. It may represent a small part of the transferor's enterprise as long as it remains 'an economic entity which retains its identity'. The bottom line is whether there is evidence that the unit transferred retains a minimum level of independence, enabling it to enjoy a separate existence either on its own, or as a discrete part of a larger undertaking.

Who is protected?

Any employee in the business or the part of the business being transferred who was employed immediately before the transfer took place is protected. Employees who can prove they were dismissed earlier for reasons connected with the transfer can also sue. Employees include not just those with a contract of service but also apprentices and workers supplied by an agency.

The rights of the employees

Both collective and individual rights are created by the regulations.

Information and consultation with employees

Both old and new employers must inform the relevant trade union or elected employee representatives of the transfer, when it will take place and why it is happening. Information as to the legal, economic and social implications of the transfer is also required, including any measures which either employer may need to take in relation to them. Consultation with union or elected representatives is generally required regarding such measures as, for example, a reduction in manpower. However, since 2014 direct consultation is possible in a business with less than 10 employees if they have no union representatives

TUPE 2006 introduced liability for failure to supply the relevant information to employees and enabled the employment tribunal to order compensation to be paid jointly or severally by the old and new employers.

Provision of employee liability information

TUPE 2014 requires the transferor to provide information to the transferee prior to the transfer about the identity and age of the employees who will be transferred as well as details of collective agreements, grievances, and disciplinary proceedings concerning them within no later than 28 days before the transfer date. This has been extended from the 14 days required by the 2006 Regulations to help ensure better exchange of information and promote effective consultation. Failure to provide information enables an employee to claim for compensation of £500 at the employment tribunal if this is considered just and equitable.

Job security

ETO:
an economic, technical or organisational reason to justify changes to workforce/conditions of service after the transfer of an undertaking.

The 2014 Regulations amend the 2006 Regulations to remove the words 'connected with' [the transfer]. Dismissal is now automatically unfair if it arises directly or indirectly from the transfer unless it is 'caused by an economic, technical or organisational reason' (ETO). Circumstances comprising an ETO have been extended by the 2014 Regulations to include an employee being required to work in a different location. However, an employee might still successfully claim that dismissal was unfair under the ERA 1996. Redundancy may be justified as an ETO.

Continuation of existing terms and conditions of employment

The transfer does not terminate the employee's contract of employment: all the existing rights, duties and liabilities of the old employer are generally transferred to the new one. The 2014 Regulations ensure that any variation by a transferee employer of a transferee will now be void if the sole or principal reason is the transfer, as opposed to merely *'connected with'* it as previously applied. The aim is to clarify the regulations and prevent unnecessary litigation.

Changes can only be justified if relevant to an ETO. Failure to comply with this may entitle the employee to claim constructive and unfair dismissal.

Insolvent businesses

TUPE 2006 makes it easier for transfer of a business which has become insolvent. The regulations prevent some of the transferor's pre-existing debts from passing to the transferee and in appropriate circumstances enable a transferee to take on a reduced workforce.

Claiming at the employment tribunal

ACAS conciliation

The E&RRA 2013 requires any employee who intends to take a case to the employment tribunal to inform ACAS of this first. No proceedings can be started until ACAS has issued an early Conciliation Certificate which proves that the parties have been informed about the process. Either party can refuse to proceed with conciliation after this point. If they decide to go through the conciliation process they may allow ACAS to help them achieve a settlement; but even then they are free to reject the proposal and proceed to the tribunal.

Claims are time limited

A claim must generally be started within three months less one day from the date of dismissal. In discrimination cases time runs from the date of the last discriminatory act.

Cost

The E&RRA 2013 gave the Ministry of Justice the power to introduce fees. Fees were introduced at the end of July 2013. A claimant must now pay £250 to start a claim for unfair dismissal or discrimination with a further fee of £950 payable if a hearing takes place. The impact was immediate and considerable. Figures released by the Ministry of Justice in 2014 showed that overall the number of single claims to the Employment Tribunal between October to December 2013 dropped by 67 per cent and by 79 per cent overall.

Judicial review proceedings instigated by the Unison trade union, which argued that the fees are unlawful because they interfere with access to justice, were unsuccessful– but leave to appeal to the Court of Appeal was granted. The case was again dismissed but Unison is seeking permission to appeal to the Supreme Court.

Remedies

1 Reinstatement: ERA 1996, s 113

This may be ordered at the request of the employee if it is a practicable option. If granted, the employee resumes the job under the same pay and conditions as before.

2 Re-engagement

The employer may be ordered to find a reasonably comparable job for the employee. The new job may be with an associated employer (ERA 1996, s 114).

3 Compensation

An employer may be liable to compensate an employee who is unfairly dismissed.

Basic award: damages intended to cover an unfairly dismissed employee's loss of income while they seek new employment.

The **basic award** (ERA 1996, s 119) is intended to protect the employee against the losses caused by a break in continuous employment and is, therefore, calculated in the same way as the statutory redundancy award with reference to the employee's age, current gross weekly pay and years of service:

- an employee aged 18–21 is entitled to half a week's pay per year of service;
- an employee aged 22–40 is entitled to one week's pay per year of service;
- an employee aged 41–64 is entitled to one-and-a-half weeks' pay per year of service.

Under ERA 1996, s 120A the basic award may be increased to four weeks' pay if the employer failed to observe the statutory dismissal procedures and the employee would otherwise receive less than four weeks' pay. The maximum for a week's pay is currently £475 and the maximum basic award is limited to 30 weeks' pay.

The compensatory award is intended to redress losses arising from the dismissal so far as these may be seen as the fault of the employer (ERA 1996, s 123). The Secretary of State may vary the minimum of the basic award and the upper limit of the compensatory award with reference to the Retail Price Index (Employment Relations Act 1999, s 29). The conduct of the employee is relevant to the size of the compensatory award. It may be reduced if the behaviour of the employee contributed to the dismissal, or failed to take reasonable steps to mitigate his or her loss. It is unlimited in discrimination cases.

Compensatory award: damages intended to compensate an unfairly dismissed employee for losses arising from the dismissal which are the fault of the employer.

The E&RRA 2013 gave the power to impose a one year cap on the compensatory award of £78,335 or 52 weeks' pay if this is lower. This power was exercised by the Secretary of State under the Unfair Dismissal (Variation of the Limit of Compensatory Award) Order 2013.

The **additional award** may be payable (ERA 1996, s 117, as amended by the Employment Relations Act 1999) where an employer fails to comply with an order to re-engage or reinstate an employee. It consists of 26–52 weeks' pay at the current rate.

Recommendations

The employer may be ordered to take practical steps to correct the situation vis-à-vis the claimant although there are no enforcement powers. In discrimination cases this originally extended to making recommendations for the benefit of the wider work-force, but the Deregulation Act 2015 abolished this power.

Penalties for non-payment of damages

Under the Small Business, Enterprise and Employment Act 2015, s 150 an employer may be fined for failing to comply with a tribunal judgment. If they fail to pay within 28 days of receiving an enforcement notice they may be fined up to 50 per cent of the total sum of damages.

18

Rights at work: protection against dismissal and redundancy

Chapter summary

Wrongful dismissal: court/employment tribunal action.

Unfair dismissal: ERA 1996 employment tribunal action.

Employee must prove:

(a) dismissal (actual/constructive/deemed);

(b) 24 months' continuous employment;

(c) use of grievance procedure.

Employer must prove: dismissal fair (grounds and procedures).

Redundancy ERA 1996

Payment: employee entitled if:

(a) 24 months' continuous employment;

(b) relevant status;

(c) dismissed because of actual/imminent redundancy.

Unfair dismissal on account of redundancy

If employer cannot prove fair procedures (selection/consultation/suitable alternative work offer).

Transfer of Undertakings (TUPE 2006)

Current employment contract terms of the relevant body of workers continue to apply after takeover/merger/sale of business/part of business subject to ETO.

Any redundancy connected with the transfer is unfair subject to ETO.

Consultation with/information for employees is required prior to transfer.

Some adjustment of liability for employer taking on an insolvent business.

Remedies

(a) reinstatement;

(b) damages: basic/compensatory/additional award;

(c) recommendations.

Quiz 17

1 Distinguish between wrongful and unfair dismissal.

2 On what grounds may Tiger Enterprises claim that they fairly dismissed the following employees?

   (a) Zebra, who was given a job as a trainee lorry driver three years ago and has just failed the HGV test for the sixth time.

   (b) Camel, who sexually harassed Ms Wart-Hog at the works' Christmas party.

   (c) Possum, a van driver who has crashed his vehicle three times.

   (d) Rhino, who was recently convicted of being drunk and disorderly one Saturday night.

3 Have the following employees been made redundant by Lynx plc?

   (a) Aardvark, who heard rumours of redundancy and resigned.

   (b) Porcupine, a senior computer programmer, whose current workplace is being closed down. He is told that he is being transferred to another branch 80 miles away.

4 What procedures should be observed by an employer before making employees redundant?

Answers to all quizzes can be found in Appendix 2.

Take a closer look

The following cases provide important examples of how the law you have studied in this chapter has developed. They are primary sources illustrating the law in action and give you more detail about their facts, as well as helping you to understand the law and to appreciate how the judges reached their decisions.

Try looking them up in the law reports or accessing them via a database, e.g. Bailli (www.bailii.org/databases.html). LexisNexis or Westlaw may be available in your university or college library, or you may find extracts in a case book. (See Appendix 1: Additional resources.)

Farr v *Hoveringham Gravels Ltd* [1972] IRLR 104

Gorfin v *Distressed Gentlefolks' Aid Association* [1973] IRLR 290

St John of God (Care Services) Ltd v *Brooks* [1992] ICR 715, EAT

Shergold v *Fieldway Medical Centre* [2006] ICR 304, EAT

Web activity

Please go to: www.acas.org.uk/index.aspx?articleid=1364 for more information about handling workplace disputes and discipline.

Assignment 16

Explain the proposition that an employee may be unfairly dismissed even though the employer had reasonable grounds for his or her dismissal.

18

Rights at work: protection against dismissal and redundancy

PART 5

Introduction to company law

CHAPTER 19

Business organisation

Introduction

Anybody setting up a business has choices about its initial structure. The majority of businesses start as a sole trader operation, with the owner reaping all the profits but entirely responsible for everything from raising capital to business liability. The partnership is a good option when two or more people want to set up a business together. Partners share the profits but like the sole trader remain personally liable for all the debts of the business. Both sole traders and partners have restricted opportunities for obtaining capital and often the only way to get a loan with the family home as security, so the financial risk may be substantial. Business owners may be able to reduce that risk by limiting their liability. The best way to do this is to set up a registered limited liability company. This makes the business corporate, an independent being from its members who stand to lose no more than their initial investment if the company fails. This makes it a much more tempting investment prospect than a partnership or sole trader business. In this chapter we will more closely examine how these different types of business may be created. First, though, it is necessary to gain understanding of three concepts which are recurring themes in the law relating to business organisation – legal personality, incorporation and limited liability.

Learning objectives

When you have studied this chapter you should be able to:

▶ define the different forms of business organisation described in this chapter;

▶ understand the concept of legal personality;

▶ distinguish between public and private companies;

▶ explain what is meant by limited liability and how it is created.

Legal personality, incorporation and limited liability

Legal personality

Legal personality: the bundle of rights and duties attaching to a human or legal/ artificial person/ corporation.

Under English law all human beings are endowed with a **legal personality** from birth until death. A person's legal personality is made up of that person's legal rights and duties. These are subject to change throughout the lifetime of the subject. A child has only very limited rights and few duties. The average adult has a complex bundle of rights and duties determined by the adult's current status: for example, as a married or single person, employer, employee, taxpayer, receiver of welfare benefit, debtor or creditor.

Incorporation

It is not just human beings who have legal rights and duties: the law permits the creation of artificial or legal persons (corporations) that have a legal personality, separate from the members.

Corporation: an office or organisation with its own legal personality distinct from holder/ members.

A **corporation** is brought into being (incorporated) by operation of law. Some form of legal process must be completed before it comes into existence. This chapter is primarily concerned with corporations created exclusively for commercial purposes by registration in compliance with the Companies Acts. However, corporations may be created by other means and for different reasons. The Crown may create corporations by royal charter for a variety of different purposes, like education (the universities) or management of a profession (the Chartered Institute of Surveyors) or public service broadcasting (the BBC). Parliament may grant corporate status to an organisation by passing a special Act; the nationalised industries were all created in this way.

All types of corporation have certain characteristics in common:

1 *Creation by operation of law.* The necessary legal process (charter, Act or registration) must take place to bring the corporation into existence. Once created, the corporation will continue to exist unless or until the appropriate legal procedure takes place. A registered company may be wound up, a chartered corporation may have its charter withdrawn, repeal of the relevant statute ends the life of a statutory corporation.

2 *One or many members.* Incorporation may create an office held by one person (a **corporation sole**), like a bishop or the Public Guardian, but most corporate bodies have at least two members (a corporation aggregate).

> **Corporation sole:** one-member corporation.

3 *Its own legal personality.* The corporation's rights and duties are conferred by the charter or law under which it was created. The company's legal personality is distinct from that of the company's members. A change in membership does not affect the existence of the company. Even if all the members of a corporation were to die simultaneously, the company would continue to exist.

4 While company officers and employees may cause breaches of its contracts, or commit tort sor crimes in the execution of its policies, it is the company which is legally liable for the wrongdoing. For example, a registered company which pollutes a river may be prosecuted and fined. Payment of the fine will come from the company's bank account, not the pocket of the managing director whose order caused the pollution.

Limited liability

> **Limited liability:** limitation of financial responsibility for registered company's liabilities enjoyed by company members.

Most registered companies limit their liability by shares but it is also possible to limit it by guarantee. The members of such a company have **limited liability** which means that, while they do not enjoy complete immunity, their liability is generally limited to the sum which they have agreed to invest, even if the company runs out of money and cannot satisfy its creditors. A minority of companies have unlimited liability and their members will be responsible for any debts which the company cannot cover.

The sole trader

> **Sole trader:** one-man/ woman business.

Any person may set up in business and trade under his or her own name or a business name. Such a **sole trader** has independent control of the business and all the profits are his or hers. He or she also has total responsibility for the legal liabilities and financial risks of the business. The sole trader provides all the start-up capital; often this will involve a bank loan secured by a mortgage on the sole trader's home. Since he or she is personally liable for all business debts, the sole trader may be bankrupted by the creditors of the business.

The partnership

Unincorporated association: organisation with no legal personality of its own.

This is like an **unincorporated association**, which simply means that it is an organisation without any legal personality distinct from its members. There are many different kinds of unincorporated associations which exist for social, educational, political and business purposes. You may belong to one: they include sports clubs, pressure groups, local chambers of commerce, trade unions and political parties, not to speak of the Scouts, Guides and Brownies. What distinguishes a partnership from these organisations is the motivation of the partners: they have joined together intending to carry on a business with a view to making and sharing profits.

Partnership: two or more people working together with a view to sharing profit.

The **partnership** is traditionally the favoured method of business organisation for many professionals like doctors, solicitors and accountants. They can share facilities which a sole practitioner would be unable to afford. It is also very common for small businesses to operate from this base, as it enables start-up capital and expertise to be drawn from a number of people. Partners, like sole traders, often raise their contributions through a bank loan and are also personally liable for business debts.

There are three types of partnership:

1 The traditional partnership.
2 Limited partnership.
3 Limited liability partnerships.

1 The traditional partnership

The Partnership Act 1890 governs the creation and regulation of partnerships.

Forming the partnership

It is usual to formalise the existence of the partnership by written agreement, which is sometimes described as the partnership deed. Writing is not essential, though. The partnership relationship may be implied from the conduct of two or more persons carrying on a business in common (as joint proprietors) with the intention of making and sharing the profits arising from their enterprise. The partnership relationship, with all its ensuing rights and duties, exists from the time when the business is up and running. Planning to run a business does not in itself create the partnership.

For clarity and for evidential purposes it is wise to have a written partnership agreement, which indicates the nature and purpose of the business, its name and address, the amount of capital invested by each partner, and how profits are to be shared and paid. If there are *sleeping partners*, whose only involvement is providing capital and taking a share of the profits, the agreement should specify which partners are actually responsible for the management.

The partnership agreement, whether written or unwritten, is a contract governed by the rules which you have studied earlier in this book. Consequently, in *Valencia* v *Lupar* (2012), the Court of Appeal held that no partnership existed between the parties as the solicitor's letters made it clear that the parties' relationship was not intended to be a partnership until a formal partnership deed was executed. There was no evidence to suggest that the parties had moved from a subject to contract position to a legally binding partnership.

Naming the partnership

The partnership may trade under the names of the partners (Glossit, Over and Dodge (Estate Agents), Bloggs Bros, Smith & Daughters), or under a business name (Speedy Cleaners). Choice of name must conform to the requirements of the Companies Act 2006 (see Chapter 20).

Numbers of partners

There must be at least two partners. Until 2001, the Companies Act 1985 imposed a maximum of 20 on commercial partnerships. It was believed that a business of such size should more appropriately be run as a registered company. However, the Partnership (Unrestricted Size) No. 17 Regulations 2001 have removed this restriction completely. No such limits have ever applied to professional partnerships such as accountants and surveyors, since the rules of their professional organisations do not permit incorporation.

The partnership relationship is a fiduciary one

This means that the partners are placed in a position of trust with each other and have the following duties:

- to make full disclosure to each other of all issues relevant to the business;
- to declare any personal financial benefit received by a partner in carrying out the firm's business;
- not to compete with the firm without the consent of the other partners.

Each partner acts as the agent of the others

When transacting business on behalf of the firm, a partner is treated as its agent. Partners can act only within their legal authority and must carry out their duties with reasonable care and skill. The Partnership Act 1890 states that partners have apparent authority to carry out any transaction relating to the business, therefore, any resulting contract is binding on the other partners whether or not they actually authorised it. Failure to perform the contract could result in an action for breach against any or all of the partners. For example, if a partner ordered headed writing paper for the firm,

19

Business organisation

the other partners will be jointly liable for its cost, even though it had previously been decided by majority at a partners' meeting that new supplies were not needed. Similarly, if a partner committed a tort while carrying out the firm's business, the other partners would be vicariously liable for it. A negligently performed job could give rise to this sort of liability.

The partners are jointly and severally liable for all partnership obligations

As the partnership has no legal existence distinct from its members, all the partners are personally liable for its debts and other legal obligations. If the firm does not have sufficient funds, the partners have to make good the shortfall out of their own pockets.

Legal action can be taken against a partnership in its own name, but the partners remain jointly or severally liable for what is owed. This means that if a judgment debt is not paid, it can be enforced against all or any of the partners. This may result in one partner having to pay the entire debt, though that partner may seek a contribution from the others.

Like a sole trader, a partner may be personally bankrupted if the assets of the business are not sufficient to cover its debts.

Dissolving the partnership

A partnership may come to an end for a number of different reasons.

1 *Lapse of time*. Most partnerships are formed in the belief that they will be continued indefinitely, but a specified lifetime may be stated in the partnership agreement. For example, two people might decide to run catering facilities for the duration of an exhibition or a trade fair.

2 *The sole purpose of the partnership is achieved*. The example in 1 above is also relevant here.

3 *Death or bankruptcy of a partner*. Usually the partnership makes provision for such occurrences, but failure to do so could result in dissolution.

4 *Illegality*. If the purposes of the partnership subsequently become illegal, the partnership contract is frustrated (see Chapter 10). A partnership created for the import of certain goods would be dissolved if the import of those goods was subsequently banned by BIS regulations.

5 *Notice from a partner*. Unless the agreement provides otherwise, the partnership will terminate if one party decides to leave. Usually provision is made for this.

6 *Court order*. A partner may ask the court to order dissolution on the grounds of mental or physical incapacity of a partner, or because of misconduct by a partner prejudicial to the business or which amounts to wilful and persistent breach of the partnership agreement. The court may also dissolve the partnership if it is just and equitable to do so. Dissolution will be ordered if the business cannot be carried on without making a loss.

2 The limited partnership

Limited partnership: a partnership with limited liability.

The Limited Partnerships Act 1907 enabled the creation of a **limited partnership**. This comprises a number of sleeping partners who must take no active part in running the business and whose liability is restricted to the amount of capital each invested. The partners running the business have unlimited liability for partnership debts. In practice, such partnerships are relatively rare, as anyone seeking limited liability was more likely to seek registration of their business as a company, though it is recognised as a useful tool for private equity and other investment funds. The Department for Business, Innovation and Skills (BIS) wished to encourage its use and brought in some minor reforms to improve regulation.

The Legislative Reform (Limited Partnerships) Order 2009 resulted in two main amendments to the 1907 Act:

- All limited partnerships must put 'Limited Partnership' or 'LP' after their names.
- The Registrar of Companies must issue a registration of partnership certificate as evidence of the date on which the limited partnership legally came into being.

Corporate status does not result from this process.

3 The limited liability partnership

Limited liability partnership: registered partnership with corporate status whose members' liability is limited to the amount of their investment. They are governed by company and partnership law.

Limited liability partnerships are governed by the Limited Liability Partnerships Act 2000 and are partnership/company hybrids. They are corporate bodies and are thus much closer to registered companies than to partnerships. Note that they are quite different from limited partnerships.

A limited liability partnership (LLP) must be registered with the approval of the Companies Registrar. An incorporation document is required. Once registered, the LLP takes on a legal identity of its own, with each partner's liability limited to the amount of his or her investment in the firm. It enjoys all the advantages of incorporation and relatively few of the disadvantages. An LLP can hold property and sue and be sued in its own name. The *ultra vires* rule, which may bind companies to their stated objects (see Chapter 20) does not affect the LLP, so that it is free to pursue any business venture with the agreement of a majority of the partners. It is not subject to the same rules as companies concerning its internal governance and may regulate its relationships with its members and make its own management rules. By April 2002, over 200 limited liability partnerships had come into existence.

Despite incorporation, the LLP is still treated as a partnership for the purposes of tax. This is a key advantage and puts partners in a better financial position than if they were company shareholders. However, certain legal responsibilities follow incorporation. The LLP must present its annual audited accounts to the Companies Registrar and the accounts are then available for public scrutiny. Insolvency procedures governing companies also apply to an LLP.

Remember, limited liability partnerships are quite distinct from limited partnerships and are thus untouched by BIS's amendment of limited partnership law.

19

Business organisation

Public scrutiny of partnerships

Unless the partnership is an LLP, its affairs, unlike those of a registered company, are not generally subject to any more public scrutiny than those of an individual trader. However, a limited partnership does require registration. Relevant tax returns must be made and the planning requirements of the local authority concerning business use of the premises must be met. Members of the public have no right to inspect the accounts of the partnership and there is no legal duty to audit them.

If a business name is used, the names of the proprietors must be displayed at the place of business and on any letterheads of business stationery (Companies Act 2006, s 1202, which repealed and replaced s 4 of the Business Names Act 1985). This enables customers and traders to ascertain the identity of the people running the business. A partner (including one in a limited liability partnership) has the same duties and rights as any other employer and employee under the Equality Act 2010 (ss 44–45).

The registered company

This is a corporation created in compliance with the registration procedures in the Companies Act 2006 (CA 2006) and monitored by the Companies Registry.

The purposes of the registration process

This serves:

- to check that, before it starts trading, a business is financially viable, has a reasonable chance of success, and is likely to be reputably managed for legal purposes;
- to provide a public record of all such businesses, which may be inspected by interested parties before trading with or investing in them;
- to guard against fraud;
- to enable continuing supervision of the company by the Companies Registrar.

A registered company is generally required to provide a regular update of the information required on registration.

Types of registered company

Public company: registered company (plc) able to sell its shares to members of the public.

The public company

Under the CA 2006, a **public company** is a company which:

1 is limited by shares;
2 has 'plc' (or its Welsh equivalent) after the company name;

3 has limited liability;

4 is registered at Companies House; and

5 in its certificate of incorporation states that it is a public company.

A public company will only be registered as such if it has at least £50,000 of allotted/issued share capital. It is called a public company because its shares may be transferred freely to members of the public. If the company is *listed* the shares may be traded on the Stock Exchange. This enables capital to be raised easily. An applicant for listing must satisfy the requirements of the Financial Services and Markets Act 2000 and the Listing Rules issued by the United Kingdom Listing Authority. In practice, only large public companies will be eligible. Most of the members of a public company will aim to share in its profits without taking any part in its management.

The private company

The CA 2006 states that any registered company, which is not a public company, is a **private company**. It must have 'limited'/'Ltd' (or the Welsh equivalent) after its name. This is the type of company usually formed by a sole trader or a partnership seeking the advantages (like limited liability) which incorporation may bring. Since the implementation of the Companies (Single Member Private Limited Companies) Regulations 1992, both private and public companies may be formed with only one member and the CA 2006 (s 270(3)) has dispensed with the requirement for a company secretary.

Shareholding in a private company is usually limited to participants in the business (and sometimes their families). Most, if not all, of the shareholders may be engaged in managing the business. Such companies are sometimes described as 'quasi-partnerships'. The transfer of the shares will be controlled by the company rules. If a member leaves, he or she may have to sell back his or her shares to existing members of the company, or obtain the company's permission before selling them to a third party.

A private company may later re-register as a public company if it grows to the point where this is appropriate.

The Companies Act 1989 began the process of deregulation of private companies to remove unnecessary bureaucracy and to lessen the administrative burdens of small businesses. The process of registration did not change, but a private company was enabled to choose by a unanimous vote of its members to opt out of certain obligations, like holding an annual general meeting or appointing auditors. This is clearly a sensible choice for a company incorporating a previous partnership of three or four people. The CA 2006 continues this process of simplification (reference will be made to these changes as relevant in the next three chapters).

Private company: registered company (Ltd) not able to sell shares to the public.

19

Business organisation

Real life

Horace was recently left £20,000 in his great uncle Maurice's will. He is undecided about how to invest it. His friend Cyril, who has just applied to patent a mouse trap which he has invented, would like Horace to join in partnership with him. He paints an optimistic picture of all the resulting profits in which Horace would share in the future.

Horace should be cautious. While Cyril may ultimately be very successful, Horace's money will be tied up and he will not see any return on his investment unless and until sufficient profits come in. Unless it is a limited liability partnership, he has no security if the business fails. He might not only lose his entire investment but, in a worst instance scenario, find he has to pay out more, since he has joint liability for business debts.

If he wants a safer business investment, he would be much better off buying shares in three or four limited liability public companies. Then, at worst, he can lose only what he has invested. If he chooses well, the shares will gain in value and he may even get dividends (bonus payments) in a good year. He will also be free to sell shares at any time he needs some liquidity, or reinvest elsewhere if a particular investment is not doing well.

Holding and subsidiary companies

During the latter half of the twentieth century, it became increasingly common for public companies to operate in groups. One (the holding company) controls the others (subsidiary companies). Such a relationship exists where the holding company has the capability to control the voting majority within the subsidiaries. Under the Companies Act 2006 there is a duty to disclose this relationship to ensure that members of the public are not misled in their dealings with any of the members. The holding company is also obliged to present group accounts as well as its own (s 487).

The consequences of incorporation

Once registered the business is said to be incorporated. This has an effect on the financial and general legal liabilities of the company, its directors, its shareholders and any outsiders who have dealings with the company or are affected by its actions.

The company is a separate entity distinct from its members

Veil of incorporation: protects the company from the liabilities of its members.

Once registration has been successfully completed a new legal person is created: its legal liabilities are entirely separate from those of its members. What the courts have described as a **veil of incorporation** prevents the members from being held responsible for the company's liabilities, however close their connections with it. This is clearly illustrated in the following case.

Salomon v *Salomon & Co. Ltd* (1897, HL)

Mr Salomon had a boot factory. He set up a company and sold the business to it for £39,000. He was paid £9,000 in cash and £20,000 in shares, the remaining six shares being held by members of his family acting as his nominees. Mr Salomon lent the company the remaining £10,000 of the purchase price, and this debt was secured by a charge on the company's property. In due course, the company got into financial difficulties and had to be wound up, leaving unpaid debts. As a secured creditor, Mr Salomon recovered what he was owed in full, but there were insufficient assets left to satisfy the other creditors. They argued that the company was a sham used by Mr Salomon as a front for his own business activities, and that he should have to pay off the creditors personally.

Held: the company had been created properly in accordance with the Companies Act and was a separate entity on whose behalf Mr Salomon acted as agent. It was irrelevant that after incorporation ownership and management stayed in the same hands as they had before. The company had borrowed the money and was legally liable to pay it back to its secured creditor who took preference over the other creditors.

Generally, the *Salomon* v *Salomon* approach has been strictly adhered to, though to a very limited extent the courts have created exceptions to prevent fraud. In *Stone and Rolls* v *Moore Stephens* (2009), the House of Lords held that where a one-person company commits fraud, knowledge of that fraud is automatically imputed to the company. However there was no evidence of fraud in *Salomon* v *Salomon*. Although Mr Salomon may seem to outward appearances to have been sailing rather close to the wind, he did not deceive anybody because his fellow shareholders knew what was going on. The charge on the company's assets was appropriately registered; the creditors could have found out about it before dealing with the company had they chosen to do so. In law they had notice of it.

The court may, however, be prepared to question whether a company owner is personally liable for its debts if it appears that the alleged company is a mere façade for the fraudulent activities of the owner. This is known as 'lifting the veil of incorporation'.

Jones v *Lipman* (1962)

Mr Lipman contracted to sell some land to Mr Jones and then changed his mind. He set up a company and conveyed the land to it to defeat Mr Jones's attempt to get a decree of specific performance.

Held: since Mr Lipman had absolute control and ownership of the company and had set it up specifically to defraud Mr Jones, he was personally liable and must perform the contract. The veil of incorporation did not protect him.

If the company is used as a front to conceal criminal activities the court will hold that piercing the veil is justifiable.

Re K and Others (2005)

Under s 41(1) of the Proceeds of Crime Act 2002, Customs & Excise sought to restrain the assets of two companies as part of an investigation into a smuggling conspiracy involving the defendants. The companies argued that this could not be done, since the defendants did not control them and so it was not justifiable to pierce the corporate veil. Control of the companies was in the hands of the family of the defendants.

Held: although the defendants had no formal connection with the companies, they were clearly being used to assist the defendants' fraudulent activities in evading customs duty. Therefore, it was justifiable to pierce the corporate veil.

Where a director uses their company intentionally to cause loss to a third party the court may be prepared to make them personally liable.

Omnibill (Pty) Ltd v Egpsxxx Ltd and Another (2014)

The defendant was the sole director and shareholder of a company which owned a website that advertised escort services. Photographs which breached the claimant's copyright were displayed on the site.

Held: the defendant was personally liable as well as the company because he had used his position as a company officer and shareholder intentionally to commit a tort on the claimant.

A director may be personally liable for negligent advice given on behalf of the company provided that a 'special relationship' exists under the principle in *Hedley Byrne* v *Heller* (1963). (See Chapter 14 for a full explanation of the *Hedley Byrne* principle.)

Williams and Another v Natural Life Health Foods Ltd and Mistlin (1998, HL)

Natural Life was a very small company consisting of Mr Mistlin, the director, who owned all the shares except his wife's nominal holding. Apart from Mr Mistlin, there were only two company employees. Mr Williams and his partner bought a franchise to run a health food shop from Natural Life. They were given a brochure which described the company and Mr Mistlin's knowledge and expertise in glowing terms. They also received some financial projections of the potential of their franchise. All this information was compiled by Mr Mistlin, but he had no personal dealings at all with Mr Williams, who negotiated the sale with one of Mr Mistlin's employees. The turnover of Mr Williams's shop always fell substantially short of the projected levels and he went out of business within 18 months of opening. Mr Williams claimed that he had been negligently advised by Mr Mistlin.

Held: Mr Mistlin was not personally liable. The veil of incorporation could only be lifted in very exceptional circumstances, particularly where one-person companies were concerned, otherwise their owners would unreasonably be deprived of the protection of incorporation. Negligent advice by a director to an outsider dealing with the company could only give rise to personal liability of the director if the necessary special relationship under *Hedley Byrne* principles existed. This required a voluntary assumption of responsibility by the director and reasonable reliance by the recipient upon it.

Postulate a food expert who over ten years gains experience in advising customers on his own account. Then he incorporates his business as a company and he so advises his customers. Surely, it cannot be right to say that in the new situation his earlier experience on his own account is indicative of an assumption of personal responsibility towards his customers. In the present case there were no personal dealings between Mr Mistlin and the respondents. There were no exchanges or conduct crossing the line which could have conveyed to the respondents that Mr Mistlin was willing to assume personal responsibility to them. Contrary to the submissions of counsel for the respondents, I am also satisfied that there was not even evidence that the respondents believed that Mr Mistlin was undertaking personal responsibility to them. Certainly, there was nothing in the circumstances to show that the respondents could reasonably have looked to Mr Mistlin for indemnification of any loss (*per* Lord Steyn).

A voluntary assumption of responsibility by Mr Mistlin could not be presumed merely because he compiled the relevant literature: in any one-person company the owner was likely to be the individual with most of the skill and knowledge relevant to the running of the company. Mr Mistlin had no personal dealings with Mr Williams and there was no evidence that he or anybody on his behalf conveyed 'directly or indirectly to the prospective franchisee that the director assumed personal responsibility towards the prospective franchisee' (*per* Lord Steyn).

Objective assessment of the evidence indicated no grounds for reasonable belief by Mr Williams that Mr Mistlin was assuming personal responsibility, given the lack of direct dealings or undertakings to this effect.

There are several statutory exceptions to the separate entity rule, mainly relating to tax and insolvency law. For example, under s 213 of the Insolvency Act 1986, if during the liquidation of a company it becomes evident that the directors were trading fraudulently, they may be required personally to contribute to the payment of the company's creditors. (Fraudulent trading in this context includes continuing to trade when the directors are or should be aware that the company is unable to meet its current debts.)

Company members may enjoy limited liability for the company's debts

The company has unlimited liability to its creditors, but the liability of its members may be limited.

Company law does not permit a company's members to be completely free of financial liability, as this would promote irresponsible trading. Members' liability for company debts may, on registration of the company, be limited to the value of the capital which they have agreed to invest. Limitation of liability is seen to be in the public interest since it encourages investment in business enterprise and, therefore, promotes the economy.

Liability may be limited by shares or by guarantee.

1 *By shares.* The majority of companies raise their capital this way. If the company is unable to meet its debts, the maximum amount that any shareholders can be asked to contribute is the amount, if any, which they have still to pay for their shares. Their loss is therefore limited to the value of their shares when they joined the company.

2 *By guarantee.* A minority of companies limit their liability in this way. These companies generally exist for educational or charitable purposes, like private schools or museums. Since they are not formed for the purpose of making a profit, it is not appropriate for them to have a share capital. The liability of such a company's members is limited to the amount which they have agreed to contribute if the company is wound up. The guaranteed sum is usually minimal.

Exceptionally, a company may be registered with *unlimited liability*. Its members agree to subsidise the company to an unlimited extent in the event of liquidation. This liability is owed, therefore, by the members to the company rather than to the company creditors.

The company may be legally liable

Criminal offences

There are certain crimes, like rape and bigamy, which a company cannot by its physical nature commit. Apart from these obvious exceptions, a company may be prosecuted for any crime which is committed in the course of carrying out the company's business. For example, prosecutions are common for using false trade descriptions, and for breach of health and safety regulations and anti-pollution controls.

After the Zeebrugge ferry disaster in 1987, it was established that at common law a company could be charged with manslaughter. The Corporate Manslaughter and Corporate Homicide Act (CMCH) 2007 s 1 creates a new offence of corporate manslaughter and came into force in April 2008. The offences may be committed by an 'organisation' if the way in which its affairs are managed (a) causes a person's death, and (b) amounts to a gross breach of a relevant duty of care owed by the organisation to the deceased. An 'organisation' includes both a corporation and a partnership (s 1(2)). The 'relevant duty of care' covers an employer's duty to employees and contractors, occupiers' liability, and duties arising from sale and supply of goods, construction and maintenance operations, use or keeping of plant or vehicles and any commercial activity of the organisation (s 2). Proceedings are taken against the company but its managers and other employees may be called to give evidence. Prosecution is reserved for the very worst cases of corporate mismanagement leading to death for which senior managers are substantially responsible. The offence is punishable by an unlimited fine.

The first proceedings under the Act were started in 2009 when Cotswold Geochemical Holdings was committed for trial for the unlawful killing of an employee who died while collecting soil samples for the company in a trench on a building site. It took two days for rescue workers to find his body buried in the several tonnes of mud that subsided upon it when the trench collapsed. At trial in February 2011 Cotswold Geo-chemical Holdings was found guilty of corporate manslaughter and fined £385,000.

There were two more convictions for corporate manslaughter in 2012. JMW Farms Ltd (Co. Armagh) was convicted for corporate manslaughter and fined £187,000 plus £13,000 costs in May 2012 after one of their employees died as a result of being hit by a large feed mixing bin that fell from a forklift loader driven by one of the company directors. The bin was balanced on the forks instead of the forks being inserted in the bin 'sleeves'. The forks of the loader were too large and incorrectly spaced to enable the bin to be correctly joined to the loader.

In July 2012 Lion Steel Ltd in Manchester was convicted and fined £480,000 for cor-porate manslaughter after Steven Berry tragically died after sustaining injuries resulting from his fall through a fragile roof panel at the firm's premises in Manchester. Mr Berry was employed as an odd-job man at Lion's works. He fell through the leaky roof which he was mending on his employer's instructions. He had received no training nor been provided with any special equipment.

Four more successful prosecutions followed from 2013–14; two others resulted in a not guilty verdict, though the defendants were fined for breaches of the Health & Safety at Work Act 1974.

In the news

Employer convicted for death of employee trapped in factory oven

In March 2015 Pyranha Mouldings and its director who was responsible for supervising production were convicted of corporate manslaughter after an employee, Mr Caterall, died from acute burns after becoming trapped in one of the ovens used in the manufacture of plastic kayaks. He had been working in the oven when another employee, not realising he was there, switched it on causing the doors to close automatically. His cries for help could not be heard through the noise on the shop floor and the heavy oven insulation. There was evidence of previous near-miss events and employees were fearful of getting trapped.

The director was given a suspended sentence of nine moths and a £25,000 fine.

The company was fined £200,000.

Source: CPS website http://www.cps.gov.uk/news/latest_news/pyranha_mouldings_ltd/

Tort

The company is vicariously liable for the torts of its employees and agents commit-ted in the course of their employment. Where the law imposes a non-delegable duty (for employee safety, for example) on the company, it remains personally liable even though the damage was caused by a third party.

Breaches of contract

Generally, a company is liable on its contracts in the same way as any other person. (This is dealt with in detail in the next chapter.)

Ownership and management

The company is owned by its members and managed by its directors. In a very small company, membership and management may be synonymous, but generally company membership does not give rights to dictate how the company is run on a day-to-day basis; it may not even entitle a member to vote at company meetings, since the rights of holders of some classes of shares may be limited under the internal rules of the company.

Public accountability

Once the company has been registered, certain information about it is open to public scrutiny through the Companies Registry. This information must generally be updated yearly through the *annual return*, though unlimited companies are exempt from this. Other company records may be inspected by the public at the company's registered office. The Department for Business, Innovation and Skills has wide statutory powers to investigate companies where malpractice is suspected. It is legally entitled to obtain a warrant to search premises. A department inspector may require company officials to produce and explain any company document. A report of the investigation is usually made public.

Continuous succession

Once registered a company continues to exist until the legal process of liquidation brings its life to an end. 'Liquidation' means the realisation of the company's capital and other assets. These are distributed to creditors and shareholders according to strict rules of priority. The shareholders often lose much, if not all, of their investment.

There are two kinds of liquidation: compulsory and voluntary.

1 *Compulsory liquidation* by court order under the Insolvency Act 1986. This most commonly occurs where the company is unable to pay its creditors who then petition the court. The Official Receiver is appointed as liquidator.

2 *Voluntary liquidation*. Here the process depends on whether the company is still solvent. If so, the members control the liquidation process. If the company has become insolvent the creditors appoint a liquidator to distribute the company's assets.

The advantages of incorporation as a registered company

Turning a business into a registered company may be a sound move for its proprietors.

Limited liability of investors

Investors in a limited liability company are able to restrict their financial responsibility to the company. They cannot be personally bankrupted to pay business debts.

Worth thinking about?

Why did limited liability develop?

Suggested solutions can be found in Appendix 2.

Transferability of shares

When a member ceases to belong to the company, this does not affect the existence of the business, although it might destroy a partnership. The member's interest in the business can be transferred by sale or other means to a new member. In a listed public company such rights of transfer are unfettered and a sale of shares may take place under the auspices of the Stock Exchange. A private company's rules may impose considerable restrictions in order to protect the close personal relationship of the small number of members all actively engaged in running the business.

Tax

Incorporation and the subsequent separation of the financial interests of the business from the personal financial interests of the members may prove advantageous for tax purposes.

Separate property rights

The assets of a business become its own property on incorporation. This is advantageous in a number of ways. For example, a member who leaves cannot disrupt the business by claiming any particular asset as his or her own; he or she is entitled to recover only his or her financial stake at its current value. Similarly, if the company goes into liquidation members cannot be personally bankrupted when the company's assets are exhausted before all its debts are satisfied. All they will lose is their financial stake in the business.

Raising capital

Unincorporated businesses are very restricted as regards obtaining new capital. The only options are to increase the number of members or obtain a bank loan. Recruitment of new members, while increasing capital, results in business profits being spread more widely and perhaps more thinly. Bank loans involve large interest payments and usually are unobtainable without the security of a mortgage on the members' own homes. A company may be able to borrow money secured by a charge on its own assets. A public company may advertise publicly to attract loans through an issue of debentures (see Chapter 21).

This advantage is likely to be enjoyed only by a company with large enough assets to secure the loan. The members of very small private companies (quasi-partnerships) are usually required personally to secure the debt by mortgages on their homes.

Continuity

Once registered the company's existence continues regardless of any changes in membership. Only winding-up proceedings can bring the company to an end.

Changing the company law map: the Companies Act 2006

This massive piece of legislation (1,300 sections) consolidated most existing company law legislation, in particular the Companies Act 1985. The new Act introduced a number of reforms but also restated, without change, much of the previous legislation by putting it into plainer English. The law has been simplified in some respects in order to benefit small businesses and to reflect the way they operate, for example by abolishing the obligation to hold AGMs. One of the most important changes is the codification of directors' duties and other measures to encourage greater transparency in company dealings. The Act also seeks to encourage more participation by shareholders in running the company. (We shall look more closely at these changes in Chapters 22–3.)

The Act received Royal Assent in November 2006 and has been implemented in stages. Implementation was completed in 2009. All relevant references in this book are to the Companies Act 2006 unless otherwise stated.

The impact of the Human Rights Act 1998 (HRA 1998) on business organisations

Businesses directly bound by duties under the European Convention on Human Rights are those designated under the HRA 1998 as 'public authorities'. However, any business may have rights which can be protected by action under the HRA 1998 against state or other public authority interference. Additionally, the court, as a public authority itself, has a duty not to infringe any Convention rights of any party. This informs how decisions are reached and remedies awarded.

Property rights

A business may be able to protect its property by reference to Protocol 1, Article 1. This states that every human and *legal* person has a right to the peaceful enjoyment of property. This right is not absolute and interference may be justified in the public interest or where necessary to the collection of debts owed to the state. The right is breached if the interference prevents a fair balance being maintained between the rights of the claimant and the public interest. For example, a compulsory purchase order of business premises without adequate compensation would probably be judged to be in breach of the right.

Privacy

As an employer, an organisation may be subject to Convention duties regarding employees, such as Article 8, which protects respect for privacy and family life. A business may need to adjust working practices to accommodate requests by employees for more flexible working hours. Article 8 may also restrict employer access to employees' emails and phone conversations. Article 8 also protects business privacy, since the court must take care that it is not breaching this Article when granting search orders to premises in civil proceedings. The court must consider carefully whether the terms of the order are fairly balanced between the competing interests of the parties and that it is a proportionate response.

Fair trial

A business and its members enjoy the right to a fair trial under Article 6. This includes right of access to the courts and an impartial hearing. However, this right may be waived in civil proceedings where an arbitrator is used and in most cases where the parties settle out of court (see Chapter 4). Article 6 also includes the right to avoid self-incrimination. In *Saunders* v *UK* (1997) the ECtHR held that by subjecting Saunders to coercive questioning (refusal to answer was itself a criminal offence) DTI fraud investigators had breached his rights under Article 6.

Freedom of speech

Advertising, publishing, film, journalism and other media businesses may be protected by Article 10 (freedom of expression). The court, when granting an injunction to prevent publication, must ensure that it is not itself in breach of its Convention duties. Any restriction should be no more than is necessary in a democratic society to protect national security, public safety, health and morals, reputation or rights of others, or against breach of confidence. In *Venables* v *News Group Newspapers* (2001) the High Court issued a gagging order to prevent the press publishing information about the murderers of James Bulger. This was held to be justifiable, to prevent them being identifiable and thus in danger once they left prison. It can be seen from the examples above that, directly and indirectly, business organisations are just as likely to be affected by human rights law as any individual.

Conclusion

By now you should be aware of the different legal consequences of operating a business in the three forms described in this chapter. Before you move on to study in more detail the formation and operation of a registered company, it might be wise to go back and check that you understand the concepts of legal personality, incorporation and limited liability (these underpin much of the content of the next four chapters). To assist you, a comparison of partnerships and registered companies follows.

The differences between a partnership and a registered company

The partnership	The company
Creation	
A written partnership agreement is usual but not essential. The parties' conduct (jointly doing business with a view to profit) will create a partnership.	The company does not exist until the registration procedures of the Companies Act have been complied with.
Numbers	
Minimum: at least two.	A one-person private company is possible.
Maximum: Not prescribed.	No maximum is prescribed.
Legal personality	
The partnership has no separate legal personality of its own: partners are vicariously liable for any breaches of civil law caused by a fellow partner in the course of the business.	Once registered, a company has its own legal personality separate from that of its members. Members cannot be made liable for its illegal activities.
Any partner may be personally liable for crimes relating to the business.	
Limited liability	
Partners have unlimited liability for the debts of the business, unless registered as a limited liability partnership.	The company's liability is unlimited.
Supervision and publicity	Members may have limited liability for company debts.
The running of a partnership is not supervised by any outside authority.	A limited liability company is monitored by the Companies Registrar through its annual return. Particulars and accounts are open to public inspection.
Partnership accounts and other documentation are confidential to the partners unless the partnership is an LLP.	The Department for Business, Innovation and Skills has wide investigative powers.
Termination	
Completion of object, lapse of time, partner leaves, bankruptcy, mental disability or death of partner.	Once created, a company has continual succession. It will not cease to exist unless or until the legal processes involved in winding up are complete.

Chapter summary

Sole trader

Personal liability for business.

Partnership

Fiduciary relationship.

Partners are each other's agents.

Joint and several liability: limited liability possible.

Dissolution: lapse of time, purpose achieved, death/bankruptcy, illegality, resignation, court order.

Registered company

Process of incorporation regulated by the Companies Acts.

Public/private.

Incorporation by registration gives it legal personality distinct from members.

Limited liability (shares/guarantee).

Human Rights Act 1998

Action by company is possible (property rights, privacy, fair trial).

19

Business organisation

Quiz 18

1 How may incorporation take place?

2 In relation to incorporation, what is meant by:

(a) limited liability?

(b) continuous succession?

(c) a corporation aggregate?

3 What is the main difference between a partnership and an incorporated association?

4 Thames, Dover and Wight are members of a partnership called Outdoor Adventures. What is the legal position if:

(a) Thames, without consulting the others, bought two new four-wheel drive vehicles from Humber; and

(b) as a result of Thames's purchase, the partnership now has insufficient sums to pay its creditors?

5 What are the main differences between a public and a private company?

Answers to all quizzes can be found in Appendix 2.

Take a closer look

The following cases provide important examples of how the law you have studied in this chapter has developed. They are primary sources illustrating the law in action and give you more detail about their facts, as well as helping you to understand the law and to appreciate how the judges reached their decisions.

Try looking them up in the law reports or accessing them via a database, e.g. Bailli (www.bailii.org/databases.html). LexisNexis or Westlaw may be available in your university or college library, or you may find extracts in a case book. (See Appendix 1: Additional resources.)

Jones v *Lipman* [1962] 1 WLR 832

Salomon v *Salomon & Co. Ltd* [1897] AC 22, HL

Re K and Others (2005) *The Times*, 15 March

Williams and Another v *Natural Life Health Foods Ltd and Mistlin* [1998] 2 All ER 577

Web activity

Please go to: www.bytestart.co.uk/index.shtml

There is a wealth of information here for small businesses. Check out the guides to setting up as sole trader, partnership and registered company.

Assignment 17

Jackie and Simon run the Good Hair Day hairdressing salon, which is prospering. They would like to expand their premises and staff and hope ultimately to open other salons in different locations. They are debating whether to continue to trade as a partnership or set up a limited company.
Advise Jackie and Simon.

CHAPTER 20

Forming a registered company

Introduction

From your studies of Chapter 19 you already know that if a sole trader or partnership wishes to incorporate its business and seek the advantages of limited liability which this can bring, it will need to comply with a statutory registration process. In this chapter we examine this process which is currently laid down by the Companies Act 2006 (CA 2006). This Act largely consolidates the Companies Act 1985 and other previous relevant legislation. All section numbers cited in this chapter are from the CA 2006 unless otherwise indicated.

Learning objectives

When you have studied this chapter you should be able to:

▶ describe the process by which a company is registered;

▶ define the functions of the memorandum and the articles of association;

▶ explain how a company's objects are determined;

▶ understand the rules governing a company's capacity to contract.

Promoting the company

The **promoters** of the company are the people who actually set it up, who may employ a solicitor, accountant or other professional providing services to assist the process.

The promoters' role varies, but it always involves the formalities of registration. It may also involve finding directors and obtaining premises, plant and equipment. However, these latter functions may not be required of promoters, since large numbers of companies do not start from scratch on being registered. They have their origins in an established small business for which incorporation is the next logical step. The promoters of such a company will usually move from being partners to directors.

Promoters' liability for pre-incorporation contracts

Section 51 of the CA 2006 makes promoters personally liable for all contracts entered into before the company has completed the registration process, even if made in the name of the future company. This is entirely logical since the company does not exist as an independent being until its registration is complete. While it may be essential for the promoters to make contracts on behalf of the business before incorporation, they cannot be treated as the agents of the company since it has no independent existence at this point. Therefore, it cannot legally authorise the making of a contract. Even when it is incorporated it cannot ratify any contracts made before incorporation brought the company into being. Thus, it is fair to give the other party to the contract the right to sue the promoters if the contract is not performed. The promoters may sue or be sued on such contracts regardless of whether the other party knew that the company did not yet exist. In *Phonogram* v *Lane* (1982, CA), the claimant contracted to supply finance to the defendant for the purposes of a company to manage a pop group called 'Cheap Mean and Nasty'. The claimant knew that the company was still at pre-registration stage, but this did not prevent him from suing the defendant for breach of contract.

Section 51 of the CA 2006 allows a promoter to avoid personal liability by express agreement with the other party to the contract. Such agreements fall into two kinds:

1 the contract may stipulate that the liability of the promoter will cease once the company has been registered and has entered into a contract on the same terms;

2 a gentleman's agreement: the promoter may enjoy complete immunity if the other party agrees to enter into a gentleman's agreement from which the intention to form a legally binding relationship is excluded. This means that in reality the pre-incorporation contract does not have the status of a contract at all.

Forming the company

Memorandum of association: statement of intent by promoters to set up a company.

Section 7 states that a company is formed by one or more persons signing a **memorandum of association** and complying with the registration process as prescribed by the Act. Note that it is possible for a company to consist of one member, which helps small businesses to register.

The memorandum of association: s 8

The purpose of the memorandum is to state the intention of the subscribers to form the company and to become members of it. If the company is limited by shares, it must specify that they each hold at least one share.

The CA 2006 makes the memorandum much simpler and shorter than before. It used to contain some information like the objects of the company which may now be found in the articles of association of companies set up since the CA 2006. The memorandum no longer forms part of the company's constitution and has been relegated to being merely a historic document indicating who set the company up. It cannot be amended after registration.

The registration process: ss 9–13

The following documents must be delivered to the Companies Registry with the appropriate fee:

1 the memorandum of association;
2 the application for registration, which includes:

Registered office: the company's official contact point.

   (a) the company's name; choice may not be as simple as it sounds. See below for more detail.

   (b) the company's domicile (England/Wales/Northern Ireland);

   (c) the address of the company's **registered office**; this is the official contact point for the company (s 86). It is here that official notices may be sent, or claim forms served. Information which may be inspected by members of the public is kept here (s 87). This includes the registers of members, directors and debenture holders.

Articles of association: document identifying the company and its officers indicating its purpose and rules for transacting company business.

   (d) the **articles of association**;

   (e) whether the company is limited or unlimited;

   (f) if limited, whether this is by shares/guarantee;

   (g) a share statement (if the company is limited by shares) indicating the amount of share capital, how it is to be divided and initial share holdings;

   (h) the terms of any guarantee;

   (i) names and addresses of the proposed officers (director(s), company secretary);

   (j) a statement of compliance with the registration procedure.

The company's name

The registrar will refuse to register a name if its use would constitute an offence or if it is offensive (s 53). For example, 'Hookers Ltd' has been rejected (*R v Registrar of Companies, ex parte Attorney-General* (1991)). The chosen name must not be the same as or to similar to an existing company (s 66). It also should not mislead the public about the company's purpose. The Company, Limited Liability Partnership and Business (Names and Trading Disclosures) Regulations 2014 have somewhat simplified requirements regarding the issue of similar names to remove for example 'exports', 'holdings', 'international' and 'services' and their Welsh equivalents.

Some names and expressions can be used only with permission from the Department for Business, Innovation and Skills (BIS). These include any which suggest a connection with a government department or local authority. In 2013, as part of its 'Red tape challenge' aimed at removing unnecessary regulation in the business world, BIS suggested that the list of over 160 names and expressions should be reduced to remove for example 'Accredited', 'British', 'Benevolent' and 'University'. After consultation the Company, Limited Liability Partnership and Business (Sensitive Words and Expressions) Regulations 2014 were passed and came into operation in 2015. They include a considerable list of words (and their Welsh and Gaelic equivalents) no longer regarded as inappropriate, but interestingly none of those listed above as examples feature. The list does include 'authority', 'international', 'pregnancy termination', 'registry', 'United Kingdom', and 'watchdog'.

Section 82 enables the Secretary of State to make regulations concerning publicising the company's name and other information. Previous legislation required the company's name to be displayed outside the business premises, and on all business stationery and on the company's seal. This has been extended. Since January 2007 a company is additionally required to list its name, registration number, country of registration and registered office address on its website and emails. The Company, Limited Liability Partnership and Business (Names and Trading Disclosures) Regulations 2014 simplified the display requirements concerning multi-occupancy business premises. Where six or more companies use the same building it is now only necessary for the name of each company to be displayed in a register available for inspection by any visitor to the building. In buildings accommodating less than six companies all the company names must still be displayed at the entrance to the building.

Failure to comply may result in criminal proceedings against the company and a fine. The officer responsible for the company's failure to display may also be personally liable for any transaction not honoured by the company, because the company was not clearly identified as being a party to it (s 83).

Where a company has limited liability this must be made evident by placing 'plc' after the name of a public company (s 58) and 'Ltd' or the Welsh equivalent after the name of a private company (s 59).

To protect use of a company name on the internet, it is wise to register its website's 'domain' with its internet service provider. Registrations are accepted on a 'first come first served' basis. Failure to act quickly could prevent a company from using its company name for internet purposes. Worse still, another company could use the name, and the only possible protection would be an action under the Trade Marks Act 1994 (see Chapter 24) or a passing-off action (see Chapter 25).

The effect of registration: ss 14–16

The registrar will register the company and issue the certificate of incorporation provided that the legal formalities have been complied with and the company is intended to pursue a legal object. This makes the subscribers to the memorandum members of it and the named officers are deemed to be appointed. The company is now legally capable of exercising its functions stated in its constitution.

In the news

Streamlining the registration process

The Small Business, Enterprise and Employment Act (SBEEA) 2015 commits the government to streamlining the process by which companies are formed. Section 15 requires the minister to have a system in place by the end of May 2017 and to give annual reports to Parliament to indicate the progress of this reform (s 16) until completion. This process will enable one person to provide once and in digital form all the necessary registration information to the Registrar, including registration for tax.

The company constitution: the articles of association: s 17

Before the CA 2006, both the memorandum of association and the articles of association contained different aspects of the company's constitution. The memorandum contained matters governing the relationship of the company to the outside world, while the articles were purely concerned with rules governing the internal management of the company.

Under the CA 2006, the constitution is comprised by the articles and any special resolutions and shareholder agreements amending them (s 17). The articles of new companies include the information previously found in the memorandum. This reflects the recommendations of the 2005 White Paper. This called for reforms to make company formation simpler for small businesses and to ensure greater transparency in all company management and affairs. Under s 32, the company has a duty to provide copies of constitutional documentation to any member on request.

Section 19 enables the Secretary of State to prescribe draft model articles by regulation. A company may adopt all or some of these. They automatically apply by default to any company on formation if the promoters do not choose to register especially composed articles. Private companies often adopt draft articles, but public companies usually draft their own.

Under s 28, such provisions of the memoranda of existing companies, formed before implementation of the CA 2006, which are not relevant to the new-style memorandum will be treated as part of the articles of those companies.

Contents of the articles

These cover information relevant to all dealing with the business including the objects of the company.

Rules governing internal conduct of the company's business

These will include, for example:

- the number of directors;
- the method of their appointment;
- powers of directors;
- the procedures for calling and conduct of meetings;
- voting rights of members;
- keeping of accounts;
- the payment of dividends.

The company may, therefore, empower itself within the confines of the law. The Companies Act prohibits some activities (e.g. shares cannot be issued at a discount (s 580)) and permits others subject to compliance with certain procedures such as altering the articles (see below).

Let us now look at some of the contents of the articles in more detail.

The objects clause

Ultra vires: in excess of legal authority. Describes behaviour by a company which is not permitted by its objects clause.

Historically the law required a precise statement of the objects to be pursued by the company, including the powers relevant to the fulfilment of the objects and specifying related transactions which the company might enter into. A contract exceeding the company's objects was totally void because it was *ultra vires* (see contractual capacity of a registered company, below, page 495). In *Ashbury Railway Carriage* v *Riche* (1875, HL) it was held that a company registered to manufacture, sell and hire railway stock was not empowered to build railways.

Promoters consequently often resorted to long, vague and complex objects clauses to avoid restrictions on later business development. As time went on, the courts adopted a more flexible approach, provided that the new enterprise was capable of being linked to the main purposes of the company. In *Bell Houses* v *City Wall Properties Ltd* (1966, CA) the court validated a clause giving a company the power to 'carry on any trade or business whatsoever which can in the opinion of the directors be advantageously carried on in connection with or ancillary to any of the above businesses and the general business of the company'.

The *ultra vires* rule became much less important after entry to the EC. The European Communities Act 1972 largely rendered it ineffective in actions for breach of contract *against* a company. Much greater flexibility was introduced by the Companies Act 1989. This amended the Companies Act 1985, providing (s 3A) that an objects clause might state that 'the object of the company is to carry on business as a general commercial company'.

The CA 2006 relaxes this requirement still further and s 31(1) provides that 'unless a company's articles specifically restrict the objects of the company, its objects are unrestricted'. Under s 31(2) any change to the objects must be reported to the company registrar.

The articles of the company represent contractual terms

Under s 33 the company's constitution (which comprises the current articles of a company) acts as a binding contract between the company and its members. It is as if the company and each of its members had promised to observe its provisions. Any money payable by a member is a debt due from the member to the company.

Failure by one of the parties to carry out its obligations under the constitution is actionable as a breach of contract by the company. The parties are bound by these terms, though the company is in the stronger position since it makes the rules and has the power to initiate their alteration.

Hickman v Romney Marsh Sheep Breeders Association (1915)

The articles of the association stated that in the event of a dispute between a member and the association, the matter must be referred to arbitration. Mr Hickman was expelled from the association and sued it, claiming breach of contract.

Held: he could not take court action until the arbitration process had taken place as required by the terms of his membership contract with the association.

A personal action by one member against another is possible.

Rayfield v Hands (1958)

The articles required the directors who were also shareholders to buy a retiring member's shares at a fair price.

Held: refusal to do so entitled a retiring member to obtain a decree of specific performance against the directors.

Members' capacity to sue on the terms imposed by the constitution is limited to enforcing their rights as members. The fact that a breach of the articles results in damage to them in their personal capacity does not allow them to sue for that breach.

Eley v Positive Life Assurance Co. (1876)

The articles stated that Eley would be the company's solicitor for life. When the company dismissed him, he unsuccessfully attempted to sue for breach of the articles.

Held: the interest which he was attempting to protect was a personal employment right, not one related to his status as a company member.

The articles may, however, provide evidence of terms to be implied in a separate contract giving rise to personal rights. For example, this enables directors to sue for remuneration owed to them under the terms of the articles. They must sue on the contract which appoints them, but its terms may be clarified by reference to the articles if necessary. In *Soden v British Commonwealth Holdings plc* (1997) it was held that the rights and obligations imposed by the Companies Act may also be implied terms within the contract. The court may be prepared to imply a term into a contract to give it business efficacy.

Cream Holdings Ltd v Davenport (2011, CA)

Cream's articles of association stated that on a transfer of shares the transferor was entitled to fair value, as determined by a third party accountant. Cream dismissed Mr Davenport, a director. Mr Davenport retaliated, refusing to agree to the appointment of the accountant chosen by Cream Holdings from the list of three that he had nominated, unless C Ltd disclosed certain documents.

Held (affirming the decision of the High Court): the company's articles represented contractual terms between the company and its shareholders and must be construed in the same way as any other contract in their entire context and having regard to any relevant commercial considerations.

On the grounds that it was better that the contract should function rather than fail, a term would be implied that a shareholder could not unreasonably withhold consent to the appointment of an accountant. D's actions in withholding consent and demanding disclosure were unreasonable as nothing in the articles gave him a right to do so.

Changing the articles of association

The articles may be amended by a special resolution (s 21). This must be put to the vote and requires a majority of at least 75 per cent of the company's members. A copy of the amended articles must be sent to the registrar.

Provisions in the articles may be entrenched. Such provisions are not capable of amendment unless any conditions or procedures specified in the articles are complied with.

Provision for entrenchment can be made in the articles before registration from later amendment passed unanimously by the company's members, or result a court order.

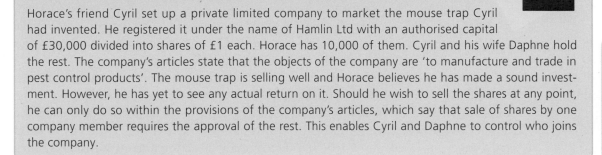

Real life

Horace's friend Cyril set up a private limited company to market the mouse trap Cyril had invented. He registered it under the name of Hamlin Ltd with an authorised capital of £30,000 divided into shares of £1 each. Horace has 10,000 of them. Cyril and his wife Daphne hold the rest. The company's articles state that the objects of the company are 'to manufacture and trade in pest control products'. The mouse trap is selling well and Horace believes he has made a sound investment. However, he has yet to see any actual return on it. Should he wish to sell the shares at any point, he can only do so within the provisions of the company's articles, which say that sale of shares by one company member requires the approval of the rest. This enables Cyril and Daphne to control who joins the company.

The contractual capacity of a registered company

Constructive notice: exists where a party is deemed to be aware of relevant issues even though he or she may not actually have that information.

A company makes many contracts as part of the running of its business and these are enforceable by and against it. Before the UK's entry into the EC, a company might avoid its liability for a contract by hiding behind its objects clause and claiming that the contract exceeded the objects of the company and was therefore *ultra vires* (beyond its powers) and void. The other party could not plead ignorance of the limitations on the company's objects since it was deemed to have **constructive notice** of the memorandum of association because it is a public document which the other party could have inspected.

Re Jon Beauforte (London) Ltd (1953)

The company's objects were stated as dressmaking, but it had abandoned this and taken up manufacturing veneered panels. The company became insolvent, and those who had been supplying it with goods were unable to claim money owed.

Held: the creditors could not claim their money as the contracts with the company were *ultra vires* and they had notice of this. Orders had been placed on writing paper describing Beauforte as veneer panel manufacturers which gave the suppliers *actual* notice that the company had departed from its authorised objects. They had *constructive* knowledge of the true objects since the memorandum of association was open to their inspection.

When the UK entered Europe, reform was necessary for the law to conform to the First Company Law Directive. The European Communities Act 1972, s 9(1) stated that in favour of a person dealing with the company in good faith, any contract decided upon

ors should be deemed to be within the company's capacity. This meant
company was sued for breach of contract it could not use the *ultra vires*
in its defence. Although this was a step in the right direction, it was heavily
. First, it was restricted to contracts initiated by directors which in practice cov-
few made by public companies. Secondly, it did not provide equal protection
company which sued a defendant for breach. That defendant could still plead that
as not bound to perform the contract because it was *ultra vires*.

Consequently, the Companies Act 1985 was amended by the Companies Act 1989,
which stated (s 35) that the company should be treated as having the capacity to make
any contract even if it exceeds its objects clause. The good faith of the other party was
irrelevant. The CA 2006, s 39 effectively re-states this unchanged.

The provisions introduced by the CA 1985 concerning the powers of the directors
to bind the company are also unchanged. CA 2006, s 40 states that the power of the
directors to bind the company or enable other people to do so is not restricted by the
articles of the company. A third party which has dealings with the company in good
faith need not worry about whether the company is acting unconstitutionally. They
have no duty to enquire whether any restriction exists. Their good faith is presumed.
Even if the third party knows that the contract does exceed the objects clause, this
alone is not evidence of bad faith.

The company can sue for breach if the third party fails to perform the contract, as
well as being liable for breach itself if it fails to perform.

The *ultra vires* rule still operates *within* the company

Section 40 does not prevent the operation of the *ultra vires* rule in the relationship of
the company to its members. Where the directors have planned to exceed their authority but have not yet done so, a company member who finds out in time may seek an
injunction to stop them.

The shareholders may ratify (confirm) the *ultra vires* activity by resolution. This
absolves any director who authorised the transaction from liability for breach of duty.
We must contrast this with the situation when shareholders merely affirm the transaction. That has the effect of making the transaction binding on the company but it does
not acquit the director who may be liable to pay compensation for breach of duty.

Although directors have a duty to act in good faith in their company dealings, there
is still a danger that they may, in their personal capacity, enter into potentially fraudulent transactions with the company. To guard against this, s 41(2) provides that if the
purported transaction by the company is made with:

1 a director of the company or its holding company; or
2 any person connected with the director or any company with which the director is
   associated, the transaction is *voidable* by the company.

This gives the company a choice not to go through with the transaction. Whether or
not the company avoids the transaction, the director can be required to account for
any profits arising and must indemnify the company for any damage caused to it.

Re-registering a company

It is possible to change the status of a company by re-registering it in accordance with the requirements of Part 7 of the CA 2006, ss 89–111. This makes it possible to change a private company into a public one and an unlimited company into a limited one and vice versa.

If a private company has done well and business is expanding, 'going public' may be advantageous as it permits the company to sell shares to the public at large, thus making it easier to raise capital. This is the commonest registration change.

The CA 2006 states that a private company (limited or unlimited) may apply to be registered as a public company limited by shares if its members have passed a special resolution to that effect (s 90) and it fulfils the minimum share capital requirements (s 91). Application is made to the registrar (s 94) including relevant accounts information, an auditor's report, a copy of the special resolution and a statement of the new name if relevant. If the registrar is satisfied that all the necessary requirements have been complied with, a certificate of incorporation on re-registration is issued.

Buying a company 'off the shelf'

Instead of going through the registration process, the promoters of a company may buy a ready-made company from a business specialising in providing such a service. The seller registers companies and then renders them dormant, relieving them of a duty to appoint auditors or prepare annual accounts. When the company is sold, the shares are transferred to the buyers, who then register themselves as the new directors and secretary. The name and objects of the company may have to be changed to fit the needs of the buyers' business. Apart from saving the promoters time and effort, buying a company off the shelf is generally cheaper than completing the registration process.

Worth thinking about?

Can you see a downside to making company formation so easy?

Suggested solutions can be found in Appendix 2.

20

Forming a registered company

Chapter summary

Forming the company

Promotion

The practicalities of starting up the business and preparing to register.

Off-the-shelf purchase possible.

Registration

The companies registrar must receive and approve key documentation from the promoters: e.g. memorandum of association which includes Articles of Association, details of officers, registered office, authorised share capital, limitation of liability.

Registrar issues certificate of incorporation legally creating the company.

Re-registration possible later to change company from public to private, unlimited to limited, etc.

The articles of association

The company's identity card and internal rule book.

May be changed by 75 per cent majority vote at a company meeting.

The objects clause

Since CA 2006, objects unlimited except so far as restricted by the articles.

Company contracts

Contracts made in the company's name are binding. *Ultra vires* does not apply outside the company, though shareholders have remedies against the directors to protect company interests/may ratify an *ultra vires* contract.

Quiz 19

1 What documentation must be received by the Companies Registry before a company can be registered?

2 What difference has EC law made to the contractual capacity of a company?

3 Dogger and Portland are the directors of Maritime Pursuits Ltd. They want to change their company to one with public status. What will they have to do?

4 How has the Companies Act 2006 changed the memorandum of association?

5 How may changes be made to a company's articles?

Answers to all quizzes can be found in Appendix 2.

Take a closer look

The following cases provide important examples of how the law you have studied in this chapter has developed. They are primary sources illustrating the law in action and give you more detail about their facts, as well as helping you to understand the law and to appreciate how the judges reached their decisions.

Try looking them up in the law reports or accessing them via a database, e.g. Bailli (www.bailii.org/databases.html). LexisNexis or Westlaw may be available in your university or college library, or you may find extracts in a case book. (See Appendix 1: Additional resources.)

Phonogram v *Lane* [1982] QB 939, CA

R v *Registrar of Companies, ex parte Attorney-General* [1991] 2 QB 197

Rayfield v *Hands* [1960] 1 Ch 333

Soden v *British Commonwealth Holdings plc* [1997] 4 All ER 383

Web activity

Please click on: www.companieshouse.gov.uk/

to explore the resources at Companies House.

Assignment 18

(a) What is the purpose of the objects clause in the company's articles of association and to what extent may the wording restrict the trading activities of a company?

(b) How far does the objects clause affect the ability of a third party to enforce a contract against the company?

CHAPTER 21

Running the company
Raising and maintaining capital

Introduction

In general terms, the company's capital includes all its business assets, including premises, equipment, stock in trade and goodwill. This chapter is concerned with capital in more specialised terms: that which can be raised through getting additional investors or through obtaining loans.

Capital therefore may be raised in two ways:

1 By selling shares (share capital): the buyers become company members. Their investment may be seen as a bit of a gamble, since its value is dependent on how well or badly the company fares. Shareholders risk losing their entire investment if the company fails.

2 By obtaining loans (loan capital) through issuing debentures. Debenture holders do not become members of the company. They will obtain interest on their debenture and provided the loan is secured by charges on the company's property which require registration under the Companies Act 2006, will be sure of recovering their investment if the company fails.

This area of the law is largely unchanged in substance by the Companies Act 2006, which restates the existing principles.

Learning objectives

When you have studied this chapter you should be able to:

▶ distinguish between the different types of share capital;

▶ define ordinary/preference/redeemable/deferred shares;

▶ appreciate how shares may be bought and sold;

▶ understand how a company may obtain loans.

Share capital

Until implementation of the CA 2006, a company limited by shares was required to have an authorised share capital. This specified the capital which could be raised by shares, although it might be increased by an ordinary resolution passed by a simple majority of members. The CA 2006 abolishes this requirement from October 2008. This means that the directors can issue shares without limitation, subject to any permission from members required by the company's articles. Each share must have a specified nominal value (s 542).

There are different categories of share capital:

Issued capital: the number of shares issued.

1 **Issued capital.** This refers to the number of shares issued to members and represents some guarantee of progress for the company's creditors.

Called-up capital: funds from payment for shares when requested after issue.

2 **Called-up capital.** The amount of capital raised by a call on shares. A shareholder, on being allotted shares, may not have to pay for them at once but may be called on to do so at a later date.

Paid-up capital: identical to called-up capital unless a shareholder has failed to pay.

3 **Paid-up capital.** This should be the same as the called-up capital unless a shareholder has failed to pay what is due. The amount of paid-up capital is a good indicator of the company's financial health.

Uncalled capital: the difference between the called-up capital and the face value of the shares.

4 **Uncalled capital.** The difference between the called-up capital and the nominal value of the shares.

Classes of shares

The articles prescribe the rights derived from the shares issued. For example, they might specify that the company may issue shares with whatever rights or restrictions may be determined by the passing of an ordinary resolution. Different classes of shares may give rise to different rights. A shareholder's rights are also to some extent governed by the size of its shareholding: this will govern the amount of dividend payable and the strength of the shareholder's voting power.

There are different classes of shares which a company might choose to issue.

Ordinary shares

A company may choose to issue only **ordinary (equity) shares**. They commonly carry most of the voting rights.

Preference shares

If the company chooses to declare a dividend, the members with **preference shares** are entitled to payment at a fixed rate promised to them when the shares were allotted to them. It will represent a percentage of the value of their shares. How great an advantage they enjoy is dictated by the fortunes of the company. They may be the only shareholders to receive a dividend, or may be paid at a higher rate than the ordinary shareholders. If the company is doing well, the ordinary shareholders may do better than the preference shareholders, since the latter, having received their dividend at the prescribed rate, are not entitled to share with the ordinary shareholders in the distribution of any surplus profits. The articles may entitle them to other benefits: they may take priority over ordinary shareholders with regard to recovery of capital during a winding up.

Redeemable shares

Redeemable shares are issued on a short-term basis. The holder takes them for a specified period of time, after which the company buys them back (redeems them). This can be a useful means of raising capital for a new small business. These shares may have preference or non-preference status. Section 684 permits the issue of any class of shares on a short-term basis.

Deferred/founders' shares

Deferred (founders') shares may be held by the promoters of the company. They carry increased voting rights but rank below **ordinary shares** for payment of dividends and the return of capital.

Treasury shares

Treasury shares are shares purchased by the company from its own stock (see page 528). No dividends can be issued and no voting rights attach to them.

The issue of shares

The first issue of shares can only be made on registration of a public company and is made to subscribers. Subsequent issues may be made provided that there is compliance with any procedures in the company's articles. A public company may make also

Rights issue:
new sale of
shares restricted
to existing
shareholders.

Prospectus:
issued by
company to
encourage
investment
in shares/
debentures.

make a **rights issue**, which is a sort of special offer, restricted initially at a favourable price, to existing shareholders.

Any company which intends to issue shares may issue a **prospectus** to describe the venture. A public company may advertise its shares for sale to the public, but that does not mean that it has an automatic right to sell through the Stock Exchange. The right to sell on the Stock Exchange is governed by rules administered by the Financial Conduct Authority under the Financial Services and Markets Act 2000.

A large public company may have the financial stature required to qualify its securities for admission to the Financial Conduct Authority Official List. The information given by the company in its listing application then becomes public knowledge and the shares may be marketed through the Stock Exchange.

The Companies Act places a number of restrictions on share issue. These exist to prevent the company reducing its capital to the prejudice of its creditors, for whom the company's share capital assets represent some security. The principal restrictions relate to the price of shares and a company's acquisition of its own shares.

Price

Under s 582, the company can generally transfer shares only in return for *money or money's worth*. Shares can be given in return for services rendered to a private company. A public company is prohibited from doing this.

Under s 580, on first issue the shares cannot be sold at *less than their face value* as stated in the memorandum, unless the sale is to underwriters when a discount of up to 10 per cent as commission is permissible (s 553).

Shares can be issued at a *premium*, i.e. at more than their face value. Any money so raised is counted as part of the company's capital, not profits, and it must be treated as such. Funds from the premium issue must be kept in a separate account and may be used for certain purposes only (s 610):

1 paying up unissued shares for issue as bonus shares to members;

2 writing off the expenses of the issue of the shares and any commission paid.

A company's acquisition of its own shares

In the interests of capital maintenance, the *general* rule is that a company cannot acquire its own shares since a likely (and undesirable) result is that Peter is robbed to pay Paul: the shareholder would be paid from the company's assets but, since the shares would be cancelled after purchase, the company's share capital would be reduced.

Under the CA 1985 a company might buy its own shares if its articles authorised this. Section 690 of the CA 2006 has changed this, enabling purchase as long as the articles *do not* impose restrictions and the provisions laid down in Part 18, Chapter 4 of the Act (Purchase of own Shares) are complied with. These require that the company can purchase its own shares only if they are fully paid up and payment is immediately made on purchase (s 691). There are restrictions on how the purchase may be financed (s 692). The purchase can only be made if authorised by the shareholders (s 693). Share buyback schemes can be beneficial to company and remaining shareholders alike as it can be used to reduce permanently the number of issued shares with a consequent rise in the value of their shares. However, success is not automatic. Next plc consistently employed a share buyback policy for 10 consecutive years, and reduced the shares in issue by 50 per cent. The value of its shares rose dramatically in consequence. In the company's Annual Report in 2013 Lord Wolfson, the chief executive, gave some guidance on how to employ a buyback strategy successfully. He pointed out that a business should always prioritise investment and only buy shares back if there is surplus cash available. The scheme must enhance earnings and produce an equivalent rate of return in the remaining shares. It is only successful if the business is experiencing long-term growth.

Unless the purchase is made in accordance with s 690, the general rule (s 658) applies. This states that the company may *not* acquire its own shares by sale, subscription or any other means unless:

1 no valuable consideration is paid for the shares; or
2 the purchase is to effect a formal reduction of capital which has been approved by the court; or
3 the court orders the purchase of shares to protect the interests of a minority of shareholders; or
4 shares are forfeited or surrendered as required by the articles, by a shareholder who has failed to pay.

Worth thinking about?

Why do you suppose the law relating to a company purchase of its own shares has been changed?

Suggested solutions can be found in Appendix 2.

Becoming a shareholder

Acquiring shares from the company

Allotment: assignment of shares.

When the shares are first issued by the company, an interested party which could be a company or an individual may apply to buy some. This is an offer which the company may accept by a letter of **allotment**. At this point a contract for sale of the shares comes into existence. However, the shareholder does not become a member of the company until his or her name is placed on the company's register of shareholders. The company must issue a certificate of registration which is evidence of the shareholder's title to the shares. Under s 769, the company has a duty to do this within two months of the issue of the letter of allotment.

Acquiring shares from an existing shareholder

A shareholder in a public company may freely transfer his or her shares; restrictions may be imposed by private companies. Section 776 requires the transfer to be formally

Running the company: raising and maintaining capital

21

notified to the company. The company must register the change of shareholder and issue a new certificate of registration within two months of receiving the instrument of transfer (s 776).

Once registered, the buyer of shares acquires all the rights attaching to that class of shares as dictated by the articles. In a limited company the buyer's liability for the company's debts is limited to the value of its shares. The shareholding makes the shareholder part owner of the company. Unless the company is wound up a shareholder cannot withdraw his or her capital investment from the company, but may transfer his or her shares to somebody else.

The rights of shareholders

To be paid any dividend declared by the company

Dividend: bonus payment for shareholders which the company may pay out of its profits.

A **dividend** is a bonus payment which can only be paid out of profits (s 263). Dividends are declared at the company's discretion, so the shareholders have no automatic right to a dividend unless the company chooses to issue one.

To vote at company meetings

Shareholders may vote at company meetings provided that their shares attract voting rights. This is determined by the articles. Voting rights may be used for the personal benefit of the shareholder and do not have to be exercised in the best interests of the company.

To recover the capital value of their shares if the company goes into liquidation

This right can be exercised only subject to the superior rights of the company's creditors. The shareholders do not necessarily have equal rights in relation to each other. Those with superior status have a right to be repaid before others. The articles determine the status of shareholders in this respect.

To transfer their shares

Shareholders may transfer their shares subject to any restrictions laid down in the articles. Restrictions are usual in the articles of a private company. Disputes regarding interpretation of such restrictions may be brought to court. The court will interpret any ambiguity in favour of the shareholder. To be legitimate the restriction must be used in the best interests of the company; evidence of bad faith by the directors would invalidate it.

Loan capital

Section 3A of CA 1985 gives a company powers to borrow money to further the business; these are usually made explicit in the company's articles, which indicate how far the company's assets may be used as loan security. When it obtains loans in this way the company creates a mortgage of its property. This is described as issuing **debentures**.

Debentures: written evidence of secured loans to the company.

Debentures

A debenture is the written evidence of a secured loan to the company. There are three forms of debentures.

Single debenture: secured loan to the company from individual/ organisation like a bank.

The single debenture

A **single debenture** is a loan to the company from any person or organisation prepared to lend it the money. In practice such loans most often come from a bank.

Series debentures: multiple debentures offered to existing shareholders.

Series debentures

The company may look to its own members for loans and issue a **series of debentures** to participants who have equal rights to repayment. They are generally protected by a trust in the same way as holders of debenture stock.

Debenture stock

Public companies are entitled to issue **debenture stock**, which may be offered to the public through the Stock Exchange in the same way as shares.

In order to protect the debenture holders, the company creates a trust with control over the company's assets, with the power to appoint a receiver. The trustee, which is often an insurance company, has the status of a company creditor, with the legal duty to act on behalf of the debenture holders. The terms of the trust deed may require the company to take certain precautions to protect the lenders' interests, including insurance of company assets and limiting its borrowing powers.

The debenture holder agrees to lend a specific sum of money repayable with interest after a certain length of time. Extra perks may also be offered as an inducement to buy debenture stock. When the facilities for the Wimbledon tennis championship were being expanded, the company responsible raised the capital through an issue of debentures.

Investment entitled the debenture holders to special facilities at the ground and priority booking rights. In 2005, Welsh Rugby Union Ltd issued debentures on the 125th Anniversary of Welsh Rugby. For £6,000 each debenture holder got the right to book a designated seat in the Millennium Stadium and the right to purchase tickets for the Six Nations matches, all Welsh Rugby Union matches and UEFA qualifying matches involving Wales. The debentures will be redeemed in 2030, when the privileges will cease.

A debenture is a transferable security and may therefore be disposed of in the same way as shares. The company is required to keep a list of debenture holders and issue registration certificates which are evidence of ownership for the registered holder.

Charges: the security behind the loan

If the company does not have the funds to repay debenture holders at the appointed time, the company's assets securing the loan will have to be realised to honour the debt.

The **chargeable assets** of the company include its premises, plant, machinery and goods (including stock in trade). As well as this tangible property, intellectual property like patents and copyright are also chargeable assets, as are book debts and business goodwill.

Registration of charges

All charges issued to secure debentures must be registered with the companies' registrar within 21 days of being created. Failure to register within this timescale renders the charge void. This does not relieve the company from liability to pay the debt, but it prevents the debenture holder from having any enforceable security for its loan.

Types of charges

Two kinds of charges are possible: fixed and floating.

1 *Fixed charges*. Specific assets to the value of the loan link with it as soon as the charge is created. Such a charge prevents any disposal of the assets over which the charge

exists and, therefore, only a limited variety of assets are suitable to being charged in this way. Land and large items of plant and machinery are the assets which are most appropriate for a **fixed charge**.

> **Fixed charges:** like floating charge but attached to particular assets.

> **Floating charges:** attached to the company's assets in general, to provide security for debenture holders.

2 *Floating charges.* Here the charge relates to the company's assets at large. At the point the loan is created the security enjoyed by the debenture holder does not attach to any specified assets, but the debenture holder will be entitled to repayment of its loan from any of the assets held by the company at the time of repayment. A **floating charge**, therefore, may relate to any of the company's more fluid assets which are subject to constant change, like stock in trade. This facility, which is available only to registered companies and limited liability partnerships, is helpful to businesses with few fixed assets.

Any of the following circumstances will cause the floating charge to *crystallise* and attach to particular assets:

- the company ceases trading;
- winding up is commenced;
- the company fails to repay the debenture holder at the due date;
- the occurrence of any other event specified in the charge deed as triggering crystallisation.

A debenture holder is better protected by a fixed charge than a floating charge. The value of a floating charge is likely to fluctuate. In the event of a winding up, the fixed-charge holders or statutorily protected creditors (employees, for example) take preference over the floating-charge holder.

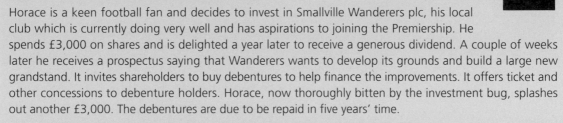

Real life

Horace is a keen football fan and decides to invest in Smallville Wanderers plc, his local club which is currently doing very well and has aspirations to joining the Premiership. He spends £3,000 on shares and is delighted a year later to receive a generous dividend. A couple of weeks later he receives a prospectus saying that Wanderers wants to develop its grounds and build a large new grandstand. It invites shareholders to buy debentures to help finance the improvements. It offers ticket and other concessions to debenture holders. Horace, now thoroughly bitten by the investment bug, splashes out another £3,000. The debentures are due to be repaid in five years' time.

Three years later, Smallville Wanderers are in trouble: two disastrous seasons have resulted in relegation to Division Two, and two of their key players are in prison for causing serious injuries to a referee after a disputed penalty decision. The current value of the shares has dived to 25 per cent of their original value. Horace is not unreasonably despondent about his investment. His debentures should be safe, as they are secured against the company's assets out of which he can be paid if necessary. However, things do not look good with the shares. Should the club slide further into financial difficulties, it may be faced with liquidation. If that happens, he may well lose his entire share investment as the company's creditors take priority over its members.

Summary of the differences between shares and debentures

Shares	Debentures
The shareholder is a member of the company with voting rights.	The debenture holder is a company creditor; he or she does not have voting rights.
Dividends are not payable out of capital. Since dividends are issued from profits at the company's discretion, a shareholder does not know if he or she will get any dividend, or what it will amount to.	The debenture holder must be paid interest on the loan, and this is payable out of capital. Debenture holders know how much interest they will get.
Risk: the entire value of the shareholding may be lost.	Since the loan is secured by a fixed or floating charge, the debenture holder has security.
The company cannot usually buy its own shares.	The company can buy its own debentures.
Shares cannot be issued at a discount.	Debentures may be issued at a discount.

Chapter summary

A company may have share and loan capital.

Share capital

This may be: issued, called up, paid up, uncalled.

Classes of shares: ordinary/preference/redeemable/treasury.

Issue of shares

May be advertised by prospectus.

Private companies may not advertise for sale to the public.

Rights issue possible.

Shares can only be transferred for money/money's worth of at least their face value.

Issue at a premium possible.

Issue must be registered at Companies House.

The company can only buy its own shares subject to the provisions of the CA 2006.

Shareholders have the right to:

1 dividends (if declared);
2 vote at company meetings (subject to nature of their shares);
3 recover the current value of their shares on liquidation of the company;
4 transfer the shares (subject to articles).

Loan capital

Single/series debentures

In effect, these are mortgages since they are loans secured on the company's assets by a fixed or floating charge.

Debenture holders

Lend the company money for a fixed term in return for interest and other benefits.

Unlike shareholders, they are not company members and have no voting right.

Quiz 20

1 What is the difference between issued and called-up capital?

2 Why might a company issue redeemable shares?

3 In what circumstances may a company acquire its own shares?

4 Silver, Gold, Copper and Brass all own shares in Metals plc and seek your advice on the following problems:

(a) Silver complains that he has never received a dividend.

(b) Gold, a preference shareholder, has just discovered that he has no right to vote at a company meeting.

(c) Copper, a preference shareholder, has heard rumours that Metals may soon be wound up and is worried about his investment.

(d) Brass, a debenture holder, is also worrying about whether he will recover his investment.

Answers to all quizzes can be found in Appendix 2.

Web activity

Please go to: www.londonstockexchange.com/home/homepage.htm

Please click on 'For companies and advisers' then click on 'AIM market' for information relevant to smaller companies considering going public.

Assignment 19

Rashida has won £1,000 in a raffle and wants to invest it in a company. She seeks your advice on whether she should buy shares or debentures. Explain the differences between the two investment methods to her, indicating the advantages and disadvantages of each.

CHAPTER 22

Daily management of the company

Functions of directors, secretary and auditors

Introduction

The company is an independent legal entity, but manages its business through its staff. The key management figures are the directors who through their decisions determine the policies, culture, and ethos of the company. Their powers and duties are largely governed by statute but an independent Code of Practice issued by the Financial Reporting Council encourages good governance. The company secretary has important administrative duties, while the auditors are responsible for monitoring financial accountability.

In this chapter we will examine the work of these officers.

Learning objectives

When you have studied this chapter you should be able to:

▶ distinguish between the different types of director and their functions;

▶ explain the duties of directors;

▶ appreciate the impact of the CA 2006 on directors' duties;

▶ understand the functions of the company secretary;

▶ describe the work and legal liability of an auditor;

▶ give examples of how insider dealing may occur.

The directors

A private company must have at least one director and a public company must have at least two (s 154). The articles of the company state the means by which a director may be appointed. Usually this is by vote at an AGM. Nobody under the age of 16 may act as a director (s 157). The company must keep a register of directors (s 162) containing their particulars (s 163).

The directors are the agents of the company; they are primarily responsible for the daily management of the company and development of company policy. Decisions on such issues are made by the directors at **board meetings.**

A large company may have a correspondingly large board of directors. A number of these may be **lay (non-executive) directors**, who provide their services on a voluntary basis and whose primary function is attendance at board meetings. They do not play any direct role in the day-to-day management of the company, which is in the hands of its executive director(s). The value of lay directors is controversial: it is argued that their presence is important to ensure independent decision-making and an objective view of company policy. A more cynical view is that their lack of relevant knowledge and experience may render their contribution largely useless. It is also said that they are likely to be too readily influenced by **executive directors**.

These concerns led to publication of the Stock Exchange Combined Code: Principles of Good Governance and Code of Good Practice 2008, Article 13 aimed to tackle this problem by requiring that lay directors have regular meetings with the chair of the board without any executive directors present. Article 14 required them to meet annually to appraise the managing director's performance. They also had responsibility for ensuring that the minutes of meetings record their concerns about company business which they believe were not satisfactorily resolved.

Good governance by all directors was encouraged by successive Combined Codes published by the Financial Services Authority (now the Financial Conduct Authority) from 1998, each aiming to make further improvements to directors' performance. The UK Corporate Governance Code 2010, published by the Financial Reporting Council, replaced and enhanced these. It provides new guidance on corporate governance for all directors but comprises principles rather than actual rules. This was updated in 2013 and again in in 2014.

The UK Corporate Governance Code

The Code stresses the need for a rise in standards by boards of companies to ensure value for money for their shareholders and the general good of the company. For example:

1 On appointment directors should conform to a role description prepared by the company's nomination committee and appointments to the board should be made on merit, judged against objective criteria

2 Appropriate regard must be given to diversity on the board, including gender.

Board meeting: a meeting of the company's directors.

Lay/non-executive director: attends meetings but is not actively involved in running the company.

Executive director: responsible for the day-to-day management of the company.

3 New directors should receive full, formal and appropriate induction on joining the board.

4 All directors should be able to give sufficient time to the effective fulfilment of their duties.

5 No non-executive director should be proposed for re-election by the shareholders without a performance evaluation indicative of his or her commitment and effectiveness in the role, since they are expected to challenge and help develop the company's strategies constructively.

6 Remuneration of executive directors should be regulated to ensure the long term success of the company; and remuneration committees should clearly explain to shareholders how this is being done.

7 Remuneration committees are also required to take a robust line when determining the size of golden handshakes for retiring managing directors to ensure that they are proportionate.

8 The Code emphasises the responsibility of the board of directors for determining what and how much risk is involved in the company's dealings: this provision clearly reflects the concerns which emerged from the collapse of various financial institutions during the credit crunch which preceded the publication of the Code.

Appointing the directors

The first directors are named in the application for registration when the company is set up. Subsequent directors are appointed by ordinary resolution passed by a simple majority at a company general meeting. The articles of association state the procedure for replacement of a director who leaves or dies before a general meeting is due to be called. Directors need not be shareholders of the company, but the articles may require them to hold qualifying shares. To promote independence and transparency in the company's dealings the Small Business, Enterprise and Employment Act (SBEEA) 2015, s 87 abolished the appointment of corporate directors. From 2016, subject to certain limited exceptions, only human persons can hold office.

In the news

Women FTSE 100 directors on the rise

One of the aims of the Davies Report in 2010 was to increase the number of female directors on the boards of FTSE 100 companies to 25 per cent by 2015. Figures for 2015 are not available at the time of writing.

According to statistics published by BIS in October 2014, there are no longer any male only boards among the FTSE 100 companies and representation by women has increased overall from 12.5 per cent in 2011 to 22.8 per cent in 2014. This is encouraging, but to fulfil the Davies aim another 24 women needed to be appointed during 2015.

22

Daily management of the company

Executive (managing) directors

Since they are responsible for the day-to-day management of the company, executive directors work for the company full-time and have expertise and experience relevant to the company's business. They may be engaged by the company under a contract of service. Provided the articles do not state otherwise, a person may be both an employee and a director of a company, subject to some restrictions:

1 a contract of employment for more than two years cannot be offered to any person who is already a director without the approval of the shareholders in a general meeting (s 188);

2 company articles generally prohibit directors from voting on their terms of employment at a directors' meeting;

3 directors' service agreements are open to public inspection at the company's registered office.

In a small private company (quasi-partnership) all the directors will be full-time managers but will decide informally how much the company can afford to pay them.

To prevent a conflict of interest for executive directors and to discourage malpractice in listed companies, the Combined Code introduced a requirement that companies put in place open and transparent procedures for appointing executive directors and formulating their remuneration. A company's annual report should state the relevant policies for the information of shareholders. The Code also requires that a committee of non-executive directors should decide, within agreed terms of reference, a company's policy for paying its executive directors. This committee is also responsible for determining the specific remuneration rights for each executive director, including pension entitlement and compensation payment.

Alternate directors

Alternate director: somebody nominated by an existing director as their representative at a company meeting.

If the articles permit, a director may appoint an **alternate director** to represent him or her at a board meeting if unable to attend. In practice, this function is usually exercised by another director.

Shadow directors

Shadow director: a company member who uses their voting power to manipulate directors' decision-making.

A **shadow director** uses their voting power to manipulate the directors and is defined (s 251) as 'a person in accordance with whose directions or instructions the directors of a company are accustomed to act'. They are bound by the general duties for directors (s 170(5) as amended by SBEEA 2015 s 89) (see below).

A person who merely gives professional advice to the board on which it acts is not a shadow director. The next case illustrates that there is a difference between giving advice and encouraging and cooperating in dishonest practice since such behaviour may result in liability as a shadow director.

Vivendi SA & Centenary Holdings III Ltd v Richards and Bloch (2013)

The defendant consultant Richards entered into a contract which bound him to faithfully serve Centenary Holdings and use his best endeavours to promote its interests. He and Bloch, the sole director of Vivendi, while knowing that the company was in financial difficulty, made it procure payments of over £10 million over several years. The company subsequently went into liquidation and the liquidators took action against Richards and Bloch for breach of their fiduciary duty, in particular their duty of good faith as directors. Richards argued that he was not a director.

Held: Richards must be deemed to be a shadow director of the company since he had contractual obligations to Centenary Holdings and he knew that Bloch relied upon his judgement and acted on his instructions. He must be assumed to have a fiduciary duty because of this and because he carried out similar functions to any *de jure* director. The interests of the company's creditors must be considered and the actions of Bloch and Richards were clearly in breach of their fiduciary duty as they had been dishonest and acted prejudicially to the creditors. Their motive was to extract as much money as possible from what they knew to be an insolvent company before it failed.

De facto directors

A person who, while not formally appointed as such, performs the functions of a director is bound by the same statutory duties as any other director and owes a duty of good faith is a de facto director. It may sometimes be difficult to detect whether someone should be treated as a de facto director.

Smithton v Naggar (2014, EWCA)

Naggar was a director of Dawnay Day International, a holding company with just over half the shares in Smithton Ltd, a joint venture company. Clients introduced to Smithton by Naggar defaulted. Smithton claimed that Naggar, as a director of the holding company had, when bringing in new business, acted as a de facto director of Smithton and should therefore indemnify it for the losses resulting from his actions.

The High Court held that he had not acted as de facto director. The joint venture agreement governing the relationship between Smithton and its holding company specifically stated that Naggar was not a director. When he had introduced clients he was 'wearing a different hat' and representing his own rather than Smithton's interests.

Smithton appealed.

The Court of Appeal held: The appeal must be dismissed. There was no absolute test to be used here to determine the de facto director question. The court needed to decide on objective and contextual evidence whether Naggar had 'formed part of the corporate governance structure of the company'. Close examination of all Naggar's actions did not suggest any greater involvement in Smithton's affairs than might be expected of someone who was acting both as a major client and chair of the majority shareholding company.

The powers of the directors

These are indicated by the articles but basically involve managing company business. Examples of directors' powers include issuing shares and borrowing money on the security of the company's assets.

Limitation on the exercise of powers

The directors' powers must be exercised subject to the company's objects clause; they are the agents of the company and their powers are limited to those of the company.

The Companies Acts impose restrictions on the way directors may use their authority, and this may also be limited by the articles. The powers must be exercised in the best interests of the company to fulfil the purposes for which they were given.

Protecting third parties against abuse of directors' powers

If the directors exceed their power the company may be bound by a resulting transaction. The third party may enforce the transaction as long as he or she acted in good faith under s 40 (see Chapter 20 for detail). The law of agency also provides some limited protection: if the company board knows that a maverick director is exceeding his or her authority but does not disown that behaviour, the company is bound by any resulting contract with a third party. In law the directors are estopped from denying that the contract was authorised. The director acts with apparent authority. (This is a good point at which to refresh your memory on these principles (see Chapter 12) and look at *Newcastle International Airport Ltd* v *Eversheds LLP* (2012), which provides a good example.)

Freeman & Lockyer v *Buckhurst Park Properties (Mangal) Ltd* (1964)

The articles of the defendant company permitted the appointment of a managing director. None was appointed, but one of the directors was known by the others to be conducting business with outsiders as if he had these powers.

Held: the director had abused his authority and the company was held liable on the resulting contracts; the board had been fully aware of the director's behaviour and could not deny his apparent authority after the event.

The duties of directors

The directors have a number of duties arising from the exercise of their powers. Such duties are owed primarily to the company and the shareholders but also include the company's employees and creditors. Before the CA 2006 these were both statutory (under the CA 1985 and related legislation) and common law duties.

Directors' common law and equitable duties before the CA 2006

These duties fell into two categories:

A duty of care

The common law of negligence requires a director to act with reasonable care and skill when carrying on the company's business. However, the fact that damage has been caused by their behaviour is not in itself evidence of lack of reasonable care and skill provided that the directors have not acted *ultra vires* or fraudulently.

Re City Equitable & Fire Insurance Co. Ltd (1925)

Due to fraud by a managing director, the company suffered major losses resulting in its liquidation. The other directors were held not to be negligent in failing to notice the managing director's misconduct. The court laid down criteria for judgement of what is a reasonable standard of care.

Held:

1 the director must act honestly for the benefit of the business;

2 what is reasonable care must be judged with reference to the experience, knowledge and skill of the relevant director. Directors cannot be expected to exercise greater care than these qualities equip them for. Less would be demanded of a lay director than of a managing director;

3 a director is not generally expected to give continuous attention to the company's affairs, since directors' duties are essentially intermittent in their nature (today it is unlikely that any court would excuse a managing director who failed to exercise continuous attention);

4 delegation of duty by a director to an appropriate company official is not evidence of a breach of duty provided it is in accordance with business practice and does not infringe the company's articles.

Where it appears that a director has breached the duty of care, an action in negligence may be started, after members at a general meeting have voted in favour of such action. A director who is found to have been negligent must personally indemnify the company for its losses.

It is possible for the directors to be informally excused (without passage of a resolution) as concerns their negligent conduct by unanimous agreement of members with voting rights. This may be done even if the negligent directors themselves control the voting.

Fiduciary duty

This is imposed by the law of equity and requires directors to act with the *utmost good faith* in dealings with the company.

This has three consequences.

1 Directors must avoid any conflict between their own financial interests and those of the company. If they breach this duty, they must account to the company for any resulting profit.

2   Directors must make full disclosure of any personal interest which they have in company business. Generally the articles provide that as long as directors fully declare their interests they may retain them, but they must not vote at a board meeting on any issue relating to those interests.

3   Directors must exercise their powers in good faith and for their proper purposes.

IDC v *Cooley* (1972)

Cooley was an architect employed as managing director of IDC. He was put in charge of negotiations with a gas board, which had approached IDC concerning the design of a gas holder. During the negotiations it became clear that the gas board was unwilling to place the contract with IDC. At this point Cooley resigned, falsely pleading ill health. Then he obtained the design contract with the gas board.

Held (Roskill J): Cooley must pay the profits from the contract to IDC, since he had abused his position as agent of the company and used his inside knowledge to obtain the contract, creating a conflict of interest. 'Information which came to him while he was managing director and which was of concern to the [company] and relevant for the [company] to know, was information which it was his duty to pass on.'

It was irrelevant that his behaviour had not necessarily caused IDC to lose the contract.

Hogg v *Cramphorn Ltd* (1967)

Hogg put in a bid to take over Cramphorn Ltd. The directors, who honestly believed that a threatened takeover was not in the company's best interests, issued 5,000 additional shares to a trust made up of employees to enable the bid to be outvoted.

Held: this was a misuse of the directors' powers. Their action had diluted the value of the company's stock. A shares issue could only be undertaken to raise capital, not to defeat a takeover bid.

If a contract is made in breach of the directors' fiduciary duty, the contract is voidable, and, therefore, the company is able to choose whether to go through with it or not. Provided that the directors have not acted fraudulently or in breach of the law, under the law of agency the shareholders might vote to ratify their actions. For example, in *Hogg* v *Cramphorn* it was held that, provided that the employees were excluded from the vote, the remaining shareholders could vote to ratify the directors' action.

Directors' duties since the CA 2006

The CA 2006 is intended to clarify directors' duties by codifying the obligations described above. These are now described as 'general duties' and comprise in effect a detailed analysis of the common law and equitable obligations.

These duties are owed to the company alone (s 170(1)) and replace the common law and equitable principles which form their basis. The Act indicates that they should be interpreted in that light and 'regard must be paid to the corresponding common law rules and equitable principles' (s 170(4)). Previous case law in this area therefore remains relevant unless and until changed. The new wording may have an impact on the interpretation of the scope of the duties.

The general duties: ss 171–177

These duties are not mutually exclusive so more than one may arise in any one case. A director has a duty to:

1 *Act within his or her powers (s 171)*. A director must comply with the company's constitution and only use their powers for the purposes for which they are conferred. This enacts the *ultra vires* rule.

2 *Promote the success of the company (s 172)*. A director must in good faith promote the success of the company to benefit 'its members as a whole' (s 172(1)).

    This re-states the director's duty to act in the company's best interests which is implicit in the original fiduciary duty. The wording appears somewhat contradictory as, although the duty initially sounds as if it is owed to the company, the Act continues by requiring the director to carry it out for the benefit of the shareholders which could give rise to a conflict. However, any contradiction is arguably resolved by the criteria for decision making in s 172(1) which require a well-rounded approach.

    A director should take the following into account when making decisions:

    (a) likely long-term consequences;

    (b) interests of the company's workforce (replaces the CA 2006 duty to have regard to the employees' interests);

    (c) the need to foster good business relationships with all who deal with the company;

    (d) environmental and community impact of the company activities;

    (e) the desirability of the company's maintaining a good reputation for business conduct; and

    (f) the need to act fairly as between company members.

3 *Exercise independent judgement (s 173)*. The directors' fiduciary duty has always required the exercise of unfettered discretion. Section 173(1) indicates that this duty is subject to any provision in the company's articles that authorises a restriction of discretion. Parliamentary debate during passage of the legislation indicates that it does not preclude delegation to committee or seeking expert advice where appropriate.

4 *Exercise reasonable skill, care and diligence (s 174)*. This re-states the common law duty of reasonable care and skill as applicable to company directors and does not represent any real change.

22

Daily management of the company

Previously the standard of care had been defined by the Insolvency Act 1986, s 214 which added an initial objective assessment to the existing subjective test in *Re City Equitable & Fire Insurance Co. Ltd* (1925) (see above).

Section 174(2) adopts a similar definition. It provides that the duty requires:

the care, skill and diligence that would be exercised by a reasonably diligent person with:

(a) *the general knowledge, skill and expertise that may reasonably be expected of a person carrying out the functions . . . [of] the director in relation to the company, and*

(c) *the general knowledge, skill and experience that the director has.*

Part (a) measures performance objectively to but (b) requires a subjective approach examining the skill, knowledge and experience of the director in question. The objective test therefore relates to the minimum standard of care required of the average reasonably competent director. The subjective test assesses whether, given their particular knowledge and experience in the particular circumstances, a higher standard should reasonably be expected of them.

Students who have studied the tort chapters will recognise this as a specialised *Bolam* test. (See Chapter 14)

5 *Avoid conflict of interest (s 175).* This general duty, which applies to the exploitation of the company's property, information or opportunity, is identical to the existing equitable duty as applied in *IDC* v *Cooley* (above). A director may be held to be liable for a breach regardless of the fact that the company suffered no loss and the director had no improper motive. (See *Towers* v *Premier Waste Management Ltd* (2011).)

6 *Refuse third party benefits (s 176).* This is another aspect of conflict of interest made specific by the Act. Benefits include bribes and gifts from those seeking to obtain business opportunities or advantageous terms. (See the *Towers* case below.)

Section 176(1) prohibits a director from obtaining a benefit from a third party which was conferred because he or she is a director or doing/not doing something as a director. A third party is defined (s 176(2)) as a person other than the company, its subsidiaries or any person acting on behalf of the company or subsidiaries. Benefits for services provided to the third party by the director are excluded (s 176(3)).

No breach occurs if the benefit could not reasonably be expected to give rise to a conflict of interest or duties (s 176(4) and (5)).

7 *Declare an interest in any proposed transaction or arrangement with the company (s 177).* Directors had a statutory duty to declare any interest in any proposed or existing contract with the company under s 317 of the CA 1985.

The CA 2006 splits this duty but the substance of the law remains the same. Existing contracts are now covered by s 182 which is explained below and s 177 concerns proposed contracts only.

Section 177(1) requires a director to disclose the nature and extent of any direct or indirect interest to all the other directors. An interest may arise indirectly if, for example, the director's spouse is involved in the proposed transaction. Provided the director has not breached his duties under s 175 and s 177, the transaction is not voidable without the approval of company members unless the articles of the company require this (s 180(1)).

A director is not in breach of this duty unless he should reasonably have been aware of the conflict of interest.

8 *Declare an interest in an existing transaction or arrangement.* Section 182(1) requires a director to disclose to all the other directors the nature and extent of any direct or indirect interest which he or she has in any transaction or arrangement which the company has entered into.

If the director has made a relevant declaration under s 177 at the point when the transaction was proposed, there is no need to make a second one (s 182(1)). He or she is not under a duty to declare an interest of which he or she could not reasonably have known (s 182(5)).

Failure to make a disclosure under s 182 is a criminal offence punishable by fine or imprisonment (s 183). Note that this does not apply to a breach of any other of the directors' duties (s 178); those are sanctioned by civil law only. Any contract involving an undeclared conflict of interest may be voidable and the director may be required to account for any profits.

Guinness plc v *Saunders* (1990)

During a takeover bid a payment of over £5 million was made to a director who had disclosed a relevant interest to a committee of the board consisting of only two other members and himself.

Held: this was not sufficient to discharge the duty because disclosure must be made to the whole board.

Case law indicates that the courts interpret these duties stringently even in the case of relatively minor breaches.

Towers v *Premier Waste Management Ltd* (2011, CA)

Mr Towers was a director of Premier. One of the company's customers offered him free loan of plant and equipment for his use in renovating his house. He did not disclose this advantageous arrangement to his company. When it became known, the company took action against him for breach of his duties.

Held: Mr Towers had breached his fiduciary duty to the company by failing in his duty of loyalty and by failing to avoid a conflict of interest. He had been disloyal in preventing the company from considering whether it objected to the diversion of a possible benefit from it. It was irrelevant that the company suffered no resulting loss and that he did not make a valuable profit, act in bad faith or that he would not have hired the equipment commercially had the offer of loan not been made.

A director may remain bound by their duties even after leaving the company.

22

Daily management of the company

Killen v *Horseworld Ltd* (2012)

Ms Killen, a director of Horseworld, was involved in negotiating a contract on behalf of the company to supply media broadcasting services to the organisers of the Badminton Horse Trials in 2009. Ms Killen then left Horseworld and set up her own company (Horse & County Ltd) and exploited the information she had secured at Horseworld to get a contract to supply internet broadcasting services for the 2009 Horse trials.

Robinson J held: she was in breach of her duty to avoid conflict of interest and must account for the profits to Horseworld Ltd. 'Section 175(1) requires a director to avoid a situation where there is even the possibility of a conflict of interest, and Section 175(2) makes particular reference to the exploitation of an opportunity.' It was irrelevant that she was no longer a Horseworld director, as on leaving that company she had immediately engaged in negotiations in direct competition with it. Also '. . . she knew that Horseworld Ltd wanted the very broadcast rights that were included in the package obtained by Horse and Country.'

Directors' duty to creditors

Insolvency Act 1986 s 214: if the directors should be aware that the company cannot reasonably avoid going into liquidation they have a duty to take reasonable steps to minimise losses to creditors of the company.

Transactions by directors which require shareholder approval

Certain transactions by the board of directors on behalf of the company require approval by ordinary resolution of the shareholders. The relevant transactions involve the possibility of unfair advantage accruing to a director. They include the following.

Substantial and material property transactions: s 190

Unless the shareholders have given their approval they may avoid any transaction involving the sale or acquisition of a non-cash asset by the company to or from a director of the company or a person connected with him or her where the value of the property exceeds £5,000 and is in excess of 10 per cent of the company's net assets. Unless shareholder approval for the transaction is given, the director, or any connected person, is liable to the company for profits arising from the contract; and any directors who gave their approval may also be liable.

Persons connected with the director are stated in s 252 to include family (e.g. spouse, civil partner, children, step-children) and a company in which the director can control 20 per cent of the shareholder vote.

Worth thinking about?

Before the CA 2006, directors considering two competing takeover bids could perform their duty of acting in the company's best interests by accepting the lower bid, if that was ultimately going to be more beneficial for the business. Arguably, this might be less financially beneficial to the shareholders.

Does the wording of s 172(1), which seems to suggest that the shareholders' benefit is paramount, prevent directors from legitimately opting for the lower bid?

Suggested solutions can be found in Appendix 2.

Directors' long-term service contracts: s 189

Without shareholder approval any provision in an executive director's employment contract restricting the company's rights to terminate the director's employment is void.

Loans to directors: ss 197–214

Subject to certain exceptions no loan can be made to a director without the company's approval and any loan is voidable without it. Exceptions cover expenses directly related to carrying out company business.

Golden handshakes: s 217

Compensation for loss of office of director or payments on retirement cannot be paid without approval from the shareholders. The UK Corporate Governance Code recommends that these should not be excessive (see above).

Reporting to shareholders

Shareholders need to be kept properly informed about the work of the company to enable them to play an effective role. As part of its campaign to promote transparency and to ensure compliance with existing legislation, the Companies Act 2006 (Strategic Report and Directors' Report) Regulations 2013 came into operation on 31 October 2013. These are aimed at making directors provide better information to shareholders about how well the directors have performed their duty to promote the success of the company (CA, s 172) during the past year. They apply to companies quoted on the Stock Exchange and require greater clarity and detail in reporting than was imposed previously.

Directors must now make a much fuller disclosure of the principal risks and uncertainties confronting the company. Overall the report should involve a fair and balanced review of the company's performance over the year.

The reports must now contain:

(a) Analysis of business trends showing the main factors in the business world affecting the company's operation

(b) Environmental reporting to show the impact of the company's business.

(c) Gender diversity with reference to the company's employees and directors.

(d) Social community and human rights issue showing how the company's policies affect such issues and take them into account.

(e) A description of the company's policy.

(f) A description of the company's business model.

The rights of directors

Fees and expenses

Executive directors' remuneration is determined by the terms of their service contracts. Lay directors' entitlement is specified in the articles, but they are entitled to expenses.

The removal and retirement of directors

Removal by ordinary resolution with special notice: s 168

A director may be removed from office before the expiry of its term. This is done by passing an ordinary resolution of the company, for which special notice is given (see Chapter 23). This might occur, for example, in the event of a serious breach of duty by a director. The director must be given a copy of the special notice prior to its distribution to the shareholders so that the director can attach a written statement to it. Under s 169 the director is entitled to address the meeting and make representations in his or her defence.

Directors are entitled to use weighted voting rights even if these have been created specifically to prevent removal. Thus, in *Bushell* v *Faith* (1970, HL) a company's articles stated that in the event of a resolution to remove the directors, their shares would carry three votes per share instead of one. Mr Faith, a director, who held 100 shares, was able to use this measure to defeat his two sisters who held 100 shares each.

Although executive directors may be removed in the same way as any other director, the company may have to pay damages if the removal is in breach of an executive director's contract of employment (s 167(5)).

Real life

Horace owns shares in Smallville Wanderers plc. He has been invited to an extraordinary general meeting of the company and given special notice of a resolution to remove Cecil, one of the directors, from office. There is evidence that Cecil was wined and dined by a sales representative of Fleetfoot Sports Shoes plc just before a meeting of the board voted by a majority of only one, to place a large order with Fleetfoot and make it their preferred supplier. Cecil is also a shareholder in Fleetfoot but did not tell his fellow directors about this prior to the vote. Fleetfoot has now gone into liquidation before fulfilling an order worth £5,000, which Wanderers are very unlikely to recover.

It is alleged that Cecil has breached two duties: first, by accepting third party benefits; and, secondly, by failing to declare an interest in a proposed company transaction.

While accepting Fleetfoot's hospitality alone would not seem to justify removing Cecil, the shareholders may reasonably feel that this, combined with his failure to declare his interest in the deal with Fleetfoot, reflects very poorly on Cecil's integrity, particularly if Cecil spoke in favour of trading with Fleetfoot at the board meeting. If, in addition, Cecil should have been aware of Fleetfoot's perilous financial situation the shareholders would seem to be even more justified in getting rid of him, as this would seem to be a breach of his duty to act independently and with reasonable care and skill. Cecil may speak in his defence at the meeting.

Retirement and resignation of directors

Retirement and resignation rules are found in the company's articles. These may provide for retirement in rotation, at the AGM, for a proportion of the board after the lapse of a specified period of service. However, this is not practicable for many small private companies and in large listed companies directors will be required to stand for election every year.

Any circumstances preventing a director from being able to carry out his or her duties (for example, ill health or failure to attend company meetings without permission of the board) may be grounds for seeking their removal.

The disqualification of directors

Company Directors Disqualification Act 1986

Any person (not just an existing director) may be disqualified by order of the court from being a director, liquidator, administrator, receiver or manager of a company's property or from being in any way directly or indirectly concerned in running a company. Such an order may be made in the following circumstances:

(a) *Conviction for an indictable offence in the Crown Court.* The offence must be connected with setting up or managing a company. The maximum disqualification period is 15 years.

(b) *Persistent failure to make the annual return.* Persistent means three times over a five-year period. The maximum disqualification period is five years.

(c) *Fraudulent trading.* The maximum disqualification period is 15 years.

(d) *Unfit conduct by a director of an insolvent company.* Unfit behaviour includes:

- breach of directors' duties;
- misapplication or wrongful retention of company property;

- failure to comply with Companies Act requirements concerning accounts and annual returns;
- failure to co-operate with the liquidator in accordance with the requirements of the Insolvency Act 1986.
- bankruptcy: an undischarged bankrupt is disqualified.

The maximum period for disqualification is 15 years.

The company secretary

All public companies must have a company secretary but since the CA 2006 this is no longer obligatory for private companies (s 270).

Company secretary: the principal administrator of a company responsible for ensuring compliance with the Companies Acts.

This is a key post, since the **company secretary** is the company's principal administrative officer. The company secretary has a wide range of duties with responsibility for ensuring that the company fulfils its obligations under the Companies Acts. The secretary is not involved in managing the company or in carrying on its business, but has responsibility for running the registered office. In a large company, the company secretary's job may involve hiring staff, buying office equipment and administering a pension scheme, as well as carrying out any functions designated by the articles or statute.

Qualifications for office

In *private companies*, no specific qualifications are needed. In public companies the directors must be satisfied that their appointee has appropriate skills and experience to do the job (s 273). In addition, the appointee must satisfy one of the following requirements:

1 for three of the last five years have been the secretary of a public company; or
2 be called or admitted as a barrister/solicitor/advocate in the UK; or
3 be a member of an approved organisation (e.g. ICA, ACCA, ICSA, ICMA, CIPFA); or
4 appear to be capable of acting as a company secretary because of experience gained as the holder of another office or membership of an appropriate body.

The directors are responsible for appointing the company secretary.

The functions of the company secretary

Ensuring compliance with the Companies Acts

The secretary must make sure that all the documentation open to public inspection is kept in order and up to date. This includes the registers of share and debenture holders. The secretary is also responsible for supervising the completion of the annual return.

Annual return: current information which the company secretary must file every year at Companies House.

The **annual return** updates the information about the company which was required for registration, so that most of the information which may be obtained by looking at the register can be found in the return. Sections 855 and 856 require the following information to be included:

1 the names and addresses of the current directors and secretary;

2 particulars of other directorships held by board members;

3 the address of the registered office;

4 particulars of the company's share capital.

Further requirements may be imposed by the Secretary of State by regulation (s 857).

The return should be delivered to the Companies Registry every year on the anniversary of the company's incorporation or delivery of its last annual return. It may also be filed online under s 858, and failure to deliver it is a criminal offence by the company and its directors and secretary. However, the SBEEA 2015, s 92 amends the CA 2006 to enable a company to opt out of filing a return annually. Instead, any change of relevant details must be notified to the Companies Registry once a year.

The secretary has authority to act as the company's agent

Company secretaries have authority to make a wide variety of contracts incidental to their functions. These include engaging office staff, buying or hiring office equipment, and purchasing such other goods and services as are necessary to running the company office. As long as the other party acts in good faith in the reasonable belief that the company has authorised the contracts, they will be enforceable against the company whether or not the secretary had actual authority or not.

Panorama Developments v *Fidelis Furnishing Fabrics Ltd* (1971, CA)

The company secretary of Fidelis Furnishings hired cars, claiming that they were to be used to transport customers to the company premises. In fact he was putting them to his own use.

Held: the company was liable on these contracts, which came within the scope of the secretary's apparent authority. The status of the company secretary had become greatly enhanced in the twentieth century and carried much greater responsibility than the largely clerical role of the office in the nineteenth century.

Some activities, however, do not come within the secretary's authority. These include borrowing money and making a trading contract, as these actions are not incidental to the administration of the company.

The role of the company secretary

In larger public companies the role of the company secretary has, in the last half century, grown considerably from the basic administrative role described so far to something much more complex and multifaceted. When performed well this enables them to make a substantial contribution to the success of the company. When they have been in post a long time they can provide useful continuity to the board as directors come and go; their wealth of background knowledge of the company's trading history is also valuable. They can play a significant role in aiding the success of the company by ensuring that all board members are appropriately supplied with the current information necessary to good decision-making; this is particularly important to keep non-executive directors in the loop and ensure the effectiveness of their role. The secretary may also provide a necessary link between executive and non-executive directors to enable good communication between them.

Annual report: comprehensive information on the company's activities and performance issued to shareholders.

Since the implementation of the Cadbury Report in 1993, the secretary's duties have become even more challenging. An **annual report** is sent to shareholders to give them a comprehensive review of the company's performance over the year. The secretary of a listed company must ensure that it includes a review of how far the company has complied with the requirements of the UK Governance Code issued by the Financial Reporting Council. Failure to declare progress to the Financial Conduct Authority on conforming to the code may result in the company having its listed status removed by the Stock Exchange.

The auditors of the company

The CA 2006 re-states this area of the law largely without change.

The duty to appoint an auditor

Auditor: accountant appointed by the company to check on the company's accounts and report on them to the shareholders.

Every company must generally appoint an **auditor** for each financial year, but the procedure is now different for private companies. A public company appoints its auditor during an accounts meeting at which the company's annual accounts and reports are laid (s 489(2)). If a public company fails to appoint an auditor, the Secretary of State has the power to appoint one (s 490).

Under the CA 2006, private companies are relieved of the obligation of holding meetings, therefore a private company must generally appoint its auditor by ordinary resolution within 28 days of the accounts being issued (s 485(2)). If it fails to do this the existing auditor is deemed to be reappointed (s 487(2)) though this can be blocked by members (s 488).

A small private company, the turnover of which does not exceed £5.6 million in the current year, is completely exempt from the requirement to have an annual audit (s 477).

The auditor must be a member of a recognised accountancy body. This includes the Institute of Chartered Accountants and the Chartered Association of Certified Accountants.

Under the Companies (Audit Investigations and Community Enterprise) Act 2004, the Professional Oversight Board for Accountancy has responsibility for monitoring the audits of all listed companies.

The functions of the auditors

The functions of the company's auditors are to check that the company's accounts genuinely reflect its actual financial position and to issue a report on the accounts to the shareholders. To perform these functions efficiently, the auditors will have to do more than just check the in-house accountant's arithmetic; the company's stock in trade and money-handling procedures will have to be inspected and the company advised of any undesirable practices taking place in the management of the business.

The powers of the auditors

Auditors have considerable powers to help them acquire the necessary information to perform their functions. They have access to all the company's books and records and may question company officials (s 499). It is a criminal offence knowingly or recklessly to make a misleading or materially false statement to an auditor.

The liability of the auditors

Contract

The auditors' contract with the company must be performed with reasonable care and skill. Failure to do so can make the auditors liable for breach of contract. Only the company has the right to sue, as there is no privity of contract between the auditors and individual shareholders.

Tort

Negligence liability will arise if the auditors do not act with reasonable care and skill, but this duty is owed only to the company, not to existing or potential shareholders. (See Chapter 14 and the House of Lords' decision in *Caparo Industries plc* v *Dickman* (1990).)

Insider dealing

Insider dealing: secretly using inside information about a company's share value for personal profit.

Anybody with inside information about the present or future value of the company's securities, who uses that information for their own profit and without disclosing it to any other relevant parties, may be guilty of **insider dealing**; this is a criminal offence. Insiders include the company's directors, shareholders and employees, and any other people who have access to relevant information about the company because of their office or professional status. Therefore, an auditor who bought shares in the knowledge that a takeover was imminent which would increase their value would be guilty of insider dealing if that information was not public knowledge.

Such dealing has been an infringement of the Companies Acts since 1980. The current law is to be found in the Criminal Justice Act 1993, Part IV, which was prompted by the need for the UK to comply with EC Directive 89/92 on insider dealing. It is an offence to deal in securities while in possession, as an insider, of inside information and if the price of securities is affected by this information. Defendants may avoid liability if they can prove that when they entered into the transaction they did not do so with the intention of making a profit or avoiding a loss.

The CA 2006 does not create civil liability for insider dealing, therefore the company or individual shareholders do not have any right to recover damages for the losses which they have suffered. Where the insider is a director, the profits from the deal are technically recoverable by the company, as by dealing in this way the director will have acted in breach of their duties. There are no reported decisions where such action has been taken.

Chapter summary

Directors

All companies must have at least one director.

Larger companies have a board consisting of one or more executive director(s) plus lay directors.

Work of the board takes place largely at company meetings but the executive directors are responsible for the daily running of the company.

Duties of directors

Act within powers.

Promote success.

Exercise independent judgement.

Exercise reasonable care, skill and diligence.

Avoid conflicts of interest.

Not accept benefits from third parties.

Declare interests in proposed/existing transactions.

Transactions between company and directors requiring shareholder approval

Long-term service contracts.

Substantial property transactions with directors/connected persons.

Loans to directors.

Golden handshakes.

Payment of directors

Executive directors: under the terms of the employment contract.

Lay directors: only so far as the articles permit.

Disqualification of directors

CDDA 1986: e.g. fraudulent trading, conviction of an indictable offence, bankruptcy.

22

Daily management of the company

Retirement

Articles indicate length of service.

Removal by resolution of the shareholders

Ill health.

Failure to attend board meetings.

Quiz 21

1 Bombazine was approached by Linen, a director of Textiles plc, and asked to supply catering services for Textiles' hundredth anniversary party. She incurred costs in preparing for the event, but has now been told that Linen had acted without the authority of the board of directors who had vetoed his proposal. What are her rights?

2 Textiles plc is having severe financial problems. What duties does it owe to:

(a) its creditors?

(b) its employees?

3 Textiles' board has proposed that the company will employ Threads Ltd to carry out an efficiency study. The principal shareholder and managing director of Threads is Taffeta; she is married to Cotton, a director of Textiles plc. Cotton fails to mention the connection. What is the legal situation?

4 What is the legal position of the following Textiles directors?

(a) Tweed, who has gone bankrupt.

(b) Denim, who has not attended a board meeting all year.

(c) Twist, who was so consumed with worry over Textiles' affairs that he has become clinically depressed, refuses to communicate in any way with any of his fellow directors and sits silently weeping during board meetings.

Answers to all quizzes can be found in Appendix 2.

Take a closer look

The following cases provide important examples of how the law you have studied in this chapter has developed. They are primary sources illustrating the law in action and give you more detail about their facts, as well as helping you to understand the law and to appreciate how the judges reached their decisions.

Try looking them up in the law reports or accessing them via a database, e.g. Bailli (www.bailii.org/databases.html). LexisNexis or Westlaw may be available in your university or college library, or you may find extracts in a case book. (See Appendix 1: Additional resources.)

Caparo Industries plc v *Dickman* [1990] 1 All ER 568

Guinness plc v *Saunders* [1990] 2 AC 663

IDC v *Cooley* [1972] 1 WLR 443

Panorama Developments v *Fidelis Furnishing Fabrics Ltd* [1971] 3 WLR 440, CA

Web activity

Please go to: www.iod.com

Find out what resources the Institute of Directors provides for its members.

Assignment 20

'The changes to directors' duties under the Companies Act 2006 will in practice make little difference to corporate governance.'

Discuss.

CHAPTER 23

Company meetings and shareholder participation

Introduction

This chapter is primarily concerned with the interaction of the company with its shareholders at meetings. The day-to-day management of the company is in the hands of the directors and usually there is little that the shareholders can do to influence this. However, the directors are accountable to the shareholders. The CA 2006 requires every public company to hold an annual general meeting to which shareholders must be invited to get an overview of the company's progress in the previous year. A general meeting may have to be called if business has arisen that is too urgent to wait until the AGM. Occasionally shareholders may call such a meeting. At meetings share-holders generally are entitled to speak and vote on resolutions presented to them by the board. In certain circumstances they may be able to present a resolution themselves to get a matter aired when the directors may be reluctant to do so.

The CA 2006 contains some measures that may be taken by minority shareholders who are concerned that the directors are in breach of their duties and all other measures to control them have failed. We shall examine these at the end of the chapter.

Learning objectives

When you have studied this chapter you should be able to:

▶ know when and how a general meeting of a company must be called;

▶ describe the conduct of a general meeting;

▶ distinguish between the different types of resolution which may be passed by company members;

▶ assess how far the law protects the rights of minority shareholders.

General meetings

The annual general meeting (AGM)

Annual general meeting: yearly meeting of company to which all members are invited.

Resolution: a proposal to be voted upon by members.

The purpose of the **annual general meeting** is to allow the shareholders to question the directors about the annual report, to vote on any **resolutions** put before the meeting and to elect new directors.

Every public company must hold its annual general meeting (s 336) within six months of its accounting reference date (the end of its financial year). This is to help the shareholders to make the directors account for any problem showing up in the annual accounts and auditor's report. Twenty-one days' notice must be given.

A private company no longer needs to hold an AGM. This takes into account the 'think small' philosophy of the reforms which preceded the CA 2006. Large numbers of private companies are small businesses maybe consisting of only one, or at the most a few, members working together on a daily basis. An AGM for such companies is clearly redundant. Where a private company chooses to hold an AGM it is obliged to give 14 days' notice (s 307).

Additional general meetings may be called

General meeting: meeting to which all members are invited.

It may be necessary to call a **general meeting** if something occurs which is so urgent that it cannot wait until the next annual general meeting. The CA 1985 described this as an 'extraordinary general meeting' but this concept no longer exists under the CA 2006. The directors' powers to call a general meeting are stated in the articles, but a duty is imposed by law in certain situations. Unless otherwise stated, 14 days' notice is required.

The CA 2006 requires a general meeting to be called in the following circumstances.

Serious reduction of capital

A director of a public company must call a meeting within 28 days of discovering that the company has suffered a serious loss of capital (s 656). A serious loss occurs where the company's net assets amount to half or less of its share capital. The meeting must be held within 56 days of notice being given.

The members requisition a meeting

The directors must call a general meeting if required to do so by members who hold at least five per cent of the paid-up share capital (s 303). Notice of the requisition, explaining why the meeting is needed, must be delivered to the company's registered office. It must be signed by the relevant shareholders. Within 21 days of the delivery, the directors must issue notice of the meeting. This must take place no later than 28 days after the date of issue of the notice.

Meeting by order of the court

A director or shareholder may ask the court to order that a meeting be convened with a specified agenda and a quorum of one when it is impracticable to call a meeting in the usual way or to conduct the meeting as prescribed by the Act or the company's articles (s 306). This is intended to resolve deadlock in a two-person company.

Requisition by retiring auditors

An auditor who has retired because of concerns about the financial management of the company may requisition a meeting to allow the members to consider the reasons for the auditor's resignation (s 518).

Rules concerning meetings

Notice of meetings

The length of notice

This varies according to the type of meeting and the nature of the business to be transacted. It may be reduced by agreement of the shareholders. An AGM of a public company generally requires 21 days' notice, but 14 days is sufficient for that of a private company (s 307).

Any other general meeting requires only 14 days' notice.

These notice periods may be reduced subject to agreement from the majority of the shareholders holding 5 per cent of the shares. The majority required is 95 per cent of the shareholders in a public company and 90 to 95 per cent in a private company (or as prescribed in a private company's articles). If a company does not have shares, members holding at least 95 per cent of the voting rights must agree (s 307).

How notice may be given: s 308

Notice may be given in the following manner:

- hard copy;
- email;
- company website; or
- by a combination of any of those means.

Electronic and website communication are changes introduced by the CA 2006. Since every member must be given notice (s 310) electronic means or a website notice alone would only be appropriate if all members have the relevant facilities. In practice, hard copy is likely to remain the most reliable method of communication in a company of any size.

Contents of the notice: s 311

The notice must contain the following information:

- the date, time and place of the meeting;
- the general nature of the business of the meeting (agenda).

Conduct of the meeting

Chairing the meeting

The articles usually specify who is to take the chair. If they do not, or if that person is not present, any nominated member may be chair. Usually this will be a director. The duty of the person in the chair is to run the meeting, but the permission of members must be sought before adjourning the meeting unless it becomes disorderly.

Quorum

Quorum: the minimum number of members required to be present before a meeting can take place/ continue.

The **quorum** is the minimum number of people who must be present to enable the business of a meeting to be legitimately transacted. This is usually specified in the articles; if not, two people are sufficient or one if the company has sole membership (s 318).

The meeting cannot take place if it is not quorate within 30 minutes of its starting time. If during the course of the meeting numbers drop below the required minimum, the meeting must be adjourned.

Resolutions

These are the proposals on which members may vote. Information regarding them may be circulated by email as well as hard copy since the CA 2006.

There are three categories of resolution:

Ordinary resolution: requires a simple majority.

1 *Ordinary resolution.* An **ordinary resolution** requires only a simple majority of members who vote to support it. This type of resolution is required, for example, to increase share capital or to remove a director.

2 *Special resolution.* A 75 per cent majority of members present and voting is necessary for a **special resolution** to be successful. This is required to make any change to the articles or to re-register a private company as a public one. Twenty-one days' notice is required though the Articles may specify 28 days.

Special resolution: requires a 75 per cent majority.

Resolutions requiring special notice

The following resolutions cannot be put before the meeting unless the company received **special notice** of them at least 28 days before the date of the meeting:

Special notice: 28 days' notice, which is required when certain types of resolution are to be voted on.

1 a resolution for the removal of an auditor or to appoint a new one (s 510, s 515);

2 a resolution to remove a director (s 168).

When the company receives the special notice it must take the necessary steps to inform the members. Usually this accompanies notice of the meeting. Where a director or an auditor is threatened with removal, he or she must be sent a copy of the special notice and is entitled to defend him- or herself by circulating a written statement to members and to address the meeting.

Avoid confusion! A special notice is notice which must be given to the company, not to the members. A special notice has nothing to do with a special resolution. 'Special' in that context refers to the size of majority required for the resolution's success (75 per cent). Only an ordinary majority is necessary to remove a director or to appoint/remove an auditor.

Passing written resolutions

The CA 2006 distinguishes between private and public companies with regard to the passing of resolutions. Private companies may now pass most resolutions in writing while a public company can *only* pass a resolution at a general meeting (s 281). This reform is aimed at simplifying business for small companies, by reflecting their practical needs which may not involve meetings as such. A written record of decisions is all that is generally required. However, a **written resolution** is not sufficient to remove a director or auditor before the end of their term of service (s 288(2)).

Written resolution: a written proposal to which members of a private company agree by signing it rather than voting at a general meeting.

Written resolutions proposed by the directors must be circulated in advance to all members (s 291). Members may propose and circulate a written resolution provided those representing at least 5 per cent of the total voting rights (or any smaller percentage specified in the articles) request this (s 292). It may be accompanied by a 1,000-word explanatory statement. The members are responsible for the circulation costs unless excused by the company.

A written resolution is passed if the appropriate majority of company members communicate their agreement to it in writing within the appropriate time limits.

Passing resolutions at a general meeting

This is the only way a public company may pass a resolution. A resolution at a meeting is passed provided notice of the meeting and resolution was given to members and the meeting and voting were appropriately conducted (s 301).

Resolutions are often proposed by directors but a group of shareholders may do so too.

Section 338 enables shareholders of a public company to propose a resolution for an annual general meeting. The company must circulate the proposed resolution to all members if sponsored by at least 5 per cent of the total members with relevant voting rights, *or* by at least 100 members holding shares on which they have paid up at least £100 on average per member. While such motions are not necessarily successful, they do allow discussion to be opened up publically with the board and sometimes to get wider publicity for the issue.

Resolutions may be amended at the meeting provided that this does not take them out of the scope of the notified business.

Voting at meetings

This may be by show of hands or by poll. A show of hands does not take into account the possible variation in voting strength of members specified in the articles.

Shareholders may register disapproval of company policy by voting against resolutions put forward by the board. Even though they may not succeed in defeating a resolution, a substantial minority vote will indicate significant objection and send a clear warning message to the board as well as attracting adverse publicity for the company.

In the news

Shareholder revolt

Since the end of the twentieth century a trend has developed for the UK's shareholders to become more militant by voting in substantial numbers against company proposals at the AGM. The main bone of contention has been remuneration packages for directors and chief executives. Substantial numbers of shareholders have voted against these on the grounds that they are disproportionately high in the context of the performance of the company and the record of the CEO or other office holder.

The biggest revolt so far was at the Royal Bank of Scotland in 2009, when there was a 90 per cent vote against a very generous pension award to Sir Fred Goodwin, seen by many as the author of the near collapse of the bank, which led to its rescue by the taxpayer.

In 2012, shareholders voted down awards in six companies. At the advertising agency WPP close to 60 per cent voted against a proposed pay award for the chief executive.

In 2013, shareholders scored a notable win against the oil exploration company Afren when 80 per cent voted against a £3.4 million pay rise for the CEO. Other substantial though less successful objections were raised including a vote of 36 per cent at Immarsat, a telecommunications company, against the size of remuneration packages. This trend continued in 2014 when WPP was back in the firing line, while Standard Charter's board was given pause for thought in the face of its narrow win over a 50 per cent vote against its pay policies.

At the time of writing in 2015 the climate continues stormy for some boards. In the face of a likely defeat at its AGM, Aviva decided to reduce its proposals to award shares to its CEO which could have taken his 2015 earnings to £6.7 million.

While there have not been many outright wins by shareholders, such protest hopefully helps to keep companies aware that their shareholders are watching pay awards and other company policies critically.

Sources: Widely reported in the business media, including www.bbc.co.uk 2/05/12, www.guardian.co.uk 2/04/13, 11/06/2013 and 18/04/13; *Daily Telegraph* 9/04/13; www.guardian.co.uk 10/06/14 and thisis money.co.uk 31/5/2015.

23

Company meetings and shareholder participation

Proxy:
a person voting on behalf of a member at a general meeting.

Proxies may be appointed by any shareholder to vote in their place on their instructions. The articles may exclude the use of a poll to select the chair or adjourn a meeting. Otherwise, voting must be conducted by poll on the request of:

1 a minimum of five persons (proxies included); or

2 a member or members holding at least one-tenth of the voting rights; or

3 a member or members holding shares to the value of at least one-tenth of the paid-up capital.

Protecting the rights of minority shareholders

The decisions of the directors may successfully be challenged by a majority of shareholders who disagree with their proposals. Problems may arise if the directors are also the majority shareholders, since this permits them to make decisions with which the minority disagree.

Shareholders may be able to bring a **derivative action** to protect the company.

Derivative action:
claim by minority shareholders to protect the company's interests from being harmed by mismanagement by directors.

The common law approach: the rule in *Foss* v *Harbottle*

The courts were generally reluctant to assist a minority of shareholders even where damage to the company's interests was alleged. The rule in *Foss* v *Harbottle* stated that, since only the damaged party can sue, the individual shareholder has no right to sue on the company's behalf, and that the court should not interfere with the internal management of a company acting *intra vires*. Three exceptions were acknowledged permitting an individual shareholder with permission from the court to intervene if:

1 the directors made an illegal or *ultra vires* decision;

2 the directors acted fraudulently;

3 the directors disregarded the procedures laid down in the articles.

The Law Commission's report of 1998 (*Shareholder Remedies* (Law Com. No. 246)) criticised this rule as being 'complicated and unwieldy' and commented that there were situations that fell outside the scope of fraud where nonetheless protection should be offered to shareholders. Reform has now been implemented by the CA 2006.

Statutory protection of minority rights

The CA 2006, s 260(1) in effect abolishes the rule in *Foss* v *Harbottle*. It states that, a derivative action may be brought by a member of a company using only the procedures specified by the Act.

There are two of these:

1   proceedings under Chapter 11 of the CA 2006, ss 260–264, which is new;

2   proceedings under s 994, which replaces s 459 of the CA 1985.

Chapter 11 proceedings

Section 260 states that a member may issue a claim against a director regarding an 'actual or proposed act or omission involving negligence, default, breach of duty or breach of trust by a director'. The inclusion of negligence expands the grounds on which action can be taken as compared with those which could have been taken at common law.

A two-stage procedure must be negotiated before a claim will actually be heard (s 261):

● *Stage 1*. The member must first apply to bring the claim (s 261). Unless there is prima facie evidence to support the claim it will be dismissed immediately. At this stage only the member's evidence is heard. Otherwise, the case proceeds to the next stage.

● *Stage 2*. The hearing: evidence from both sides is heard and the court comes to its decision.

Under s 262, a shareholder may request that a derivative action started by the company but stalled, be fully heard. If the court is satisfied by evidence from both sides then the claim will continue.

When deciding whether permission should be given, the court must take into account (s 263) whether the member is acting in good faith and whether the claim is really for the benefit of the company, rather than for the shareholder personally. A claim cannot continue if problematic conduct was authorised or subsequently ratified by the shareholders in accordance with required procedure. For example, s 239 requires that conduct by a director amounting to negligence, default, breach of duty or trust can be ratified by an ordinary resolution of the members of the company.

The CA 2006 has clarified the law in this area and potentially facilitated claims by shareholders. Concern has been voiced by some directors that they are now more vulnerable to claims due to the introduction of the new procedure (see directors' duties in Chapter 22) plus the many factors which must now be taken into account in taking duty-related decisions.

Worth thinking about?

Do you think the CA 2006 has got the balance of interests between directors and minority shareholders right? How does the CA 2006, Chapter 11 protect directors?

Suggested solutions can be found in Appendix 2.

Shareholder rights to petition the court on the grounds of unfair prejudice: s 994

This section is transferred unchanged from the CA 1985.

Unfair prejudice is a broad principle; it may exist even where the directors did not act intentionally or in bad faith, but a decision unfairly militates against the interests of a minority of shareholders.

In order to take action under s 994:

1 the petitioner must be a member of the company;

2 the petitioner must have evidence that the company's affairs have previously been carried on in a way that is unfairly prejudicial to the interests of members, or at least to himself; or

3 the petitioner must have evidence that a proposed act or omission of the company would be similarly unfairly prejudicial (as in 2 above).

Whether or not unfairly prejudicial behaviour has actually occurred is a matter for the court to decide on the particular facts of each individual case. It may exist without the directors being negligent or acting in bad faith.

Petitioners may succeed even though not entirely without spot or sin themselves; but the morality of their behaviour is relevant to judging whether they have been unfairly treated.

Petitions have most commonly been sought on the following grounds:

- exclusion of the petitioner from the management of a small private company where the members are also directors and it is easy to vote someone off the board;
- failure to lay accounts before members;
- reduction in voting power;
- insufficient information and advice about a proposed takeover bid.

Under s 996, when a petitioner is successful, the court may make any appropriate order to give relief. This might include:

1 regulation of, or restrictions on, those eligible to manage the company;

2 an order requiring the company to purchase shares from a minority shareholder;

3 amendment of the company's articles, which can then be changed only with permission from the court.

Unfair prejudice: running the company in any way which unfairly affects the interests of a minority of shareholders.

23

Company meetings and shareholder participation

The following case provides a useful example of the use of s 994.

Kohli v *Lit and Others* (2009)

Mrs Kohli was a minority shareholder in Sunrise Radio. She applied to the court for an order requiring the directors, who were majority shareholders, to buy her shareholding because their behaviour had allegedly been unfairly prejudicial to her under the Companies Act 2006, s 994.

The defendant directors had:

1 Issued shares for a nominal price to a company in which one director had an interest.

2 Failed to disclose their remuneration when compiling the company accounts.

3 Been late in filing the accounts and company return.

4 Failed to get the agreement of shareholders before selling company property to one of the directors.

Held: the discounted shares sale was a breach of fiduciary duty; the defendants had not obtained the true and higher price of the shares and thus failed to promote the interests of the company or its shareholders.

Although the failure to disclose remuneration was unintentional, it was 'improper accounting', which might well destroy Ms Kohli's faith in the integrity of the board, making it unlikely that she would ever trust it again. The accounts, albeit prepared by accountants, remained the responsibility of the board.

Occurrences 2, 3 and 4 taken together clearly evidenced unfair prejudice and made it reasonable for Ms Kohli to feel that it was intolerable to continue as a shareholder in Sunrise.

The company must purchase her shares without a discount.

Such orders have been used successfully by minority shareholders of small private companies, but the procedure is less likely to be helpful to shareholders in large public companies who, in practice, are likely to remain largely powerless.

Shareholders' powers to initiate intervention by the Department for Business, Innovation and Skills

Where serious abuse of corporate powers is suspected, the shareholders may be able to instigate an inquiry by the Department for Business, Innovation and Skills inspectors. The relevant statutory provisions (which were *not* repealed by the CA 2006) are as follows:

1 under the CA 1985, s 431, a minority of at least 200 shareholders, or those holding at least one-tenth of the issued shares, may apply to the Secretary of State for an investigation to be carried out;

2 under the CA 1985, s 432, the Secretary of State may initiate an investigation in any circumstances suggesting that the company's members have not been kept appropriately informed, where there is evidence of fraud, unlawful behaviour by the company or misfeasance or misconduct towards members.

The Companies (Audit, Investigations and Community Enterprise) Act 2004, ss 21–24 give the Secretary of State considerable investigatory powers regarding production of documents, disclosure in a formal inquiry and the power to enter/remain on premises.

The following consequences may result from an investigation:

1 Under the Insolvency Act 1986, s 124A the Secretary of State may, if justified by the results of an investigation, petition for the company to be wound up on the grounds that it is just and equitable for this to happen.

2 Under the CA 2006, s 995 the Secretary of State may, if satisfied by an inspector's report that there is evidence of unfair prejudice to shareholders, petition the court for an order under s 994, in addition to/instead of an order to wind up the company.

Real life

Horace is a shareholder in Smallville Wanderers plc and was recently summoned to a general meeting to vote on a resolution to remove Cecil, a director, from office for malpractice. Unfortunately, Cecil used his influence to gather support from sufficient shareholders to defeat the motion.

However, the shareholders who had been responsible for raising concerns about Cecil's conduct refused to be beaten and are taking advice. Chapter 11 proceedings might provide the answer. Permission to bring and continue the claim would be very likely to be given since there was no shortage of prima facie evidence. The shareholders seem to be acting in the interests of the company. Behaviour like Cecil's was likely to have brought his company into disrepute and undoubtedly attracted undesirable publicity. This was evident from reports published in the *Smallville Bugle* and subsequently in the business and sports sections of some national papers. However, the claim will not be allowed to proceed if the directors have ratified Cecil's conduct. Given that he survived the resolution to remove him, it looks as if a resolution to ratify his conduct would probably also succeed.

If sufficient shareholder support is forthcoming, they could ask the Department for Business, Innovation and Skills to carry out an investigation. This might result in the company being wound up.

Chapter summary

General meetings

Company members are invited to these to debate and vote upon resolutions which have been circulated in advance.

A public company must hold an AGM. Other general meetings may be called where there is urgent business that shareholders need to vote upon. All resolutions must be passed at a general meeting.

Private companies are largely free of any duty under CA 2006 to hold general meetings of any kind and may pass written resolutions instead.

Notice of meetings

AGM of public company: 21 days.

AGM of private company: 14 days.

Other general meetings: 14 days.

CA 2006 has added email and company website as means by which notice and other company communications may be circulated to members.

Quorum

A meeting must have a minimum of at least two members present (one if company has only one member) before official business can be effectively transacted.

Voting on resolutions at the meeting

A resolution can be passed only by majority.

Some resolutions require special notice (28 days).

Ordinary resolutions: require only a simple majority and are used to transact most business.

Special resolutions: require a majority of 75 per cent and are needed to transact some business.

Proxies may be appointed by members to vote on their behalf and according to their instructions.

Written resolutions: are only effective if used by private companies. Certain business cannot be transacted this way, e.g. removing a director before his or her period of office expires.

Protecting interests of minority shareholders

Common law procedure:

Foss v *Harbottle* exceptions effectively abolished.

Three types of statutory procedure:

Under CA 2006

Chapter 11 proceedings: permission from the court required (a) to bring and (b) to continue a previously existing claim.

Section 994: unfair prejudice claims.

Under CA 1985

Department for Business, Innovation and Skills reform investigations.

Quiz 22

1 What is a general company meeting?

2 In what circumstances does the Companies Act 2006 require the directors of a company to call a general meeting?

3 Titan is an auditor of Atlantis plc who has just been sacked by Medusa the managing director. What procedures must be fulfilled before Medusa's order can become effective?

4 Consider the rights of the following shareholders in Vulcan Ltd:

(a) Brunhilde, who is unhappy about the company's decision to become a public company.

(b) Siegfried, who believes that the directors of Vulcan are trading fraudulently.

5 What is meant by a 'derivative' action by a shareholder?

Answers to all quizzes can be found in Appendix 2.

Web activity

Please go to: www.rbosaction.org/home

to explore the website of a group representing shareholders in the Royal Bank of Scotland, who are taking legal action against directors at the bank who allegedly misrepresented the bank's trading potential in the prospectus for a rights issue in 2008. The group claims that as a result shareholders lost money because they bought shares at an inflated price. Trial is now scheduled for 2016.

Assignment 21

'Despite recent changes to the law, the minority interests of shareholders are still largely unprotected.'

Discuss.

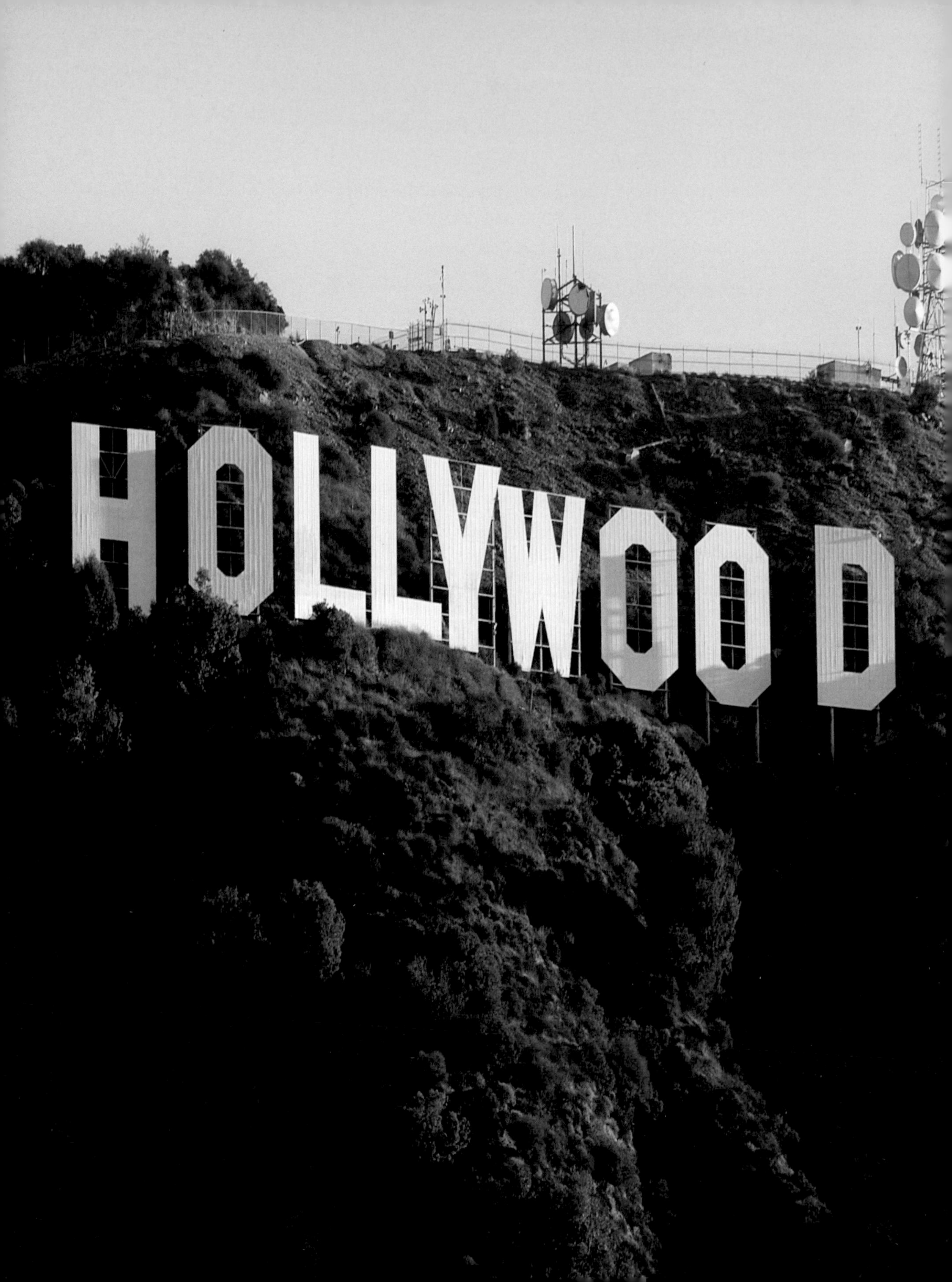
HOLLYWOOD

PART 6

General principles of intellectual property law

CHAPTER 24

Statutory intellectual property protection
Copyright, designs, patents and trade marks

Introduction

The law gives rights not only in relation to tangible property, i.e. goods capable of physical control like a car, but also in relation to the ownership of the intangible fruits of your labours arising from the use of mental as opposed to physical energy. This is called *intellectual property* and enjoys both statutory and common law protection.

Mental effort is obvious in the creation of a book, film, piece of music or the invention of a 100 per cent efficient mousetrap. It is just as important in developing a successful business through original marketing strategy, or a novel way of packaging or labelling your goods. This chapter explains statutory intellectual property rights including copyright, patents and registered trade marks.

Learning objectives

When you have studied this chapter you should be able to:

▶ appreciate the nature of the different types of intellectual property protected by statute;

▶ describe the scope of copyright protection;

▶ explain in outline the registration process for designs, patents and trade marks;

▶ be aware of the legal sanctions imposed for breach of statutory intellectual property rights.

Statutory regulation of intellectual property

Copyright

Copyright: protects ownership of original literary/ artistic/dramatic work recorded in any tangible form.

Copyright is regulated by the Copyright, Designs and Patents Act 1988 (CDPA 1988). The scope of copyright is very wide and includes (s 1):

- original literary, dramatic, musical and artistic works;
- sound recordings, films, TV and radio broadcasts and cable programmes;
- typographical arrangements of published works.

These terms have been defined in the Act or by the courts.

1 *Original: s 2.* This means 'not copied' rather than 'unique'. The issue of originality concerns the way an idea is expressed rather than the idea itself. It is also measured by the amount of independent work and effort which it required. A famous person may be the subject of a number of biographies. Information conveyed in the first biography does not become the exclusive property of the author and may well appear in subsequent works by different authors. The original author has rights to the 'copy' (the form of words or other form of expression used), not to the information which was conveyed. Commonly available knowledge may be 'original' because of its form of presentation. For example, in *McMillan & Co.* v *Cooper* (1923) a street directory was held to be original for copyright purposes.

2 *Literary: s 3.* This is not nearly as grand as it sounds and includes anything written, spoken or sung (other than a dramatic or musical work) if recorded in some tangible form. It covers tables, compilations and computer programs and their preparatory designs. Writing of any sort, including letters, lists of customers, reports and business plans may, therefore, attract copyright. To a limited extent copyright therefore protects privacy.

Prince Charles successfully used copyright to restrain publication of private journals in which he had recorded personal views and impressions during overseas tours (*HRH Prince of Wales* v *Associated Newspapers Ltd* (2007)).

3 *Artistic: s 4.* Again, the scope is wide. As well as covering works of 'artistic craftsmanship', like sculpture and paintings, textile patterns and clothing designs, it includes more prosaic items.

Charts, maps, plans, graphs and diagrams may also be protected. It also covers buildings and models for buildings.

In *Lucasfilm* v *Ainsworth* (2011), the Supreme Court held that the defendant, who was the designer of the Imperial Storm trooper helmet for one of the films had not breached Lucasfilm's copyright by marketing helmets to the public. They were not items of sculpture as Lucasfilm claimed but merely utilitarian items incidental to the production of the film.

To attract copyright the item must be more than a scheme or idea existing in the mind of the creator; it must be in a *tangible form* like a book, film, audio tape or a piece of writing, or a musical notation. If you tell somebody your scheme for a business plan or

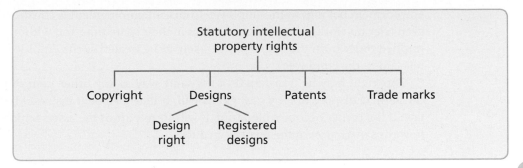

Figure 24.1

sing them your jingle before it is written down, they may possibly be liable for breach of confidence (see Chapter 25) if they steal your idea, but not for infringement of copyright.

Performers enjoy similar rights to copyright owners in relation to their work, under Part II of the Act. A bootleg recording at a pop concert would involve breach of copyright in the songs and breach of the performance rights of the members of the band.

Acquisition of copyright: ss 154–158

No formal process exists. Copyright is automatically acquired provided that the qualification criteria laid down in the CDPA 1988 are fulfilled.

A work will attract copyright if there is sufficient connection between it and the UK It is sufficient that the author has British citizenship, or is domiciled or resident in the UK, or if the work is first published in the UK Copyright also applies to works created or published in other countries to which the Act applies. This covers foreign states with which Britain has reciprocal copyright links.

The duration of copyright: ss 12–15

How long the copyright period lasts depends on the type of work. Literary, dramatic, musical or artistic works enjoy copyright for 70 years from the end of the calendar year in which the author dies. Films are protected for 70 years from the end of the calendar year in which the last of the following die – director, writer, musical composer. Broadcasts and cable programmes enjoy copyright for 50 years from the first broadcast. Copyright in sound recordings lasts 70 years from the end of the calendar year in which they were released.

Crown copyright: s 163

The copyright in works created by civil servants and other Crown employees belongs to the Crown and lasts for up to 125 years.

The ownership of copyright: ss 9–11

The author (creator) of the relevant work is also generally the owner of the copyright. However, the copyright in any work created by an employee in the course of employment belongs to the employer. Course of employment is construed widely, and even relevant works created by employees in their spare time and without an express or implied order from the employer are likely to be treated as the employer's property, if relevant to the employee's job.

Copyright may be transferred in the same way as any other item of property. The owner may dispose of it by sale, gift or will. It may also be transferred by operation of law: if the owner becomes bankrupt, it will form part of the assets which may be sold towards satisfaction of the owner's creditors.

The rights of commissioners of photographs and films: s 85

This is relevant to anybody running a photography or video-making business. The photographer or film maker is owner of the copyright in the photograph or film, but the party who commissioned it has the right to prevent its publication without that party's consent. This only protects commissions for domestic use. In *Williams* v *Settle* (1960) wedding photographs commissioned by the claimant included pictures of her father. He was subsequently murdered and the defendant photographer sold copies of the photographs to the press. It was held that this was a breach of the claimant's moral rights since she had not given permission for sale of the photographs which she had commissioned.

A person who is the subject of an unsolicited photograph (for example, by a street photographer) has no moral rights under the Act since the work was not commissioned.

Worth thinking about?

Do you have any rights in law if an unsolicited photograph is taken of you?

Suggested solutions can be found in Appendix 2.

The rights of the copyright owner

Copyright owners have exclusive rights to copy, adapt or present the work publicly.

Infringement of copyright

Any exercise of the owner's exclusive rights by a third party without lawful authority is a *direct infringement* (ss 17–21). It is irrelevant that it is being done for private use and that no profit is being made. Not surprisingly, thousands of such infringements take place every day as many people copy CDs or 'pirate' their friends' computer software. It is highly unlikely that any action will be taken against them. However, where copyright materials are being used in public places greater caution is required: for example, where a business uses background music to soothe (or irritate) its customers.

Secondary infringement (ss 22–26) occurs if the copyright is exploited commercially, and includes importation or sale of infringing items.

The CDPA 1988 provides some limited defences (ss 29–40). Where these apply, use of copyright material will not amount to an infringement: for example, making a copy for research or private study, limited use of quotations for the purpose of critical review or inclusion in a current affairs programme. Libraries and educational institutions also enjoy some limited protection. A new defence was introduced by the Copyright and Rights in Performances (Quotation and Parody) Regulations 2014/2356 to cover parodies and pastiches of existing copyright protected works.

Licensing

The copyright owner, or a collecting organisation like the Performing Rights Society, may grant permission to do something which would otherwise be an infringement. The licensee may be required to pay royalties for this privilege. A business wishing to use background music on disc or tape should apply to the Performing Rights Society for a licence.

If owners of copyright unreasonably refuse licences, they may be ordered compulsorily to grant them by the Secretary of State: for example, on the recommendation of the Competition Commission (s 144) where the public interest is prejudiced.

Sanctions

Breach of copyright entitles the owner to take civil action (s 96). Some forms of secondary infringement (including those mentioned above) also give rise to criminal liability (s 107) provided the defendant should reasonably have known that copyright existed.

Rights in performances and recordings

A composer of a piece of music is protected by copyright as explained above. Part II of the CDPA 1988 and the Copyright and Related Rights Regulations 1996 similarly protect the rights of performers and recording companies. Bootleg audio or video recordings of, for example, a rock concert will therefore breach the performers' rights as well as those of a company legitimately recording the event. Breaches also arise from the illicit copying of existing recordings.

Copyright and internet users

Everybody who accesses the internet should be aware of the copyright implications. If you download or reproduce materials you find on a website, you may be infringing the copyright of the author, or the performance or recording rights of other people. If you are the proprietor of a website, you will have copyright in the design of the website and materials on it, provided that these are your own original work, but you may be infringing the rights of others if you reproduce their materials on your site without a licence. Internet service providers may also be infringing copyright if they are unable to show that they took reasonable steps to monitor the contents of the websites which they facilitate.

European Community Directive (2001/29/EC) was implemented in the UK through the Copyright and Related Rights Regulations 2003. Their purpose is to harmonise the basic rights of authors of materials transmitted through e-commerce and the information society. The details of these regulations are outside the compass of this text.

Protection for design owners: the design right and registered designs

Design right: protects ownership of an original design for a three-dimensional functional item excluding surface decoration.

The **design right** (governed by Part III of the CDPA 1988) attaches *automatically* to any sufficiently *original* design of three dimensional objects, and gives similar protection to copyright. An *inventive* design may also be registered under the Registered Designs Act 1949. The registered owner obtains a monopoly on the design similar to a patent.

The design right

The author of a design acquires copyright of that design, but that gives protection only against infringements of the copy (wrongful copying and publication). Ownership of the design right enables the owner to control the use of the design for manufacturing purposes. Nobody else may make items to that design without the owner's consent.

The design right protects a huge variety of items. Some qualify for registration under the Registered Designs Act 1949 (see below). Others might qualify for copyright protection as works of artistic craftsmanship. Where these other rights exist the design owner may rely upon them rather than on the more limited design right.

The implicit intention of the Act is to ensure a limited protection for owners of sufficiently original designs for items capable of mass production. Such items are often functional, not necessarily visually attractive, and include a multitude of items in everyday use. The limits to design right protection are intended to prevent undesirable restraint on industrial development. Some areas of industrial design are very fast moving, but would be frozen in a time warp if adaptations were an infringement of an existing design right. Also it is unfair to restrict other designers unreasonably in the exercise of their creative skill.

Section 213(2) of the CDPA 1988 defines 'design' as: 'the design of any aspect of the shape or configuration (whether internal or external) of the whole or part of an article.' Only designs for *three-dimensional articles* are covered. Therefore, designs for surface decoration are not protected by the design right but may be protected by copyright. The design *must be original*. Original is described as 'not commonplace' in the relevant design field at the time of creation (s 213(4)). This is interpreted much more stringently than the originality test for copyright, but the design need not be unique.

The right does not exist unless and until it has been recorded in a design document, or an article has been made to the design (s 213(6)). Like the law of copyright, it does not protect ideas. The design may be computer generated.

The person who creates the design is first owner provided that the design was not created in the course of employment or in carrying out a commission (s 215). If it was, the employer or commissioner will be first owner.

The right lasts for a maximum of 15 years from the end of the year when the design was created in tangible form. If goods made to the design are marketed within five years of the year of creation, however, the design right will last for only 10 years from the marketing date (s 216).

The design right is acquired in the same way as copyright (ss 217–220). It is part of the owner's personal property and may be sold, given away, or disposed of by will or by operation of law (s 222). The owner has exclusive rights to exploit the design for commercial purposes, either by reproducing the design document or by making articles to the design (s 226).

The provisions of ss 226–227 concerning infringements mirror those explained above in relation to copyright. Infringement gives rise to civil liability only (s 229) and the remedies are the same as those of a copyright owner.

Licences may be granted by the owner to third parties enabling them to exercise any of the exclusive rights to exploit the design (s 222). During the last five years of the right, anybody is entitled to a licence (s 237). Licences may be compulsorily ordered if it is in the public interest to prevent unreasonable restriction of competition (s 238). The Crown may, without a licence, use the design to supply articles for the use of the defence and health services. Compensation for loss of profit may be paid (ss 240, 243).

The community design right

Since 2002 designers in the UK have a two-year right to protection throughout the EU and this covers two- and three-dimensional designs.

Registered designs

Some designs may qualify to be registered under the Registered Designs Act 1949 (RDA 1949) as amended by the Registered Designs Regulations 2001, Registered Designs (Amendment) Rules 2001 and the Registered Designs (Fees) Amendment Rules 2001. This amending legislation was necessary to implement the Designs Directive (98/71/EC) which aims to harmonise registration requirements across the EC, in order to eradicate differences which may adversely affect trade. This legislation, implemented in December 2001, has extended the scope of the right and made the process more flexible.

The rights arising from a **registered design** relate to the appearance of the product, its shape and any patterns or design on it. Registered design is not concerned with its function, unlike a patent which is concerned with how a product works. In order to be registered the 'design' must relate to a 'product', which is 'new' and has 'individual character' as defined by the RDA 1949, s 1.

1 *Design.* This is the appearance of the whole or part of a product resulting from 'the lines, contours, colours, shape, texture or materials of the product or its ornamentation'. To be registered the design must therefore be visible to the user when the product is being used.

Registered design: protects ownership of original design of three-dimensional items with individual character and capable of being produced industrially or as a handicraft.

2 *Product*. This includes 'any industrial or handicraft item' except a computer program. It covers three-dimensional designs such as lamps, door furniture, water-filter jugs or one-dimensional designs such as patterns for wallpaper, floor covering, or clothing fabrics.

3 *New*. The design must differ materially from any existing 'publicly available' design. This is more generous to the designer than the old law, which required 'substantial' difference. 'Publicly available' means products being currently marketed as opposed to museum exhibits.

4 *Individual character*. The overall impression of the design on the user of the product must be different from that of any similar publicly available design. Under the old law 'eye appeal' was required which meant that the design had to be aesthetically pleasing. While this may be relevant to determining the existence of individual character, it is no longer essential. Designs for components of other products may be registered as long as they fulfil the above criteria.

Protection for spare parts remains very limited. The directive proved very contentious on this issue and member states were unable to agree on its operation. This part of the directive is suspended from operation currently, so the UK's existing law is retained. The design for a spare part must be for a product which is capable of standing alone. The product must not rely in its shape or configuration on another item. This is aimed at preventing unreasonable hindrance of development in the design field; it also prevents a designer of spare parts from acquiring a monopoly (*Ford Motor Co. Ltd and Iveco Fiat SpA's Design Application* (1993)). In *Ford Motor Co. Ltd*, designs for car doors, bonnets, boot lids and windscreens were held to be excluded.

The person who created the design is generally the owner, unless acting in the course of employment or carrying out a commission when ownership lies with the employer or commissioner respectively (s 2). Only the owner can apply for registration. UK citizenship or resident status is not necessary. Applications are filed with the United Kingdom Intellectual Property Office (UKIPO). The procedure is complex so the owner of the design may use the services of a design agent to prepare the application.

The registrar will register the design if searches indicate that the design is new, and the other statutory criteria are satisfied. Modifications may be required. Registration generally takes about six months. It must be completed within a maximum of 15 months from the time of application. A fee, currently £60, is payable for registration.

A design will initially be registered for five years, which runs from the date of registration. This may be renewed for up to five further five-year periods on application to the registrar with payment of further fees (s 8). Most designs become outdated within about six to ten years as fashions and technology change, making it unlikely that renewal applications will be made more than once.

The owner of a registered design has the *exclusive rights* of commercial exploitation of the design (s 7): this entitles the owner to manufacture, import, sell or hire items made to the design. Items made to the design should be appropriately marked with the number under which it is registered. This is a clear indication of registration. Failure to do so may provide an infringing party with the defence that they acted innocently without knowledge that the design was registered. These rights are infringed by anybody who exercises them without a licence granted by the owner. Civil proceedings may be taken by the owner. The Intellectual Property Act 2014 introduced criminal penalties similar to those for infringement copyright or trade marks for breaches of rights relating a registered design. The Act also set up an opinions service to provide expert advice to owners and others on whether infringement has taken place.

The owner may issue *licences* to use the registered design. To protect unreasonable restrictions on the development and exploitation of designs, the registrar has powers to grant *compulsory licences* (s 10) if, having registered the design, the owner fails to exploit it. The registrar may also be ordered to issue licences on the recommendation of the Monopolies and Mergers Commission, where the owner is unduly restricting the issue of licences (s 11A).

The Crown is given rights to use the registered design under Sch 1 to the Act. These are similar to those concerning the design right (see above).

It is a *criminal offence* to falsify the register (s 34) to register a design. Under s 35, it is also an offence to claim falsely that a design has been registered.

Registered community designs

A registration process enables design owners in EU countries to obtain protection in all member countries.

Patents

Patent: protects ownership of original invention of a product or process.

Patents are regulated by the Patents Act 1977 (PA 1977) as amended by the Patents Act 2004 (PA 2004). (All further references are to the PA 1977 unless the contrary is indicated.) The registration of a patent enables an inventor to obtain a monopoly over its exploitation. The invention may be a *device* (such as a mouse trap, an electric can-opener, or a solar-powered heating system) or a *process* (for example, making glass or waterproofing fabrics). The possibilities are manifold.

The criteria for registration of a patent are stringently interpreted (ss 1–4):

1 *The invention must be new*. It must not currently form part of the state of the art in the UK or elsewhere (s 2). This means in effect that only the inventor and close associates must know of it and the information must clearly be confidential. Publication of information in, for example, a trade or academic journal anywhere in the world may put the invention into the public domain. Similarly, if the invention is already in use industrially its novelty is lost. Once an unpatented invention becomes part of the state of the art, it enables other people to develop it; the public interest would not be well served by the grant of a patent, as this would put a stranglehold on technological development already initiated by others.

2 *It must be an inventive step*. This is defined as something which would not be 'obvious to a person skilled in the art'. It must involve originality of thought and represent a new development in the relevant industry. It may be something deceptively simple, but which solves a problem which has existed for some time. It might cause even a lay person to say 'Why didn't I think of that?', for example in *Parks-Cramer Co.* v *Thornton Ltd* (1966, CA).

The invention of an overhead vacuum cleaner with long vertical tubes reaching almost to the floor for cleaning narrow spaces between rows of fixed machinery was held to be original. It solved a problem which had vexed the textile industry for many years.

3 *It must be capable of industrial application.* The invention or process must be capable of being produced or used under industrial conditions, which includes agriculture. Plant and animal varieties cannot be patented nor can biological processes which could be used to produce plants or animals. Micro-biological processes and the products of these processes may be patented. This includes genetic engineering processes.

Some inventions will not be registered: for example, those encouraging 'offensive, immoral or anti-social behaviour'. Current taste dictates what is appropriate here, but presumably ingenious instruments of torture are excluded. Public policy also plays a part. The Patents Act 2004 s 1 states that a patent is not to be granted for the invention of a surgical or therapy process. Registration of such processes would not be in the public interest given the cost implications for the NHS.

Certain things are not 'inventions' for the purposes of the 1977 Act. These include some things like computer programs and literary works which are protected by copyright. Scientific discoveries and theories also do not qualify; they are not directly capable of industrial application.

Real life

Horace is a member of a small private company called Hamelin Ltd which sells a mouse trap which was invented and successfully patented by Cyril.

The mouse trap is very ingenious. It consists of a small plastic box which gives off an infra-red beam. If a mouse comes within the field of the beam this triggers a tiny disc player inside the box to play at mouse-ear frequency a little tune quite irresistible to mice. The creature is lured into the box, at which point a small but powerful hammer neatly disposes of it by a swift blow to the head. The mouse remains can later be removed hygienically in the replaceable lining of the trap.

With the help of a patents agent, Cyril was able to convince the Patents Registrar that this invention fulfilled the registration criteria. Fortunately, he acted swiftly and applied for the patent before publicly releasing any information about it or attempting to market it, so it is a *new* invention. It represents an *inventive step* as it is indeed an original concept in the vermin control trade. Finally, it is capable of mass production so is capable of *industrial application*.

The right to register a patent

The inventor is usually entitled to apply to patent the invention. This right is transferred to the employer, however, if the invention was created by an employee in the course of the employee's normal, or specially assigned, duties (s 39). Employers may try to protect themselves by putting a term in employment contracts claiming ownership of employees' inventions. This will not be applicable if an employee's duties do not involve potentially inventive activity. *Electrolux* v *Hudson* (1977) illustrates this well: Mr and Mrs Hudson invented an adaptor which allowed any brand of vacuum cleaner using disposable bags to be used with any brand of vacuum bags. Mr Hudson worked as a storekeeper for Electrolux, who tried to claim ownership. It was held that the invention belonged to Mr and Mrs Hudson and had been developed in their home. The nature of Mr Hudson's job did not cover such creative activity.

The inventor is entitled to be named in a patent application being made in some other person's name (usually an employer) (s 13).

If the patenting of the invention is of 'outstanding benefit' to the employer, the employee is entitled to be compensated by them (s 40). Section 10 of the PA 2004 extends the scope of compensation for employees. Before 2004, 'outstanding benefit' was only relevant to the patent itself, i.e. royalties from its being licensed, not the invention per se. A patent owner, however, may manufacture the invention itself and derive considerable profits. Under the PA 2004 these must be taken into account when computing the employee's compensation. The Comptroller of Patents or the court may order compensation if the employer does not voluntarily provide it.

Kelly and Another v *GE Healthcare* (2009)

Duncan Kelly and Ray Chiu, employees of GE Healthcare, were the co-inventors of a highly successful cardiac imaging agent that was patented by their employer. Marketed as Myoview, product sales are estimated at over £1.3 million, representing a hefty proportion of GE Healthcare's profits.

Held (Floyd J): that the invention was an 'outstanding benefit' to GE Healthcare, particularly as it had protected the firm against generic competition and enabled it to make highly profitable deals. 'The benefits went far beyond anything which one could normally expect to arise from the sort of work the employees were doing.' Dr Kelly and Dr Chiu were entitled to £1 million and £500,000 respectively, based on the value of the patent estimated at £50 million.

The registration process: ss 14–19

This is a lengthy and highly complex business. A patent agent is usually employed. The different stages of the process have to be completed within certain time limits. Unless these are adhered to and the necessary fees paid, the application will be rejected. Here is an overview of the process, which concentrates on key features:

1 *The application.* An application for a patent must be made to the UKIPO in the required form and must include a full description of the invention. This must convey sufficient information to enable a reasonably skilled person in the relevant field to make the item or to carry out the process. It will involve lengthy written instructions and any necessary drawings. The inventor must indicate the specific purposes which the invention is intended to fulfil. The claim must not be too wide or it will be rejected, or at least require amendment. Some devices and processes have a very wide field of potential application, but the patent when granted may not necessarily

cover them all. Some uses may not even exist yet as a twinkle in a technologist's eye, and it is not in the public interest to allow an inventor to monopolise their development.

2 *Search and publication.* Once the application has been received, initial checks and searches are carried out and the UKIO publishes the application in its journal. This has two consequences:

(a) the published invention is now part of the state of the art; subsequent applications for a similar patent may fail the novelty test. If the application fails it cannot be re-submitted;

(b) on registration the applicant will be entitled to take action for any infringements occurring after the publication date.

3 *Substantial examination and registration.* Full examination of the specification and claim now takes place. Final checks are made against searches and any other information received since the publication date. Further amendments may be required. Provided the invention still meets the registration criteria, the patent will be granted. Notice of this appears in the *Patents Journal.*

Duration of patents

Patent rights exist for up to 20 years. Renewal fees are payable.

Ownership rights

A patent is the personal property of the owner and can be disposed of by operation of law or in any way the owner chooses: for example, sale or will. It can also be security for a mortgage (s 30).

Infringement

Protection under the PA 1977 is very wide: a large number of activities carried on without the consent of the patent owner are actionable. Infringements include the manufacture of patented products and the use of patented processes; they also arise from import into the UK of such products manufactured in breach of a patent (s 60). The owner of the patent may take civil action against infringement.

Defences to infringement include non-commercial use of products or processes and scientific investigations for the purpose of testing them.

The Intellectual Property Act 2014 implemented proposals to expand the patents advisory service so that anyone can approach the Intellectual Property Office for advice about the validity or possible infringement of a patent. It is hoped that this will assist small businesses and encourage innovation, as well as preventing the necessity for expensive litigation.

Licensing

The owners of patents can grant licences to whomever they choose. The owner may request that the UKIPO indicates in the register that licences are available as of right (s 46), which could be a useful move if the owner has not been successful in marketing licences privately.

After three years the UKIPO may grant licences either if the patent is not being worked, or if demands for relevant products are not being met (s 48). Wide Crown exploitation of certain patents by government departments is permitted (s 55), in connection with defence, health and nuclear energy policies.

Criminal liability

Under ss 109–113, offences include falsification of the register and false claims that a patent exists or has been applied for.

The Intellectual Property Act 2014 required a Patents Opinion Service to be set up to advise patent owners on potential patent validity.

Trade marks

The purpose of trade marks

Trade mark: protects ownership of distinguishing marks used to advertise goods and services.

Trade marks are used as a marketing strategy to enable providers of goods or services to ensure that their products are immediately clearly recognisable by their potential customers. A competitor who markets a similar product in a similar way may be breaking the law. If the distinguishing feature has been registered as a trade mark under the Trade Marks Act 1994, the competitor may be sued for infringement. Registration creates rights of ownership in the mark which can then be disposed of in the same manner as any other personal property.

Not all distinguishing characteristics are registrable, but the tort of passing off may provide a remedy for the misuse of unregistered marks and other distinguishing features. (Passing off is covered in Chapter 25.)

The law relating to trade marks was updated and expanded by the Trade Marks Act 1994, which replaced the 1938 Act. The 1994 Act implements an EC directive aimed at harmonisation of trade mark law throughout the European Union.

The marks capable of registration

Section 1 of the Act defines a trade mark as any sign capable of being represented graphically which is capable of distinguishing the goods or services of one undertaking from another. 'Represented graphically' means capable of being represented in the form of pictures, words or numbers. This has greatly extended the scope of trade mark law. As well as designs, letters and numerals (which were all covered previously) it is now possible to register shapes of goods or their packaging (like the Coca-Cola bottle). Moving images clearly come within this definition, as do advertising jingles, and even perfumes since these can be graphically represented by their notation or chemical formulae, respectively.

A mark must be distinctive. It may be verbal or non-verbal in form. Verbal marks include the following:

1 *Names of people*. Names can be trademarked but will have to be represented in some way that makes them distinctive and immediately recognisable as that of one trader alone. This can be achieved by a signature (Walt Disney), or by a very distinctive style of lettering (McDonald's, Marks & Spencer). A business may prefer to trade under a made-up name (Kwikfit) to ensure a distinctive character.

2 *Names of products*. To prevent other businesses from being unreasonably restricted in the advertisement of their products, names will not be treated as distinctive if they relate to the character, quality, geographical origin, intended use or any other characteristics of the product. 'Wholemeal Flour' or 'Best Butter' could not be registered, but 'Floss Mill' and 'March Hare' would not offend. Invented words may well be distinctive for registration purposes: in themselves they convey no clear and ordinary meaning to the average person. 'Snickers' and 'Hovis', for example, without their associations with chocolate bars and bread, are completely meaningless. In this way monopolisation of the use of ordinary words is avoided.

Non-verbal marks include emblems, symbols and other pictorial representations, as well as combinations of letters or numbers. This enables eau de cologne to be marketed under the 4711 trade mark. Advertising jingles come within the definition, which also embraces distinctively shaped goods or packaging: for example, Jif lemons.

A mark will not be registered if it is insufficiently distinctive, against the public interest or public morality, or identical or too similar to an earlier trade mark.

1 *Insufficiently distinctive*. As determined by the above rules. Thus, in *Phillips Electronics NV* v *Remington Consumer Products* (1998) it was held that a drawing of one of the heads of a three-headed electric razor was not sufficiently distinctive, because it did not sufficiently identify the manufacturer but merely referred to the function of the goods.

A trade mark, therefore, must be sufficiently distinctive to enable the public clearly to identify the origin of the product and not confuse it with others. In *Interlego AG's Trademark Application* (1998) the court refused to register a Lego brick shape on the grounds that it was insufficiently distinctive.

2 *Against the public interest or morally offensive (s 3)*. These criteria are interpreted in the light of current taste and attitudes. 'Hookers' or 'Hustlers' condoms might prove problematic.

3 *Identical or too similar (s 5)*. Marks which are identical or very similar to an earlier trade mark and applied to the same or similar goods or services. In *Berlei (UK) Ltd* v *Bali Brassiere Co.* (1969) both parties manufactured brassieres and corsets. Berlei successfully claimed that the use of the name Bali would lead to confusion with its product.

Some emblems enjoy special protection. These can be used as a trade mark only with permission from the registrar (s 4). They include royal coats of arms, pictorial representations of members of the royal family, and any of the flags of the UK The use of any device or words suggesting that the product has been patronised or authorised by royalty is similarly protected.

The registration process

The applicant for registration must own the mark. There is no nationality or residence qualification. Application is made to the Trade Mark Registry. It must include a representation of the mark and state the product to which it may apply. A fee is payable (s 32). The registrar decides whether the mark is sufficiently distinctive and carries out any necessary searches (s 37). If the application is acceptable, the registrar must publish notice of the application to enable interested parties to raise objections (s 38). Provided no objections are sustained, the registrar will on payment of a fee register the trade mark (s 40), for use in relation to a particular class of goods or services.

Duration of protection

Registration lasts 10 years and renewal is possible every 10 years.

Infringements: s 10

Infringements may be committed only in the course of trade. They may arise from the wrongful application of an identical or similar mark in connection with identical or similar goods for which use of the mark is registered.

Phones 4u Ltd v *Phone4u.co.uk Internet Ltd* (2006, CA)

Phones 4U Ltd had a registered trade mark consisting of a red, white and blue logo including the words 'Phones 4U' in stylised form and had registered a domain name Phones4U.co.uk. It claimed that the defendant company had infringed its trade mark by registering and using the domain name phone4u.co.uk to sell mobile phones.

Held: no infringement had occurred. The defendant was merely a similar name in a form not identical to or sufficiently similar to the claimant's registered trade mark, which involved the use of specific colours.

The defendant in the above case was, however, guilty of passing off (see Chapter 25).
'Application' of the mark includes not only putting it on the product or its packing, but also offering products for sale under the sign, or using it on business papers or in advertising.

Cosmetic Warriors Ltd and Lush Ltd v *Amazon.co.uk Ltd* (2014, HC)

Amazon manipulated its search facility so that if anyone typed 'Lush' into Google it displayed a sponsored advertisement for Lush on the Amazon website. However, Amazon did not sell Lush products and nor did it openly state that it did not on its website. Lush alleged that Amazon infringed its trade mark rights in three ways:

1 Customers who continued the search on the Amazon site found some pages carrying the Lush trade mark, showing products which closely resembled some of Lush's products like soap bombs.
2 Other pages illustrated goods similar to Lush products but did not carry its trade mark.
3 People who typed 'lush' into the site search facility found a drop down menu displaying various goods resembling or equivalent to those from Lush.

Held: Claim (1) did infringe Lush's trade mark, since the average shopper who saw the trademarked page would expect to find Lush products on sale by Amazon at a discounted price.

Claim (2) did not infringe the trade mark because the average customer using the Google search would not expect an un-trademarked page to be displaying Lush's products.

Claim (3): the onsite drop down menu did breach the trade mark because the average consumer would believe that he or she was being led to goods specifically produced by Lush and there was no indication that real Lush products were not available through the site.

Therefore an implication that a product is connected to a trademarked product may be sufficient to constitute infringement.

Ate My Heart Inc v *Mind Candy Ltd* (2011)

Ate My Heart is Lady Gaga's company and owns the trade mark LADYGAGA. Mind Candy is an online computer game company which had created a number of characters which parodied real people. One of these was Lady Goo Goo, an animated cartoon baby who resembled Lady Gaga and sang one of her songs. The song was very successful on YouTube and Mind Candy wanted to promote it on iTunes.

Ate My Heart claimed breach of its trade mark and sought an interim injunction to prevent the song being promoted on YouTube and released through iTunes.

Held: Mind Candy had breached the trade mark and had diluted its effect. Evidence of comments made in blogs on the game and on YouTube showed that members of the public had been confused, as there was great similarity in appearance between Lady Gaga and Lady Goo Goo. Tags planted by Mind Candy relevant to Lady Gaga website tags prompted search engines to go to the YouTube listing of the Lady Goo Goo song. Searching for 'Lady Goo Goo' brought up the Lady Gaga trade mark, which gave the impression that Lady Gaga approved of this use of it. An injunction was granted to prevent the song and character of Lady Goo Goo being exploited via YouTube and iTunes, but its use in the computer game was allowed to continue.

Using the mark merely to identify the relevant goods in accordance with honest commercial or industrial practice is not an infringement. Provided that your business is selling or servicing a particular product, it is perfectly legal to use the name on your own advertising materials. Thus, Currys legally advertise that they stock Hotpoint and Hoover washing machines.

Licensing the use of trade marks

Only the owner may grant licences for use of the mark by others (s 29). The licence may impose restrictions on the range of products to which the mark may be applied, or the manner of its use, or the locality within which the licence may be exercised.

Assigning the right to use a trade mark

Like all other intellectual property, a trade mark is part of the proprietor's personal property. It is transferable by assignment (in writing), by will or by operation of law.

Remedies for infringement of statutory intellectual property rights

These are largely similar whichever type of intellectual property is involved.

Injunction

An injunction may be granted to prevent the commission or continuance of the infringement.

Damages

Damages may be awarded to compensate for consequential losses to the proprietor.

Account of profits

Any profit on the sale of relevant goods may be forfeit. This prevents the defendant from retaining any financial gain resulting from the illegal behaviour.

Seizure, delivery up or destruction orders

These remedies are relevant to infringement where goods have been manufactured or marked in breach of patent or trade mark rights.

The impact of EC law and international treaties on intellectual property rights

Intellectual property rights have considerable implications in relation to international trade. Consequently, their operation and development have been considerably influenced by EC law. A number of internationally binding treaties to which the UK is signatory are also important.

The EU context: conflict with English law

EC law takes precedence over English law in the event of conflicting rights (see Chapter 3). The Treaty of Rome imposes obligations to promote free trade within the Community. Thus, free movement of goods must be encouraged, restrictive trade practices are prohibited and a dominant trading position must not be abused. Discrimination against nationals of other member states is also prohibited. It is easy to see that the exercise of some rights like licensing could be a breach of the treaty; the European Court of Justice has had to decide on issues like this in a number of cases.

In addition to the UK's treaty obligations, any relevant directives must be complied with. For example, the Trade Marks Act 1994 implements a directive aimed at harmonising this area of law throughout the Community; it has greatly widened the scope of trade mark protection in this country.

The EU's Protected Food Name scheme instituted in 1993 has been beneficial to some food producers. There are three marks under this scheme: the PDO (Protected Designation of Origin); the PGI (Protected Geographical Indication); and TSG (Traditional Speciality Guaranteed). Once registered with the EU, these protect the names and reputations and quality of a whole range of foods taking their names from the locality where they have originated or been traditionally manufactured often with a particular recipe, and prevents those names being used for foods not manufactured in the relevant locality. Champagne and Parma Ham are famous examples internationally. In the UK there are currently 62 protected names, including Melton Mowbray Pork Pies, Stilton Cheese, Whitstable Oysters, Jersey Royal Potatoes and Anglesey Sea Salt.

In the news

Scotland seeks PGI for Dundee Cake

A 2014 application for registration as a PGI concerned the Dundee Cake. A famous dark fruit cake made to a traditional recipe and decorated with whole blanched almonds, it was first manufactured in Dundee during the 1700s. The European Commission is considering the application at the time of writing and a decision is expected in 2016.

Source: http://news.scotland.gov.uk/News/A-slice-of-recognition-3cf.aspx

A number of recent changes to copyright law have been the result of EC directives. The length of copyright was extended to its current limits in 1995 in compliance with EC law. Additional rights to protect copyright in databases were also added in response to EC requirements by the Copyright and Rights in Databases Regulations 1997.

Currently, under the European Patent Convention a proprietor may register their patent with effect in any member state specified in the application. An application may be filed directly with the European Patent Office or through the UKIPO in London. Infringements must be pursued in the courts of relevant state(s).

However, under the Unitary Patent Court Agreement signed by most EU countries in 2013, a Unified Patent Court will be established to enable enforcement of a patent across Europe in a single legal action. A unitary patent will be created which will be automatically enforceable in all the signatory EU states, unlike the European patent, which requires validation in each relevant state. The European patent will continue to exist. Owners of inventions will have a choice as to whether to opt for a European patent, which will protect them in any named state, or a unitary patent, which will protect them in all the signatory states. The Intellectual Property Act 2014 amends the Patent Act 1977 and gives the Secretary of State the power to implement the Agreement in the UK and to set up a branch of the Unitary Patent Court in London.

The Registered Community Design enables designers in EU countries to register their designs and thus protect them throughout the EU.

The wider international context

The UK is signatory to a number of treaties with a large number of other countries, both in and outside the EU. These treaties give reciprocal rights to protection of intellectual property in signatory states. For example, through the Berne Convention and the Universal Copyright Convention, UK citizens and residents enjoy copyright protection of their work in any of the signatory states. Almost all countries are signatory to one or other of these. The Patent Cooperation Treaty enables patent holders from the UK to apply for registration in any signatory country.

International registration of trade marks has been possible since 1995 for members of states which are signatories to the Madrid Protocol.

Chapter summary

This chapter has examined how English statute law classifies and protects certain types of intellectual property. This is summarised in Figure 24.2, which provides a useful checklist of the principal legislation in this area, which has been gradually amended to bring it into line with a number of EC directives and treaty law.

	Copyright	Design right	Registered design	Patents	Trade marks
Statute	Copyright, Designs and Patents Act 1988, Parts I and II	Copyright, Designs and Patents Act 1988, Part III	Registered Designs Act 1949 (as amended 2001)	Patents Act 1977 (as amended by Patents Act 2004)	Trade Marks Act 1994
Scope	Original, literary, dramatic and artistic works	Original design for 3D items excluding surface ornamentation	New design for any industrial or handicraft item, includes shape, pattern and ornamentation	New things/process, inventive step, industrial application	Distinctive identifying symbol for goods or services
Acquisition	By owner on creation, no formalities	By owner on creation, no formalities	Registration: UKIPO	Registration: UKIPO	Registration: UKIPO
Duration	Max: 70 years from author's death	Max: 15 years (No renewal)	Max: 25 years (5-year renewal)	Max: 20 years	Renewable indefinitely
Property rights	Personal property: transferable by assignment, will, intestacy, operation of law				
Licensing	Voluntary, compulsory, Crown	Voluntary, compulsory, Crown	Voluntary, compulsory, Crown	Voluntary, compulsory, Crown	Voluntary only

Figure 24.2

Quiz 23

1 Advise Pipit whether she has copyright in the following works:

(a) a piece of music which she has composed;

(b) an idea for a short story which she and Bunting discussed in the pub and which Bunting has now written;

(c) a flow chart which she produced at work and which is now being used by her employers in publicity leaflets;

(d) a booklet of mathematical tables.

2 Heron has designed a series of figurines representing different types of fish. He would like to know his legal rights over this design.

3 Puffin, who works for Fulmar Fish Foods, has designed a new fish-smoking process.

   (a) What criteria will the process have to satisfy if it is to be patented?

   (b) Who will own the patent?

4 (a) Nuthatch Products advertise a peanut spread with a musical jingle.

   (b) Bullfinch plc markets fruit pies which it calls 'Yummies'. Jackdaw plc has registered its trade mark 'Yum-Yums' under which it markets lollipops.

   (c) Merlin Ltd wants to market a game pie called 'Queen's Favourite'. The wrapper bears a picture of Windsor Castle.

   Will these parties be allowed to register their trade marks?

   Answers to all quizzes can be found in Appendix 2.

Take a closer look

The following cases provide important examples of how the law you have studied in this chapter has developed. They are primary sources illustrating the law in action and give you more detail about their facts, as well as helping you to understand the law and to appreciate how the judges reached their decisions.

Try looking them up in the law reports or accessing them via a database, e.g. Bailli (www.bailii.org/databases.html). LexisNexis or Westlaw may be available in your university or college library, or you may find extracts in a case book. (See Appendix 1: Additional resources.)

Berlei (UK) Ltd v *Bali Brassiere Co.* [1969] 2 All ER 812

Electrolux v *Hudson* [1977] FSR 312

Parks-Cramer Co. v *Thornton Ltd* [1966] RPC 407, CA

Williams v *Settle* [1960] 1 WLR 1072

Web activity

Please go to: www.ipo.gov.uk/

Explore the site and check on current news.

You might also find the website below interesting:http://webarchive.nationalarchives.gov.uk/20140108134321/http://www.ipo.gov.uk/news.htm

Check out the famous cases section and take a look at the IP newsletters for the most up to date developments.

Assignment 22

What types of work are protected by the Copyright, Designs and Patents Act 1988 and what rights does this give the owner?

CHAPTER 25

Common law protection of intellectual property

Passing off, malicious falsehood and breach of confidence

Introduction

The common law of tort protects certain aspects of intellectual property and the rights occur more informally, unlike those arising from statute.

The tort of passing off protects a business from loss of sales or reputation if another business imitates the appearance of a product, its packaging or advertising by for example, using a very similar name. There is some overlap here with the law protecting trade marks.

The reputation of a business is readily damaged by bad publicity. Where this is untrue and done intentionally with the aim of damaging a business the owner may find a remedy through the tort of malicious falsehood.

The tort of breach of confidence was initially developed to protect a business owner from losses arising from the inequitable peddling of information, given in confidence to an employee who then breached the trust of the employer for personal gain. However, its scope has gradually become much wider under the influence of the ECHR and the HRA 1998 so that it is now sometimes used by celebrity figures seeking to protect personal privacy.

Learning objectives

When you have studied this chapter you should be able to:

▶ define the torts of passing off, malicious falsehood and breach of confidence;

▶ distinguish between passing off and malicious falsehood;

▶ appreciate the scope of the tort of breach of confidence and its relationship to the Human Rights Act;

▶ explain the legal remedies for the above torts.

Passing off

Passing off: selling goods/ services in such a way that they appear to be the product of another party's business.

Goodwill: custom/ customers/ customer appreciation.

The tort of **passing off** protects the **goodwill** and reputation of a business. It is committed where the defendant falsely attributes to its own product some distinctive feature (for example, packaging, logo, definitive or distinctively presented name) likely to persuade members of the public that it is associated with the claimant's business.

The tort may be committed in a number of different ways:

1 The defendant presents its goods or services in a distinctive get-up similar to that used by the claimant for a similar product.

White Hudson & Co. Ltd v Asian Organisation Ltd (1964, PC)

The claimants had for five years marketed their cough sweets in distinctive red cellophane wrapping labelled 'Hacks', and people buying them often asked for 'red paper' cough sweets. The defendants started to market their brand of cough sweets in similar wrapping paper labelled 'Pecto'.

Held: the defendants were liable for passing off; the public associated that sort of packaging with the claimant's product.

(See also *Numatic Ltd* v *Qualtex* (2010) below.)

2 The defendant uses a false description imputing a definitive characteristic of the claimant's product to its own.

> ### *Erven Warnink BV* v *Townend & Sons (Hull) Ltd* (1979)
>
> The defendants marketed a drink made of eggs and sherry under the name of 'Keelings Old English Advocaat'; this competed very favourably with the more expensive Warninks Advocaat which carried a heavier excise tax as it was made of brandy and eggs.
>
> **Held:** the defendants were liable for passing off what should properly have been described as egg flip as Advocaat. Real Advocaat was recognised by the public as an entirely distinct drink because of its spirit base.

3 The defendant claims the claimant's work as its own.

Thus, in *Bristol Conservatories Ltd* v *Conservatories Custom Built Ltd* (1989) the defendants were held to have acted illegally when they showed prospective customers photographs of conservatories constructed by the claimants, as evidence of the defendant's own work.

4 The defendant falsely suggests that the claimant vouches for the defendant's work.

For example, in *Associated Newspaper Holdings* v *Insert Media Ltd* (1991) it was held that the insertion of an advertising leaflet between the pages of a newspaper would be likely to make readers believe that the newspaper approved of the products advertised. The context of the defendant's behaviour may be crucial to proof of liability.

In the news

Fenty v *Topshop/Topman Ltd* (2015, CA)

In this case the claimant was Rhianna, the pop star, whom many people regard as a fashion icon.

Topshop sold a T-shirt with an image of Rhianna which had been used to publicise her most recent album. Previously Topshop had run a competition with a shopping trip and lunch with Rhianna as the prize; it had frequently referred to her in publicity including Tweets about her visit to their main branch.

Rhianna claimed Top Shop's use of her image had implied that she had approved and authorised this, which would encourage people to believe that she was endorsing its products. Topshop argued that she was merely claiming rights to her image which English law does not support and appealed when the High Court found in her favour.

The Court of Appeal held (upholding the High Court decision): Topshop was liable for passing off. Although selling a garment with an image of a pop star was not in itself sufficient to create liability, it became so in the context of Topshop's related publicity campaign. This was likely to confuse members of the public and make them think that, as a celebrity known for her interest in fashion, she approved of their product.

To succeed in an action the claimant must prove the following:

(a) *The defendant made a false statement.* The statement must be untrue, but the defendant need not have known this. The motive of the defendant is irrelevant.

The statement may be express or implied from conduct, e.g. by using a similar name to the claimant or packaging goods similarly. The next case provides a very clear example.

Numatic International Ltd v Qualtex Ltd (2010)

Numatic, the claimant, manufactures the well-known Henry vacuum cleaner. It is red and tub-shaped, decorated with a cheerful face surmounted by a black bowler hat-shaped lid.

The defendant, Qualtex, produced a prototype of a very similar shape in blue with the same black bowler hat lid, though without a face. Numatic claimed passing off and sought an injunction to prevent Qualtex marketing its model.

Held (Floyd J): the injunction should be granted. Numatic's protectable interest and goodwill in the shape and features of the Henry model were indisputable. A customer survey indicated that there was a real danger that members of the public might buy Qualtex's model mistaking it for Numatics's. It was not sufficient for N's model merely to lack the facial characteristics of the real Henry: It 'does not mean that it necessarily follows that the absence of one or more of these features is sufficient to distinguish a replica product from the original'.

(Note: For additional clarity, check the following web reference for pictures of the two models side by side: www.bailii.org/ew/cases/EWHC/Ch/2010/1237.html.)

(b) *The statement was made in the course of trade.* 'Trade' has been defined widely by the courts and includes non-profit-making organisations.

(c) *The statement must be published to the claimant's customers.* The law of passing off exists to protect the goodwill of the claimant. Therefore, the claimant must currently be engaged in running an established business with the same catchment area as the defendant. Where a business organisation enjoys only very local goodwill, the use of a similar marketing technique 200 miles away will not be seen as illegal. However, the court may take into account likely geographical expansion.

(d) *Damage to the claimant's business must be reasonably foreseeable.* The claimant does not have to prove that the defendant intended to cause damage. Where the public is not reasonably likely to connect the claimant's business with the defendant's activity, no liability exists.

Granada Group Ltd v Ford Motor Co. Ltd (1973)

Held: Ford Motors could not legally be restrained from marketing a car under the name 'Granada' merely because the claimant traded under the same name. The parties were not engaged in a similar field of business activity; therefore, it was unlikely that the public would be confused about the origin of the car and associate it with Granada TV.

Compare the outcome in:

NAD Electronics v NAD Computer Systems (1997)

Held: the public might well be confused by the use of the name NAD by these two companies. The claimant manufactured high-quality hi-fi equipment while the defendants were computer manufacturers. There were, therefore, similarities in their respective products since many computer systems include CD players and loudspeakers. Their products were also likely to be sold alongside each other in the same retail outlets.

(e) *Damage or sufficient probability of damage must result.* Any of the following may evidence actionable damage:

1 loss of sales to the claimant because customers believe the defendant's product was manufactured by the claimant;

2 loss of business reputation: the defendant's goods are inferior and people are likely to associate them with the claimant;

3 the unique character of the claimant's product is being eroded or its status diminished by the defendant's conduct.

Taittinger SA v Allbev Ltd (1993, CA)

Held: the limitation imposed by EC law on use of the name 'Champagne' to wines produced in the Champagne area of France gave the name a distinctive character. The defendant, by selling a soft drink described as 'Elderflower Champagne', was marketing its product in a way which would inevitably lead to an erosion of the distinctiveness of the name Champagne.

(Note that 'Champagne' now enjoys protected status from the EU under its Protected Food Name scheme and can only be used to describe wine made in that area of France (see Chapter 24).)

Note the relationship of registered trade mark protection to passing-off actions.
If a product is marketed under a registered trade mark, the proprietor who alleges infringement merely has to prove that:

1 the mark is registered in relation to a relevant product; and

2 the conduct of the defendant amounts to an infringement within the definition of the Trade Marks Act 1994.

The mark is protected immediately on registration, even if, as yet, the product has not been marketed. So, it may be easier to assert your rights under a registered trade mark than to commence a passing-off action. However, an action in passing off may be brought where the relevant product does not have the protection of a registered trade mark. Not all products are sufficiently distinctively marketed to qualify for registration. A passing-off action may also arise from conduct which does not amount to an infringement of a registered trade mark.

Real life

Horace has shares in Hamelin Ltd which produces an ingenious type of mousetrap. This is marketed in yellow and black packaging marked with the company's registered trade mark, which is a black and yellow drawing of a mouse dressed like the Pied Piper and playing a pipe. Horace recently came upon an advert for Pied Piper Bait, a new brand of mouse and rat poison sold in yellow and black drums. He reported this to Cecil, the company's managing director, who is considering taking proceedings against Wilfred Piper, the owner of Pied Piper Bait, for trade mark infringement and passing off.

The packaging and name of Wilfred's product does seem likely to encourage people to think that the two products are both Cecil's and permit Wilfred to take advantage of Cecil's existing reputation to boost sales of a product that has a similar purpose. However, Wilfred will argue that his packaging contains no mouse drawing and that he is using his own name. This might well defeat trade mark infringement proceedings as the dancing mouse image is a crucial part of the trade mark. Nonetheless, the appearance of the two products does sound very similar and this may be good grounds for a passing-off action.

To succeed, Cecil will need to prove that there really is a danger that he will lose trade as a result of Wilfred's behaviour. Evidence that his customers are confused (e.g. if some have sought to order the rival bait) would be helpful. The geographical area in which the two products are marketed is also relevant. If Cecil's product enjoys nationwide goodwill, it will be no defence for Wilfred to argue that his sales are confined to one part of the country. Proof of damage is also crucial. Unless Cecil can prove that he has lost or, on the balance of probability, will lose sales as a result of Wilfred's marketing methods, his claim will fail.

Passing off on the internet

If you have a website you may obtain exclusive use of this *domain* by registering its address through your internet service provider. However, if it bears a close resemblance to the name of another business, which has not sought registration and which the public might confuse with yours, you may be liable in passing off. In *Marks & Spencer plc* v *One in a Million Ltd* (1998) the defendant registered the domain name, marks & spencer.co.uk, and then offered to sell it to the claimant. This was held to be a threat to pass off by the defendants. The claimant obtained an injunction that required the defendant to transfer the domain name to the claimant.

Malicious falsehood

Malicious falsehood: intentional or reckless statement causing damage to business interests.

Like passing off, an action for **malicious falsehood** protects a claimant against false statements damaging to the goodwill and reputation of its business. The claimant must prove the following:

1 *A false statement published by the defendant relating to the claimant's business.* The statement must be untrue and likely to cause damage to the claimant's business. It may

consist of an express attack on the claimant's business reputation, but an untrue statement of an apparently innocent kind may give rise to liability.

Ratcliffe v *Evans* (1892)

The defendant untruthfully stated in a local newspaper that the claimant had ceased to trade from a particular address. He knew this was untrue, but wished to get the claimant to abandon his business premises.

Held: liability existed here since the statement was likely to deprive the claimant of customers.

Conduct may amount to a statement.

Wilts United Dairies Ltd v *Thomas Robinson & Sons Ltd* (1958)

Condensed milk manufactured by the claimant was bought and stockpiled by the government during the war. Years later when its quality had deteriorated, it was sold to the defendant on the condition that it was to be used only as animal feed. The defendant sold it for human consumption.

Held: the inferior quality of the milk sold suggested that this was the normal standard of the claimant's product and, therefore, the defendant was liable in malicious falsehood.

2 *Damage must be reasonably foreseeable.* It must be reasonably likely that potential customers will be influenced. Comparative advertising, where the defendant merely 'puffs' its goods by claiming that they are superior to those of the claimant, is unlikely to give rise to liability. In *White* v *Mellin* (1895) it was held that no liability existed where the defendant attached labels to the claimant's product, which the defendant sold in his shop, claiming that his own brand was superior.

The defendant will be liable if it has infringed normal business practice. In *De Beers Products Ltd* v *International General Electrics* (1975) apparently weighty statements about the accuracy of the claimant's instruments, backed up with reference to plausible, but actually specious scientific data, amounted to malicious falsehood.

Malice: Intentional/ reckless behaviour aimed at causing harm to someone.

3 *The statement must be made with* **malice**. The defendant must have made the statement either knowing it to be false or not caring whether it was true or false, or believing it to be true but publishing it because motivated by the intention to cause the claimant damage. An untrue statement made in good faith will not give rise to liability.

4 *The claimant must suffer damage as a result.* Proof of a general drop in custom will be sufficient.

Note the relationship between malicious falsehood and passing off:

1 *Dual liability may exist.* Where passing off involves the sale of inferior goods, this is also an implicit assertion that the claimant produces goods of poor quality and, therefore, may also be malicious falsehood.

2 *Both parties to a passing-off action must be in competition.* A passing-off action is limited to situations where both parties are engaged in competing businesses. Malicious falsehood can be pursued against any defendant who attacks another party's business reputation.

If the claimant has a choice it is easier to succeed in a passing-off action. It is hard to prove the malice and falsity crucial to success in malicious falsehood.

Breach of confidence and protection of privacy

This area of the law gives some protection to privacy in private and business life. If one party confides information to another, a legal duty may be created not to reveal that information to anyone else. Traditionally liability for **breach of confidence** existed only where the following criteria were completely satisfied:

> **Breach of confidence:** revealing information to a third party, after it had been imparted by another party in circumstances indicating that it should be kept private.

1 the claimant expressly or implicitly reveals confidential information to another person;

2 a relationship of trust already exists between the parties or is created as a result. It will be apparent from the circumstances that this information is private and that the confidant is being relied upon to keep it confidential;

3 the confidant makes use of the information or passes it on to a third party;

4 as a result the claimant suffers damage.

However, since the end of the twentieth century, due in part to the implementation of the Human Rights Act (see below, page 586) the strict criteria of breach of confidence have been relaxed particularly in relation to proof of a relationship of trust. See *Campbell* v *MGN Ltd* (2004, HL) (see below, page 586). In *Max Mosley* v *News Group Newspapers Ltd* (2008), Eady J held that the law protected privacy rights even where no existing relationship of confidence existed, provided that it was reasonable for a claimant to expect his or her privacy to be respected. This development of the scope of breach of confidence to give wider protection of privacy will be evident from the recent cases which are described below.

What information is confidential?

It is very difficult to define what information will be treated as confidential: it is a question of fact in every case and is judged objectively by the courts. Personal information may enjoy protection. In *Stephens* v *Avery* (1988) the claimant, Mrs S, confided in the defendant, Mrs A, details of her previous sexual relationship with Mrs T. This information was newsworthy because Mrs T had recently been murdered by her husband; Mrs A leaked the story to a newspaper and was held liable for breach of confidence.

In 2007, an injunction was granted to protect Prince Charles's private journals containing his personal accounts of royal tours from publication in the *Mail on Sunday* (*HRH Prince of Wales* v *Associated Newspapers Ltd* (2007)).

In the context of business, confidential information includes trade secrets which do not enjoy statutory protection: for example, plans for an invention or industrial processes peculiar to the claimant's business. It may cover ideas and information not yet protected by copyright. It could also include information forming the subject of a competitive tender prior to its submission; leakage of such information could cause the claimant to lose the contract. For example, in *PSM International* v *Whitehouse & Willenhall Ltd* (1992), drawings, price quotations and business plans were treated as confidential.

Equitable principles are very influential here; the moral justification for secrecy or revelation and the issue of public interest will be relevant to determining whether liability exists. However, even information that would have been treated as confidential ceases to be so once it enters the public domain.

Attorney-General v *Guardian Newspapers (No. 2)* (1990)

Memoirs of an ex-secret service officer were published in a book called *Spy Catcher* leading to a claim of breach of a confidence clause in his contract of employment. The information would have been regarded in law as confidential because of its national security implications.

Held: *The Guardian*, which published details from the book, was not liable for breach of confidence as the book had already been widely published and commented upon in the media abroad and, therefore, a duty of confidentiality no longer existed.

When does a duty of confidence arise?

This will be determined by reference to the nature of any relationship or legal obligation already existing between the parties. Such a relationship is capable of arising as a result of an informal request, or by operation of law or a contract term.

Informally

An informal duty of confidence exists between friends, family members or business colleagues, employer and ex-employee. The confidant may be told of the need for discretion, or this will be obvious given the nature of the information and any other attendant circumstances. Recent cases involving the media indicate that no previous personal or business relationship between the parties is required, provided that the information published is clearly confidential. (See above, *Mosley* v *News Group Newspapers*.)

Operation of law

In the past a duty of confidence did not arise by operation of law unless the relationship of the parties was treated as fiduciary: for example, solicitor and client, and doctor and patient. In such relationships there is an automatic duty of confidence. The fiduciary relationship exists regardless of whether or not the parties are joined by a contract. A National Health Service doctor or a solicitor acting under the Legal Aid scheme is in a fiduciary relationship with the patient or client.

However, the courts indicated in the late twentieth century that a fiduciary relationship is not essential. This has widened the scope of the tort of breach of confidence, giving greater rights of privacy to claimants who in the past would not have been able to sue. In *A-G* v *Guardian Newspapers* (*No. 2*) (1990, HL), Lord Keith held that 'breach of confidence involves no more than an invasion of privacy . . . the right of privacy is one which the law should in this field seek to protect'. Potentially, this enables the bringing of claims by any person whose private life is exposed by a third party who passes on information about them without their consent.

Every case ultimately turns on its facts and not every breach of confidential information is actionable, however embarrassing the revelations may be for the claimant.

A v *B, sub nom Garry Flitcroft* v *Mirror Group Newspapers Ltd* (2002, CA)

A professional footballer who had had a one-night stand tried to obtain an injunction to prevent a report from the woman concerned being published in the press. His application was refused.

Held: breach of confidence had not occurred here. A transient sexual relationship may not be treated as confidential by the courts, if it involves an element of public interest and a party to such a relationship other than the claimant does not want it to remain confidential. A technical approach to the law was not required in such cases. A balancing of all the interests involved in the light of the particular facts was required.

While the court is unwilling to allow celebrities to use breach of confidence as a means of unfairly suppressing true information damaging to their reputation, some limited protection may be given to prevent publication of unnecessarily intrusive information, which is over and above what public interest requires. Not everything that the public may find interesting is actually deemed to be in the public interest.

Campbell v *Mirror Group Newspapers Ltd* (2004, HL)

Held: a report by the *Daily Mirror* that Naomi Campbell had taken illegal drugs and was seeking treatment for addiction was not a breach of confidence, given her previous untrue assertion to the contrary. However, a photograph of her leaving a Narcotics Anonymous meeting and other details of her drug history was more information than the public interest required, so damages could be awarded for this.

The issue of how far the privacy of celebrities should be protected is controversial and even the judges themselves may disagree. This is evident in a succession of cases involving Michael Douglas and Catherine Zeta Jones.

Douglas and Another v *Hello! Ltd* (*No. 3*) (2007) has ended the saga of 12 cases triggered in 2000 by the 'spoiler' photographs of the wedding reception for Michael Douglas and Catherine Zeta Jones, published by *Hello* magazine in breach of the exclusive publication rights which *OK* magazine bought from the Douglases for £1 million.

In 2000, the Court of Appeal (*Douglas and Another* v *Hello! Ltd* (2001, CA)) held that an arguable case for damages in breach of confidence existed, but quashed an injunction previously ordered by the High Court, since by allowing publication of the photographs by *OK* they had surrendered their rights to the full privacy that such an event would normally enjoy.

No fewer than nine cases followed, before another Court of Appeal decision (*Douglas and Another* v *Hello! Ltd* (2005, CA)) approved a High Court award of £14,760 damages to the Douglases, on the ground that the photographs clearly related to their private life and therefore came within the protection of breach of confidence law.

However, it quashed an award to *OK* of £1 million, on the ground that it had *not* suffered breach of confidence just because the exclusivity contract had given it some proprietary interest in the photographs.

OK appealed to the House of Lords (*Douglas and Another* v *Hello! Ltd* (*No. 3*) (2007)) which, by a majority of only three to two, decided that *OK* had suffered a breach of confidence in relation to commercial information. The photographs were confidential since the opportunity to publicise them had been restricted to *OK* by the Douglases, in their sale of exclusive rights. This information was protected by the law because it was information of commercial value over which the Douglases had sufficient control to allow them to impose a duty of confidence. Lord Hoffmann commented that: 'being a celebrity or publishing a celebrity magazine are lawful trades and I see no reason why they should be outlawed from such protection as the law of confidence has to offer.'

Worth thinking about?

Lord Walker, one of the two dissenting Law Lords in *Douglas and Another* v *Hello Magazine Ltd (No. 3)* (2007), said that breach of confidence law should not be employed to make a spectacle exclusive: '*The Douglases were content to have wedding photos published, for a handsome fee, so long as they had strict control over the selection of the pictures.*'

What do you think about this controversial decision?

Suggested solutions can be found in Appendix 2.

Contract

In a business context it is very common for a confidence clause to be an express term of any consultancy contract, and in some other contracts for the provision of services where access to confidential information is involved. Such a term might also be implied in a contract of service as part of the duties of good faith and trust and confidence (see Chapter 16). This obliges both employer and employee not to reveal confidential information about each other to outsiders.

Lady Archer v *Williams* (2003)

Ms Williams was engaged as personal assistant to Lady Archer (Jeffrey Archer's wife) under a contract requiring her to work confidentially. After the contract was terminated, the defendant gave details of her employment with Lady Archer to a Sunday paper. Later it published an article saying that Lady Archer had had plastic surgery.

Held: an injunction would be granted to restrain Ms Williams from publishing any details which she had directly obtained through working for the claimant. The disclosure of such sensitive personal information as she had acquired was not in the public interest.

The nature of the employment is crucial to determining what will be treated as confidential. Ms Williams' contract was one of personal service. It is much harder to prove that information in a commercial contract is confidential, so a confidentiality clause does not give blanket protection to an employer, regarding all their business activity. Thus, in *Faccenda Chicken* v *Fowler* (1986) it was held that lists of the claimant's customers' names and details of van rounds compiled by the defendant (an ex-employee of the claimant) to assist him to set up a competing business were held not to be confidential information.

Tillery Valley Foods v *Channel Four Television* (2004)

Tillery manufactured and supplied foods for the public service market. A reporter working on a programme for Channel Four posed as a worker at Tillery's factory. The resulting programme contained allegations about lack of hygiene and also footage of production practices secretly filmed at the factory.

Held: an employee filming in the workplace did not in itself amount to a breach of confidence unless confidential information was revealed. Tillery was unable to prove that any secret process which would attract confidentiality had been filmed. The blanket clause banning the employee from revealing information gained at work did not assist the employer, as no confidential information had been revealed.

Even a specific confidentiality clause will not be effective if it amounts to restraint of trade. (See also Chapter 10.) Breach of confidence may arise commercially without a breach of contract.

What sort of damage is actionable?

A claimant will have to prove that the breach of confidence operated to the claimant's detriment. Economic loss may have been suffered, but the courts also acknowledge the distress attendant on loss of privacy.

The public interest defence

As is evident from the *Flitcroft* and *Campbell* cases above, a defendant who can show that there was a duty to reveal the confidential information in the public interest may avoid liability. This defence does not just apply to celebrity cases. In *W* v *Edgell* (1990) a doctor, who informed the Mental Health Review Tribunal about his patient's psychopathic tendencies, was held not liable for breaching doctor–patient confidentiality, since this information was revealed in the interest of public safety.

The impact of the Human Rights Act 1998

Article 8 of the European Convention on Human Rights and Fundamental Freedoms (ECHR) gives the right to respect for privacy and family life, so an action under the HRA 1998 may be taken to enforce this right, providing an alternative to a breach of confidence action, if the defendant is a public authority. ECHR rights are not absolute. Article 8 states that interference by a public authority with the privacy of the individual may be justified so far as necessary 'in a democratic society to ensure national security, public safety or the economic well-being of the country, for the prevention of crime, the protection of health and morals or for the protection of the rights and freedom of others'. The court as a 'public authority', therefore, must balance the rights of the claimant against the right to freedom of expression of the defendant and the public interest in receiving the information.

The court as a public authority is bound by the ECHR. This means that in *every* case, not just those brought under the Human Rights Act, it has a duty to ensure a fair trial under Article 8 and have regard to the ECHR where relevant to the issues raised by the facts of the case. In *Douglas and Another* v *Hello! Ltd* (2001, CA) the Court of Appeal held that the ECHR required English law to respect a right of privacy and upheld their breach of confidence claim on that ground. The HRA 1998 is always likely to impact on cases involving breach of privacy, since the court must maintain a balance between the competing requirements of Article 8 (right to privacy) and Article 10 (freedom of information).

The following case provides a practical example of how the court balances the interests of each party.

Murray v *Big Pictures UK Ltd* (2008, CA)

David Murray (DM), son of Harry Potter author J. K. Rowling, appealed against a High Court decision which struck out his claim for breach of his rights of privacy against a photographic agency which had covertly obtained pictures of him in the street and sold them to Express Newspapers. The High Court held that since the pictures were taken in a public place and recorded a mundane activity, no right to privacy under ECHR Article 8 had been infringed.

Held: the action should not be struck out.

When deciding whether Article 8 had been breached two questions must be decided:

1 Was there a reasonable expectation of privacy? This must be decided objectively taking into account the facts of the case including the particular attributes of the claimant and the activity in which he was involved, and the means by which the defendant obtained the information.

2 If there was reasonable expectation, then a balance must be struck between the claimant's right to privacy and the defendant's right to publish.

> It could be argued that DM, as the child of a famous parent, might reasonably expect not to be pursued by the press, since a child whose parents were not well known would not have been similarly targeted. Subject to the facts, children should be protected from unnecessary media attention. Consequently, David Murray was entitled to continue his case.

(See also *Douglas and Another* v *Hello! Ltd* (2001, CA); *A* v *B*, sub nom *Garry Flitcroft* v *Mirror Group Newspapers Ltd* (2002); and *Campbell* v *Mirror Group Newspapers Ltd* (2004) (above).)

Conclusion

There will therefore always be a potential conflict in privacy cases between the claimant's rights to privacy and the freedom of information. It may be argued that cases of the celebrity 'kiss and tell' kind may be more about reputation management than preserving privacy, with the claimant actually more concerned about loss of income than their privacy as such. However, it is often the tabloid press who protest the loudest in such cases and it is those papers that are most inclined to employ intrusive means to obtain such stories and portray them in the most lurid terms to boost sales. Motivation here is more about making money than keeping the public appropriately informed. The use of so-called 'super injunctions' which prevent the media reporting even that an injunction has been applied for, let alone the name of the applicant, have unsurprisingly proved controversial, even though applications often fail or are overturned on appeal and, if granted, are only in use in the short term. The Neuberger Report published in 2011 recommended that, in the interest of open justice, the Ministry of Justice should collate the numbers of such applications every year so that the number can be readily known. It also recommends that, before an application is heard, the relevant branch of the media should be informed so that it or any interested member of the public is able to contest the application. No implementation appears to have occurred at the time of writing.

Remedies for passing off, malicious falsehood and breach of confidence

Account for profits: judicial remedy requiring a defendant to hand over any financial advantage gained from their illegal activity.

The following remedies are available for each of the three torts:

1 *Injunction*: to prevent publication and/or require the defendant to hand over relevant goods or documentation.

2 *Damages*: to compensate the claimant for loss and damage.

3 *Account for profits*: the defendant may be required to **account for profits** by handing over the fruits of his or her wrongdoing.

Chapter summary

Passing off

The defendant:

(a) presents its goods or services in a similar, distinctive get-up to those of the claimant's similar product; or

(b) falsely describes its product and suggests that it has the same definitive characteristics as the claimant's product; or

(c) presents the claimant's work as the defendant's own; or

(d) falsely suggests that the claimant vouches for the defendant's work.

Claimant must prove:

(a) misrepresentation by the defendant;

(b) published in the course of trade;

(c) to the claimant's customers;

(d) which reasonably foreseeably would/did cause damage to the claimant.

Malicious falsehood

Claimant must prove: malicious publication of a false statement concerning the claimant's business and resulting in reasonably foreseeable damage.

Breach of confidence

Claimant must prove: information relating to the claimant was revealed by the defendant to a third party/parties in circumstances when privacy could reasonably be expected and resulted in damage to the claimant.

Public interest may be a defence.

Remedies

Account for profits.

Damages.

Injunction.

Quiz 24

1 What torts may have been committed in the following situations?

  (a) Rockall told Dogger, a fellow inventor, of his plans to develop a voice-activated tin opener. Dogger has now patented the item.

  (b) Wight, a professional photographer, discovers that Lundy has been using samples of Wight's work to help him obtain photographic commissions.

  (c) Fairisle, an opera singer, discovers that Plymouth, a professional rival, told Bight that Fairisle was temperamental, unreliable and given to cancelling engagements at the last minute.

2 What must a claimant prove in a claim for breach of confidence?

3 What remedies are available to a victim of malicious falsehood?

4 Why may a party seek to register a trade mark rather than rely on the common law protection of a passing-off claim?

Answers to all quizzes can be found in Appendix 2.

Take a closer look

The following cases provide important examples of how the law you have studied in this chapter has developed. They are primary sources illustrating the law in action and give you more detail about their facts, as well as helping you to understand the law and to appreciate how the judges reached their decisions.

Try looking them up in the law reports or accessing them via a database, e.g. Bailli (www.bailii.org/databases.html). LexisNexis or Westlaw may be available in your university or college library, or you may find extracts in a case book. (See Appendix 1: Additional resources.)

A v B, sub nom Garry Flitcroft v Mirror Group Newspapers Ltd [2002] 2 All ER 545

Douglas and Another v Hello! Ltd (No. 3) [2007] 2 WLR 920

NAD Electronics v NAD Computer Systems [1997] FSR 380

Fenty v Topshop/Topman [2015] EWCA Civ 3

Web activity

Please go to: www.carter-ruck.com/

This website belongs to a well-known firm of lawyers whose caseload includes media and privacy cases. Click on 'News' to get see some recent cases it has handled. You might also like to have a trawl through 'Media Law' to get an overview of the scope of Carter Ruck's work.

Assignment 23

Discuss how far it is true to say that application of the Human Rights Act 1998 has expanded the scope of breach of confidence actions?

APPENDIX 1

Additional resources

Additional resources

Your studies will be more rewarding if you look beyond what is in this book. Coursework assignments may require some research from specialist textbooks. The internet is a very useful research tool. Here are some suggestions.

Background information

Apart from quality newspapers, TV and radio programmes are a useful source of information about current legal topics. 'You and Yours' and 'The Money Programme', and 'Law in Action' on Radio 4 all deal interestingly with a variety of topical legal issues. *Which?* magazine is published monthly by the Consumers' Association and provides a lot of very accessible information on consumer rights.

Specialist texts

The English legal system

The English Legal System: Elliott and Quinn, Pearson, 16th edn, 2015.
English Legal System: Essential Cases and Materials: Elliot and Quinn, Longman, 2nd edn, 2009.
Law of Contract: Richards, (Foundations) Premium Pack, Pearson, 12th edn, 2015.
Casebook on Contract: Poole, Oxford University Press, 11th edn, 2012.
For reference: *The Law of Contract*: Cheshire, Fifoot and Furmston, Oxford University Press, 16th edn, 2012.

Consumer law

Consumer Law and Practice: Woodroffe and Lowe, Sweet & Maxwell, 9th edn, 2013.

The law of tort

Law of Tort: (Foundations) Premium Pack, Cooke, Pearson, 12th edn, 2015.
Casebook on Torts: Kidner, Oxford University Press, 12th edn, 2012.

Employment law

Employment Law for Business Students: Nairns, Longman, 4th edn, 2011.
Cases and Materials on Employment Law: Pitt, Longman, 3rd edn, 2009.
For reference: *Selwyn's Law of Employment*: Emir, Oxford University Press, 18th edn, 2014.
Employment Law: Davies, Pearson, 2015.

Company law

Smith and Keenan's Company Law: Wild & Weinstein, Pearson, 17th edn, 2016.
Cases and Materials on Company Law: Hicks and Goo, Oxford University Press, 7th edn, 2011.
For reference: *The Principles of Modern Company Law*: Gower and Davies, Sweet & Maxwell, 9th edn, 2012.

Intellectual property

Intellectual Property: Bainbridge, Pearson, 10th edn, 2014.
Intellectual Property Law: Davis, Oxford University Press, 4th edn, 2012.

Useful websites

Subject to any specified copyright restraints, you may download and print off documents for your personal study use. Websites also often have useful links to other relevant sites.

Name	Nature of resources	Contact
ACAS (Advisory, Conciliation and Arbitration Service)	Good employment law resource	**www.acas.org.uk**
Advice Guide	Consumer advice from the Citizens' Advice Bureau	**www.adviceguide.org.uk/**
BBC	Useful background information for many of the topics in this book	**www.bbc.co.uk/**
British and Irish Legal Information Institute (BAILII)	Large database of cases	**www.bailii.org/databases.html**
Business and Human Rights Resource Centre	Lots of useful information and news about business with a human rights perspective	**www.business-humanrights.org**
Bytestart	Advice on setting up and running a small business	**www.bytestart.co.uk/index.shtml**
The Carbolic Smokeball Company	Information about the famous case	**www.carbolicsmokeball.co.uk/**

Name	Nature of resources	Contact
Carter Ruck Media and Human Rights Lawyers	Useful articles and information about current cases	www.carter-ruck.com/
Commission for Equality and Human Rights	Non-departmental government body responsible for promoting equality, monitoring anti-discrimination law and ensuring its effectiveness	www.equalityhumanrights.com
Department of Business, Innovation & Skills	Consumer and employment law resource	www.gov.uk/government/organisations/department-for-business-innovation-skills
Europa	EU website: lots of news and information about the EU and how it works plus databases of legislation and cases	europa.eu/index_en.htm
Health & Safety Executive	Practical information about workplace safety and the law	www.hse.gov.uk/index.htm
Insolvency Helpline	Consumer debt advice	www.insolvencyhelpline.co.uk/
Institute of Directors	Information and resources for company directors	www.iod.com
The Liberty Guide to Human Rights	Lots of useful information about the ECHR, and the HRA 1998	www.yourrights.org.uk/
Parliament	Information about forthcoming legislation, Acts of Parliament from 1988, House of Lords cases	www.parliament.uk/
The Society of Motor Manufacturers and Traders	Useful example of ADR procedure	www.smmt.co.uk/
The Stock Exchange	Useful information about the operation of the stock market	www.londonstockexchange.com/en-gb/
Trading Standards Institute	Trading Law information and enforcement	www.tradingstandards.gov.uk
UK Intellectual Property Office	Lots of news and information about copyright, design right, patents and trade marks	www.ipo.gov.uk/
Wikipedia law portal	A variety of resources including access to law reports of leading cases	en.wikipedia.org/wiki/Portal:Law

Worth thinking about? and quiz solutions

Worth thinking about? and quiz solutions

The idea behind these questions is to get you thinking and to prompt discussion, not just to test your knowledge, so there are not right and wrong answers to all of them.

Chapter 3

There are a number of possibilities here, the most obvious being that a case may have become so outdated that it no longer reflects current attitudes. In *British Railways Board* v *Herrington* (1972) where a child trespasser was badly injured by a live electric rail, the House of Lords departed from its previous decision in *Robert Addie & Sons Ltd* v *Dumbreck* (1929) in order to increase the duty of care owed by an occupier to trespassers, to reflect the more humane attitudes of the late twentieth century.

On occasion, the House of Lords has been prepared to acknowledge that a previous decision was misguided. In *R* v *Shivpuri* (1986) it departed from *Anderton* v *Ryan* (1985) which contained a statutory interpretation of attempt to commit a crime, which had been widely criticised. Lord Bridge described it as a serious error which should be corrected quickly.

Chapter 4

Out-of-court settlements work well if both parties are equally powerful. However, in many cases concerning personal injury or consumer problems the defendant is an insurance company or large business concern and the claimant, unless very well advised, may be squeezed into accepting an unprofitable deal for much less than would have been awarded by the court. Where small claims are concerned, the claimant will usually not be represented and have received a minimum of legal advice. The only real advantage to the claimant in cases like these is that at least they get some money; if the case had gone to court they might still have lost.

Chapter 5

The post rule was developed to prevent uncertainty about when a contract, made at long distance, came into being. Acceptance is fixed at the earliest possible time in the communication process to ensure that a party cannot change its mind once a letter is posted. Once a letter is posted, any attempt on the part of the offeror to revoke would be a breach of contract.

Chapter 6

It is possible to see an element of potential duress in *Stilk* v *Myrick*. Also that case was decided at a time when mutiny at sea was greatly feared, so the court would have been inclined to take a strong line against the sailors. No threat was imposed by Mr Williams; in fact, the suggestion that the terms be varied seemed to come from Mr Roffey; who was concerned about avoiding a sanction imposed by a third party (the Housing Association). It is common business practice for the parties to vary the terms of a contract and happily go along with the change. This decision is in line with other current decisions on similar facts where lack of consideration has not been questioned and the outcome has been determined on the presence or absence of economic duress. (See Chapter 8.)

Chapter 7

Where the contract terms are incomplete or even unclear but one of the parties has embarked on performance by paying money or carrying out work prior to a dispute the court may use a purposive approach to imply a meaning to keep the contract alive and prevent one party unfairly gaining an advantage.

Chapter 8

Here we have two contracts in one. The 'buy one get one free notice' amounts to a unilateral offer which the customer accepts through making the contract to buy one of the products. This brings into being a collateral contract which the shopkeeper must perform by handing over the second product. Buying the first product forms the consideration for the second contract. The reality is that the customer in such situations is not getting a free item they are just getting it more cheaply than usual. They are entering a contract and providing consideration for the goods. They are not getting anything free just (maybe) a good bargain.

A shop which refuses to allow such a sale would, apart from any contractual liability, be breaking trading standards law and be liable for criminal prosecution.

Chapter 9

Here the contract has become impossible to perform. Provided this is not due to the fault of the seller, the contract is said to be discharged by frustration. (See Chapter 10.)

Chapter 10

The sale of a very basic mobile phone to a minor is arguably a contract for necessaries in our security-conscious age, so an excessive price could be challenged. However, the very fancy pieces of kit brandished by many children today would be likely to be treated as non-necessaries.

A monthly contract to supply phone services would be one of continuing obligation and therefore voidable by the minor at any time. You will find that phone companies are wise to this and refuse to enter into such contracts with anybody under 18 years of age.

Chapter 11

Mrs Beswick could sue John Beswick under the Contracts (Rights of Third Parties) Act 1999, as the contract between John and Peter was made for her benefit. (See Chapter 6.)

Chapter 12

Spearmint Rhino might try to argue that the contract with the lap dancers is illegal and void because it promotes sexual immorality, so it has no duty to pay. (See *Pearce* v *Brooks* (page 225).) In practice, however, it is unlikely to do so as presumably lap dancers encourage custom at the clubs and it makes some money directly for them as well. Many potentially illegal contracts go unchallenged while both parties are happy with the arrangement.

Chapter 13

Mr Piper has a potential action in negligence against the hospital which owes him a duty of care. He might try to claim that the hospital damaged the prosthesis when implanting it, thus breaching its duty of care.

Chapter 14

Since *Hambrook* v *Stokes* it was the rule that a successful secondary victim must have witnessed the relevant accident through their own senses, not filtered through a third party, so in *Alcock* the House of Lords was affirming this principle. This was the first case of an accident directly injuring hundreds of victims which had been witnessed by countless people through TV. Their lordships held that the victims would not be sufficiently identifiable in the TV pictures. Maybe this was influenced by policy considerations concerning freedom of information in simultaneous broadcasts and the need to remove threat of litigation to broadcast media.

Chapter 15

First, vicarious liability provides an identifiable defendant when this might be any one of many faceless employees. Secondly, the average employer is in a better financial position to meet the claim than the employee, since the employer should be fully insured against such losses.

Chapter 16

Perceptive students may ask why Ms Reid did not sue the landlord under the Occupiers' Liability Act 1957 as the occupier of the building. While she would have had a cause of action, she would have needed to ascertain who the occupier was, while the regulations led her straight to the employer. Further, under the OLA 1957 the occupier's duty is to take reasonable care to ensure reasonable safety. The regulations require the employer 'to ensure' safety, which imposes a higher level of duty. It was also more advantageous to sue the employer for breach of the regulations than at common law for breach of non-delegable duty, where only reasonable care is required and liability could be avoided if the employer could not reasonably have known of the state of the lift.

Chapter 17

Serco would appear to be a public authority and therefore under a duty (HRA 1998) to act compatibly with the ECHR Mr Redfearn could argue that under Article 10 (freedom of expression) he is entitled to hold opinions. He was, after all, not even attempting to express them at work. *Redfearn* v *Serco Ltd* (2012) indicates that is a successful argument.

Like most of the Convention rights, this is not absolute and conditions and restrictions may be imposed upon it in the interests of public safety. Serco would no doubt have raised this argument, but, given where he actually worked and his good relationship with other staff, sacking him might be argued to be disproportionate. While most of us (author included) abhor the BNP, stopping its members from earning a living in the circumstances of this case seems a rather extreme response which should be corrected by the court.

However, since the amendment of ERA 1996, s 108, following the ECtHR decision in *Redfearn* v *Serco Ltd* (2012), which held that his rights to freedom of speech and association had been breached, he could take the much simpler route of suing for unfair dismissal, regardless of how long he has been employed there. His employer will have to show that he was fairly dismissed for other legally recognised reasons and that the procedures used to dismiss him were also fair.

Chapter 18

The employer's policies are the key here. These should be reasonable and clear so that the employee can understand in advance what behaviour will/will not be tolerated.

The amount of time spent during working hours, apart obviously from breaks may be an issue but appropriate warnings should be sufficient and it is highly unlikely to be a sacking issue. It's a sad fact of the modern workplace that employees often don't take the breaks they are entitled to and may be doing extra work from home, so sensitive treatment of this issue may be necessary. If there is no issue with the employee's output and efficiency a light touch is probably wise.

Any gross breaches involving harassment of colleagues or other people, defamatory comments or any other behaviour implicating the business and likely to bring it or the employer into disrepute may justify dismissal provided all appropriate disciplinary and appeal procedures have been used prior to the dismissal.

Chapter 19

Limited liability promotes investment. It is good for business, as it gives some guarantee of safety for investors in what is essentially a gamble: 'the value of your investment may go down as well as up'.

The history of limited liability is long, diverse and sometimes shameful. Dubious and often disastrous speculation protected by it, led to the Joint Stock Act 1844, which provided a registration system for companies which did not permit limited liability. However, public opinion aided by a disastrous slump in the economy led to a re-think and in 1855 the Limited Liability Act permitted it subject to certain controls.

Chapter 20

Company formation has become increasingly easier over the years, as successive governments have tried to help small businesses. However, this does promote opportunities for fraud, assisted by the ease and cheapness with which one can buy a company 'off the shelf'. Try Googling that phrase and you will find hundreds of firms ready to help, sometimes for as little as £30. All too often we hear of companies being set up as a cover for scams which enable the rogues behind the name to take the money and run. They may then cease trading or just disappear without trace or shelter behind limited liability in the event of proceedings being brought against them.

Chapter 21

This reform clearly reflects the policy behind the Act that seeks to simplify the transaction of company business and give greater flexibility to management. This is one less thing for company promoters to consider when drawing up the company articles, as it will not be necessary to include permission. The relaxation of the rule is arguably balanced by adequate protection for shareholder democracy.

Chapter 22

A decision to accept a lower bid may be justified once reference is made to the qualifying criteria in s 172(1). The directors must, for example, have regard to the long-term effects of their decision and how it will impact on the company employees. Maybe the lower bidder is offering a better long-term deal for them. The only real change made by the CA 2006 is to spell out decision-making criteria.

Chapter 23

The two-stage test will surely act as a powerful filter. If the directors are also major shareholders they will be able to support each other against a minority. Finally, given that a shareholder may be a company, there is the likelihood that a board of directors under threat may be able to rely on such institutional support, motivated by sympathy for a predicament which any board might face.

In practice, it seems likely, given its built-in protection for directors, that minority shareholders will be no better protected by the CA 2006 than they were by the rule in *Foss* v *Harbottle*. Directors' rather than the company's interests are arguably better protected by Chapter 11 proceedings.

Chapter 24

If the photograph is taken in a public place, the law generally regards you as fair game to any passing photographer. It may be irritating to individuals who feel that their privacy is being invaded, but restricting the activity would in most circumstances be incompatible with the ECHR (rights to free expression/information). It is sad that the paparazzi so often abuse this. Photographs taken on private premises may in some circumstances amount to breach of confidence. (See Chapter 25.)

Chapter 25

We live in an age where celebrity has been described as a 'trade' by the courts (*per* Lord Hoffmann in this actual case) so in that context maybe it is reasonable to treat its 'products', such as a wedding, as a marketable entity. Any of us less famed human beings would probably prefer to control who takes photographs of us on such occasions. Maybe the Douglases thought that, as their wedding was going to attract a lot of media attention, the least disruption might be caused on the day by giving an exclusive to one magazine. These are reasonable wishes that deserve legal protection. When looking at a legal problem we have to try not to take the biased (though not necessarily unreasonable) view that Catherine Zeta Jones should 'get a life' and stop worrying about bootleg pictures of her engulfing a piece of cake, entering the public domain.

OK did pay £1 million for the exclusive photographic rights and it is arguable did not get their money's worth since some people wanting to see the pictures would doubtless have bought *Hello* instead if that was their celebrity magazine of choice, so this would affect *OK*'s sales figures even though they got their pictures out first. Again, we need to have regard to the legal principle involved.

Quiz answers

Quiz 1

1 Source: the state; scope: geographical limitations; sanctions: imposed by or with the authority of the state.

2 Retribution and protection for society through containment, deterrence, rehabilitation.

3 Compensation for damage caused by defendant; possibly an equitable remedy to make the defendant alter behaviour.

4 Sparrow may be prosecuted for drunken and careless driving. He may also be liable in negligence to Finch and breach of contract to Wren.

Quiz 2

1 European law, parliamentary legislation, case law.

2 Regulations have immediate effect and aim at uniformity. Directives require state legislation and aim at harmonisation.

3 First and second reading; committee and report stages; third reading; transfer to the other House; procedures repeated; Royal Assent.

4 Two of the following: Orders in Council, statutory instruments, regulations, bye-laws.

5 Literal rule: face-value meaning of the statute's words. Mischief rule: purposive approach.

6 General words take their meaning from any preceding specific words.

7 A precedent may be binding if it was decided by a court whose decisions bind the current court and the facts are sufficiently relevant to the current case.

8 *Ratio decidendi* may be binding. An *obiter dictum* is always persuasive.

9 Its decisions are merely persuasive, though its membership consists of Law Lords.

10Where the claimant alleges that their rights under the ECHR have been breached by a public authority.

Quiz 3

1 (a) Crown Court. (b) Court of Appeal Criminal Division. (c) Crown Court/Divisional Court of QBD. (d) County court. (e) High Court: QBD. (f) Employment tribunal. (g) County court.

2 A freezing order prevents the defendant from transferring his or her assets abroad or otherwise concealing them.

3 Arbitration: arbitrator's decision binding. Conciliation: conciliator may suggest a solution. Mediation: parties reach their own decision.

4 Tribunals have specialist lay members. They are less formal, cheaper (but generally no legal aid), quicker and not necessarily bound by precedent. They have wide discretion.

Quiz 4

1 (a) No: invitation to treat. (b) No: invitation to treat. (c) Yes: unilateral. (d) No: lacks communication. (e) Counter-offer by Esther. (f) No: offer revoked, if P knew of sale.

2 (a) No: conditional. (b) No: failure to communicate. (c) Yes: if the postal rules apply. (d) No: failure to communicate.

Quiz 5

1 (a) Gratuitous: past consideration. (b) Binding: adequacy irrelevant. (c) Gratuitous: existing contractual duty. (d) Binding: exception to *Pinnel's* case. (e) Provides a defence under *High Trees* if Pink tried to repudiate.

2 The Contracts (Rights of Third Parties) Act 1999 may assist Grey, since the contract is made for his benefit.

Quiz 6

1 Conditions: major terms, innocent party may repudiate and claim damages. Warranties: minor terms, damages only.

2 Capable of being breached in a number of ways, some serious enough to justify repudiation.

3 The *Cehave* criteria indicate (a) Does contract indicate the consequence of the term? (b) Using the words condition/warranty does not give them specific status. (c) Is there a statutory right to repudiate? (d) Is there commonly accepted commercial practice? (e) If none of the above apply then assess status from the extent of the damage.

4 Limitation clause: limits financial liability. Exclusion clause: exempts the party in breach for legal and therefore financial liability for the breach.

5 (a) Yes, if it should be visible to customers before they enter the contract. (b) Yes, regardless of whether the signer read or understood it. (c) No: contract concluded at reception. (d) No: too late, contract already concluded.

6 This rule means that any unclear wording in the contract will be interpreted to give the meaning most favourable to the party who did not impose it.

Quiz 7

1 Seller is able to pass title, goods match description, are of satisfactory quality, are suitable for their purpose and conform to sample.

2 Buyer may reject goods within a reasonable time if the seller has breached any of the implied terms under the SGA 1979.

3 In a contract between businesses UCTA 1977, s 2 applies: negligence liability cannot be excluded for death or personal injury, damage to property may be excluded if reasonable.

4 CRA 2015 and the CC(IC&AC)R 2013.

5 Assuming that this is a consumer sale, Rosanna is entitled to reject the goods (s 22) or request repair or replacement under the CRA (s 23) within 30 days of delivery. If repair

or replacement is not carried out within a reasonable time she then has a final right to reject.

6 This term may be voidable under the CRA 2015.

Quiz 8

1 (a) Voidable. (b) Void. (c) Voidable. (d) Voidable. (e) Void.

2 (a) Misrepresentation. (b) Mistake: subject matter. (c) Misrepresentation, mistake: identity. (d) Undue influence.

Quiz 9

1 A contract for an illegal purpose (breaking the law) is completely void. Property is not generally recoverable. Severance is impossible. Under a contract perceived as merely undesirable to the public interest, property is recoverable and severance possible. Any void portion may be severed.

2 (a) To commit a crime. (b) Sexually immoral. (c) Dangerous to international relations.

3 (a) Necessary goods: reasonable price payable. (b) Non-necessaries: not enforceable. (c) Yes, if for his benefit. (d) No: contract of debt.

Quiz 10

1 (a) (i) Yes: divisible contract. (ii) Yes: acceptance of part performance. (b) Yes: full performance prevented.

2 Chambray committed an anticipatory breach. This would have entitled Linen to repudiate the contract but, as he did not exercise this right, it was lost when the contract was frustrated by destruction of the car. If the car was destroyed before the contract was made, the contract is void for mistake if neither party was aware that the goods no longer existed.

3 Remoteness: limits the amount of actionable damage. Quantum: concerns the amount of damages payable by the defendant to compensate for the actionable damage.

4 Specific performance will not be granted to enforce an employment contract, or one requiring continuing supervision. Discretionary: will not be granted to enforce any contract unless this is deemed fair to both parties.

Quiz 11

1 (a) Actual express authority. (b) Actual implied authority.

2 Yes: Starboard failed to notify Compass about Port's dismissal and is estopped from denying Port's apparent authority.

3 If the third party wished to contract with the agent personally.

4 When the principal agrees/trade practice/routine tasks not requiring special skill.

5 When an irrevocable/enduring/lasting power of attorney exists.

Quiz 12

1 Duty, breach, consequent damage.

2 Reasonable foreseeability, proximity, justice and reason.

3 Lapse of time, third-party interference.

4 Basil has rights in contract against Tarragon. Basil and Rosemary also have rights in negligence and under the Consumer Protection Act against Marjoram.

5 Liability: Negligence; fault: CPA 1987. Strict: Defendant: Negligence: manufacturer; CPA 1987: producer/marker/importer/supplier. Property damage: limited to claims over £275 under CPA 1987, no limitations in negligence.

Quiz 13

1 (a) Yes: negligent statement (*Hedley Byrne* v *Heller*). (b) No: pure economic loss (*Muirhead* v *Industrial Tank Specialities*). (c) Yes: nervous shock (*Alcock* v *Wright*). (d) No: damage caused by the third party (*Smith* v *Littlewoods Organisation*).

2 Reasonable care.

3 An exception to the remoteness of damage rule, which makes a defendant liable in a personal injuries case for all the injuries flowing from the negligent act if they are due to some illness or condition suffered by the claimant, even if not reasonably foreseeable.

Quiz 14

1 (a) Public nuisance affecting the highway: non-delegable duty. (b) Under the Occupiers' Liability Act 1957, no liability if notice sufficient to discharge duty. (c) Lymeswold is a trespasser (Occupiers' Liability Act 1984). Red likely to be liable, as he could easily have prevented a child from obtaining access to his storeroom and should have foreseen Lymeswold's likely presence if children regularly visit his shop. (d) Private nuisance.

2 Contributory negligence if Wensleydale suffered head injuries.

3 Employers are vicariously liable for torts committed by an employee if incidental to the job. Generally there is no liability for independent contractors unless the employer's personal duty is non-delegable.

Quiz 15

1 Employer is responsible for paying employees' NI contributions and sick pay and deduction of income tax. No such responsibilities for contractors, who also have no rights to claim for unfair dismissal or redundancy. Lesser duty to contractors under the HSAWA 1974 than that owed to employees.

2 (a) Good faith: conflict with Juniper's interests. (b) Lack of reasonable care and skill. (c) Good faith: failure to account for profits.

3 Common law duties: competent staff, safe work systems. Criminal liability under the HSAWA 1974.

4 Prosecution, improvement/prohibition notices.

Quiz 16

1 (a) Ms Antelope may claim that her work is of equal value under EA 2010 and that she is being treated unfavourably on the grounds of her protected characteristic of sex.

2 (b) Mr Buck may be able to claim sex discrimination under the EA 2010, s 11 for direct discrimination (s 13) unless the occupational qualification (Schedule 9, para 1) is applicable.

3 Direct: overt restriction of employment opportunity resulting in unfavourable treatment of people with a protected characteristic under EA 2010. Indirect: conditions imposed which are less likely to be fulfilled by people with a relevant protected characteristic.

4 If race or sex is deemed an occupational qualification because the employer can show that it is essential to the job and a reasonable and proportionate response.

5 Ms Rabbit has been subjected to unfavourable treatment because of being on maternity leave (s 18(2)). She is entitled to equal pay and therefore can claim the bonus under the EA, s 74. Ms Hare can claim victimisation (s 27) because she encouraged Ms Rabbit to exercise her rights and maybe have been unfairly made redundant as a result.

Quiz 17

1 Wrongful dismissal: breach of contract; no qualifying period of employment; common law action in the courts; remedy – damages determined by the court.

2 Unfair dismissal: employer has not necessarily breached the contract. One year's continuous employment; statutory rights, hearing: employment tribunal, compensation regulated by statute, reinstatement/redeployment possible.

3 (a) Lack of qualification. (b) Misconduct. (c) Negligence/incapability. (d) Conduct, but only if it reflects on Rhino's suitability for the job.

4 (a) No: he was not dismissed. (b) If a contract term requires acceptance of relocation, not redundant; otherwise distance is likely to be too great to be reasonable.

5 Fair selection procedures, warnings, consultation procedures, redeployment offers.

Quiz 18

1 Royal charter, Act of Parliament, registration.

2 (a) Financial liability of corporation members may be limited to their investment. (b) Once incorporated, corporation continues to exist until extinguished by relevant legal process. (c) At least two members.

3 A partnership is formed to make profits.

4 (a) Partners jointly bound if T had apparent authority. (b) All partners personally liable for partnership debts.

5 A company is public if: specified in the memorandum, limited liability, plc suffix, and it has at least £50,000 authorised capital, 25 per cent of which is paid up. Any other company is private.

Quiz 19

1 Memorandum and articles, details of directors and secretary, domicile of registered office, authorised share capital, whether/how liability is limited, statutory declaration.

2 Company may be bound by a contract which exceeds its objects clause.

3 This resolution must go to a meeting of the company: 75 per cent majority. Re-registration required.

4 Memorandum is merely evidence of the intention of the promoters to set the company up. It is no longer part of the company's constitution.

5 By a vote at a company meeting passed by a 75 per cent majority.

Quiz 20

1 Issued capital: potential profit raised so far by the shares issued. Called-up capital: money actually raised by calls on issued shares.

2 As a short-term measure to raise capital.

3 No valuable consideration/court-approved reduction of capital/court order/shares forfeited.

4 (a) Company has no obligation to issue dividends. (b) Company's articles define voting rights: not all shareholders necessarily entitled. Preference shareholders enjoy no privileges in this respect: their preferential rights may compensate for lack of voting rights. (c) Any shareholder may lose all/some of investment on winding up: rank below the company's creditors. Preference shareholders may be paid before the equity shareholders if the articles so require. (d) Brass has made a loan to the company which is secured against its assets and should recover his investment.

Quiz 21

1 Bombazine has rights in agency law: CA 2006, s 39.

2 (a) Insolvency Act 1986, s 214. (b) CA 2006, s 172(1).

3 Cotton: in breach of his duty under CA 2006, s 177 to declare an interest in a proposed transaction: contract voidable.

4 (a) Tweed is disqualified. (b) Denim is disqualified unless he has permission. (c) Twist's ill health entitles the company to remove him from office.

Quiz 22

1 General meeting: all members.

2 (a) AGM. (b) Serious reduction of capital. (c) Shareholder requisition. (d) Court order. (e) Retiring auditor requisition.

3 Resolution requires special notice to the company 21 days prior to meeting. Titan may address meeting/circulate defence to members. Resolution must pass (ordinary majority).

4 (a) Section 98: petition to court if at least 50 shareholders/those who hold 5 per cent of shares agree. (b) Chapter 11 proceedings, s 994: if he can prove unfair prejudice, Department for Business, Innovation and Skills intervention.

5 Derivative: shareholder acts in the company's interests. Right to sue is derived from the company's rights.

Quiz 23

1 (a) Yes: if written. (b) No: not a tangible form. (c) Employer owns the copyright. (d) If format sufficiently original. If created incidentally to her work, employer owns it.

2 Copyright: design drawings and figures (if works of art). Design right under CDPA 1988. Possibly design registrable: Registered Designs Act 1949.

3 (a) New, inventive step, capable of industrial application. (b) Owned by Fulmar. Puffin may get compensation.

4 (a) If sufficiently distinctive it is registrable: capable of graphical representation. (b) Not if too similar. (c) Not if it unjustifiably suggests royal family endorsement.

Quiz 24

1 (a) Breach of confidence. (b) Passing off. (c) Malicious falsehood.

2 (i) Confidential revelation. (ii) Relationship of trust between the parties. (iii) Information used by confidant/third party. (iv) Resulting damage.

3 Damages, injunction, surrender of profits.

4 Greater protection: goodwill need not yet exist. Simpler to prove.

Index